The Librarian's Career Guidebook

Edited by
Priscilla K. Shontz

The Scarecrow Press, Inc.
Lanham, Maryland • Toronto • Oxford
2004

SCARECROW PRESS, INC.

Published in the United States of America
by Scarecrow Press, Inc.
A wholly owned subsidary of
The Rowman & Littlefield Publishing Group, Inc.
4501 Forbes Boulevard, Suite 200, Lanham, Maryland 20706
www.scarecrowpress.com

PO Box 317
Oxford
OX2 9RU, UK

British Library Cataloguing in Publication Information Available

Library of Congress Cataloging-in-Publication Data

The librarian's career guidebook / edited by Priscilla K. Shontz.
    p. cm.
  Includes bibliographical references and index.
  ISBN 0-8108-5034-6 (pbk. : alk. paper)
  1. Library science—Vocational guidance. 2. Librarians—Employment. 3.
Library education. 4. Career development. I. Shontz, Priscilla K., 1965–
Z682.35.V62L53 2004
020'.23—dc22

                                                    2004008537

©™ The paper used in this publication meets the minimum requirements of
American National Standard for Information Sciences—Permanence of
Paper for Printed Library Materials, ANSI/NISO Z39.48-1992.
Manufactured in the United States of America.

To Laura and Sophie,
who make me laugh every day

Contents

Section 1 Career Planning

Section 2 Education

Section 3 Employment

Section 4 Experience as an Entry-level Librarian

Section 5 Experience as an Experienced Librarian

Foreword

When I first read Priscilla Shontz's *Jump Start Your Career in Library and Information Science* (2002), I appreciated the straightforwardness of that practical entry-level guide for potential and newer librarians. So often, we tend to focus on librarianship only as it pertains to our institutions, rather than as it pertains to ourselves and our professional careers. This welcome follow-up title builds on *Jump Start*, collecting the contributions of librarians and information professionals at various points in their careers, work environments, and professional thinking. You will find both big names and new names represented here; the range of topics is reflected in the range of contributors — who themselves reflect our diverse field.

We have all heard the curse "May you live in interesting times." Today's librarians live in most interesting times indeed, with the corresponding need to adjust their profession and their workplaces to meet changing technological and societal expectations. You will see a range of discussion in the following pages, addressing various practical aspects of how to be a library professional today.

At any stage in our library career, we work best in collaboration with others, building on the wisdom of our collective experience. On e-mail lists, at conferences, in one-on-one conversation, we share our perspectives and experiences with one another in an effort to make sense of our profession and of where it — and we — are headed.

Shontz has collected the contributions of a number of participants in this ongoing conversation, providing advice for those at different points in their careers. Contributors maintain a welcome focus, not on "how we did it good," but rather on what to expect, how to decide, where to turn, and how to contribute. In a changing field, we need to concentrate on personal professional issues as we chart our own career paths.

From beginning to end, topics range from the most basic questions of why and how to become a librarian to the most pressing of why and how to stay a librarian. Contributors touch on a variety of issues along the way, from career options and job hunting, to becoming a manager, to exploring related careers, to publishing and self-marketing. Each chapter provokes readers to think further on these issues, inspiring them to join in the professional conversation and to explore their many options.

Rachel Singer Gordon
rachel@lisjobs.com
Webmaster, Lisjobs.com
Coauthor of *The Information Professional's Guide
to Career Development Online* (ITI, 2002)
Author of *The Librarian's Guide to Writing
for Publication* (Scarecrow, 2004)

Acknowledgments

This book couldn't have happened without the hard work of the authors who contributed to it. I've been thrilled to work with them on this project, and I am excited to share their advice and perspectives with you.

Thanks to Rich Murray, who commented on a rough draft and proofread several chapters; to Wayne Jones and Anne Brûlé, who indexed the book; to Erika James, who drew the illustrations; and to Rachel Singer Gordon for writing the foreword. A special thanks goes to my acquisitions editor, Sue Easun, for her constant encouragement and patience. As always, the support of my husband, David, helped me finish this book.

Introduction

Imagine you're sitting in a room with librarians and information professionals who are employed in a variety of positions around the world. They're all willing to share their experiences and answer your career questions. What would you ask them?

I hope that this book answers some of those questions.

In *The Librarian's Career Guidebook*, sixty-three information professionals from diverse positions, workplaces, and locations offer practical advice on a wide variety of career issues. The book examines career options, education, job searching, on-the-job experience, professional development, essential skills, and strategies for enjoying your career. The advice is aimed at librarians in various stages of a career, from prospective librarians to MLS students to entry-level librarians to experienced information professionals.

Should you become a librarian? Is librarianship right for you? Why did you choose this career? Section 1: Career Planning begins by addressing the question, "Why be a librarian?" Are you curious about career options? This section describes career alternatives, including working for a public library, academic library, school library, special library, library consortium, or library association. The section discusses careers as an LIS faculty member, vendor, or publisher. Alternative career options such as freelancing and working in nontraditional environments are also covered.

Section 2: Education is aimed at students entering or already enrolled in an MLS program. Have you asked yourself, "Is the MLS worth the time and money I'm spending (or will spend)?" After discussing this question, this section advises students on choosing an MLS program, selecting classes, and participating in distance education programs. Authors also share strategies for getting practical experience while in school and preparing yourself to be as marketable as possible when you graduate.

Section 3: Employment covers aspects of the job-hunting process. How do you find jobs? How can you evaluate a potential workplace before you accept a job? How do you begin to write your cover letter and resume? How can you prepare for your interview? Can you negotiate if you are offered a job? How can you maximize your chances of being hired? If you must leave a job, whether voluntarily or involuntarily, how can you do that without hurting your reputation? How can you keep your career alive when you are unemployed, whether by choice or not? Is it possible—and is it a good idea—to switch career paths?

If you are beginning your first job after earning your MLS, you have many challenges and transitions ahead. Section 4: Experience as an Entry-level Librarian shares practical advice for surviving your first year on the job and familiarizing yourself with your new work environment and supervisors' expectations. Authors also offer perspectives on practical skills you might not have learned in school. The section discusses how to develop a professional image as you make the transition from student to professional. Performance reviews are a stressful experience for almost everyone; how can you prepare for your own review and use these reviews to improve your performance? If you have to review others, how can you do it in a fair and constructive manner? Would you be comfortable in a tenure-track academic library environment? Authors discuss how to thrive in a tenure-track position and how to make the most of the performance review process.

Section 5: Experience as an Experienced Librarian addresses challenges facing seasoned or midcareer librarians. How do you get promoted? How can you prepare for a promotion review or apply for promotion? If you are entering a management position, how can you be a good supervisor? How do you stay relevant to avoid becoming stale, bored, or out of touch? How can you use your experience, professional involvement, research, and other activities to develop an expertise in a specific area? How can you prevent or cope with burnout? How do you stay enthusiastic about the profession?

Section 6: Skills provides advice for improving many essential career skills, including interpersonal, communication, computer or technical, organizational, time and project management, public speaking, teaching, writing, and leadership skills.

Section 7: Professional Development answers questions you may face when developing your career. What is considered professional behavior? How can you communicate and present yourself professionally online? How do you find relevant conferences, how can you afford to attend them, and how can you make the most of your time there? Why should you join professional associations? Should you become actively involved in association commit-tees, and if so, how do you begin? How can mentors help you? How can you find a mentor? Can you mentor others? How do you keep up with all the news and issues in the field? If you would like to—or need to—publish, how can you begin doing this? How can you market yourself, your experience, and your skills to advance your career?

Section 8: Enjoying Your Career includes strategies for coping with stress, adapting to change, and maintaining a positive attitude. This section also presents advice for achieving a healthy balance between work, personal life, and family demands. To conclude the book, librarians share personal accounts of what they love about their jobs and our profession.

I hope this book can serve as a guidebook at various stages in your career. This book is meant to be quite practical. You'll notice differing perspectives, opinions, writing styles, and tones as you read this book. You'll also see some overlap between chapters. This is intentional. The authors come from various types of jobs, work environments, and locations (including Canada and Aus-tralia). The diversity is intended to provide a variety of perspectives and to al-low you to hear different voices. You may not agree with all of the advice; sometimes the authors don't even agree with each other! Consider this book a conversation between you and sixty-three professionals in the field. Enjoy the dialogue.

Please feel free to e-mail me with your comments and suggestions. Please visit LIScareer.com at www.liscareer.com, and contact me if you'd like to contribute an article sharing your career advice with others.

I hope that this book provides some practical strategies and ideas that help you design a career that you love.

Priscilla K. Shontz
pshontz@liscareer.com

Companion Website

LIScareer.com offers career development resources for librarians, information professionals, and students. The goal of the site is to help new and prospective librarians and information professionals manage a successful and satisfying career. Though the site is primarily aimed at newer librarians and students, the resources may be helpful to a librarian at any stage of his or her career. The site includes practical advice contributed by information professionals, links to online resources, and information about print resources. LIScareer.com welcomes contributed articles and suggestions. Please visit www.liscareer.com for more information.

1

CAREER PLANNING

1

Why Be a Librarian?

Sarah Ann Long

Choosing a career is a momentous decision. Once made, the decision usually requires an expenditure of money and time in preparing for the career. The decision can be defining in terms of lifestyle, friends, associates, and even where you will live.

People choose librarianship for a variety of reasons. Real-life stories from six librarians are included here with the hope that you will find resonance that will help you make this important decision.

This chapter concludes with reasons why librarians love their career choice even after the first blush of enthusiasm has faded. Again, the hope is that you will find resonance in the words and stories of others

As a child, Nancy Pearl wanted to be a librarian. When she was ten years old, the librarian at her local branch library was her mentor and heroine. Pearl, already an avid reader, spent many hours at the library. Despite her tender age, she decided that librarianship was her goal in life, and she achieved it. Today, Nancy Pearl is the director of Children's Services and the Washington Center for the Book in Seattle. She has her own radio show where she reviews books and talks about a variety of subjects of interest to her clientele. She is a published author. Her most recent book, *Book Lust,*[1] is an eclectic collection of Pearl's reading recommendations. Most recently she became the first library action figure—a six-inch plastic figure of a woman raising her finger to her mouth in a shushing motion. Pearl explained that librarians have been accused of lacking a sense of humor. "This action figure proves we can laugh and have fun with our own stereotypes," she said.[2]

Pearl is an exception to the rule. Most librarians come to their career decisions later in life, often after considering or even entering another profession.

Chadwick Raymond, director of the Northbrook (Illinois) Public Library, became a librarian when his original career plans fell apart. He had planned to go to law school, but his marriage and family responsibilities required a reliable income. "I took a job in a library simply as a way to make money," he said. "I always had a strong desire to help people. The longer I worked in the library, the more apparent it became that librarianship would be a better career fit for me than the law."[3] Since then, Raymond has worked in a number of outstanding public libraries, and he has successfully directed two libraries in the suburban Chicago area. Several impressive library construction projects are concrete testimony to Raymond's effectiveness. When asked why he stays in librarianship, Raymond said:

> I like being in a position where I can make a difference. Libraries do change lives and build community. While I enjoy the sense of achievement that comes whenever I am able to find the right resource for a library customer, it is really a team process. Without the board to guide in the development of new policies and programs, the library would wither and die. Collaboration and resource sharing are crucial to good service. Effective teamwork that engages the staff, board and library administration can turn even a poor library into a dynamic place. I like the collaborative approach; not everything is on my shoulders. Having been active in the Northbrook community for many years, I feel I have credibility. That's been useful especially when the library has had to take controversial stands or even make the case for a new library.[4]

Carol Bartlett is reference and audio visual specialist at the Ela Area Library District in Lake Zurich, Illinois. She caught the library bug in elementary school. "I liked to read and our school library was open in the summer, so I read all year long. I liked those nice pencils the librarian had with the date stamps on the end. The librarian was friendly and there were ALL those books." In junior high, Bartlett volunteered in the library, and she was assigned to the elementary school to put things in order. She became a library aide in high school, and this experience further increased her commitment. In college she majored in literature and music, since she believed these liberal arts courses would strengthen her skills as a librarian. After that, Bartlett read what was required for the master's degree in librarianship and decided that music would be easier. After twenty-five years as a music teacher, a fifth-grade teacher, a stint working in a newspaper office, and helping her husband with his master's degree, Bartlett declared, "I am going to be a librarian!" With her husband's support she took a year off and earned her MLS from Simmons College in Boston. "I love being a librarian," she said. "If you like libraries and people, there is no better opportunity."[5]

Mike Ragen, chief deputy director of the Illinois State Library, came to librarianship after more than twenty-five years on the staff of the Illinois General Assembly.

I chose to work in the Illinois State Library because I had always been interested in information and the role that manipulation, massaging, and managing of data play in policy development. After I had worked in the library for about a year, I wanted to know more, so I enrolled in the School of Library and Information Science at the University of Illinois and earned my MLS. Being in the program expanded my horizons. I thought I had a global view, but the MLS experience greatly enhanced my concept of the possibilities.[6]

Ragen noted that career specialists have long said that most people have more than one career during their working life. He touted librarianship as a great second career because it is information based. "The MLS is a versatile credential," he said. "It doesn't typecast you. It's a rapidly changing field that allows you to grow and change as your interests evolve. On the other hand, the MLS is great foundation for a career in law, technology, teaching or public administration. You gain research skills that enhance your ability to move on to something else."[7]

Many librarians made their career decision because someone recruited them to the profession. It might have been a relative or another librarian. In a study reported by Kathleen Heim in 1991, many librarians cited a formal or informal recruitment as the primary reason for choosing librarianship.[8]

When Judith Mayzel, professor of library services at Oakton (Illinois) Community College, was getting her teaching degree, she took a course in children's literature from an inspired librarian who mentored her. Mayzel liked working with children, so she went straight into the classroom. But, as she put it, "the library was still tugging at my heart." She borrowed the money to enter library school on a part-time basis, and she soon earned her MLS. Since then, Mayzel has held several different jobs in the Oakton Community College Library. She especially enjoys bringing people and information together. Mayzel noted that the introduction of the computer and the World Wide Web into the information environment has greatly expanded the information possibilities. "It's a powerful feeling," she said, "to have all this information at your fingertips."[9]

Patti Kuhl is in charge of Information Resources at Hewitt Associates, a major human resources consulting firm, but she came to librarianship because of William Shakespeare. It happened at a small college where Kuhl was finishing her bachelor's degree. She signed up for a course on Shakespeare and the teacher just happened to be a librarian. "He made Shakespeare come alive for me," she said. "And he just knew so much. I asked him how he had become so knowledgeable and he said he got it all from the library. He gave me not only a passion for Shakespeare but also the career tip that the library was a place for learning." Kuhl didn't act on her library tip immediately. She worked for a bank for a while and then earned a master's degree in teaching, followed by an MLS. While her children were young, she worked in several different public libraries and school libraries. Now working as an information specialist in a corporate setting, Kuhl says, "At the public library I loved helping people—loved linking people up with information. I felt honorable. But after awhile, I needed a change. At Hewitt I have been challenged and have learned a whole new body of knowledge complete with new concepts, new terms, and most importantly firsthand experience of how business works. I feel like I have made it in a tough world." Kuhl made the distinction between working at a public library, where the emphasis is on helping people, and working at a special library, where the emphasis is on content or a body of knowledge. "I might want to be a medical librarian next," she said, "just for the content challenge!"[10]

The example of good service lured Frances Roehm, SkokieNet librarian at the Skokie (Illinois) Public Library. "I was working part time as a page and the demonstration of service inspired and encouraged me," she said. "The librarians spotted my interest and said, 'Honey, why don't you get a library degree?' As a child, I was turned off by the grumpy, frowny librarian at school. But these women were just so helpful. I wanted to be part of that." Roehm went on to say that she finds her job in helping people meaningful every day. "I get feedback," she said. "Every day, people tell me how much they appreciate my help. Doing something that matters nourishes my soul," Roehm said.[11]

I make it a habit to ask my librarian friends why they became librarians. From my experience, almost all librarians are happy they found librarianship. According to my unofficial survey, here are the top six reasons why:

1. "Librarianship is a calling. It is the means of fulfilling my personal life mission."[12] Libraries are the "People's University" and librarians support everyone's freedom to read. In the words of one librarian, "I am one link in the long chain of equal access and opportunity for all Americans that stretches back to the founding of our country." Being a librarian means doing important work. It makes you feel that, every day, your work makes a positive difference in our society.

2. Librarianship is infinitely variable. Speaking personally, I chose librarianship because I liked children and books. But since then I've worked in academic, public, and special libraries and have taken on many different tasks. For the last fourteen years I have been the director of the North Suburban Library System in Wheeling, Illinois. My job changes regularly and I especially cherish this aspect of it. For those who like to continually learn, change, and grow, librarianship is a perfect career choice. Think how much libraries have changed since the Internet became ubiquitous. David Bishop, university librarian of Northwestern University, recently told me that he had been a librarian for forty years

and that this was the best time to be a librarian, because it was the most exciting time.

3. Libraries are nice places to work. Most libraries are clean and well-lit and there is the lure of all those books and ideas as a backdrop. People who work in libraries are interesting. They represent many different backgrounds and conversation in the staff room is never dull. A furniture salesman who sold to libraries as well as to other professional groups told me that librarians were among his favorite clients because they were sharp and lively, but also sincere, dependable, and ethical.

4. Librarianship means great life skills. A graduate degree from a school approved by the American Library Association is the necessary credential for a professional librarian. A friend of mine said, "In library school I learned to think and use tools that have dramatically increased my problem-solving ability. In our society, problem solving becomes more important every day."

5. Librarianship means access to the best books. This is especially true if one works in the public library. Not only do you see and hear about the newest and most interesting new materials, but you may also choose to be a reviewer for a professional journal and get advance personal copies along with the power surge of sharing your opinion with others. In a library there are always colleagues and patrons who like to read, too. That means not only access to the best books but also conversations with others who have read them. As the Internet continues to grow and change our world, librarianship means access to new ideas, whether in traditional print-on-paper books or online.

6. Librarianship is satisfying work. How much is a small boy's smile worth, or the gratitude of an adult who has at long last found illusive and important information? Librarians receive smiles and gratitude every day from their patrons. And if you like the hunt and the chase of finding illusive facts, that can be satisfying, too. On the other hand, if you have a job like mine that is more managerial, satisfaction might not come on a daily basis, but it comes. I have never been more personally satisfied than when a program or initiative of North Suburban Library System (NSLS) is useful to the librarians in this community.

Are you hooked yet? Want to become a librarian? Read on in this book, but also check out these websites for many links that will answer questions and give you valuable information for pursuing a career in librarianship:

- NSLS Library Career Center—www.nsls.info/librarycareers
- Becomealibrarian.org—www.becomealibrarian.org/

- "Career Planning," LIScareer.com—liscareer.com/careerplanning.htm
- "Careers in Libraries," American Library Association—www.ala.org/
  Content/NavigationMenu/Our_Association/Offices/Human_
  Resource_Development_and_Recruitment/Careers_in_Libraries1/
  Careers_in_Libraries.htm
- "Career Information," Canadian Library Association—www.cla.ca/
  careers/careerinfo.htm
- "Library Science as a Career," LibraryHQ.com—www.libraryhq.com/
  libcareer.html

NOTES

1. Nancy Pearl, *Book Lust: Recommended Reading for Every Mood, Moment, and Reason* (Seattle, Wash.: Sasquatch Books, 2003).
2. Nancy Pearl, interview with the author, 8 October 2003.
3. Chadwick Raymond, telephone interview with the author, 16 September 2003.
4. Raymond, telephone interview.
5. Carol Bartlett, telephone interview with the author, 16 September 2003.
6. Michael Ragen, telephone interview with the author, 17 September 2003.
7. Ragen, telephone interview.
8. Kathleen Heim, *Opportunities in Library and Information Science* (New York: McGraw Hill, 1991).
9. Judith Mayzel, telephone interview with the author, 18 September 2003.
10. Patti Kuhl, telephone interview with the author. 18 September 2003.
11. Frances Roehm, telephone interview with the author, 19 September 2003.
12. Mary Pergander, "Can't Help Lovin' That Job of Mine," *The Shy Librarian* (Summer 2003): 10.

ABOUT THE AUTHOR

Since 1989, Sarah Ann Long has been the director of the North Suburban Library System, an organization of over 650 academic, public, school, and special libraries in the north/northwest suburbs of Chicago. Prior to this position, she was the director of the Multnomah County Library in Portland, Oregon. She also directed the Dauphin County Library System in Harrisburg, Pennsylvania, and the Fairfield County District Library in Lancaster, Ohio. She was a consultant at the state Library of Ohio and was an academic librarian in England. Sarah began her career as a school librarian. Having held a number leadership positions within the American Library Association, Sarah served as president in 2000–2001. She also is a past president of the Public Library Association.

2

The Public in Public Libraries

Erika James

At orientation for my master's degree in library and information science, one of the professors asked the room of over a hundred students what kind of library they expected to work in after graduation. A group of hands went up for each type—school, public, academic, special, and so on. When she finished with her poll, the professor informed the packed room, "Whatever library you *think* you will work at, 60 percent of you will begin your career in a public library."

I was convinced she was not referring to me. At the time I was a reference assistant at a university library and, in my mind, destined for an academic career as a librarian with faculty status. My attitude quickly changed when I graduated eighteen months later and relocated to northern Texas. Public libraries were suddenly more appealing as they were the only libraries in the area hiring full time.

Many of my public library colleagues have shared similar stories with me about planning different career paths. Although school libraries actually employ more librarians, most MLIS students' first job after graduation is in a public library. I was pleased to find working at a public library was as rewarding as an academic library, with a wide range of job responsibilities and opportunities for professional growth.

TYPES OF PUBLIC LIBRARIES

In the broadest definition possible, public libraries are supported by public funds and are intended for use by the general public. Their goal is to serve the needs of the community. Public libraries fall into three categories: city/county, state, and federal.

City/county libraries can range from a storefront in a small town all the way to a network of libraries, referred to as a system, serving millions of people. Not all systems are run by a single governmental entity. Several libraries in an area may get together to form a system, each specializing in a different subject area with patrons having privileges at all locations. Several systems can join together to form a consortium to gain access to resources otherwise out of their reach. Also becoming more common are joint-use facilities, pairing a city/county library with a school or academic library to create a combined library.

Each state operates a state library system serving the needs of the state's agencies and officials as well as the general public. Among their many functions, state libraries set standards and direct aid to support local libraries. They work to improve and share resources among all libraries in the state with programs such as interlibrary loan and electronic resource access.

Technically, federal libraries are public libraries, although they operate as special libraries. They serve the federal agency of which they are a part, and the public may have restricted access or none at all. The largest federal library, the Library of Congress, is considered a collection of special libraries. Federal libraries include overseas agency information centers and libraries on military bases.

WHAT IT MEANS TO BE SUPPORTED BY PUBLIC FUNDS

Public libraries are primarily funded by federal, state, and/or local government. Statutes authorize a city, county, or state to levy taxes to establish and support a library department. Some communities vote to designate a library system as a separate taxing entity. This gives the library a stable funding source that is not as vulnerable to the fluctuating economy. When working at a public library, you will find yourself taking more of an interest in taxes as well as the politics that factor directly into library services, your salary, and even your retirement fund.

YOUR SALARY

Salary ranges for entry-level positions are not negotiable. Thriving communities may offer lucrative salaries or do midyear cost adjustments to attract and retain employees. If an area's sales tax revenues sharply decline or a local large business goes under, employees run the risk of not receiving cost-of-living increases or raises or even the possibility of losing their jobs. Benefits for full-time government employees tend to be generous, with employees receiving paid holidays, the ability to carry over unused leave from one year to the next, and retirement saving accounts.

CITY COUNCIL AND THE LIBRARY BOARD

Many decisions impacting the library, such as filters for public computers and fine policies, are decided outside the library by an elected or appointed body such as a city council or county commission. The most important of these decisions is approval of the budget. During lean economic times, libraries are often the first on the chopping block when cuts need to be made. As a result, libraries are constantly trying to demonstrate their worth to the community. It is to your benefit to know the names and faces of board members as well as all politicians in the area, especially those living in the neighborhoods surrounding your library.

In addition, your library or system may also have its own advisory board or commission that advises elected officials in matters relating to the library. The board may recommend a study about which services are not cost-effective or may review floor plans for a new library. Typically meeting once a month, they advise the council on library matters and advocate for money and improvements.

I GET BY WITH A LITTLE HELP FROM MY FRIENDS: FRIENDS, GROUPS, AND FOUNDATIONS

Most libraries have a Friends of the Library group. These are nonprofit organizations that raise money and increase awareness of library programs, services, and activities. They may be vocal in legislative issues that affect library resources, such as campaigning for continued state funding of electronic databases. Funds raised by Friends organizations are reinvested in the library for materials, furniture, programs, special needs, and the educational support of staff. For librarians this means the Friends may pay all or part of their costs to attend conferences.

Some libraries also have a Foundation or Endowment Trust whose purpose is strictly financial. The Foundation seeks monetary gifts from businesses and individuals and invests those funds. While anyone can join a Friends group, usually for a small fee, members of the Foundation are most often appointed and sometimes paid. Money raised by the Foundation is funneled into a trust that accrues interest. Typically the money is used for large expenses such as funding a special program, building a computer room, or purchasing a major piece of art.

JOB POSITIONS

As the library tries to be all things to all people, the librarians are the ones who make much of it happen with the cooperation of library assistants, clerks, and pages. Like any organization, the size of your library or system determines the range of your job responsibilities. At a small library you may be the lone librarian responsible for administration, circulation, acquisitions, cataloging, and reference. In a larger library or library system, your position is more defined. You may work on the business floor of a central library, answering only business-related questions. There are specialists such as catalogers, with only one function, and generalists, often with the universal title of librarian, who perform several job functions.

Librarians are most often associated with the traditional reference services they provide on the library floor, over the phone, and now more frequently through e-mail or online. However, librarians actually provide many other services that take place in the workroom, in classes, and at outreach locations.

BEHIND THE SCENES

Most of the job responsibilities that take place in the public library workroom are similar to their counterparts at other types of libraries. Cataloging, collection development, acquisitions, and serials are often a part of a technical services department that operates out of public sight. Although they do not interact with patrons, they are aware of the wide spectrum the library serves.

Catalogers handle a wide variety of books and media ranging from Barney videos to chemistry workbooks. They also are responsible for repairing or replacing items in the collections, such as videos left in hot cars or board books, dubbed "teethers" by those in the circulation department who handle the gnawed remains.

Collection development and serials librarians must know the makeup of the community and be familiar with who uses the library. For example, books about curtains are one of the most popular titles in my library because of the many new homeowners in the area. The librarians observe circulation rates and listen to the public's suggestions for new titles and areas in which to expand the collection. This is done in an effort to maximize the available resources. In doing so, they have to consider many factors such as the cost of cataloging popular paperback romance novels versus the fact they will fall apart after relatively few check outs.

Acquisitions is accountable for allocating the public's tax dollars. Purchases over a certain amount may need approval by a board or financial officer outside of the library. In addition, certain procedures need to be followed in accordance with city, county, or state laws when handling public funds.

WHAT TO EXPECT ON THE LIBRARY FLOOR

The library floor is where the question "Are you a people person?" comes to life. At the reference or information desk you will work with all ages, backgrounds, and temperaments. Patrons will have varying needs and reading interests including some students who will inform you, "I hate to read!"

The public library offers services to a large amount of people. Despite the number of people they help, librarians strive to provide hands-on help to all patrons. Whereas an academic librarian focuses on an instructional approach to reference, public librarians are more likely to come into contact with patrons who need more guided help for various reasons. Many public library patrons have time on their hands to explore, browse, and chat online all day long, in contrast with school or special libraries whose patrons tend to have very specific reasons for being there.

READER'S ADVISORY

Reader's Advisory is a necessary skill at the reference desk and one that takes time to develop. Whatever your opinion is of mystery, romance, action, or science fiction, you will need to stay on top of the latest books and most popular authors in these genres because patrons will ask you for recommendations. The public library is where many devoted best-seller readers stock up. They request their favorite author's latest title before it is published, and you will know the release dates of the new Janet Evanovich or Harry Potter better than your birthday.

COMPUTERS AND THE INTERNET

Each year more people discover computers at the public library, where they have not only free access but also assistance by trained professionals. Overseeing the public computer terminals can be a time-consuming task. A lot of time is spent helping patrons with basic computer skills or troubleshooting computer malfunctions. However, there are instructional opportunities such as teaching information literacy to a class or illustrating the difference between search engines and databases to individual patrons.

Even if you are fortunate enough to be supported by an information technology services department, you may still be responsible for installing, testing, and changing hardware and software. Areas of concern associated with computers are filtering and security measures, not to mention irritating problems such as pencils stuck in the A drive.

PATRONS

You will run into difficult people anytime you work with the public. Irate and impatient patrons as well as homeless, mentally ill, or inebriated patrons are among those you will encounter. Developing strong customer service skills will help you deal with these situations. Many problem patrons are regulars and once you get to know them you can anticipate their eccentricities and learn to work with them as individuals.

Unpleasant situations, such as patrons viewing objectionable websites, frequently crop up in the news and library literature. These tend to be problems more associated with larger library systems in big cities, although even smaller libraries have their share of problems with pornography and the Internet. Be clear on your library's procedures for handling these incidents. Federal, state, and local provisions that require the use of filtering software, often in order to qualify for certain types of funding, have reduced these.

If you have qualms about your personal safety, ask questions about security during your interview. In many areas, the police and library staff have amiable relations since they work for the same entity. I've run into fewer problems with patrons at the small to midsize libraries I've worked in over the years than I've had to deal with on a weekly basis working at a bookstore in a larger city. Public libraries are full of appreciative, well-mannered patrons who don't make the news.

NON-NATIVE ENGLISH SPEAKERS

Public libraries have long been hailed as a place where new immigrants can learn to assimilate into the American culture. Speaking another language is a plus for anyone working in a library. Understanding cultural differences is necessary when working at the reference desk where you will encounter patrons from a variety of countries and cultures. This goes beyond a culture's reluctance to ask for help; you may unknowingly affront a patron by asking their child to stop running. This brings us to a public library's greatest challenge: children.

CHILDREN AND CHILDREN'S LIBRARIANS

Introducing young readers to books they are guaranteed to fall in love with and easing students' apprehensions by finding the perfect resource for homework assignments are some of the rewards of working with children. The downside is that you will spend a good deal of your time reminding children to speak in their "inside voice" and not to run. Rowdy and unattended children can be hazardous to patrons, the order of your shelves, and your blood pressure.

Children and young adult positions are excellent opportunities for those who want to work with children and children's literature outside a school environment, or for those who may not have the teaching certificate required of many school librarians. Even when you work at a library with a children's librarian or department, you will undoubtedly still handle some children and young adult questions. It is often helpful to shadow a children's librarian to learn about juvenile resources and fiction.

Storytimes and summer reading programs, staples of public library programming, are time-consuming responsibilities of children's librarians. The planning and promoting of summer reading programs keep librarians busy throughout the year. Storytimes challenge librarians to entertain toddlers and preschoolers (not to mention their parents) while introducing them to books, songs, and stories.

Children's librarians strive to attract both ends of the youth spectrum, creating programs for infants and teens. Reading programs for infants and their parents, with colorful names such as Bouncing Babies and Mother Goose, are gaining popularity. Attracting teenage and preteen "tween" patrons is another idea that resurfaces every few years. Current trends include creating a teen area in the library, forming a teenage library advisory group, and circulating graphic novels.

YOUR SCHEDULE

The library is open and the reference desk is staffed as many hours as the budget can accommodate. This includes nights, weekends, and holidays. Libraries fill many of these hours with part-time employees but even full-time employees will find themselves on a night- and weekend-shift or rotation.

MOVING ON UP: ADMINISTRATION

Public libraries offer opportunities for advancement up to the administrative level. At many libraries managers and directors must have a master's degree in library and/or information science. Other libraries expect only a years of library experience. It is rare to find a director of a library who did not work in a library prior to taking that position. Many cities may have leadership classes that librarians can take to better prepare themselves to move up. A business background is helpful, as at this level you are working more with budgets than bestsellers. Directors and branch managers spend most of their time handling personnel, financial, and building issues. A lot of time is spent in meetings with staff, city council, advisory boards, and professional organizations.

CONTINUING EDUCATION

Most library systems require some form of continuing education. Large organizations may have their own training program specifically for librarians while smaller organizations may require attendance at city classes or regional training workshops. Continuing education hours are required by some library systems. Regional library groups and state library organizations offer many of these classes and workshops that include the number of credit hours you will receive for attendance. Don't try to sneak out of them; certificates stating you attended the session aren't given out until the very end!

PUBLIC LIBRARY ASSOCIATION (PLA)

Involvement in the Public Library Association connects you with other public librarians through programs, advocacy, continuing education, and publications. PLA is a division of the American Library Association (ALA) focusing on public library issues and legislation. ALA conferences, both national and state, are geared toward all types of libraries, and some public librarians may feel there is at times less emphasis on public libraries. At PLA conferences, held every other year, all programs are relevant to public library staff from the latest laws on filtering to how to introduce a coffee bar at your library.

SEE FOR YOURSELF: GAINING LIBRARY EXPERIENCE

For the most part, patrons are only exposed to half of the library. To gain an insight into what goes on in the workroom and to understand how the public library functions as a whole, you need to volunteer at a public library. Almost all public libraries have volunteer opportunities. At some libraries many services and programs would not take place without volunteers. Another way to gain public library experience is to work as a clerk or page while in graduate school. When you are a librarian your job may involve supervising these groups and this will give you an insight into their point of view.

Working at a public library offers librarians a wide choice of job responsibilities and positions. Public libraries give you the opportunity to work with children and adults or, if you prefer, to work in the back room with less public contact. Last but not least, public libraries are numerous, spread out across the country, and employ many new graduates despite their planned career tracks.

ONLINE RESOURCES

Become a Librarian—www.becomealibrarian.org

Libraries on the Web: USA Public Libraries—sunsite.berkeley.edu/Libweb/Public_main.html

Occupational Outlook Quarterly Online Librarians—www.bls.gov/opub/ooq/2000/Winter/art01.pdf

Public Library Association—www.pla.org

RELATED READINGS

Eberts, Majorie, and Margaret Gisler. *Careers for Bookworms and Other Literary Types*. Chicago: VGM Career Books, 2002.

Fourie, Denise K., and David R. Dowell. *Libraries in the Information Age: An Introduction and Career Exploration*. Greenwood Village, Colo.: Libraries Unlimited, 2002.

Hall, Matthew L. "Reflections for Librarians who are Considering the Switch." *Public Libraries* 42, no. 3 (May/June 2003): 154–55.

Institute for Career Research. *Career as a Librarian, Public Libraries: Managing Knowledge and Information, Making It Available to Everyone*. Chicago: Institute for Career Research, 2001.

ABOUT THE AUTHOR

Erika James is a senior public services librarian at the Maribelle M. Davis Library in the Plano Public Library System, Plano, Texas. She received her MLIS at the University of Texas in Austin.

3

Career Options in Academe

Mary Anne Hansen

Many academic libraries, but certainly not all, require a master's degree in library or information science from an institution accredited by the American Library Association (ALA). Frequently, librarians seeking a position in an academic library will have taken coursework in library school geared toward academic librarianship. However, it is not unusual for librarians without formal coursework or experience in academic librarianship to make the transition from public, school, or special librarianship to an academic library position.

SECOND MASTER'S DEGREE

To degree or not to degree, that is the question. Many librarians pondering a career in an academic library wonder if the second master's degree is necessary. The answer is: It depends. Some academic libraries require a second master's degree for employment and some do not. The second master's degree is beneficial in that it provides an area of expertise, especially if you are seeking a position as a subject specialist. Many institutions filling subject-specialist positions will require a master's degree in the respective area of specialty; for example, a business librarian may be required to have an MBA in addition to the MLS.

FACULTY VERSUS NONFACULTY STATUS

Just as some academic libraries require the second master's degree and some do not, some academic libraries hire librarians into faculty positions, while others do not. If an academic librarian has faculty status, she or he is typically required to fulfill responsibilities in the areas of service and research and creative activity, in addition to responsibilities in librarianship, in order to fulfill the requirements of tenure and promotion expected of all faculty across campus. The requirements of tenure and promotion for librarians are similar to other teaching faculty, yet specific to unique functions and responsibilities of librarians. The requirements for achieving tenure and promotion often include teaching, which for librarians includes duties such as reference desk transactions, bibliographic instruction sessions, and occasionally credit courses; service to the library, the campus community, and professional library associations; and research and creative activities, which often take the form of presentations at state, regional, and national conferences, as well as publications in academic journals, both in librarianship and in other areas of interest and expertise. Faculty status for librarians can also put them at equal rank with other teaching faculty across campus.

Academic librarians in positions without faculty status are typically considered support professionals on campus. Depending on the campus climate, they may or may not receive the same recognition and consideration as teaching faculty, that is, nonfaculty librarians may or may not have a voice in much of the politics on campus, depending on the culture at that particular campus.

TYPICAL POSITIONS

Reference Librarian

What skills are necessary for academic reference librarians? The requirements are essentially the same as for reference positions in other types of libraries, except the clientele is different, and thus the types of patron questions vary among library types. Necessary skills for academic reference librarians include any or all of the following, depending on the position description: excellent interpersonal communication, presentation, and organizational skills; ability to work constructively, creatively, and energetically both autonomously and in a collaborative, collegial, and often team-based environment; strong commitment to user-centered services; strong knowledge of and recent experience with traditional and electronic reference resources; ability to handle multiple responsibilities in a rapidly changing environment; facility with computers, technology, and presentation software; experience with issues related to user assessment of library services; and knowledge of emerging issues related to teaching, instructional design, learning technologies, and information literacy standards for higher education.

The primary clientele in academic libraries include students, faculty, and staff of the institution and, as mentioned earlier, may include the general public if the institution is public. The variety of questions fielded by academic reference librarians tend to be geared toward the specific programs of study offered at the respective institution. Academic reference librarians must have strong communication skills, the ability to instruct others on relevant information resources in both traditional and electronic formats, and an understanding of academic research processes in an academic environment.

Depending on the institution, a reference position may require a person to be either a subject specialist or a generalist. Often, but not always, those institutions that require the second master's degree will have reference positions for subject specialists in areas such as maps, music, art, engineering, humanities, the sciences, and the like. Reference positions requiring one to be a generalist are typically at smaller institutions that do not have enough positions to warrant subject specialists. Yet as is the case in this author's institution, while each reference librarian is considered a generalist, consideration for employment may require a second master's degree; thus, each reference librarian, though a generalist, has an area of expertise by virtue of the second master's degree. Additionally, generalists often develop additional areas of expertise, depending on instructional and program needs across campus. For example, at this author's library, each generalist reference librarian serves in one or more instruction liaisonships to various departments, such as engineering, business, chemistry, education, psychology, and so on. Liaisons generally provide specialized reference assistance, instruction, collection development, subject guide preparation, collaboration, and communication of all issues between the library and assigned liaison departments.

Just as more and more public libraries are offering digital reference services, so are academic libraries. These services include asynchronous and synchronous, or e-mail and chat. Those academic librarians serving as digital-chat reference librarians typically work traditional reference desk shifts as well. However, some libraries are hiring digital-only reference librarians, but this is still rare. Additionally, many academic libraries that provide digital reference services will make digital reference shifts optional rather than required for their reference staff, recognizing that not every librarian has the aptitude or the skills to provide digital-chat reference service.

Many academic reference positions require both reference and instruction responsibilities, while some institutions still separate these two functions into distinct positions. Additionally, most reference positions will have a certain percentage of the position description devoted to collection development, sometimes with a purchasing budget, sometimes without (in which case, the collection development and management librarian makes the final purchasing decisions from reference staff recommendations).

Outreach/Distance Education Librarian

Academic librarians in outreach or distance education positions function similarly to academic reference librarians, but their focus is on the library user at a distance. Responsibilities include the development, evaluation, and management of library services and instruction for remote users. Librarians in such positions often have a more intensive liaison role than the typical departmental liaison roles held by reference librarians. Outreach and distance education librarians must work closely with the designers and providers of remotely delivered courses, including teaching faculty and technical support personnel.

Bibliographic Instruction Librarian

As noted earlier, some academic institutions hire librarians to serve in a dual role as both reference and instruction librarian, while others hire librarians into separate reference and instruction positions. The trend in position descriptions over the past decade seems to be a combination of the two, rather than separate positions functioning in isolation. The rationale for this trend is that bibliographic instruction enhances one's reference work and vice versa. Instruction librarians, often in a liaison capacity with specific departments on campus, work with other teaching faculty as well as library colleagues to establish instructional programs and integrate information literacy skills into course content. These collaborative efforts often involve the codesign of assignments that integrate library research and may even result in team-teaching situations with the librarian and faculty member serving complementary roles in the teaching-learning process of library research.

Cataloging Librarian

Catalogers in every type of library are evolving beyond the traditional duties of classifying and organizing materials, describing and indexing resources, developing controlled access to information from a user-centered point of view, and working out of the public eye with materials and/or systems. As is the case in this author's library, the two catalogers in our medium-sized academic library are increasingly involved with the design and functionality of the online catalog. Additionally, it is more important than ever that catalogers possess excellent interpersonal communication and negotiation skills because there must be so much necessary communication and collaboration among catalogers, technical services staff, systems staff, and reference librarians in making electronic resources, especially the online catalog, a resource that functions as effectively and efficiently as possible.

Depending on the size of the library, cataloging positions may be all-inclusive or specialized in nature. In large academic libraries, positions often exist for the cataloging of a variety of specialized items and formats: foreign language cataloging specialists and media catalogers (including videos, DVDs, and CDs).

Collection Development and Management Librarian

Academic collection development and management librarians serve as negotiators and facilitators for incorporating new models of access over ownership of library materials. They often direct the allocation and expenditures of the library materials budget, and, in the absence of an electronic resources librarian, they negotiate licensing and contracts for electronic information resources. They also develop and manage approval plans, coordinate the assessment of information resources and user needs through the analysis of statistics and data, and participate in cooperative collection development efforts and consortia at the local, state, regional, and national level. Collection development and management librarians must stay abreast of publishing trends and electronic resources in order to make cost-effective purchasing decisions involving print versus electronic or subscription versus document delivery.

Electronic Resources Librarian

More and more academic libraries are creating electronic resources librarian positions in order to dedicate a position to the acquisition and management of electronic resources with the goal of ensuring continuous and seamless access. This position is usually created in addition to the collection development librarian position because the exploding electronic environment has complicated the nature of collection management. Electronic resources librarians manage issues related to licensed electronic content; serve as the point person for electronic resource inquiries from faculty, staff, and students; and assist in the assessment and marketing of electronic resources, often in tandem with reference staff.

Library Webmaster

Many academic libraries hire librarians into webmaster positions in order to have someone with the requisite knowledge and expertise in librarianship to effectively design, maintain, and program the library website. This is especially true in large academic libraries where there are more librarians and thus more specialized positions. In small- to medium-sized libraries, librarians assigned in this capacity often assume this responsibility in addition to another position, such as systems, cataloging, or reference librarian; the webmaster piece is only a percentage of the position description. In such instances, it is also often the practice to assign several librarians to a web team in order to give enough time and attention to what is a full-time position in larger libraries.

Special Collections Librarian or Archivist

Special collections librarians and archivists manage archival collections, including the processing, arrangement, description, and cataloging of materials. They also perform a variety of other responsibilities: assist and instruct patrons in accessing and using materials housed in the archives, disseminate information about archival holdings, appraise papers and records for addition to the collections, provide bibliographic instruction to classes, prepare and update print and online reference tools, and develop exhibits. Archivists also perform outreach activities to various clienteles, as well as initiate donor contacts. Many archival positions require extensive technological knowledge in order for the archivist to create Internet accessible collections and finding aids. Knowledge of archival descriptive practices often required of archivists includes USMARC and electronic access tools such as HTML, Encoded Archival Description (EAD), and SGML.

Archivists typically need an ALA-accredited MLS, a master's degree in archival administration, or a master's degree in history or another related humanities field with an emphasis on archival administration. Additionally, some positions require certification from the Society of American Archivists.

Systems Librarian

Systems librarians manage integrated library systems, CD-ROM networks, and PC computing environments. They are often involved in the design and maintenance of the library's website. Systems librarians should stay abreast of developing technological trends in information delivery and service, and they should have some familiarity with library and information services for support of distance education. Systems librarians work in collaboration with other librarians to plan and implement the efficient delivery of electronic resources to users. The ability to collaborate, communicate, and negotiate effectively with staff in all areas of the library is essential.

Government Documents Librarian

While most federal information is available electronically via the Internet, there remain more than 1,200 depository libraries throughout the United States that assist with the dissemination of government information and ensure free access to citizens. Academic, public, and special libraries alike recognize the need to provide information specialists to assist users with statistical datasets, geographic information systems, and both electronic and traditional access to government information.

ADVICE TO ASPIRING ACADEMIC LIBRARIANS

If you are interested in academic librarianship, do your homework to learn as much as you can about various types of positions and institutions. If you are still in library school, take internships in academic libraries and/or seek paraprofessional or student employment in your campus library. Formally or informally interview academic librarians. Attend conferences and workshops focusing on academic librarianship and join professional associations, such as the Association of College and Research Libraries (ACRL). Read the professional literature, such as *The Journal of Academic Librarianship*. Join one or more discussion lists. Extend your inquiry beyond academic librarianship to the realm of higher education in general. The more you know going into an interview, the better you and your potential employer will be able to ensure a good match for your employment future.

RELATED READINGS

Fourie, Denise K., and David R. Dowell. *Libraries in the Information Age: An Introduction and Career Exploration*. Greenwood Village, Colo.: Libraries Unlimited, 2002.
Johnson, Timothy J. "Making it to the Major Leagues: Career Movement between Library and Archival Professions and from Small College to Large University Libraries." *Library Trends* 50, no. 4 (Spring 2002): 614–33.

ABOUT THE AUTHOR

Mary Anne Hansen is an associate professor and reference/instruction librarian at Montana State University—Bozeman; she recently completed a one-year appointment as interim associate dean. She has a master of library and information resources from the University of Arizona's distance education program, as well as a master of education in Adult and Higher Education, with a counseling emphasis, from Montana State University. Her undergraduate degree is a BA in modern languages, French, and English, also from Montana State University. Her professional and research interests include leadership, mentoring, library instruction, information literacy, Native American issues, and distance education. Each summer she cofacilitates an annual weeklong professional development institute at her campus for tribal college librarians from the United States and Canada.

4

Never a Dull Day in the School Library

Linda Rowan

- Do you have any books about the rain forest?
- Do you know a website the class can use for the Solar System unit?
- When can the students do research for their "great events" reports?
- Why do we have to learn about the Internet? We already know how to use it.
- My overhead projector needs a new bulb, and I need it for the first-period class.

These are just some of the questions you might be asked on a typical day as a school librarian. Whether the questions are from students or teachers, it is your job to assist them all while managing the library. Sound interesting? Yes, I would say there is never a dull day in a school library.

LIBRARY SCHOOL

I began working on my master's degree in library science with school library media certification because I wanted a career that was in demand. I already held a bachelor's degree and certifications in early childhood and elementary education, however, the job market was tight. As I perused the classifieds, I noticed many school library positions listed. I investigated the local colleges that offered school library media certification. Some colleges and universities offer school library media certification, but not all of those programs are accredited by the American Library Association (ALA). It is desirable to earn your degree and certification through an accredited program because many employers favor it. I had two options: I could earn a master's degree in education with the school library media certification from a college that was not accredited by the American Library Association, or I could earn a master's degree in library science with school library media certification from an accredited university. The master's degree was more comprehensive and would prepare me to work in all types of libraries not just a school library. The master's degree in library science proved to be more marketable in my case, as I was offered a job in a private school before completing my degree.

Here is a sample of courses you will take while earning a master's degree in library science with school library media certification:

- Information and Society
- Reference and Information Services
- Cataloging and Classification
- Management of School Library Media Centers
- Resources for Children
- Resources for Young Adults
- Collection Management
- School Library Fieldwork or Internship
- Instructional Role of the Information Professional

There may be required education classes for those who are not already certified teachers.

As a candidate for school library media certification, you will need to complete student teaching, also known as educational media center fieldwork. You will be assigned to work with a school librarian to gain practical experience in planning lessons and managing a school library on a daily basis. A word to the wise: You are not the clerical helper for the time you are assigned to the school. You should be interacting with the faculty and students in the school to assist with their information needs. If there is a shortage of school librarians, you may be able to bypass this student-teaching phase by getting a school library position. I would not recommend this path for someone who does not already have a background in education. The job of managing a school library can be challenging at the start, and if you also have to learn classroom management skills and lesson planning, it could be overwhelming. In any case, as a new school librarian you should be assigned a mentor, who is a librarian, to provide guidance and support in your first year.

The certification process involves more than completing courses and student teaching. Many states require you to take the Praxis Exam, which is a national teacher certification test. You should discuss the process with your college advisor to determine which tests are required. It is important to consider all the states where you may seek employment so that you can take the appropriate tests required for certification. When you have completed all the courses and passed the certification exam, the college or university will submit your certification application and the required documentation to the state department of education. Finally, with the certificate in hand you will be ready to look for your first job.

TYPES OF SCHOOLS

Attaining a master's degree of library science and school library media certification will qualify you to work in any school library, kindergarten through grade twelve. This has its advantages because there is some diversity among school libraries. In fact, there is much to consider in seeking a job. Some options to explore include whether you want to work in a private or a public school, and with which age level you prefer to work.

In a private school you will most likely be the only librarian. You will have to join local library associations to meet other librarians. There are a variety of electronic discussion lists available on the Internet for librarians, but nothing beats sitting down with others in your profession to share ideas. One advantage to working in a private school is that there is less bureaucracy than in a public school.

In a public school you will find yourself as one librarian among many serving that particular school district or system. There will be periodic meetings that will enable you to meet the other librarians. You will not be the sole decision maker. Requests for materials and equipment for your school will be channeled through the bureaucracy and it may take some time before your request is approved or denied. In both types of schools the ability to acquire the items needed to benefit the students and teachers is contingent upon the available budget for the library. One advantage to working in a public school district is that there may be some flexibility that will allow you to change schools or grade levels periodically.

The three basic categories of schools are elementary, middle, and high school. Elementary schools seem to offer the widest range of grades. Some schools are the traditional kindergarten-through-grade-eight configuration. This is often the case in private schools. Another common configuration is kindergarten to grade five or six. The range of grades in an elementary school will determine the type of activities you will be doing in the library. Those schools that are kindergarten to grade four will be using the library to learn about the genres of literature and to be introduced to information literacy skills. If it is a kindergarten to grade eight school, you will be sharing literature and collaborating with classroom teachers on projects. The students will be developing their skills in locating and using information. When considering work as an elementary school librarian, be sure to find out the grade structure of the school. If you know that you prefer working with young children, you may not be happy in a kindergarten-to-grade-eight school. One advantage of a kindergarten through grade eight school is the diverse grade levels. You can be the storyteller for the youngest students, the teacher who introduces them to lifelong literacy skills, and the guide who helps them refine their skills. If you do your job well you will have students of all ages who love literature and can locate and use information.

The middle school structure is often grades six through nine. It will vary based on the local or state structure for schools. This grade level can be challenging. You will be working with students in their early teens, which can be a trying time for them and those who teach them. You may find that in the middle school you do less work in the area of literature and more in research. You will need to stay informed about the best search engines and be prepared to instruct in the use of periodical databases.

The high school level will find you doing activities similar to the middle school level, but with older students. You will need to be prepared to assist as they research careers and colleges as well as required class work. In both the middle and high school there is often less demand in the area of literature because there is less time for leisure reading.

So how do you decide where you belong? That decision may be easy if your undergraduate work was in education and you have worked in schools. However, if you are changing careers you will want to explore the schools. You will have a course that is a field study or practicum scheduled toward the end of your coursework. This will be a good opportunity to gain experience. You may want to observe in some schools prior to this so that you know what to expect. Try to find out if there are any schools offering internships or volunteer opportunities. The best way to understand what it is like to work with a particular age group is to experience it firsthand.

SCHOOL LIBRARY SCHEDULES

School library schedules have been a hot topic for some time. For many years there was only one type of schedule, the fixed schedule. The schedule that is popular today is the flexible schedule. In some schools you will find a combination of the two that I call a modified flexible schedule.

The fixed schedule is one that gives each class an allotted time to go to the library. Usually this time will be the prep time for the classroom teacher. One advantage to this type of schedule is that every class visits the library regularly. The time in the library can be used for information literacy skills lessons, selecting books for leisure reading, or research. What takes place depends upon the amount of collaboration between the teachers and librarian. The disadvantage is that in a large school the librarian's time may be completely taken up with these scheduled classes, leaving little time for collaboration or library management.

In a library with a flexible schedule there is no prescribed time for a class to use the library. In this situation the librarian needs to be very proactive, frequently talking to the teachers to learn what units are being taught and then advising them on the resources available in the library. In this scenario it is helpful to have a large blank calendar so teachers can sign up for times to bring their students to the library. It is helpful to have forms available for the teacher to note what type of work they will be doing so that you can plan the lesson together. Schools using this schedule may also have blocks of time at the beginning or end of the day for students to borrow and return books. The disadvantage to this type of schedule is that there may be some classes that never come to the library. It will be up to the librarian to try to work with those teachers to encourage them to use the library, even if it is just to get books for book reports.

The modified flexible schedule is what I like to think of as the best of both worlds. There are times set aside for classes to visit the library on a regular schedule. Depending on the size of the school, these times may be weekly or biweekly. There are also large, open time blocks that will allow the teachers to bring classes for additional library time. The librarian and the teacher will usually collaborate on the goals and objectives for these visits.

I have a modified flexible schedule in my library and feel that it works very well. My school is pre-kindergarten to grade eight. There is a morning and afternoon pre-kindergarten class and one class of each other grade. The pre-kindergarten through grade five students have a scheduled weekly library time. Each of those classes will have a lesson and time to select books to borrow. Often the lesson is something that I have arranged in collaboration with their teacher. The sixth- through eighth-grade classes do not have a scheduled library time. I work with the subject-area teachers to encourage the use of the library. I schedule one of these classes during each trimester. It is during that trimester that I have specific goals and objectives to meet. These goals and objectives are linked to topics the students are studying in one or more subject areas. The sixth-grade curriculum includes the use of the Internet and searching skills. The seventh grade completes a guided research paper. I teach bibliographic citations and assist in developing search terms and locating information and materials. This is truly a project that involves collaboration across the curriculum. The eighth-grade students hone their research writing skills as they complete an independent research paper on a topic of their choice. Once again I teach and reinforce the bibliographic citations and search skills learned the previous year.

There are many benefits to the modified flexible schedule. It allows one to see the younger children regularly, at an age when it is important for them to become familiar with the library and how to locate books and information. It also gives one an opportunity to collaborate with the teachers. The open blocks of time in the schedule allow the librarian time for managing the library. This is where flexibility is important. I have made it a rule that student and teacher use of the library comes first. There are times when an opportunity to use the library arises serendipitously. Even if I was planning to do some weeding or work on a book or magazine order, I will reschedule my plans so that a class can use the library. There will always be more time later for mundane library tasks.

OTHER RESPONSIBILITIES

All teachers find out that they have some responsibilities beyond their own classroom. The same is true for school library media specialists. School administrators will ask faculty and staff members to serve on committees. The committees can serve a variety of purposes, from planning a special event to revising the curriculum to reviewing current trends or policies in education. It is important for school library media specialists to be involved, especially in areas of curriculum and technology. You need to be aware of curriculum changes in order to maintain a library that is an integral part of the school. Technology plays such a big role in the way students and teachers access and use information that your input on any technology committee is essential. Committee work is also an opportunity to establish yourself as a leader in your educational community.

Many schools, both private and public, request that teachers and staff members perform a number of duties during the school year. These assignments may include supervising such things as lunch, recess, or dismissal if there are no paid monitors for these jobs. These routine duties are things you must do for the health and safety of the students.

PROFESSIONAL DEVELOPMENT/CONTINUING EDUCATION

The amount of information available increases regularly. The variety of means to access information changes almost as rapidly. For these reasons one must continue to monitor changes in the profession and to learn about current trends. One of the best ways to do this is to become a member of a professional organization, such as the American Library Association (ALA). Within the ALA there are many divisions. The American Association of School Librarians is the division that focuses on the concerns of school librarians. One alternative to joining a national organization is to join your state library association.

Conferences offer great opportunities for networking, attending workshops, meeting authors, and seeing demonstrations and exhibits by vendors associated with libraries. This is especially important to school librarians working alone in private schools who don't have the built-in network afforded by positions in school districts.

If you cannot attend a conference, it is important to be aware of local professional development opportunities that are offered in the form of workshops. These workshops may be offered by the local school district, another educational agency, or a business.

While the main reason to continue your professional development should be intrinsic, there is another reason. Many states mandate that educators fulfill a required number of continuing education credits or hours over a period of time to maintain certification. These credits and hours can often be earned by attending conferences and workshops. In the area of school library work this is important because the type and means of accessing information is constantly evolving. You will want to be able to share the latest innovations with your students and faculty members.

A TYPICAL DAY

I open the doors of the library at 8 A.M. The library server is up and running. I turn on the printer and computers. At 8:10 the students go to the classrooms. They will have twenty minutes to unpack and get organized for the day. Fourth and fifth grade will have library today, so they stop by to return and renew books. Occasionally a student will come in to use a computer to print an assignment. They know that they can e-mail a document to school or bring it on a disk to print if they have printer problems at home.

During homeroom, I print out overdue notices to distribute to the students later. I check my lesson plan book and get the folders that have been prepared with materials for each class. It will be a busy day: one pre-kindergarten class, two fourth-grade groups, a Reading Olympics team meeting, and two groups of fifth-grade students. When the first class period starts, I collect the attendance folders to deliver to the office. This is one of my nonlibrary duties. As I collect the attendance folders, I look for books that teachers and students have waiting to return. Many of the primary-level teachers have a designated place for books being returned to the library. As I drop off the attendance folders I check my mailbox. I find the usual: catalogs, magazines, and teacher requests for materials. I stop in the pre-kindergarten classroom to collect their library books.

Back in the library I check in all the books that I gathered. Then I run the reports of materials checked out for the pre-kindergarten, fourth-, and fifth-grade classes. Theses lists will be used to write reminder notes for books that were forgotten. The parent volunteer who will assist with the pre-kindergarten class arrives around 9:30. I explain what I will be doing with the class this morning. While she shelves books that have been checked in, I log in the magazines. Magazines for students will have a sign-out card attached; they are placed in the magazine rack. Professional magazines will have a routing slip attached for circulation to faculty and staff members. These magazines will be placed in the teacher mailboxes later. The first-grade class has requested resources available about spiders. I have a bibliography for spiders already printed, and the volunteer will locate these books while I read to the pre-kindergarten class. Next I place a variety of fiction and nonfiction books on one of the tables for selection by the pre-kindergarten class. I put out about fifteen books for the ten students because no child wants to have to take the last book. During the first half of the school year it is easier to have them select from a small group of books rather than go directly to the shelves.

Pre-kindergarten arrives at 10:00 and will stay for one half hour. I get them seated on the floor in the story area. We talk about Halloween, which is only a week away. Today the story is one that has a lot of class participation. Each child has a picture of an item from the story that they will place on the magnetic board at the appropriate place in the story. As I read aloud, they join in with a few lines that are repeated throughout the story. By the end of the story they find that all the parts they placed on the board make a scarecrow. They want to hear the story again, but now they only have ten minutes to select books. I take them to the table to look at the preselected books. As usual some students take the first book they look at, while others can't decide which one they want. One child is upset because his friend took the frog book. While I go to the shelves to locate another frog book, the parent volunteer is checking out the students' books at the computer. When all the children have selected and checked out a book, they line up to go back to their classroom. While I take them back, the volunteer shelves the books that were left on the table before she leaves. I am grateful for volunteers helping with the younger children.

I place the magazines in the teacher mailboxes and check my mailbox again before getting a quick cup of coffee. In one half hour I will be working with the fourth-grade students.

The fourth grade is divided into two groups. I will have half the class for forty-five minutes, while the other half is in the computer lab. Then we switch. In the next ninety minutes, I will teach the same lesson twice. As the class arrives I distribute reminder notes to those students who forgot their library books. Today the lesson is about using the encyclopedia. We will review the rules for locating people by last name in preparation for research they will do tomorrow on a famous person from Pennsylvania. After the lesson, which lasts twenty to thirty minutes, the students have time to select library books or magazines. Some browse the shelves, and some use the computer card catalog. I roam around the library to offer assistance when not checking out books at the circulation desk. As students select and check out books, they go back to their seats to read. Sometimes this is not as quiet an activity as I would like it to be. At 12:30 when the fourth-grade library class is finished, they leave to go to lunch, and the fifth-grade Reading Olympics team arrives. No lunch or recess duty for me today! For the next half-hour we will discuss the books the students are currently reading as we eat lunch together. The team will meet every other week in preparation for competition in the spring.

Now I have a break for a half hour—time to use the restroom, check the mailbox, and chat with a few teachers in the faculty room before returning to the library to get ready for the fifth grade. The last ninety minutes of the day are spent with the fifth grade. We follow the same routine as the fourth grade. Today the lesson is an introduction to the ten main Dewey Classes. Then they will select books. I encourage the Reading Olympics team members to bring their books to read while others are selecting books. Some browse the books and magazines while others use the card catalog. If they have an assigned book for their class, very few students will borrow books.

As the day ends, I check e-mail. I assess what was accomplished today in all the classes and turn to the next week in my lesson plan book. I write down what we will be doing the next time we meet. Then I turn back to the present week to see what tomorrow will bring. I have scheduled classes for first and second grade tomorrow. As I leave for the day I will put a bin in their classrooms for their library books to be collected. I get out the folders for the classes scheduled to see if all the materials have been prepared. I close the online card catalogs and shut down all the computers. Tomorrow will be another busy day in the library.

RELATED READINGS

Fox, Carol J. "Designing a Flexible Schedule for an Elementary School Library Media Center." *Library Talk* (January/February 2001): 10–14.

ABOUT THE AUTHOR

Linda Rowan has a BA in early childhood education from Holy Family University, and a master's in Library Science from Drexel University. She is employed as a school library media specialist at Grey Nun Academy in Yardley, Pennsylvania, and an adult reference librarian at the Margaret R. Grundy Memorial Library in Bristol, Pennsylvania. In her spare time she is an avid bird watcher.

5

From Makeup to Missiles: Special Libraries Mirror the Diversity and Complexity of Today's Business Economy

Regina H. Lee

With fluctuating economies, globalization, and an enriched technological environment, today's corporations exist in a world of continuous change. Most of the current workforce is information savvy; employees have been exposed to and have access to more information through technology than any preceding generation. Instant gratification is expected. Connectivity is the norm. Continuous learning is a basic life skill. Expectations for quality are high.

The current social and business milieu offers challenge and opportunity for managers of information organizations that cater to the needs of a specialized clientele. Information professionals are challenged to provide quick, accurate responses to the demands of a workforce that expects specific, targeted, and practical data necessary for informed decision making. No matter what you call it—information services, knowledge resources, content management/deployment, or competitive intelligence—special libraries are as complex and diverse as today's digital business economy.

WHAT IS A SPECIAL LIBRARY/LIBRARIAN?

Special libraries vary in size from the solo librarian to large enterprises resembling academic libraries. Clients or users exist throughout an organization and vary depending on the industry, but they may belong to such diverse operations groups as manufacturing, market analysis, information technology, purchasing, media relations, research and development, and executive administration. Corporate information centers are found in industries such as:

- Cosmetics, toiletries, and personal care
- Food and beverage
- Finance
- Pharmaceuticals and healthcare
- Architecture
- Advertising
- Oil and gas
- Engineering
- Aeronautics and defense

The *Occupational Outlook Handbook* lists libraries maintained by government agencies, law firms, museums, professional associations, and religious organizations as some of the employment opportunities available for special librarians.[1] Nonprofit organizations supporting the arts and humanities should also be added to the list, as well as any other special-interest business or organization, whether for profit or not for profit, that relies on information or knowledge to operate successfully in today's entrepreneurial climate. According to Guy St. Clair, specialized librarianship involves a particular or "special" subject or field of interest, "special" customers for whom services are provided, and/or a collaborative relationship between information provider and the information customer.[2]

Information brokers or independent information professionals are also considered special librarians, but they own and operate businesses to provide information services on a contractual basis to more than one client. These objective intermediaries serve industries not heavily reliant on information but with an occasional need to embark upon an information quest to support a key project, organizations that outsource their information service function as a whole, or information centers that have determined outsourcing some functions enables them to focus on higher priority demands and maximize limited resources.

Vanishing resources and troubled economic times require reengineering the organizational structure to focus on core business functions and implies that outsourcing noncore functions may be a necessity. Frequently viewed as a high overhead support function, information centers have become victims of outsourcing. In addition, with the proliferation of electronic content and the ability to increase access and service to remote users, the need for housing on-site information sources has diminished. In a recent *Outsell Inc.* industry update, analysts declared that the "corporate library is dead."[3] They quickly clarified that it is the corporate library as a physical place that is dead, but "the bottom line is that in the eyes of corporate information users and other observers, the value of information professionals is in the services and expertise they provide. The corporate *librarian* lives!"[4]

WHAT DO SPECIAL LIBRARIANS DO?

Corporate librarians "strategically use information . . . to advance the mission of the organization. [They] harness the current and appropriate technology tools to deliver the best services, provide the most relevant and accessible resources, develop and deliver teaching tools to maximize clients' use of information, and capitalize on the library and information environment of the 21st century."[5]

What the earlier, well-crafted summary statement from the Special Libraries Association does not imply is that in the current economy, information center managers must also:

- Strategically align the services of the center with the primary mission of the parent organization
- Manage the center as a business within the organization
- Make the center visible to key administrative personnel
- Identify critical performance measures
- Anticipate the need to demonstrate value

Services must be targeted to the key drivers of the business and to the interests of the managers responsible for leading the organization. "It is vitally important that library managers have needs assessment, user benefit, and loyalty research at hand so they can, without undue delay, effectively craft a value proposition that carries weight with executives" (*Outsell Inc.*, April 2001).[6]

The current reality for corporate information professionals is:

- Tracking vendors, products, pricing, technologies, and applications
- Negotiating contracts and licensing agreements
- Leveraging budgets to maximize realistic acquisition strategies
- Benchmarking best practices
- Organizing and retrieving information
- Defining market segments of information users within the organization
- Developing market plans

Today's corporate culture is information-centric and promotes proactive, client-centered services. Information managers are required to provide more service with fewer resources. This requires an in-depth knowledge of the available information products, realistic pricing strategies, acceptable use constraints in licensing agreements, and the required infrastructure to push the products to the users' desktops.

The information-seeking behaviors of Generation Xers and millennials—who are quickly becoming the new workforce leaders—have been shaped by the information glut of the Internet. As a result, the profile of the information user is changing as radically as the information environment. Librarians encourage and teach clients to be self-sufficient. Users perform initial research at their desktops but still come to librarians for the more complex searches and in-depth information. The basic information search, as a result, is more complex and requires greater skills and more efficient techniques for searching out the obscure.

To create vested partnerships, to develop user appreciation of the service, and to determine user recognition of the value of the service, some special librarians actively solicit financial commitments from other departments for products purchased in support of their specific information needs. Other librarians try to anticipate users' needs by providing current awareness services tailored to individual profiles and delivered via email. Traditional services such as information searching and research services, provision of access to external or secondary information, and management of the physical library continue to be essential functions; however, they are yielding to the provision and dissemination of digital content as well as managing internal information resources. Special librarians may also serve as webmasters and advisers for design and navigation of the digital landscape. In addition, they may use company intranets to deliver products and services and to identify user needs. Capitalizing on the visibility of the company intranet is one strategy successfully used by many corporate libraries to keep users aware of what libraries have to offer.

WHAT COMPETENCIES/SKILLS DO SPECIAL LIBRARIANS NEED?

It may be hard to believe because of the recent Enron and Martha Stewart scandals, but corporate America has become value-driven. Employers require honesty, integrity, and personal ethics. Human resources and management organizations tout the description of the ideal candidate for jobs in the new millennium as "passionate," "dedicated to excellence," and "energetic." Note that none of these characteristics are specific to the theory and practice of information science or any other profession for that matter. While it is generally understood that a master's in library or information science is the basic credential for a professional position in any library career, the multidimensional role of special librarians demands a full complement of well-honed management and interpersonal communication skills as well as a broad-based set of professional competencies.

In the current workplace, being well educated and technically competent in your chosen field is often not enough. The successful information professional must demonstrate:

- Adaptability and willingness to embrace change
- Accountability
- Creativity, resourcefulness, and imagination
- Courage and risk taking
- Understanding of diversity
- Persistence
- Positive attitude
- Curiosity and dedication to learning

To effectively respond to workforce demands for specific, targeted, and practical data, information professionals must be fully engaged in time-management, multitasking, written and oral communications, marketing, and management. Analyzing vendors, products, pricing, technologies, and applications requires the use of critical thinking and deductive reasoning. Negotiating contracts, staying involved by participating in companywide project teams, and developing interdepartmental alliances requires the ability to influence, motivate, and persuade with oral and written communications, but it should be emphasized that effective communication in the digital arena requires a significantly different style than the traditional print media. Finally, budgeting, planning, and personnel management skills also are essential for operating as a business within the parent organization.

Developing marketable personal attributes and managerial skills does not replace the need for a solid education in library and/or information science from one of almost sixty schools accredited by the American Library Association. Key findings in the executive summary of the KALIPER Report (Kellogg-ALISE Information Professionals and Education Renewal Project) show that in addition to the word *library* being removed from the name of the schools, current education and curricular trends include:[7]

- Transforming traditional courses to incorporate concepts with broader application
- Examining information problems across environments
- Increased interdisciplinary studies
- Stronger emphasis on information technology infrastructure
- Distance learning

Unless you are a recent graduate, you probably perform many daily tasks that use skills you never learned in school. Traditional courses such as cataloging and classification are still valuable, but today's librarian must evolve to embrace information usability and metadata. By examining information practice and theory across environments, new graduates are empowered to seek employment throughout the information industry, including such areas as market research, competitive intelligence, and information technology. Frequently, today's programs incorporate studies from the schools of business, humanities, behavioral sciences, computer sciences, and cognitive studies. Topics such as web page design, script languages, intranets, multimedia design, and telecommunications are emphasized now, while they were barely considered relevant to the field ten years ago. Distance education caters to the flexibility needs of the GenXers and millennials but, it also opens the door for the midcareer professionals who can retool their skill sets through continuing education.

Ultimately, the best education is experience. No matter where you are in the career cycle, a mentor will provide valuable insights for problem solving, improving job performance, and leadership. The mentoring relationship is reciprocal. While providing a protégé with advice and encouragement based on actual practice, the mentor also receives the benefit of the mentee's fresh perspective and is challenged to stay on top of the current trends of the profession.

HOW DO I FIND A JOB?

Mentors may be your best way of opening doors into the job market. A trusted advisor can help you evaluate your skills, pinpoint your character strengths, define your values, identify potential employers, and introduce you to contacts in the profession. Whether you are a student or making a career change, just knowing people is a key strategy for finding the right job. Capitalize on contacts made during internships and on informal relationships with faculty or colleagues. Get actively involved in professional associations such as:

- Special Libraries Association (SLA—www.sla.org)
- American Society for Information Science and Technology (ASIST—www.asis.org)
- Association of Independent Information Professionals (AIIP—www.aiip.org)
- Association for Information Management Professionals (ARMA International—www.arma.org)
- Library and Information Technology Association (LITA—www.lita.org)

Most of these organizations have student chapters. Make yourself visible by presenting papers or poster sessions. Accept committee appointments and nominations for office to develop your leadership skills. Demonstrate your knowledge and communication skills to as broad an audience as possible. You never know who your next champion will be.

Career planning requires a fundamental understanding of yourself, the industry in which you are seeking employment, and your potential employer. As a special librarian you will most likely need to perform market research, and there is no better time to begin than when you are personally invested in the outcome of the analysis. Identify an industry that is of interest to you. Study market projections to determine if the industry is growing and determine whom the key players are. Knowing how long a company has been in business and its current financial status can help you identify companies with job stability and potential for promotions. Read company annual reports and trade journals in addition to surfing the Internet to determine which organizations' missions and goals are strategically aligned with your own and what the corporate climate is.

Classifieds in professional newsletters, association and corporate job lines, and online job boards will list available jobs. Tailor your resume to the industry and to the job in which you are interested. You should also include a cover letter, written for your target audience. A bright, snappy, informal cover letter works for an advertising firm, but it is probably not the best option for a highly technical industry or a business that is committed to a formal, conservative corporate culture. Your cover letter should highlight the value you will add to the company that invests in you (e.g., foreign language skills, additional degrees, professional certifications or licenses).

Remember that job titles and ads often do not tell the whole story. Read between the lines to determine whether a specific skill set is critical or if the position can be mastered by someone who can creatively adapt previous experiences to the current situation. And finally, prepare for the interview. Know how to respond to open-ended questions, discover the dress code, and understand your worth when salary is discussed.

WHAT FUTURE IS THERE IN SPECIAL LIBRARIES?

With the graying of the profession, many experienced librarians will be leaving it over the next decade. Estimates vary from 20 percent to 60 percent. This exodus creates a shortage at a time when the media reports that jobs for librarians are in "hot demand." *CNNMoney's* "Hot Jobs Now" article lists corporate librarians with an average salary of $60,000 to $65,000.[8] A headline from *The Wall Street Journal*'s (wsj.com) *CareerJournal* states, "Demand Explodes for Librarians with High-Tech Research Skills."[9] But recruiting may be difficult since all librarians are still fighting the stereotypical images perpetuated by librarian action figures and commercials where readers "shush" the gregarious salesman. The SLA Competencies statement projects that now and in the future, with the amazing growth of the Internet and the rise of electronically available communications and storage media, information professionals are needed more than ever to filter and customize information to the needs of the user.[10] Once again, *Outsell Inc.* hits the nail on the head: "Innovative librarians never die; they just adapt to the newest reality and press on."[11]

NOTES

1. "BLS career information. Librarian," *Occupational Outlook Handbook*, U.S. Department of Labor, Bureau of Labor Statistics. stats.bls.gov/k12/text/red_003t.htm (last accessed 15 September 2003).

2. Douglas Newcomb, "Knowledge Services and SLA's History: An Interview with Guy St. Clair," *Information Outlook* 7, no. 9 (September 2003).

3. Mary Corcoran, "The Corporate Library is Dead," *Outsell's e-briefs*, 15 August 2003. www.outsellinc.com/outsell/news/030815CorpLibDead.html (last accessed 25 September 2003).

4. David Curle, "In Outsell's Opinion: The Corporate Librarian Lives," *Outsells e-briefs*, 5 September 2003.

5. "Competencies for Information Professionals of the 21st Century," Rev. ed., Special Libraries Association, Special Committee on Competencies for Special Librarians (June 2003). www.sla.org/content/learn/comp2003/index.cfm or www.sla.org/PDFs/Competencies2003.pdf (last accessed 25 September 2003).

6. Shelva Suggs, "More Than One Way to Learn," *Information Outlook* 7, no. 5 (May 2003).

7. Association for Library and Information Science Education, *Educating Library and Information Professionals for a New Century: The KALIPER Report* (July 2000). www.alise.org/publications/kaliper.pdf (last accessed 15 September 2003).

8. CNN "Hot Jobs Now." money.cnn.com/2003/08/28/pf/saving/hotjobsnow/ (last accessed 15 September 2003).

9. Maura Rurak, "Demand Explodes for Librarians with High-Tech Research Skills. National Business Employment Weekly," *Career Journal Wall Street Journal* (1998). www.careerjournal.com (last accessed 15 September 2004).

10. "Competencies for Information Professionals."

11. Curle, "In Outsell's Opinion."

RELATED READINGS

Axiometrics International, Inc. *Professional Competencies Assessment (120)*. www .axelrodlearning.com/professionalcompetency.pdf (last accessed 15 September 2003).

Bernbom, Gerry. "The Information Professions and the Information Professionals." *Beyond the Beginning: The Global Digital Library, An International Conference.* (UKOLN on behalf of JISC, CNI, BLRIC, CAUSE, and CAUL. Queen Elizabeth II Conference Centre, London, UK, June 16–17, 1997.) www.ukoln.ac.uk/ services/papers/bl/blri078/content/repor~11.htm (last accessed 15 September 2003).

Boiko, Bob. "Understanding Content Management." *Bulletin of the American Society for Information Science and Technology* 28, no. 1 (October/November 2001).

Career Options 2002/2003. *Canadian Association of Career Educators and Employers (CACEE)*. www.cacee.com/coptions/2002/c5.asp (last accessed 15 September 2003).

Cates, Jo. "CKO Wanted." *Bulletin Business & Finance Division* (Fall 2000).

Chadwick, Terry Brainerd. "Career Planning." Presentation for the "Plan is Not a Four Letter Word" program of the Oregon Chapter Special Libraries Association. 28 September 2001. www.tbchad.com/career_planning2.html (last accessed 15 September 2003).

"The Changing Roles of Content Deployment Functions: Corporate Information Professionals." 6, no. 14 *Information about Information Briefing Outsell, Inc.* (6 June 2003).

Donald, Roslyn. "Marketing: A Challenge for Corporate Librarians." www .insitepro.com/donald3.htm (last accessed 15 September 2003).

Find/SVP "Checking in with the Future (Are We There Yet?)." *Information Advisor* 15, no. 3 (March 2003).

Gordon, Rachel Singer, and Sarah L. Nesbitt. "Market Yourself Online!" *M.L.S. Marketing Library Service* 15 (October/November 2001).

Gross, Margaret. "Competitive Intelligence: A Librarian's Empirical Approach." *Searcher* 8 (September 2000).

IRN Research. "Brief No 4: Should Information Centres be Outsourced? Why, When and How." Free Research Brief. www.irn-research.com/globalframe.htm (last accessed June 2002).

Jones, Alyn. "Corporate Intranets: The Last Tool of Survival for Corporate Library?" jimmy.qmuc.ac.uk/usr/im94jone/ (last accessed 15 June 1998). In: Hall, Hazel, and Alyn Jones. "Show Off the Corporate Library." *International Journal of Information Management* 20 (2000).

Murphy, Teresa. This article was published in the fall of 1995 in the Special Libraries Association, Western Canadian Chapter's *Chapter 8* with the title "Cold Call Your Way to Job Success." The article is reprinted with permission of the author under the new title: "Finding Good Jobs in Tough Times." *Provenance: The Electronic Magazine* 1 (March 1996). www.netpac.com/provenance/vol1/no2/features/findjobs.htm (last accessed 24 September 2004).

Paul, Cheryl J. "Special Library Intranet Sites: Trends and Issues." www.libsci.sc.edu/tephen/students/paul/intranetsites.htm (last accessed 15 September 2003).

Primary Research Group. *Corporate Library Benchmarks*: *2002–2003* (July 2002).

Rosenstein, Bruce. "99 Words or Fewer: Advice for New Special Librarians from Some of the Top Practitioners in the Field." *Course Information. LSC #818 The Special Library/Information Center.* slis.cua.edu/courses/818/adv4h.htm (last accessed 15 September 2003).

Sklar, Jeannie, and Karen Trimberger. "Advice for Future Information Professionals." www.si.umich.edu/library-cultures/special/corporate/advice (last accessed 15 September 2003).

Sykes, Jan, and Richard Fletcher. "Global Study of Information Professionals: Emerging Issues and Trends" (2000). www.factiva.com/infopro/globalwhitepaperlet.pdf (last accessed 15 September 2003).

"The Value of Libraries: Justifying Corporate Information Centers in the Year of Accountability." *Information about Information Briefing Outsell, Inc.* 4, no. 10 (23 April 2001).

Weaver, Susanna. "Non-Traditional Jobs for Special Librarians." www.libsci.sc.edu/bob/class/clis724/SpecialLibrariesHandbook/non-traditional.htm (last accessed 15 September 2003).

ABOUT THE AUTHOR

Regina H. Lee, senior information research specialist, has been at Mary Kay Inc. since 1998. For almost twenty-five years, Ms. Lee worked in the public sector as a health sciences librarian. In addition to experience in both hospital and academic health sciences center libraries, she served as the associate director of the South Central Region in the Regional Medical Library Program of the National Library of Medicine (currently the National Network of Libraries of Medicine). Currently serving as an officer for the South Central Chapter of the Medical Library Association, Ms. Lee has been actively involved in national, regional, and state library associations including the Special Libraries Association. Outreach to and education for colleagues and constituents are a central theme in her career.

6

A Bird's-Eye View: Working for a Library Consortium

Kim Armstrong

Library consortia are plentiful in the United States and throughout the world. Beyond that they share really only one commonality among them: to serve a group of libraries, alike or diverse, near or far. An instructor's note for a course on library consortia at the University of Washington Information School says, "For our purposes, a library consortium is any organization that helps libraries collaborate" (libweb.uoregon.edu/orbis/iSchool/). As a profession, librarians are among the most cooperative because the sharing of work and expertise enhances the collections and services that libraries can provide to their users. Cooperatives can also provide a cost savings to their members and save duplication of staff time and effort. Consortia were designed to exploit the power of collaboration among libraries.

A DEFINITION OF CONSORTIA AND NETWORKS

Consortia are formed and grouped by several formulas. The first is by type of library. There are academic library consortia such as the CIC (Committee on Institutional Cooperation) whose members are twelve research universities in the midwestern United States. There are public library consortia, such as OPLIN in Ohio, which serves every public library in Ohio. There are special library consortia, school library consortia, and multitype consortia that include public, academic, and/or special libraries, such as SEFLIN in Florida. Geographic location is also a common grouping for cooperatives. Consortia have been formed based on all the members being in the same city or larger urban area, which is the case with the Triangle Research Libraries Network in the Triangle region of North Carolina. There are statewide consortia such as GALILEO in Georgia. Consortia can also span the same geographic region, as NERL does in the Northeast. There are even consortia that cover an entire country like the Canadian National Site Licensing Project. Recently a number of libraries have banded together to form "buying clubs." The purpose of these consortia is to license or purchase electronic content at the lowest price based on a bulk-purchase model. There are real advantages to such an arrangement, but these consortia, or clubs, can't necessarily be defined by any of the traditional groupings.

Online Computer Library Center (OCLC) networks are another type of cooperative environment with employment opportunities for librarians. OCLC is a nonprofit, member-based library cooperative based in Dublin, Ohio. It has over 45,000 member libraries worldwide. Libraries use OCLC services to "locate, acquire, catalog, lend, and preserve library materials" (www.oclc.org). OCLC has seventeen service centers whose mission is to provide OCLC services to a specific geographic region in the United States. An example of an OCLC network is the MINITEX Library Information Network that serves all library types in Minnesota, North Dakota, and South Dakota. The networks usually have larger staffs than library consortia described above. Librarians who work in these service centers, or networks, sell OCLC services to member libraries, provide training on OCLC services to members, offer technical support, and manage administrative and fiscal services for library payments for OCLC services. In addition, networks often provide other non-OCLC services such as interlibrary loan document delivery, storage facilities, and shared or group purchasing for products and resources. The types of jobs held by librarians currently working in these networks include preservation specialist, consultant to libraries, digital services librarian, training librarian, and electronic resources coordinator. To read more about the OCLC Networks and Service Centers, see www.oclc.org/memberscouncil/documents/directory.pdf.

THE WORK ENVIRONMENT

The work environment in a consortium can be very different from the library environment. Some consortia are housed within libraries, on university campuses, or near the institutions they serve. Others have staff that work in independent office settings. A consortium office can employ between one and hundreds of employees. Librarians employed by consortia generally serve the librarians and staff of their member libraries as their primary clientele and often have little or no contact with library users.

Consortia staff work very closely with staff from the libraries, often through committee structures, so that much of the work is accomplished through collaboration rather than individually. Since the planning and decision making happens in a distributed environment between the consortium and its members, communication is critical to shaping the direction and services of a consortium. Consortia use the Web, e-mail, and teleconferencing technologies to streamline interaction with members. Depending on the geographic coverage of a consortium, staff may not be able to meet face to face with library staff very often. Meetings often require travel and significant planning. Sometimes libraries designate individual staff to spend a percentage of their work time on consortial projects or priorities. Most frequently, consortial staff work with library "volunteers" who take on committee assignments and program responsibilities in addition to their regularly assigned duties.

Because the work that is available to a librarian in consortia spans library functions, the preparation for such work will vary based on your desired career path. However, the best preparation for a consortium office is to work in a library. All libraries share similar functions that translate well to consortia. Since consortia staffs interact most often with library employees instead of the users of the services, an understanding of the library environment, administrative structures, budget practices and cycles, and priorities can be an important component to being well prepared for consortial work. A few staff at consortium can serve many staff at libraries, so a broad familiarity with different types of job functions and responsibilities can be an advantage.

HELPFUL JOB SKILLS AND RELATED WORK EXPERIENCE

Consortia jobs require skills that can be directly developed and harvested from job positions in correlating library units. Knowledge of technology (IT) administration and systems department management would be useful in a consortium that runs shared bibliographic systems, union catalogs, and Internet applications. Librarians and nonlibrarians hold technical and programming jobs at consortia. The technical infrastructure at some consortia is quite extensive, while other consortia provide little or no technical or computing services to library members. Technology librarians at consortia work closely with vendors to acquire and provide information systems for their libraries. In some cases the consortium leads negotiations for the purchase of integrated library systems that will be hosted and supported centrally. And some consortia actually create new technological tools and services for members or market and sell to the library community as CARL in Colorado did with their Gold Rush product (grweb.coalliance.org/).

To pursue a position with training responsibilities, experience in library instruction programs would be good preparation. An instructional services librarian comes into contact with all types of library users and must be able to consider a variety of learning styles and methods for the delivery of instruction. That experience is directly relevant for consortial trainers. In some instances, librarians at the consortium design training for member libraries. In the case of OCLC networks, training may be designed externally or centrally by OCLC, and the regional network employee delivers the training to staffs of the member libraries. Finally, consortial trainers may identify external consultants or trainers to come and deliver a "pre-packaged" program to the consortium for a fee. Reference work would also be relevant, since there is an educational function tied to assisting patrons with their questions and research.

Resource sharing is often one of the core reasons for a consortium's existence. Library members want streamlined, automated, and often expedited processes for sharing their material with their partners. The work of interlibrary loan and circulation departments is a good basis for understanding how libraries serve their patrons from remote collections. Consortial support for resource sharing may involve the creation of a union catalog that lists all members' holdings, development of shared policies and performance goals for a delivery service, and negotiation of contracts with delivery services such as UPS or Lanter. Consortia also acquire software for direct patron ordering of books from remote library locations and software to manage scanning of material for digital delivery directly to users.

Each of these areas in a consortium includes the task of keeping up to date on new and emerging products and systems that have application in a multilibrary setting. Consortia also gather and evaluate statistics to determine whether products and services are being used.

Many consortia now negotiate contracts for the purchase or license of information and products on their members' behalf. Licensing coordinators for consortia might find a background in an acquisitions or collection development department particularly relevant. In collection development, there is the opportunity to develop a familiarity with collection evaluation processes and techniques that take into account the program strengths and priorities of a library. There is also a high level of collaboration with other library units and library users as they do decision making. Having business skills, such as negotiation expertise and familiarity with accounting, budgets, and contracts, can be useful, too. Often a consortium office is more like a business environment than a library environment. Workshops, such as "Licensing Review and Negotiation" offered by the Association of Research Libraries, are very helpful introductions to the licensing and legal issues involved.

Consortia that are funded by state agencies and legislatures have staff members who work to educate politicians about the value that consortia bring to libraries through centralized funding. All consortia report to their funding bodies, boards, or governing committees. While this job falls mostly to the director of a consortium, staff with skills in marketing, public relations, and even lobbying can provide needed advice to help formulate the message the consortium wants to promote.

Digital libraries are currently a strong focus of both libraries and consortia. Many consortia are currently taking advantage of national and private grant funding to create shared digital libraries for their members. There are many components to a digital library. Grant writing to gather the necessary financial support for the project is a skill that can be learned through direct experience but also through workshops or online courses. The content selected for digitization and inclusion in these repositories is often culled from special collections and manuscripts held by member libraries. Work in special collections or archives can be a good introduction to the unique nature of these materials. Preservation of materials, both print and digital, is also a component of digital libraries. Hands-on experience with preservation or with the migration of information across formats is a needed skill for staff.

EMERGING ROLES IN CONSORTIA

Consortia are constantly developing new services in conjunction with their libraries to maximize services for the investment of cost and human resources. Some cooperatives have built shared storage facilities to save members the cost of constructing new facilities on their campuses. The staffs that work at these facilities support resource sharing and sometimes have preservation facilities and labs. Shared facilities require agreement on the deposit and handling of print collections. Shared virtual reference is another emerging area for consortia, because libraries can share the cost of the software and distribute the online staff time dedicated for the service across multiple institutions. Consortia play a role by acquiring the software and helping to manage the staffing schedules. In addition, a consortium staff member may help facilitate the development of policies and service standards. Professional development and continuing education can be a significant activity for a consortium, both as a service to libraries that cannot afford costly training or travel for staff on their own and also as a way for the consortium to generate revenue. Central staff may help identify the types of training or programs desired, but the libraries identify and negotiate the delivery of such programs.

The work in a library consortium is exciting, challenging, and dynamic. New roles are constantly emerging. The types of jobs and services offered in support of the member libraries are ever changing. Opportunities to move into new areas with libraries, to offer new services, and to take advantage of technological advances abound. Consortia employees are creators, problem solvers, facilitators, and communicators. As Tom Peters, editor of the column Consortia Speaking in the *Journal of Academic Librarianship,* writes, "Library consortia are fascinating, occasionally frustrating creatures. They tend to be highly energized, very efficient organisms."[1]

NOTE

1. Tom Peters, "Consortia Speaking," *Journal Of Academic Librarianship* 27, no. 2 (March 2001): 149.

ABOUT THE AUTHOR

Kim Armstrong is a program officer at the Triangle Research Libraries Network (TRLN) based in Chapel Hill, North Carolina. She received her master of science in library science from the University of Illinois at Urbana–Champaign.

7

Association Careers

Stephen A. Kershner

When choosing a career or profession, most people think of becoming a doctor, lawyer, teacher, librarian, fireman, or cowboy. One would not guess "association professional" would be high on the list. Ah . . . but once one moves further into a career attending, participating in, and eventually planning or presenting at professional development training sessions, retreats, seminars, and conferences, one may ask, "Who is responsible for maintaining this juggernaut of activity?" The answer is association professionals.

Many associations draw from individuals who have worked in the profession or area of interest to hire staff to perform the many functions necessary to provide services to members. In the case of library associations, many librarians undertake a career change. This is true for this author, who worked in public libraries in positions of librarian to middle manager to director during a twenty-four-year career and decided to venture into the corporate world to help create a new entity, a high-tech professional training and development center. After accomplishing and enjoying that challenge, former colleagues called, encouraging another change: a return to the library profession via directorship of the state library association. The decision to make the change was really an easy one. Having knowledge and experience working in the profession, one knows the areas of priority and range of services and activities to undertake. The skill transfer of abilities and expertise needed to work in the association environment from work in the profession can be very compatible.

This chapter outlines and discusses library and related association career opportunities, the types of jobs available, and sources of training in preparation for association work. Other chapters discuss continuing education and association involvement. The American Library Association (ALA) and state library associations first come to mind as sources for careers. The ALA is a large, complex organization while most state association staffs are small work teams. Other not-for-profit associations with opportunities are organizations such as OCLC and OCLC's state and regional groups that offer OCLC services. Trade associations also offer opportunities to serve companies providing services to libraries from book publishers to information and computerized services.

WHAT ASSOCIATIONS?

Librarianship is a service profession, as is association work. Some librarians work in positions serving the general public and others work in more specialized positions with targeted audiences. The same is true of associations. A quick Internet search or check of published association directories produces what seems like an association for anything and everything. If one has a particular interest or expertise, targeting associations serving those audiences is a good choice when making a career change or when starting one's career.

A place to start is the American Library Association. The ALA is a microcosm of the library profession with an association, division, or operating unit for each specialty of librarianship. Whether one is interested in academic, public, school, or special libraries, ALA has staff working with each division. If one has worked in academic libraries, the Association of College and Research Libraries would be a logical choice to pursue. The same advice would follow for the Public Library Association or the American Association of School Librarians. Under the large umbrella of ALA, other divisions target even more specific areas of librarianship. Ranging from management, information technology, children's and young adult services, special and cooperative libraries, technical services and special collections, library trustees, reference and user services, and more, ALA has an association unit specializing in service to each audience. Navigate through the ALA website (www.ala.org) to peruse the scope of career opportunities.

At the state level, one finds a library association or a multistate association, which are usually chapters of ALA. There is an advantage to working at the association when one has worked in that state. Being a member, volunteer, and/or an office holder in the association, or working with association staff members is important. Active association work at the state and national levels should provide a good perspective on the range of work responsibilities and tasks of association staff. There is also the opportunity to interview and speak with association staff about their work experiences.

The same is true for trade organizations that serve various professions with crossover increasingly related to technology and information services. As librarian job duties change, so will memberships in allied associations and the opportunity for positions in those associations. If you have an interest in the expanding world of technology, do not forget such associations that parallel many of the activities and interests of the library world.

ASSOCIATION JOBS: A VARIETY

Let us turn our attention to the types of jobs involved with association work. Management and administration are an obvious positions, but the range of jobs can vary widely for a large association. Professional development, conference management, advocacy work, marketing and public relations, publications and technology, and information systems specialists are some of the key areas offering challenging and rewarding career opportunities.

The executive directorship of an association is the most visible position with the responsibility of overall management and administration. Work in a large association, such as in the American Library Association (ALA) will entail the executive director supervising other staff with deputy directors and division and department heads. A check of the ALA website staff directory shows the wide variety of staff positions. A small association may have a single-person office where that person must deal with all aspects of the association, relying upon member volunteers to undertake many tasks and/or outsourcing services. The former situation relies upon a veteran executive with abilities to delegate and work with complex staffing levels and multiple boards and committees. In the latter situation, the person must be a jack-of-all-trades. Your work style and interests will determine your choices. Work in a smaller association or organization may be a wise path to take in order to gain a wide range of experience and later to move to a middle-management position in a large association.

The American Library Association offers a full range of management opportunities, as mentioned earlier, with executive directors of associations and divisions and department heads of offices within ALA. The divisions, units, and offices offer the opportunity to work closely with a segment of the profession while working within a large organization. Positions range from upper-management, middle-management, and entry-level supervisory positions.

Professional development and continuing education represent major components of most associations' activities, and staff is needed to plan and conduct such programs. Staffs also work with members to plan workshops and seminars. Frequently, certifications and CEU (Continuing Education Unit) programs are involved and association staffs often administer these programs.

Online coursework is emerging as a viable long-distance education option and association staff will certainly be involved in the creation, delivery, and administration of this service.

Professional development is also a component of conferences, institutes, and academies. Conference planning utilizes major components of association resources, and staff with experience and expertise with conference planning is essential for success. Other essential skills for success include long-range planning; the ability to work with members, vendors, and conference sites and local hotels; intricate scheduling and event planning; and financial management.

Associations would not be associations without members. Membership recruitment, development, and retention comprise core elements, and individuals who like to work closely with a variety of individuals will enjoy membership work. In addition to marketing and public relations activities, there is close work with membership development committees. Telecommunications permit the use of online surveys to receive input and feedback on services, to plan for new services, to eliminate services of lesser value, and to contribute greatly to the strategic planning efforts of the governing board and management.

Communications require staff with expertise in newsletters, journals, and even magazines in larger associations. Besides traditional print publications, associations now offer online newsletters, e-journals, and media publications in such formats as DVD and CD-ROM. Directories and subject-specific monographs have long been produced, along with proceedings of symposia and conferences. Individuals with writing and editing skills will have opportunities in associations. If one has already written professional journal articles in one's profession, he or she is familiar with the writing process.

Associations quite often become involved in the political process within the bounds of 501c3 or 501c6 organizations, and "advocacy" efforts range from regional and state to national levels. The ALA has a sophisticated system of advocacy, including an office in the nation's capital; they have established a separate advocacy organization. State library associations, such as chapters of ALA, work with ALA on national legislation and advocacy issues. Many state associations also hire governmental relations firms—lobbyists—to check on the daily pulse of state lawmakers and governors as full-time legislatures pass more laws affecting libraries and associations. Individuals with political savvy and experience are needed to work with association public policy and legislative committees in developing legislative agendas, writing position papers, and doing liaison work with lobbyists. Conducting media and advocacy training for association members and planning and conducting legislative days are becoming increasingly important association activities.

Another area of staff positions in associations, as is true for libraries, is technology positions. From managing in-house systems to websites to the increasing array of online member services and publications, technical expertise is increasingly at a premium. To reduce overhead costs, associations turn to online delivery of services, including membership directories, newsletters, journals, continuing education opportunities, information for workshops and conferences online, and registration via the Internet. Association technology staff enable associations to conduct more business online 7 days a week, 24 hours a day, 365 days a year, ranging from holding elections to surveying members to offering electronic discussion lists to members.

WHERE DO I GO FROM HERE?

A comprehensive source for association career information is the American Society of Association Executives (ASAE). The website (www.asaenet.org) provides information about its educational programs, such as Certified Association Executive (CAE) designation and Partner Allied Societies, including state chapters.

If you desire to remain in the world of libraries and enjoy working with professional colleagues, developing continuing education and professional development programs, publishing, doing advocacy work, and/or managing organizations, association work may be in your future. George Needham, currently vice president for Member Services at OCLC in Dublin, Ohio, and formerly executive director of ALA's Public Library Association, is a veteran of career work in libraries, associations, and not-for-profit organizations such as OCLC. When I spoke recently with Mr. Needham, he stated, "The skills you learn from working in a library translate quite well into an association setting. In a library, you focus on your clientele, making decisions that improve their experiences with the library so they'll continue to use your services and support you at budget time, balance demands and resources, and keep the board or provost informed and satisfied. This is also a definition of what an association executive does for the group's members." He continued, "The first advice I'd give to anyone interested in moving from a library to an association is to get actively involved in the associations to which you belong. Getting active in a regional library consortium, state association, an OCLC network, or ALA will help your understanding of the way organizations work while introducing you to other member leaders and leverage your field experience. It will also help determine if this type of work is right for you."

Mr. Needham also recommends seeking support for career development from Meeting Planners International (MPI) and ASAE. The ASAE Allied Societies have supported him in his work by offering a network of nearby executives who provided insight and assistance. The MPI and ASAE certification programs can further one's career and provide a reminder of what was accomplished through the process of getting one's MLS degree. Needham also believes that moving back to libraries from association work is a viable option. The experiences gained in creating coalitions, lobbying, and using committees to further association goals apply equally well to library directors. Contacts you'll develop in association work ensure that one will always have experienced executives to act as a sounding board for one's ideas, a pool of candidates for future job openings, and people who will be of benefit to your library.

Be active, be involved, and check out association work. It just might offer the type of career challenge you seek.

ABOUT THE AUTHOR

Stephen A. Kershner worked in public libraries in Illinois, Ohio, and Michigan for twenty-four years as a librarian, department head, and middle manager, including eighteen of those years as a library director. After a career change to the corporate world in 1997 to work in professional development and training, he became executive director of the Michigan Library Association in 2000.

8

Passing It On: A Career as a Full-Time Educator

Elaine Yontz

If our precious enterprise is to continue, the knowledge and skills that are the heart of librarianship must be transmitted to the next generation. One way to contribute to this effort is to make a career shift and become a full-time educator.

The role is vital. The need is great. The demands on the educator's life are substantial.

A former supervisor of mine encouraged us to "look for what you can uniquely contribute." If you possess a combination of personal circumstances, academic interest, and inspiration that might enable you to pursue this path, please consider it very seriously. You can learn more about his career path by exploring the website of the Association of Library and Information Science Educators (ALISE) at www.alise.org. A particularly helpful part of the site is the "New Job Postings" at www.alise.org/jobplacement/index.shtml, where you can see the qualifications that are being sought. The ALISE Doctoral Students Special Interest Group offers useful resources at www.fims.uwo.ca/organizations/dsa/sig/index.html.

WHY DO IT?

Simply put, we do it to make a difference.

Most people hunger to know that they make a real difference. I know that I do; don't you? We are so lucky to be part of a profession that offers many ways to make a positive difference in the lives of people around us. The joys of daily library work are real and just as important, and I miss them. But if the life is right for you, the satisfactions of being an educator are like no others.

On the "macrolevel," I know that I'm helping to preserve librarianship for all future generations. Wow! To feel that my individual effort will help to make life better for countless others whom I will never meet and who may not even be born until after I'm gone is a thrill that I never expected to have. Librarianship has both a history and a future, and I'm contributing.

At the "down-on-the-ground" level, there are many fulfilling experiences as well. Here are some of the moments that make the life worthwhile for me:

- Seeing people set previously unimagined goals and reach them.
- Sharing the "aha" moments when new insight dawns or new skills are realized.
- Hearing a former student say, "I can't believe I get paid to do this!"
- Shaking hands with former students who are now librarians.
- Reading messages that say, "I enjoyed the last class and look forward to the next one." (Maybe they're kidding, but I enjoy reading it anyway!)

WHAT IS REQUIRED?

Necessary building blocks include a doctoral degree, teaching ability, comfort with writing, and strong time-management skills.

Doctoral Degree

A doctoral degree is required for a full-time appointment in almost every case. The experienced educators and deans whom I queried for this chapter resoundingly confirmed the need for a terminal degree. The few educators who may be able to carve a path without a doctoral degree will probably work on campuses where a terminal degree is considered standard and a rite of passage. In short, a doctoral degree will almost certainly be required and will make a substantial difference in your effectiveness as an academic.

Planning for Your Doctoral Degree

Find what works for you. People have decided not to follow these suggestions and have still succeeded.

Attend school full time if you can. You will be able to begin your new career sooner. There are more opportunities for financial aid. In addition, you will sidestep the difficulties that arise from working against what might be called the "Ph.D. culture."

In most institutions, the process of preparing new scholars assumes that the doctoral student will spend a concentrated period sequestered from other life priorities. Expectations and processes are heavily biased toward these assumptions. "Swimming against the tide" is draining and time consuming. I earned my Ph.D. as a part-time student, so it can be done. Based on that experience, I urge you to try to go full time.

If you are place-bound, consider the doctoral programs near you. As a result of the assumptions about concentration and sequestering, distance education options for doctoral students are slim or nonexistent. The bright spot here is that LIS programs are hiring candidates with a wide variety of degree types. As you will see in the vacancy announcements, most ads require doctoral degrees in LIS or a related field. Look for a near-home program in which you can do a library-related dissertation.

Choose your dissertation topic carefully. Points to consider include intrinsic interest to you, easy availability of resources, faculty support for the topic, possibilities for grant funding (now and later), and applicability to future publications. In his book, *How to Complete and Survive a Doctoral Dissertation,* David Sternberg offers helpful advice about the dissertation process.

Finish your dissertation before you accept a full-time faculty position.

Teaching Ability

Teaching ability has two components: a basic liking for students and a knowledge base in pedagogy.

How many times have you said to a classmate, "That professor is really knowledgeable but just can't get the information across?" Understanding the material you are teaching is essential but insufficient. Coursework in education, workshops, and tools such as McKeachie's *Teaching Tips* may help.

Capacity for Service and Creative Activity

Most professors have three areas of responsibility: teaching, research, and service. How much of each is required, what types of activities "count" in each category, and how much bearing each area has on your continued employment depends on where you work.

"Service" can mean service to the department, campus, profession, or community. These activities may be similar to many things you have done as a librarian.

"Research" is called "research and creative activity" on some campuses. In some situations, published books or refereed journal articles are expected. In other places, a wider range of creative products may be acceptable. Choosing a dissertation topic that can be the basis of subsequent publications is a wise move.

Comfort with Writing

Writing, whether of books, articles, lesson plans, or committee reports, will be a large part of your life. Joseph Michael Moxley's book *Publish,*

Don't Perish offers good advice on academic publication. To improve basic writing skills, consider systematic study of Diana Hacker's *A Pocket Style Manual*.

Strong Time-Management Skills

You must either have or acquire Herculean time-management skills. Lee Tobin McClain's article "Lessons in Time Management" on this topic is aimed at new professors.

HOW IS IT DIFFERENT?

The life of a full-time educator is different from that of the practicing librarian in ways that I couldn't appreciate until I had experienced it. I am showing signs of making a successful transition (this week, anyway!), but the first two years were very difficult.

It's harder, especially at first. As an academic librarian, I always wanted to roll my eyes when my faculty friends lamented about how hard they worked. Little did I know! Teaching, research, and service draw on very different energies, and the demands to excel in each area are continuous.

It's more time consuming, particularly during the pretenure years.

You have more control over how the work time is organized. This can be a strong advantage. It's also true that planning one's own schedule and sticking with it takes effort.

It's more solitary. Class planning, grading, writing, and study are solo activities in most cases. Though excellent interpersonal skills remain essential, you must also be able to tolerate working alone and be able to motivate yourself.

Sometimes the money gets better and sometimes it doesn't. Salaries are attractive in comparison to what some "line" librarians make. The other side of the coin is that some librarians, particularly administrators, might have to take a pay cut.

It's more entrepreneurial. Being a college professor has strong similarities to being self-employed. Two manifestations are the necessities to be self-motivating and to be responsible for organizing most of your work time. It's also true that higher education in the current era is a market-driven enterprise, whether rightly or wrongly. Academic departments must be able to demonstrate that they contribute to the "bottom lines" of their institutions. In many situations, the bottom lines are grant funding and student credit hours. There are departments in which you won't be hired unless you can attract outside funding for your research. Strong contributors to student credit hours are people who can teach subjects nobody else in the department can teach, people who teach required courses, and people who teach classes that draw large enrollments.

There is tension between "librarianship" and "information science" in some programs. Kathleen McCook's article discusses the moves on some campuses to join education for librarianship with other disciplines, often information science. In some situations, educators who focus on librarianship feel like second-class citizens. In other places, library educators feel strongly valued. This depends entirely on where you work. The job interview process is a time to probe carefully to determine whether you can be happy and effective in that particular culture.

SOME ADVICE FOR YOU

In preparation for this chapter, I asked LIS deans and educators what advice they would give to potential educators. I hope their comments will help you decide whether this path is for you.

- Lorna Peterson, associate professor of Library and Information Studies, State University of New York at Buffalo: "Some days will be better than others. The real matter is what contribution you are making to the world, not how much happiness you are withdrawing from it."
- Martha Hale, dean, Catholic University of America School of Library and Information Science:

  Anytime someone is changing careers/directions, one of the most difficult things is to realize that that you aren't being disloyal to the former career by grasping the new one. The practitioner's career will enrich teaching and open doors to learning more than you knew in your former place of employment. But the faculty position is very different. To be a success and maybe happy, you must grasp the traditions, values, and demands of the new position. It is often hard to know what "being a scholar" means in your particular place of employment, but it is critical to find that out.

- Kathleen de la Peña McCook, distinguished university professor, University of South Florida School of Library and Information Science: "Read widely and across disciplines. Span boundaries. Spend time in the field, spend time in other fields. Assume leadership roles in state and national organizations. Work to recruit people of color."
- Louise Robbins, professor and director, University of Wisconsin-Madison School of Library and Information Studies:

  Just as libraries are not a refuge for people who wish to hide and read, so library education is not a place for people who want to hide out and work by themselves. Our field demands high-quality instruction and high-quality research, as well as interaction with folks in professional information practice. It also requires, now more than ever, people who can articulate the importance of what they do, both in terms of balancing the demands within the university and in terms of why librarianship is an important profession requiring an advanced degree.

I will end by mentioning a strong advantage that is less than obvious. Full-time educators are paid to think about what would be best and to move practice forward by disseminating their thoughts. Though professors are sometimes accused of being "out of touch" with reality, it's part of their job to contribute to improvement by thinking, writing, and speaking about the ideal. Professors can help practitioners reach for the stars, which increases the chance that we'll land on the rooftops. This mandate to think about the ideal is a privilege given to relatively few of us.

The path is demanding. For the right people, the potential satisfactions are very great. Please think about whether this direction might be right for you.

RELATED READINGS

Hacker, Diana. *A Pocket Style Manual*, 4th ed. Boston: Bedford/St. Martin's, 2004.

McClain, Lee Tobin. "Lessons in Time Management." *Chronicle of Higher Education*, December 19, 2003.

McCook, Kathleen de la Peña. *Using Ockham's Razor: Cutting to the Center.* www.ala.org/ala/hrdrbucket/1stcongressonpro/1stcongressusing.htm (last accessed 7 August 2004).

McKeachie, Wilbert J. *Teaching Tips: Strategies, Research, and Theory for College and University Teachers*, 9th ed. Lexington, Mass.: D.C. Heath, 1994.

Moxley, Joseph Michael. *Publish, Don't Perish: The Scholar's Guide to Academic Writing and Publishing*. Westport, Conn.: Praeger, 1992.

Sternberg, David. *How to Complete and Survive a Doctoral Dissertation*. New York: St. Martin's Griffin, 1981.

ABOUT THE AUTHOR

Elaine Yontz is associate professor in the Master of Library and Information Science Program at Valdosta State University in Valdosta, Georgia. She formerly taught in the School of Library and Information Science at the University of South Florida in Tampa. Before becoming a full-time educator, she was a catalog librarian and manager in the George Smathers Libraries of the University of Florida.

9

Looking at Libraries from Both Sides: Librarian-Vendors

Karen J. Cook

WHAT IS A VENDOR, ANYWAY?

The word "vendor" comes from Latin *vendere* by way of the French, *vendre*, "to sell": A vendor is one who sells, exchanging goods or services for money. In common usage, the term vendor typically brings to mind a street peddler hawking cheap wares ("Hey, buddy, want a watch?"), the hot-dog man at a ball game ("Hot dogs! Get yer hot dogs here!"), or a vending machine ("Insert bill"). The word can, with equal propriety, describe those delivering high-quality products or professional services on a cost basis.

Those who sell to libraries are collectively referred to as vendors, perhaps because no other term is adequate to cover the myriad for-profit companies, nonprofit organizations, and individuals providing library goods and services. Bibliographic utilities, independent library consultants, publishing houses, serial and book jobbers, library architects, freelance writers or editors working for libraries and library associations, integrated library system software companies, retrospective-conversion services, manufacturers of library supplies, companies producing assistive technologies, temporary professional staff agencies, and firms selling bookmobiles are all vendors.

Librarianship is a service profession, dedicated to free and open access to information whenever and wherever possible. Librarians often choose to work for minimal recompense themselves as part of the price paid for the privilege of serving others. Many lack business experience, denigrating vendors who expect to be paid for library goods and services as greedy, foreign to the library profession, and an obstacle to be overcome. To the contrary, vendors are essential partners in the business of operating libraries and providing information services. Vendors are the source for many of the tools we librarians need to do our jobs, including but not limited to the raison d'être of libraries, the physical and virtual materials in our collections.

LIBRARIAN-VENDORS

It surprises traditional librarians to learn that many vendors are themselves librarians, possessing the MLS or MLIS degree and often years of experience working in traditional library settings as well. It shouldn't come as a surprise—the skills and knowledge that librarian-vendors have pertaining to libraries and librarianship enable vendors to design and market products and services that assist libraries to fulfill their missions efficiently and well. In a 1994 survey of emerging opportunities for LIS professionals, Forest Woody Horton pointed out that, just as accountants don't always work for accounting firms or lawyers in law firms, librarians should not be stereotyped as fit for work only in library and information institutions.[1]

Some vendor companies were created by librarians who experienced a need for a particular product or service and set out to fill it. One noteworthy example is Serials Solutions, cofounded in 2000 by Peter McCracken, a full-time academic reference librarian.[2] Other vendor companies employ librarians to work with librarian customers. Barbara Herzog, writing of her work in vendor relations, says, "I have seen librarians' eyes widen with surprise, and their shoulders relax, when they see the MLS after my name on my business card. . . . 'Ah, you're a librarian; you understand what I am talking about.'"[3]

Some librarian-vendors are employees working for multinational corporations or small, mom-and-pop businesses, while others run their own companies. Some work alone as freelancers, solo entrepreneurs, or consultants. A few librarians straddle the divide, running a library-vendor business while maintaining a professional job in a traditional library setting. The range of possible vendor positions is limited only by librarians' imaginations. In fact, the number of librarians working as vendors appears to be increasing—part of a general trend toward nontraditional careers as opportunities outside libraries become more abundant than those inside libraries.[4]

Librarian-vendors may do much the same type of work in a corporate or commercial environment that they could do in a traditional library setting, for example, creating online cataloging records while employed by a bibliographic utility or other company that provides cataloging services to libraries, alone or in conjunction with the sale of books or serials. Likewise, librarians utilizing professional skills work for indexing and abstracting services relied upon by libraries. For forty years or more, enterprising librarians have sold their skills to libraries as "information brokers," providing fee-based research and reference work.

Other librarians do work that is quite unlike any traditional library job. Librarian-vendors' knowledge and understanding of libraries and library operations, rather than specific professional skills, is what they bring to the table in this type of nontraditional employment. Librarians are salespeople and customer account managers; others write marketing literature; some edit technical manuals for customers; still others interface with programmers on product design; a few work as exhibits managers. My own experience as public library product manager at SIRSI involved aspects of all the above and more.

PROS AND CONS

There are copious short- and long-term benefits to working as a librarian-vendor. Naturally, as with any career, there also can be some not-so-great features that should be carefully weighed. Please keep in mind that "your mileage may vary." Just as all library jobs are not fungible, not all of the potential good—or bad—aspects of a librarian-vendor career apply to every library-vendor company or librarian-vendor position.

The Good Things

Pecuniary Benefits

Vendors are in the business of selling things, after all, so they tend to enjoy better financial rewards than librarians employed by libraries, particularly those librarians working in nonprofit public-sector libraries. Salespersons on commission selling big-ticket items—for example, corporate vendors selling large integrated library systems—have the potential for earning *very* nice incomes. Even those on straight salary may net an immediate 10 to 20 percent (or more) "pay raise" by moving from a traditional library employment to a vendor position.

In addition to better salaries, and possible commissions, corporate employees typically receive great benefits packages, annual bonuses, stock options, and other direct financial rewards. Less obvious but no less valuable are other types of indirect financial benefits, for example full reimbursement for expenses that colleagues in traditional library employment often must bear themselves in whole or in part, such as professional dues and costs of travel to conferences.

Better Toys

A one-time coworker of mine, a former academic systems librarian then enjoying a career as a library system sales representative, explained his happy career transition to skeptical librarians by saying, "Vendors have better toys!" While not all vendor employees have the opportunity to work with cutting-edge products as part of their daily routine, many do. For the technophile, this can be a significant perk. Certainly, librarian-vendors often enjoy the excitement of observing—if not actively participating in—the conception, development, and birthing of new products.

Travel

Frequent travel is a common aspect of a librarian-vendor's life. Sales staff, account managers, customer support representatives, or trainers visit prospective or current customers' libraries, getting to see the country—or, for those employed by multinational corporations, more exotic parts of the world—in the process.

A Climate of Innovation

"Moving at the speed of business" is part of a librarian-vendor's life. Vendors continuously strive not only to build better mousetraps but also to market, package, produce, and deliver them as efficiently as possible, and certainly before the competition does so! Successful vendors employ creative, innovative, energetic, and imaginative people and provide them with ample opportunities to utilize those abilities.

New methods, new products, new services, and new job descriptions can be approved and implemented rapidly with little or none of the bureaucratic process or rounds of tedious and repetitive committee meetings so often required prior to making the smallest changes in library procedures, particularly within academic libraries or library networks. Of course, similar pro-innovation climates are found in many libraries, but perhaps less commonly than the less risky penchant for the tried-and-true "we've always done it that way" approach.

Far-Reaching Impact

Working in a library, the ability of a given librarian—no matter how innovative, brilliant, or talented—to have an impact beyond the confines of his or her own library or system is typically limited to what can be accomplished indirectly through service in professional associations or via scholarly publication, an essential and worthy effort but one that may bear fruit with excruciating slowness. By contrast, an entrepreneur or corporate vendor who develops a new product, service, or feature that enhances the ability of thousands of library customers to meet the needs of their patrons may have precipitated rapid improvements in library services to hundreds of thousands, or even millions, of people. For example, vendors of preservation products have worked together with librarians to develop high-quality tools, equipment, and supplies. At the opposite end of the technology spectrum, eBook vendors have been actively involved in planning metadata standards and with the Program for Cooperative Cataloging.

Learning New Methods and Skills

Library school training provides novice librarians with a starter-kit of skills, knowledge, and job expectations. Once employed in a professional library position, that starter-kit is enhanced by personal on-the-job experiences and observations of coworkers in action, hopefully supplemented by professional reading and continuing education through attendance at workshops and conferences. Inevitably this learning process is substantially limited by one's specific job circumstance and library environment.

A librarian-vendor visiting and assisting many library customers has the opportunity to learn from the collective experience of many librarians working in a variety of library settings, observing firsthand instances of successful solutions to thorny problems and likewise observing other situations where theory has not worked out altogether well in practice.

This rich, vicarious experience can add breadth and depth to professional knowledge, improving a librarian-vendor's immediate job performance and quality of service to his or her company. It can also be of long-term value to the librarian beyond the scope of current employment, in a possible future career in a traditional library setting or even as library school faculty. Additionally, librarian-vendors may have the opportunity to learn skills not taught in library school, such as marketing and public relations or technical writing, which can be advantageous when seeking or performing certain library positions.

Learning to appreciate vendors' business realities can cause a former librarian-vendor to be a more knowledgeable consumer and a better customer upon return to library employment, as it is easier to work effectively in partnership when each partner understands the needs of the other.

Safety Net

During hard economic times when libraries may be experiencing hiring freezes or job losses, working as a vendor may be an attractive interim solution for those having trouble finding or retaining a traditional library position. Carol Berger, president of C. Berger and Co., founded her business providing temporary library staff in 1982 after she lost her special library position as a result of corporate restructuring.[5] Different budget cycles and the relatively more rapid hiring process for corporate entities can mean immediate employment with a vendor as opposed to a six-month or year-long job hunt to find a school, academic, or public library position.

Not-So-Good Things

Pace and Pressure

The for-profit world moves along at a swift pace. The popular business expression "Time is money" applies to library vendors just as it does to other types of businesses. New products are never ready soon enough.

The unquestionable value of many library activities is difficult if not impossible to measure, at least in the short run, so librarians tend to take the long view when evaluating outcomes. By contrast, business is very good at determining a bottom line, and many decisions are driven by it. When coworkers' jobs (as well as one's own) depend on the effectiveness with which one works, there may not be any predictable "quittin' time" or regular eight-hour days. Stress can be high, and the hours are often long.

On the Road Again

Travel—even to exotic places—can get old.

Regular business travel is nothing like vacation travel. Quite apart from the obvious—that it involves working rather than lounging on a beach sipping tropical drinks with little umbrellas, or enjoying the sights or relaxed hours with a good book—business travel doesn't just happen once or twice a year at a time, place, and duration of the business traveler's choosing.

Some librarian-vendor jobs involve being on the road 50 percent of the time and may include trips to Minneapolis in January and El Paso in August. Traveling 50 percent of one's life often includes long hours waiting in—or frantic minutes dashing through—airport terminals, futile attempts to sleep in strange beds, desperate efforts to remember (without one's glasses on) which way the shower faucet in the hotel turns to increase—or *decrease! Ouch!*—the flow of hot water, eating a continuous diet of restaurant food, and simply being away from family, friends, and the familiar haunts and regularly scheduled activities at home.

Job Insecurity

While it is not unknown for university, public, or school libraries to eliminate positions by lay-offs during times of budget constraints, personnel costs are more likely to be reduced gradually through attrition and hiring freezes. In some instances, employment contracts provide some level of job security. It is almost unheard of for the library itself to shut down or cease to exist, because the acknowledged importance of libraries to their communities would not allow that to happen. There are seldom, however, guarantees of continued employment for those working in the for-profit sector. A business downturn, reorganization of a company's business model, or a merger may result in the abrupt evaporation of one's position, department, or company.

Missing the Library Environment

Librarian-vendors may suffer "library withdrawal." Even if the librarian-vendor's job provides substantial support for libraries and effectively promotes the highest principles of librarianship—which it may well do—it seldom entails working in a library. For those initially drawn to the field through a love for books, the contemplative (or at least intellectually stimulating) atmosphere of libraries, and the joy of serendipitous discoveries made browsing the stacks, working outside a library environment just isn't the same.

Professional Activities

Vendors have long been essential partners with library associations. The American Library Association (ALA), for example, works with vendor-exhibitors through the Exhibits Round Table to ensure that exhibits are an integral part of each annual conference and midwinter meeting. Typically, income from vendors' rental of exhibit space covers a major portion of the conference costs, thereby reducing the price of registration fees that must be paid by attendees. Many ALA and divisional awards and programs are funded in whole or in part by vendors.

Becoming a vendor does not require renouncing one's professional identity. It is not only possible but also advisable for library vendors to be involved in professional library association activities.

First, librarian-vendors make excellent representatives for their companies to library organizations, as they understand the professional interests and concerns of librarians. The ALA has numerous units that explicitly or implicitly rely upon vendor members' participation. For example, the bylaws of the Exhibits Round Table require that a certain number of executive board positions be reserved for conference exhibitors, who are principally vendors. Standards development groups depend upon vendor involvement and cooperation in their ongoing work. Several ALA divisions recognize the unique perspective and expertise that vendors can share, and make provision for vendor participation in regular conference programming, as speakers and panelists, or by establishing designated vendor presentation venues for informational programs. This pattern is repeated at the state level as well, providing ample opportunities for librarian-vendors to represent their company through association activities.

Second, librarian-vendors can maintain personal memberships in professional library organizations.

Being active is not always easy. There can be grueling demands on the librarian-vendor's time at conferences, attending committee meetings and programs, mentoring, and visiting the exhibits, as well as a full menu of corporate obligations, including hosting customer receptions, serving "booth duty," and so forth.

"Librarian" members on occasion may be hostile to participation on committees or boards by a "nonlibrarian." This "us-versus-them" mentality can generally be overcome with patience, proving oneself through solid contributions and gentle education, such as wearing an "I'm a Librarian, Too!" button. Librarians who are customers of a competitor may be uncomfortable initially working on a committee with a librarian-vendor. This may arise from concern that the vendor will harbor bad feelings at loss of business or, more commonly, from a fear that the librarian-vendor will attempt to make a sale. The librarian-vendor can diffuse this situation by behaving in a professional manner, refraining from any conduct that smacks of advertising or sales promotion, being willing to carry his or her weight, and exhibiting knowledge of and concern for professional activities and values. This will, in time, reap good public relations for the vendor's business while at the same time the librarian-vendor is able to maintain a personal presence in professional associations.

On the other hand, it may be easier for librarian-vendors than those employed in a library setting to participate on an executive board or task force that requires substantial commitments of time, money, or travel. The librarian-vendor may have more freedom to use work time for association activities, more flexibility for travel, and more institutional support for supplies, copying, postage, and travel expenses.

A librarian-vendor can be in the wonderful position of being able to work from within his or her company to do good for the library community by encouraging and facilitating vendor-funded sponsorships, scholarships, awards, and other financial support for library school students, deserving librarians, and professional programs. Of course, this can contribute to good public relations or advertising for the vendor, but this does not negate the tremendous value of vendor dollars "given back" in this manner to the library profession.

Staying on top of issues, concerns, and developments within the field by participating in professional workshops, conferences, and programs and reading professional publications, the librarian-vendor is in a position to keep his or her company informed and thereby to help steer development of products and services into optimum channels.

FINDING A JOB

Finding job opportunities as a vendor is a bit different than locating traditional library jobs.

Job-hunting resources for librarians, not surprisingly, primarily list jobs for librarians in libraries. A very few include a category for vendor jobs. For example, the classified advertisements in *American Libraries* includes available listings under the heading "Vendor/Utility." There are seldom more than a few positions shown, if any. Some job boards may actually list openings for vendor jobs, but those will be interspersed with library jobs in regional listings rather than broken out by category, making the search tedious.

Most vendors list available positions on their websites, under obvious entry points such as "Employment Opportunities," "Career Options," or, more to the point, "Jobs!" Sometimes a bit of sleuthing is required to find openings displayed more discretely under "About Us." Of course, not all those positions will be specifically for librarians. In many cases, however, an enterprising librarian will be able to make a case for being an ideal candidate for the job by demonstrating how the librarian and information science skill set adds competencies appropriate for the work.

There are tools to help locate vendors that might be particularly good employers. One good starting point is to identify vendors who are attuned to and appreciate libraries and librarians. On the ALA website is a searchable list of library vendors who have exhibited at previous ALA conferences; some of these companies have a long track record, having done business with libraries for more than 100 years. Exhibiting companies often arrange interviews through the placement services at library conferences. *Library Journal* provides an online directory of companies that sell library products and services, accessible by company name or category of product or service. Another excellent finding aid is *The Librarian's Yellow Pages*, available free in a print version or accessible online, with keyword searching for products and companies and browsing by category of product or service. *Information Today's* "Library Resource Guide" is a website with alphabetical lists by category and vendor name. Library school websites sometimes list vendors that have previously hired their graduates; a list of all accredited library schools in the United States and Canada is available through the ALA website. University libraries often maintain lists of publishers and suppliers used by the library.

In addition to researching companies online and via traditional library resources, take advantage of conference exhibits for picking up information, become familiar with products, and chat with company representatives.

Don't forget that if you are working in a library, you already have relationships with a number of library vendors. You may have a good sense for whether a given company would be good to work for by the way its representatives interact with you as a customer.

CONCLUSION: A NEW CONNOTATION FOR "VENDOR"

Working as a librarian-vendor can be challenging, exciting, and a great opportunity to expand personal and professional horizons. It may begin as an interim move, undertaken of necessity when traditional library work is unavailable and abandoned when an opportunity in a library setting is available once more. In many cases, however, the temporary stop-gap employment turns into a lifelong career path. It is a road less traveled, but one that can be professionally as well as monetarily rewarding for those comfortable in a fluid business environment.

NOTES

1. Forest Woody Horton Jr., *Extending the Librarian's Domain: A Survey of Emerging Occupation Opportunities for Librarians and Information Professionals.* SLA Occasional Papers Series, no. 4 (Washington, D.C.: Special Libraries Association, 1994), 3.

2. Norman Oder, "Peter McCracken: Librarian as Entrepreneur," *Library Journal* (August 2001): 44–46. Peter was a speaker for an ALA/New Members Round Table program, "Places Your M.L.S. Can Take You: Alternative Careers for Librarians," at the ALA/CLA Annual Conference in Toronto, June 2003.

3. Barbara Herzog, "Working for a Library Vendor," in *What Else You Can Do With a Library Degree: Career Options for the 90s and Beyond,* ed. Betty-Carol Sellen (New York: Neal-Schuman, 1997), 75–79.

4. Betty-Carol Sellen, "Preface," in *What Else You Can Do with a Library Degree: Career Options for the 90s and Beyond* (New York: Neal-Schuman, 1997), x; "Librarians: Job Outlook," *Occupational Outlook Handbook*, 2002–2003 ed. www.bls.gov/oco/ocos068.htm (last accessed 29 September 2003).

5. Wilda W. Williams, "You *Can* Take Your M.L.S. Out of the Library," *Library Journal* (15 November 1994): 43–46.

JOB-FINDING RESOURCES

ALA Vendor Finder—vendors.ala.org/
Internet Library for Librarians: Library Vendors—www.itcompany.com/inforetriever/vendors.htm
The Librarian's Yellow Pages—www.librariansyellowpages.com/
Library Journal 2003 Buyer's Guide and Website Directory—sourcebook.cahners1.com/libjrn/

RELATED READINGS

The Personal Experiences of Librarian-Vendors

DeCandido, GraceAnne A. "Hanging Out My Shingle: From Librarian to Consultant." *American Libraries* (March 2000): 46–48.

Oder, Norman. "Peter McCracken: Librarian as Entrepreneur." *Library Journal* (August 2001): 44–46.

Sellen, Betty-Carol, ed. *What Else You Can Do with a Library Degree: Career Options for the 90s and Beyond.* New York: Neal-Schuman, 1997.

Shontz, Priscilla K. "Career Planning." In *Jump Start Your Career in Library and Information Science,* 1–25. Lanham, Md.: Scarecrow Press, 2002.

Williams, Wilda W. "You *Can* Take Your M.L.S. Out of the Library." *Library Journal* (November 15, 1994): 43–46.

Two (of Many) Examples of Vendor-Library Community Partnerships

Connaway, Lynn Silipigni. "Librarians, Producers, and Vendors: The netLibrary Experience." Paper delivered at the Bicentennial Conference on Bibliographic Control for the New Millennium: Confronting the Challenges of Networked Resources and the Web, Library of Congress, November 15–17, 2000. www.loc.gov/catdir/bibcontrol/connaway_paper.html (last accessed 20 May 2003).

Schrock, Nancy Carlson. "Welcome Allies: Vendors, Librarians, and the Public." *Abbey Newsletter* 20 (August 1996). palimpsest.stanford.edu/byorg/abbey/an/ an20/an20-3/an20-309.html (May 20, 2003).

What Librarians Working as Vendors May Miss

Sheehy, Carolyn A. "Who Says It's Always Greener on the Other Side?" *American Libraries* (September 2000): 52–54.

ABOUT THE AUTHOR

Karen J. Cook has had a diverse library and information science career encompassing both traditional library environments and "alternative" settings. Her background includes circulation, reference, technical services, and systems positions in academic and public libraries, four exhilarating years as public library product manager for SIRSI Corporation, and two years as team lead for NASAexplores.com, a K-12 teacher resource from the Marshall Space Flight Center. Currently, Karen is serving as adjunct faculty and pursuing doctoral work in Information Studies at the College of Communication and Information Sciences, University of Alabama.

10

Beckoned by Darth Vader: Careers in Publishing

Trudy Lindsey

It was the end of my second day on my new job as a library representative for John Wiley & Sons. I was walking with a group of my colleagues as we left the Special Library Association exhibit hall, where I'd spent a dizzying day ostensibly working, but mostly observing—and repeatedly apologizing to the librarians who asked me questions I was too green to answer—in the Wiley booth.

As we walked through the hall of the large conference center, one young man from Wiley asked me where I had previously worked. I gave him a thumbnail description of my twenty years of library experience and then he asked me if I'd enjoyed being a librarian. "Yes, very much," I answered.

"So," he asked, "what made you come over to the dark side?"

PROFIT VERSUS SERVICE

I had never heard publishing referred to as "the dark side" before that day, but it certainly made me stop and think. And during the four years that I have worked in publishing, I've come to see why it's possible that many librarians might see publishing as the somewhat "evil" version of what libraries do.

Libraries and publishing houses are both in the information business. Both want to disseminate as much information to as many people as possible. Libraries, however, generally do so as a service. Publishers do so to make a profit. It sometimes makes for an uneasy alliance, but the world of publishing nevertheless offers an attractive option to those with a library degree, and especially to those with library experience.

THE WILEY STORY

The director of the Library Sales Department (and my boss) at John Wiley & Sons, John Chambers, and I sat down one afternoon to talk about the genesis of Wiley's unique approach to library sales. John explained that, at one time, Wiley had a tradition of sending out representatives to visit libraries, but it wasn't a formal program and Wiley representatives spent most of their time meeting with vendors.

John had previously worked at Simon & Schuster where there was a slightly similar program, but it was really "an afterthought," according to John, and budget cuts ended the program before it had a chance to succeed. That program was a copy of yet another program, begun at Pergamon Press, where about twenty librarians had been hired as part-timers. Their role was to visit libraries, bringing samples of reference works, journals, and similar materials. These representatives were called "library consultants" who were viewed by the publishing house as an affordable way to maintain close contact with a large number of libraries.

In 1993, John Chambers collaborated with others at Wiley to restructure the Wiley library sales program. They decided that Wiley library reps would no longer visit the vendors, but would instead speak directly with librarians. More importantly, Wiley library reps would be graduates of library school who had worked as librarians. Instead of being located in-house, the library reps would be in the field. Their full-time job would encompass visiting libraries and meeting with librarians. In the ten years since the formation of this program, library sales at Wiley have gone up most years, whereas prior to that time period, library sales had gone down.

I asked John why he thought it was important to hire librarians to be Wiley's library reps. "It's critical," John answered. John believes that a "subtle" approach is greatly appreciated by librarians who are repelled by a spiel that is focused only on making and closing a sale. People with library experience know the issues, and hiring former librarians to talk to working librarians shows a respect for the library world. "It's simply good business practice," John told me, "and we also view it as a *service* to the librarians." Wiley library reps are available to serve in a customer service capacity to any librarian who calls upon them for help. "I want to emphasize," John continued, "that the Wiley library representative program is about forming relationships. Ninety percent of library sales are made through vendors." The Wiley program is not a platform for a sales pitch. It's designed to keep the communication flowing between the library world and Wiley, and it is the sincerity of the program that makes it successful.

Successful indeed—the top three sellers in terms of volume of business with Yankee Book Peddler are Oxford University Press, Cambridge University Press, and Wiley. This is impressive when you consider that the first two "out-volume" Wiley and also account for numerous standing orders. So when it comes to library sales, Wiley is clearly doing something right. Perhaps in some ways it's about empowerment: The librarians are asked for feedback on format, content, price, and marketing, and in turn Wiley gains knowledge about the daily issues and concerns librarians are confronting.

MY OWN PERSONAL JOURNEY

So how did I end up on this so-called dark side? I suppose in one way it's because I have always been fascinated by publishing. In library school I took a publishing course that turned out to be one of my favorite classes of all time. I suppose my fascination with publishing arose naturally out of my lifelong love affair with books. I remember when I was applying to library school, I had to write an essay about why I wanted to become a librarian. "Don't say it's because you love books!" warned more than one graduate of the library school. I can't recall what I wrote, but the truth was I did become a librarian because I love books. To me, becoming a librarian was an incredible honor. When I received my degree I felt as if I'd been inducted into one of the finest professions in the world. I was thrilled to be able to call myself a librarian — a keeper of books. I felt as if I might as well have a gigantic neon sign above my head that stated "I LOVE TO READ."

For my first ten years of librarianship I labored in a tiny research facility on a college campus, earning a miserly salary but loving what I did. Unfortunately, all of my salary was dependent upon grant money so when hard times hit and the grant money began to dry up, I saw everyone who was hired after me lose their jobs. After I was laid off, I spent a year working as a substitute teacher before finally landing a job as a branch manager in a public library. Once again, I wore that glorious appellation: "Librarian."

I was, however, ill prepared for public library work. To all public librarians out there, my hat is off to you! Yours is a tough job. You are babysitter, social chairman, teacher, janitor, reader's advisor, marketing director, committee worker, policy maker/enforcer, and social worker. Add in the extra duties at a full-service branch library and you are doing collection development for adults, children, and teens — including selecting in all formats: books, magazines, videos, DVDs, CDs, and toys. You work a circulation desk, create and run programs and, if you're the manager, you supervise people as well.

Being a public librarian was one of the most challenging and stimulating things I've ever done, but after nearly ten years, I was seriously burned out. At an in-service meeting one day, our library director made a statement that gave me pause. He said he hoped everyone on the staff really enjoyed working at the library, and that they awoke each morning and looked forward to coming to work. That, he said, is what makes a library great. It made me think back to my first several years on the job when I'd felt *exactly* like that. But I had to face the fact that I no longer glowed with pride about my job and often came home after work feeling exhausted and drained. I knew then it was time for a change.

Completely changing the course of my career was not my initial plan. At first, I took a close look at other library jobs. I thought about moving back into the academic realm or possibly finding a special library job similar to the job I'd held in the research facility. I updated my resume and began to scan the classifieds in the library literature. One day, looking through the ads in *American Libraries*, I spotted an ad for a library representative for John Wiley & Sons. The job description was incredibly appealing precisely because of the lack of emphasis on selling. What the heck, I thought, and I sent in my resume.

When several months passed and I had not heard from Wiley, I crossed them off the list of potential employers I'd sent resumes to, assuming that I simply hadn't made the initial cut. Too bad, I thought—it had sounded like a great job! Then, one lovely spring morning one of my branch staff came into my office to tell me I had a phone call. "It's a gentleman from John Wiley & Sons," she said. "Well, how do you like this," I thought. "I applied for a job with these folks and never heard so much as a thank you, and now some guy is calling me to try to sell me something." I was all set to politely tell him we only buy from vendors when he asked me if I recalled sending in my resume and was I still interested in the job? Once I recovered from my initial surprise, we talked briefly, arranged to meet for an interview in a coffee shop near O'Hare Airport, and three months later I was no longer officially a librarian. Darth Vader had crooked a black-gloved finger at me and I caved. But hey!— I'm not the only one. Read on for more publishing career stories.

OTHER JOURNEYS—AND A LITTLE ADVICE

Besides myself, there are two other library representatives at John Wiley & Sons. Both of them shared their personal stories with me about their transition from librarian to library representative. Athena Michael was Wiley's very first library representative, and she brought to the job many years of diverse library experience. Prior to joining Wiley, she had spent twenty-five years in the information industry—half in libraries (academic, public, corporate, and even as a ship's librarian for Semester-at-Sea), and the other half working for vendors.

In library school, Athena had set her sights on the role of a traditional librarian: Her goal was to become a fine arts librarian in either an academic or museum setting. Although her career has taken her far afield from that original plan, she believes that library school provided her with the fundamentals that enable her to work well in the publishing world. "The principles of librarianship— collecting, organizing, managing information," she said, "gave me the best foundation possible to work with librarians." Her varied work experience has given her the background necessary to understand librarians' needs.

I asked her if she thought publishing is a good career choice for librarians. "Definitely, yes!" she responded. "What librarians bring to the table is really important and helpful to publishers, so it's a win-win for both parties in my opinion." She said she hopes more librarians choose to work in publishing because it's a great match. A variety of tasks within publishing are ideal for librarians, she said: developing products, managing electronic information, creating databases, editing, indexing, to name just a few. Athena recommends that library students take a traditional publishing class in order to learn the terminology and to get a basic understanding of the industry. "It's all about disseminating information," she said, "a natural choice for librarians."

Wiley's West Coast library representative is Barry Champany. Barry began library school with the idea of becoming an academic librarian, but as he worked toward his degree he became instilled with "idealism for public libraries" and began his career by working for nine years as a reference librarian at the Baltimore County Public Library. In 1979, the siren song (and mild winters) of California beckoned him and he moved. Because library jobs were scarce in California at that time, Barry's first job there was working for an information broker, providing document delivery service. He spent seven years in that position before becoming a marketing manager for CLASS (Cooperative Library Agency for Systems & Services). After seven years with CLASS, Barry again felt the need for change. A friend referred him to Wiley and Barry has now been with the company for nearly ten years.

Barry feels that his experience in the library world has served him well in preparing him for his role as a library representative. As a librarian, he told me, he has learned to get a feel for what the patrons want, and this experience is very useful to him in providing service to his library customers. He knows what the librarians are looking for, as well as what their issues and concerns are. He also believes that librarians can relate more easily to a former librarian.

Barry thinks publishing is a good career choice for those librarians or library students who are "more interested in the book end of libraries." For those who are interested in publishing, Barry suggests getting to know the company you're interested in, "to make sure you're a good fit. Make a list of questions to ask *them*." For example, how committed are they to libraries and librarians?

PUBLISHING SOUNDS COOL . . . BUT WHAT IF I DON'T WANT TO BE A LIBRARY REPRESENTATIVE?

Jane White, now a senior account manager in the Scientific, Technical, and Medical (STM) division of Wiley, was my predecessor in the Library Sales Department. In library school, Jane set out to be a corporate librarian. Her first job was at Unisys in Detroit, but when the company headquarters moved east, Jane decided to move to Chicago where she again worked as a corporate librarian. Then Jane was bitten by that idealism bug that seems to affect so many librarians and she made the jump to the public library sector, working for three years as a children's librarian. "I went from corporate meetings one day, to Little Ducky Storytime the next," she told me, "quite a transition!" Jane very much enjoyed working in the children's department and especially enjoyed the young adults. So when the library created a new position—YA librarian, plus adult reference—Jane took that on. Two years later Jane then became head of reference services at Rolling Meadows Public Library, but then she began to feel the need for new challenges. Wiley was looking for a library representative to handle the central United States and hired Jane. Three years after joining Wiley as a library representative, Jane became a marketing manager in Wiley's STM division and was soon promoted to senior marketing manager.

Jane feels that her years of experience as a librarian in a variety of settings certainly prepared her for her current work. In addition to being familiar with all kinds of libraries, "I speak the language, and I'm familiar with the issues," she explained. "I can pass along important information to Wiley," she continued, because her contacts in the library world give her a deeper understanding of what's needed, wanted, and valued.

Her advice for those interested in a career in publishing:

> Get as broad an experience as possible—look for internships in the publishing field. Keep up with current trends because publishing follows the trends of the day. Keep up with technology. Get to know a lot of practical—as opposed to theoretical—information. That basic cataloging course will be immensely helpful because MARC is an issue in both the library and publishing worlds.

As an example, Jane posed this question: "What are the implications of journals' name changes?"—just one of many issues that publishers (and librarians) must deal with. Jane thinks publishing is a good career choice for librarians because "you are still working with knowledge and information. You're just selling it instead of classifying it!"

THE PUBLISHER'S LIBRARIAN

I've discussed the myriad ways in which someone with a library degree might find success within the publishing environment, yet I've left out what is perhaps the most obvious role for a librarian who would like to work for a publisher: the company librarian. What does a publisher's librarian do? To answer that question, I interviewed two librarians currently working in those roles.

Tzofit Butler is a librarian at HarperCollins. In library school it had been her goal to work as a special librarian doing research for a company or a consulting company or a law firm. She told me that when she found the job of Corporate Librarian for HarperCollins, "it was exactly what I was looking for because it allowed me to work as a librarian doing research in a small special library environment." As the director of the Information Center at Harper-Collins, Tzofit is responsible for anything related to the budget, staffing, and administrative issues of the library, including negotiating contracts with research vendors. She also provides research services to the Information Center's users, who are both employees and the public. "We typically handle between 75 and 100 research requests per month," she explained. Other responsibilities include overseeing the corporate archive, the book archive, and their records management program, as well as creation, development, and maintenance of their website on the corporate Intranet.

When I asked Tzofit if she thinks publishing is a good career choice for librarians or library students, this is what she had to say: "I think it is great for someone who loves books and the publishing process. However, it truly depends on what department you are working in. There is a library marketing department, which works directly with librarians [for] marketing our books. That might be a good choice." However, Tzofit warned that a career in publishing can be stressful and, in some areas, the pay is not great. She also feels that getting into the field via the marketing department might allow for more advancement opportunities than you would find in traditional entry-level positions, such as editorial assistant.

At Wiley, Nicole Luce Rizzo is responsible for providing competitive intelligence, creating an environment for business literacy, providing material in a timely manner, researching and evaluating content for various divisions to help them reduce costs, as well as working with teams to assist them in the creation of Wiley products. "There's lots of team work," Nicole told me, "and lots of variety." The Wiley Information Center provides an assortment of resources to the Wiley staff, including biographical information about people who have established reputations in a variety of fields, company and competitor information (e.g., corporate structures, SEC filings, merger and acquisition activity, stock market quotes), federal government information (e.g., research and development spending, National Science Foundation data, copyrights, demographic data), industry information (e.g., forecasts, trade publications, professional associations), and statistical information (e.g., publishing industry statistics, college enrollment figures for selected disciplines, number of industry practitioners). The center's collection is made up of books, periodicals, newsletters, electronic resources, and clippings.

Nicole's advice to those interested in pursuing a career in publishing is to gain "exposure to different research environments and methods, by freelancing in research libraries or even in companies without libraries, in all types of settings—not-for-profit, venture capital, investment banking." Nicole emphasized that having experience is paramount to getting a toe-hold in the industry. When I asked Nicole if she thought publishing to be a good career choice for librarians, she answered with an enthusiastic, "Yes! Publishing is a unique place to be," she went on, "because it's where an interesting group meets: author/librarian/publisher."

If you are interested in those areas, then the world of publishing may just be for you.

IS IT REALLY ALL THAT DARK?

One of the many things I loved about being a librarian was working with other librarians, who are terrifically nice people. One of the many things I love about my job at Wiley is that I spend so much time meeting and talking with librarians. But I've met some similarly terrific people at Wiley, too—people who are just as dedicated to disseminating information and knowledge as are librarians; people whose values, integrity, and ethics I admire and respect; people who are caring and honorable and decent—just like many librarians. Publishing, like librarianship, is not something you go into to get fabulously rich.

So is it really fair to call it the dark side? I don't think so. Besides, as we all learned in *Return of the Jedi,* even Darth Vader had a warm and fuzzy side.

ABOUT THE AUTHOR

Trudy Lindsey, a native Chicagoan, received a double bachelor's degree in elementary education and in education of the deaf and hard-of-hearing from the University of Illinois at Urbana–Champaign (UIUC) in 1969. She taught deaf children in Champaign, Illinois, for several years. In 1977 she returned to UIUC for her master's degree in library and information science and received her MLS the following year. She worked for ten years as a librarian/research associate for the University of Illinois Housing Research and Development Program, a multidisciplinary research department that studied low-income housing and housing for the elderly. In 1989 she became branch manager of a small community public library located in an African American neighborhood in Champaign. Following what seems to be a "new job every decade" pattern, she then turned to a career in publishing, becoming the John Wiley & Sons library representative in the central United States. She had thought that she'd like to stay with Wiley until she retired, but the governorship of California looks mighty inviting.

11

You Want Me to Put What Where? Freelancing Librarianship as Job, Hobby, and Passion

Jessamyn West

> You can take the girl out of the library, but you can't take the library out of the girl.

> —Marylaine Block

When I was still in library school, I got married and moved to Romania for a year. My student job had been night and weekend reference at one of the university's libraries. The pay was lousy, and when it got slow at the desk one of the senior librarians would bring out her typing for me to do. I foresaw a long and demeaning career ahead of me.

In Romania, the fact that I had even been to library school excited people. One of the early Freedom Forum libraries was being set up in Bucharest. The organization, saturated with money from *USA Today*, hired me to help them organize its collection and develop library procedures, thus beginning my entry into freelance librarianship. The pay was exceptional—well, it was almost the same as in school, but the standard of living was much lower—and a lot of my suggestions were ignored, but no one treated me like a temp worker or begrudged me an extra five minutes on my break.

Since then, when I haven't been working in an actual library, I've called myself a freelance librarian. To me, this meant lots of little jobs, varied assignments, sleeping in, and wearing overalls. Or, to put another way, a little work and a lot of 1099 forms. Some of the work I did was for pay, some wasn't. Almost all of it is listed on to my resume in one way or another. It's not what I would call lucrative work, but it is never dull. Freelancing involves certain realities. There's a built-in amount of scutwork you need to do. And as with everything, some personality types are more suited to the work than others.

CERTAIN REALITIES

Success usually comes to those who are too busy to be looking for it.

—Henry David Thoreau

A question I dealt with a lot was "What does a freelance librarian do?" My general explanation was that I had a library degree and I did library work (or "information work" as I like to call it) but did not have a regular job in a regular place. As many librarians can tell you, this sort of work is often more of a calling than an actual practice anyhow. We need to help people find information. We love to answer questions. We organize things the way some people watch TV. People ask us questions in department stores.

I have had many different jobs since graduating from library school that I have felt were tied in to my education and skill set. Some of these are business researcher, textbook writer, standardized test scorer, conference speaker, book editor, information booth worker, magazine writer, VISTA volunteer, computer instructor, web designer, encyclopedia article writer, tech support consultant, and technology project coordinator. I have worked for the Educational Testing Service, Houghton Mifflin, Amazon.com, the City of Seattle, Seattle Public Library, and the University of Washington. Some of these jobs were volunteer, some paid handsomely. It almost doesn't matter which ones; they're all on my resume. Other librarians I know who have freelanced have performed 24/7 reference work, phone support for library vendors, information architecture for library websites, or management consulting for libraries.

While freelancing is a good route to a varied career, it's not for everyone. I have good news and bad news lists, which I have assembled from my own advice; freelance writer, speaker, and trainer Marylaine Block; Douglas Lord, who works 24/7 reference part time; Karen Schneider, the director of lii.org; and my mom, the first freelancer I ever met.

Seven Good Things

1. You can set your own schedule (within deadline parameters).
2. Taking time off is easier.
3. There are more relaxed dress codes.
4. There are "no pointless meetings."
5. The "pay is f-ing great" (or can be).
6. It takes lots and lots of self-determination, also known as the "sink-or-swim" syndrome.
7. Life is never boring, although it is sometimes wretched.

Seven Bad Things

1. Quarterly tax payments, and higher taxes at that.
2. There is no built-in work social scene.
3. There is no guaranteed income.
4. Looking for work takes a lot of time.
5. Dealing with suspicion from 9-to-5 friends that you don't work very hard.
6. There is no one to blame but yourself if things don't work out.
7. You still need to suck up to bosses, but now they're called "clients."

Freelancing requires that you do your job and also manage your budget, juggle your engagements, and keep your space(s) organized. The trade-off is an ever-changing schedule, a good deal of self-determination, and an opportunity to really learn a lot about many different things. Additionally, you'll get a lot of suspicious looks from nonfreelancers who will view your freelancing as an attempt to avoid "real work."

In all honestly, the freelancers that I know work more than almost anyone else. This is partly because when they're not working at one job they are frequently looking for the next one. And if their project succeeds or fails, it's all on their shoulders. This can necessitate extra hours, even the dreaded nights and weekends. On the other hand, once you've handed in an assignment or finished a task, you can turn off your cell phone, quit checking your e-mail, leave the house, and not come back for weeks. IF you know where your next paycheck is coming from, that is.

Librarianship is not thought of as a risky profession. I see many of the free lance librarians and other information workers I know as people who are interested in the work but dislike the routine. They need to always be working on something new, encountering new people, and trying new things. Sometimes they have specialized skills such as indexing or rare book repair that keeps them hopping from job to job. Other times they have other family or life commitments that keep them from regular jobs. Sometimes they just value leisure time. Others can't work well with other people. Often it's a mixture of those and many other reasons. It's important when you're freelancing to make sure you're doing it because you like it, not because you can't manage elsewhere. This is one of the best ways to make sure you can grapple with the necessary scutwork.

SCUTWORK

It's not very pleasant in my corner of the world at three o'clock in the morning. But for people who like cold, wet, ugly bits it is something rather special.

—Eeyore

Seven Scutworks of the Self-Employed

1. Sacrifice

    It's easy to think about the things one would enjoy about freelancing, but it's important to be aware of the less-enjoyable bits. Working for yourself can be taxing both emotionally and physically. Having odd hours can make it difficult to juggle family and community responsibilities and last-minute deadlines always throw everything into a tizzy. Make sure you feel comfortable making the decision to freelance not only for you but also for your entire social and familial network.

2. Sucking Up

    While most of my freelance jobs have been delightful, some were not. When you are contracted to do a freelance job and find your client very difficult to work for, it can be a challenge since there is really no conference room to hide out in and no coworkers to blame. Since you often work both for the job you're on and the promise of getting more similar work in the future, you need to really adopt a customer-is-always-right policy, which can be grating. I have had clients who wouldn't let me finish a sentence, some who would call be me before 7 A.M., and the one odd client who demanded endless rewrites. Sometimes you can say "screw the good reference" and tell the client what you really think, but more often than not it's a fine line of diplomacy that needs walking. Be sure you're ready for that.

3. See Ya, Sleep!

    Depending on what sort of freelance work you do, your schedule may not be your own. My mom finds that in the textbook writing business, there are often shifting deadlines based on the many layers of production a book has to go through. I like working at night on the West Coast, but this can mean sleeping through my client's entire day in the East Coast. Giving clients your home phone number can be great for last-minute design changes, but it can be really tough for last-minute snooze-button pressing. Having an odd schedule in general can make you a bit of an oddball when your friends all make plans for the evening and you still have a few hours of work left to do.

4. Sam, Uncle

    Taxes are a whole new kettle of fish when you are self-employed. You must not only keep current with all the year's employers so they can mail you your tax forms, you are also obligated to report earnings even if you did *not* get tax forms from them. Since you have no employer paying their share of your social security, the entire burden is on you. I generally estimate that 25 percent of my freelance earnings go straight to taxes before deductions. You will also be responsible for state and local business licenses and corresponding taxes. While there are many good information sources and websites to help you figure this all out, you must find the initiative to go find them.

5. Self-Discipline

You need to be able to keep yourself on task even though other people aren't telling you to get stuff done. If you work at home, you may have the added curse of the phone, e-mail, family, friends, or just Other Things to Do. Or, as Greg, who has been observing my freelance work at home for the past year or so says, "It's tough when you want a beer at two in the afternoon and there's no one there to tell you not to have one."

6. Seepage

When you work in an office and live in a house, the two places have very little in common, so it's easy not to conflate the work you do in each place. If your office *is* your house, this is not so simple. Having a home office is not only a tax deduction under some circumstances, but it can be an essential way of keeping your work life and your home life separate as well.

7. Secretary, Lack Thereof

This doesn't just mean lacking someone around to do typing and filing, it means all the support staff in a normal office or library environment. When I began freelance writing, I was amazed at how much time making copies, sending resumes, copying disks, burning CDs, sending query letters, and sending clip files took. Not that I ever had anyone to do that for me before, but since I was working only for myself now I saw the time as time I wasn't working for pay.

PERSONALITY PARADE

Opportunity is missed by most people because it is dressed in overalls, and looks like work.

—Thomas A. Edison

I'm not saying if you're not outgoing you can't freelance, but it's a better career choice for people who like people. Since the work isn't always lucrative, it's important to seize opportunities when they come up. This can require a bit of the go-getter mentality. It's also very important to be able to talk about things that are difficult for some people, such as money, your abilities or lack thereof, or contractual obligations. While I'm not entirely into the idea that you have to always be "selling yourself" to get work, the truth is you do need to be able to not sabotage yourself when discussing your abilities or your rights. While aggressive self-marketing is often a turn off—ever have some-one give you his business card on the bus?—knowing the proper way to in-troduce yourself and your skills is crucial.

A large part of being a successful freelancer is being able to promote your-self not only accurately but also strongly. There are a few areas that you must be prepared to discuss, and discuss well, with potential clients.

Money

I became a happier freelancer when I raised my rates and quit doing cut-rate work for friends. Now, if I work for friends, I do it for free, and it's clear who is doing whom the favor. If I do work at full rates, I give it my full attention and I fit in nonpaying work as I can. Remember, libraries don't have a lot of money, but they do have budgets. The same goes for library organizations. Often, especially with speaking engagements, people won't offer money un-less you ask, but I have rarely been turned down when I ask for travel or lodg-ing expenses to be covered. Remember to save all of your receipts; much of your travel and work expenses as a freelancer can be written off your taxes. I've even written off parts of my vacations if I was doing research that wound up as part of a magazine article.

Similarly, assume that there may be certain cash outlays that are an impor-tant part of the freelancing world that were not part of the 9-to-5 world. You pay for a lot of your own postage, long-distance calls, travel, Internet access, office supplies, and coffee. All of these expenses should be built into your fees; make sure you don't just translate your hourly rate from your old job to your new one.

When you're new at working for yourself and you don't have a lot of money, it's tempting to skimp on things like health insurance that are very rarely built into work-for-hire contractual arrangements. Many organizations like the American Library Association have been looking into group coverage for their members. The National Writers Union also offers group coverage for their members in New York. See if there is an organization that you are al-ready involved with that can help you get a lower rate on necessary expenses like health care and childcare. Be sure to reflect these costs in your fees. A li-brarian friend of mine talked about her first job, which was half time and paid 10K a year (this was in the 1990s). She said the assumption was that whoever was doing the job was either retired and didn't need the income or had a hus-band with a better job who handled most of the bills. The job was considered philanthropy to the town. Be sure the work you do isn't philanthropic, unless you intend it to be.

Contracts

Contracts protect you as well as your employer. Before you do a lot of writing or speaking for hire, make sure you understand the various kinds of work-for-hire contracts and be prepared to do some negotiating. This can be tough. It is generally in your employer's or publisher's best interest to imply or otherwise let you know that the contract is standard, non-negotiable, or otherwise set in stone. Why are contracts so important? I'll cede the floor to Karen Schneider, chief of lii.org, member of ALA Council, and experienced freelancer, to give you her opinion.

"Seven Reasons Contracts Matter" by Karen Schneider

1. Contracts clarify what you're doing and what they're expecting. Nothing is worse than completing a project only to hear, "Oh, you really wanted. . . ."
2. Contracts give you diplomatic tools for getting paid on time. It's really only fair to the contracting organization to spell out to them how much you want and when you want it.
3. Contracts give you a tool to go after offending third parties.
4. Contracts can be used to take control. If you're even thinking about writing a book, you not only need a contract, you need a lawyer to review that contract and help you get a good deal. A lot of us are so eager to see our name in print the first few times we don't even ask what the terms are. Down the road, you don't want to find out you can never, ever publish another book about, say, Internet hamster sites because your contract for that really neat book owns all future rights. You will never make enough money from a title in library science to justify relinquishing that control unless you know you will never publish on that topic again.
5. Contracts communicate your intentions to the world. Look at the GNU "license." That's really a tool for explaining the expectations established by open source developers.
6. Then there's the self-esteem issue. If a magazine publisher thinks your work is worth publishing, it's worth paying for. They are not doing you a favor by publishing your work; good writers are much harder to find than you realize. We all have "freebie" exceptions, such as case studies in scholarly books to help a friend get tenure.
7. Finally, as fun as it is to get published, remember when you write for free or cheap, you make it that much harder for others to get paid for their work. My best experience here comes not from the publishing world but from my brief experience as a freelance Internet trainer. I set very reasonable prices and pitched my services to local library consortia, only to be beaten out for jobs by librarians all too willing to donate services on personal time. I couldn't compete with "free regardless of the quality," and ended up earning my living from jobs with school districts and non-profits.

You

At the very least, you'll need a phone number, mailing address, home address, and e-mail address. Helpful additions are business cards, letterhead, a website, a cell phone, and a big smile. I have had trouble in the past because I didn't have ready access to a fax machine or had given an editor my P.O. Box when they needed to send something UPS. My mom keeps several versions of Microsoft Word on her computer at home to accommodate editors who use older versions. This is, of course, not a necessary accommodation, but a service she provides. The more ways you can show you are easy to work with, the better. This changes over time, certainly, as your reputation grows, but making an eager first impression, I believe, is important. An honest, informative website and a nice thank-you note for an interview go farther than you could imagine.

You'll need to be able to chat people up about your experience and skills and why you are better for the job than someone else. You'll find it helpful to learn to explain what you do in a thirty-second bit, a five-minute bit, and lengthier explanations for bigger jobs. Since the library world is a bit mystifying to people, you may need a way to explain why you aren't working in a library, why you chose freelancing, or how your skills are useful outside of the library world. Learn to stress your strengths and don't hesitate to brag a little, especially if you can do so truthfully. When you tell people, "I've been in the biz fifteen years and never missed a deadline!" they pay attention.

IN TOTO

> Everything is part of it.
>
> —Tom Robbins

For a freelancer, life and work are not two distinct entities, they are inexorably linked. You can't leave your job at work, but you also don't have to keep your personal life at home. Manuel Castells argues in the book *The Hacker Ethic* that we are seeing a rise of informationalism that will challenge a lot of our previously held assumptions about the nature of work and the nature of jobs. Freelancers and librarians will be on the forefront of that movement. Now is a good time to get ready for it.

NOTE

1. See marylaine.com/personal.html (last accessed 20 May 2004).

ONLINE RESOURCES

National Writer's Union, info on contracts, freelance jobs, and union issues— www.nwu.org/.

NWU tips for a better work-for-hire contract—www.nwu.org//bite/tipswfh.htm.

Are you an Employee or a Contractor? an IRS form to help you determine your status—www.irs.gov/pub/irs-pdf/p15a.pdf.

List of Gnu Licenses—www.gnu.org/licenses/licenses.html.

The Hacker Ethic, a manifesto for the modern-day freelancer—www.hackerethic.org.

Electronic Rights: Copyright Law & Collective Works, a good article from the Publishing Law Center—www.publaw.com/erights3.html.

RELATED READINGS

Himanen, Pekka, with Linus Torvalds and Manuel Castells. *The Hacker Ethic and the Spirit of the Information Age.* New York: Random House, 2001.

ABOUT THE AUTHOR

Jessamyn West runs the weblog librarian.net and has just recently started a job as an actual librarian. On her way to landed librarian bliss, she has written for *American Libraries*, *Computers in Libraries*, and *Searcher* magazine, and coedited *Revolting Librarians Redux.* She has worked in special, academic, public, and weird libraries. She lives in Vermont.

12

Countless Opportunities: Alternative Career Paths for Librarians and Information Professionals

Selma Permenter

When most students enroll in library school, they envision themselves working in a traditional library environment, perhaps as a reference librarian, a children's librarian, or even an archivist or a cataloger. But as the role of traditional librarians evolves, the number of career opportunities for librarians outside the traditional library environment is growing as well. More and more companies and organizations are recognizing the benefits of employees with a library school education. And more and more librarians are taking advantage of this trend and applying their abilities outside of the library.

Library and information science students and traditional librarians who are ready for a career change should consider all of the possibilities—both inside and outside the traditional library environment—when determining their next career path. It is important to realize that many of the same skills and traits that make a successful librarian are also some of the same skills and traits that make an excellent database manager, bookseller, researcher, information architect, or even professional fund-raiser. Some of these opportunities pay significantly more than many traditional librarian positions. More importantly, however, if you consider these options in your job search, you will open a whole new world of opportunities.

TECHNOLOGY-RELATED CAREERS

Libraries have always been among the first to utilize emerging technologies. Therefore, it should come as no surprise that the librarians who helped implement these technologies are highly skilled and capable of applying these skills to a number of positions outside the traditional library setting.

Information and Database Manager

Over the last several years, the information management field has exploded with career possibilities. At no time in our history has more information been so readily accessible to the general population. As a result, there has never been a greater demand for expert information professionals who can plan, manage, and implement the organization and dissemination of this information.

All databases, whether a student database at a university, a patient database at a hospital, or an employee database at a Fortune 500 company, need to be managed by someone who understands how information is organized and how that information needs to be retrieved. Library and information professionals with an expertise in technology are vastly qualified to help fill this need. Librarians are educated and trained in the organization and retrieval of information. Librarians who are able to apply this skill to information found outside the walls of a traditional library are prime candidates for positions in the private sector, government agencies, nonprofit organizations, and academic institutions. All of these organizations depend on sophisticated databases to manage their day-to-day operations.

Database managers are responsible for maintaining the integrity and security of the database. They analyze system capabilities and recommend and plan for upgrades and improvements. In addition, they often train end-users, design reports, and verify the accuracy of output. The database manager need not be a computer programmer, but he or she does need to have a working understanding of computer programming to better communicate needs to the programmers.

Network Administrator

Many libraries utilize large computer networks. In many cases, it is a librarian who serves as the library's network administrator. As a result of this on-the-job training, these librarians are immensely qualified to fill similar roles outside of the library. And many of the positions in the private sector pay significantly more than those in a library setting.

Network administrators monitor and evaluate the performance of local and wide area networks. They are responsible for installing and maintaining hardware and software on the network and providing technical support to users. Network administrators are also responsible for overseeing nightly backups of servers and preparing a disaster-recovery plan. Because network administrators are also responsible for troubleshooting to solve network problems as they arise, they are often on call and can put in long hours.

Information Architects

Because of the increasing use and importance of websites, a growing number of companies and organizations are looking to information architects to support the design, development, implementation, and maintenance of their website. And because of the strong organizational and technical skills of librarians, they are increasingly being looked to as candidates for this important position.

A well-planned and well-designed website targets a specific audience and plays an integral role in a business's success. It is the information architect's job to ensure that web content is well organized and presented in an easily accessible interface. To accomplish this, information architects typically work with a team that includes end-users, web designers, graphic designers, and content writers. They use Visio or a similar diagramming software program to diagram elements of the website and help the design and programming teams implement this structure.

Other Technical-Related Positions

There are many more technical-related positions that you may want to consider in your job search. Listed below are such positions that surfaced during a search of Monster.com and HotJobs.com.

- chief information officer
- data information analyst
- data manager
- database administrator
- database analyst
- database consultant
- database designer
- database manager
- database specialist
- information architect
- information engineer
- information management specialist
- information manager
- information security engineer
- information site architect
- information specialist
- information technology manager
- knowledge management coordinator
- knowledge manager
- medical records administrator
- network administrator
- reporting analyst
- systems analyst

- systems consultant
- systems network engineer
- technology services specialist

RESEARCH CAREERS

If you have an insatiable curiosity, enjoy working independently, and are process and detail oriented, you may want to consider a career in research. With the vast and growing amount of information available, countless organizations worldwide rely on researchers to retrieve and analyze the information that is relevant to them. All types of organizations—businesses, government agencies, academic institutions, and nonprofit organizations—need qualified researchers.

The researching and reference skills librarians possess are extremely helpful in research-related careers. Other traits of a good researcher include the ability to meet deadlines, effective communication skills, strong organizational skills, and attention to detail.

Business Research

Companies in all industries need individuals to conduct research to support their business operations. Business researchers utilize online databases, internal records, the Internet, and other resources to track information on customers, competitors, and industry trends. They support sales efforts by providing information on prospects and help businesses succeed by providing detailed market reports and competitive intelligence.

Successful business researchers must be self-motivated, flexible, and able to manage multiple projects simultaneously while meetings tight deadlines. An interest in business and a general knowledge of the industry is helpful.

Prospect Research

Prospect researchers are fund-raising professionals who gather, analyze, and disseminate information, better enabling universities and nonprofit organizations to raise private support. In their research, they use in-house records, on-line services, public records, library resources, and the Internet. They analyze the information gathered to help identify a prospective donor's philanthropic interests, giving capacity, and inclination to give. They also use the information they gain to identify and qualify new donors. Prospect researchers summarize the information they collect in a report, or profile, that front-line development officers use when cultivating and soliciting prospects.

Colleges and universities were among the first organizations to hire professional researchers to conduct this type of research, but more and more nonprofit organizations are turning to prospect researchers to help them raise private support in an increasingly competitive fund-raising environment. For many, prospect research can lead to a long-term career in fund development.

Other Research Opportunities

A number of other research opportunities are out there waiting for you. Since the opportunities in this field are so varied, it is wise to look at your personal interests and goals when searching for the perfect research position for you. Looking to your undergraduate degree may help define the path you should take. For instance, if your undergraduate degree is in business, you may enjoy working for a large corporation conducting product and industry research. If your undergraduate focus is in social services, you may be more skilled at gathering and analyzing information for a nonprofit agency. If you have a background in science, you may be excellent at medical research.

Listed below are a few research-related positions you may want to consider in your job search.

- administrative research analyst
- business research analyst
- database researcher
- development research associate
- donor research
- knowledge manager
- library researcher
- prospect researcher
- research assistant
- research manager
- researcher
- strategic research consultant

BOOKSELLERS

Librarians and booksellers share so many common skills and interests that it is only natural for librarians ready for a career change to consider bookselling. Like librarians, booksellers enjoy reading and sharing books with others. They enjoy the variety of topics covered in the books they provide and have a natural curiosity and love for learning. Like librarianship, bookselling can be a very broad field. It is best to consider your personal interests and goals when determining the type of bookseller you want to be.

Bookstore Owner

If you have an entrepreneurial nature and a strong business mind, you might consider opening your own bookstore. As with any small business, running a bookstore requires excellent planning, reporting, budgeting, and management skills. You will also find that the cataloging and classifying skills you learned as a librarian are useful when organizing your inventory.

Owning your own business does come with a number of risks and requires a significant financial investment. To be successful, it is important to do your homework. Research and learn about the trade. Visit as many different bookstores as possible. Attend book fairs and pour over book catalogs. And above all, develop a solid business plan. Owning a bookstore can be very rewarding, but it will also require hard work and long hours.

Out-of-Print Book Finder

If you like the idea of being your own boss but do not want to take the risk of opening your own store, you may want to consider becoming an out-of-print book finder. As an out-of-print book finder, you will use your reference skills daily to locate out-of-print books for your customers. You can market your services to used bookstores or directly to the public. Since you will undoubtedly acquire an inventory, another way to earn revenue (and make room for more books) is to sell your collection through print or Internet-based catalogs.

Antiquarian Bookseller

If you love finding and acquiring beautiful, old books and are not afraid of the risks involved with self-employment, you may want to consider becoming an antiquarian bookseller. Antiquarian booksellers sell fine and rare books and other printed materials, often specializing in a particular subject, author, or genre. Many antiquarian booksellers have stores where they sell their collections. Others sell their books through book fairs, catalogs, and Internet stores while holding down other full- or part-time jobs.

Antiquarian booksellers often travel throughout the country searching for books for their collection. They meet and network with others in the trade through involvement in the Antiquarian Booksellers Association of America and numerous local bookseller associations. Few get rich in this business, but those who chose this career path do it for the love of the books.

Bookstore Manager

If you have excellent managerial skills, love the idea of being a bookseller, but do not want to take the risk of opening your own store, you should consider a career with a large corporate bookstore like Barnes & Noble or Borders. These stores offer their employees excellent benefits and opportunities to advance. They, like public libraries, promote a community environment by organizing events such as poetry readings, books clubs, craft nights, game tournaments, and children's events.

Store managers are responsible for managing the day-to-day operations of the store, achieving sales goals and building an inventory that is reflective of the needs of the community. Since the manager hires, develops, coaches, motivates, and evaluates staff, excellent supervisory skills are important.

CONCLUSION

The alternative career options discussed in this chapter are just a few of the many options available to librarians and information professionals. In most cases, the job postings for these positions do not list a MLS or MIS among the required degrees. In fact, most do not. Therefore, it is important to be creative and open to new ideas when looking to apply your skills to a nontraditional career path. If you take an active and aggressive role in applying your skills to all of the positions you feel you are capable and qualified to fill—both inside and outside the traditional library environment—you are likely to be successful in your job search.

ONLINE RESOURCES

ABAA.org—Antiquarian Booksellers' Association of America
APRAHome.org—Association of Professional Researchers for Advancement
ARMA.org—The Association for Information Management Professionals
Bookweb.org—American Booksellers Association
HotJobs.com
Monster.com

RELATED READINGS

Cohen, Sacha. "Becoming an Information Architect: Work as a Web Site Strategist." *Monster Technology* (2003)— technology.monster.com/articles/infoarchitect.

Eberts, Marjorie, and Margaret Gisler. *Careers for Book Worms & Other Literary Types*, 3rd ed. Chicago: VGM Career Books, 2003.

Horton, Forest Woody. *Extending the Librarian's Domain: A Survey of Emerging Occupation Opportunities for Librarians and Information Professionals*. Washington, D.C.: Special Libraries Association, 1994.

McCook, Kathleen de la Peña, and Margaret Myers. *Opportunities in Library and Information Science Careers*. Chicago: VGM Career Books, 2002.

Sellen, Betty-Carol, ed. *What Else You Can Do with a Library Degree: Career Options for the 90s and Beyond*. New York: Neal-Schuman Publishers, Inc., 1997.

Wodtke, Christina. *Information Architecture: Blueprints for the Web*. Indianapolis: New Riders, 2002.

ABOUT THE AUTHOR

Selma Permenter is director of development for annual giving and advancement services at the University of Texas at Arlington where she manages the university's alumni database and directs the annual fund with a goal of more than $1 million. She began her career at the University as a prospect researcher in 1992. She received her undergraduate degree in English from the University of Texas at Arlington in 1991 and a master's in information science from the University of North Texas in 1993.

2

EDUCATION

13

Choosing a Library Program

Kevin O'Kelly

GRADUATE SCHOOL RANKINGS:
NOT AS IMPORTANT AS YOU THINK

Many people contemplating graduate or professional school turn to the *U.S. News & World Report* annual rankings. Take a look if you want, but certainly don't let the rankings settle any questions for you. A high *U.S. News* ranking reflects that a library school, and the university of which it is a part, has prestige. And it would be foolish, in our world, to say that prestige doesn't matter. But there's a lot that a *U.S. News* ranking doesn't tell you, such as what it's like to sit in a class at a given school or how supportive the faculty are. A *U.S. News* ranking gives you no insight into availability of financial aid that will help you pay for library school or of student work opportunities that will give you a leg up when you enter the job market.

"There really isn't any particular source that reliably ranks professional programs," notes Louise Sullivan, the education reference librarian at Spokane Public Library. "The problem is that the criteria for ranking are usually not disclosed," Sullivan adds. "The only recommendation that I can make is to contact the professional organizations that oversee the various professions."

Sullivan is right: Professional organizations don't rank schools. But you should *definitely* check out the American Library Association (ALA) list of accredited library school programs in the United States, Puerto Rico, and Canada. Go to www.ala.org, click on the "Education and Careers" button at the top of the page, and then click on "Accredited Programs" in the left-hand frame. And note the word *accredited*. The minimum qualification for employment as a professional librarian in most libraries is an MLS or MLIS from a library school accredited by the American Library Association. It doesn't matter how "prestigious" a given school is; the University of California at Berkeley, for example, has a School of Information and Systems Management—but it's not ALA accredited.

DO YOUR RESEARCH: IN OTHER WORDS, START ACTING LIKE A LIBRARIAN *NOW*

The ALA site listing provides links to library school websites and all the information you need to contact them and request course catalogs and financial aid information. The websites usually list the current semester's course schedule. Some sites even have the school prospectus available in PDF. While reading the published information is worthwhile, don't stop there. Talk to people. Make an appointment to speak to someone in a supervisory position at the type of library you might like to work for one day. Ask them what library schools they recommend—what schools on a resume make them take a second look, and why. Or contact someone who's doing the sort of job you would like to have after you graduate. Ask them where they went to school, and what they did in library school that best helped them get where they are now.

Katie Barrett, a reference librarian at the Boston Public Library, said her background reading and interviews were invaluable in preparing her for library school and a job. "When I was looking at the programs and classes offered by the different schools, I talked to librarians who had been in the field for some time," Barrett said. "They gave me advice as to what kind of classes I should take for both my personal and professional development, and most importantly what classes would get me hired. They specified reference courses and cataloging courses."

Barrett looked over course catalogs from different library schools, and noted the schools with substantial reference and cataloging course offerings. "On a side note," she added, "they were right about the cataloging courses. These courses got my foot in the door for a few jobs [after library school] and gave me something to talk about in interviews. Even for reference jobs!"

To sum up: the more you know, the better off you are.

MAKING LIBRARY SCHOOL AFFORDABLE

Let's face it: None of us is going to get rich on a librarian's salary. According to the ALA's 2002 salary survey, the mean salary for public and academic librarians with an MLS was $49,866; the median was $46,600. According to the SLA's 2002 salary survey, the median pay for special librarians was $56,500 (the mean was not specified).

I encourage you to think very hard before incurring significant debt to attend library school. At some schools, it's quite easy to rack up $25,000 in debt. Fortunately, many library schools in the United States are at public universities. Some students move to a place where they think they would like to go to library school, get a job (ideally in a local library), and then apply, so that they're qualified for in-state tuition.

Richard Giersch was working in a library at West Virginia University and trying to figure out how to afford library school. "The back door approach seemed to be the best way to go about it," he said. "I applied for jobs at UNC and waited for about a year until I heard back from them, came down for an interview, and was hired a month or so later. I took a position at UNC and moved down there. Part of the deal was [that] UNC libraries had set aside graduate research assistantships if you were an employee."

Giersch, now chief operating officer of Zen-Bio, a biotechnology firm in North Carolina's Research Triangle Park, concedes that his approach to library school takes a long time. But his method has its rewards: "To avoid coming to UNC as an out-of-state student and paying out-of-state tuition and other bills for two years I invested a little time and saved $40,000 in the process."

When Katie Barrett was considering her library school options, she realized it would be cheaper to go to McGill University in Montreal than it would be to attend the only U.S. library school where she had in-state tuition—the University of Washington at Seattle. "At the time (1999–2001) the U.S. dollar was much stronger than the Canadian dollar," she noted. "Also the cost of living in Montreal was pretty low as well."

Other library schools offer substantial assistantships. Dora St. Martin, now director of reference at the Somerville Public Library in the Boston area, decided to attend the University of Michigan when she was accepted into their University Library Associates program. "You get a two-year assistantship working in one of the university libraries that provides a small stipend, a tuition waiver, and health insurance."

I was lucky: I was already living in Chapel Hill when I decided to apply to the UNC School of Information and Library Science (SILS), which meant I already had in-state tuition. I had also applied to several other library schools, among them the University of Michigan. I was accepted into their program but got no financial aid. Out-of-state tuition at Michigan was over $16,000 a year at the time. Then UNC SILS notified me that I had received a fellowship waiving tuition and fees for the first year.

I was going to UNC.

Do your homework: there's a good bit of money out there to help you. The American Library Association provides more than $300,000 annually in scholarships for master's students in library and information science (see the "ALA Scholarships Program" in the Awards and Scholarships section of the

ALA website). The ALA also publishes a guide called *Financial Assistance for Library and Information Studies* (also available in PDF on the ALA website in the "Awards and Scholarships" section). And directly contact any school you are considering about financial aid opportunities.

THINKING AHEAD: WORK EXPERIENCE

Not to belabor the obvious, but the reason you're going to library school is to have a library job after you graduate. Any work experience you can get while still in school can only help you later. One factor in my choice to attend SILS at UNC was the libraries—the University of North Carolina has over thirty university and departmental libraries and special collections, and they all need part-time help of some sort. Job opportunities abounded. SILS also offered course credit for internships, so I could earn three of the course credits I needed for graduation at the same time that I was getting useful work experience.

The opportunity for work experience helped Giovanna Gossage decide to attend the University of Western Ontario. "One of the reasons I chose Western was they offered a co-op program. It made a lot of sense to me to be able to get work experience while I was in school," said Gossage, now a reference librarian at the National Library of Canada. Her get-it-done and get-on-the-job attitude also played a factor in her decision to attend Western: "They have a more condensed program than some library schools, so I could do it in three terms rather than two years. It gets you out into the workforce sooner and gets you qualified sooner."

The University Library Associates program at Michigan not only paid Dora St. Martin's rent and tuition—it helped her get her first real job. "The Library Associates offered me a job in Michigan's Engineering Library," she explained. "I worked there for two years. It led to my first professional job as a Science Librarian at the Toledo Lucas County Public Library."

As an international student, Katie Barrett faced some difficulties in Montreal; as a foreign student she couldn't get work-study (or work off campus) the first year. Fortunately, her savings went pretty far in Montreal, and she got an on-campus non-workstudy job in March. During the summer, she moved back across the border and interned at the Maine Historical Society. It sounds like a lot of hassle, but she has no regrets: "I had a great time," she reflected. Her second year at McGill, she was eligible for work-study and took a position at a reference desk. "I had the autonomy to make it a real work experience, and it really helped me after graduation."

LIBRARY SCHOOL CAN BE MORE THAN JUST THE MLS

Most librarians—or people planning to become librarians—have diverse interests. One of the great things about library school is that many programs offer you the opportunity to indulge those interests and prepare for your career at the same time. Think about your interests and how to combine them into a job. The school listings on the ALA website list the joint degrees offered by each library school. Are you a news junkie? The University of Indiana offers a joint master's degree in journalism and library science—ideal preparation for a news librarian. Are you fascinated by business? The University of California at Los Angeles offers a joint MLS/MBA—perfect for a business school or corporate librarian. If you're fascinated by Latin American history, you could to go to UCLA where you can combine your MLS with an MA in Latin American studies. Some schools will help you combine an MLS with degrees in folklore, law, Eastern European Studies, divinity, or music. Think about your dream job—you can probably find a library school that will let you pursue the right combination of coursework or degrees to qualify you for it.

IT'S NOT JUST ABOUT MONEY OR JOBS: IT'S ABOUT YOU

All of us have preferences, crotchets, quirks, and tastes that indicate we would be happier in some places than others. Do you thrive on urban life? Maybe you should think about the University of Washington at Seattle, Catholic University of America (DC), or Drexel (Philadelphia). Do you hate hot weather? The University of Texas might not be the best place for you. Do you love the beach, the forest, or the mountains? Whatever your preferences are, take them into account if you can.

I liked living in Chapel Hill and wanted to continue living there for a couple more years. Similarly, one of the reasons Dora St. Martin applied to the University of Michigan was that it's in Ann Arbor. "It's a very nice town—an important consideration when you're taking a partner along," she said. "[It's] home to the Ann Arbor Art Festival, the Ann Arbor 16mm Film Festival, the original Borders bookstore, and many good late night cafes and beer bars."

In addition to the strong course offerings and financial advantages, Katie Barrett had an additional reason for wanting to study at McGill: its location. "I have to admit that one of the biggest factors in my choice of a library school was its location. I chose McGill because it was in French-speaking Montreal. I have always been passionate about foreign languages, particularly French," she continued. "I studied it as an undergrad and taught it in high school for a time. Although the decision to go to a school in a French-speaking city seems arbitrary, in retrospect it really wasn't, because I think that being bilingual is an important skill for librarians and I saw myself working as a bilingual librarian in the future."

And once you've sorted out issues like what kind of degree(s) you want to pursue, the likelihood of financial aid, and where you are willing to live for a couple of years, then you're ready to apply. And when some schools have admitted you—go visit. Sit in on classes. Meet with faculty. Talk to students.

And ask yourself: Would I like working with these people? Is this school my best chance at helping me get where I want to be in a couple of years?

RELATED READINGS

Guidelines for Choosing a Master's Program in Library and Information Science. (Go to www.ala.org. Click on the "Education and Careers" link at the top of the page. Then click on "Accredited Programs" in the list of links on the left. Click on "ALA-Accredited Master's Programs." The "Guidelines" link is just below "Distance Learning Opportunities").

U.S. News and World Report Graduate School Rankings. It can't tell you which library school is the best (whatever that means), but it often includes stories on issues facing graduate students—such as how to pay for school.

ABOUT THE AUTHOR

Kevin O'Kelly is a cataloging and reference librarian at Somerville Public Library in Somerville, Massachusetts. He received his MLS from the University of North Carolina at Chapel Hill.

14

The MLS: What Is It Worth?

Chrissie Anderson Peters

The MLS is often a debatable issue across the various segments of the information profession. While some maintain that it is essential to the true "professional" in terms of obtaining a specific core base of knowledge, theory, and practicality, others hold that hands-on experience can be far more useful and advantageous than studying hypothetical scenarios and other scholars' thoughts on the vast scope of areas covered under the library or information science umbrella. I have worked with people with degrees and without degrees who were impressively knowledgeable about the field. I have also worked with people with and without degrees who were completely lacking in any social skills or library know-how. In fact, before my first job in an academic library, it never occurred to me that there was a very significant difference between those with and without master's degrees. I had been taught many skills as a paraprofessional that others entering the field may not have experienced. Situations such as these are still rather commonplace and only add to the confusion and misunderstanding of the degree and what it means as a professional endorsement.

Learning how to perform adequately in a library or information environment can be accomplished in large part without having ever taken a master's-level course in library or information studies. Landing a job in such an environment is also quite possible without anything more than a bachelor's degree. As a matter of fact, it is even possible to land a professional-level library position without the MLS (although these positions are not as plentiful as positions requiring "an (American Library Association) ALA-accredited master's degree"). Whether to pursue the degree is more an issue of personal preference than a strictly "right or wrong" decision. Many wonder whether pursuing such a degree is "worth" it to those wishing to enter or further their careers in the profession. In other words, "How badly do you want it?" This chapter addresses two different types of "worth" that people may want to consider in their decision-making process—financial and time commitment.

IT'S ALL ABOUT THE MONEY

Perhaps it's unfair to imply that it's *all* about the money, but realistically, money can play a huge part in your decision whether to pursue the MLS—or even *where* to pursue the degree. How much does a typical ALA-accredited master's program cost? Are there financial aid opportunities? How much money can you expect to earn once you finish the master's program and land your first professional position? Which types of library or information environments pay the highest entry-level salaries? Does geography matter in terms of pay? The list of potential "money" questions could go on and on.

MONEY CHANGES EVERYTHING

In early 2000, I had decided that the time was right for me to find a graduate program and begin work on my master's degree. I had researched materials available from ALA, had meticulously studied the graduate school rankings in *U.S. News & World Report*, had researched the area to which I would be relocating, and had wondered how in the world I would afford the tuition at this well-respected, highly ranked, private institution and the cost of living in this exciting, historic city. But I was single, in my early twenties, and full of confidence. Once I took off the rose-colored glasses, I realized that I was full of other things, too! When I realized I had accumulated quite a bit of credit card debt in the years since finishing my BA, still had undergraduate student loans to be paid off, had no savings or investments to speak of, already had trouble making ends meet in central Virginia, and was moving to a faraway city and enrolling in a program that would cost approximately as much as my annual salary once I completed the program, I faced the fact that it was time to stop and reevaluate my choices.

I decided to consult people "in the know"—directors and other supervisors in various types of libraries across the country. I started with folks I knew in my own library system and regional affiliates. My supervisor had graduated from a school somewhere about halfway down the *U.S. News* rankings ladder, and he told me that, while attending the program of my choice would be important to my own happiness and possibly my performance (the logic being that, if you are happy, you will probably perform better), what matters most to potential employers is the fact that you graduated from an ALA-accredited institution and are competent in the area(s) for which you are seeking employment. One of my coworkers, who was at that time in a paraprofessional position in our system, had graduated from the top program in the nation. Her advice was to do what made me happy in terms of selecting a school accredited by ALA, but not to feel compelled to spend a huge amount of money if I didn't have to. Although she wouldn't have traded her experiences at her alma mater for anything, she admitted that she did have a rather significant student loan to repay.

Consulting colleagues through e-mail discussion lists and my state library association ties, I heard the same thing over and over: Just get a master's from an ALA-accredited institution, regardless of how it ranked on the *U.S. News & World Report* list. Of course, this made me stop and wonder what the point of ranking the programs was. Thus, I began more research, starting at the source of the rankings. I found a brief article in the April 10, 2000, issue of *U.S. News & World Report* that explained their rankings more in-depth:

> Our analysis is based on data collected last fall in more than 13,000 surveys; to rank schools, we use objective quality measures such as test scores and research expenditures and reputation ratings drawn from inside and outside of academia. Deans and faculty members, for example, were asked to rate each program with which they are familiar on a scale of 1 ("marginal") to 5 ("distinguished"). Experts have long considered reputation a valid measure of quality in higher education, and we believe a diploma from a school known for excellence offers graduates a powerful edge in the competition for good jobs.

So this ranking of graduate schools offering library/information science programs ranked the ALA-accredited programs on the recognition of the programs from others inside and outside of the field. It was based—at least, in part—on the reputation of the program. While that made sense to me, it also indicated that these rankings, much like any other type of "popularity contest," might not take all factors into consideration (for example, larger or older, more established programs already have certain reputations and a considerable amount of clout among professional colleagues). I decided that the *U.S. News* rankings might certainly be helpful and valid to an extent, but that it also might have overlooked *some* aspects of importance along the way. I could still use the rankings as a guideline, but they weren't necessarily the whole yardstick by which I would choose to measure. (John Berry's article "Choosing a Library School" in the November 15, 1998, issue of *Library Journal* also served useful.)

I decided to apply to two more programs: one that was ranked in the top five in the nation and would charge me out-of-state tuition—which would be expensive, but still less than the private school I had been considering, and in a city where I already knew someone and where the cost of living was more manageable; and one that ranked just inside the top one-half of the *U.S. News & World Report* list, where I would qualify for in-state tuition through something called the "Academic Common Market" because my home state didn't offer an equivalent program to the one in the neighboring states (see more details at www.sreb.org/programs/acm/acmindex.asp). After being accepted into all three programs and being turned down for any sort of federal aid, and not having heard anything yet from the numerous scholarship applications I had sent out, that bottom line of "total cost" became an even more significant factor. That midranked program with in-state tuition began to look better and better as my checkbook and meager savings account began to prepare for the University of Tennessee.

MONEY MATTERS

When you're still paying off undergraduate student loans, the price tags on ALA-accredited master's programs can seem daunting. Researching the links to the forty-nine ALA-accredited programs in the United States, there is a wide range of tuitions out there for prospective students in library/information science disciplines. Strictly speaking, there are three basic options: a private institution, a state-funded institution that charges residential or "in-state" tuition, or a state-funded institution that charges out-of-state tuition. There are exceptions to these rules (for example, the Academic Common Market/ Regional Contracts offered by SREB and the New England Board of Higher Education; see www.nebhe.org/tuition_assistance.html), so students should always ask about such programs through both the specific programs and the graduate schools to which they apply.

Looking again at the three basic types of programs, then, strictly in terms of money, without considering factors such as rankings, reputations, student satisfaction, academic respectability, or any other terms of "quality" that might be applied, the private institutions typically have the highest price tags. The least expensive programs tend to be the state-funded institutions located in a prospective student's state of residence. This is not to say that private institutions or state-funded programs outside of your state of residence should not be considered; rather, it is to alert those just beginning to think about pursuing the MLS about factors to consider as they start their research into the program(s) that might best suit their career goals. Many of the more expensive programs have very specific specialties that might appeal to a certain kind of student, and the reputation of that specialty might be important enough to the student to persuade him or her to select that program, regardless of the cost. To that student, graduating from that program and finding a job in that particular specialty might very well be "worth" the money invested in himself or herself to achieve the MLS from that program.

Another money matter to consider is the average starting salaries of librarians/ information specialists. Unlike some other professional graduate programs, there is not always an immediate "big payday" at the end of an MLS program. According to the 2002–2003 Annual Salary Survey of the Association of Research Libraries (ARL), "ARL librarians' salaries are barely keeping up with inflation," only increasing 1.8 percent over the previous year's figures to $51,636. In the 2002 salary survey conducted by the Special Library Association (SLA), there was a significant increase in the salaries of professionals working in special or nontraditional libraries: "The U.S. median pay for full-time information professionals as of April 1, 2002 was $56,500." The 2002–2003 edition of *Occupational Outlook Handbook* reports the 2002 median salary for librarians working in "local government (except education and hospitals)"—a group likely dominated by public librarians—to be $38,370 and $43,320 for librarians or media specialists working in elementary and/or secondary schools. ALA's 2002 annual salary survey showed an overall increase in salaries in the profession of 4.2 percent "with a mean of $49,866 and a median of $46,600."

There are separate figures available for "new" librarians. Library Research Service (LRS) reports these salaries in its 1999 release, "A Salary Comparison of Library Agencies": $28,767 for medium public libraries; $30,443 for larger public libraries serving populations of 100,000 or more; $30,386 for two-year colleges; $29,293 for four-year colleges; $30,236 for universities; $35,843 for special librarians with two or fewer years of experience; no data given for school media specialists. *Library Journal*'s (*LJ*) 2002 Annual Placements and Salaries study reveals that "the average starting salary for 2001 LIS graduates is $36,818, a 5.49% increase over the 2000 average of $34,871." While geography can certainly affect it, salary seems to be driven largely by the *type* of information environment in which graduates pursue employment. This same *LJ* study shows that, despite a 5.3 percent increase, public librarians' salaries still rank the lowest at an average of $33,345; academic librarians fared a little better at $35,883; school librarians or media specialists weighed in at $39,371; government librarians averaged $39,538; those working in special libraries reported an average salary of $40,293; and the two 2001 graduates surveyed who landed jobs in library cooperatives or networks ranked highest at an average of $41,500 per year.

While availability of positions varies, the outlook for the profession as a whole looks bright for librarians entering the profession in the next few years. It is estimated that a large portion of the profession will be retiring from the profession by the end of this decade. An article in the June 2003 issue of *University Business* cites the percentage of elementary and secondary school librarians/media specialists retiring at 50 percent. In an article published in the November 2002 issue of *Curriculum Review*, ALA puts the statistic for the overall predicted shortage at a lower figure—about 25 percent of public, school, and college librarians becoming eligible for retirement by 2009. *Library Journal* columnist Roy Tennant maintains that public, school, and college libraries aren't the only places that will be hit by such a mass retirement in the profession. In his "Digital Libraries" column in March 2002, Tennant says:

> Recently both First Lady Laura Bush and the Institute of Museum and Library Services pledged support for librarian recruitment in response to a shortage of library professionals. Nowhere is that shortage more acute than in positions that require a high degree of technical knowledge and experience. Very few librarians . . . can explain . . . ASP and PHP (both methods of creating dynamic web pages) and why you may want to use one or the other.

Gordon Flagg cites estimated statistics from the U.S. Institute of Museum and Library Services (IMLS) in the September 2002 issue of *American Libraries*: "As many as 58% of our nation's librarians will reach retirement age between 2005 and 2019." Of course, it is also wise to realize that "reaching retirement age" does not automatically ensure that 58 percent of those eligible to retire will *immediately* do so. It would also be wise to take note that money for many publicly funded libraries is not in abundance in a slumping economy and that hiring freezes currently impact openings that may become available (and may continue to do so in the future).

However, the prospects look relatively bright in terms of *potential* positions in the profession. Whether those positions become available where you live may be another case entirely. As Matthew David recently expressed on NEWLIB-L, "As for jobs, the availability has everything to do with your local economy and your willingness to relocate." This may be especially true for those who live in or near cities where graduate schools in information studies are located. The *Occupational Outlook Handbook* advises, "Applicants for librarian jobs in large metropolitan areas, where most graduates prefer to work, usually face competition; those willing to work in rural areas should have better job prospects. Opportunities will be best for librarians outside traditional settings."

TIME WON'T GIVE ME TIME

Time is another factor that can figure heavily into the decision-making process for those considering pursuit of the MLS. Is the pursuit of the MLS "worth" it in terms of the amount of time you will spend getting through your master's courses? If you are an older person, possibly exploring a career change, will your age be held against you once you earn your degree? If you go straight from a bachelor's degree to your master's, will potential employers see you as too inexperienced to consider you seriously against others who may have more experience in life and in the field? Is it possible to commit the necessary amount of time to your studies and still have a job to help pay the bills or to continue developing your on-the-job skills if you're already working in an information environment? Is it better to go full time than to try to juggle so many other factors? How long will it take you to land that first position after earning your MLS? Time is something that most of us never feel that we have enough of, so it is not surprising that issues of time management might weigh heavily in the decision to pursue the MLS.

HOW LONG HAS THIS BEEN GOING ON?

By the time I enrolled in the distance education (DE) component of the University of Tennessee's SIS at the age of twenty-nine, I had vast library experience. I had worked with children's and young adult's services, reference, interlibrary loan, course reserves, publicity, acquisitions, and budgets; had worked with an opening day collection of $1 million; and had been a supervisor in both public and academic library settings. It was in my first academic position that I decided I would indeed pursue the master's degree. I had been working in libraries for over three years and this was the first time that I had ever been treated differently because I did not have an MLS. Prior to that, if I wanted to learn something new, someone was more than happy to teach me how to do it so I could help. In that particular setting, however, I was told that I was not qualified to assist our patrons in certain ways because of my lack of a degree. That status of inequality got under my skin in such a way that I knew I would not be satisfied until I had an MLS. Yet it was ultimately my seven and a half years in these different environments and positions that convinced me that I loved the profession and wanted to move upward and onward in the field.

I enrolled in University of Tennessee's new distance education cohort, their first DE group since 1996. I found myself moving to Bristol, Tennessee, to continue working in a public library while beginning my 'master's degree in fall 2000 as a DE student, taking my courses online. SIS had designed the 1996 cohort's program to take about six years to complete the forty-three credits required for the program; most students took just one course each semester for fourteen semesters (including summer sessions). When the Pioneers began in 2000, we were advised to cut that time to three years by taking two courses during each of the first fall and spring semesters, then one in the first summer session; then repeat the same cycle for the second year of the program; the third (and final) fall and spring should include two courses each semester, for a total of forty-two credits. During the final semester, students could opt to take written comprehensive exams or defend a thesis.

After the first semester (which is almost always the toughest because there is so much to adjust to, learn, or relearn), some of my classmates decided that two classes plus a full-time job plus (in many cases) the responsibilities of family was just too much, so they dropped down to a more manageable one class per semester. Some of us decided that we would like to finish the program earlier, and took three courses some semesters.

Completing the MLS at thirty-one meant that I would likely be in my chosen profession for a long time before retirement. That very fact was, in part, what led me to decide that the time was right for me to begin graduate school when and where I did. As long as I enjoyed what I was doing and I wanted to continue doing it, there was no reason to put off returning to graduate school to get the degree underway. I knew that I wanted to continue in the profession, but not necessarily where I was working at that point. I knew that not every library system would hire me as a professional-level employee without the master's degree, so getting the MLS made the most sense to me. Besides that, there was the incentive of a bigger salary at the end of the program—and any of us would admit that making more money in any profession would be a welcome change!

A HARD DAY'S NIGHT

In my case, the timing seemed perfect. I was in my twenties, was single, had no children except my two faithful feline companions, Mel and Reid, had some great background experience, and had even lucked into a DE situation where I could continue working in the profession while going to school. Some of my classmates were choosing second or even third careers, though, and were in their early fifties when they began the program. Generally speaking, it was more common to come across people who had been working in the field for at least a few years before deciding to take the plunge and go back to school for a master's degree in the DE contingency of the program's population and to find younger folks either straight out of bachelor's degrees or just a very few years out of undergraduate work in the on-campus portion of the SIS population. Neither option can be considered "right" or "wrong," but both must be evaluated by the individual. Different people respond differently to stress, workloads, and the rigor of juggling careers, projects, papers, and relationships. Because of this, having the flexibility to work at your own pace in a graduate program is an amazing benefit. This is another example of how time can figure into the equation when you're trying to decide how or when to pursue the MLS. Know the program's requirements and decide which route—part time, full time, or somewhere in between—will likely be most advantageous to you in your own particular situation. While each ALA-accredited program can differ from others, most of them require either thirty-six or forty-two semester hours to complete.

RIGHT ON TRACK

Why do different programs have different requirements in terms of time commitments? Probably for the same reason that some programs require applicants to take the Graduate Record Examination (GRE) and others don't. In other words, it is simply because that is how that particular program feels that it can best prepare you for the profession once you leave its classrooms and educational experiences. Some programs require just two or three "core classes" and then allow students to either choose a particular "track" (i.e., school/media specialist, academic, public, special, technical, youth services, etc.) or encourage the students to follow their own interests. Taking a predesignated track typically offers very little wiggle room in terms of other electives that might be of interest to the student. The plan is there in front of students and they know from the moment they begin what the requirements are to complete the graduate program. If the student changes his or her mind somewhere along the way, there are three basic options: continue the track to finish the program more quickly, veer to another track, or just take a couple of classes that are enjoyable. For students who choose the nontrack option in the first place, their schedules after the core courses are completed could be compared to the popular "Choose Your Own Adventure" books that I loved as a kid (see www.gamebooks.org/cyoalist.htm if you're unfamiliar with the series). "If you like working with people, take Reference Services. If you prefer to be behind the scenes, take Cataloging. If you adore working with teens, jump into Young Adult Programs. If you are totally into saving important documents, sign up for Archiving." Then each of those choices might lead to another course of interest, and soon, students may find that they have been exposed to several different areas of the field. However, the point of core courses in graduate school curricula is not only to give students a solid overview of the theory and history of the profession, but also to help students identify potential professional areas of interest through such exposure.

Sometimes students take courses because they know very little about the topic. These classes might prove most valuable as they open up a whole new area of exploration. For example, someone who never dreamed of being a school librarian/media specialist might decide that doing so would be the experience of a lifetime after taking a course or an independent study requiring working with younger students. Someone who considers himself or herself a total "public services fiend" might learn not only that abstracting and indexing is fascinating, but also that the concepts covered in the coursework help explain much about researching in databases or indexes. Therefore, taking more time to complete a program—or even taking extra time to explore different types of classes—is not necessarily a bad thing. As long as you factor the time and money issues into the overall graduate education, taking more time to discover a particular facet of the field that you love can actually save you time, money, and lots of frustration later (i.e., taking time to do a practicum or independent study in public libraries might show you that there are countless variables involved with serving the general public and can help you determine whether it is the best environment for you to grow professionally).

WRAP IT UP

For anyone considering a long-term commitment to the library/information environment, there are several issues to research and weigh when deciding whether to pursue the MLS. Money is one of the obvious factors—the cost of the graduate program of your choice, how to finance it, starting salaries, and realistic salary increases are among them. Money impacts many of the basic decisions that anyone considering educational endeavors will need to evaluate. Another issue to factor in is time—how long it will take to complete the master's degree in terms of the number of courses required for the program and how many courses you can feasibly take at one time, how long you have already been in the field, how long you intend to remain in the field, whether you intend to work part time or full time while in graduate school, and so on. If working full time, an MLS program will take longer than if you were to attend grad school full time. If you have already devoted time to the profession and intend to continue working in libraries while pursuing the MLS, you may not mind the extra time involved to manage your full-time job and your part-time educational endeavors.

Recently, I surveyed library supervisors to get feedback on the opportunities and perceptions of employees with the MLS versus employees without the MLS. The survey asked what these supervisors consider to be the most significant differences between those two groups. More than one supervisor commented that those with the MLS tend to show a greater "depth of background and commitment" or "a basis for understanding the profession." Suresh Ponnappa (past president of the Tennessee Library Association and the assistant dean for Learning Resources and director at the James H. Quillen College of Medicine Library in Johnson City, Tennessee) remarks, "I think the 3 R's—Responsibility, Reliability, and Respectability. Once [students go] through an MLS . . . they are more dependable on those 3 R's as a part of their 'professional' behavior. During a professional degree program, there is a focus on being a 'professional'. . . and that influences the attitude of such a person. That does not mean that a non-MLS person cannot be like that . . . most of them [can] but it is hard to expect that of them." He concludes, "It's most likely that a person with an MLS degree has decided to make library work as their professional goal and that should explain the difference in attitude." Opportunities seem to be increasing opportunities for those holding the MLS. Making the decision to "enlist" professionally may very likely open more doors for library employees.

THE HEART OF THE MATTER

While there is nothing wrong with being a paraprofessional, earning the MLS and becoming a librarian/information specialist has marvelous merit. If you have picked up this book, chances are you're considering a career in librarianship or information science seriously enough to begin research on the matter or to hear other people's stories about decisions they have made throughout their professional careers in the field. This means that you are interested in what makes the profession what it is, and that you may want to be part of what will make the profession what it remains or evolves into in the future. I have found it to be most rewarding in countless ways. I cannot imagine doing anything other than what I do, even though it was not what I envisioned immediately after college. The profession is wide open in terms of work environments, job titles, responsibilities, professional development opportunities, and more. It is an ever-changing field, impacted by technology and the human touch. It is a profession that has its ups and downs, but it is also one that stands strong in terms of its past and its possibilities. Pursuing the MLS is just the first step to what I hope you will find to be the adventure of a lifetime.

RELATED READINGS

American Library Association. "Why Should I Go to an Accredited Program?" *Accreditation Frequently Asked Questions*. August 13, 2003. www.ala.org/Content/NavigationMenu/Our_Association/Offices/Accreditation1/faq1/faq.htm#q7 (last accessed 6 September 2003).

Association of Research Libraries. "Annual Salary Survey for 2002–2003 Published." *ARL Announces . . .* March 24, 2003. www.arl.org/arl/pr/salary_survey2002-03.html (last accessed 6 September 2003).

Berry, John. "Choosing a Library School." *Library Journal* (November 15, 1998): 36–39.

David, Matthew, in message to NEWLIB-L e-mail discussion list, "Re: Today's Technology" (last accessed 15 September 2003).

Flagg, Gordon. "I.M.L.S. Grants Address Librarian Shortage." *American Libraries* (September 2002): 14.

Garrett, Gayle, Robert J. Morse, and Samuel M. Flanigan. "How U.S. News Ranks Graduate Programs." *U.S. News & World Report* (April 10, 2000): 59.

Goral, Tim. "Quiet: Studying for a Career! School Aims to Fill Predicted Librarian Shortage." *University Business* (June 2003): 15.

Katz, Demian. "Choose Your Own Adventure." *Demian's Gamebook Web Page.* 2003. www.gamebooks.org/cyoalist.htm (last accessed 16 September 2003).

Library Research Service. "A Salary Comparison of Library Agencies." *Fast Facts: Recent Statistics From the Library Research Service.* www.lrs.org/documents/ fastfacts/161salary.pdf (last accessed 6 September 2003).

Lynch, Mary Jo. "Librarian Salaries: Annual Increase Above National Average." *American Libraries* (September 2002): 93.

New England Board of Higher Education. "Tuition Assistance." *New England Regional Student Program.* www.nebhe.org/tuition_assistance.html (last accessed 6 September 2003).

"On the Lookout for Librarians: What the Numbers Say." *Curriculum Review* 42, no. 3 (November 2002): S3.

Ponnappa, Biddanda, past president of the Tennessee Library Association, assistant dean for Learning Resources, and director, James H. Quillen College of Medicine Library, in e-mailed survey response, September 15, 2003.

Southern Regional Education Board. "SREB Academic Common Market." *SREB Academic CommonMarket/Regional Contract Program.* www.sreb.org/programs/ acm/acmindex.asp (last accessed 6 September 2003).

Special Library Association. "Salary Survey Index." *Virtual SLA.* August 6, 2003. www.sla.org/content/memberservice/researchforum/salarysurveys/salsur2002/ index.cfm (last accessed 6 September 2003).

Tennant, Roy. "The Digital Librarian Shortage (Digital Libraries)." *Library Journal* (March 15, 2002): 32.

Terrell, Tom. "Salaries Rebound, Women Break Out." *Library Journal* (October 15, 2002): 30–35.

U.S. Department of Labor, Bureau of Labor Statistics. *Occupational Outlook Handbook*, 2002–2003 ed. Indianapolis, Ind.: JIST Works, 2002.

ABOUT THE AUTHOR

Chrissie Anderson Peters is a fall 2002 graduate of the School of Information Sciences at the University of Tennessee, a program that she participated in as a distance education student. A member of the Tennessee Library Association, the Virginia Library Association, the Boone Tree Library Association, ALSC, NMRT, and YALSA, she is a librarian for Northeast State Community College in Blountville, Tennessee. Her interests include writing, music, reading, traveling, *Buffy the Vampire Slayer*, watching football on weekends, her feline "children" (Mel, Reid, Xander, Willow, and Ella), and spending as much time as possible with her husband, Russell Peters, who makes her life a joy each day.

15

Now That I'm Here, What Do I Take?

Tanzi Merritt

You've not only decided that an MLS is worth having, you've also applied and been accepted to a program, and it's time to register for your first semester's courses. What courses are you going to take? The answer to this depends on a number of factors. Do you want to do whatever it takes to make sure you get a job in a particular type of library? Are you positive that you never want to work at a reference desk and instead dream of spending your days immersed in the world of cataloging? Are there any courses that you have to take in order to graduate? Are there courses that you know you want to take someday that have prerequisite courses? These questions are a few of those that you need to ask as you decide what to take that first semester, and they will help you develop a path for your coursework that will take you where you want to go.

TO SPECIALIZE OR TO GENERALIZE

The decision to specialize your education toward one particular type of library or one particular area of librarianship is one that not all students face, and whether it is a question often depends on your background. Maybe you were a student worker in your college library and your experience convinced you that you're no longer interested in using that accounting degree but instead want to work in an academic library. Maybe you loved your part-time job as a page at your local public library and now that the kids are all in school you want to get your degree so that you can get hired on full time. Maybe you've gotten tired of working the long hours of a lawyer but want to use that knowledge as a law librarian. A background in library work or some other profession can definitely influence your idea of what you want to do when you've got that MLS in hand. On the other hand, maybe you're more like I was when I started graduate school. I was an avid library user, and with an undergraduate degree in history, I had spent a lot of time doing research. However, I had never worked in a library, so I had little knowledge of the different types of libraries or the variety of jobs from which I would be able to choose someday. Because I had no firm idea about the type of position that I would seek after completing my MLS program, I decided to approach course selection from a general perspective.

The most compelling argument for getting a general education is flexibility. As Priscilla Shontz states in *Jump Start Your Career in Library and Information Science*, "You never know what your job may require of you, or what type of job you may hold ten years after you graduate."[1] A librarian with a general education may have an easier time finding a position. Staying general in your coursework can keep you from being pigeonholed when you seek a position— a factor that can be important depending on your situation. Billie Ann Gebb, reference librarian at Midway College, states, "You may be prepared to take a different type of job [than the type you had originally been seeking] for location or salary reasons, and it's better to be prepared for different positions." This is especially important for anyone for whom location is a restriction due to a spouse or other family obligations. With a general education a librarian isn't restricted to applying for only one type of position. A generalist could be qualified for reference, cataloging, collection development, technical services, interlibrary loan, or any of the wide variety of positions available in a library, and he or she may be a more attractive candidate than a specialist because of flexibility. What library wouldn't love to have a cataloger who can fill in at the reference desk in a pinch or assist with development of the library's website?

For those who are planning to work in some type of special library, such as a law library, a medical library, or a corporate library, the flexibility one obtains from a general education can be a great benefit. Special libraries are often small, and special librarians may find themselves working alone. In these cases the librarian will be performing reference, evaluating and choosing print and electronic materials, handling the technical issues related to online database subscriptions, and budgeting for the library. A librarian with a broad education will know more about each of these duties than a librarian who has focused his or her coursework on one particular subject area.

What happens if you start your dream job as a technical services librarian and within a short time discover it's not really what you want to do? If your coursework has centered completely around technology, you may have a difficult time moving into another type of position without gaining experience in another area. A librarian with a more general education can move from one type of job to another with less difficulty because he or she will have a background in many different areas of librarianship. This same flexibility will also help you as you climb the career ladder. As you move up, you're likely to change job duties. These new duties may require you to fall back on information from your classes, as some of your new duties may be things that you haven't done in previous positions.

SO WHAT MAKES UP A GOOD GENERAL EDUCATION?

Reference

Libraries and librarians are here to provide the best possible information to those who need that information. Reference work is arguably the most important work in the library and is the reason that all other areas of librarianship exist. No matter what type of job you end up with, there's a good chance that you might be expected to spend some time manning the reference desk. A working knowledge of how to use common reference sources will come in handy! In addition to reference, another course to look for on your school's schedule is a class on database searching. Database searching is one of a reference librarian's most basic duties and is one area in which we should all be proficient. A good course in this will teach you all about Boolean operators, limiting and expanding your searches, and so on. In the end it doesn't matter what database you spend the most time searching in class. What matters is that you learn the major concepts of retrieving information from electronic sources. Most databases are constructed using these same basic concepts.

Cataloging

Many students of library science who are interested in public services think that cataloging must be the most solitary and tedious job in the library and are positive that a cataloging class will be not only boring but also a waste of time. These students couldn't be more wrong! The organization of knowledge is the foundation of librarianship, and an understanding of the rules of classification is essential for those who want to retrieve information for patrons and researchers. James Manasco, coordinator of liaison activities at the University of Louisville's Kornhauser Health Sciences Library, says, "Cataloging is at the heart of what we do: organizing information. Having a basic understanding of cataloging is essential to truly *getting* how databases work, especially our own electronic card catalogs." I couldn't agree more! While working on my MLS, I took all the cataloging classes that were available. I wasn't sure I wanted to work as a cataloger, but I noticed that the farther along I went in cataloging, the better I was at reference work. (Plus I really liked cataloging.) I found that when students had trouble finding information using keyword searches, I could use my knowledge of subject heading construction to locate what they needed. It was exciting to see myself getting better at both skills at the same time, and I couldn't wait to get to class so that I could learn something that was going to help me at my job.

Technology

I once heard a fellow student argue that she saw no need for the one technology class that was required in our graduate program. She believed that, as a children's librarian, she would never use technology. She honestly believed that she'd spend all her time planning children's programs and leading story hours and would never use a computer. The administration didn't buy her argument and she had to take the class, and I trust that by now she's learned how wrong she was! Carol Tenopir, in her article *I Never Learned about That in Library School*, correctly states, "The Web has made information access an expectation in the workplace, schools, and at home." No librarian can escape technology, and why should any librarian want to? Technology has revolutionized the landscape of information storage and retrieval. Before the widespread use of computers and the Internet, information requests were limited to the information that patrons could learn about in their library. How many libraries, especially public libraries, relied on the *Reader's Guide to Periodical Literature* for article indexing? Now, with the Internet so widely available, patrons can find references to an infinite amount of publications and studies, and with electronic databases becoming more affordable to many libraries through statewide cooperative purchasing and consortium memberships, there is relatively no information source in existence to which a patron cannot find a reference. Increased knowledge of information sources leads to increased requests for that information, and it's the librarian's job to use technology to find that information, whether it be through a database or through an interlibrary loan request. Libraries have embraced technology, and there are a number of technological issues with which librarians must deal.

Do you know how a computer is put together? Do you know how computers are networked? Do you know anything at all about a proxy server or a firewall, or anything about how the many ways computers can connect to the Internet? If you don't, this is the time to learn! Many library schools offer classes covering the basics of technology, and taking this course is a wise choice for anyone entering the field. As with all other duties in the library, you never know when you will be called on to extract a diskette that's stuck in the floppy drive, or when you will have to adjust settings on a proxy server or firewall so that your patrons can access your database collection. An added benefit of these basic technology classes is that they will often cover software such as word processing and spreadsheet programs as well as basic Web development. Advanced Web development is another technology course that your school might offer. Take it! Libraries are under increased pressure to have a Web presence and to provide access to information resources from patrons' homes and offices. The more you know about developing your library's website, the more exposure your library will receive, and the patrons will be happy!

Collection Development

Knowing how to evaluate the needs of your service community and how to choose materials appropriately is important. If you make decisions about what materials are appropriate for your library, you are entrusted with money. It's your job to make sure that your collection fits the needs of the individuals you serve and that the money is being used in the best way possible. For example, in a college or university library your acquisitions process should be geared toward supporting the academic programs offered. Or, at a public library located in an area with a large Hispanic population, it would be important to acquire materials in Spanish. Understanding how to determine needs such as these, as well as how to survey your collection to see how well it currently meets the needs of the community, are essential to being a good custodian of the funding provided by your service community, whether that be through taxes, tuition, or other sources.

Management

Like every other profession, if you move up you will probably be managing personnel, budgeting, and writing job descriptions and mission statements. A course in library management will come in handy when that happens. Management can also help if you start your career in a special library where you are the only librarian, as you will be responsible for all management functions.

Government Documents

Not everyone would agree that a course in government documents needs to be part of a good general education, but the U.S. government is one of the largest publishers of information in the world, and large amounts of information are coming from international governments as well. This information can be tough to locate, even for those who work with government publications frequently, and this course is invaluable to any librarian who might be performing reference work in a major research library.

WHAT ELSE?

In addition to these core areas of which you need to have some knowledge, there might be other classes that are interesting to you. Take them! You never know in what manner these courses might be useful or where the knowledge will lead. I took a course in preservation management because my background in history had taken me into many archives and special collections, and I was personally interested in learning about this topic, although I planned to pursue positions where I would be heavily involved with technology. The course was fascinating, and while little that I learned in it has been relevant to my current position (although we did spend some time discussing preservation of electronic formats and the implications of rapidly evolving and changing technologies), a paper that I wrote for this course became my first published work and led to an invitation to sit on a panel at a regional library conference. Plus, who's to say that someday I might not want to change paths? Preservation is still very interesting to me and is something that I might want to pursue professionally in the future. While you might not have time for a lot of elective, after taking all your required courses plus courses in the above areas, make the time that you have available count!

Additionally, add an internship or practicum to your coursework, especially if you've had no experience working in a library or if you're not working as a paraprofessional or a graduate assistant while in school. This experience can put you one step ahead of the competition during the job search. Lesley Wolfgang-Jackson, interlibrary loan/document delivery services librarian at the University of Kentucky's Chandler Medical Center Library, said, "I was actually working full time in a library while I was taking classes, therefore very few of the concepts or lingo presented in class were really new or foreign to me." Lesley benefited from her experience with a greater understanding of what she learned in class because she was putting many of those concepts into practice every day. Another advantage of an internship or practicum is determining that a particular type of library or area of the profession is not what you enjoy. Laura Hall, senior library technician in Reference and Information Services at the University of Kentucky's William T. Young Library, had a field experience assignment that was different than the one that she had originally wanted, but, as she says, "I did learn a great deal from the one that I did do (mainly that I never want to work in a consumer-health library)!" An experience such as Laura's can help you avoid accepting a position that is just not for you.

EXCEPTIONS TO THE RULE

The list of courses I recommend for all students of library science differs greatly for one special group: those interested in children's services and in working in school libraries. While I believe that a student hoping to work mainly with children will benefit from taking many of the above courses, it goes without saying that working with children requires more specialized knowledge of literature, appropriate reference sources, and programming for children.

FITTING IT ALL IN

At this point you might be wondering how you're going to fit all these classes into what is most often a one- to two-year program. Some of these courses may be required. Many schools require basic courses in reference, cataloging, management, and technology. Other courses may not be offered. In those cases the decisions are made for you. While no group of librarians will completely agree on a list of courses that make up a good general education, chances are in any group you will hear each of these classes recommended many times, as those in the field have learned from experience what they were happy they learned in school and which classes they wish they had taken.

NOTE

1. Priscilla K. Shontz, *Jump Start Your Career in Library and Information Science* (Lanham, Md.: Scarecrow Press, 2002), 71.

RELATED READINGS

Shontz, Priscilla K. *Jump Start Your Career in Library and Information Science.* Lanham, Md.: Scarecrow Press, 2002.
Tenopir, Carol. "I Never Learned about That in Library School." *Online* 24, no. 2 (2000). scarch.epnet.com/ (last accessed 7 October 2003).

ABOUT THE AUTHOR

Tanzi Merritt graduated from the University of Kentucky's School of Library and Information Science in 2001, and has worked in reference, instruction, and electronic resources. She is very involved in ALA's New Members Round Table as well as a number of organizations in her local community.

16

Replacing Classrooms and Carrels with Keystrokes: Distance Education of Library and Information Science Professionals

Amanda J. Roberts

Distance education (DE) of librarians and information science professionals is not as recent a development in U.S. higher education as one may think. Since the 1880s, librarians and library faculty have shared their knowledge and skills through correspondence courses, driven or flown to remote areas to meet with students, and used telecommunications equipment and services to communicate and offer library services to students living hundreds or thousands of miles from campus. Since the advent of the World Wide Web, however, library and information science (LIS) distance education has grown dramatically. On its website, the American Library Association (ALA) lists thirty-eight LIS schools that offer the ALA-accredited master's degree through some form of DE technology.

There are many models of LIS distance education programs, as well as types of distance education technologies. As early as 1888, there were correspondence courses for special library and small library service. This grew into LIS extension efforts, which consisted of summer sessions, compact sessions, weekend courses, evening classes, institutes, and traveling LIS faculty. With the advent of telecommunications technologies, the twentieth century saw a rise in the use of radio and television for delivery of academic courses and continuing education. The American Library Association delivered its first satellite conference on copyright in 1978, and satellite videoconferencing continues to be a choice for LIS continuing education. Today, LIS schools employ a variety of technologies in course delivery. For cxample, students take courses via compressed video and on the Web using course software such as BlackBoard and WebCT.

The most exciting things about distance education technologies are their seemingly endless opportunities. Through a Web-based LIS course, a student in Alaska can theoretically complete a group assignment for a course with students in Florida, Kentucky, and Hawaii, without ever having to meet face to face. However, while technology may streamline and improve our lives, its newness tends to raise our expectations to levels that are not always practical. For those of you who are still considering an LIS distance education program, take a few moments to ask yourselves some critical questions that will help determine if you are ready for distance education.

CRITICAL QUESTIONS

Why Do You Want to Obtain Your Graduate Degree via Distance Education?

Most people would answer this question with one word: convenience. Indeed, distance education programs, whether they offer completely online or compressed video courses or they send professors to teaching locations in your area, attempt to extend instruction to geographic areas than cannot be reached by the traditional model. One of the primary goals of the DE model, if not to increase enrollment, is to fill an educational gap. This goal, however, is slightly different than the potential DE student's dream of convenience. Institutions broaden their geographic range not to streamline the workload of coursework or make things easier for you because you work full time, but to offer alternatives to commuting or the life-altering relocation that is necessary in the traditional model of education. The explanation of this point is not meant to turn you away from distance education; it is meant to suggest that you examine your definition of "convenience." If you do work full time, have you examined your schedule to ensure that you have adequate time to prepare for your classes? Distance education courses take at least as much (if not more) time to complete than courses taught in physical classroom settings. If you are excited about the freedom and mobility of the virtual "anytime, anywhere" learning, have you considered the external technological learning that will be required of you? All online DE courses require a much greater degree of technological competence than traditional ones due to their electronic format delivery. Have you examined the library resources and services of the LIS institution's library, and do you live within driving distance of an academic library that provides a graduate-level research collection? Sometimes public libraries have collection arrangements and scholarly resource-sharing agreements with research institutions, so the collection of your local public library may be able to complement the library resources you have access to.

Is the Master's Program in Library and/or Information Science Accredited by the American Library Association?

There are many online programs out there that offer you certificates of advanced studies, but the only certificate that will get you a job as a public, academic, or special librarian is a master's in library and/or information science degree accredited by the ALA. (Note: Some LIS schools call the degree an MLS, MA, or MS.) Library science courses taken at institutions that are not accredited by the ALA will *not* count toward the master's degree in library and/or information science. In addition, it is important that you consider the reputation of the host institution. If you think that the institution may not be reputable, follow your instincts and critically evaluate the program. For a complete listing of ALA-accredited institutions that provide DE courses, see "ALA Accredited LIS Programs that provide Distance Education Opportunities," available at: www.ala.org/Content/NavigationMenu/OurAssociation/Offices/Accreditation1/lisdir/disted.htm.

Have Your Initial Experiences with the LIS Distance Education Program Department(s) Been Positive and Supportive?

We've all been there: standing in line at the university registrar's office, waiting for an important document that turns out to be incomplete, then walking across campus to another office, only to find that the office is closed. Such is the experience of on-campus students every fall, and DE students are not immune. In your preliminary examination of the LIS school's admissions information, did you feel that the procedures for DE admission and registration were adequately explained? Did the information presented about the LIS distance education degree appear to be an afterthought on the school's website, or was there a complete section of the website dedicated to the distance education component? Is there a toll-free number offered for distance education students? Is there a contact person dedicated to the needs of distance students? Finally, how easy is it to get in touch with administrative personnel? Are you on hold on the phone for a long time? Did they appear too busy to help you, or did they spend extra time with you to make sure your questions were answered? When you are enrolled as a DE student, and you are not able to interact in person with your professors or LIS school staff, you will need a sufficient communication alternative to help you cope with potential issues or problems that will undoubtedly arise.

Are Extracurricular Professional Opportunities Extended to Distance Education Students?

Since the master's in library/information science is not only an academic but a professional degree, it is helpful to engage in professional activities and communication while attending school. If the LIS school has student chapters of national organizations such as the ALA, Public Library Association (PLA), Special Libraries Association (SLA), American Society for Information Science and Technology (ASIS&T), other LIS professional organizations, or the school's student organizations, are DE students allowed to serve as officers in these student organizations? Also, hands-on experience is crucial to new LIS graduates entering the workplace. Does the LIS program offer apprenticeship or assistantship opportunities in libraries in your geographic area? How many opportunities are available and what types of libraries are they in? In addition to these considerations, it would be very helpful if you could converse with some of the alumni of the LIS DE program. Sometimes the LIS school will provide that contact information if you request it.

Where, When, and What Will Be Required of You?

Some distance education programs require all students to attend an orientation that may be one day to one week long. Others have a residency requirement of a semester or more. Do you have adequate freedom in your schedule or family commitments to meet these requirements? Do you have reliable transportation? To meet the needs of working students, many LIS schools offer distance courses during weeknights and on Saturdays. While this is a blessing to you and your employer, this may lengthen your time in school. Have you determined the requirements you need to complete the MLS degree, and have you examined when, where, and how these courses are taken? For example, it is possible to earn the MLIS offered by Louisiana State University's School of Library and Information Science (LSU SLIS) completely at a distance, but it does take approximately five years to complete the requisite forty hours of graduate credit. In addition, some traveling is required, at least to universities across the state of Louisiana that host the satellite-video courses. Also, many required core courses are repeated within a period of a few years, but elective courses may not be. To help DE students plan their academic futures, many schools such as LSU SLIS plan their DE schedules years in advance. Be sure to request this course schedule if you are seriously considering a program.

EXAMPLES OF LIS DISTANCE EDUCATION PROGRAMS

From the thirty-eight LIS programs listed on the "ALA Accredited LIS Programs That Provide Distance Education Opportunities" web page, I have selected four of these DE programs to describe: (a) FastTrack MLIS program at the University of Pittsburgh, (b) Online Degree Program at the University of Tennessee, (c) Distance learning option available at the University of Iowa School of Library and Information Science, and (d) LEEP program at the University of Illinois at Urbana–Champaign.

FastTrack MLIS program at the University of Pittsburgh

The Fast Track MLIS (FT/MLIS) program is based on the cohort group concept. According to Darrel L. Hammon and Steven K. Albiston in the introduction to *Graduate Survival Skills: Completing Graduate School Long Distance*, a cohort group is a "group of students who enroll in the same distance education program you do . . . who become, in essence, your surrogate family."[1] In the FT/MLIS program, students begin the program as a part of a cohort group, and this group attends an on-campus summer orientation for technology training and to meet their cohort peers and the program faculty. In addition to this orientation, students meet again with their instructors for one weekend of each semester. The FT/MLIS program consists of thirty-six credit hours divided into six terms, which is approximately two years, and it is separated into three tracks: school librarianship, medical librarianship/informatics, and public/academic/special librarianship. Courses are delivered using four instructional delivery methods: Web-based, asynchronous courses; CD-ROMs containing course and program materials; real-time conferencing; and on-campus learning experiences. Students in the first three FT/MLIS cohorts lived in nineteen states and were an average age of thirty-nine.

Online Degree Program at the University of Tennessee

The Online Degree Program at the University of Tennessee is also based on the cohort concept. This degree program requires forty-two semester hours and is divided into three years. Those who earn the MS degree in information science from the program will be prepared to work in all library and information professional settings. Admitted students will begin their program with a required week-long orientation in Knoxville preceding the first fall semester, and they will return to campus at the end of their program to take comprehensive exams or to defend a thesis. Course delivery includes e-mail, electronic discussion groups, net forum applications, and Web methods using software provided by the University of Tennessee. Chrissie Anderson Peters, a student in the pioneer cohort, describes using a variety of multimedia and software programs: "web safaris," text chat, virtual group "rooms," and at least one virtual "town meeting." In addition to the advantages of technological innovations, Chrissie, who is now a reference librarian at Northeast State Technical Community College, reports that her SIS instructors maintain contact with her.

University of Iowa School of Library and Information Science: Distance Learning Option

Unlike the FT/MLIS and the University of Tennessee's Web-based programs, the principal method of course delivery at the University of Iowa School of Library and Information Science is the Iowa Communications Network (ICN), which links students at remote sites located in the state of Iowa. The ICN uses fiber optic technology to deliver real-time interactive video and audio sessions of classes. The Web is used as a tool to enhance these live class sessions. The Louisiana State University School of Library and Information Science offers a similar course-delivery method called compressed video, which is broadcast simultaneously to various sites all across the state of Louisiana. Students in these LSU SLIS compressed video classes meet during the same class time as the "home site" class, and students at the remote sites watch a video version of the class and are able to participate in class discussions by pressing a button and making comments. The University of Iowa offers at least two ICN courses per semester, and it is possible to complete the degree program in three years via the ICN network, plus a required eight hours of on-campus residency, which can be met through one- and two-week summer courses.

LEEP Program at the University of Illinois at Urbana–Champaign

According to its website, the LEEP program at the University of Illinois at Urbana–Champaign is a "scheduling option" that combines short periods of on-campus instruction with the Internet and "independent learning." During live, Web-based instruction, students can hear the faculty, see slides and graphics, hear audio files, and chat with all the participants in the class. Students can earn the MS degree by completing forty semester hours of credit, which includes a "CAS project," described as a "substantive investigation of a problem in librarianship or information science." The LEEP program offers fairly flexible course credit options. Here is an example of one scenario: one unit (four semester hours) of graduate coursework not in library and information science, one half unit practicum carried out at an information center near one's home, one unit of independent study, one and a half units of thesis work, and six units of LEEP coursework.

TECHNOLOGICAL AND INFORMATION LITERACY COMPETENCIES

Due to the increasingly technological nature of LIS course delivery, as well as librarianship itself, no chapter about the education of librarians, information scientists, or other types of information professionals is complete without a discussion of technological competencies. Before you enter an LIS degree program, and particularly one that is distance education, you should have a basic knowledge of office software and hardware. Because many of your classes may be offered via the Internet, you should know how to access the Web using an Internet browser such as Internet Explorer or Netscape Navigator, and you should understand how to access pages with a uniform resource locator (URL). You should know how to send and receive e-mail; use a word processing program and its features, such as copy, cut, and paste; open PDF documents using Acrobat Reader; send and receive attachments via e-mail; and understand file structure and management, including extensions. Some programs require more advanced skills, such as HTML coding and knowledge of spreadsheet, database, and presentation software, as well as how to use ftp and telnet. Since many LIS programs assume that its students know the basics of library research, it would be useful for a potential LIS distance education student who is not already working in a library setting to review how to find books and other materials using an online library catalog. If you have access to a local public library, it would be helpful to log on to one of its databases to try to find some popular as well as scholarly periodical articles on various subject matters. Because DE students sometimes live too far from a college or university library, or their local library doesn't usually collect scholarly materials in library science, they rely heavily on the full-text articles and e-books that are available in the databases subscribed to by the library of the LIS host institution.

HARDWARE AND SOFTWARE REQUIREMENTS

Since many of your classes may be offered via the Internet, it is important that you have access to a personal computer, preferably your own. Some distance education students try, not without a large degree of frustration, to use their computer at work or computers in public libraries to conduct research or to complete their assignments that require word processing, spreadsheet, web page authoring, or presentation software. Most computers in office environments are connected to a local area network that is protected by security software. Many online research resources, such as subscription databases offered by the LIS institution's library, are protected by authentication software that is not compatible with security software on local area networks, making it nearly impossible to log on to these databases from a computer at one's place of employment. Public libraries do offer many computers with Internet and e-mail access, as well as a variety of software programs; however, sometimes there is a time limit on computer usage, making it difficult for the LIS DE student to compose long, graduate-level research papers. Nonetheless, if you do opt to purchase your own computer, public libraries offer many free classes and training programs on how to use software programs. Remember that while many librarians and libraries are Windows-based computer environments, it is not crucial that you purchase a personal computer with a Windows platform. The Macintosh platform, as well as the Linux environment, is just as online-database-friendly as the Microsoft products. Note that an Internet browser that is very popular among the American public does offer problems. The AOL (America Online) browser has been known to be incompatible with the off-campus authentication software of libraries' online databases. You may use AOL as your Internet service provider, but you will probably be required to use Internet Explorer or Netscape Navigator browsers to actually access online databases from off campus. Some LIS DE programs require that you not only own your own computer, but you subscribe to an Internet service provider that provides broadband Internet access as well. Instead of dial-up, which tends to be slow, dedicated Internet access such as DSL or cable is very fast and can handle large multimedia files, .PDF documents, and course web pages easily.

SUPPORT SERVICES OF THE
LIS SCHOOL'S HOST INSTITUTION LIBRARY

One of the most important and probably most overlooked considerations by potential distance education students is the DE support service of the LIS host institution's library. Support services may consist of the following: free or low-cost document delivery services to one's home, Web or e-mail reference services, remote access to full-text databases, toll-free number to the library's reference desk, librarian-provided instruction, online tutorials, guides to library research, and a web page or portal on the library's website dedicated to the research and service needs of distance education students.

In a 1999 survey of DE students, University of Iowa librarian Stephen Dew reported that the three most important library services among distance education students in all disciplines was Web and/or e-mail reference services, remote access to full-text databases, and home delivery of books and articles. In general, DE students were not interested in library instructional services. MBA students were more concerned with access to Internet and electronic sources, while library science students were more interested in document-delivery services. Keep in mind that document-delivery services' efficiency will vary from institution to institution. Students at Nova Southeastern University enjoy a fast turnaround time of fewer than ten days because NSU specializes in distance education. Michele Lanclos, a librarian at Jesuit High School in New Orleans, Louisiana, attended a primarily traditional institution to pursue her MLIS, but she took many of her LIS courses in a DE format from its library science school and reports a high level of frustration with the document-delivery service at the host institution's library.

EMOTIVE ASPECTS

One of the most common complaints of distance education students is the feeling of isolation one may experience as a result of not meeting regularly in a physical classroom. Consider the following comment of one DE student: "The course I took totally online was not satisfying. I missed the interaction with professors and peers, and felt little involvement with the subject matter. I completed all the assignments . . . but I feel like I achieved very little." However, Lori Albrizio, a reference and instructional librarian at Nova Southeastern University, attended the University of South Florida (USF) School of Library and Information Science and reports that she enjoyed the freedom of her online classes. She chose USF's program because of its mixture of online and in-person classes, and she did not feel too "disconnected" from the host institution. In addition, some students attempt to overcome this isolation or disconnected feeling by meeting between sessions at a local public library, someone's home, or a coffee shop. Of course, not all students have this sort of extracurricular time.

Many distance education LIS schools recognize their students' need for human interaction and have built a proactive response into their program. For example, the School of Library Information Management at Emporia State University employs site coordinators at each program location. These site coordinators serve as student advisors, hold office hours, are available for in-person consultations, and track the return of students' work by faculty. While distance education LIS schools do work to offer a more personalized touch for their students, it is important to note that distance education students have an important role to play in their own education. The USM School of Library and Information Science website warns that online courses are not "as simple as pointing and clicking for academic credit." Students must be proactive, self-motivated, and responsible.

WILL THE DEGREE LOOK "BAD" ON YOUR RESUME?

Many potential library professionals worry that courses or programs taken in a distance education format will be viewed in a negative light by employers. Often, these individuals will send inquiries to library listservs such as the ALA New Members Round Table NMRT-L, and these inquiries contain a common element: Will the distance MLIS look bad on my resume? Answers to these inquiries are a resounding "no." As long as your master's degree is accredited by the ALA, which means that it meets certain educational standards and criteria for on-campus and off-campus programs, your degree obtained via distance education will be just as legitimate as a degree obtained on campus. In fact, a master's degree certificate looks the same and is signed by the same people, so many potential employers will not know the difference if you do not tell them. However, you may want to divulge this information because it may actually make you more marketable. For example, many institutions of higher education are in the early stages of implementing DE programs, and their libraries need librarians to develop DE library instruction and resource-delivery programs to their off-campus patrons. In addition, your experiences and the specialized training or software that you may learn as a distance education student will be useful for all library and nonlibrary settings. Library vendors, for example, need insights on the needs of DE students so that they can perfect and sell their electronic products to libraries.

CONCLUSION

Distance education of librarians, media specialists, information scientists, and other information professionals will continue to grow and evolve to keep up with trends in the information science field. As with all innovations, new distance technologies will go through a period of growing pains until time perfects their processes. In the meantime, this growth gives LIS students and professors a unique opportunity to collaborate with their professors as well as influence the future of education. If you do decide to embark on a virtual educational journey, try to keep an open mind. If you experience difficulty on your path, remind yourself that the end justifies the means. Pursuing one's master's degree is only one part of being an information science professional. Remember: There is an exciting career in library and information science waiting for you!

ACKNOWLEDGMENTS

I would like to thank Stephen H. Dew for providing the results of his survey of distance education students at the University of Iowa.

NOTE

1. Darrel L. Hammon, and Steven K. Albitson, "Introduction," in *Graduate Survival Skills: Completing Graduate School Long Distance*, ed. Bruce A. Thyer (London: Sage Publications, 1998), 5.

RELATED READINGS

American Library Association. "ALA Accredited LIS Programs that Provide Distance Education Opportunities." *Accredited Institutions.* 2001. www.ala.org/Content/NavigationMenu/OurAssociation/Offices/Accreditation1/lisdir/disted.htm (last accessed 22 September 2003).

Anderson, Chrissie. "Earning Your M.L.S. Online." *LIScareer.com: The Library and Information Science Professional's Career Development Center.* 2001. www.liscareer.com/anderson_msonline.htm (last accessed 23 April 2003).

Association of College and Research Libraries: A Division of the American Library Association. "ACRL Guidelines for Distance Learning Library Services." *Guidelines for Distance Learning Library Services (Draft Revision).* 2003. www.ala.org/Content/NavigationMenu/ACRL/Standards_and_Guidelines/Guidelines_for_Distance_Learning_Library_Services1.htm (last accessed 22 September 2003).

Barron, Daniel D., ed. *Benchmarks in Distance Education: The LIS Experience.* Westport, Conn.: Libraries Unlimited, 2003.

Barsun, Rita. "Postsecondary Distance Learners and Public Libraries: Challenges and Opportunities." *Indiana Libraries* 21, no. 1 (2002): 11–17.

College of Communication and Information, University of Tennessee. "School of Information Sciences: Distance Education Program." *The School of Information Sciences: Distance Education Program.* 2003. www.sis.utk.edu/programs/distance/ (last accessed 29 September 2003).

Department of Library and Information Science, School of Information Sciences @ University of Pittsburgh. "Cohort Concept." *FastTrack M.L.I.S.* 2003. fasttrack.sis.pitt.edu/academics/cohort.htm (last accessed 29 September 2003).

Department of Library and Information Science, School of Information Sciences @ University of Pittsburgh. "FAQs." *FastTrack M.L.I.S.—FAQs.* 2003. fasttrack.sis.pitt.edu/academics/cohort.htm (last accessed 29 September 2003).

Department of Library and Information Science, School of Information Sciences @ University of Pittsburgh. "Overview." *FastTrack M.L.I.S.—Overview.* 2003. fasttrack.sis.pitt.edu/academics/overview.htm (last accessed 29 September 2003).

Dew, Stephen H. "Knowing Your Users and What They Want: Surveying Off-Campus Students about Library Services at the University of Iowa." *Journal of Library Administration* 31, no. 3/4 (2001): 177–93.

Graduate School of Library and Information Science, University of Illinois. "Programs." *Library and Information Science Online Master's Degree at the University of Illinois.* 2003. alexia.lis.uiuc.edu/gslis/degrees/leep.html (last accessed 29 September 2003).

Hamilton-Pennell, Christine. "Getting Ahead by Getting Online." *Library Journal* 127, no. 19 (2002): 32–35.

Hammon, Darrel L., and Steven K. Albitson. "Identifying an Appropriate Institution." In *Graduate Survival Skills: Completing Graduate School Long Distance*, edited by Bruce A. Thyer, 14–22. London: Sage Publications, 1998.

———. "Introduction." In *Graduate Survival Skills: Completing Graduate School Long Distance*, edited by Bruce A. Thyer, 1–5 . London: Sage Publications, 1998.

Oder, Norman. "LIS Distance Education Moves Ahead." *Library Journal* 126, no. 16 (2001): 54–56.

Raphael, Laura B. "Far and Away: The Pros and Cons of a 'Long-Distance' MIS." *American Libraries* 33, no. 9 (2002): 50–52.

School of Library and Information Science, University of Iowa. "Distance Education at SLIS." *Overview: SLIS Distance Learning.* 2003. www.uiowa.edu/~libsci/distanceed.html (last accessed 29 September 2003).

School of Library and Information Science, University of Southern Mississippi. "SLIS Online." *USM SLIS.* 2003. www.usm.edu/~slis/SLISonline.htm (last accessed 29 September 2003).

ABOUT THE AUTHOR

Amanda J. Roberts is the instructional librarian of Florida Atlantic University's S.E. Wimberly Library in Boca Raton, Florida, and serves as editor of *Footnotes*, the ALA New Members Round Table newsletter. She earned her MLIS in 2001 from the Louisiana State University School of Library and Information Science, where she took approximately one third of her courses in a distance education format.

17

Library Work Experience: Get Some!

Tom Bahlinger

Let's face it: library school is not that difficult. Yes, library school is time consuming and requires dedication and commitment, but chances are if you work reasonably hard you will earn As and Bs in your classes . . . as will nearly *all* of your classmates. Come job hunting and graduation time, what will separate your resume from those of your classmates: A 3.5 GPA . . . a 3.7 . . . a 4.0? No! Just about every graduate will have a high GPA. Experience will make your resume stand out, so my advice to library students is: *Get some library work experience!*

The benefits of acquiring library work experience are huge. The experience will help you succeed in graduate school and when interviewing for and working in your first professional job. Working in a library setting may help you discover the setting (such as academic, public, special, or school) in which you will ultimately prefer to work. This in turn can help you decide what classes to take in graduate school. Furthermore, depending upon what kind of experience you acquire, you may determine if you are better suited for or will enjoy more a public-services position, such as reference or instruction, or a technical-services position, such as a cataloging or systems job. Where better to learn about the profession of librarianship than by working and talking with librarians? The contacts made while working in a library are extremely important, too. Library work enables students to fill their resume with relevant work experience and create a list of librarians willing to write letters of recommendation.

MY EXPERIENCE

I am convinced that my work experience during graduate school is the primary reason I landed an excellent tenure-track, faculty-status position upon graduation from library school. Here is how that happened.

I graduated from college with a history major and a minor in English and had absolutely no thoughts about working in a library. Instead, I worked retail at a local bookstore, starting as a sales clerk and working up to a management position. (Bookstore work or any job involving extensive customer service is excellent preparation for a public-services librarian job, by the way.) After three years of long hours and low pay in the retail sector, I seriously began considering switching to a library setting. To see if I enjoyed that particular environment, I accepted a full-time clerk job at a medical library. Yes, a clerk job. I had a bachelor's degree and I accepted a position that did not even require a high school diploma, and in hindsight, this is the move that jump-started my career.

As a clerk I did a little of everything: opening and closing the library; troubleshooting computers, printers, and copiers; pulling items for interlibrary loan; shelving books and journals; working the circulation desk. This brings me to another excellent reason to gain library work experience before you earn your graduate degree. If you've done the grunt work of a library clerk, page, volunteer, or student worker, you will appreciate the work these vital employees provide when you become a librarian, and you will never take them for granted. In the article "How Library School Prepared Us for the Profession," Lisa Spillers and Doug Bates state, "By performing these tasks (of a student worker), I gained some insight into how the library was organized and maintained. While I was not aware of all the job responsibilities of the librarians in the department, I had at least a vague idea of their duties" (1989, p. 212). Now, this is not to say librarians must have "been there, done that" in order to appreciate the work of clerks, but such experience helps individuals appreciate staff as well as understand some of the inner workings of a library.

An added bonus of having gone through the clerk experience is that as a librarian I feel I can describe my past experience as an example for hard-working and promising library clerks who may want to become a librarian. ("If I used to shelve books for a living and now I'm a librarian, then you can do it, too!")

I was eventually promoted to library assistant in the reference department where my responsibilities increased and I began doing more of the kind of work the librarians were doing. On a typical day, for example, I worked the reference desk for four hours beside a librarian, and on Saturdays I was the only person staffing the reference desk. That's right, eight hours of solo reference work. Needless to say, I gained excellent experience during my tenure as a library assistant and during this time I decided to attend library school. I could earn a master's degree in library science and essentially double my library salary. I continued working full time and attended library school part time.

Obviously, working full time and attending graduate school part time took me longer to graduate than if I'd attended school full time, but by working full time I earned enough salary to pay tuition without taking out loans. More importantly, my work experience greatly helped me in my class work. I felt light-years ahead of students who had never worked in a library, making the assignments and papers much easier for me.

Slated to graduate from library school in December 1998, I searched and interviewed for jobs early in my final semester. Before I even had diploma in hand, I had two job offers at nearby academic libraries. There is no doubt in my mind that the interviews for these positions went beautifully and job offers followed due in great part to my extensive job experience and knowledge gained before and during graduate school. I declined these two offers and continued working as a library assistant until a position opened at the college where I wanted to work. I interviewed, was hired, and began work in August 1999.

In all honesty, there is a great deal of luck involved in landing the job you want. Much has to do with timing. The job simply must be available in order for you to fill it. But although timing is vital, there must be something outstanding about your resume that sets it apart from the others when jobs become available. That something, in my opinion, will almost always be experience. In the article "Gaining Library Work Experience While You're a Student," Susanna Van Sant (2003) writes, "I strongly believe that being able to send out a resume with as much recent, highly relevant, and varied library employment history as I was able to gather as a student made a very positive impression on the people who read my resume as I began applying to professional academic library positions."

GETTING EXPERIENCE

I worked full time in a library while attending graduate school, but this may not be possible, practical, or ideal for every library student. Fortunately, numerous opportunities exist for students trying to gain valuable experience. In "Working Knowledge," Elisa F. Topper (2003) recommends improving your marketability to an employer by completing an internship (or independent study) as part of your coursework to gain on-the-job experience. Establish a work history with a part-time job at the university or local public library. If paying jobs are unavailable, Topper suggests volunteering at your local library. Regardless of the type of library experience, Van Sant reminds us that individuals should *always* behave professionally and responsibly. Furthermore, be inquisitive, offer to do more than you are asked to do, and say yes to opportunities to take on additional projects and responsibilities.

INDEPENDENT STUDY AND INTERNSHIPS

Independent study and internships (or practicums) provide excellent and challenging methods for MLS students to gain practical experience and, in some graduate programs, earn credits toward graduation. An independent study requires a game plan in the sense that the student must generate his or her own course of study in conjunction with a graduate advisor. Ultimately the graduate advisor must approve and oversee the successful completion of the independent study.

Independent studies are as varied as the students themselves, but ideas for study may include analyzing a segment of a collection, compiling and analyzing usage or circulation statistics, or conducting user satisfaction surveys. Permission to conduct an independent study, of course, must be granted at the library where the work will occur, which puts the student in contact with the library director or librarian responsible for that particular part of the collection.

Upon successful completion of the independent study, the student earns graduate credit and library experience, and has connected with librarians who may be willing to write letters of reference. The written report of the study, if extremely well done, may be publishable. Finally, if the student performed admirably, he or she may have opened the door to being hired at the library where the study was performed.

Internships differ from independent studies in that they are jobs where students gain real-world work experience and may earn graduate credit simultaneously, depending upon the program. An intern may work alongside librarians at the reference desk or behind the scene with catalogers, for example, depending upon the specified internship. According to Peter Hepburn in his *Feliciter* article, an internship "precedes the degree and is usually quite short term. Internships do not necessarily pay well, if at all" (2001, p. 142). An article in *Library Personnel News* (1996) states, "An internship is a short-term work experience with an employer in a field of interest to you. It emphasizes learning on the job rather than earning. It provides a chance to observe the work, to gain on-the-job experience and to learn how you like the field" (1996, p. 4).

Library science schools do not always offer internships as part of their program, as was the case with my graduate school, and this is unfortunate. In *Library Journal*, John Berry states, "As a laboratory, a place to gain experience through internships/student assistantships, and an example for study and experimentation, the library is ideal. It could provide the connection to the practice that graduate LIS programs so often lack" (2003, p. 8). An intern in Cindy Mediavilla's *American Libraries* article writes, an internship "reveals whether a person is suited to the work or not. It is also a situation that a library school, and even clerical work in libraries, cannot hope to simulate" (2003, p. 61). And in "Five Steps to an Effective Internship Program," Barbara Quarton observes, "Top-notch graduate students in library and information science (LIS) programs can become effective reference interns to lighten the workload at busy reference desks. The key is in providing excellent training" (2002, p. 109). Internships offer students real-world library experience and training, and if the opportunity to participate in an internship presents itself, students should pursue it.

STAFF AND STUDENT WORK

Paying library jobs offer students perhaps the best avenue for gaining valuable library experience. In her LIScareer.com article, Suzan Lee states, "Some M.L.S. students are fortunate in that they are currently employed either full time or part time (short-term or long-term) in a library environment. For these M.L.S. students, completing a library internship may not be as important, particularly if they are employed in the library field of their choice." The jobs can be part time or full time, depending upon what is available. Possible jobs include being a student worker at a college or university library, or being a page, clerk, or library assistant at a public or other type of library. The responsibilities are extremely varied but tend to be more involved than volunteer work. Responsibilities may include shelving books and periodicals, shelf reading, staffing the circulation desk or reserve desk, photocopying articles for interlibrary loan, assisting with cataloging duties, and perhaps assisting at the reference desk. No matter how tedious the work may be or how few hours you work per week, the experience and work history look great on your resume.

Library students should be aggressive in trying to get a job in the library. Arrive in town earlier than the other students and apply for the jobs before anyone else even thinks about it. Van Sant advises, "Apply for almost any library job, performing almost any task just to get your foot in the door." Student jobs tend to be flexible, so holding a part-time job should not interfere with your graduate classes. Yes, the work may be boring and the pay may be low, but the experience may help you land your first professional job.

VOLUNTEER WORK

If paying jobs are unavailable, Topper states that volunteering at your local library is a good method of gaining experience. Contact the library director or individual responsible for volunteers; chances are, they will be delighted to have you help in their library. Keep in mind that volunteer work can be tedious and monotonous. Carol Smallwood (1999) explains in her article "Training Student and Adult Assistants, Interns, and Volunteers" that volunteer duties may include working with the library's vertical files, shelving books, arranging displays, or evaluating donated material.

I once volunteered at a public library where I spent hours peeling old labels from book spines. Not glamorous, but it had to be done. When volunteers perform duties like this, it enables paid staff to do more involved work, while providing the student volunteer with relevant work experience.

CONCLUSION

Library students should acquire as much library work experience as possible. Through internships, independent study, staff, student, or volunteer work, students enhance their marketability to employers. Additionally, library work experience may help students decide what courses to take in graduate school, as well as determine what type of job and what work environment they are best suited for. High GPAs are very common among library school graduates, and students need something that distinguishes their resume from their classmates'. Experience will make your resume stand out, so my advice to library students is: *Get some library work experience!*

RELATED READINGS

Berry, John N, III. "We Must Unify Practice and Research." *Library Journal* 129, no. 8 (2003): 8.

Hepburn, Peter. "Residency Programs as a Means of Nurturing New Librarians." *Feliciter* 3 (2001): 142–44.

"Key to a Job: The Internship." *Library Personnel News* 10 (1996): 3–4.

Lee, Suzan. "Internships or Practicums—Does it Matter?" www.liscareer.com/lee_internships.htm (last accessed 1 June 2003).

Mediavilla, Cindy. "FILLing in the Public Librarian Ranks." *American Libraries* 34, no. 6 (2003): 61–63.

Quarton, Barbara. "Five Steps to an Effective Internship Program." *College & Research Libraries News* 63, no. 2 (2002): 109–111.

Smallwood, Carol. "Training Student and Adult Assistants, Interns, and Volunteers: Tips for New Librarians Servicing Small Libraries." *Book Report* 17, no. 4 (1999): 24–26.

Spillers, Lisa, and Doug Bates. "How Library School Prepared Us for the Profession." *Journal of Library Administration* 11 (1989): 211–22.

Topper, Elisa F. "Working Knowledge." *American Libraries* 34, no. 1 (2003): 96.

Van Sant, Susanna. "Gaining Library Work Experience While You're a Student." www.liscareer.com/vansant_studentexperience.htm (last accessed 2 June 2003).

ABOUT THE AUTHOR

Tom Bahlinger is a reference/instruction librarian and the liaison to the nursing and allied health departments at San Antonio College. He received his MLIS from the University of Texas at Austin in 1999.

18

Get Hired Soon! Improving Your Postgraduation Employability

Elaine Yontz

If you are like most of the students I have taught, you are eagerly anticipating graduation and the thought of getting a new J-O-B. You are investing significant amounts of money, time, and energy in your degree, and you look forward to putting your new knowledge to work as soon as possible. If you are helping to support a family, you may feel special urgency.

There are things you can do while you are in school that will help you to enhance your postgraduation employability. Here are some suggestions.

> *Excel at what you do.* Ann Landers wrote, "If you have love in your life it can make up for a great many things you lack. If you don't have it, no matter what else there is, it's not enough."[1] The same can be said for excellence in your chosen field. Learn as much as you can in every class, which is *not* necessarily the same as getting high grades. Be curious. Pay attention. Visit as many libraries and information centers as you can. Meet as many people in the profession as you can, and try to learn something new from every one.
>
> Do you feel that you have the potential to become one of the best in the world at this work? If you don't, keep looking until you find a line of work where you do. The sense of purpose and satisfaction that comes from doing the work that is truly right for you is a joy that you will not want to miss. Your conviction that you are spending your energies in the right place will sustain you through the challenges and difficulties that come to everyone, during school and beyond.
>
> *Nurture collegial relationships.* Another way to say this is, "Be easy to get along with." I have a button in my office that says, "Be nice to other

people. They outnumber you 6 billion to 1." LIS is a small world. You
will encounter your fellow students, your teachers, and current practitioners again and again throughout your career. Behaviors of respect
will be remembered, and so will the opposite. There's no way to act
badly and keep it a secret. The chance that a prospective employer
knows one of your teachers or classmates, or knows someone who does,
is huge.

One of the major library vendors, Demco, uses the slogan, "It's still
about people." This profession places a high value on relationships.
Learning to work well with others is a lifelong journey, and none of us
will ever completely "get it." If you are satisfied with your current level
of skill in dealing with other people, you will be much happier in a different field. If, on the other hand, you think are up to the challenge, study
Dale Carnegie's *How to Win Friends and Influence People.* This is the
best tool I know for sharpening interpersonal skills and for learning how
to build strong relationships.

Read job ads, starting now. Even if this is your first semester, start a regular practice of reading vacancy announcements for jobs that might interest you. Notice the qualifications and salaries listed. You will get a realistic idea of what kinds of jobs and salaries are available. Seeing the
qualifications desired while you are still in school will give you time to
assess yourself against the qualifications and to look for ways to gain the
needed skills. Knowing what employers want can help you to choose
classes, workshops, and internships that will prepare you to be a strong
candidate.

When you read job ads, distinguish between "responsibilities" and
"qualifications." Responsibilities are what you will do in the job, after
you have been trained. Nobody expects you to know how to do all of
them before you start, so don't panic! What you need before you are hired
are the qualifications.

There are two types of qualifications: "required" and "preferred." Required qualifications tell you what is minimally expected of candidates
for that job. In some hiring processes, you won't be considered unless
you show evidence of possessing all the required qualifications. Preferred qualifications are optional but desired. From among the applicants
who have all the required qualifications, the person who has the greatest
number of preferred qualifications will be in the strongest position.

Participate in professional organizations. This means professional organizations within your school, at the state or regional levels, nationally, or
internationally. Join. Attend their conferences. Do a poster session, a relatively painless and enjoyable way to begin presenting at conferences.

Colorado State University's Writing Center provides a useful website with advice for creating poster sessions. Volunteer for committees. Run for office. These activities will help you to learn, grow, meet new people, and hone your interpersonal skills. In addition, professional organizations often have job-placement services. Consult the list of professional organizations in LIS at LibraryHQ.com. Also look at Priscilla Shontz's useful suggestions in her LIScareer.com article, "Involvement in Professional or Community Associations."

Participate in electronic discussion lists. Thoughtful, substantive contributions will help to "get your name out" to people who may be hiring or who know someone who is.

Get practical experience. Having hands-on experience gives you an edge over applicants who don't. There are several ways to accomplish this. See Tom Bahlinger's chapter in this volume for specific suggestions.

Learn to write. To reach your professional potential, you must learn to write well. Writing skills will make a difference in your job hunting, as you compose your cover letters and resumes. Every professional position requires writing documents, including memos, news articles, annual reports, and grant applications. Your university probably offers writing classes or labs. Take advantage of them. As you write papers for classes, look for chances to create publishable manuscripts and submit them.

Understand that landing a new job will take time. Many of the students I have taught spent six to eighteen months seeking their first postgraduation job. This has been especially true for place-bound students, unless the place is a major metropolitan area. Some of them began this process before graduation. Others waited until they were finished with school and turned the time they had previously spent on class work over to job hunting.

Researching openings, writing resumes and cover letters, responding to queries, and attending interviews are time consuming. If you feel that it's essential that you have a job immediately after graduation, you will have to "crunch" the time necessary and work on it before you graduate.

Some students say, "If there's a librarian shortage, why does it take so long to find a job?" It's true that nationally there are more jobs than graduates. But the openings are not evenly distributed geographically. In addition, you probably don't want to take "just anything" after all the work you've done on your degree. Finding a job that you really want, especially if you are choosy about the geographic location, will take time and effort.

If you are geographically limited, think broadly about type of library or job. The more restricted you are in one aspect of job hunting, the more open-minded you should be in the others. If you know that you will be place-bound after graduation, prepare yourself to be open-minded about the type of library or information center and about the kind of work. While you are in school, look for ways to learn about all the kinds of work settings that exist in your chosen community. This will help you to be a viable candidate for any job that is open when you graduate.

Consider a lateral move that will help you advance later. This is especially applicable if you must work in a particular geographic location. Some paraprofessional and outside-library positions can give you a "foot in the door" at the institution or in the community where you want to work. The most effective way to get a job is to be personally acquainted with the person who has the power to hire you. Look for positions that might provide the opportunity to become known by people who can hire you into a professional position later.

When you evaluate a paraprofessional position, ask these questions: Will this job enable me to expand my professional contacts? Will I increase my knowledge and skills? Does the management support continuing education and involvement in professional organizations?

If you accept a job that does not require your degree, commit yourself to behaving with integrity. The work is important to the functioning of the institution or company. During the interview, ask, "What is an honorable length of time for someone like me to remain in this job?" If you take the job, stay that long. Perform your tasks to the best of your ability. Comply with regulations and customs cheerfully.

At the same time, you must continue to grow as a professional, even if the job doesn't require it. Participate in professional organizations by attending conferences and volunteering for committees. Read professional literature. Write for publication. Consult Sarah L. Nesbeitt and Rachel Singer Gordon's book, *The Information Professional's Guide to Career Development Online* for suggestions on using the Internet to further your professional growth.

Maintain a positive attitude. Positive people are attractive. If you can't keep a sense of joy about this profession, find something else to do. Your positive outlook will enhance your employability, brighten the lives of your family members and coworkers, and give you the best chance for a happy, fulfilling life.

NOTE

1. Ann Landers, "Ann's Definition of Love," in *The Ann Landers Encyclopedia A to Z* (New York: Ballantine Books, 1979), 694.

RELATED READINGS

Carnegie, Dale. *How to Win Friends and Influence People*. New York: Pocket Books, 1998.

"Library Organizations and Associations." LibraryHQ.com. www.libraryhq.com/orgs .html (last accessed 30 September 2003).

Nesbeitt, Sarah L., and Rachel Singer Gordon. *The Information Professional's Guide to Career Development Online*. Medford, N.J.: Information Today, 2002.

"Poster Sessions." Writing@CSU. writing.colostate.edu/references/speaking/poster/ (last accessed 30 September 2003).

Shontz, Priscilla. "Involvement in Professional or Community Associations." LIScareer.com. www.liscareer.com/shontz_involvement.htm (last accessed 30 September 2003).

ABOUT THE AUTHOR

Elaine Yontz is associate professor in the Master of Library and Information Science Program at Valdosta State University in Valdosta, Georgia. She formerly taught in the School of Library and Information Science at the University of South Florida in Tampa.

3

EMPLOYMENT

19

Hunting and Gathering: Finding Jobs

Suzan Lee

So you're looking for a job. Whether you are just out of a MLS program or seeking to find new employment, the most difficult part of job searching is summoning up the strength/courage to begin looking. Before the actual job searching begins, ask yourself the following questions.

Why am I looking for a new job? Is it because:

(a) I just need to get away from my current position. I am miserable.
(b) I want to work in a different field. The current job is no longer stimulating.
(c) I do not see any new responsibilities or promotions forthcoming.
(d) I cannot work with my current/new boss or peers.
(e) I cannot live on my salary.

If you answered (a), your motive for seeking a new job may not lead you to landing a "better job." Take a weekend to think about why you are unhappy in your current job. You may wish to speak to trusted peers or your manager about some solutions you have thought of to improve your work environment. Communicating with your manager and peers is crucial. No manager or peer wants to lose a fantastic information professional. If at all possible, you should give your peers and/or manager the opportunity to help improve your situation.

If you answered (b), you have a legitimate reason. However, you should speak with your manager or department head first. They may have job transfer opportunities that will interest you. Give your manager the opportunity to help you. You may be offered new responsibilities that you never thought of.

If you answered (c), you may have a sound reason to seek new employment that would serve as a promotion. If you have explored all avenues with your manager about future promotions with little or no success, then it is time to move on. If you have a good relationship with your manager, he or she may know of promotion-equivalent opportunities and may serve as a good reference.

If you answered (d), you're in a difficult predicament. Your relationship with your manager may be poor. One option is to inquire with human resources to see if there are any job transfer opportunities. Short of that, the only remaining recourse would be to seek new employment.

If you answered (e), you should speak with your manager. Your job is what feeds and clothes you. If you feel that your compensation is low, bring it up with your manager. You should speak of your pay in terms of adequate compensation, not as a personal financial dilemma. Don't phrase your request for a raise as "I cannot live on what I make," but rather, "I do not feel that my salary adequately reflects my value to the company. I have taken on several new responsibilities and I feel that those responsibilities should be reflected in my salary."

Now that you have some idea of why you are looking for a new position, you need to uncover your list of dos or don'ts. This step will cement for you what you are *ideally* looking for. It is best to spell it out for your own clarification so that during an interview, you know when to stand firm on certain issues and when you can be flexible on others. For example:

- Am I willing to relocate?
- Am I willing to travel frequently (more than three times a month)?
- Am I willing to work nonconventional business hours (e.g., evening or weekend shifts)?
- What type of work environment am I looking for? It is a
  - traditional library
  - small library (one to five staff members)
- What type of location would I like to work in? It is in a
  - non-U.S. location
  - metropolitan area location
  - suburb
  - rural
- What type of employer is most ideal?
  - public corporation
  - partnership (e.g., law firms)
  - medical

o arts and humanities
o nonprofit organizations or associations
o public library
o academic library

Ultimately, whatever the reason you have for seeking a new position, once you have made the choice to move on, the following tips and techniques will help guide you.

SOURCES OF JOB POSTINGS

The most difficult step in the job-searching process is knowing where to start. There are a variety of sources of job postings such as newspapers, trade journals, jobs online, discussion lists, placement agencies, or word of mouth. What differentiates them from each other? It is the employee pool or the target audience toward whom the ad is geared. As with any decision we make, every individual has his or her own approach to job searching.

Some will begin with placement agencies. For those who are looking for for-profit employers, contacting placement agencies first makes sense. The human resources (HR) departments of for-profit or large public conglomerates will frequently outsource their recruitment of professionals to placement agencies. For such large corporations, placement agencies serve to screen out unqualified applicants and present to the HR department a short list of qualified and talented candidates. Those that are seeking positions in the academic field may do the same but will also turn to positions posted or advertised on academic jobs online or the wanted ads of trade journals.

Whatever field you are seeking positions in, the following sources should be looked into as a vital component in job searching. With which source should you begin? My suggestion is to cast a narrow net by first focusing on the source that will most likely yield the largest number of relevant jobs. If the yield is small, then I would cast the net slightly wider. The job-searching technique that I recommend is to begin at the center or target point and search wider and wider. Note that the further you search away from your center or target point, the fewer jobs you will likely encounter.

Newspapers. Often when one does not know where to look (i.e., for entry-level positions), a job seeker will usually start with the Sunday paper. No one should discount the value of the Sunday "Wanted" ads, but it should not be one's only source. Remember that the Wanted ads will be seen by thousands of job seekers. So for each ad, the odds are you will be one of hundreds applying for the same information professional job. The aim of the employer is to cast the candidate net wide and to be an Equal Opportunity Employer.

Trade Journals. For every library or information association, there are monthly magazines or journals containing job wanted ads. For example, the American Library Association publishes *American Libraries.* As is the case with newspapers, the ads will be seen by hundreds of applicants.

Jobs Online. There are several information professional job posting websites.

- lisjobs.com/—for a small fee, you can post your resume. Lists global job postings
- www.libraryjobpostings.org/postings.htm—chronological list of jobs by date of posting
- www.fedworld.gov/jobs/jobsearch.html—job postings by the U.S. federal government
- http://sla.jobcontrolcenter.com/search.cfm—job postings in special libraries
- www.asis.org/Jobline/—Association for Library Collections and Technical Services

Other reliable sources of job postings are placement agency websites and professional association websites. Placement agencies generally serve clients in a specific geographical area. For example, for job postings in the Washington, D.C., and New York metro areas, one of the placement agency websites you would visit is www.infocurrent.com; in California, you would visit www.libraryassociates.com/index.html.

Professional association websites that you might visit should be based on the type of library you are interested in. For example, if your interest were in for-profit libraries in the New York tri-state area (including parts of New Jersey and Connecticut), you should visit the New York, New Jersey, and Connecticut chapters of the Special Libraries Association as well as the headquarter website, www.sla.org. In addition, I would also visit the online job postings by the regional or state/provincial library associations. Just to name a few:

- California Library Association—http://www.cla-net.org/
- Eastern Canada SLA Chapter—www.sla.org/chapter/cecn/chapterinfo/ Employment/index.html
- Massachusetts Library Association—www.masslib.org
- Newfoundland and Labrador Library Association—www.infonet. st-johns.nf.ca/providers/nlla/

- New Hampshire Library Association—www.state.nh.us/nhla/
- Pacific Northwest Libraries—www.pnla.org/jobs/index.htm
- Texas Library Association—www.txla.org/

Please visit the association websites listed below for their job postings.

- Association of College and Research Libraries—www.ala.org/acrl
- American Medical Library Association—www.mlanet.org/
- American Records Management Association—www.arma.org/
- Art Libraries Society of North America—www.arlisna.org
- Canadian Library Association—www.cla.ca/careers/careeropp.htm
- Canadian Librarians and NAFTA—www3.sympatico.ca/derekgsmith/canlib/
- Canadians Librarians in America—www.geocities.com/cdn_moose/CanLib.htm
- International Federation of Library Associations and Institutions—www.ifla.org/
- American Association of Law Librarians—www.aallnet.org/
- Music Library Association—www.musiclibraryassoc.org/
- Special Libraries Association—www.sla.org
- Association for Library Collections and Technical Services—www.ala.org/alcts/
- SLA Information Technology Division—www.sla.org/division/dite/index.html

Discussion Lists. Associations and MLS programs have discussion lists that facilitate mass e-mail distributions to their members and students. Discussion lists are invaluable sources of employment opportunities. When employers wish to target a specific pool of qualified candidates, posting jobs on discussion lists will accomplish just that. As most discussion lists are free with membership, there is no reason why you shouldn't subscribe.

- Global Info Jobs—to subscribe, send a blank e-mail to subscribe@globalinfojobs.com
- Libjobs-L—to subscribe, visit infoserv.inist.fr/wwsympa.fcgi/subrequest/libjobs
- Newlib-L—to subscribe, visit www.lahacal.org/newlib/
- Buslib-L—to subscribe, visit www.willamette.edu/~gklein/buslib.htm
- Greater New York Metropolitan Chapter ACRL—to subscribe, send an e-mail to join-acrlny-l@forums.nyu.edu

- Libjobs—to subscribe, visit www.ifla.org/II/lists/libjobs.htm
- LIS-JOBLIST@AC.DAL.CA—to subscribe, visit liblists.wrlc.org/LiblistsQueries/TDetail.idc?LisID=170

Placement Agencies/Agents. Placement agencies are used by employers as a screening tool. Placement agents will post job ads in newspapers, journals, or online discussion lists, and then screen the incoming applicants. A select small group of qualified applicants will be provided to the employer, their client. From the select group, the employer will arrange interviews with the placement agent who will serve as the intermediary. On the flip side, placement agencies are a boon for job seekers. They can simplify your job-searching process by noting your requirements for a potential employer and fair compensation, as well as making the necessary arrangements for interviews. There will be overlaps between placement agencies and the job postings you have found on your own, but it's worth signing on to more than one agency in order to cover all bases, especially if you have yet to form a comfortable relationship with a specific agency.

Word of Mouth. In the job market, there is nothing more valuable than the word of mouth. In order to be privy to them, networking is necessary. What is networking? It is when one person meets with another and forms an acquaintance that is of mutual benefit. Interlibrary loan is a form of networking. When one library needs a book, they will ask another library for a temporary loan. The request for the temporary loan is granted as both sides are fully aware that this favor or borrowing privilege will be reciprocated in the future. Networking is based on the same principle. Where can you network? You can begin at your workplace. Also, membership to associations and alumni groups will open doors to professional and social events where you can meet and get to know your peers. If the thought of networking makes you apprehensive, invite a friend or a mentor for support.

COMPREHENSIVE WORK HISTORY AND LEGAL DOCUMENTS

To respond to a job posting, you will need the following documents: a cover letter, resume, references, comprehensive work history, and legal documents such as a working visa, U.S. passport, U.S. driver's license, social security card, or photo ID.

Other chapters in this book will deal with cover letters, resumes, and references. I highly recommend that you compile a comprehensive record of your work history. For each position that you have held, your work history record should contain the former manager's name, company address, telephone number, and/or e-mail address. In addition, keep your legal documents, such as a working visa, U.S. passport, U.S. driver's license, social security card, and photo ID, handy at all times during your interviewing period. Advance preparation will save you a lot of precious time.

As most interviews are held during the day, you will no doubt be scheduling interviews before or after work or perhaps even during the middle of your day. Interview processes vary. Some organizations will require you to meet with their human resources representative before meeting with anyone in the library. Should this be the case, it would be to your advantage to arrive early and to complete any application forms necessary. Application forms will be lengthy and may require up to ten years of work history or the years since your undergraduate education. Having your work history and legal documentation with you allows you to minimize the time spent on paperwork. This level of preparation will permit you to squeeze in as much time with the interviewer as possible, without allowing your job search to compromise your current position.

RELATED READINGS

Dewey, Barbara I. *Library Jobs: How to Fill Them, How to Find Them.* Phoenix, Ariz.: Oryx Press, 1987.

McCook, Kathleen De La Pena, Margaret Myers, and Blythe Camenson. *Opportunities in Library and Information Science Careers.* New York: McGraw-Hill, 2001.

Nesbeitt, Sarah I., and Rachel Singer Gordon. *The Information Professional's Guide to Career Development Online.* Medford, N.J.: Information Today, Inc., 2002.

Shontz, Priscilla. *Jump Start Your Career in Library and Information Science.* Lanham, Md.: Scarecrow Press, 2002.

ABOUT THE AUTHOR

Suzan Lee is a senior research librarian at UBS. Prior to UBS, she has worked for JPMorgan and Credit Suisse First Boston. She conducts seminars and workshops relating to job searching for MLS students and New York chapter members of the Special Libraries Association, where she has served as the outreach chair for more than six years. Suzan Lee has been named a 2004 Mover and Shaker by *Library Journal*.

20

Avoiding the Landmines: Evaluating a Potential Workplace

Nancy Cunningham

Evaluating the workplace before you accept a job is one of the most important aspects of a job hunt. It is exciting to be asked to interview at the workplace of your choice, but your quest doesn't end there. Beyond developing your resume, applying, and preparing yourself for the interview, this aspect of the search places you in the center of the process. You are the final decision maker in accepting or rejecting a job based on your evaluation of the workplace and job offer. Evaluation is an active process of determining whether the position and workplace will support your goals and objectives. This does not mean for the rest of your life but at least for the intermediate term. You will need to do research with "due diligence" on the workplace environment to unearth the character of the organization's culture. Regardless of how promising the position is, problems in a workplace environment may create obstacles to your realizing your goals and may result in frustration and disappointment. While you will never know everything about a workplace without actually working there, there are steps you can take to gather enough information to make the best decision possible.

DEVELOP CAREER GOALS AND OBJECTIVES

Part of the hunt for the right job is to know what you want to gain from the position. Every library and work environment is different and every position within the organization offers both opportunities and challenges. If your goal is to work directly with the public in a small community, one of your objectives may be to find a reference position at a public library in a small town.

If your goal is to work with librarians but not as a librarian, you may wish to seek a position with a book vendor or information publisher. Your goal should be broad and contain a vision of what type of environment you see yourself working in. Your objectives can be more concrete and measurable. To determine your goals and objectives, ask yourself the following questions:

- What type of library or organization do I want to work in?
  - Academic, public, special, school, other type of library
  - Vendor (information publisher, book vendor, database provider, etc.)
  - Small business (consulting firm, etc.)
- What size organization do I want to work in?
  - Large (i.e., with large staff, multiple locations)
  - Medium
  - Small (i.e., one or two person library)
- What kind of community do I want to live in?
  - Big city, with lots of cultural activities
  - Medium city with easy access to larger cities
  - Small town in a environmentally beautiful place
  - College town outside an urban area
- What kind of work environment am I looking for?
  - Relaxed, informal, easy-going
  - Fast-paced, competitive, formal
  - Traveling weekly to different libraries or businesses
- What type of position?
  - Administrative
  - Direct service to the public
  - Working with collections and acquisitions
  - Behind-the-scenes operations, technical or computer services
  - Sales, marketing, public relations
  - Mix of many types of jobs
  - Tenure- or nontenure-track (i.e., academic libraries)
- What salary range meets my needs?
- What kind of experience am I looking for from the organization?
  - Direct mentorship
  - Solo experience
  - Great collegiality between coworkers
  - Ability to advance in the organization
- How do I want to be managed?
  - I want to be given projects and left alone.
  - I want a lot of feedback and direct mentoring.
  - I want a team experience and a lot of collaboration.

Answers to these questions will guide you as you scan the Web and print sources for job announcements. The goal is to look for a match between the position description and your needs. It does not have to be a perfect match and it is important to have some flexibility. Many times new aspects of the job and the workplace will reveal themselves in the interview process. However, if you really hate supervising, don't apply for an administrative job with implied supervisory duties even though it is in your favorite city. Likewise, if you love the big city and serving the public in a busy, fast-paced environment, a main branch reference position in a large city may be the job for you.

EVALUATING THE WORKPLACE BEFORE YOU APPLY

Doing some early reconnaissance before applying is a good way to save time and energy in the application process. It may result in the realization that this workplace is not a fit for you. Before you apply, here are some steps to take when you see an attractive job announcement:

- Check out the organization's website.
  - If it is a college or university library, check out the institution's website.
  - Check out the organization's human resources website for further information about benefits, and so on.
- Evaluate the website like any source of information.
  - Are there errors?
  - When was it last updated?
  - Is there information on the staff (i.e., organizational chart, staff web pages, etc.)?
  - Is it easy to navigate?
  - What impression does the organization present with its web page?
- Do a search in the literature for any news about the organization.
- Contact colleagues, friends, or mentors to determine if they know anything about the library or business and the community it serves.
- Ask yourself if you still want to apply.

VISITING THE WORKPLACE BEFORE THE INTERVIEW

If you live within a reasonable distance from the organization, or fly in the day before the interview, drop in to tour the grounds or facility. If the organization is a library, visit it as if you were a patron. Ask questions of the staff, search the website, browse the collections, and take note of your findings. Write down any impressions and questions you may want to ask during the interview. If the organization is in an office building, take note of the surrounding area, parking, distance from your home, or whether it is a new or old building.

HOW TO EVALUATE THROUGH A TELEPHONE INTERVIEW

Some organizations, especially academic libraries, choose to conduct telephone interviews before deciding to bring a candidate in for an on-site visit. This is usually the case when a short list of candidates has been selected from a larger list. Usually academic libraries pay the cost of travel for a candidate and want to make sure the selected group represents the best fit for the position. For the candidate, a telephone interview provides the first real opportunity to evaluate the library through the telephone question and answer process. Before you answer the telephone, have a list of questions ready to ask the search committee. Keep a notebook handy to write down your impressions and any questions that arise. Remember, you are evaluating them just as much as they are evaluating you. Here are some questions to ask yourself after you have completed the telephone interview:

- Was the interview organized? Was it informative?
- Was I introduced to the people in the room listening to the interview?
- Did the questions seem clear and well reasoned or redundant and irrelevant?
- Was I offered the chance to ask questions?
- What were my impressions of those asking the questions?
- How would I characterize their reactions to my responses?

There are no correct behaviors or right answers, only information to help you decide to continue the process or decline the next step. If the interview seemed disorganized, this could reflect on how serious they are about the position or the skills of the committee chairperson. If the interviewers made you feel at ease and you seemed to develop a rapport with them, this may be a positive sign about those with whom you will be working.

CHECKING WITH YOUR REFERENCES

Your references may provide an objective viewpoint that will help you evaluate the workplace. If you know your references have been checked, you may wish to contact them and ask about their impressions of the questions and the person conducting the reference check. The types of questions asked and how they asked them, even if it is by e-mail or post, can tell you a lot about what they consider important in a candidate.

INTERVIEW DAY

The day of the interview is the best opportunity you have to evaluate the workplace. It will build on all the other steps you have taken to determine if this workplace is right for you. But you also have to interview, right? Exactly right, but this does not mean you spend all your time trying to please the committee and neglect to observe or ask questions. For example, you will probably have several opportunities to observe the behavior of those interviewing you. Notice how they treat you. Do they seem to listen well? Are they polite? Notice how they treat each other. How do they interact? Do they seem bored with the interview process, anxious, or engaged?

Sometimes the interview process is an all-day affair lasting into the evening or even the next day. You may have the chance to lunch or dine with the search committee. If so, be especially observant. Many times this is when committee members let their guard down. You may observe or hear things that will give you more clues about the people and the workplace. Pay attention to the flow of the conversation and note if you are included in the discussion. For example, I attended a candidate luncheon at one of my jobs where one of the search committee members opened up a newspaper at the table and started reading it in front of the candidate, while another librarian was desperately trying to signal her to stop. You want to pay close attention to these signals and what they reveal about the behavior of key personalities. Did the committee members discuss things about the workplace without including you or explaining what they were talking about? Did they seem genuinely interested in you and your interests? Were they asking you questions to get to know you or only talking about themselves?

The day of the interview, gather as much information as time allows. Here are some things you can do:

- Observe everything, notice the little things, and make mental notes (this may help your nervousness).
  - What is the physical layout of the facility where you will be working? Easy to navigate or confusing?
  - Is it busy? Relaxed? Informal or formal?
  - If it is a library, is there visible customer service?
  - Who will be present during the interviews? Who will be left out? Why?

- o If it is not a library, what is the office space like?
- o Does the staff project a positive attitude?
- o How does staff communicate with each other?
- o If it is a library, is signage clear or non-existent?
- o Do search committee members interact well?
- Ask questions, when the opportunity arises, of as many people as you can.
  - o Search committee members
  - o Staff not on the search committee
  - o Patrons or customers
  - o Administrators or managers
- Get the names and titles of everyone you interviewed with.
  - o Were there some staff you did not interview with? Why?
- If possible, get some time by yourself either by going to the bathroom or during breaks in the interview day. Take this time to reflect on what you have heard and seen.

ASSESSING ORGANIZATIONAL CULTURE

A key element of evaluating the workplace is assessing its culture. This can be difficult given the limited contact you have with the search committee and the time you are allotted for the on-site interview, but it is not impossible. Remember, a healthy work culture will help you achieve your career goals as long as they are congruent with the organization's mission and objectives. An unhealthy culture will present obstacles and may result in frustration and disappointment, no matter the salary or level of position. There are a number of aspects that comprise the corporate culture of any workplace.

The following questions may help you discern characteristics of the workplace culture. Your job is to gather information in the interview process and use the questions to develop a profile of the organization that will help find the right workplace fit for you.

1. Organizational Culture
   - What is the organization's structure? To whom do you report?
   - Who will evaluate you and how?
   - If this is a tenure-track position in an academic library, how are the faculty librarians governed? Do the librarians govern themselves? If so, how is this done?
2. Management of Operations
   - How smoothly do things seem to run?
   - How are problems handled? Is the organization crisis driven?

- Is the smooth running of operations a priority?
- What is the level of technology used to run the operations?

3. Leadership
   - Who are the actual leaders in the organization? (it may not be the ones you think)
   - Who are the project leaders?
   - What is the management style of the key people in the organization?
   - Are there opportunities for everyone to develop leadership skills or only a few?
   - Do the same people chair all the committees?

4. Communication
   - How is information shared?
   - What are the standing meetings? How often do they meet?
   - Is there a librarywide meeting or a meeting during which most of the staff attend?
   - How do staff and librarians participate in the decision making?

5. Professional Development
   - What is the attitude toward participation in professional activities? Is it supported?
   - Are there funds available to support development? How are decisions made regarding who gets funded?
   - Are there efforts to train within the organization? Does everyone get the training they need?

6. Decision Making
   - How are decisions (major and minor) made?
   - How are decisions about policies and services communicated?
   - Who decides work priorities? Who decides which projects should be initiated?

7. Work Life
   - What is the general pace of the library or organization?
   - What is the attitude about work hours and dress? Is there pressure to work late, or a martyr complex among those who always seem to work late?
   - Do staff members (librarians, library assistants, managers, technical personnel, etc.) socialize together? Is there pressure to socialize after work hours?
   - Is there a discernible morale problem? Do there seem to be cliques or camps?
   - Is there a sense of mutual support among different levels of staff (i.e., librarians, library assistants, etc.)? Or is there complaining about covering for others or helping a patron when it is not in a job description?

QUESTIONS TO ASK YOUR INTERVIEWERS

The following are some questions that you may wish to ask during the interview process to unearth characteristics of the workplace culture. Feel free to modify them to fit your situation.

- Can you give me an example of a typical week in terms of hours? Are there times or cycles when there is a need to work late or on weekends?
- What happens when there is overload at the reference desk, in reshelving materials, or on a specific project? Do others pitch in?
- Has there been a situation where staff from one department had to pitch in to help another department? If so, how did that go?
- How long has the staff been here? What has been the staff turnover rate?
- How long has the library director or head manager been here?
- What is the management/leadership style?
- How many committees do you have? How do they communicate with the rest of the organization?
- How do the departments communicate with each other?
- How are major decisions made and communicated?
- Every organization has communication challenges. What are the challenges here?
- Can you describe a crisis situation and how it was handled?
- How is the morale among the staff? What are their concerns?

POSTINTERVIEW DAY

Immediately following the day of the interview, spend some time reflecting on the experience. Share your experience with friends, mentors, and other trusted colleagues. If you are interviewing at a library, share your experiences with someone outside the library world who may have a different reaction to what you experienced during the interview process. Sharing with different sets of people sometimes recalls more details and memories of the event. Always ask for feedback on your impressions. Note any questions you may still have. You may wish to e-mail your contact with more questions. Debrief yourself with the following questions:

- Overall, did the interview seem organized and well presented?
- Did I get my questions answered?
- Was the process informative for me?
- What are my overall impressions, both positive and negative, of the librarians and/or staff?

- Did they seem engaged and interested in their work?
- Did they seem engaged and interested in what I had to say?
- Did they say when a decision would be made?
- Did I get to meet most of the staff or only a select few?
- Did I feel comfortable with the people with whom I will be working? My manager? My library director?
- After interviewing, would I recommend this organization to a close friend as a place to work?
- Is there anything that makes me uneasy?

LANDMINES TO WATCH OUT FOR

There are definite landmines that you may uncover during the search process by practicing careful observation and asking the right questions. Certain landmines, or too many, may reveal symptoms of a problem workplace or a workplace to avoid. The following provides examples of landmines and the unhealthy symptoms they reveal about the work culture. Don't ignore them. Make mental notes and discuss them later with friends, trusted mentors, and colleagues.

1. Lack of healthy and competent leadership and management
   - Invisible management or library director
   - Eye rolling or joke making at the mention of a manager's or library director's name
   - Job responsibilities and performance standards are not clearly outlined or explained
   - Professional involvement is not supported and may be discouraged
   - Inability on the part of management to articulate a mission and set of objectives for the organization
   - Constant reference to the "good old days;" lack of a vision for the future
   - Expectation that you will do anything anytime to be "part of the team"
   - Too many meetings without good facilitation
   - Pervasive negativity about any kind of change
2. Poor communication (external and internal)
   - Disorganized interview process
   - Conflicting information about salary, duties, or performance expectations
   - Visible patron or customer confusion about services or products
   - Long delays in responding to your queries
   - Lack of visible and helpful signage
   - Confusing or poorly designed web page or literature

3. Lack of desire or inability to identify and solve problems
   - No meetings or too many meetings that are not well facilitated
   - Blaming attitude toward administrators, users, or nonprofessional staff
   - Denial or downplay of challenges or problems
   - Inability to identify problem areas and provide examples of problem-solving process
4. Secrecy, favoritism, cliques
   - Certain key staff are excluded from interview process
   - You did not get to meet the staff you will be supervising
   - Inside jokes without explanations
   - Visible discomfort by search committee when certain questions are asked
   - Narcissistic or negative personalities that seem to dominate the work environment
   - Negativity about certain departments
   - Eagerness of one group to have you share their views on certain issues

FINAL TIPS AND WORDS OF WISDOM

Today there is a real recognition of and support for networking and mentoring in the professional world, especially in librarianship. When you evaluate a potential workplace, there are many sources you can draw from and much support you can request. You don't have to make the decision in an information vacuum. Use friends, teachers, colleagues, and objective outsiders to help evaluate the information you gather. Regardless of whether the new workplace is across the street from your house or across the country, you will spend a tremendous amount of time and energy making the transition. You want to find the right fit. To do this, you will need to compare and weigh a number of factors. An unhealthy or problematic workplace can dilute your best intentions or, at worst, break your enthusiasm for the job. No workplace is perfect. However, a workplace where most of the staff is taking antidepressants just to cope with the director is not a healthy place to launch a career or develop one. Here are some final tips from someone who, if she had to do it over again, would definitely do it differently!

- Be clear and honest with yourself about what you want from the position and the organization.
- Don't jump at the first bite unless you really feel you have done your homework, thought about it, talked with friends and family, and feel "in your gut" it is the right workplace for you.
- Don't get swayed by a big salary to the exclusion of other factors.

- If you are aware of the negative aspects of the workplace and want to accept the position, do not expect them or the personalities who created them to change overnight. Healthy organizational change is a slow process.
- If you sense there are difficult personalities with whom you will need to work, there probably are. If you don't want to deal with them, don't take the job.
- Do try to assess the leadership and management capabilities of the leader of the organization. An invisible or problem library director or manager can present a formidable obstacle to attaining your goals and feeling comfortable in the organization. The director may have serious handicaps that no one says anything about.
- Don't apply for or interview at jobs you don't really care about or where you know in advance that you would hate the work environment. It wastes everyone's time.
- Don't override your gut feeling. If it doesn't feel right, don't take the job.

RELATED READINGS

Biggs, Debra R., and Cheryl T. Naslund. "Proactive Interviewing." *College and Research Library News* 48 (January 1987): 13–17.

Challenger, J. E. "Six Key Questions to Evaluate a Job Offer." *Women In Business* (May/June 1991).

Cunningham, Nancy. "In Search of an Emotionally Healthy Library." LIScareer.com. 2001. www.liscareer.com/jobhunting/ (last accessed 14 December 2002).

"Hiring On Versus Fitting In." *Psychology Today* 26 (September/October 1993): 20–21.

La Guardia, Cheryl, and Ed Tallent. "Interviewing: Beware Blogging Blunders." *Library Journal* (September 15, 2002): 42, 44.

Mort, Mary-Ellen. "The Info Pro's Survival Guide to Job Hunting." *Searcher: The Magazine for Database Professionals* 10, no. 7 (2002): 42.

ABOUT THE AUTHOR

Nancy Cunningham is director of the learning resources center at Southwest Florida College in Ft. Meyers. She received her MLIS from the University of California, Berkeley, in 1986 and an MBA in 1997 from St. Mary's University in San Antonio, Texas. Throughout her career she has worked in a number of academic and corporate libraries where she has held both reference librarian and administrative positions in public services.

21

Cover Letters: Tips for Making a Good First Impression

Sarah L. Johnson

As the cliché goes, you only have one chance to make a good first impression. When you are in the market for a library job, the first impression you make on employers will be with your cover letter. Although many job seekers focus exclusively on the content of their resume, the material in their cover letter will be equally as important. Not only will your cover letter be the first thing employers see when they open up the envelope (or e-mail), but it will be your first chance to present yourself and show your enthusiasm for the job.

THE PURPOSE OF A COVER LETTER

A well-composed cover letter can demonstrate a number of factors all at once. These include your organizational abilities, writing proficiency, neatness, and, last but not least, why you would be a good match for the job. It's a lot for a single piece of paper to accomplish! This is why you should prepare your cover letter just as carefully as you do your resume.

Think of your cover letter as an opportunity to introduce yourself and your skills. Rather than repeating information verbatim from your resume, your cover letter should serve as a bridge between your resume, the job ad, and your skills and accomplishments. Like a preface to a book, your cover letter should pique employers' interest, giving them a reason to want to continue reading—and find out more about you and your expertise.

PARTS OF THE COVER LETTER

Use the following template as a guideline when composing your cover letter, realizing that each one should be different. The cover letter should reflect the specific job that you are applying for.

Your name
Home (not work!) address
City, state, zip
Telephone number(s)
E-mail address
(skip one line)
Today's date
(Leave three or four blank lines between the date and the inside address, below.)
Your addressee's name
Your addressee's job title
Name of library, institution, or company
Street address
City, state, zip

1. *Salutation.* Use the form "Dear Ms. (or Mr.) Last Name:" here. It is always best to address your letter to a specific individual whenever possible, rather than using the generic "Dear Sir or Madam." Most position announcements will provide the name of a person to whom you should address your inquiry. If this isn't given, use the research skills you learned in library school to find out who the appropriate person is. Make a brief phone call to the library to ask to whom your application should be addressed. Use resources such as the *American Library Directory* or the library's website to find the library director's name. In the case of a job ad posted on a mailing list, drop a polite e-mail note to the person who posted the ad.
2. *First paragraph.* Briefly mention the job title you are applying for and how you heard about it. Be as specific as possible here. Your source may have been an ad in *American Libraries*, a posting on your library school's bulletin board, a colleague who will be known to the employer, or an ad posted on a mailing list. Not only will this give employers feedback on what advertising venues work best for them, but it can also help demonstrate how familiar you are with the library literature, print or electronic. If you found out about the job via an online source, for example, employers will take note of the fact that you are technology-literate or that you subscribe to a certain library mailing list.

3. *Second and/or third paragraphs.* This is the place to explain to the employer why you are the right person for the job—and why the job is the perfect one for you. The amount you write in this section depends on how much you need to say, but in general, include no more than two paragraphs.

Use this section to expand upon your most important skills and accomplishments. Rather than simply repeating information from your resume, use this space to clarify how you would apply your past experience to the new position. Read over the required and desired qualifications listed in the job ad and explain how your skills fit the criteria. If you are a new graduate without previous professional experience, it is appropriate for you to use student projects or course assignments to illustrate these points. In addition, tell the employer why you want to work for his or her organization. Why did the job interest you? Why do you feel it would be a good match for your skills?

At this time, you should also address any potential concerns employers may have in reading your resume. In particular, if any of the following situations apply to you, it will be to your benefit to speak about them in your cover letter.

- Are you switching library types or roles, such as from academic to public librarianship? Explain briefly why you're looking for a career change. Focus on the positive aspects of the type of library you would like to work in, rather than dwelling on the unpleasant aspects of your current job.
- Are you hoping to relocate to a specific geographic area? If you're currently employed and taking this new position would mean moving a significant distance, briefly explain why you are looking to move.
- Did you hold your previous position for a year or less? This will be obvious from the dates listed on your resume, and it's something that employers will notice. If your last position was a short-term contract or temporary job, mention this, either in your cover letter or in your resume. If your current job simply wasn't a good match, briefly explain this without expressing any negative opinions about your workplace. Most employers will understand your desire to return to the type of work you're most interested in. However, the more frequently that you change jobs (with the exception of temporary or contract positions), the harder it will be for you to get new ones; employers won't want to hire you if you can't seem to hold a job for any length of time.
- Are you lacking any required experience? If so, explain how your background would nonetheless make you a strong candidate for the job. For example, an employer's ideal may be for a new hire to come

in with five years of post-MLS experience. Even so, the search committee may be willing to consider applicants with less, or with a combined five years of paraprofessional and professional experience, if their other qualifications were strong enough. One exception to this rule is possession of the MLS; if the job requires the degree, only those candidates who have it should apply.

4. *Last paragraph.* Thank the employer, and state that you look forward to hearing from him or her. Many general job-hunting books, particularly those geared toward the corporate sector, will advise you to state your intention to follow up by phone within a certain period of time. This is advisable if you are looking for a position in a corporate setting, with a recruiter, or if you are sending in an application that is not in response to a specific ad. However, following up by phone within a short time-frame may not be practical or even advisable if you're applying a position that is likely to use a search committee for candidate selection, such as in academic or larger public libraries. In such cases, the search process can take weeks or even months. Most libraries already have formal procedures in place during a search to notify candidates about the status of their applications, and repeated phone calls inquiring about the status of the job search can be unwelcome.

5. *Closing.* The phrase "Sincerely yours" is simple and to the point.

6. *Your signature* (in black or dark blue ink).

7. *Your full name* (typed).

Naturally, your cover letter will be shorter than this section, but it should include most if not all of the points listed above. In all, your cover letter should fit on a single page or page and a half, though lengthier letters are acceptable if you are expected to go into detail on your management or teaching philosophy, such as for a high-level administrative position or a faculty position in a library school. Longer cover letters are also appropriate if the position announcement asks you to respond to specific questions within your letter.

COVER LETTER DOS AND DON'TS

When writing your cover letter, it is important to remain professional. This will ensure that you make a positive impression on the employer. Use the following as a checklist while writing, making sure that you avoid any common problems noted below.

1. *Watch for spelling and grammatical errors.* Employers can be notoriously critical when they find typos or other errors in applicants' cover letters—

justifiably so, because they expect that applicants will be putting their best foot forward. Employers will be reading your cover letter not only to see how you qualify for the position, but also to see how you present yourself in writing. Most library positions require some sort of writing component, whether it be in creating brochures and bibliographies, applying for grants, or even composing e-mail messages to vendors, sales reps, and other library employees. Word processors come equipped with spell- and grammar-checking software for a reason; use them! In addition, carefully read over your cover letter after using the built-in checker programs. While they are generally reliable, they won't catch everything, particularly if you mistake one correctly spelled word for another. Best of all, have a family member or good friend read over your cover letter before you send it. Other people may find mistakes that you missed.

2. *Pay attention to presentation.* Use the same high-quality paper that you are using for your resume and print your letters using a laser printer. The paper should be white or off-white; stay away from fancy colors or patterns. Stick to standard fonts, preferably ones that use variable widths, such as Arial or Times New Roman, rather than a fixed-width font such as Courier. This will make your letter easier to read. Make sure your cover letter fits evenly on the page, with 1" margins all around. Also, while it may seem common sense to avoid sending cover letters with coffee or other stains, you may be surprised how frequently employers receive them.

3. *Tailor your cover letter to each job that you apply for!* Yes, this takes extra time, but it will make a big difference. If you apply for multiple positions using one generic cover letter, it will give employers the impression that you are either desperate, unfocused, or that you simply don't care enough about the job to bother. You may be applying for more than one job simultaneously, particularly if you're just out of school, and employers will realize this. Why should employers spend time on your application if you don't explain why you want to work for them specifically?

4. *Ensure that your cover letter is consistent with your resume.* If you don't update your resume or cover letter frequently enough, old information can creep in. For example, if you were promoted during the course of your last job and are now supervising ten employees instead of five, make sure this change is reflected in both your resume and cover letter. Avoid making employers wonder which is correct.

5. *Vary your sentence structure.* Your letter will be more interesting to read if you deviate from the usual Subject-Verb-Object construction now and again. Also, although the point of a cover letter is to sell yourself and your skills, beginning every sentence with the word "I" will make it appear that you can't communicate well in writing or that you enjoy

bragging about yourself—neither of which is a good thing when job hunting.

6. *Use an appropriate tone.* Even if you know the addressee personally, your cover letter should use a professional tone, one appropriate to workplace communication. Keep humor to a minimum. Chances are that your cover letter will be read by more than one person; avoid overly personal comments.

7. *Avoid repeating, word for word, the qualifications listed in the job ad.* While you'll want to provide examples of how your expertise fits the employer's requirements, avoid simply cutting and pasting sections of text from the ad into your letter. Instead, focus on particular keywords from the advertisement and illustrate how your accomplishments fit their needs. This will demonstrate good writing and organizational skills.

8. *Keep your tone optimistic and positive.* Whatever your reason for leaving your current job, avoid bad-mouthing your current employer or workplace. For all you know, your current employer may be an acquaintance—or good friend—of your possible future employer. The library world is smaller than you might think!

9. *Focus on your accomplishments and provide examples, particularly if they are relevent to the position you're applying for.* Rather than simply outlining your responsibilities in previous jobs—most of which can be gathered from your resume—tell the employer about the results of your activities. How many staff members did you oversee? Did you obtain any major grants to improve library services? If you are an experienced instruction librarian, how many instruction sessions did you provide, and for what types of courses? New graduates can focus on the results of their internships, student jobs, and other activities, such as web-page creation or committee leadership roles.

10. *Use library jargon judiciously.* Using jargon in your cover letter can have one of two effects: it can either demonstrate to employers that you're very familiar with the job and its requirements, or—if the person reading the letter isn't familiar with the terms—it can make it seem like you're trying too hard to impress. If you're applying for a systems librarian position, for example, mentioning your expertise with XML, RSS, C++, and Windows XP proves to the employer that you know the lingo. If this expertise isn't immediately relevant to the job description, though, leave it out of your cover letter.

11. *Include only relevant information about yourself.* Remain focused on your qualifications and the job ad. While it may be tempting to include personal information such as hobbies, marital status, or family life, keep this information out of your cover letter (and your resume). In addition,

avoid including every single detail of your work history. Be concise and focused, mentioning only information that explains how your skills and accomplishments make you an excellent candidate for the job.

SENDING A COVER LETTER ELECTRONICALLY

More and more libraries and library organizations are accepting electronic applications and resumes. If you decide to take the opportunity to send your resume to an employer via e-mail, make sure to include a cover letter as well. Although electronic communication is frequently more informal than written communication, in the job hunt nothing could be further from the truth!

Sending an electronic resume without an accompanying cover letter will not only make employers wonder who you are and what job you are applying for, but it may cause them to perceive your message as spam—particularly if you send your resume as an attachment. If this is the case, chances are that your carefully prepared resume will be deleted, unread. To prevent this from happening, always include a cover letter, using the format shown above, but typed within the text of the e-mail message. This way, employers will know the purpose of your e-mail immediately upon opening it. A subject line of "Application for Reference Librarian Position" (or something similar) will also help in this regard.

Your typed name should conclude your electronic cover letter. If you include a signature file, keep it basic: name, home address, home phone, and e-mail address only. Although it may be tempting to include a more personalized signature, avoid doing so. Jokes or quotes may demonstrate your sense of humor, but in the job search, they can easily be construed as unprofessional. Likewise, signature files containing your work address and phone number are not appropriate in a cover letter designed to help you get another job!

RELATED READINGS

There are many cover letter books in print, and chances are that your local library or bookstore will own a fair number of them. There are also a large number of websites dedicated to the subject. Most focus on job hunting in the corporate sector, but at the same time, they should give you further insight into the writing process as well as examples of successful cover letters. The following sources, listed below, provide additional tips and insight into writing cover letters for the library profession. Best of luck in the job hunt!

Allen, Tiffany Eatman, and Richard A. Murray. "Making Your Cover Letter Work for You." LISCareer.com. March 2002. www.liscareer.com/allenmurray_ coverletters.htm (last accessed 20 September 2003). This short article outlines the main functions of a cover letter and provides some positive suggestions on what to include (and what to leave out).

Nesbeitt, Sarah L., and Rachel Singer Gordon. *The Information Professional's Guide to Career Development Online.* Medford, N.J.: Information Today, 2002. Chapters 11 and 12, "Your Electronic Resume" and "Library Job Hunting Online," provide useful tips on applying for library jobs electronically.

Newlen, Robert R. *Writing Resumes That Work: A How-To-Do-It Manual for Librarians.* New York: Neal-Schuman, 1998. While the author concentrates on resume writing, he also includes a brief section on writing cover letters for library positions.

The Guide to Basic Cover Letter Writing, 2d ed. New York: Public Library Association/ VGM Careers, 2003. Though written for a general audience, this source—overseen by the Job and Career Information Services Committee of the Public Library Association—contains library-friendly advice on writing great cover letters.

ABOUT THE AUTHOR

Sarah L. Johnson is librarian and assistant professor at Booth Library, Eastern Illinois University, Charleston, Illinois. Since 1995, she has compiled Library Job Postings on the Internet (www.libraryjobpostings.org), an online employment guide for librarians. Her other publishing credits include the library career book *The Information Professional's Guide to Career Development Online* (as Sarah L. Nesbeitt; coauthored with Rachel Singer Gordon).

22

The Resume: A Short Story about You

John Lehner

WHAT'S THE PURPOSE OF THE RESUME?

A resume is the short version of your professional life. It includes your relevant educational background, your work experience, and information about your qualifications for a professional position. It's your opportunity to present yourself to an organization that's recruiting employees. You get to shape the presentation of yourself. As you do this, remember that most organizations are pretty conservative and expect you to follow established conventions. Preparing a resume is probably not the time to unleash your most creative urges. You need to present a coherent, well-organized picture of yourself that is professional and dignified. The resume serves to document and describe the aspects of your background that are relevant to the hiring decision. It is a tool with which job seekers present themselves to hiring organizations, and it is a tool hiring organizations use to review applicants for positions.

RESUME CONTENT

Your resume should convey employment, education, and professionally related information about you in a concise and structured way. I believe that the need for brevity has probably been far overstated. Academic libraries, especially, don't expect a one-page resume. In fact, for a librarian with any post-MLS experience, a one-page resume would be considered much too brief. The corporate world's rule about extremely brief resumes may be applied only in the corporate world (i.e., special libraries in corporations). However, your resume should be as long as it needs to be to convey useful, relevant information to a potential employer. Just keep in mind that your resume is a short story not a novel. Public librarians probably don't need to be as rigorous as private-sector special librarians about trimming down their resumes. The conventions are different for academic librarians and there is an expectation that applicants for academic library positions will have more detailed and lengthy resumes.

Note that the academic curriculum vitae (CV) is different from a resume and is not really used much even for academic librarians. You might need to prepare one if you're in a true faculty-status librarian position and are entering the promotional and tenure process, or are an experienced academic librarian negotiating tenure as part of a job offer. It typically details research activities and the actual content of major publications undertaken by an individual. The term CV is sometimes used casually and interchangeably with resume, but in its true form it's a bit different.

THE BASIC RULES

Your resume begins with your name and the information needed to contact you. Phone numbers and an e-mail address should be there, as well as a correct mailing address. It's wise to include a phone number that has voicemail or an answering machine on it. (It's also wise to remove any overly personal or cute greetings from your answering machine.) If you're someone who uses a mobile phone for most of your communication, include that number on your resume. If an organization wants to contact you to set up an interview or request references, it doesn't want to play a lengthy game of phone tag. You should also include your e-mail address. Many organizations may wish to use e-mail for routine communication with you.

The most basic categories for your resume are Education and Work Experience. Additional possible categories are Professional Memberships, Awards (or Honors), Continuing Education, and Publications. The categories or sections you use for your resume must, of course, be determined in part by your own background. For example, if you had a career prior to entering the field of librarianship, you may wish to have a section titled "Library Experience" and a section titled "Other Professional Experience" or "Other Work Experience." There isn't a single template that's going to work for everyone's resume and you're going to have to think about what makes the most sense for presenting your personal career history.

You need to convey your education and work experience in the resume, and the convention is to always use reverse chronological order. Your first job appears last in the list and your most recent job first. Academic credentials are treated the same way, with the latest graduate degree listed first and your bachelor's degree last in the listing.

As you describe your work experience, the usual approach is to simply list each job, the organization, the position title and the dates held, with a short description of your job activities. The description of your responsibilities may be text or may be bulleted items. It's helpful to review your job description, the position announcement that you were hired with, or your last performance appraisal to identify the major elements of your current job so you can describe it on your resume. Keep in mind that you shouldn't just recite the job description. You need to convey what you did and should pay attention to important accomplishments. Were there special projects that you completed? Did you introduce any innovations? Were you part of a team that successfully undertook a major project for the organization? These things should be briefly described as part of the job you held.

Your educational background is usually detailed degree by degree, giving the name of the degree received, the major area or concentration, the name of the granting institution, and the month and year the degree was received. The name of the degree may be abbreviated, such as BA, BS, or MLIS. You may include the location of the institution if it's not a widely known school. For a professional position requiring a master's degree, information about where you attended high school isn't relevant. Although it's not necessary to include grade point averages, it's good to indicate degrees awarded "with honors," "cum laude," or "magna cum laude."

If you are currently enrolled in a degree program and it's clear when you will be receiving your degree, the date of conferral indicated on your resume should say "expected" or "anticipated." It's also certainly appropriate to list significant coursework undertaken that did not culminate in the granting of a degree. You should name the degree program or discipline, indicate graduate or undergraduate, state the number of credits completed, give the name of the institution where the coursework was completed and give the dates.

BEYOND THE BASICS

Many employers will be interested in your efforts to stay current with our fast-changing field. It is often appropriate to include a section in your resume on continuing education. Whether you've attended institutes given by a library consortium, training classes on a particular database given by a vendor, or workshops sponsored by one of the library associations, you should certainly consider including that information on your resume. It can convey your commitment to your own ongoing education and professional development.

For academic librarians, activities such as publications and conference presentations are important and there should be resume sections for these endeavors. In addition, academic librarians are frequently expected to engage in service activities within the library, at the university level, and with the professional organizations, so they may wish to include categories for these activities.

Many resumes include an opening statement of the applicant's objective. These are useful only if the resume is going to be used in a blanket mailing, not as part of the application for a particular position. When applying for a particular position, your cover letter addresses your interest in the specific position and the statement of the objective at the beginning of the resume serves little purpose. Sending a resume with an irrelevant or inappropriate objective when applying for a specific job should always be avoided, of course. If your resume includes the objective of "working in a service-oriented public library and addressing the information needs of a diverse user group," you will look silly using it to apply for a job in a corporate special library. Unfortunately, I have seen librarians apply for specific positions with such oddly discordant job objectives on their resumes.

It may be useful to create several resumes, emphasizing different aspects of your education and experience, depending on the types of jobs you're seeking. You may also wish to customize your resume for a particular position. Some of the task of specifically addressing the particular position you're applying for is accomplished by carefully drafting your cover letter. For more experienced librarians with diverse work experience, it may be helpful to custom-craft a resume for a particular position that emphasizes the most relevant aspects of your background. Given the ease of word processing and the ubiquity of good laser printers, it's not too hard to maintain several resumes or to customize a resume for a particular job.

The best way to learn about resumes is to see resumes of other librarians. Ask your colleagues if they will share their resumes with you. If you're still in a library and information science graduate program and are putting together your first professional resume, you need to see the resumes of recent graduates and early-career-stage librarians. The resume of someone with twenty years of experience may not help you understand how to present yourself appropriately. In addition, even experienced librarians would do well to have a colleague review their resumes simply to gain an objective opinion. Someone else will bring a fresh eye to your resume and will notice things that didn't occur to you.

SOME SPECIAL CONCERNS

Some job applicants who are concerned about age discrimination don't include the dates of academic degrees. If you choose to delete dates for important job criteria such as degrees, make sure you're not raising unnecessary questions about what you're trying to hide. I think many academic institutions and public entities are sensitive to discrimination issues and avoid considering age in the employment decision. Many employers are going to probably require a transcript showing the granting of the required degree at some point in the hiring process anyway.

Eliminating dates for positions listed in your employment history can also raise questions about what you're trying to hide. One useful approach is to exclude dates for positions held more than ten years ago. If you can show a good job history for more recent years, few questions are likely to be raised about what you were doing more than ten years ago. This approach puts the focus on your recent accomplishments and takes the focus off the length of your work experience.

Most of us probably do not need to address citizenship or U.S. work authorization on our resumes. However, if you have information on your resume that suggests that you may not be a U.S. citizen, such as an undergraduate degree from abroad, you need to address this. If you hold foreign credentials, but are a U.S. citizen or have permanent resident status, you should probably include that information on your resume. Canadian nationals applying for positions in the United States would be well advised to include a mention of "Canadian citizen" on their resume. Many U.S. employers know that Canadian librarians holding the appropriate master's degree are professionals who specifically qualify for the easily obtained TN visa. Be aware that although U.S. employers may not discriminate on the basis of national origin, they may inquire about and consider whether potential employees have U.S. work authorization and whether an applicant will require sponsorship for it in the future.

SOME FORMATTING CONCERNS

The advice on cover letters—white paper, standard font style—is even more important for your resume. Your resume is likely to be extensively photocopied and distributed around an organization. If you're selected for a position, more photocopies of it will be made for processing your hiring paperwork. The version that finally ends up in the human resources department personnel file may be a third- or fourth-generation photocopy. So avoid anything that doesn't photocopy well.

If you're sending your resume electronically (such as an attachment to an e-mail message), it's even more important to use a standard font and simple formatting. It may be appropriate to ask the recipient of the resume if there are certain file types that are preferred for electronic submissions. Be wary of using "zipped" or compressed files, or anything else that may complicate the opening and printing of your resume on the recipient's end.

THE "SKILLS" RESUME

There are some alternative approaches to the typical chronological model for a resume. One is the "functional" or "skills" resume, which lists skills you've acquired and treats education and employment history as brief secondary sections. Be wary of using these—it can look like you're trying to hide something. Employers want to see if you have a coherent career development path and want to be able to associate the skills you are touting with the particular positions in which these skills were developed. Academic and governmental institutions are usually pretty conservative. They're not going to hire you just because your resume asserts that you're a whiz at PERL script and Java and have "outstanding organizational and interpersonal skills."

The "skills" resume is sometimes used by applicants who've had interrupted career paths. If you are someone who has had an interrupted career path, perhaps because of health problems or family responsibilities, it may be preferable to simply state that in your cover letter. Going through elaborate resume machinations to avoid addressing that issue will often cause potential employers to carefully scrutinize your resume and to assume the worst. You don't want employers to assume that you didn't work for two years because you can't hold a job. If you didn't work for a while because of a health problem, child-rearing responsibilities, or caring for elderly parents, it's probably better to briefly mention that in your cover letter. You don't need to, and probably shouldn't, provide details. With the Family Medical Leave Act and other legal protections in place, employers are more attuned to these employee concerns than they have been in the past and, in many instances, workplaces have become much more open about these issues.

SOME TIPS FOR NEW GRADS

New graduates from library and information science programs have some unique concerns in assembling their resumes. Presenting yourself for your first professional-level job takes you into some unfamiliar territory. I offer these suggestions for new graduates:

- The best place to start may be with the Education section of your resume, especially if you don't have much work experience. Your graduate degree in library and information science and bachelor's degree may be your strongest credentials, so put them up there at the top of your resume, right after your name and contact information.

- Do list the library school courses that you took that are relevant to the sort of positions you're applying for. If you're applying for cataloging positions, it would certainly be appropriate to list the names of the cataloging courses you completed in your degree program. For public-services positions, courses in database searching, reference services, and information literacy and instruction are probably relevant.
- Do include details of work done in a library school internship or practicum. Don't just say "Reference Internship, North Winston Library, Summer 2003." Include the name of the librarian who supervised the internship, the supervisor's job title, and include a description: "Internship under the direction of the Head of Reference Services. 10 hours per week on the reference desk. Assisted library users with library databases, Internet searching, and use of the reference collection."
- Don't leave off pre-professional experience. If you had work experience in a library before receiving the MLS, detail the position(s). Such experience is a big advantage that many other new grads won't have. Even student jobs in the university or college library where you got your undergraduate degree are a big plus. It means you know something about the work environment you're seeking to enter.
- Don't underplay seemingly unrelated experience. If you've supervised employees in any workplace, that's valuable experience and should be included on your resume. For public-services positions in libraries, retail experience can be a real plus.
- List your associations. It's good to be a student member of SLA or ALA or your state library association, and they offer bargain deals for student members. Your membership indicates that you have an interest in and commitment to your chosen profession.
- Any teaching experience should be included and described. Library reference service often involves teaching people to use information resources, and even if you taught soccer, CPR, or bridge, it's a potentially helpful experience. Academic librarians are frequently required to do instructional work, so any teaching experience will be especially valued for many academic librarian positions.

SOME RESUME "DON'TS"

It's always hard to come up with hard and fast rules. Different employers will have different expectations about how resumes should be constructed. I've reviewed hundreds of resumes over the last five years, however, and there are some things that I think everyone should avoid. Here are a few rules that I'd suggest:

1. *Don't forget to spell check and carefully proofread your resume.* Proofread your resume again and again and again. And that's after you've used the spell-checking and grammar-checking functions in your word processing program. Failing to use the spell-checking function in your word processing application is inexcusable. Remember, too, the spell checker won't capture a properly spelled word used incorrectly. After you've proofread your resume, ask someone you trust to carefully proofread it, too. Errors in a resume do get noticed by search committees, interview panels, and hiring officials, and they reflect poorly on the applicant.

2. *Don't include a photo on your resume.* It's inappropriate and harkens back to the days when this was a tool to help employers discriminate on the basis of race. You're not in a beauty contest; you're applying for a professional position.

3. *Don't include your age, marital status, or information about children.* These have nothing to do with your qualifications for a position and may touch on legally protected statuses that are not to be considered in an employment decision.

4. *Don't include your hobbies and personal interests.* This is one that a lot of people seem to think is useful or appropriate. When an employer is reviewing applications for an interlibrary loan specialist, the fact that you enjoy fly-fishing, snowboarding, or quilting isn't relevant or useful; it's just clutter on your resume.

5. *Don't ever lie on your resume.* Many academic, governmental, and other organizations will consider a material misrepresentation in your application documents to be grounds for subsequent dismissal. In many organizations, your resume becomes part of your official application, so don't assume you can lie on your resume as long as you don't lie on an official application form. You can only get away with a little puffery. A resume is indeed a marketing tool; however, any significant misrepresentation is a serious problem. For example, don't ever claim to possess a degree you don't hold, even if you're only several credits short of having completed it. Stating that you have a degree that you don't really hold is clearly a material misrepresentation and, if revealed, could get you fired. The same goes for jobs. Don't ever say you held a job you didn't hold. Seriously, your mother was right when she taught you to tell the truth. Don't lie.

KEEPING IT UP TO DATE

Finally, it's really useful to keep your resume up to date, even if you're not looking for a new job. Your career in librarianship is an ongoing process and the resume that documents your career should also be an ongoing work in progress. It should be a process of continuous updating, revision, and improvement. As your career evolves, your resume should evolve, too. Allowing your resume to lie fallow for three, five, or ten years and then trying to update it can be an onerous task. The pressure to quickly update your resume so that you can make a timely application for a new job will cause you to forget and overlook important aspects of your professional background. As you develop new skills, undertake new tasks at work, and pursue new opportunities in continuing education, you should be updating your resume to reflect these things. Then when it's time to pursue a new job opportunity, you need only do a little editing and polishing to quickly have a great resume ready.

RELATED READINGS

Ireland, Susan. "A Resume That Works." *Searcher* 10 (2002): 98–109.
Newlen, Robert R. *Writing Resumes That Work: A How-To-Do-It Manual for Librarians*. New York: Neal-Schuman Publishers, 1998.
Ream, Richard. "Rules for Electronic Resumes." *Information Today* 17 (2002): 24–25.

ABOUT THE AUTHOR

John Lehner holds an MBA in human resources management and a labor relations degree; he is also an attorney. He received his MLS from the University at Albany-SUNY. He is the library human resources director at the University of Houston Libraries.

23

Interviews in Libraries: Planning, Preparation, and Perfection

Tiffany Eatman Allen

Congratulations! Your perfectly written cover letter and resume were a success and you have been invited for an interview. What should you expect? And most importantly, how should you prepare?

TYPES OF INTERVIEWS

There are several types of interviews. Public libraries, for example, more commonly employ a panel interview, while academic libraries use on-site interviews, meeting with multiple search participants, for as long as a day or two. When you are invited for the interview, ask about the interview format. That information will help you prepare for the big day. The following are the more common types of interviews employed by various libraries.

Telephone Interviews

In order to expedite the search process, many libraries use telephone interviews to narrow a large pool, to gather more information, and ultimately to help with the decision about whom to invite for an on-site interview. Most often the telephone interview is a prescreening interview and is usually the first, but not the last, opportunity a candidate will have to speak with members of the hiring institution. A successful telephone interview may be your ticket to the more formal, structured, on-site interview. The preparation for a telephone interview is much like that for an on-site interview, which will be discussed in more detail later. While it may be difficult to establish a rapport with an interviewer via telephone, here are a few strategies for a telephone interview:

- If given advance notice of the telephone call, ask to whom you will be speaking. You will get an idea of the size of the group and you may be able to research the individuals you will be speaking with, their role in the organization, and their relevance to the position for which you are interviewing.
- Have your prepared notes and a copy of your application materials in front of you so you can refer to them as needed, but try not to read from them directly. You want to sound animated and excited about the position, not like you are reading from a script.
- Have a quiet space to speak with the interviewer or search committee. If you cannot hear the question, always feel free to ask the interviewer to repeat it.

Panel, Board, and Team Interviews

In the panel interview, you will be interviewed once by a group of between four and six people in the library system, usually at the library or other organizational building. Each member of a panel of interviewers is a stakeholder in the outcome of this search. This panel may consist of the supervisor, department head, or board of directors for a position, as well as potential coworkers. The good news about a multiple-interviewer situation is that you would probably need to meet with all of these people at some point during the interview; in this situation, you meet with them all at once.

When dealing with multiple interviewers, the best strategy is to treat each person on the panel as an individual. While they may be a panel of interviewers, each member is a stakeholder in the outcome of this search. That is, each person has his or her own agenda and personal interest in mind when determining the best person for the position. Make eye contact with each member of the panel, treat each person equally, and answer his or her questions clearly and concisely, providing relevant examples of how your education and experience closely match the duties and responsibilities of the position.

On-Site Interviews

On-site interviews, most common in academic libraries, can be as short as a half-day or as long as two days. You will travel to the campus library and meet with different groups and individuals who represent departments throughout the library and sometimes across the campus or larger organization. You will most likely have the opportunity to meet with the search committee, the human resources professional of the organization, and the supervisor for the position. You may have an open meeting with library staff or, in some cases, a public presentation on a given topic. On-site interviews are long and can be very tiring. Preparation and rest prior to the interview are your keys to success. You should be familiar with the area, the campus, and the library. Be prepared to meet a number of people and shake a lot of hands. Greet each person enthusiastically and answer each question as though it were the first time you had been asked (even if you get the same question a hundred times). When answering questions, instead of giving general responses, try to employ the STAR strategy described by Barbara Reinhold in her article "Isn't an Interview Just an Interview?"

- S = name a SITUATION facing you or
- T = a TASK you had to complete
- A = describe what ACTION you took
- R = tell the RESULTS of your actions

It will be a long day. If traveling, try to arrive the day before your interview so you are well rested. Wear something professional but comfortable. In his work "The On-Site Interview—A New and Different Experience," Walter Vertreace (2003) advises, "Conservatism in dress, speech and demeanor is the order of the day when making your first impression."

THE INTERVIEW

With any type of interview, preparation is most essential to success. From first impressions to follow-up letters, the sections below will offer guidance for before, during, and after the interview.

Preparing for the Interview

The best preparation for an interview is interviewing. If you are still in school, take advantage of career fairs. Career fairs are an opportunity to introduce yourself to representatives from different institutions, learn more about activities in a particular organization, practice your selling skills, or to have a screening interview.

Mock interviews are another helpful tool when preparing for an interview. With the vacancy announcement for the position in mind, fellow colleagues or classmates can role-play as members of a panel or search committee, and they can ask you questions similar to those you will be asked on the day of your interview. By practicing your answers, you can receive feedback from the group about the type of information you should or should not include on the day of your real interview. Members of the mock interview panel will also be able to coach you on your performance. In addition to the feedback and coaching, you will gain practice and self-confidence in your interviewing abilities through role-play.

Research ahead of time is extremely important to the success of your interview. Prepare yourself for the interview first by analyzing what they are looking for in the position and what you have to offer. Make two lists. On the first, using the vacancy announcement, list the needs of the employer and the required and preferred qualifications of the position. On the second, list the qualities, experience, and education you possess that match the needs of the position.

You also need to know more about the library than where it is located and the number of staff employed. You should know how the position for which you are interviewing fits into the larger organization. Look for people within the organization who will have contact with this position. Check out the library's and the department's web pages. See if you can find monthly or annual statistics. Research the types of activities the library offers and the type of clientele they serve. Research will not only help you prepare your answers for typical interview questions, but it will also help you formulate the questions you have for the interviewer or search committee throughout the day.

There are some interview questions that are easily predictable. You should think of answers to these questions and, using the research you have done on the organization, be prepared to answer the questions providing relevant examples from your education and experience. Be prepared to talk about yourself and be sure that you are able to answer such questions as: "Tell us about yourself and about your interest in this position," "What are your strengths and weaknesses?" and "What makes you an effective team member?" You should also be prepared to answer specific behavioral questions, such as: "Tell me about a situation when . . ." or, "Give me an example when you . . ." One example: "I see from your resume that you have worked in a team environment. Could you please tell me about a time when you had to accomplish a task as a group and your role in the group?"

An interviewer should avoid questions that have more to do with personal lifestyle than job experience. Questions should focus on the requirements of the position, not the individual's personal characteristics or situation. The following list of topics, compiled by the Society for Human Resources Management, should not be asked about or discussed in an interview. If a question should be asked that falls into one of these categories, try to answer in a way that brings the interviewer back to a relevant topic such as the duties of the position or your relevant experience.

- Age
- Arrest record
- Association with present employees

- Bankruptcy and credit affairs
- Citizenship (unless required by law or regulation—a potential employer may ask if you are authorized to work in the United States)
- Disability
- Driver's license (unless a requirement of the position)
- Educational attainment
- Emergency contact information
- English-language skills (again, unless it is a requirement of the position, i.e., an English teacher)
- Height and weight
- Marital status/name changes/spouse/children
- Organization or club membership
- Race, color, religion, sex, or national origin
- Union affiliation
- Veteran status/military records (unless the question is based on business necessity or job-related reasons)
- Weekend work/shift changes

Equally as important as preparing for questions you will be asked is preparing questions you should ask the potential employer. During the interview, you will be given an opportunity to ask questions. When asked "Do you have any questions for us?" your answer should never be "No." Asking the right questions shows you have done your research, you are listening during the course of your interview, and you are genuinely interested in the position and the organization. Also beware of asking questions that focus on "What's in it for me?" Initiating questions about benefits, such as vacation time or the number of holidays, before the employer initiates the subject is premature and may be seen as a bit self-centered. Unless prompted, concentrate on questions about the position and the organization.

When preparing for your interview, use your research to formulate several questions that you can take with you. Ask more about preferred qualifications for the position, challenges of the position or the library, or opinions on future trends in the profession. You should also use your judgment about the number of questions and the best time to ask. Consider this a conversation and share the time.

On the day of the interview, take extra copies of your resume with you, along with a portfolio or pad of paper to take notes. Also be sure to take directions to the interview and any interview packet that may have been sent in advance.

During the Interview

First impressions are very important in an interview and you want to present yourself in the best way possible. Arrive a few minutes early and check your appearance one last time. Nonverbal communication will be the first noticed. Be sure you have good posture, smile, make eye contact, and give a firm, but not crushing, handshake. During the interview, focus on your prepared points and questions, and relay your thoughts with a calm, pleasant demeanor. Relax, listen, and ask questions that are relevant to the conversation. Good communication is listening and letting the interviewer know you heard what was asked by responding to his or her questions and bringing in relevant examples from your education and experience. Stay poised and consider each aspect of the interview a meeting between professionals. Even social events, such as lunch or dinner with the interviewer or search committee, are considered part of the interview and you should conduct yourself professionally. Remember manners and etiquette; time spent with institutional representatives is always evaluated.

Be sure to ask the questions you prepared in advance and any other questions you noted throughout the interview. Asking questions will demonstrate that you have been listening and paying attention during the course of the interview and that you are interested in the position. It will also further engage you in the process. At the same time, you will get the information you need to evaluate the organization. While it may not feel this way, remember that you are interviewing them as much as they are interviewing you. Your questions should reflect your interest in the organization and the organizational culture of the library and the institution. Observe body language and facial expressions when listening to the answers to your questions. Your questions should focus on the needs of the library and the supervisor. This information will help you during your evaluation of the position and the potential workplace. Additionally, if you are offered the position, you will be in a better position to negotiate if you understand the needs of the organization and how your accomplishments can address those needs.

After the Interview

After the conclusion of your interview, go home and relax. Put your feet up, take a deep breath, and spend a few minutes reflecting on the day. How do you think you did? Did you enjoy the people you met? Does the institution feel like a good fit? Are you still excited about the position? The answers to these questions will help you with your decision should you receive an offer. If you do not receive an offer for this position, at the very least you will have met some interesting people and may have gained insight into things you could do to better prepare for your next interview.

A few days following the interview, send thank-you letters to people with whom you met during your interview. Thank them for their time and express appreciation for their hospitality. If you are still interested in the position, be sure to express that. Even if you are no longer interested in the position, send a thank-you note. The kindness reflected in a thank-you note extends beyond this position, and you may be kept in mind if another position better suited to your abilities and experience becomes available.

If time elapses and you are still interested in the position but have not heard back from the institution, be sure to contact the human resources representative of the organization. Ask him or her how the search is progressing. If the position is still unfilled, let him or her know you remain interested in the position and would be happy to provide any additional information. If you have another offer, you can also ask what their anticipated timeline is so you can plan accordingly.

CONCLUSION

Interviews can be a long and stressful process. They can also be excellent opportunities to meet other professionals in the field and to visit different organizations and institutions. With the proper preparation and rest prior to the interview, you will be well equipped for the day (or days) ahead. Do your research, ask your questions, and the get the information you need to do your best in the interview and make the best decision regarding your successful career in libraries.

RELATED READINGS

Alleyne, Sonya. "The Resume, The Pitch, The Close. What You Need to Know Now About Finding a Job." *Black Enterprise* 33, no. 7 (February 2003).

Martin, Carole. "Nonverbal Communications: Escape the Pitfalls." *Monster Interview Center*. interview.monster.com/review/actions (last accessed 3 September 2003).

Reinhold, Barbara. "Isn't an Interview Just an Interview?" interview.monster.com/rehearsal/interviews/ (last accessed 3 September 2003).

Society for Human Resources Management. www.shrm.org (last accessed 3 September 2003).

Vertreace, Walter C. "The On-Site Interview—A New and Different Experience." *The Black Collegian Online*. www.black-collegian.com/career/interview2003-2nd.shtml (last accessed 3 September 2003).

ABOUT THE AUTHOR

Tiffany Eatman Allen is a graduate of the University of North Carolina (UNC) at Chapel Hill, with a BS in psychology and political science and an MLS from the School of Information and Library Science. She held a support-staff position in the catalog department of the UNC Chapel Hill Academic Affairs Library while attending library school and currently serves as the assistant personnel librarian at the University of North Carolina at Chapel Hill.

24

Negotiation

Mari Marsh

You got the job! You are exhilarated and the search committee is waiting for you to say "YES." But wait! Before you say "yes," say "thank you," and ask for twenty-four hours to think it over. And *then* get ready to put your best research skills to work. Sit down with pencil and paper to organize your thoughts and figure out how to maximize your total compensation for the best deal possible.

SALARY NEGOTIATION IN LIBRARIES

Most of what you will read on salary negotiation is focused on the corporate arena where salaries are fluid and flexible. Since we know that most librarian salaries are funded through controlled systems, that is, by federal, state, county, or city government agencies, we *assume* that compensation cannot be negotiated. We also know that some libraries have a policy on fixed salaries for new librarians or fixed salary ranges that cannot be negotiated. Get the courage to ask no matter what you assume. There are many situations where flexibility exists and you don't want to miss any opportunities to negotiate for exactly what you want.

WILL THIS BE AN INCREASE IN MY TOTAL COMPENSATION?

First of all, assess whether the salary *should* be negotiated. While the salary may seem low, when combined with benefits and perks the total package can add up to a substantial sum.

To do that, determine the total compensation for your current job and compare it with the total compensation of the job offer. The total compensation is the annual salary added to the cost of the benefits. To determine the cost of benefits, find out the percent of salary allotted to benefits for library employees. This is specific to each library, but it is a standard number used in fiscal circles. You can get this information from human resources or from library administration. What you want to do is estimate the total compensation for a job offer, so ask what percentage of librarian salaries is allocated for benefits in that institution or agency.

For example, imagine you are offered a position at $40,000 and the cost of benefits is 28 percent. The calculation would look like this:

$$\$40,000 \text{ [salary]} + (\$40,000 \times .28 \text{ [cost of benefits])}$$
$$= \$51,200 \text{ [total compensation]}$$

For this offer to represent a significant promotion for you, the total compensation should be a 15–20 percent increase over your current total compensation. If the compensation for the new position is not satisfactory, consider negotiating the salary and benefits to get a higher level of total compensation.

BUT CAN I SURVIVE ON THIS SALARY?

While total compensation is important, no amount of benefits will translate to cash money; your new salary should enable you to earn a living wage at a comfortable level. You will want to negotiate the salary before you discuss benefits. Salary is the most important part of the negotiation, especially if you cannot live on the salary offered.

First, calculate your needs based on how you spend money and how your current cost of living compares with the cost of living in the new geographical area. There are a variety of websites that estimate cost of living from one geographical location to another. When using print data, Sherry Chastain (1990), in *Winning the Game: Salary Negotiation for Women*, advises adding an 80 percent annual cost of living increase to the recommended salary.

Once you know how much money you will need in your new location, do some market research. Review salary surveys to determine the salaries of librarians performing similar jobs in your geographical area. You can also find this information from human resources, college placement offices, and colleagues familiar with the local market.

Using this information, you should have a good idea of what you need in terms of an annual salary and how much you can expect given your education and work experience. Generally, the counteroffer you will propose will hover around 5 percent more than the original offer, but no more than $5,000 higher than the original offer. If you find that the offered salary is significantly out of range, you may want to discuss these concerns with the hiring administrator before making a counteroffer. In his article "Negotiating the Best Deal Requires a Poker Strategy," Myron Leibshutz cautions candidates to be aware of overnegotiation. He says that, "asking for too much, even if you get it, may cause you to be viewed with resentment and can hinder you in future salary reviews" (1997, p. B1). A frank conversation about your concerns before you make a counteroffer that is too high will prevent the hiring administrator from making inaccurate assumptions about your motives.

WHAT ELSE CAN I NEGOTIATE?

Now that you know how the offer looks after considering salary needs, determine whether you want to negotiate benefits as a way of making the total compensation more attractive. The following is a list of benefits and perks that may be negotiable:

- Relocation expenses
- Home-buying trips
- Lodging between homes
- Computer equipment
- Title
- Office space
- Parking
- Voicemail
- Professional travel
- Spouse travel
- Professional association dues
- Educational reimbursements
- Continuing education
- Tuition assistance
- Flex time
- Vacation
- Voluntary insurance program reimbursement

WHAT ARE MY SKILLS WORTH?

The next step in preparing to negotiate your salary offer is to determine how you will persuade the hiring administrator that your skills are worth more than was offered. To do this, pull out your notes and remind yourself how well you will fit into this organization. Remember what you heard during the interview about expectations and organizational values.

Make a list of reasons for a higher salary based on your knowledge, skills, and abilities; level of responsibility in the job; people you will supervise; market value of the position; or the perspective that you see this as a promotion from your current position. Be able to articulate how your reputation, skills, and work will contribute overall to the success of the organization.

Reasons based on personal need will have no value to the hiring administrator. Do not go into the fact that you need more salary because you will need to relocate, your spouse does not work, or you will need another car to travel to the job on a daily basis. It is acceptable to discuss the differences in cost of living expenses, but be sure that you have facts and figures to relay should you want to use that as a reason to negotiate.

If you have a higher offer for a similar position from another library and want to use this as part of your negotiation, it is acceptable for you to tell the hiring administrator from Library A that you are considering the other position at Library B, but if Library A could meet your salary requirements, you would accept Library A's offer. DO NOT bluff about a counteroffer. Library A may tell you to take Library B's offer, and if there is no such offer, you will have missed the opportunity for negotiation and lost the job offer from Library A as well.

MAKING THE CALL

It is natural to be a little nervous the next day when you make your call to the hiring administrator. Preparation and practice will build your confidence.

If you did not set a time to return the call, ask if this is a convenient time to discuss salary concerns. Tell the person that you have given the offer a great deal of thought, that you remain enthusiastic about the position, and that you would like to talk further about the salary. If you also want to negotiate benefits, say that you are also concerned about benefits, but you want to get the salary settled first.

If the administrator is open to discussion, start by clarifying your understanding of the job responsibilities and reaffirm that you believe you can benefit the library, but do note that you think the offer is a bit on the conservative side. Remind the administrator about your experience in the field (if you have significant years of experience) and highlight the knowledge, skills, and abilities that will complement the responsibilities of the position. Make it clear that you believe that you will be a valuable asset to the library. Stay calm, fixing your thoughts on worth and the skills you offer to the library.

If you want to focus on market value or cost of living as a reason to negotiate your salary, it is time to cite facts and figures. Of course, you can combine all of these reasons for asking, but you don't have to if it feels awkward.

Give the administrator the salary you have in mind. Again, some good advice from Liebshutz: "Remain silent for about 30 seconds. By remaining quiet, you invite the other person to mention a higher salary figure or talk about flexibility" (1997, p. B1). At this point a number of things may happen. The hiring administrator may have more questions for you or may ask for some time to think over your proposal.

If the administrator accepts your proposal, graciously thank him or her and accept the offer. If you still have questions about benefits, tell the administrator that you have more questions and make your case for those based on total compensation needs.

On the other hand, the administrator may already know that he or she cannot meet your proposed figure. He or she may tell you that your proposed salary is over budget, that it will negatively affect employee equity, or that the proposed figure is too much more to ask in light of your present salary. Remember that your proposed salary should be no more than 5 percent of your current salary (unless this position is a significant promotion) or no more than $5,000 over the offer. Since you did ask if the salary could be negotiated in the initial telephone call, and the answer was "yes," ask if there is any room for negotiation and proceed accordingly.

If the hiring administrator gives you a figure that is within close range of your proposed offer, ask if you can accept the lower figure with a guarantee that you will get the balance at raise time. Or, break the difference into a weekly figure. For example, if the difference between your proposal and the administrator's proposal is $3,000 a year, break the difference down to a weekly, not annual, figure. Instead of an extra $3,000/year, you really want an extra $60/week.

If the hiring administrator firmly denies your request for a higher offer, ask then if benefits can be negotiated. If so, ask for what you want and the reason for wanting it. For example, if you are moving from another state, you might want to ask if you could be reimbursed for relocation expenses. Or, if you noticed that the computer equipment in your new office is outdated, you may want to ask for a better computer that will assist you in your work.

The negotiation can end at the point at which you feel you have a fair offer and you are willing to accept the position based on those points.

If the hiring administrator gives you a final "no," and you do not get what you want, decline the offer *gracefully*. Thank the administrator for the offer and willingness to negotiate with you, but state that you do not think this position is a good alternative to what you are doing at this time and that you regret you will have to decline the position. Stay positive and nondefensive; you may have other opportunities for employment in this organization and will want to maintain an amicable relationship.

HAPPY NEGOTIATORS

Your willingness to negotiate a salary will improve your chances for better pay and benefits in your professional career. Each negotiation builds confidence in your ability to negotiate and affirms your worth to the organization and the profession. And there is nothing like feeling that you got a really good deal!

RELATED READINGS

Chastain, Sherry. *Winning the Game: Salary Negotiation for Women*. New York: Wiley, 1990.

Leibshutz, Myron. "Negotiating the Best Deal Requires a Poker Strategy." *Wall Street Journal*, June 8, 1997, p. B1.

Lewicki, Roy J., Alexander Haim, and Karen Wise Olander. *Think Before You Speak: The Complete Guide to Strategic Negotiation*. New York: Wiley and Sons, 1996.

Lewicki, Roy J., David M. Saunders, and John W. Minton. *Essentials of Negotiation*, 2d ed. Boston: McGraw Hill, 2001.

Wendleton, Kate. *Interviewing and Salary Negotiation*. Franklin Lakes, N.J.: The Career Press, 1999.

ABOUT THE AUTHOR

Mari Marsh holds a bachelor of social work and a master of library science from Florida State University in Tallahassee, Florida. She served as the library personnel officer at the University of Florida in Gainesville from 1992 to 1997 and currently serves as director of library personnel at the University of North Carolina at Chapel Hill.

25

Standing out from the Crowd: Maximizing Your Hirability

Richard A. Murray

Much has been written about certain aspects of job searches in general and library ones in particular: creating the perfect resume, complementing it with a strong cover letter, performing well in an interview. These are all crucial parts of a successful job hunt, without a doubt. There are a number of other things you can do to make yourself a strong candidate, however, that may not be as obvious. In any pool of applicants, the odds are that there are going to be a lot of people with good cover letters, resumes, and interviewing skills. So what can you do to make yourself stand out from the crowd? How can you maximize your "hirability"?

Whenever an organization is searching for someone to fill a vacant position, it's very likely that most of the candidates are going to be quite similar. Daniel Ryan summarizes the situation like this:

> For any position that is posted there will be a small number of applicants who do not meet the minimum qualifications for the job. Those résumés or applications are usually discarded quickly. The ones that remain are quite likely to be more similar to the remaining applications than dissimilar. The differences between applicants tend to be at the margins—one candidate will have more experience in one particular area, or a combination of experiences that will differentiate them somewhat from other candidates.

This chapter is designed to give you ideas on how you can accentuate the special qualities and achievements that will differentiate you from the other candidates or, in other words, how you can make yourself stand out from the crowd.

IDENTIFY YOUR "TARGET JOB"

This step is particularly important if you're just finishing library school and are looking for your first professional position. You don't need to be extremely specific, and, in fact, you don't want to limit yourself too much, but it's useful to have a fairly clear idea of what you're looking for, or your "target job." Decide whether you're interested in working in an academic, public, school, or special library. Larger academic libraries usually have staffs that are big enough that some specialization is appropriate (e.g., reference, technical services, information technology), while public, school, and special librarians often have to do a little bit of everything. The important thing is to give your job search some focus: It's more efficient to go after particular types of jobs rather than to throw everything at the wall and see what sticks. For their part, employers would rather interview candidates who say, "I'm really interested in being a children's librarian" or "I'm looking for a systems position in an academic library" than "Oh, I don't care what I do, I just want a job." (The latter may be closer to your actual state of mind, especially if your job hunt has been going on for a while, but don't broadcast that fact to potential employers.)

It's a good idea to be a specialist *and* a generalist. This statement, as with many things in life, is somewhat contradictory. It boils down to this: It's great to have a particular area of expertise or goal in mind, but the more specific it is, the less likely you are to find it. Don't give up on your dream job, but don't limit yourself to only one thing, especially in the early stages of your career. It *is* possible to find your ideal position, but most people have to work toward it over a number of years rather than falling into it immediately. You might be lucky enough to find your dream job right off the bat, especially if you're geographically mobile; otherwise, look for jobs that are in the ballpark of where you want to end up and go from there.

SPECIAL SKILLS

Technology

Keeping your technology skills up to date is one of the most important things you can do to maximize your hirability. Unfortunately, technology changes so quickly that this is often easier said than done. There are many technical skills that are more or less universal no matter what kind of job you're looking for, like word processing and general Windows savviness. If you don't already have these skills, you should definitely go about acquiring them as soon as possible, whether by a formal class, a how-to book, an online tutorial, or just by sitting down at a computer and teaching yourself the basics. Potential employers don't want to hire people whom they will have to teach how to use a mouse.

Once you have the basics down pat, there are a number of other skills that are often very attractive to employers. Being able to create a web page is an extremely valuable skill, even if it's just a simple, static page with descriptions of collections or links to resources. Added bells and whistles like Java or dynamic pages are nice but not essential. Even if you're not a computer whiz, it's important to let potential employers know that you're not a technophobe.

Find out what the most common technical skills are that people in your target job need. If you want to be a cataloger, try to gain familiarity with OCLC or RLIN. If you're looking for reference jobs, play around with some of the major databases like Academic Search Elite or ProQuest. There's no way you can become an expert at the key resources or software without actually doing the job on a day-to-day basis, but you'll impress potential employers if you can at least discuss them in an intelligent manner. In other words, prospective catalogers don't need to know every function key and search strategy OCLC offers, but you also don't want to go into your interview and ask blankly, "OC-what?"

Foreign Languages

There are few skills that can increase your hirability more than knowledge of one or more foreign languages, particularly if you're going into academic librarianship. Before you sign up for a Berlitz class, though, keep this in mind: generally speaking, the important skill is to be able to *read* the language, not speak it. This isn't to say that speaking another language isn't helpful, but nine times out of ten, reading the language is what you're going to be called on to do. There are exceptions to this rule, of course; for example, it's extremely beneficial to speak Spanish if you're looking for public-service positions in communities with sizable Hispanic populations.

If you don't feel comfortable with your language skills, do something about it. Brush up on your high school or undergraduate French by reading French newspapers and magazines at your local library or online. If you're still in library school, ask your advisor if you can take a foreign language class as an elective. Most universities offer reading courses for graduate students, which are ideal for academic librarians; rather than spending all your time learning to conjugate irregular verbs and pretending you're ordering croissants and Orangina in a café, these courses will give you the ability to *read* texts in the language.

Reading knowledge of one or more languages is especially valuable for technical-services librarians. It's rare to see a job posting for a cataloger or acquisitions librarian that doesn't require or strongly prefer reading knowledge of a language other than English. In fact, technical-services positions that specialize in one or more foreign languages frequently have trouble attracting qualified applicants. There have been numerous programs and meetings at recent American Library Association (ALA) conferences specifically about the predicted shortage of foreign language catalogers that academic libraries are expected to face in the next decade.

It's hard to go wrong with languages in which research libraries typically collect extensively, such as Spanish, French, and German. Asian languages — particularly Chinese and Japanese — are also very useful. The odds are good, though, that if you know any foreign language, you will find a library somewhere that's desperately in need of people who understand it.

Happily, if you already know one language, it's often relatively easy to achieve proficiency in other related languages. For example, if you have a solid reading knowledge of Spanish, you'll probably find it reasonably easy to learn to read texts in French, Portuguese, and Italian. Every language you add to your repertoire increases your hirability exponentially.

Science, Business, and Geographic Information Systems (GIS)

Backgrounds in some disciplines always seem to be in short supply among librarians. Most libraries never have enough staff who are comfortable with the sciences, which means if you have an undergraduate degree (or just a personal interest) in something like biology or physics, it will work to your advantage. Colleges and universities normally have any number of librarians with backgrounds in literature or history, but they frequently have trouble filling positions such as the head of a chemistry library or a reference librarian in a geology library. If you're just naturally bad at or disinterested in the sciences, there's not much you can do about it at this point, but if you *do* have a background in math and science, you'll probably find less competition for jobs involving those disciplines.

A background in business can also open many library doors for you. Academic libraries frequently need staff members who specialize in business reference but find it difficult to attract qualified candidates. Public libraries also provide a great deal of reference assistance in matters of business and economics and therefore need librarians who are comfortable working in those disciplines.

Finally, there is a growing need for librarians who are familiar with geographic information systems technology and applications. Universities and large public libraries are facing a growing number of patrons who specifically request help with GIS software or who ask questions that can be answered using GIS even if they don't know what GIS is. It's often difficult to find librarians with a background in this area, however, which means that those who are familiar with it have a big advantage over those who aren't.

Many library schools offer specialized electives in science librarianship, business reference, or GIS technology, often taught by librarians who work in those fields. If you're still in library school and are looking for electives to earn your required credits, you may want to consider these kinds of courses. If you're no longer a student, you may be able to take such classes through continuing education programs as a way of preparing yourself for future job hunts.

THINGS TO DO ON THE JOB

If you already have a job—even as a student assistant or a temp—you're ahead of the game. Many new MLS graduates have little real experience *working* in a library. Every bit of experience you have will help you rise above the masses applying for your target job. In fact, your job history will almost certainly have more to do with your employment prospects than your graduate or undergraduate grades. As long as you have a degree from an ALA-accredited library school, most employers aren't going to care what your grades were. If you have a choice between spending all your time and energy earning straight As or working a part-time library job and getting As and Bs, go for the latter.

Besides giving you the skills real live librarians need to do their jobs and teaching you to play well with others, your work experience will make it easier for you to "talk the talk." Hiring committees love candidates who are familiar with the major issues and trends in librarianship. It's a turn-off if you get to your interview and have no idea what your potential coworkers are talking about when they say "OPAC" or "AACR2" or "ALA." You don't have to be an expert—but you don't want to appear completely unprepared.

There are also a number of things you can do in your current job that will help pave the way for your future.

Ask for New Opportunities and Challenges

You may feel that you already have enough on your plate with your current responsibilities. However, it's very beneficial to broaden your work horizons by tackling varying tasks and getting involved in new projects. Depending on your relationship with your supervisor, you may feel comfortable asking him or her if there's anything new you can work on, assuming you've attained a certain mastery of your current duties. Frequently the department you're working in will have a number of projects on the "to do" list that no one has had the time or energy to tackle. A reference department may need some of its web pages checked for dead links or outdated content. A cataloging department may have a particular collection that has been waiting for attention or a group of items that has never been entered into the online catalog. Perhaps there's a section of the stacks that's notoriously out of order and could benefit from some shelf reading. Even if it's a project that doesn't seem particularly appealing, you'll be gaining new experience, and you will probably also earn brownie points for being willing to tackle something nobody else wants to do. You may also be able to be cross-trained in another unit or department, which will give you new skills as well as giving you a better grasp on the big picture of how various functions fit together to make the organization run smoothly.

Projects with a tangible end product are especially valuable. Once you finish them, you'll have a nice sense of satisfaction and will also have great new resume fodder. Potential employers will be impressed if you can say "I created this web page" or "I cataloged this collection."

It's very important, however, to make sure that your new projects don't cause you to neglect the duties you were hired to perform. Asking for new opportunities can broaden your horizons and keep your job interesting, but don't overextend yourself or make others do the work that you're supposed to be doing.

Document Your Life

Once you've gotten your new projects underway or have begun to pick up new skills, make sure you keep a record of what you're doing. It can be difficult to remember everything you've accomplished at a job after a year or two. Many people find it useful to keep a journal or to write a report at the end of each month detailing tasks completed, meetings attended, and other accomplishments. Spending ten minutes once a month will save time in the long run, especially if you're expected to write an annual self-evaluation or provide other documentation of how you've been spending your time. It's much easier to write a "What I Did This Year" report at the end of the year if you can look back on notes you made each month rather than having to scratch your head and puzzle over what you did back in February.

The other benefit of documenting your activities is that you can build a portfolio of your accomplishments that will aid you when you go job hunting. Make printouts of web pages you've designed or updated, since Internet resources frequently change or disappear. Take photographs of exhibits you may have helped install or children's storytimes you may have done. Some job announcements actually ask the candidate to submit or bring a portfolio, but even if this isn't the case, your potential employers will like it if you bring something tangible to your interview that you can show them and say, "I did this." (This is another reason that it's particularly beneficial to work on projects with an end product.)

GRAB BAG: OTHER THINGS YOU CAN
DO TO MAXIMIZE YOUR HIRABILITY

There are many ways you can make sure you stand out from the crowd that don't fall into the neat categories of "your skill arsenal" or "on the job activities." Remember, anything you can do to separate yourself from other applicants in a positive way will help you find the job you want.

Be Active Professionally

The value of professional involvement can't be stressed enough. Libraries like to see potential employees who have done more than the bare minimum and who have expressed interest in bigger issues. It's especially important to demonstrate that you have the skills and self-motivation to earn tenure if you're applying to institutions at which librarians have faculty status.

Look for opportunities to write and have your work published. It's impressive to have something you wrote appear in a book or a refereed journal, of course, but there are also many opportunities to be published in newsletters, online publications, and other outlets. Being able to list works you've published on your resume will demonstrate to potential employers that you're active in the profession and that you have excellent written communication skills.

Join committees or organizations in your field of interest. If you've currently got a job in which serving on library committees is a possibility, try to get involved. Not only will you have extra activities to put on your resume, but you will meet new people and learn more about "the big picture" as well. If you're still in library school, investigate student organizations that will present new opportunities.

One of the best ways to stand out from the crowd—and a possibility that many people don't consider—is to become active on a larger level through state and national library associations. There are many ways you can become involved in ALA even if you can't attend the Annual Conference or Midwinter Meeting. For example, ALA's New Members Round Table (NMRT) guarantees a committee appointment to any member who wants one, and many committees don't require conference attendance because work can be done online, by phone, and so on. ALA's committee rosters frequently list "virtual members" who may never attend a conference but are actively involved in the organization's work nonetheless.

Many students and new librarians are intimidated by ALA or assume that they don't have enough experience to have anything to offer, which is absolutely not the case. If a committee or round table is working on a project you find interesting, do your homework and contact the chair to ask if there's a way you can get involved. Many committees are desperate for interested and enthusiastic volunteers.

Besides giving you new accomplishments to put on your resume, getting involved professionally will open many new doors for you in terms of the people you meet. The library world can be a surprisingly small one; even though an organization like ALA has thousands of members, the number of people who are actually *active* is much smaller. Once you get involved, you'll probably find that you start running into the same people again and again. This is nice because it makes it possible to make some great friends, but it also means that once you get your foot in the door, the sky's the limit. Once you prove that you're dependable and hardworking, people you've worked with on Committee A will often approach you later on to ask if you're interested in being involved with Group B or Project C.

All this said, don't make commitments you can't keep. Many state and national association activities will require surprisingly little work on your part, especially when spread out over the course of a one- or two-year term, but don't overextend yourself. You don't want to develop a reputation of being someone who doesn't keep his or her promises or who is deadweight on a committee. Start out with one or two projects you're interested in and then add more later if you find that you still have the time and energy.

Networking Is Not a Four-Letter Word

Networking is a concept that in recent years—whether deservedly or not— has gotten something of a bad reputation. Many people think of superficial schmoozing when they think of networking, and while there often *is* some of this, networking can actually be a very positive (and fun) part of your career. One of the best things about librarianship is that it's full of fascinating, intelligent, genuinely nice people from a huge variety of backgrounds. If you get involved in an organization like ALA, you'll never run out of fun and interesting new people to meet, some of whom will become lifelong friends. But besides the fact that making new pals is always a good thing, it's important from a career standpoint to develop a circle of professional relationships.

Don't think of networking just as "What can this person do for me?" Keep in mind that you never know where your friendship (or acquaintanceship) with someone will lead you. If the relationship doesn't go beyond a simple friendship, at least you've made a new friend. But this new friend could also become someone with whom you write an article, someone who gives you a lead on the job of your dreams, or someone you start a business with somewhere down the line. Remember, the library world is a surprisingly small one.

Be a (Positive) Presence Online

For many librarians, online mailing lists, bulletin boards, or other electronic forums are a vital part of their professional life. They're useful, they're educational, and frequently they're fun. It's possible to do some serious networking without ever leaving your desk.

Use those skills you picked up in your reference class to identify electronic mailing lists related to your target job. Subscribe to the group and watch the traffic to see what kind of things people are talking about. You can begin participating if you have something to ask or contribute, but only after you've spent time as a "lurker" watching the group to see how things work. By joining in on the list's conversations, you can establish yourself as a valuable member of the virtual community and become a positive presence.

Be very careful, however, about what you say and how you behave on the list. Never, ever say anything about your current job that you wouldn't feel comfortable saying directly to your supervisor. People frequently use mailing lists to air their dirty laundry, which often has a way of eventually getting back to their supervisor. You should also be very careful not to get a reputation of being argumentative, negative, or rude; the people you're insulting (and the audience who's watching you do it) may be on a hiring committee some day when you're applying for a job, and you don't want them to remember you for a spectacle you made of yourself on some mailing list in the past.

Hit the Road, Jack

Geographic mobility can be one of the biggest positives you have going for you as you begin your job hunt. There's no question that your odds of getting a job are much, much better if you're not limited to one locale. Since you'll have more choices, you'll also be more likely to be able to find a job that's close to your dream job, even if it may not be in your dream location.

Once again, this is another one of those things that can be particularly important if you're looking for your first professional position out of library school. There *are* jobs out there; they just may not be exactly where you want them to be. Many people operate under the assumption that they can't possibly relocate, but then have trouble thinking of legitimate reasons why they really can't move. Is inertia the only thing keeping you in your current location? The job market can be especially tight in cities with one or more library schools; many graduates don't want to leave after they get their degrees, which means there's a glut of applicants for every job in the area. It's definitely a buyer's market in places like Austin, Madison, and Chapel Hill.

It's much easier to get your second professional position than your first one. Many new librarians find that they have to make sacrifices to get their first job, but then can be pickier when they go looking for the next one. If you're willing to relocate for a year or two to get good experience in your first professional position, you'll have much more leverage when it comes to getting your second one. Frequently, librarians choose to move away for a couple of years and then find it much easier to get a job "back home" once they've got some years of strong experience under their belts.

Do What You Love

If you've become a librarian for the money, you're probably going to be disappointed. Since librarians tend not to be highly paid, most people who enter the profession (and stay in it) do so because they love the job. Find a position in which you can spend the majority of your time doing things you enjoy. No position is going to be perfect—every one has its faults—but the important thing is that, all things considered, you love what you're doing.

Applying and interviewing for jobs you're genuinely excited about will certainly help your chances of getting an offer. Libraries want to hire people who are enthusiastic about the position and the organization. If you're applying for a job as a school librarian and you don't like children, that's going to come out in the interview, and chances are you're not going to get the job. (And even if you do, you'll probably be miserable.) Don't get carried away with your enthusiasm, but if you're energetic and excited about the job, your positive energy will carry over to the people who are interviewing you.

WHAT HAVE WE LEARNED?

By now you may be overwhelmed by the possibilities, but hopefully you've thought of some ways in which you can fine-tune your job hunt and add more arrows to your proverbial quiver. Do what feels right to you, but don't be complacent. The librarians' employment market may not always be dog-eat-dog, but it's also not "dog-lies-around-and-waits-for-somebody-to-give-it-a-job."

And, of course, all this advice will probably be useless if you don't take the time to write a good cover letter and resume. Don't forget the fundamentals when you're looking for ways to make yourself stand out from the crowd. Preparing yourself for a job search is a like doing a jigsaw puzzle with a lot of pieces, all of which are important to the finished picture. It's difficult, but if you take the time to put the pieces together correctly, the end result is well worth it.

RELATED READINGS

Beile, Penny M., and Megan M. Adams. "Other Duties as Assigned: Emerging Trends in the Academic Library Job Market." *College & Research Libraries* 61, no. 4 (July 2000): 336–47.

Kellsey, Charlene. "Crisis in Foreign Language Expertise in Research Libraries: How Do We Fill This Gap?" *College & Research Libraries News* 64, no. 6 (June 2003): 391–92.

Khurshid, Zahiruddin. "The Impact of Information Technology on Job Requirements and Qualifications for Catalogers: Review of Job Advertisements in *American Libraries* and *College & Research Libraries News*." *Information Technology and Libraries* 22, no. 1 (March 2003): 18–21.

Lack, Adina R. "'People Skills' and Technological Mastery: What U.S. Academic Libraries Require of Catalogers in These Areas." Master's thesis, University of North Carolina at Chapel Hill, 2001.

Murray, Richard A. "Geography 101: See the World, Get a Job." LISCareer.com. www.liscareer.com/murray_mobility.htm (last accessed 14 October 2003).

O'Connor, Lisa, and Stacey A. Marien. "Recruiting Quality Business Librarians in a Shrinking Labor Market." *The Bottom Line* 15, no. 2 (2002): 70–74.

Peterson, Christina A., and Sandra Kajiwara. "Scientific Literacy Skills for Non-Science Librarians: Bootstrap Training." *Issues in Science & Technology Librarianship* 24 (Fall 1999). www.library.ucsb.edu/istl/99-fall/article3.html (last accessed 14 October 2003).

Ryan, Daniel. "If It Were Me . . ." BuffaloJobFinder.com. www.buffalojobfinder.com/CAStoryTemplate.asp?CatID=1&StoryID=57 (last accessed 14 October 2003).

Saunders, Laura. "Professional Portfolios for Librarians." *College & Undergraduate Libraries* 10, no. 1 (2003): 53–59.

Singleton, Brett. "Entering Academic Librarianship: Tips for Library School Students." *College & Research Libraries News* 64, no. 2 (February 2003): 84–86.

White, Gary W. "Academic Subject Specialist Positions in the United States: A Content Analysis of Announcements from 1990 through 1998." *Journal of Academic Librarianship* 25, no. 5 (September 1999): 372–82.

Yeager, H. Jamane. "Career Resources for Librarians/Information Professionals." *North Carolina Libraries* 61, no. 1 (Spring 2003): 33–36. www.nclaonline.org/NCL/ncl/NCL_61_1_Spring2003.pdf (last accessed 14 October 2003).

ABOUT THE AUTHOR

Richard A. Murray is catalog librarian for Spanish and Portuguese languages at Duke University in Durham, North Carolina. Previously, he was a catalog librarian at Vanderbilt University and a library assistant at the University of North Carolina at Chapel Hill. A native of Raleigh, North Carolina, Rich earned a BA in international studies and an MS in library science from the University of North Carolina at Chapel Hill.

26

Leaving a Job: It Really *Is* a Small World

Madeline A. Copp

Today, it is unusual to find a person who has had only one position in the same institution for his or her entire professional life. Many factors play a role in our lives, so we may find ourselves looking for another job at some point in our career. Whether we leave voluntarily or involuntarily, it is important to remember that the library world is very small, so the manner in which a person leaves a position may be as important as how they begin or what kind of jobs they hold during their tenure. The following chapter discusses why people leave a job, how to plan for a good departure, dealing with voluntary and involuntary termination, and the importance of being professionally active.

WHY PEOPLE LEAVE A POSITION

There are numerous reasons why a person leaves a job. These may include:

- Accepting a new position (e.g., a promotion, new challenge, or different career direction)
- Spouse/partner needs to move (or a family member needs care requiring you to move)
- Dissatisfaction with your current position
- Unhappiness with the geographic location
- Tenure bid is rejected
- Being laid off or fired from your current position
- Being asked to leave after an evaluation period
- Retiring (voluntarily or involuntary)

Some of these circumstances can increase our enthusiasm and love of our profession, while others leave us depressed and wondering if we have chosen the best career after all. Depending on why you are leaving a job, there are several strategies that will help you make a smoother transition. A very important and often stated rule of thumb is expressed by Gail Audibert and Mary Jones in "Time to Move On? Leaving a Job Gracefully" when they note that "regardless of the reason you're leaving a job and whether it's on good terms or bad, it is always crucial to leave in a professional manner. Avoid burning bridges, because you never know when your professional path will intersect with a former supervisor or colleague" (2002, p. 33).

Voluntary Termination

When the decision to leave a job is your own idea, the transition typically is easier than if you are asked to leave a position; however, leaving a job to venture into the unknown is always stressful.

Applying for and Accepting a New Position

There are many reasons why a person leaves a position for another one. Accepting a promotion; being dissatisfied with your current working environment including geographic location, coworkers, boss, or institutional environment; or accepting the "dream" job and/or location are among the most common. No matter why you are leaving your current position, this is usually a thrilling period filled with anticipation and excitement.

Although this is an exciting time for you, your current colleagues and supervisor may not feel the same enthusiasm. Shontz notes: "Don't be surprised if people are upset with you when you announce you are leaving. You have just said you no longer want to be part of their organization. Some bosses feel personally rejected (whether or not they realize it) when their employees quit" (2002, p. 55). Your colleagues will need to take up the slack after you are gone and before another person can be hired (*if* someone else will be hired), so you will need to be considerate of their feelings. Share your bliss with close friends and family and minimize your elation with colleagues.

Before you leave, try to finish up projects, organize your files for your replacement, clean your office and work area, and leave useful information for the next person (e.g., change the password for your voicemail and leave the new password on your telephone; leave keys to your desk, file cabinet, and office with a supervisor or somewhere visible in your office, etc.). Think about what you would like to find in your new office when you start a position and emulate that situation (and, if appropriate and possible, leave your contact information for your successor so that he or she may call you if there are questions).

Moving with a Spouse, Partner, or Family

When you are leaving a position because of other factors (e.g., your spouse or partner is moving, you need to be near a family member, etc.), finding a position may be more difficult. My husband accepted a position in Washington, D.C., so we moved (from California) even though I did not have a job. I hadn't been out of work since I graduated from library school, but I felt that I had a lot of very good, diverse experience and was moving to a location with many libraries. As a result, I wasn't too worried about obtaining another position. I was unemployed for about six weeks, which turned out to be a very long and stressful time. I had arrived with three very good prospects, but one didn't start for six months, one was a temporary appointment, and one that I interviewed for did not result in an offer. Sitting in an empty apartment (our furniture was still en route) in a Washington, D.C., suburb was incredibly discouraging. Luckily, I soon started a temporary position and afterward found a permanent job.

If anyone experiences this situation (or if I ever am in this position again), I would try to keep more active and get out of the house as much as possible. Although job hunting is a full-time job, it is important to be good to oneself. Most people in this situation don't have much extra cash, but there are many activities that are free. Depending on your interests, visit museums, libraries, and parks, or volunteer at an institution or association (local library, SPCA, etc.). Investigate temporary job agencies in your area (both for librarians and other workers) and try not to feel too dejected.

If you need to find another position (whether you are out of work or unhappy in your current position), don't be afraid to apply for or accept a job that pays less than your previous job, is a lateral move, or is even a demotion. As long as there is promise in the position and the institution, and if you are moving to a better work environment for you, it is worth looking at taking a cut in pay. Sometimes a pay cut can be made up in the benefits package, so it is important to look at the offer and the institution's benefits carefully. Although I don't recommend making a habit of taking less pay or a position that is a demotion, I have never regretted the times I have been in this situation and have accepted less pay and/or less responsibility for happiness and peace of mind.

Retirement

I think that most people have an ideal image of retirement. Personally, I imagine myself traveling, attending fun classes, relaxing, and concentrating on the areas of life that I enjoy. According to Christopher Farrell (2003) in "Re-tired—To a New Job," "Retirement is increasingly regarded as a transition to another work life, although at a more relaxed pace." I am not certain if every-one would agree with the phrase "at a more relaxed pace," but retirement may present opportunities that are unavailable in our pre-retirement phase of life.

A person I worked with retired from an academic library and then volun-teered in her local public library; she succeeded in being successful in an area she hadn't excelled at in her previous job. She learned new skills, worked with a different clientele, and ended up with a paying, satisfying part-time job.

If, after you retire, you want to continue working and contributing to the library profession, other possible types of work include volunteering at your previous place of employment (perhaps in another department), volunteer-ing at your local school or public library, or writing publications for pro-fessional literature. Retirement can be a time of renewal and regeneration for those who want to keep active and try new areas (either professional or personal).

Involuntary Termination

If we are asked to leave a job, it is very normal to ask some of the following questions: Am I in the wrong profession? Where should I go? Can I get an-other job? What did I do wrong? How could my boss let me go? Could I have saved the situation? Although it is important to analyze your situation, it is also essential to do so as objectively as possible. Unless it is absolutely ap-parent that one party is to blame (and this is sometimes, although rarely, the case), try to look at the situation objectively and without bias. It is easy to lay blame on someone (yourself, your supervisor, your colleagues, etc.), but typ-ically these situations are complex and consist of many factors.

If possible, when you find out that you will not be hired permanently at a job, try to leave as soon as you can without breaking any legal requirements. Register with a temporary agency, talk with a headhunter if applicable, send out resumes, and let friends and colleagues know that you are looking for a new position. Although you are the one losing your job, it is an awkward and demoralizing situation for all concerned when a person is terminated invol-untarily. Marigold Cleeve, in "Up the Junction: Some Advice for the Older Unemployed Professional," makes a good point when she says, "If any for-mer colleagues seem to avoid contact for a while try not to judge them too harshly. They are probably terribly worried about their own position after what happened to you, or quite simply do not have any idea what to say in cases of job bereavement" (1996, pp. 32–33).

Tenure Bid Is Rejected or Contract Is Not Renewed

Seeking tenure is a long process with several steps leading to a person achieving tenure. If your goal is to achieve tenure at your current institution, be proactive in your goal. Keep track of everything you do, meet regularly with your supervisor, read all of the tenure documentation, and make sure that you are following the procedures. Find a mentor to guide you through the process (ideally from the same institution, but a person from another tenure-granting institution will also be able to help and advise you). Typically there are signs indicating that tenure is not going to be awarded—pay attention to these signs and ask your supervisor, human resource manager, and colleagues for advice.

Laid off from Current Position

Being laid off is not a sign of failure, especially in the current, uncertain work environment. Many for-profit companies and nonprofit institutions are laying off employees. In "If You Lose Your Job" (2003), Lynn Brenner outlines several tactics to consider when you are laid off. Find out what happens if you're laid off (e.g., will your firm pay severance, can you keep your health insurance using COBRA?). Rather than telling your former boss what you really think, get the best possible severance package you can, get the deadline for applying for COBRA, and file for unemployment insurance.

Fired or Asked to Leave after Review/Probation Period

Cleeve notes that "for anyone, being out of a job is a frightening time" (1996, p. 32). This concept is even more apparent if you have been fired. Even though this is an upsetting and horrible experience, it is still important to leave professionally. Besides finding out about any kind of benefits, ask someone (your boss, if possible, or the head of human resources) for a general letter of recommendation that will outline your responsibilities. When interviewing for another position, leave your anger at home. Eric Wahlgren, in "Smoothing a Rough Patch" (2001), also recommends, "Whatever you do, don't lie. Repeat: Don't lie, either about whether you were fired or about the details of the dismissal."

Regardless of how you are asked to leave a job, do not share your anger and frustration with your boss or coworkers; save this venting for your personal friends and family. Since you will be looking for another job, it's important to try to leave on good terms and deal with your anger before you start interviewing with other organizations. Find other ways to deal with your resentment such as joining a support group, physical recreation, connecting with friends, or other activities that will take your mind off the situation.

PREPARING FOR DEPARTURE

It may seem curious, but it is wise to start planning to leave your current position when you begin it. We tend to start a new position with optimism and enthusiasm, but for many reasons, the position may not work out. If you keep this in mind when you begin a new job, you will be prepared for almost any contingency. Priscilla Shontz notes in *Jump Start Your Career in Library and Information Science* that "environments and organizational cultures change, sometimes very rapidly. The job you sign up for may be very different two months later. Your boss or coworkers may leave; your company may be bought by another company; your job duties may change" (2002, p. 65). There are additional personal factors that may influence our decision to leave a position, including unhappiness with the physical/geographic place, lack of friends and family in the area, or the feeling that we are fish out of water.

It is important to try to adapt to changes, but it is also important to be satisfied in your current position. Before you turn in your resignation, consider the following questions:

- Have you been at your current job for at least a year?
- Have you tried talking with your supervisor to see if there are other opportunities for you at the institution?
- Have you made the most of the geographic location (are there activities you may enjoy but haven't tried)?
- Have you invited friends and family to visit, or have you visited them or taken a vacation?

Giving the position time, including giving yourself time to adjust to a new place, is one of the most important factors when deciding to leave a job. A person typically goes through various adjustment stages after starting a new job and it's important to recognize where you are before deciding to move on. These stages may include: (1) everything is new (and exciting) and there is an emphasis on learning about the job and your colleagues, (2) a person is getting more familiar with the position and starts feeling more comfortable, (3) a point where a person feels like he or she should know more, and (4) a level of confidence that allows a person to be comfortable and secure with the job and in the environment. I believe that it is important to try to stay at a new job for at least one year; this should allow you the opportunity to learn your responsibilities, discover if you like what you are doing, and make adjustments to your personal life.

We will never know *everything*, but there eventually will be a time when we feel comfortable in our positions and know enough to ask relevant questions and give appropriate responses. If after a year, a realistic amount of confidence does not set in, it is time to analyze your position, your working environment, and yourself to discover if you and your job are a good match.

IMPORTANCE OF BEING PROFESSIONALLY ACTIVE

In "Fired . . . ," Martha Neil states that "it is networking more than anything else that may hold the key to a successful job hunt" (2003, p. 56). When you are ready to leave a position or if you have been asked to leave a position, colleagues from professional associations and other institutions can be invaluable. Whether they are from state, local, or national professional organizations, colleagues can provide references, perspective, and advice if you are out of a job or looking for a new position.

If your library school still exists, contact the department staff for advice or job leads, or contact another library school or university, school, or public library in the area. Often these locations have job postings, career development information, or temporary and permanent positions available.

CONCLUSION

It is important to figure out what makes you happy and what kind of job and environment is a good match for you. Shontz reminds us that "not everyone will like you, and you won't like everyone. Focus on the work, not the people. Try to remain neutral with people you don't like" (2002, p. 107). In addition to the people, you won't always like all of the tasks that you need to do. If you find yourself out of a job or looking for another one, remember that other professional literature (e.g., business, law, medicine, teaching, etc.) can be very useful in helping us through tough times. And remember that there are always options. Some options are more attractive than others, but we always have choices. Think about the options available to you and choose the best one for you.

Although every minute at work cannot be perfect, it is possible to find a job that makes you happy and allows you to express your ideas and creativity. If your current position does not make you happy and you've tried to make it work, then you need to consider looking for another job. But when you leave your current job, remember that the library world is very small, so the way that you leave an organization can make an immense impact on your future career.

RELATED READINGS

Audibert, Gail, and Mary Jones. "Time to Move On? Leaving a Job Gracefully." *USA Today* 131, no. 2686 (July 2002): 32–33.

Brenner, Lynn. "If You Lose Your Job." *Parade Magazine,* 7 September 2003, p. 16.

Cleeve, Marigold. "Up the Junction: Some Advice for the Older Unemployed Professional." *Librarian Career Development* 4, no. 3 (1996): 32–36. Available from ABI Inform: proquest.umi.com (Ann Arbor, Mich.: ProQuest Company, last accessed 21 September 2003).

Dickinson, Gail K. "A New Look at Job Satisfaction." *Library Administration & Management* 16, no. 1 (Winter 2002): 28–33.

Farrell, Christopher. "Retired—To a New Job." *Business Week,* no. 3843 (28 July 2003), p. 99. Available from Academic Search Premier: http://search.epnet.com (Boston, Mass.: EBSCO Publishing, last accessed 20 September 2003).

Jansen, Julie. *I Don't Know What I Want, but I Know It's Not This: A Step-by-Step Guide to Finding Gratifying Work.* New York: Penguin Books, 2003.

Neil, Martha. "Fired . . ." *ABA Journal* 89, no. 6 (June 2003): 52–57. Available from Academic Search Premier: search.epnet.com (Boston, Mass.: EBSCO Publishing, last accessed 20 September 2003).

Shontz, Priscilla K. *Jump Start Your Career in Library and Information Science.* Lanham, Md.: Scarecrow Press, 2002.

"Six Secrets to Being Happy at Work." *Library Personnel News* 155, no. 4 (Fall 2002): 4.

Topper, Elisa F. "Working Knowledge: Today's Times: Surviving Job Loss." *American Libraries* 34, no. 7 (August 2003): 94.

Wahlgren, Eric. "Smoothing a Rough Patch." *Business Week Online,* 11 September 2001, pN.PAG. Available from Academic Search Premier: search.epnet.com (Boston, Mass.: EBSCO Publishing, last accessed 20 September 2003).

ABOUT THE AUTHOR

Madeline A. Copp is a librarian at Johns Hopkins University. Since earning her MLS in 1985 from University of California Los Angeles, Madeline has held eight librarian positions, has moved a total of twelve times, and has lived in four different states. She has been active in ALA since 1985 (mainly in LIRT, IS, LES, and ACRL), and at this writing, she is happy where she lives and works.

27

Make Your Own Opportunities: Staying Professionally Active While Unemployed

Colleen Simmons

Since careers do not always follow the straightest or most predictable paths, you may find yourself unemployed at some point along the way. Perhaps you chose to take some time off to be with your family. Perhaps you have relocated due to your spouse's job. Perhaps you were laid off and are looking for a new job. Whatever the circumstances, many librarians will wonder how to keep their skills current without working in a professional setting. Though a break in employment can make it difficult to find a new job, what you do while unemployed can improve your chances of finding your next job. With hard work and careful planning, you can use this time to make new opportunities.

The most important thing you can do is to plan how you will keep up your knowledge and skills. If you do nothing, then it will certainly be more difficult for you to find a job at a later time. You have to take charge of your time and truly become your own boss. For perhaps the first time in your life, your career does not depend on what your job expects but on your expectations. In an article about planning sabbatical leave, Marlis Hubbard (2002) suggests extensive planning and "taking stock of ones abilities." Use this time to be creative and brainstorm about how to use your skills in a nonwork setting. Simple activities such as reading, evaluating, volunteering, networking, and writing will help your skills survive unemployment and will help you succeed in the future.

PROFESSIONAL LITERATURE

The easiest activity to keep your knowledge current is to continue reading. Subscribe to some professional journals. If this is cost-prohibitive, stop by your local library or read them online. You may not be able to read the most recent issue in the library, but most libraries have a good selection of professional literature. If you read them online, you might not have access to every article, but it should be enough for you to stay current. You should try to read actively, which means you should take further action on what you read. You might want to take notes. You should definitely pay attention to the authors and their affiliations. Think about the articles and ask yourself questions. If you can't answer your questions about the article, research the topic further or e-mail the author. Contact former colleagues about articles that may spark their interest. Your former colleagues may be so busy working that they missed an important article. If not, you could start a discussion with your colleagues about the topic of interest. You might even pretend you are still in school and that you will have a test over the topic. Not all of these ideas are appropriate for everyone, so choose the ideas that motivate you. Active reading can help you network with new librarians, help you contact former coworkers, and help you increase your knowledge. Reading the literature is such a simple activity, but it can really make a difference in your connection to the field.

Reading the journals is just the beginning, since there are hundreds of library news websites and weblogs available. If you're not careful, you could spend hours every day just reading the blogs. In her article "Blogs: My New Addiction," Mary Ellen Bates (2003) suggests looking at LibDEX (www.libdex.com/weblogs.html) for a good list of library and information related weblogs. For those of you with limited time, you may want to try a service like Library Link of the Day (www.tk421.net/librarylink/). This site surfs the library weblogs and news sites for you and e-mails one story to you each day. Whatever your time allows, the library news sites are also an excellent way to read the current trends and ideas in the field. The strategies for active reading also apply to online literature. Since you are already online, it is very easy to post a message about a news item, e-mail the author, or start a chatroom discussion.

Along with reading library news, don't forget the discussion lists. Remember those days when your e-mail box was flooded with discussion list messages that you never had time to read? Well, perhaps now you have time to start answering those messages. Even if you are unemployed, your knowledge is still valuable, and you may be able to provide assistance to others. Pick one or two lists in your areas of expertise and make an active contribution.

You don't have to limit your reading to library literature either. As a librarian, you never know when a subject might be useful. Take advantage of this time off to explore other subjects. Do you have a passion for distance learning or creating websites? Is there a subject area where you feel your knowledge is weak? Perhaps you want to catch up on some *New York Times* best-sellers or some classic literature that you never read. Even reading the newspaper daily will help you stay current with world and local events.

Perhaps you can pick a new subject each month and research it as an in-depth reference question.

The point of all this reading is to keep your knowledge of the field current and help you network, but reading can lead you to many more activities. You may find ideas for projects you can work on while unemployed. You can develop research projects and papers based on articles that you have read. You can also use the electronic media to develop a strong online personality. Your participation in discussion lists and e-mailing authors may introduce you to future employers.

PROFESSIONAL ORGANIZATIONS

There is no law that says you must have a job to be part of a professional organization. If you do nothing else, at least maintain your memberships in appropriate professional organizations. Many have special discounts for unemployed librarians. In addition, these organizations are always looking for dedicated volunteers. Many of you, like me, never had time to volunteer for a committee while you were working, so now is a great time to start. Committee work can be an excellent way to maintain your skills, to make new contacts, and to learn new skills. The committee work will also look excellent on a resume, may provide current references, and will help you network with professional colleagues. For most committee assignments, you must be able to attend the major conferences. If travel is impossible, consider applying to be a "virtual" member or an e-member. Virtual members participate electronically in committee work without attending the conferences.

If possible, you should try to attend the conferences, since they provide good contacts and connections. The meetings, discussions, and exhibits can provide a direct connection to the field that you might be missing working on your own. New technology demonstrations will update you on the equipment and may enable you to get some hands-on experience. If cost is an issue, most of the major organizations have reduced rates for unemployed librarians. You should consider state and local associations as well since they are often less expensive. You might also consider working a conference in to your vacation schedule, which might also save money.

CAREER EVALUATION

While you are unemployed, you can take the time to reevaluate your career and goals. If you have worked for several years in one type of library, perhaps you should explore another area. After she was laid off from a corporate position, Tracy Williams explored other options. "I took advantage of my time off to talk to some librarians in different types of libraries and reevaluate where I wanted to go with my career. I went to the nearby public library during a slow time of the day and 'interviewed' the librarian about her job. I also emailed a friend at an academic library to ask her about her job." This information helped her with job interviews, and she now works at a community college library. You shouldn't be shy about talking to other librarians. Most are very willing to take some time to discuss their jobs, careers, and choices. You might find some new area that really interests you and leads to a new job. Even if you don't change your career path, the time you spend evaluating other options will help you better define what you want and why you want it. This clarity will help you on later job interviews or help you work on your own.

As part of that evaluation, you should also continue to browse job ads. Even if you are not currently looking for a job, the job ads will tell you what employers are requiring and requesting. You can use these job ads to plan your activities while unemployed. This is especially important if you would like to change your career focus. For example, when you see an ad for a job that you think you would enjoy, examine the requirements and assess your skills. Do you need to have proven written and verbal commutation skills? You might write an article or volunteer on a professional association committee. Do you need to be able to maintain a website? Create your own (professional or not) and maintain it. You might not be able to do everything the job requires, but you can use the job requirements to plan your time while unemployed.

As you evaluate your career, you may want to consider taking some training, classes, or workshops. Examine your skills and see where you might need some improvements. For workshops, try to look for offerings from groups like Amigos Library Services or SOLINET. You can ask at local libraries to see if you could join sessions they offer. You can also search for online workshops. Librarians need many different skills, so you should also consider nonlibrary-related possibilities. Community colleges and local universities usually offer classes in public speaking, marketing, business, management, computer programming, or occupational psychology. These classes help provide valuable skills for modern library work. You might even want to consider pursuing another degree. Though it requires a long-term commitment, many librarian positions request candidates with additional degrees. The classes will help improve your skills and look very appropriate on a resume.

PUBLISHING OPPORTUNITIES

Publishing tends to frighten people, but it provides an excellent medium to continue working when you are not formally employed. If the thought of writing is intimidating, try thinking on a small scale. Most people do not start with writing a book. Keep the idea of writing in mind while you plan your activities. As you read articles, weblogs, or discussion lists, look for topics that interest you. After you develop some ideas, you can start by writing for a website, reviewing a few books, or starting a newsletter. On her website, GraceAnne Andreassi DeCandido suggests that you "start by doing" to become a book reviewer. Based on her experience, she advises that you "write book reviews for your library newsletter or your local newspaper. If those publications don't have a book review section, start one." As your confidence grows, you may want to apply to a journal as a reviewer, where potential employers may read your reviews. If you want to start writing articles, but still feel intimidated, you might want to contact a former colleague with similar interests and collaborate on an article. Perhaps you even want to branch out and start creative writing. The possibilities are almost endless.

VOLUNTEERING

You can continue working by volunteering your time and skills. Many libraries and information organizations desperately need help, especially from those well trained to provide it. However, you don't have to volunteer to shelve books for hours a week or even volunteer in a library if that isn't for you. Be creative and thoughtful about volunteering as well. Are there other organizations that could benefit from your time and skills? Private companies are not always able to accept volunteer help, but you never know unless you ask. Maybe some local organization needs a website that you could create and maintain. Perhaps a hospital needs some books cataloged. While you are searching for volunteer positions, include internships as possibilities. When money is tight, many organizations are willing to accept volunteers or interns.

NETWORKING

While you are unemployed, you should spend some significant time creating and maintaining professional networks of people. First, keep in touch with former coworkers electronically or in person. Let them know what you are working on and your plans for the future. These people are familiar with your work, which can be a great asset when you search for a job. The hardest part of networking while unemployed may be branching out to find new contacts. Start by making contact with others online through weblogs and discussion groups. Then you might try contacting authors of interesting articles. You can also make great contacts through volunteer work, internships, and professional associations. Though some people may find it difficult to reach out in these ways, networks of people can really help you stay current in the field and find a job.

MAKING YOUR OWN OPPORTUNITIES

While you are unemployed, you can spend your time productively, whether you are currently looking for a job or not. This chapter only includes the basics that are fairly universal. It is up to you to plan your time and choose your activities. Tailor these ideas of reading, evaluating, volunteering, networking, and writing to fit your comfort level, time constraints, and career goals. This may be the first time you are your own boss, so act like a boss and make your own opportunities. Schedule your time. Think of the time you spend as work and try to work efficiently. Be sure to evaluate your work and adjust your plans and goals if necessary. You are in charge, so you make the rules. Don't feel discouraged if you have not been making a strong effort since the moment you were unemployed. Start where you are now and make your plans. Any effort you make now is likely to improve your chances of finding the job you want when you want it.

RELATED READINGS

Bates, Mary Ellen. "Blogs: My New Addiction." *Online* 27, no. 5 (2003): 64.

DeCandido, GraceAnne Andreassi. "GraceAnne Andreassi DeCandido: How to Write a Decent Book Review." BlueRoses Consulting. www.well.com/user/ladyhawk/bookrevs.html (last accessed 3 September 2003).

Droste, Therese. "Reenter the Workplace Easily." Monster.com. www.adminsupport.monster.com/articles/highlight/ (last accessed 3 September 2003).

Hubbard, Marlis. "Exploring Sabbatical or Other Leave as a Means of Energizing a Career." *Library Trends* 50 (2002): 603–13.

Kinghorn, Lynne. "How to Keep Your Career Skills Up-to-Date at Home." At Home Mothers.com. www.athomemothers.com/infoguides/41a.htm (last accessed 3 September 2003).

McKay, Dawn Rosenberg. "Stay at Home Parents: A Career Crossroads." Career Planning About.com. www.careerplanning.about.com/library/weekly/aa072799.htm (last accessed 3 September 2003).

"Re-Entering the Job Market." Fiftysomething Jobs.com. www.fiftysomethingjobs.com/reenter.html (last accessed 3 September 2003).

Shontz, Priscilla. "A Librarian without a Library: How to Stay Professionally Active While Unemployed." LIScareer.com. www.liscareer.com/shontz_active unemployment.htm (last accessed 3 September 2003).

———. "Writing and Publishing." In *Jump Start your Career in Library and Information Science*. Lanham, Md.: Scarecrow Press, 2002.

Stevens, Jen. "Making Non-Library Experience Work for You." LIScareer.com. www.liscareer.com/stevens_nonlibraryexperience.htm (last accessed 3 September 2003).

Writer's Weekly.com—Freelance writing jobs, markets, self-publishing, courses. www.writersweekly.com/ (last accessed 3 September 2003).

ABOUT THE AUTHOR

Colleen Simmons is a former academic and special librarian. She is currently a stay-at-home mom who is working on a website, becoming a freelance writer, and plans to reenter the job market soon.

28

When You Come to a Fork in the Road . . . Take It

Beverley Geer

YOU NEED A DEGREE TO DO THAT?

My aunt once remarked to my cousin: "I don't understand it. All those years of college and she works in a library." She was, of course, referring to me. She was not being disparaging or unkind. Like most people then (1980) and now, she did not realize that having a job as a serials cataloger in a university library required a master's degree in library science.

Another misconception is that librarians read all day. How often have you gotten this response when you tell someone you work in a library or that you are going to library school: "Oh, I just love to read. How nice to have a job where you get to read."

And then there is my mother. I'd love to hear her describe my job to her friends. In 1998 a book I coedited on notes found in serials bibliographic records was published. I proudly took it to my mother to show her, like a schoolgirl who got a good grade on a test. She opened the book to the title page, saw my name, looked at me with tears forming in her eyes, and asked, "Where did you learn to do this?"

I'm sure that people in all professions could tell similar stories. For example, I have a friend who is a programmer. If he is at a party and a stranger asks him what he does for a living, he responds that he writes creative fiction using a vocabulary of two hundred words. It is a joke, of course, but he gets that person's attention, and he achieves his goal, which is not to have the person run for cover or look cornered when he says, "I'm a programmer." Instead he has found a way to keep the person, at least momentarily, from conjuring up an image of a humorless nerd, sitting in a corner talking to his computer because he has no social skills.

In presenting these anecdotes I hope to get you thinking about what you do and how you would explain it to your mother, a stranger, or a prospective employer.

SWITCHING CAREERS, OR ALL
ENGINEERS DRIVE TRAINS, RIGHT?

"Initial career choice is usually driven by youthful dreams, personal interest, personal talents, market availability, geographic preferences, and likelihood that the career will support one's lifestyle. It is a forward-looking choice. In some ways, it is the most open of all career choices."[1] However, the decision to change one's career is often driven by more prosaic forces: burnout, family concerns, lay-off or dismissal, dissatisfaction, a need for more money. But not all career changes are caused by negative influences; for many it will be a normal part of life in the modern world. In her article on career planning, Vicki Casey proposes that "the norm for those entering the workforce will likely be a job and/or career change four, five or more times over the course of a working life."[2] A career or job change can mean moving to another position within the same library, to another library, or out of libraries altogether. Whatever the situation, switching careers involves performing self-assessment, adjusting your approach to job hunting, taking a few chances, and maybe having a bit of dumb luck.

SELF-ASSESSMENT

Casey suggests conducting a skills and interests inventory during which you will ask yourself simple but important questions such as, "what do I enjoy doing most?"[3] Such an exercise will help you recognize your strengths and weaknesses, determine what skills you should acquire, and discover what interests and aptitudes you have. You can design your own inventory or take advantage of structured tests offered by career counseling centers. And in this wonderful age, you can find sources on the Web such as:

- Oklahoma Department of Career and Technology Education—www.ok careertech.org/guidance/intinv.htm
- Career and Personality Tests Online—www.discoveryourpersonality .com/index.html
- Pennsylvania State University, Division of Undergraduate Studies— www.psu.edu/dus/md/mdinti.htm)
- Psychometrics.com—www.psychometrics.com
- Alternative Futures—www.alternativefutures.com/

In my opinion the skill set that a person develops reveals the most about potential. The programmer friend I mentioned earlier told me many years ago that he thought I'd make a good programmer. His reasoning went like this: "You are a cataloger. Catalogers, like programmers, process and organize data. Therefore, you could be a programmer." I was amazed by his statement, but these many years later I realize that he was not suggesting that I stop being a cataloger and become a programmer; he was merely pointing out that I had skills and aptitudes that were applicable to other fields, or that I had transferable skills. In an article on barriers to library career development, Peter Dalton, Glen Mynott, and Michael Schoolbred wrote that "many skills are common to all or most sections of the profession. In general these include basic LIS [library and information science] skills, communication and interpersonal skills, information and communications technology (ICT) skills, and self-management skills."[4] There is ample proof that a librarian's skills and experiences can be applied outside of the library work environment. Just ask anyone who has moved into a nonlibrary job. Or survey any of the several articles on alternative careers for librarians published in the past few years. All of the authors state in some form or another that their library skills and experiences were transferable and proved downright valuable in the new job. For example, in 2000 Maureen Johnson wrote: "Organizational skills are considered essential, but so is the ability to assess information . . . and so is the ability to communicate solutions. . . . This requires a staff member capable of liaison with systems, sales, customers, marketing, and operations. And this is what librarians do every day and have studied hard to learn to do well."[5]

NEW APPROACHES TO NEW ROLES

Many of us have been in the same job for so long that we have lost perspective on our potential for new roles, or we very simply are nervous about change. Dalton, Mynott, and Schoolbred observed that "lack of confidence in their transferable skills is, for many LIS professionals, a major barrier to career development and cross-sectoral mobility."[6] Yet librarians have become systems designers, information consultants, webmasters, subscription agents, or salesmen, just to name a few alternative careers.

Find new ways to describe your skills. In 2002 Linda K. Wallace interviewed several librarians whose library degrees had taken them to new places. One interviewee commented: "It took quite a bit of packaging to make nonlibrary folks recognize that library skills can be sliced and diced and used in many ways outside books and online searches."[7] Although he was being facetious, that is what my programmer friend did when he said he wrote creative fiction using a two hundred-word vocabulary. Many advertisements for jobs in corporations state requirements using different terminology. For example, I have a friend who started out as a cataloger in an academic library. He saw a job ad in the *New York Times* for a "director of content management." The ad used terminology such as, metadata, knowledge management, and asset management, which he determined meant that the company was looking for someone who organizes and manages information and data; in other words, a cataloger.

Another friend was recruited for a job in which she uses her collection development skills in a nonlibrary environment. She did not have to convince her employer of her potential. Rather she had to open her mind to the possibilities the job offered her: "I had been in the same position at the same institution for seven years, and was ready for a change. From my work with vendors, I was intrigued with the creation and marketing of electronic databases and products—I saw this as a great opportunity to see how this process worked from the inside."[8]

Leslie Zampetti offers excellent advice in her article about career changes.[9] She too encourages self-assessment. In addition she recommends networking, even employing a recruiter. Networking involves going to conferences, observing and talking to people whose jobs you find interesting. I suggest developing a mentoring relationship with someone whose career appeals to you. Recruiters can save you time and even money, since they usually are paid by the employer if a candidate is hired. A recruiter can help you develop your resume in a nonlibrary style, search for job opportunities, and even line up interviews. Examples of recruiters are:

- Library Associates—www.libraryassociates.com
- Employon, Inc.—www.employon.com
- InfoCurrent—www.infocurrent.com
- TFPL—www.tfpl.com (last accessed 21 September 2003)
- C. Berger Group, Inc.—www.cberger.com

Take the assertive approach and create your own job. One of the librarians Wallace interviewed got a job as an information specialist for the newly elected governor in her state. She said, "I came down one Saturday, and actually barged in and left my resume. I thought I could be helpful."[10] Or seek out temporary or contract work that allows you to test your skills in another environment and gives the employer a chance to determine your worth. Recruiters can help you find temporary or contract positions.

No matter the road taken to a new career, what each of us must understand is that it "will never be sufficient to define 'new roles' as specific technical or administrative skill sets, which can be itemized in job descriptions. . . . Instead, 'new roles' must be understood as attitudes, aptitudes, and approaches."[11]

WHAT HAVE I DONE?

If you have been working in a library environment for even a short time, then you have reached a level of comfort with and understanding of the institutional culture, your colleagues, the work pace, and your library users. You very likely will find the nonlibrary environment completely different, even a bit unnerving. In the literature I surveyed, I found these descriptive phrases: fast paced, entrepreneurial, demanding, proactive, risky, exciting. You may not have the leisure of easing into the new job; instead you will have to adapt, adjust, and evolve. But don't let the new job bowl you over. Ask questions, talk to and observe your new colleagues, and most of all, keep your sense of humor.

Be prepared to make mistakes or to be disappointed. You may find that you made the wrong career decision or that the job does not last. Zampetti wrote that she always remembers the advice she received from a colleague: "what has changed can be changed again."[12]

CONCLUSION

Librarianship is a time-honored profession. It is satisfying, enriching, and full of challenges. It is also ripe with potential. I hope you believe as I do that the skills and experiences librarians have can be applied to just about any work environment. But you owe it to yourself to approach a career change carefully, even methodically, and certainly with an open mind. Once you've analyzed your skills, talked to others, and surveyed the job market, then you'll be in a good position to take the leap into a new career. Remember: despite the economic climate, you have some control over your future. O'Leary quotes Cynthia Hill as saying "People need to recognize that they have a professional portfolio. They take their competencies with them. They don't belong to the organization."[13] I agree completely.

NOTES

1. Candy Zemon, "Midlife Career Choices: How Are They Different from Other Career Choices?" *Library Trends* 50, no. 4 (Spring 2002): 665–72.
2. Vicki Casey, "Do You Have a Plan?" *Feliciter* 46, no. 4 (2000): 167.
3. Casey, "Do You Have a Plan?" 167.

4. Peter Dalton, Glen Mynott, and Michael Schoolbred, "Barriers to Career Development within the LIS Profession," *Library Review* 49, no. 26 (2000): 271–76.

5. Maureen Johnson, "Jump In, the Water's Fine: Alternative Choices for Librarians," *Feliciter* 46, no. 5 (2000): 260–62.

6. Dalton, Mynott, and Schoolbred, "Barriers to Career Development," n.p.

7. Linda K. Wallace, "Places an M.L.S. Can Take You," *American Libraries* 33, no. 3 (March 2002): 44–48.

8. Nancy Buchanan, personal e-mail communication, 15 September 2003.

9. Leslie J. Zampetti, "Moving Up and Out," *Information Outlook* 11, no. 4 (November 2000): 24–29.

10. Wallace, "Places an M.L.S. Can Take You," n.p.

11. Mick O'Leary, "New Roles Come of Age," *Online* 24, no. 2 (March/April 2000): 20–25.

12. Zampetti, "Moving Up and Out," n.p.

13. O'Leary, "New Roles Come of Age," n.p.

RELATED READINGS

Butcher, Megan. "Sex Toys? You Bet! Librarians in Non-traditional Positions." *Feliciter* 47, no. 6 (2001): 302–3.

Fourie, Denise K., and David R. Dowell. *Libraries in the Information Age: An Introduction and Career Exploration.* Greenwood Village, Colo.: Libraries Unlimited, 2002.

Houdek, Frank G. "'Alt.lawlibrarian': New Career Paths for Law Librarians." *Law Library Journal* 93, no. 3 (Summer 2001): 375–422.

Oder, Norman. "The Competitive Intelligence Opportunity." *Library Journal* 126, no. 4 (March 1, 2001): 42–44.

Sellen, Betty-Carol. *What Else You Can Do with a Library Degree: Career Options for the 90s and Beyond.* New York: Neal-Schuman, 1997.

Weihs, Jean Riddle. "Not Everyone Can Be a Consultant." *Technicalities* 19, no. 8 (September 1999): 1, 11–13.

ABOUT THE AUTHOR

Beverley Geer started her library career in 1976 as a shelver in the University of Oklahoma Libraries. In 1980 she graduated with a master's degree in library science and spent the next nineteen years working in academic libraries in various capacities (cataloger, serials acquisitions librarian, cataloging department head). In 1999 she moved into the corporate world as a project manager for Endeavor Information Systems, Inc. Today she is a regional manager for YBP Library Services, Inc.

4

EXPERIENCE AS AN ENTRY-LEVEL LIBRARIAN

Does This Job Make Me Look Fat? Or, Making Your First Year on the Job a More Comfortable Fit

Clint Chamberlain

Your first year on the job is an exciting time. You're learning new things, meeting new people, and encountering all kinds of new opportunities. It's also quite possibly one of the most important years during your career in the library field, because it's a time when you are testing the waters, figuring out what works best for you, and laying the groundwork for what hopefully will be a long and fruitful career. Because your first year is the foundation for your career, it is worthwhile to give some thought to the kinds of things you'll need to do and pay attention to during those first twelve months in order to set a successful tone for the years to come.

YOU NEVER GET ANOTHER CHANCE . . .

Hackneyed it may be, but the expression "You never get another chance to make a first impression" is advice you should heed. "But wait," you're thinking. "I already made a first impression when I interviewed, and obviously it was a good one, because they hired me!" Well, yes and no. The first impression you make during an interview is obviously important. It's also somewhat false, because during an interview you are on your best "special occasion" behavior, and everyone you met knows it. Starting from your first day on the job forward, they'll get to see what you're *really* like, and you don't want the people you met during your interview to wonder just what they were thinking when they made the decision to hire you. You also will meet people you never even saw during your interview, much less talked to, yet these may be the people with whom you will work most often.

To ensure you put your best foot forward, here are some things to consider. Yes, they are all no-brainers, but a gentle reminder is never remiss:

1. *Dress appropriately.* Remember that the definition of "appropriate dress" varies from workplace to workplace, and even from job to job within the same workplace. You probably got a good idea of the general range of acceptable dress in your workplace when you came to interview. All the same, it's probably a good idea to dress up just a little bit at first, at least until you figure out what is considered acceptable for someone in your position. If you still have no idea of how to dress appropriately, read Jill Emery's (2003) "The Style Council: A Twelve Step Fashion Do & Don't Guide for Library Professionals."
2. *Mind your manners.* Nothing says "professional" like treating other people with respect. Remember those little social niceties that your elders tried to pound into your head when you were a child—little things like saying "please" and "thank you"? They may seem like small matters, but simply remembering to be polite and mannerly will go a long way toward establishing your reputation as a likeable, professional person.
3. *Keep your office space neat.* I hesitate to suggest this bit of advice as I survey the towering piles of paperwork that threaten to bury my own desk. It's a good idea to try to be as organized as possible though, especially during your first few weeks on the job. At the beginning you may not even have that much work to do, as you'll be learning the ins and outs of your new position, but rest assured, the river of paperwork will begin to flow into your office soon enough. Try to stay on top of it. Not only will you reap the benefits of being organized later on, you will also give the appearance of being at the top of your game. Caveat: don't be *too* neat. If your desk is too tidy, it will look as though you have nothing to do.
4. *Open mouth; do not insert foot.* Think before you speak, and try to avoid controversy as much as possible. You probably won't know any of your coworkers well enough to know what their political leanings are, what their religious affiliations are, or which topics of conversation they may find distasteful. Don't hide your opinions, but be especially tactful when expressing them at the start of your career. You never know who you might inadvertently tick off.

"YOU WANT ME TO DO *WHAT*?"

When you first start your job, you may be champing at the bit in your rush to jump right in and start doing things your way. Hold your horses there, pardner; things on the job are never as elegantly cut and dried as they may appear at first.

"Other duties as assigned." Ah, that lovely little clause that appears in so many job descriptions! Be prepared to discover that what you actually do on your job may bear little resemblance to what you thought you'd be doing. "I didn't realize that most of the Reference Desk work is signing up people for Internet computers and enforcing Internet procedures/rules, rather than assisting patrons with reference questions," says Frances "Heidi" Flythe (information specialist, Public Library of Charlotte/Mecklenburg County). If you encounter this sort of situation, accept it gracefully. In most instances, there may be little you can do about it, especially at first. Look on the bright side, it gives you a great opportunity to learn some new skills.

Realize that things may get off to a slow start. Amy Gleeson (reference/education librarian, University of Florida Health Science Center Libraries) notes, "At first I didn't have enough to do (and I thought I would never be able to fill up my days), but after about three months that was not a problem. Now I have more than enough to do." In fact, starting off slowly is a good thing, because it allows time for you to pay more attention to things like building connections, learning how things are done around your workplace, and just catching your breath before the *real* work starts. Enjoy it while it lasts.

Be prepared to admit your ignorance. As Gleeson also points out, "You are not going to know everything once you get your job—not by a long shot." Get used to it. No one expects you to know everything, or even most things. Also, each workplace does things a little bit differently. Let go of your ego and the need to be right in every situation. Often the best way to appear competent is to admit when you don't know something. Once you admit that to yourself, admit it to someone else: ask questions and find out the answers to the things you don't know.

Get involved, but not too involved. For many folks in the library field, committees are a fact of life. Although you can't avoid them entirely, be careful about which ones and how many you choose. "I did not realize that the 'new person' is the first choice for committee assignments," says Emily Jackson Sanborn (reference and digital services librarian, Perkins Library, Duke University). "I took the first several committees that were offered to me, not realizing that every committee that remotely related to my job would want my participation. Now, I get on committees that are directly related to my job or are ones that will extend me in professional directions I'm interested in—and say 'no' to the rest." Lindsey

Schell (bibliographer for English literature and women's and gender studies, University of Texas at Austin) concurs. "Be very selective and guard your time. Discuss it with your boss if the requests are too many — sometimes he/she can fend off the wolves for a few months while you get your bearings. Tell people you are interested but want to wait a year so you know what your work cycle will look like."

Keep records. "Start a file of your accomplishments, and maybe keep a log of important or impressive things you've done each month," says Lindsey Schell. "You never know when you will need to back yourself up, and it's just the kind of thing that will make writing your annual evaluation a breeze."

Push for professional development. If your workplace supports any kind of professional development (e.g., support for workshops or travel to conferences), take advantage of it. Adina L. Riggins (archivist/special collections librarian, UNC-Wilmington) points out that during her first year on the job, she pushed to be able to attend conferences and other venues for continuing education. "It is good to get into the pattern of going to these things right away — and to let your management know that you are interested." Attending these kinds of events can help you determine where you want to focus your energies during your career. "I made a conscious decision to select the professional organizations that I was interested in and to attend one of their meetings or conferences during my first year in the profession," says Sarah Sutton (serials librarian, Texas A&M University–Corpus Christi). "I wanted to meet the librarians that were active in each organization face to face before committing to participate in them myself. Doing so simplified the decision about how and where I could make a meaningful contribution to the profession." Keep in mind that there are often scholarships and other awards to assist new professionals in attending conferences and other meetings.

ORGANIZATIONAL CULTURE

Who among us has never watched one of those shows on television in which the intrepid explorer travels far into the unexplored reaches of the back of beyond, lives with people who are foreign and yet like us in so many ways, studies their culture, and returns to tell us armchair explorers about it? Your first year on the job is the perfect chance for you to be the same kind of explorer in libraryland, without having to worry about learning another language, dealing with the unpleasantness of parasites, and living in a hut that's a ten-day mule ride from the nearest town with a flush toilet. (Well, scratch the part about not having to learn another language. If you've had any exposure to librarians at all, you know that we love to talk in acronym-laden jargon.) Each library, just like every other organization, has its own culture, and, just like someone traveling to another country for the first time, your task is to figure out what *you* need to do to fit in with the locals. In other words, you need to figure out what your new workplace's organizational culture is.

When in Rome. It may be tempting to go your own way from the very beginning, but establishing an identity as a maverick during your first year is probably not in your best interest. Sure, be one later, once you've established a reputation and have earned the respect of your colleagues. During the first few weeks and months, though, watch your colleagues for cues as to what is considered appropriate behavior, and follow their lead. This is not to say that you should stifle all of your wacky, offbeat behavior, but just try to keep things like that to a minimum until you have a good feel for which of your quirks will be accepted and which are better off left at the front door.

Getting to know you. From day one, get to know your coworkers—not just the ones with whom you deal directly on a regular basis, but everyone possible. For one thing, it's always beneficial to get to know your coworkers as real individuals. That's just good sense because it's a nice, normal, and human thing to do. As it turns out, it's also one easy way to learn about what's acceptable and what is not at your new workplace. Even if you're not a very sociable person, make an effort to get to know your colleagues on an individual basis. This doesn't mean that you need to go out and socialize with them outside of work if you don't want to; making the effort can be as simple as eating in the staff lunch room with them a few times a week, going on coffee breaks, or stopping by someone's desk just to say "Hi." Also, don't just establish good rapport with your coworkers; try to do so with everyone you encounter in your workplace. Donna Nixon (reference/access services librarian, Everett Law Library, UNC–Chapel Hill) suggests, "Show humility and respect for every person you deal with (librarians, staff, non-affiliated patrons, faculty members, students, maintenance people) and cultivate good relations with them. They will remember that when there is an opportunity to help or harm you."

Tap into the office grapevine. Getting to know others will almost inevitably lead to getting to hear all of the office gossip . . . er, news. Gossip is a fact of life, of course, and it's a good way to learn about what's *really* going on. Always remember, however, to take what you hear with a grain of salt, especially when you've just started, and try to refrain from actively contributing to the rumor mill. Be careful what you say during your interactions with coworkers. "When you're listening to others gripe, don't be too open about your own complaints," says Sue Willman (reference/information literacy librarian, Texas A&M University–Corpus Christi). "The person you're complaining to (or about) might end up being your supervisor or director someday. Don't shoot yourself in the foot."

Make an effort to learn about the power and political structure in your workplace. No matter how flat the organizational hierarchy, there will be individuals who have power over one area of the workplace or another, and it behooves you to learn who these people are. Taking a quick look at the staff organizational chart will answer many questions of this nature. Some organizations, however, will have different types of power structures that may not be readily apparent in the official organizational chart. If you're in an academic, tenure-track environment, who has tenure? Who has rank or seniority? If you work in a public library, which constituencies have some kind of say in the running of the library—public officials, civic leaders, state legislators? Who else outside your organization has power over it— faculty, trustees, administrative officials, corporate executives? Flythe says that she learned a great deal about the power structure that affects her library "by observing employee interaction and by reading the procedural manual, the library directory, the library Intranet, and library publications." Making connections with others in the workplace is also a great way to learn more about the political structure. In other words, look to a variety of sources for this kind of information.

Learn about the outside bodies (state or local government, academic committees or administration, etc.) that affect your institution. Melanie Reeves (outreach librarian, City of Norfolk-Norfolk County Public Library) notes, "I wish I had begun the job with a better understanding of the processes involved in local government work." Having this kind of information handy can help you figure out whose work and agendas can affect your job, as well as where you should turn if you need help in pushing through new initiatives in the future.

Attend meetings, even if you don't have to. "This helps the newcomer to learn how things work in that institution. . . . The more informed you are, the less likely you'll make embarrassing mistakes or comments that will ruffle someone's feathers," says Sue Willman. And speaking of ruffling feathers. . . .

JUMPING IN WITHOUT MAKING A HUGE SPLASH

Ed Holton, in *The Ultimate New Employee Survival Guide,* recommends, "Keep your eyes and ears open and your mouth shut during the first six months" (1998, p. 39). By keeping a low profile at first, he says, you will be able to take time to learn about your new organization before you make any moves that may result in costly mistakes. Sounds like good advice, right? Here's what some library professionals who have been in the field for a few years have to say about that piece of advice, as well as related matters.

Stop, look, and listen. Sally Bickley (access services librarian, Texas A&M— Corpus Christi) concurs with Holton's advice. "There are many undercurrents and hidden reasons as to why things happen or don't happen. Being observant allows you to discover what some of these things are and how they affect your ability to do your job."

It's quiet out there . . . too quiet. There's a difference, however, between being quietly observant and just being so quiet that you become a nonentity. Nixon offers this bit of advice. "I think it's a good idea to look, listen and learn before you jump in with opinions and initiatives. But, I don't think you should be totally silent. People may get the first impression that you have nothing really to bring to the table. First impressions are hard to erase. I do think the focus of your 'mouth-opening' in your first six months should be asking thoughtful questions rather than strutting your stuff."

Know your audience. Getting to know your coworkers early on in the game will help a great deal. Riggins suggests, "If you have something to say, be sure to say it to the right people—folks who are open-minded themselves and won't automatically discount everything that comes out of the mouths of those 'new, young librarians.'"

Know your role. Knowing why you were hired can also help you decide whether it's better for you to speak up early and often or keep quiet for a while. "Some people get hired specifically because the administration wants a fresh perspective and someone who isn't afraid to make waves," says Schell. "That's fine if you know that's your expected role, but try to find the balance between infusing your organization with fresh ideas and stepping on the toes of others."

Slow but steady wins the race. That old adage applies to more than just the tortoise and the hare. "When I initiated changes, I did it slowly," says James M. Roth (archivist, John F. Kennedy Library and Museum).

I first asked the question why we did things. I then kept it in my mind which functions/procedures I thought I could change that would be beneficial. I broke those changes down into smaller units of change. I waited six months into the job before making those changes. Small changes can be tolerated, especially if I talked about the changes with those concerned (mostly my boss), tried to understand their concerns, backed off if they weren't receptive and thought more about it. I then went back after incorporating those concerns and presented the change in another way. After about three months, the small change was accepted as normal and I went on to my next small change. People don't like changes, whatever they tell you.

Roth continues. "They need to feel comfortable with a change and to fully understand the benefits of the change. It's not good enough to tell someone the change is good. You have to allay their fears, convince them it's easier [rather] than difficult, and you can't push, well, too much." Making changes in this way, after you're learned the history behind the current system, the personalities involved, and the concerns of those affected by your proposed changes, can help make the difference between successfully introducing new ideas and having your new initiatives fall flat.

IF IT DOESN'T FIT, IT'S OKAY TO QUIT

Sometimes, no matter what you do, no matter how carefully you researched the organization, the job, and your future coworkers before accepting the position, it becomes apparent that your new job really isn't a good fit for you at all. Perhaps the daily tasks just aren't a suitable match for your skills, abilities, or personality. Maybe you've been unfortunate enough to get a manager who is unbelievably ineffective, yet so entrenched that there's no chance that he or she will ever leave the job before you will. Or maybe you've caught your coworkers sticking pins into a doll that bears a more than superficial resemblance to you. Whatever the case, things just are not working out the way they should, and in a situation like that, it may be okay to bail.

> *Don't quit at the first sign of trouble, or even the second or third.* In fact, you should try to work things out if it's at all possible and reasonable to do so. If things are okay on the whole, it's best to try to work your way through whatever difficulty you've encountered.
> *Try to weather the storm.* Your first year may prove to be difficult on many different levels, yet if you tough it out, you may find yourself getting a lot out of the experience. "Difficult is probably not the most accurate way to describe my first year," says Melinda Deyasi (reference librarian, Coker College). "I'd say exasperating, puzzling, bewildering, and frustrating are most accurate. Oh yeah, and rewarding."

Physician, heal thyself. One of the first things to do is take a good, hard look at yourself, at your expectations, and at the way you conduct yourself in the workplace. Are there things you can do to ameliorate the problematic situation? Perhaps you can be a better manager of your own time. Maybe your expectations are a bit too high. This is not to say that you should blame yourself for whatever problems you encounter; simply making subtle adjustments to your own behavior, however, may improve a difficult situation.

Talk it out. If necessary and possible, talk with your supervisor or with your supervisor's supervisor. Often problems may be caused by simple miscommunication that is easily cleared up. If it's a bigger issue, it may be possible to talk to someone in the human resources department at your workplace. Many workplaces will have an ombudsman who can help you resolve disputes in the workplace. Also, if you can, consult people outside your current situation so that you can hear a more objective viewpoint. One librarian who has faced a particularly difficult situation at her first job (and who, therefore, asked that her comments remain anonymous) has found her outside contacts especially valuable. "Those are the people who tell you, 'When you are running your own department, you may want to do things differently than where you are now,'" she says. "They are the people who remind you that you are more than your current situation and great things truly are expected."

Hit the road, Jack. If all else fails and you truly believe you will be happier elsewhere, don't be afraid to move on. As the aforementioned anonymous librarian put it, "I would tell new librarians that guilt and the myth of loyalty are commonly used as a method to keep people from answering a higher call. But there will always be work to do." Keep an eye on those job ads. Not only will you know when a new and, hopefully, better position comes along, you'll also be able to keep your finger on what skills are needed in a rapidly changing marketplace.

Chalk it up as the proverbial learning experience. No matter what your first year experience is like, there is always something to be gained from it. "Approach your first position as a learning experience and be open to moving on if it is not what you truly want," says Clista Clanton (web development and education librarian, University of South Alabama Medical Library). "Don't lock yourself into a position either mentally or financially until you decide that it is where you really want to be."

Take the high road when you do leave. If you do decide to move on, do so in a cordial and professional manner; no back-stabbing, name-calling, or dramatic scenes required. As Clanton points out, "The field of librarianship is a fairly small pool, so best not to muddy the waters, so to speak."

CONCLUSION

These tips are just a few of the things you should keep in mind during your first year. Above all else, just use common sense: Don't be afraid to ask questions, do remember to treat others courteously, perform your job to the best of your abilities, and be patient. Build a firm foundation now, and you'll be better able to build the rest of your career to new heights.

RELATED READINGS

Emery, Jill. "The Style Council: A Twelve Step Fashion Do & Don't Guide for Library Professionals." LIScareer.com. September 2003. www.liscareer.com/emery_style.htm (last accessed 1 October 2003).

Holton, Ed. *The Ultimate New Employee Survival Guide*. Princeton, N.J.: Peterson's Guides, 1998.

Sannwald, William. "Understanding Organizational Culture." *Library Administration & Management* 14, no. 1 (2000): 8–14.

ABOUT THE AUTHOR

Clint Chamberlain is currently in his second year as e-access/serials librarian at Trinity University, San Antonio, Texas, where he is also liaison librarian to the departments of sociology/anthropology and classical studies. Regarding some of the advice offered herein, he requests of new librarians: "Do as I suggest, not as I do."

30

I Got the Job, Now What Do I Do? Or, Acclimating to the Environment and Defining Expectations in a New Workplace

Marilyn P. Lewis

In librarianship, as in other professions and jobs, one finds that fewer and fewer people spend their entire careers in one workplace, let alone in one position. That's not to say you will not encounter such an individual, or become one yourself, but the days of single-place careers are more of an exception than the rule. What does this mean to you who are beginning a new job? It means that you are almost surely not the first, nor the only, "new kid on the block." So while change may cause trepidation, one can accept this not unnatural anxiety and put it to a beneficial use. As one who has made more than a few changes, let me make the following suggestions.

YOU'RE NEW—SO WHAT?

As the song says, "Don't worry, be happy." Everybody you meet has been new at least once in their career; some people will remember how they felt and others won't; the length of the individual's tenure will have little to do with his or her empathy with you. But there are some definite pluses in starting a new job:

1. As when you began a new school year, the new job is a clean slate. What you did before may have some bearing on what you do now, but use only the positive similarities; if you made mistakes before, this is the time to let them go and begin anew. This does not mean that you should forget the mistakes from the past, but rather learn from them and bring those lessons to the new position.

2. Even if you are a fashion-conscious person, you do not require an entirely new wardrobe for your new job. The people with whom you come in contact have not seen the clothes you currently own—unless you are moving to a new position within the same organization, in which case a new wardrobe would seem a little ostentatious anyway. And if you have moved to a new location, financing your move is more important than appearing on the scene as a fashion model. More to the point, this is the time to concentrate on the job and not on how your clothes will impress the locals.

3. Don't set your goals too high right away. You're not going to change the world, nor the library, in the first few months on the job, so don't set yourself up for failure by promising yourself (or your colleagues) to accomplish something that may need changing but that, for whatever reason, others have not been able to do in years. Wait until you become more familiar with all the routines and relationships.

4. Arrange your work area to suit your sense of efficiency and your own aesthetics (if these are not too distracting to others). If you don't get this done now, you may not have another chance until the next computer upgrade or system crash because the day-to-day work may not leave time for these personally desirable options.

5. A new library is a great place to try out some of the recipes that you have collected over the years. You should know by now that librarians, professional or not, are latent gourmands and delight in trying different foods. Snacking on a new dish is an excellent way to get acquainted with your coworkers.

LEARN THE JOB!

It is quite possible that your supervisor, or whoever will be describing your duties in detail, may not have the time to sit down with you on your first day on the job. You may be given a manual to read, or some general instructions to pass the time, but however your orientation is handled, use this time productively.

1. If you don't have a written job description in hand, obtain one as soon as possible. As unlikely as it may sound, some institutions have functioned for years on the basis of a kind of "oral history" for each position. Having a written description is the best way for your supervisor and you to objectively rate your performance, and of course you can more efficiently organize your own time if you have a clearer understanding of the requirements.

2. Organize your work area. This can and should be done with your duties in mind (see earlier) and with a sense of how you like to move from one function to another. Also, it is important to accomplish this before you are so deeply involved in the work itself that it may be difficult to find the time to rearrange your materials for more efficient access.
3. If you have your own workstation (not a given, sorry to say), take the time to learn the e-mail program, addresses, and web pages. You can obtain a lot of information for later use.
4. Watch what others are doing without being a nuisance. They know you are new, and if they don't come and introduce themselves, introduce *yourself*. Ask them if there is anything you can do for them until your supervisor has time to really get you started. This is the time to show that you are not above doing some photocopying or shelving books that have backed-up in circulation due to lack of staff. Offers to assist in this way show you are a team player and that you are willing to do what must be done for the good of the entire organization. It is also a great way to learn more about the whole library and an opportunity to become acquainted with others outside your immediate assigned area.

THERE IS A TIME AND PLACE FOR EVERYTHING

Choose the time and place carefully when you want to offer suggestions. Obviously, you were hired for your qualifications, so there is no need to prove yourself again at every meeting. One of the quickest ways to get off to a poor start is to overuse the phrase: "At my last library (or workplace) . . ." or "Here's how we did it better somewhere else. . . ." These can be killer phrases for a new employee to use, no matter how true they may be. Leave any similar phrase out of your vocabulary for at least the first six months unless the system is crashing daily and people are walking off en masse. Even then, *offer* your opinion, don't *thrust* it on people. After you have been there awhile and really believe you are familiar with the operation, offer suggestions at a meeting, in a private conversation, or in an e-mail message. At any rate, realize that you may not know the entire history of that to which you are reacting, so:

1. Try to determine how the situation originated.
2. What has been done, if anything, to remedy the situation?
3. Is the organization seeking help? Are people ready to accept suggestions, or are they still in denial mode?

OTHERS HAVE BEEN THERE
BEFORE YOU AND OTHERS WILL FOLLOW

One beauty of librarianship is that basic principles have remained the same. Technology has had a tremendous impact on the outward trappings. Management methods have had to accommodate themselves to the ubiquitous computer environment, but we are still all here for the same reason: to offer our patrons access to the information they require. Sometimes we also have to remind administrators that, McLuhan notwithstanding, the medium is not always the message. There are many routes to the same port. This basic principle of service crosses all generations of librarians. Keep in mind that those who have preceded you in this library have much to offer in institutional history, in contributing to the library's mission, and in mentoring your own career.

I suspect that each generation goes through a period of believing that the previous generations are out of step with the present. It is precisely that vitality of the "young Turks" that the organization needs and yet also needs to control. The humility that comes with the realization that you may be one of these "masters of the universe" can be liberating in the sense that you need no longer fear or avoid the "lifers," but rather you can embrace and appreciate what they can offer to your own career and to the library in which you are employed. They are often just waiting to be asked their opinions, and the exchanges that take place can be profitable for all.

While one should continue one's formal education in librarianship and/or relevant fields, one can learn a great deal from simple observation. Familiarizing yourself with other areas without being intrusive is a desirable form of internship. It will broaden your background and you will find it useful in unexpected ways in years to come.

WHAT SHOULD I EXPECT DURING
THE FIRST YEAR IN A NEW POSITION?

Once you have physically settled into your work area, have a reasonable and cogent job description, and have attended a few meetings, you may ask yourself, "What now?" Consider the following:

1. Expect to be reviewed either formally or informally. Most organizations have such a review process established. (Again, this is why a written job description is so important. It is the best, if not the only, way to compare what you have done with what you should be doing.) If such a review process is not automatic, request an evaluation. Feedback is im-

portant to your own self-knowledge, and also it will indicate that you are serious about doing a good job and that you are open to suggestions.

2. If you have had previous professional commitments, such as state, local, or national organization membership and assignments, you might consider paring these external activities for a time so that you can give more attention to the job that pays your salary.

3. Work with your immediate supervisor on the progression of your training. This is slightly different from the review or evaluation process itself, although it may be incorporated into it. The evaluation process discusses what you have *done*, while the progression discussion deals with *goals* (i.e., where you hope to be in the future). If you are not both on the same page, your expectations from the position may be in conflict with your supervisor's, and this will lead to job dissatisfaction.

4. Try to achieve a balance with your professional and personal life. You know the old saying, "All work and no play. . . ." You do not want to become one very dull librarian. There are few professions that are so interesting that they can command the attention of an audience hour after hour. If you don't have a hobby, get one. Sharing your hobby with others during lunch or breaks is an excellent way to establish camaraderie. If you have a family, balance their needs with the needs of your profession; doctors and policemen are not the only groups that suffer a high divorce rate.

CONCLUSION

A new job can be exciting. You are not expected to know it all. It is a wise librarian who realizes that jobs change, people change, and nobody knows it all—even the people at the top. Have fun with your job and you will find that others will respond positively to your enthusiasm and sense of pleasure. Know what you are supposed to do, do it well, and you will look forward to going to work. You will be confident of your ability, and you will sense the appreciation of others who recognize you as a valued member of the team.

ABOUT THE AUTHOR

Marilyn P. Lewis is currently the technical services librarian at Saint Leo University, Saint Leo, Florida. Due to shifting family priorities and evolving professional goals, she was well prepared to write on this topic. She has worked in more than ten libraries in New Mexico, California, Florida, Oregon, Texas, and North Carolina in more than twenty-five years of librarianship. Her motto could be "Gather no moss."

31

It Just Doesn't Matter: What You Didn't Learn in Library School

Jill Emery

There are many opinions within the library and information science professional literature and within the LIS mind-set as to how helpful a degree in library and information science or information science from an American Library Association (ALA)-accredited institution really is. While these opinions by themselves could make up a chapter in this book, my intent is not to give validity to the arguments about whether one should or should not have to obtain a master's degree to work in this profession. Instead, this chapter is going to focus on the fact that most institutions of higher education, large public libraries, and many special libraries do still require you to have an ALA-accredited degree to hold a professional position within their walls. Working from this premise, then, do you learn everything you need to from your ALA-accredited library program to begin an entry-level professional position? In my opinion, the answer to this question is a resounding "No." However, it really doesn't matter that you do not learn everything you need to in library and information science programs. In fact, it can be said that it is a better thing that you are given only rudimentary introductions to some of the aspects of this profession.

So why does it not matter that you do not learn everything you need to for that entry-level professional job? It doesn't matter, because this is a learning profession in and of itself, and it is better to have graduates who recognize the learning aspect of their profession and are willing to find out more about the profession than to have a field of graduates who feel as though everything is already known and therefore no longer worthy of investigation and of time and self. The field of library and information science draws people into it from a myriad of backgrounds and other disciplines. This is perhaps one of the profession's greatest unembraced assets, the fact that everyone who enters into this profession brings with them unique and useful attributes from other professional careers, other professional positions held, other master's degrees, and even from their undergraduate educational experiences. This secondary knowledge often provides an individual with information that not only defines that person's professional life but also strengthens the organization into which the person is hired. For the individual, these skills can be capitalized on to make a professional experience more directed and focused. Because our environment is a learning environment, there is always room for growth and professional development opportunities that may not always be recognizable to the entry-level professional. For these reasons, it is better to come out of a library and information science program feeling as though you have a grasp on the basic tenets but that there is still much for you to learn.

RULE FOLLOWER OR PROBLEM SOLVER

At a recent North American Serials Interest Group annual conference, Rick Anderson (director of resource acquisitions at the University of Nevada-Reno and recognized LIS career pundit) divided our profession into two main character traits. These are problem solvers and rule followers. It is absolutely essential for a new library and information science professional to embrace qualities of both character types. Quite often, there is too much emphasis put on an early career librarian/information specialist to be just a rule follower and not to spend much time and effort on problem solving. This is to the detriment of our profession. The tricky task for a new professional is to navigate between the two tendencies and understand when one should follow the rules and when one should tackle problem solving. For instance, a time to follow the rules would be related to the schedule you and your boss have negotiated that you will work. A time to problem solve is when you receive an e-mail from a colleague that mentions a product or topic you are unfamiliar with; this gives you the golden opportunity to search the Web and a few databases, and perhaps begin a discussion at lunch about the topic. Being too much of a rule follower will make you feel like you never get to innovate or develop interests other than the tasks assigned to you, which can become really frustrating. However, if you act like a problem solver, take some initiative, and learn about things separately from the tasks assigned, you will indicate to your boss and your colleagues that you can be given special projects or be asked to serve on task forces or in working groups. Lastly, rule followers can become annoying because these individuals are always expecting to be told what to do either by their supervisors or by their colleagues. While it is true that problem solvers do have a tendency to step beyond their boundaries, their initiative and go-after-it attitude tends to be appreciated more in most organizations.

GET THE BIG PICTURE

Another recommended approach is learning how an organization as a whole operates. Yes, you may have been hired as an assistant archivist, an entry-level reference librarian, or a monographic cataloger, but you cannot limit your view of your working world to just the one area into which you were hired. The more quickly you catch on to how your department fits into the library and how your job relates to the organization's mission and goals, the better off you will be. In library and information science programs, it is really easy to become tracked into one line of professional activity and think that one line of study and investigation is all you need to know in the workplace. Nothing could be further from the truth. If you do not clue into the big-picture or organizational view within your first few years of employment, you will have a harder time advancing up the career ladder. Make sure you familiarize yourself with the organizational chart of your institution and how your department fits into a bigger realm of public or technical services and the library. Depending on the type of organization you work in, you may want to meet with department heads from other parts of the library to get a better feel for what occurs in their divisions and to talk to them about how your job or role in the organization may interplay with the work that occurs in their area.

DON'T KNOW MUCH ABOUT POLITICS

One thing that is definitely not touched upon in library and information science programs is how political most library environments can be. In every organization there are office politics at play. The best way to educate yourself as to the innerworkings and unspoken relationships in a work environment is to keep your ears open. When interviewing, it is of the utmost importance to try to pick up on the political environment you are about to join. See if the members of the search committee interact well together. If there is an open forum, see how colleagues interact and if any one colleague tries to capture the focus of the group. Pay attention to the overall tone you get from people who already work within the organization. Ask questions to find out if there are larger environmental politics you should be aware of, such as: How is the library viewed on campus in general? Has the city council provided funding or bond issues for the library recently? Has there been any separate line item funding for library projects in the company recently?

Once you have been hired, not only listen to reports given at committee meetings or provided by your boss but also be aware of the tone in which these reports are delivered. Tune into who does not seem to be invited to lunch with specific groups of people as well as who does tend to get included. When you are first hired, do not immediately adopt the politics of your boss or of your area, but rather hold back and learn the dynamics first without sharing an opinion or taking sides. You will go much further in the organization the longer you are able to stay on neutral ground, and you will be respected for your impartiality. Watch out for members of the organization who seem to want to befriend you just to push their agenda or factional belief in the organization. When you are new to a position, this type of friendship or co-opting may be hard to recognize, but if a person's sudden friendliness makes you uncomfortable or you feel ill at ease around the person at work-related social events, you may want to maintain a cool distance. Whatever you do, do not become the office gossip, as this will just end up damaging your work reputation.

ACT LOCALLY—THINK GLOBALLY

It is never too early to begin to investigate and learn about your area of interest at the state, national, and international arenas. Find out what electronic lists cover the job tasks you have been assigned. If you have no one to ask or feel embarrassed asking, perform Google searches and see what comes up. You'll more than likely find web pages for organizations you may want to be involved in or electronic lists you will want to join for discussions. Ask your boss if there are particular committees or meetings that you should be aware of and attending at professional conferences. Ask your colleagues what sessions they have considered attending at national conferences or if there are speakers that they would recommend. Find out what committees your boss and your boss's boss serve on and seek out those committee programs at state and national conferences. This will help provide a track or direct you to particular sessions at conferences, which often seem huge, unwieldy, and directionless to an entry-level librarian.

SHOUT SELF-START

All of this is to say that you will appreciate your job and your new work environment more if you invest time to learn about it a bit more and to take some initiative to comprehend the bigger picture. More often than not in library and information science programs, what you are asked to do is be a rule follower. You are told what to look at, when to look at it, and how you should present it back in your classes for a grade. Out in the workday world, however, often you are left to direct the project you are given and to take the initiative to understand and comprehend complex organizations and their interoperability. These are not skills that can necessarily be taught in a classroom but rather can be seen more as life lessons. The more of a self-starter you are, the further along you will be when your first evaluation rolls around or when the first opportunity for promotion presents itself.

WHAT CAME BEFORE

More than likely you have another degree of some sort. In most cases, you have an undergraduate degree; in many cases, you also have a second master's degree or other professional certification; in some instances, you worked for a while at another career. All of these things can be capitalized on in your career as a librarian or informational professional. While you are probably becoming a librarian because you want to change your career direction, you shouldn't discard everything pertaining to your previous work life. In many instances the skills and knowledge you gained from your previous education or previous employment can and should guide your career in library and information science.

For instance, if you have a master's degree in history and have decided to pursue a master's in library and information science so that you can work with specialized collections or archives, you can capitalize on your history expertise by finding employment at a library, museum, or historical society that has holdings in the area of history in which you are most versed. One of the things that has surprised me most about early career reference librarians is that they do not always think to apply for reference jobs or subject specialist jobs that would cover the same subject matter in which they achieved their bachelor's degree, or that they are unwilling to relocate to an area of the country or even their own state where that subject specialty becomes more of an asset.

If you have held sales jobs before but want to move away from the pressures of the for-profit sales environment, you may want to look into sales jobs at nonprofits, such as societies or university presses, once you obtain your library and information science degree. Sales people who have MLIS degrees are respected by the library communities with whom they interact. Also consider jobs either in library acquisitions or a consortium, since much of the work that goes on in these jobs is tied closely to the environment from which you have had some initial training, and you can start your job with some understanding of the innerworking of the sales world.

Perhaps you worked for a while as a teacher but are now burned out on the K-12 job market. You may want to consider focusing on instruction and instructional technology while obtaining your degree as this is an area of growth in many educational and nonprofit sectors. Your background with teaching and with designing teaching tools can be great assets in this area of librarianship. Perhaps you worked in finance or in budgeting offices previously. Again, this work can be translated into useful positions in the library and information science arena.

DON'T BE BOXED IN

If you do not want to capitalize on previous work or educational experience, then make sure that you can clearly articulate your move away from that area of study and have a game plan for what you would like to learn and how you'd like to invest your career future. Make sure that most of your work in your library and information science program coincides with the new direction in which you have headed and can support your career goals once you have graduated. Be willing to downgrade your short-term career expectations and don't expect to start off in exactly the area you'd like to be, but rather in an area that might relate to where you want to end up. For instance, while you may not have a background in art, you may have a strong desire to be an art librarian. In this case you may need to take another type of position at an art library, such as being a serials librarian, and then apply for time sharing or departmental swaps to demonstrate that you can also provide reference support.

TAKE IT WHERE YOU CAN

As proposed earlier in this chapter, library and information science is a learning profession and, because of this, there are many postgraduate training and educational opportunities that arise, not to mention the perks that some libraries and nonprofit industries offer in order to have a more informed and better trained staff. When possible, you should be taking advantage of educational opportunities that come your way. Since we are in the business of information, it is mandatory that we stay informed. Many employers are willing to help subsidize training and educational opportunities when they come along. However, if your workplace does not offer funding for these types of opportunities, then you have to ask yourself if you are willing to invest in yourself, your career, and your future.

PRECONFERENCE PREP

Many state and national annual conferences hold preconference sessions that can be seen as hands-on or training opportunities. If your employer offers travel benefits but not funding for training, then here is an opportunity where you can have some of the cost for a training session underwritten by your employer. Usually preconference sessions are a half or full day in length. The topic covered is usually focused and there are more than likely hands-on exercises or small group breakout sessions to allow you time to become more familiar with the issues being covered and discussed. Usually these sessions end up being more valuable than the conference itself, due to the directed nature and intimate focus of the subject matter. Preconferences are great opportunities not only to learn something new but also to network with colleagues who share your interests.

CONFERENCES A-GO-GO, OR SIZE DOESN'T ALWAYS MATTER

Unlike lecture classes in graduate school where you are usually required to defer to the knowledge of the person at the front of the class, most library conferences offer programs that provide an exchange of ideas and topics. There are many members of the library and information science community who like to argue with one another in public forums, whether these are electronic mail lists or at professional conferences. Your attendance at national conferences allows you the opportunity to experience a variety of opinions and interact with colleagues from around the country, and in some cases internationally, to learn different ways of organizing, processing, accessing, and disseminating information. Always attend conferences with an open mind and a willingness to jump into the fray. Overcome your shyness and start a conversation over a buffet table or during a break between programs; you'll be surprised what you can learn from your colleagues. Also, do not limit yourself to the big conference experience. Seek out some of the smaller venues as these tend to attract our colleagues who are committed to specialty areas of librarianship, but who often times feel as though they cannot be heard at the larger mega-meetings. Some of the smaller conferences to consider are: American Association of Law Libraries annual conference, American Society for Information Science and Technology annual conference, Art Libraries Society of North America annual conference, Association for College and Research Libraries conference, the Charleston Conference, Joint Conference on Digital Libraries annual conference, the Medical Library Association annual conference, the North American Serials Interest Group annual conference, Society for Scholarly Publishing annual conference, various integrated library system user group meetings, and the Virtual Reference Desk Conference.

REGION TO REGION

Regional consortia are nonprofit organizations that serve the library community by offer training programs. Some these organizations, such as Solinet, Nelinet, and Amigos, offer training opportunities on a regular basis for specific library tools that may not have been covered fully in your library and information science program. Furthermore, various states and regions also have consortia established that provide training on specific resources and/or initiatives that have been funded or underwritten by the state governments or by regional cost sharing. When you are hired by a library, ask to see what consortia the library belongs to in order to find out what training opportunities may be available.

WEB-BASED OPPORTUNITIES

Many of the academic and research libraries host the Association of Research Libraries (ARL) Workshops, so if you live in an area close to an academic/research library, you may want to check their calendar or the workshop calendar at www.arl.org for training opportunities. In many instances ARL offers Web-based classes, so it is easy to take these classes as no special software is required. The University of Maryland also offers online programs that focus on copyright and intellectual property. You can find out more about their offerings at www.umuc.edu/distance/odell/cip/. Lastly, there are almost always announcements made to library and information science-based electronic mail lists about forthcoming training and education opportunities.

YOU CAN GO HOME AGAIN

Almost all library and information science graduate programs offer continuing education opportunities. These offerings can range from a one-day program on a weekend to a full week's worth of specialized training or certification. It doesn't hurt to check and see what educational opportunities are available from your graduate school or from the local university that offers a library and information science degree. Sometimes these classes or programs are marketed as three- or four-day intensive clinics on specific topics such as e-commerce, intellectual property, or new partnerships for instructional technology.

THE BEST THINGS IN LIFE ARE FREE

You may want to see what technical classes or continuing education classes are offered at your local community college, local college, or university. If you work at an institution of higher education, you may be able to take technical training classes for free or on a lottery system at a cut-rate. Often times these classes provide you with invaluable, specific training on either computer programs or technical expertise that was too focused to be taught in a class in library school. If you do work in an educational environment but feel that some of your skills are rusty, consider sitting in on an undergraduate research class to brush up on your research techniques. You could also see if there are professors who would be willing to work with you one on one to develop the specific skills you feel you need.

There are many continuing educational opportunities available to the library and information science professional. Sometimes it is just a matter of figuring out where these opportunities exist and how you can best afford them. You want to make sure that the training opportunity you are planning on taking does fit within the scope of your job requirements and will enhance your ability to perform your job better, especially if you would like these opportunities to be counted toward your overall career advancement and potential tenure review.

GET A COACH

While some library and information science programs focus on having faculty mentors for students, it's likely that you did not have the opportunity to form close ties with any specific faculty member. However, once you do have your degree, there are numerous members of our profession who are interested in mentoring newer professionals. Some organizations have formal mentoring opportunities; however, this type of relationship often begins from informal interactions at national conferences, through state organizations, or within your own workplace. Perhaps there is someone in the profession whom you find fascinating from their posts to electronic mail lists, from the papers the person has published, or through presentations you have seen them give. Do not be afraid to approach someone to see if they would be interested in providing a mentoring relationship. If you feel intimidated by the person, try to meet some of their colleagues to find out more about them, and ask colleagues if they think the person would be willing to serve as a mentor to you. If a person's time is too tied up at the moment, they will probably direct you to another individual that they feel would be a good mentor to you. We are a helping profession as well as a learning profession, and it is highly unlikely you will be turned down for mentorship.

IT REALLY DOESN'T MATTER

It just doesn't matter what you did or did not learn in your library and information science program. Once you have obtained your degree and have begun working, there are ample opportunities for educational growth in this profession. Sometimes you need to sleuth these opportunities out. Other times, educational opportunities will fall into your lap. You became a librarian for a myriad of reasons, but an underlying tenet is your love of learning new things and finding out about things you never heard of before. You have come into this profession from somewhere else and with other skill sets already in place. Capitalize on your strengths and your educational background, and keep your mind open and your willingness to learn intact.

This profession provides more training and educational development than most careers. Take advantage of these opportunities and do not be afraid to invest in yourself. If you just settle for what has been given to you, you are apt to be disappointed. The intelligent librarian and information scientist never settles for what has been given to him or her; rather, he or she continues to strive to learn more, to be more, and to develop more.

RELATED READINGS

Andersen, D. L. "Teaching Analytic Thinking: Bridging the Gap between Student Skills and Professional Needs in Information Science [at SUNY Albany]." *Journal of Education for Library and Information Science* 43, no. 3 (Fall 2002): 187–96.

Beales, D. "To Be (or Not to Be) a Librarian [Value of MLS vs. Job Experience]." *School Library Journal* 45, no. 4 (April 1999): 53.

Berry, J. N. "Students Sound off about Their Schools [Survey of Students Enrolled in Graduate Library Science Programs]." *Library Journal* 124, no. 18 (November 1, 1999): 46–48.

Buchanan, E. A., Xie Hong, and Malore I. Brown. "A Systematic Study of Web-Based and Traditional Instruction in an MLIS Program: Success Factors and Implications for Curriculum Design [at the University of Wisconsin, Milwaukee]." *Journal of Education for Library and Information Science* 42, no. 4 (Fall 2001): 274–88.

Carolina's MLIS Program. *Journal of Education for Library and Information Science* 43, no. 1 (Winter 2002): 16–31.

Douglas, G. "Speaking Out: Analysis of the Experiences and Opinions Reported by Recent Graduates of the University of South Carolina's MLIS Program." *Journal of Education for Library and Information Science* 43, no. 1 (Winter 2002): 16–31.

Emery, Jill, Rick Anderson, Adam Chesler, Joan Conger, and Ted Fons. "There Is No Forest, We're Only Hugging the Trees: Nontraditional Ways of Acquiring, Providing Access and Managing Serials: Surveying the Landscape. Augmented title: Closing Plenary at the 2003 NASIG Conference." *The Serials Librarian* 46, no. 1/2 (April 2004): 39–56.

Hildreth, C. R., and Michael E. D. Koenig. "Organizational Realignment of LIS Programs in Academia: from Independent Standalone Units to Incorporated Programs." *Journal of Education for Library and Information Science* 43, no. 2 (Spring 2002): 126–33.

Novick, K. "Negotiating the Role of University Continuing Education Programs." *Journal of Education for Library and Information Science* 42, no. 1 (Winter 2001): 59–62.

Shannon, D. M. "Effective Teacher Behaviors and Michael Moore's Theory of Transactional Distance." *Journal of Education for Library and Information Science* 43, no. 1 (Winter 2002): 43–46.

Van House, N. A., and Stuart A. Sutton. "The Panda Syndrome: An Ecology of LIS Education [reprinted from *Journal of Education for Library and Information Science,* Spring 1996]." *Journal of Education for Library and Information Science* 41, no. 1 (Winter 2000): 52–68.

ABOUT THE AUTHOR

Jill Emery is director of the Electronic Resources Program at the University of Houston Libraries. Previous job titles have included acquisitions and collections specialist and serials librarian. Jill doesn't believe that there are typical workdays anymore, just one continuous stream of issues to be addressed and problems to solve. She has never sung karaoke or traveled to Australia, but she's still seemingly young.

32

How to Look Like You Know What You Are Doing: Developing a Professional Image

Sarah E. O'Neal

Many people associate libraries with impressive brick buildings full of wooden tables, paper card catalogs, and a pervasive smell of leather and old books. Unfortunately, many people also assume that librarians are old women who wear glasses and their hair in a bun and scowl at anyone who appears to be having fun in the library. Although the vision of libraries is changing with the addition of computers, rows of videos and CDs, and coffee bars, the stereotype of the bun-wearing librarian has remained. In their article "Still Mousy after All These Years: The Image of the Librarian in the 21st Century," Jennifer Bobrovitz and Rosemary Griebel state, "The general public and even dedicated library customers fail to make the connection between technology and the professional librarian." They conclude their article by stating, "A positive personal experience with a librarian is the single most powerful influence in shaping a positive image" (2001, p. 260). So what kind of image do you have?

In their book *Five Steps to Professional Presence*, authors Susan Bixler and Lisa Scherrer Dugan state that "whenever we walk into a room, our clothing, manners, and mannerisms are on display. Others assess our self-confidence and our ability to present ourselves based on about five seconds of information" (2001, p. 7). This is especially important when we are dealing with library patrons of all ages, races, and genders who are relying on us for their information needs. Abby Kalan discusses this issue in her article "Are we Sabotaging Ourselves with Our 'Professional' Image?" She asks:

> Is the frumpy librarian the image we wish to convey? Of course not. We view ourselves as indispensable overseers, managers, and providers of information; as detectives who can find the answer; as defenders of civil liberties and intellectual freedom. Do we wear last season's clothing? Who are we kidding? Last

century's clothing. We're all guilty. It would be nice to think we dress this way
so we won't intimidate our customers. Or perhaps our workplaces are so effective at being nonjudgmental havens of serenity that we put on our most comfortable clothes so we too can relax. (2002, p. 42)

The term "librarian chic" has been coined on the website *The Word Spy*
(www.wordspy.com). It is defined as "A fashion style that uses elements of,
or is inspired by, the styles stereotypically attributed to librarians." Kalan argues that if librarians had attended business school, we would be more aggressive in selling our own image. Our image, as librarians, will be viewed
with respect if we meet patron demands with "professionalism, competence,
timeliness, convenience, accuracy and interest."

FROM GRUNGY GRAD STUDENT
TO CONFIDENT PROFESSIONAL

There is a new television show on the TLC network called *What Not to
Wear*. Friends and family members send secret videotapes of loved ones
showing them at their worst. Then fashion stylists give the fashion victims
advice and a $5,000 check to buy the right wardrobe. Although you aren't
being secretly taped, it is important that you pay attention to how you look
at the library.

WHAT CAN I WEAR?

Many libraries, whether they are public, academic, or school libraries, have
dress codes. Check with your immediate supervisor to see what is required. Remember that dress codes are in place to protect the employee and assure professionalism. This isn't school anymore. In his book *The New Professional*, author Ed Holton says, "How you dress is a very important factor in creating your
professional image. Without ever saying a word or doing anything, you make
or break your image just by your dress" (1991, p. 81). Holton suggests that your
goal as a first-year professional should be to "blend in, to wear the 'uniform'
that is widely accepted in your environment." He emphasizes that your first
year as a professional is not the time to "make fashion statements, assert your
individual style through clothing, or wear suggestive clothing" (1991, p. 82).

Each library will have its own dress code. One library system I worked at
stated that librarians could not wear jeans at all. In another system, there is a
"casual Friday" where wearing jeans and tennis shoes is acceptable. Some libraries have policies that male librarians must wear a tie, while other libraries

say that a shirt with a collar with no tie is acceptable. Ann Marie Sabath makes a list of typical dress code blunders in her book *Beyond Business Casual* (2000). These are clothes you want to avoid wearing at work:

- Sweatpants
- Sweatshirts
- Workout or jogging outfits
- Clothing with extreme or outrageous colors
- Uncoordinated clothing and color combinations
- Revealing or transparent items
- Baggy or sloppy looking sweaters
- Wrinkled clothing
- Baseball caps
- Shirts without collars
- Tops with plunging necklines
- Short skirts or dresses

Your best bet is to dress conservatively your first day of work and then ask your supervisor for a copy of the dress code guidelines at your library.

ATTITUDE AND BEHAVIOR

Being a professional at work isn't just dressing appropriately. It is having a positive attitude and demonstrating the right behavior. Pat Wagner discusses this in her article "Communication Mistakes Only Really Smart People Make." She writes:

> When I first entered the workplace, I suffered the smugness shared by many young people who have had success in college. I could write well under the pressure of deadlines and felt comfortable speaking in public. I was quick to learn new skills and could solve technical problems that baffled more experienced colleagues. I had lots of energy, loved to work hard and enjoyed succeeding at complex tasks. I was an up-and-coming star. However, despite what I thought were my superior workplace skills, no one seemed to want to work with me. During meetings, my ideas were ignored. I was passed over for a promotion with the vague explanation that I needed to work on my interpersonal skills. (1997, p. 13)

Wagner soon discovered that it was not enough to have the technical knowledge to do her job well, it was just as important to build positive professional relationships and have good interpersonal skills. This view is reiterated by Liz Hughes in her article "Don't Be a 'Lone Ranger.'" Hughes states, "Although every work environment is different, making a sustained effort to communicate effectively, honing your diplomacy skills, and projecting a polished image will help you build the solid working relationships so important to your career advancement" (2002, p. 5).

Here are some more tips on how to build positive professional relationships.

WORKING WITH YOUR BOSS

A professional librarian also is an effective subordinate. Holton gives several good tips about how to be a good employee. Two of Holton's most valuable tips are to keep your boss informed and never to surprise or embarrass your boss. It is important to keep your boss informed of what is going on in your area. Supervisors depend on you to communicate successes and problems. The problems can't be solved unless your boss knows about it. I have seen many librarians complain about problems but refuse to tell the branch manager. The manager cannot solve a problem if he or she doesn't know it exists.

It is also very important to not surprise or embarrass your boss. The key is to keep your supervisor informed of what is going on, even if you think it is trivial. Again, it is important to communicate with your supervisor. While I was branch manager at one public library, one of my librarians solicited materials from the community for a children's program. After getting the materials, she wrote thank-you letters to the businesses, signed my name, and mailed them without my knowledge. Several words in the letter were misspelled. I was shocked to receive a call from a business acquaintance pointing out the misspelled words in "my" letter! This is a good example of why it is important to communicate with your supervisor.

WORKING WITH YOUR COWORKERS

You will be a newcomer in your first position, while the rest of the staff will have been working there awhile. Some staff members might have been working there for twenty or thirty years. The librarians and the support staff at the library have created their own "culture." It will be your challenge to discover what the "culture" is and if you fit into it. Holton talks about "fitting in" in his book *The New Professional*. He says, "You have to conform to the team before you can earn the right to assert your individuality" (1991, p. 251).

So how do you find out what the culture of your library is? Holton suggests that you try these tips:

Observe your colleagues and talk to them. You will see patterns emerging regarding the library's work ethic, norms for behavior, and values.

Notice what people spend their time on. Watch how the successful people spend their time. This will tell you what their priorities are.

Listen for "heroes and legends." This happens very frequently in libraries. When I took a position as a children's librarian at a new library branch, all the other staff members, both librarians and support staff, told me how wonderful the previous children's librarian was and how sad they were that she left the library. Then the patrons and children began telling me how much they missed the previous children's librarian. I always stopped and listened to their stories about the exciting programs and complicated storytimes that this librarian conducted. I couldn't duplicate the work that she had done, but I got a lot of really good ideas. I also learned exactly what the patrons and my supervisor expected from me.

SOME DOS AND DON'TS

These are some of the issues that new professionals face when they enter the workforce.

Gossip

The workplace is a nest for gossip. You see the same people every day and you just can't *help* hearing that someone broke up with someone else. In their book *Five Steps to Professional Presence*, Bixler and Dugan say "Celebrating, or commiserating, with office staff or colleagues helps us gain perspective on both triumphs and disasters. Talking things over with others helps to humanize the work and the workplace. . . . On the other hand, companies point to idle chatter and water cooler gossip as the worst offenders that contribute to unproductive time" (2001, p. 143). Being a professional librarian means working well with your colleagues and not contributing to the library gossip. Holton states, "Gossip is like a poison. What you need here is to learn to stay away from it. Let others do it all they want, but you stay out of it" (1991, p. 84).

Telephone Manners

It always amazes me how many people do not have appropriate telephone manners at work. Remember that the library installed the phone so you can answer reference questions and assist patrons. They did not install the telephone so you can call home every hour. In libraries, where most of the staff is visible to the public, it is not a good idea to discuss your daughter's illness while patrons wait by your desk. Instead, use a private phone in the staff lounge or workroom. Also, remember to keep your calls brief. Your personal phone call could be tying up the phone line for the patrons.

"Works Well with Others"

The relationships you build with your colleagues are very important. Holton states, "The bonds you build with your fellow new hires will be the basis for a professional network that will help you throughout your career. . . . So, while you need to be careful to view the relationships as professional, not personal ones, you also need to nurture them with great care" (1991, p. 118). In her article "Don't Be A 'Lone Ranger,'" Hughes says that it important to "build solid relationships with your coworkers and managers" (2002, p. 5). Hughes suggests that to build a professional image you must "avoid the rumor mill." Just remember that you are there to work, and the relationships you build with your coworkers are usually professional, not social, ones. Holton states that "Professionals who work together do build friendly relationships, but most do not build true friendships. . . . People don't come to work expecting to develop personal relationships. The company will encourage building some level of personal rapport to make it easier for people to work together. But they couldn't care less about whether you build close friendships" (1991, p. 291).

GET INVOLVED

A great way to get involved in work and build positive working relationships is to participate in committees, groups, and professional organizations. A good place to start is with the American Library Association's website. This site offers comprehensive information about the organization and the different divisions and affiliate state chapters. In her book *Jump Start Your Career in Library and Information Science,* Priscilla Shontz discusses how to get involved in a professional organization. Shontz writes, "Reading professional literature will help you learn the terminology and key players in the field, and keep up with current trends. Scope out the various organizations by talking with friends and colleagues and reading the association's publications. Once you are a member of an organization, volunteer for involvement in committees" (2002, p. 87).

You don't have to look very far to be involved. What about volunteering for committees and groups at your library? Shontz suggests, "Volunteer for special projects or committees at work. Suppose that your library is planning a big function, or that there is a big task that needs to be done. Volunteer to participate or to head up that project, and then do a good job at it. This puts you in touch with people you may not work with every day, and it shows your coworkers how you function in teams or as a leader. You will come in contact with different people and this will expand your network" (2002, p. 91).

IT IS ALL ABOUT THE IMAGE

In his article "Rupert Giles, the Professional Image Slayer," John Cullen writes, "The history of negative portrayals of librarians in the media is a long one. We have been categorized as: murderous (*The Name of the Rose*); dizzy (*The Mummy*); absurd (the character of Ook, the orangutan librarian in several of Terry Pratchett's novels); and unhelpful and ineffective (in practically every advertisement, TV show, or movie that features a librarian)" (2000, p. 42).

As a new library professional, you have the skills and knowledge to help patrons find they information they need. But don't neglect the behavior, attitude, and wardrobe to convey the image of a professional. Kalan writes:

If we had attended business school, we would have learned the importance of selling our own image, as well as our product. (We might even have been taught that part of our job is developing our image and building our career!) . . . And as far as the wardrobe, well, simple works. Trash those fashion don'ts. But the most important item we wear is our expression, so smile! Make eye contact. Give up that dour image. Being unpleasant only devalues our product, our image, and our self-respect. (2002, p. 42)

So armed with your new degree and a smile, you can be a successful library professional.

RELATED READINGS

Bixler, Susan, and Lisa Scherrer Dugan. *Five Steps to Professional Presence.* Avon, Mass.: Adams Media Corporation, 2001.

Bixler, Susan, and Nancy Nix-Rice. *The New Professional Image.* Avon, Mass.: Adams Media Corporation, 1997.

Bobrovitz, Jennifer, and Rosemary Griebel. "Still Mousy after All These Years: The Image of the Librarian in the 21st Century." *Feliciter* 47, no. 5 (2001): 260.

Cullen, John. "Rupert Giles, the Professional-image Slayer." *American Libraries* 31, no. 5 (May 2000): 42.

Gross, Kim Johnson, and Jeff Stone. *Chic Simple: Dress Smart Women*. New York: Warner Books, 2002.

Holton, Ed. *The New Professional: Everything You Need to Know for a Great First Year on the Job*. Princeton, N.J.: Peterson's Guides, 1991.

Hughes, Liz. "Don't Be a 'Lone Ranger.'" *Office Pro* 62, no. 5 (June/July 2002): 5.

Kalan, Abby. "Are We Sabotaging Ourselves with Our 'Professional' Image?" *American Libraries* 33, no. 5 (May 2002): 42.

Liebold, Louise Condak. "Changing the Librarian Stereotype." *Library Imagination Paper* 19, no. 2 (Spring 1997): 4.

Pincus, Marilyn. *Projecting a Positive Image*. New York: Barron's Educational Series, Inc., 1993.

Sabath, Ann Marie. *Beyond Business Casual: What to Wear to Work if You Want to Get Ahead*. Franklin Lakes, N.J.: Career Press, 2000.

Shontz, Priscilla K. *Jump Start Your Career in Library and Information Science*. Lanham, Md.: Scarecrow Press, 2002.

Tobias, Jenny. "Ad Lib: The Advertised Librarian; The Image Is the Message." *Information Outlook* 7, no. 12 (February 2003): 12.

Wagner, Pat. "Communication Mistakes Only Really Smart People Make." *Records Management Quarterly* 31, no. 3 (July 1997): 13.

Wyse, Loise. *Company Manners: How to Behave in the Workplace in the 90s*. New York: Crown Trade Paperbacks, 1992.

ABOUT THE AUTHOR

Sarah O'Neal is the branch librarian at the Atascocita Branch of Harris County Public Library in Houston. She is a graduate of Austin College and the University of Arizona. Sarah has worked at libraries in New Mexico and Utah, as well as Texas. She lives with her dog in the Houston area.

33

Performance Reviews: Terror, Tedium, or Inspiration?

Frances C. Wilkinson and Linda K. Lewis

Performance reviews are variously described as hated, inspiring, paternalistic, supportive, demeaning, informative, controlling, destructive, empowering, intimidating, valuable, frightening, helpful, time consuming, draining, energizing, or useless. Some management experts regard them as crucial tools in managing and planning; others recommend abolishing formal performance appraisals completely. How can performance reviews cause such divergent reactions? Why should you conduct or participate in them? And if you use them, how can you make certain that the results are positive? Whether you are the person conducting the reviews or the employee being reviewed, you need to know how to prepare for the process.

WHAT ARE PERFORMANCE REVIEWS?

Performance reviews, sometimes called performance appraisals or performance evaluations, are usually a mandatory, annual, scheduled, face-to-face meeting between supervisor and employee to discuss the employee's performance. They should not stand on their own but should be part of a larger performance management process. Reviews are usually a structured, formal process based on goals negotiated between the employee and supervisor at the beginning of the evaluation cycle. Final, signed review documents are kept in the employee's personnel file. The organization in which the employee works determines the schedule for performance reviews, including such factors as who will be evaluated and when (i.e., each year at the same time for everyone or on the employee's anniversary date)?

WHY USE PERFORMANCE REVIEWS?

When performance reviews are done well they acknowledge achievements and good work. They provide feedback to the employee about tasks that were performed well and those that need improvement. When improvement is needed, reviews should identify the resources required for the employee to achieve that improvement, such as additional training, upgraded equipment, workload adjustment, and the like. Often organizations use performance reviews to assign merit raises or even determine the total salary increase. In large organizations, care must be taken to ensure that everyone agrees on what constitutes unsatisfactory, satisfactory, and superior work (or whatever the categories may be) and that enough money is available, above cost of living increases, to award merit.

WHY NOT USE PERFORMANCE REVIEWS?

If you have a choice about whether to do annual performance reviews, ask what you want to accomplish with them. Be sure that these reviews accomplish your goals. Before you decide, read *Out of the Crisis* by W. Edwards Demming or *Abolishing Performance Appraisals: Why They Backfire and What to do Instead* by Tom Coens and Mary Jenkins. These authors believe that performance appraisals are based on the faulty assumptions that the process can be objective and can motivate employees. Thus, if your underlying assumptions are wrong, the process can be damaging to employees and organizations, or, at best, may be a waste of time. To motivate employees toward better performance, goals must be realistic and meaningful, and they should be negotiated with the employee so that she or he has ownership in them.

WHAT DOES YOUR ORGANIZATION DO?

It depends. Just as every organization is different, the process for performance reviews is different. Your responsibility is to find out how your organization deals with performance reviews. They can be complex systems created and managed by a personnel department for a large organization or they can have no formal structure at all. If a library operates under union or civil service regulations, the procedures may be highly structured. The paperwork required can be anything from a long form to a blank sheet of paper. Knowing how your system works is the best way to prepare for a successful review.

HOW TO PREPARE

Goals

Whether you are a supervisor who will be reviewing employees, or an employee who is about to be reviewed, you need to prepare for this important process. The performance review should actually start a year in advance, when the supervisor and the employee meet to discuss goals for the coming year. Goals should not be top-down but should be negotiated and agreed upon by both parties. They should support the goals of the organization, not just the individual. These goals must be specific, have measurable results, and be achievable within the negotiated time frame because they will form the basis of the evaluation review.

Employees

The employee should keep a file that includes achievements, thank-you letters, and anything else that documents his or her progress throughout the year. Before the evaluation, she or he should review the goals and prepare a self-assessment. This step will be helpful whether it is a required part of the process or whether it is used just to aid the employee in recalling the extent to which goals were met. Be prepared to present your successes, the impact of your work on others, and to explain why any goals were not completed.

Supervisors

The supervisor should also keep a file noting the employee's progress. Before the evaluation, she or he should review the goals and the employee's self-assessment. Some organizations gather input from the employee's peers and/or subordinates (if there are any). The supervisor should consider such multirater feedback if it is available.

In some organizations, the manager will write a draft evaluation before meeting with the employee and then revise the document after the meeting; in other organizations, the document is written after the meeting. If it is written beforehand, the supervisor gives a copy to the employee sufficiently far in advance so that the employee can read it carefully.

What Training (or Help) Is Available?

This assistance also varies by the organization, but do not be afraid to seek help. Larger organizations may offer formal workshops for both employees and supervisors on how to set goals and conduct performance reviews. Local library associations, business schools, and commercial training companies often offer seminars and workshops. Courses are also available online through the American Library Association (ALA). Identify a manager whom you admire and ask him or her to mentor you. Finally, thousands of books and articles deal with performance reviews. Do not fret about the latest fad in the management literature—trends come and go—but do read a few articles and/or books so that you will be better informed.

CONDUCTING THE EVALUATION

Employees and supervisors alike often approach performance reviews with some hesitation. The goal of a performance review is to identify areas of strength as well as areas where improvement is needed. A good performance review measures the employee's success in meeting the negotiated goals, identifies areas that need improving, identifies resources needed to improve the employee's performance, and documents the employee's success in assisting the organization to meet its goals.

Several specific steps should be taken to make reviews as comfortable and useful as possible. Reviews should be scheduled, giving enough advance time for each party to prepare for them. They should be conducted in a private office or room, behind closed doors, with no ringing phones or other interruptions. The discussion must be kept confidential. If possible, reviews should be conducted at a table, which is less intimidating than talking across a desk. This is a time for both parties to engage their active listening skills, open body language, and eye contact. Both people need to be aware of the emotions, both theirs and the other party's. The challenge is to understand the emotions without falling under their influence. Never perform reviews when you are angry; reschedule the meeting if necessary. Managers should provide objective criticism to the employees, avoiding sweeping statements and generalities. Managers must concentrate on the job performance, the goals and expectations, and the extent to which goals were met. Performance reviews should be a dialogue, not a monologue on either side. These meetings are opportunities for the supervisor to mentor and coach the employee on what was done well this year and what should be improved upon next year. The employees should remind their managers of their accomplishments as well as point out what resources would be needed to improve their performance. Both parties should listen closely. In order to improve communication, they should summarize and rephrase topics in order to check for understanding and agreement. They should ask open questions that encourage discussion. Managers must evaluate the performance, not the personality. People have different styles of communication, understanding, and learning; both parties need to respect each other.

WHAT HAPPENS IN A GOOD PERFORMANCE REVIEW?

Throughout the year, the supervisor should have provided feedback to the employee about his or her performance so that there are "no surprises" at evaluation time. The best feedback is "intended to be helpful; includes positive elements (not just negative ones); deals with issues that are within the control of the receiver; specific and clear; cross-checked with the receiver for understanding; leaves the receiver free to determine their own solution and corresponding behavior; solicited, not imposed; given when it is needed; clear, concise, caring, and constructive" (Lubans 1999, p. 89).

The review is an opportunity to think about the year's activities. These reviews allow people to sit down together without interruptions to discuss the accomplishments, concerns, and the future of the position and the organization. Such discussions are infrequent in most hectic organizations; therefore, the reviews can be critical components of planning for the future.

Reviews should be encouraging, empowering, and motivating while remaining balanced and constructive. Reviews may be one of the few ways in which an organization takes time to praise employees for their performance. When organizations cannot provide pay raises or promotions, the positive evaluations can help show employees that their work is valued. When organizations can afford pay raises or promotions, positive evaluations can support such rewards.

The dialogue during reviews allows the employee to share interests and talents that may be useful in his or her specific job or elsewhere in the organization, offering a way to identify talents that can be enhanced. For example, during the review an employee may remind the supervisor that she or he took a course in Web design and is interested in designing or maintaining the organization's Web page. A review can also identify needed training or resources for the employee.

Reviews should be based on the performance and evaluated as objectively as possible. They should consider the goals and the individual's success at meeting those negotiated goals.

WHAT PERFORMANCE REVIEWS SHOULD NEVER BE

Think of all the bad performance reviews that you have had or horror stories that you have heard, and you will know what performance reviews should not be. We have all heard of monologues that attacked an individual or that had nothing to do with the job performance. Reviews should not be top-down but participatory dialogues. They are not a replacement for disciplinary processes; those must be handled separately. A good review should never be a substitute for a deserved promotion or pay raise if the organization can afford to give one. They are not replacements for regular communication and feedback that should be given throughout the year. Reviews are not tools to identify scapegoats for problems that are beyond the control of the person being reviewed; if the machines are not adequate for a person to do the job, get better equipment. Reviews must never be punishment or tools to suppress employees. Reviews must not become gripe sessions or personal attacks on individuals. Managers should never concentrate solely on recent events instead of considering the overall performance. If reviews are used to discriminate against an employee, the manager is probably violating state or federal laws.

WHEN PROBLEMS HAPPEN

Even when both the employees and managers are well prepared, and when everyone has agreed upon the goals and objectives, people can have different opinions about the results. In some cases, individuals may disagree so strongly with an evaluation that they refuse to accept it. Some organizations require that employees sign the evaluations with a statement that indicates they received it, but do not necessarily agree with it. Organizations may allow employees to attach rebuttals to the evaluations.

Depending upon the organization, the employees may have formal appeal channels. Among the possibilities may be formal or informal procedures for dispute resolution or mediation. Whether you are an employee or a manager, you need to learn the options available within your organization before you start performance reviews.

OTHER TYPES OF REVIEWS

Evaluation of Supervisors

Some organizations evaluate supervisors in addition to having their supervisors evaluate the employees. Organizations may also request input from peers, subordinates, or patrons about individuals being evaluated. Some organizations allow anonymous feedback, while many require forms be signed and promise confidentiality. The techniques vary, but they may be referred to as "peer reviews," "multirater" feedback, or "360 degree rating" where supervisors, peers, and subordinates provide input.

Evaluation of Teams

Many libraries have teams that are responsible for functions such as cataloging or systems. Some organizations are now evaluating the performance of these groups in addition to, or instead of, evaluating the performance of the individual members of the teams. Most of the guidelines concerning performance reviews are still valid, but some of the techniques will vary. Teams should be evaluated on the success of the team as a unit: Did they set their goals and meet them? Did the team meet as a unit, communicate regularly, and distribute the work among the members?

Individual team members may also be evaluated on their participation. Did all the members play an active role in the success of the project? While not all members will play the same role, all of them should contribute to the final results.

AFTER AN EVALUATION MEETING

After an evaluation meeting, the first reaction of both parties is usually a massive sigh of relief. The second reaction is frequently the thought that "I forgot to say something." Both reactions are quite normal and serve as clues for what comes next. As you enjoy the relief, you can consider what you need to do in order to make the process easier the next time. Before the final evaluation is written and signed, you can discuss the things that were forgotten.

If the manager had written a preliminary evaluation before the meeting, she or he will revise it after the meeting. The employee will reread the revision and decide whether any additional discussions are needed. If no preliminary review existed, the manager will now write the evaluation. It will be given to the employee who will have the opportunity to respond. In most organizations, the employee and manager will then sign the document to show that it was received, whether or not the employee agrees with the statements. The document should summarize the discussions and include plans for the future.

Some organizations will have central personnel offices that retain the official copies of all performance reviews. In these cases, the copies kept in the personnel offices are the only documents that will be accepted as evidence in case of legal challenges. Other libraries will keep copies in the individual departmental offices. You will need to ask your personnel department where the copies will be filed.

Once the copies are filed, the entire process starts again. You will work on any remaining questions, follow up on any needed support or training, negotiate the goals for the coming year, and continue communicating.

CONCLUSION

Personnel management is probably the most challenging part of any job, and performance reviews can be one of the most stressful parts of management. They can also be very rewarding for both the managers and the employees when they are done well. Each organization approaches performance reviews differently; you must learn how your organization functions. Everyone must take time to prepare for them throughout the year. It is an ongoing cycle in which people develop goals; communicate expectations; monitor, praise, and correct performance; evaluate results; and then repeat the sequence again. Performance reviews are opportunities to encourage, acknowledge achievements, plan, and communicate. They must be based upon respect in order to be successful. The goal of performance reviews is to improve both the individual's performance and the performance of the organization.

RELATED READINGS

Aluri, Rao, and Mary Reichel. "Performance Evaluation: A Deadly Disease?" *Journal of Academic Librarianship* 20, no. 3 (1994): 145–55.

Bacal, Robert. *Manager's Guide to Performance Reviews*. New York: McGraw-Hill, 2004.

Belcastro, Patricia. *Evaluating Library Staff: A Performance Appraisal System.* Chicago: American Library Association, 1998.

Bender, David R. "Improving Personnel Management Through Evaluation." *Library Administration & Management* 8, no. 2 (1994): 109–12.

Coens, Tom, and Mary Jenkins. *Abolishing Performance Appraisals: Why They Backfire and What to Do Instead.* San Francisco: Berrett-Koehler Publications, Inc., 2000.

Cohen, Lucy R. "Conducting Performance Evaluations." *Library Trends* 38, no. 1 (1989): 40–52.

Demming, W. Edwards. *Out of the Crisis*. Cambridge, Mass.: MIT Press, 1986.

Diaz, Joseph R., and Chestalene Pintozzi. "Helping Teams Work: Lessons Learned from the University of Arizona Library Reorganization." *Library Administration & Management* 13, no. 1 (1999): 27–36.

Edwards, Ronald G., and Calvin J. Williams. "Performance Appraisal in Academic Libraries: Minor Changes or Major Renovation?" *Library Review* 47, no. 1 (1998): 14–19.

Giesecke, Joan. "Appraising Performance." In *Practical Help for New Supervisors*, 3rd edition, edited by Joan Giesecke, 24–34. Chicago: American Library Association, 1997.

Jones, Lois W. "Making Sense of the Annual Performance Review." *Colorado Libraries* 18, no. 1 (1992): 31–32.

Kaehr, Robert E. "Personnel Appraisal, Who Needs It?" *Journal of Academic Librarianship* 16, no. 1 (1990): 35–36.

Leysen, Joan M., and William K. Black. "Peer Review in Carnegie Research Libraries." *College & Research Libraries* 59, no. 6 (1998): 512–22.

Lindsey, Jonathan A. *Performance Evaluation: A Management Basic for Librarians.* Phoenix, Ariz.: Oryx Press, 1986.

——. "Using Negotiation Theory, Conflict Management, and Assertiveness Theory in Performance Evaluation." *Library Administration & Management* 4, no. 4 (1990): 195–200.

Lubans, John, Jr. "'I Ain't No Cowboy, I Just Found This Hat': Confessions of an Administrator in an Organization of Self-Managing Teams." *Library Administration & Management* 10, no. 1 (1996): 28–40.

——. "'I've Closed My Eyes to the Cold Hard Truth I'm Seeing': Making Performance Appraisal Work." *Library Administration & Management* 13, no. 2 (1999): 87–89.

Marquardt, Steve. "Managing Technological Change by Changing Performance Appraisal to Performance Evaluation." *Journal of Library Administration* 22, no. 2/3 (1996): 101–10.

Metz, Ruth F. *Coaching in the Library: A Management Strategy for Achieving Excellence.* Chicago: American Library Association, 2001.

Osif, Bonnie Anne. "Evaluation and Assessment, Part 1: Evaluation of Individuals." *Library Administration & Management* 16, no. 1 (2002): 44–48.

Russell, Carrie. "Using Performance Management to Evaluate Teams and Organizational Effectiveness." *Library Administration & Management* 12, no. 3 (1998): 159–65.

Schwartz, Charles A. "Performance Appraisal: Behavioralism and Its Discontents." *College & Research Libraries* 47, no. 5 (1986): 438–51.

Smith, Karen F., and Gemma DeVinney. "Peer Review for Academic Librarians." *Journal of Academic Librarianship* 10, no. 2 (1984): 87–91.

Todaro, Julie Beth. "How Am I Doing?" *Library Administration & Management* 14, no. 1 (2002): 31–34.

Turner, Anne M. "Appraising Support Staff: Not Just a Silly Paper Ritual." *Library Administration & Management* 4, no. 4 (1990): 181–83.

Wallace, Patricia M. "Performance Evaluation: The Use of a Single Instrument for University Librarians and Teaching Faculty." *Journal of Academic Librarianship* 12, no. 5 (1986): 284–90.

Waters, Richard L. "Peer Review: A Team-Building Way to Evaluate Employees." *Public Library Quarterly* 16, no. 1 (1997): 63–67.

ABOUT THE AUTHORS

Frances C. Wilkinson is the associate dean of library services at the University of New Mexico General Library. She has more than twenty years of experience in administrative, public, and technical services. She has coauthored three books, authored or coauthored numerous articles and book reviews, and has served on several editorial boards. She has served on ALA and NASIG committees and presented papers, workshops, and poster sessions at library conferences.

Linda K. Lewis is the director of the collection management and resource acquisitions department at the University of New Mexico General Library. She has more than thirty years of experience in public and technical services and has authored or coauthored a book, numerous book chapters, and articles. She has served on ALA and NASIG committees and presented papers and workshops at library conferences.

34

Tenure-Track or Tenure Trap?

Christopher Nolan

When looking at articles written about academic library issues, a reader quickly notices that discussions of faculty status and tenure for librarians have occupied a prominent place. Should librarians be considered faculty when they work for colleges or universities? If so, should they be offered tenure? And if they are offered the chance to achieve tenure, how should they be evaluated? Or are faculty status and tenure things that are irrelevant to the pursuit of librarianship and unnecessary diversions from what we should be most concerned about? These questions have been answered differently at different institutions. When considering a position at an academic library, you should understand how librarians are employed and evaluated at that library and whether the situation is one that matches your interests.

WHAT IS TENURE?

Tenure is basically a lifetime contract between a teacher and an institution. Tenured professors have received a commitment from their universities that they may not be dismissed from their positions except in extreme cases (usually situations such as major financial hardship at the institution or egregious behavior by the professor). Various other benefits accrue to faculty who have received tenure: the ability to take academic study leaves, eligibility to serve on committees that may make policy, and, of course, the right to participate in the judging of future candidates for tenure.

Lifetime contracts are few and far between in our society. Why would universities and colleges offer such a benefit? The standard answer is that tenure protects faculty's academic freedom. Faculty, expected to pursue the truth in their research and teaching, may sometimes discuss or support ideas that are unfashionable, unpopular, or even considered unacceptable by others. During the early part of the twentieth century, and especially after the McCarthyism of the 1950s, tenure was widely implemented in American higher education as a reaction to dismissals of faculty for political reasons.

Of course, if a university offers lifetime contracts to faculty, it hopes to avoid hiring people who don't perform well over the years. Departmental colleagues will live with such a mistake for many years. Consequently, almost all universities and colleges offer probationary contracts to faculty for several years (usually six or seven) in order to evaluate the quality of these unproven faculty. During the probationary period, a professor will normally be evaluated on his or her teaching, research skills, and service to the community (campus, profession, and local community). For the final tenure decision, various groups at the university review the candidate's performance and make their recommendations to whatever person or committee serves as the final arbiter.

Although tenure is typical throughout U.S. universities and colleges, it does not mean that there is uncritical acceptance of its presence. Criticism has been leveled at tenure from several quarters. University administrations sometimes want more flexibility in hiring, and many have increased their hiring of adjunct professors who are not eligible for tenure. Critics inside and outside the academy are concerned that tenure prevents long-term faculty from being held to appropriate performance standards. Additionally, many faculty who have gone through the tenure process complain of vague standards and procedures and political machinations that distort the process. Proposals to eliminate tenure have come from many directions, but higher education has not developed a widely accepted replacement. As a result, new librarians should be aware that standards for tenure are in flux and may change in the future.

LIBRARIANS AND TENURE

Librarians looking for a position in an academic library will find quite a variety of ways that their professional status is delineated. Faculty status for librarians is not the rule, in spite of the Association of College and Research Libraries' strong support for it. Shannon Cary's 2001 survey showed that librarians at community or junior colleges are the most likely to receive full faculty status, while those at four-year colleges without graduate programs appear to have the least parity. Additionally, the presence of tenure or something similar to it is not necessarily tied to faculty status. There are many libraries that offer positions with faculty status but without tenure; librarians may have annual contracts or may serve at the pleasure of the administration. There are also libraries in which librarians are not faculty but have "professional" or "academic" status. Some, but not most, of these schools offer what is frequently called "continuing appointment," which is similar to tenure.

Librarians themselves have mixed opinions on the merits of faculty status and tenure. The debate over their appropriateness for librarians shows up in print on a regular basis. Arguments often center on whether such status enhances a librarian's career (in terms of higher pay or prestige) and creates better performers (by stimulating professional development) or whether this status creates librarians who try unsuccessfully to mimic teaching faculty, take time away from librarianship, and thereby diminish their usefulness to their institutions. A key issue for many has been whether the rationale for tenure even applies to librarians; do academic librarians really need the protection of academic freedom? Or is this more likely a problem for school and public librarians who face greater attempts at censorship? The inability of our profession to come to any firm conclusion on the merits of the tenure process indicates that this is truly an ambiguous area; much of one's opinion will be colored by the effectiveness of the librarians where one has firsthand experience. Where does this leave the new librarian trying to decide which positions to apply for? Let's look at the advantages and disadvantages of working in a tenure-track situation in order to understand better what you should look for when investigating a job.

ADVANTAGES OF TENURE

The most obvious advantage of tenure is the job protection that it affords. Although tenured faculty can be and are dismissed by institutions, the process is more difficult and potentially fraught with legal confrontations. Though challenges to his or her academic freedom may be rare, a tenured librarian may feel more secure when disagreeing with others about collection development, copyright enforcement, or campus governance. Tenure may also be protective in cases of discrimination or harassment.

Tenure usually offers full or almost-full integration into the campus's faculty governance structures. Librarians participate in peer review of their colleagues and strongly influence their tenure decisions. Depending on the size of a university or college and its own governing patterns, librarians may serve on important committees that review other faculty for tenure decisions, affect curriculum, recommend faculty benefits, and so on.

Tenure provides other benefits to faculty. Many institutions offer only the tenured faculty the opportunity to take an academic leave to pursue research or other professional development. Being tenured or on the tenure-track may also result in more funding to librarians for professional travel or research projects. Frequently accompanying that research support is an expectation that one's normal work hours will include time for research and other professional development. Some libraries will provide faculty librarians with designated release time in their regular schedules to pursue these other areas of faculty activity.

Aside from the personal "perks," many argue that the entire process of achieving tenure and promotion spurs librarians to greater levels of professional development than they might have achieved without that process. Librarians in the tenure-track become motivated to explore outside their normal routines. If research and publication are expected for tenure, librarians will develop the skills to find professional issues that need attention, discover ways to address those problems, and share their solutions with their campus and the profession. They stay more current on trends and technologies in their specialties; they keep the library moving forward as their environment changes. Likewise, when service is required of librarians for tenure, they get involved in campus committees and events, as well as professional organizations. This also works to keep librarians aware of the world outside their libraries, while injecting library talents and perspectives into groups that may have been unaware of what we offer. Involvement in the intellectual pursuits of scholarship and the practical efforts of campus and other groups develops better-rounded librarians who are more apt to influence their environments.

The question of whether tenure has an impact on librarians' salaries has not been settled. In the 2001 ACRL survey that Cary describes, "equivalent salaries with teaching faculty" occurred least frequently out of nine "faculty status conditions" (2001, p. 511). Yet some library administrators claim that they can hire librarians at higher salaries when they can offer tenure-track faculty positions. It may be fair to say that this issue varies considerably among different institutions. However, librarians who have taken tenure-track positions and participated vigorously in the requirements for professional and scholarly development will find that they have increased their own skill set, have achieved a greater level of visibility on the campus and within the profession, and have thereby increased their perceived value. If this does not translate into more dollars at one's current institution, it may certainly do so during future job changes, while also making one's candidacy for positions more attractive.

Some have argued that this personal development is not a result of faculty status and the tenure process—that this type of bright, motivated librarian would act that way regardless of the review system. To some extent, this is true—only motivated people would want to take on the extra requirements of a faculty position. Yet the demands of any job, especially with technological changes and the staff cutbacks, often consume our entire schedule and leave no time or energy for stepping back and thinking more broadly about what we're doing. The tenure process helps inculcate those habits that allow you to incorporate scholarship and service into your normal activities.

DISADVANTAGES OF TENURE

If there are so many advantages to accepting a tenure-track position, why would anyone not want to work in this environment? The most daunting problem with working within a tenure-track situation is the possibility of failure. The tenure decision is a major career hurdle. Jump over it and you gain many benefits; trip over it and you almost always will be forced to find a new job (and deal with the resulting resume damage and psychological scars). The atmosphere for tenure review of librarians can vary greatly among institutions, yet the final review always comes down to a yes or no from colleagues, supervisors, and other campus figures. The pressure this can put on an untenured librarian should not be underestimated.

Tenure-track positions have requirements that are not always part of other jobs, most notably scholarship, research and publication, and service. These can create a more strenuous position, because these additional duties must be juggled along with all of the other daily tasks you need to do. Teaching faculty often postpone much of their scholarly activities to summers and other breaks when classes are not in session. Librarians occasionally will have the same sort of schedule as teaching faculty, but it is probably more common for librarians to work year-round. That schedule makes it challenging, though not impossible, to complete these additional requirements.

While some librarians enjoy and look forward to these additional responsibilities, many did not choose a career in librarianship in order to do them. Tenure requirements consequently may become things that take away time from those activities for which a librarian joined the profession: reference work with users, cataloging, and so on. If you are unable to *integrate* scholarship and service into your overall career development, these activities can make a position less enjoyable.

Lack of campus support can be a problem for faculty librarians as well. Even if a librarian feels comfortable about faculty activities being a part of the job, other campus faculty may not. Sometimes this may be a status issue, since librarians usually lack the doctorate held by most teaching faculty. More often this is because teaching faculty (and perhaps administrators) believe that librarians should be available to do their "librarian-type" things all the time. Time taken to work on a publication, attend a conference, or serve on a faculty committee may be considered time ill-used, when it could have been used to get books cataloged faster or questions answered more promptly. This attitude ignores the importance of professional development for librarians, yet it is not uncommon on academic campuses.

As mentioned earlier, librarians frequently work eleven or twelve months of the year, while teaching faculty may have nine-month contracts. Besides the difficulty of completing tenure requirements while working a longer contract, librarians may feel that these disparities show them to be second-class faculty—especially if their salaries are correspondingly lower for the ranks they hold. This may not affect some librarians, but certainly many of us have heard resentment from our colleagues when teaching and library faculty workloads and salaries are compared.

Finally, tenure status can create strong ties to a particular job, both positive and negative. Once a librarian achieves tenure and then decides to look for another position, he or she may find that other jobs may not offer tenure status. Even if tenure is an option, new faculty may be required to prove themselves at the new institution before tenure is granted. This is rarely a full probationary period, but it does require a new librarian to go through a tenure decision a second time. On the other hand, if the new position does not offer the option of tenure, a librarian who has obtained it elsewhere may have to decide to give up that hard-earned status. In other words, there is no guarantee that the tenure you achieve at one library is transferable to other libraries. That doesn't mean that a prospective employer may not value the work that went into the achievement, but it does mean that the job security afforded by the process may turn out to be temporary.

QUESTIONS TO ASK BEFORE TAKING A TENURE-TRACK JOB

Interviewing for a position is a two-sided process. Not only does the hiring library staff interview you; you also are asking questions to check how the library fits with you. This means evaluating a possible tenure-track position and determining if the way the tenure process is implemented at a particular library is likely to provide a good chance for you to be successful. To aid your decision making, here are a few of the key questions that you should ask before deciding whether to accept an offer of such a position. Consider how well your answers indicate a match between your skills and interests and the demands of the institution that may hire you.

1. What are the parameters of getting tenure at this institution? That is, how does the tenure process work and how clear are the procedures? For instance:
   - If you have worked as a professional at other libraries, can you receive credit toward tenure for that experience, or will you need to go through the entire probationary period?
   - How well defined are the tenure requirements? Some libraries have detailed policy documents that carefully spell out what is expected in each category of the tenure evaluation and when these things should be completed. Candidates for tenure in these situations usually know where they stand. Other libraries provide only generalities about the types of activities and achievements expected for tenure, and candidates may have no sense of whether they have achieved enough to get tenure.
   - How frequently will you receive feedback on your progress? A negative surprise at the time of the tenure decision is the worst possible outcome. You should check to see that the tenure process includes frequent and regular evaluations of a candidate's progress toward tenure. This gives you the ability to make adjustments to meet the expectations of the tenure reviewers.
   - What factors are evaluated in making tenure decisions, and how are they weighted? Assuming that the traditional categories of librarianship, scholarship, and service are specified, how is each of those defined? Scholarship, especially, can be a difficult task for many librarians. Are only peer-reviewed publications considered appropriate to meet this requirement, or are book reviews, poster sessions, and other means of sharing your experience given any consideration? Regarding librarianship, check to see if all the major roles of the position you are considering are included within the evaluated category of librarianship. Or are only those activities that mimic teaching faculty, such as instruction or collection development, given much importance? In terms of service, is local involvement sufficient, or do your evaluators want to see that you have become an active participant, or even leader, in national organizations?
   - Who makes the decision to grant tenure to a librarian? Some larger universities, in particular, allow the tenured librarians to make the

principal decision, and an administrator, perhaps a provost or academic dean, affirms or denies this recommendation. Under this system, a candidate has a good sense of the likelihood of tenure from departmental (i.e., library) feedback and deliberations. However, if the case is then passed along to a campus review board and other academic administrators, the library's recommendation may not be as predictive of the outcome.

2. What support is given to untenured librarians to help them succeed?
   - Is time to work on the various criteria given during typical work weeks? That is, if scholarship and service are considered especially important for achieving tenure, does your supervisor permit a realistic amount of time for this work to be done, or must it usually be completed by working longer hours? For even larger projects, such as a major publication effort, is release time given? And is financial support for workshop and conference attendance provided? (These latter activities often lead to committee appointments, speaking opportunities, and invitations to write for publication.)
   - Does the library provide a support network for its tenure-track colleagues? Tenured librarians can give career guidance, help develop your research and speaking skills, offer to coauthor papers, and much more. Additionally, those who have gone through the tenure process can help you stay on schedule, seek out appropriately regarded activities, and submit the best possible portfolio for tenure consideration.

3. How successful have librarians been at achieving tenure at this library in the past? Ask your potential future employer to indicate how many librarians have achieved tenure and how many have been turned down. But even this information can be slightly misleading. Many institutions will encourage librarians to seek employment elsewhere if these staff are not considered faculty material. So an important follow-up to the first question is one about turnover: how long have the current staff been at this library and how long did their predecessors work here? A possible warning sign is a staff that consists almost entirely of long-tenured and very recently hired librarians. This may indicate that recently hired librarians are not succeeding or are being driven away to other positions before they have the chance to get tenure.

4. How active are the tenured librarians in their areas of expertise? Because of the job security that tenure offers, those with this status may decide that they can work much less diligently and still remain at that library. Do senior librarians still participate in professional organizations? Do they still pursue areas of personal research and share these

findings with colleagues through publication or presentation? Do they continue to receive promotions or do they "plateau"? An active, tenured library faculty creates a more dynamic working environment and is also more likely to help you make it through the tenure process.

5. Finally, what is the campus perspective on librarians and tenure? Do administrators and teaching faculty recognize and support librarians' status? Lack of campus support for librarians could foretell difficulties with your tenure process or future changes in librarians' working situations.

As shown above, librarians can find many pluses and minuses in a faculty-status, tenure-track position. Most important is finding a position in which you feel that personal success is possible in an atmosphere of reasonable stress. Equally satisfied librarians occupy positions with and without the option of tenure. In many cases, your decision to join a particular library may be based more on the quality of the institution and your colleagues than the particular governance system used to evaluate you. But you should always carefully consider what the expectations will be for you in the following years.

RELATED READINGS

Association of College and Research Libraries. College Libraries Section. *Criteria for Promotion and Tenure for Academic Librarians*. Chicago: American Library Association, 1997.

———. *Standards for Faculty Status for College and University Librarians*. Chicago: American Library Association, 2003. www.ala.org/Content/NavigationMenu/ACRL/Standards_and_Guidelines/Standards_for_Faculty_Status_for_College_and_University_Librarians.htm (last accessed 20 October 2003).

Campbell, Jerry D. "An Administrator's View of the Negative Impact of Tenure on Librarians." *Technical Services Quarterly* 6, no. 2 (1988): 3–9.

Cary, Shannon. "Faculty Rank, Status, and Tenure for Librarians: Current Trends." *College & Research Libraries News* 62, no. 5 (May 2001): 510–11, 520.

Cubberley, Carol W. *Tenure and Promotion for Academic Librarians: A Guidebook with Advice and Vignettes*. Jefferson, N.C.: McFarland, 1996.

Herring, Mark, and Michael Gorman. "Do Librarians with Tenure Get More Respect?" *American Libraries* 34, no. 6 (June/July 2003): 70–72.

Hoggan, Danielle Bodrero. "Faculty Status for Librarians in Higher Education." *Portal: Libraries and the Academy* 3 (July 2003): 431–45. Hoggan provides an excellent survey of the literature and the many issues surrounding tenure.

Shontz, Priscilla K., and Jeffrey S. Bullington. "Tips for New Librarians: What to Know in the First Year of a Tenure-Track Position." *College & Research Libraries News* 59, no. 2 (February 1998): 85–88.

ABOUT THE AUTHOR

Christopher Nolan is the assistant university librarian and head of public services at the Coates Library, Trinity University, San Antonio, Texas. He holds the rank of associate professor, having received tenure at Trinity in 1993, and has served on his university's Commission on Promotion and Tenure. Chris has published several articles on various aspects of reference services, reviews reference books, and has also written the book *Managing the Reference Collection*, published by the American Library Association.

5

EXPERIENCE AS AN EXPERIENCED LIBRARIAN

35

Preparing for Promotion: How to Succeed without Developing an Ulcer in the Process

Linda Marie Golian-Lui

Congratulations! After several years of consistent professional growth you have made the decision that now is the time to apply for promotion at your library. Preparing for promotion is a tedious task that requires sound judgment, strong communication skills, organized record keeping, and sturdy character. In the ideal situation, preparing for promotion is a task that takes several years of thoughtful reflection, growth, documentation gathering, mentoring, and portfolio preparation. Unfortunately, for many librarians, preparing for promotion is a task that is often undertaken with little preplanning and only a few weeks devoted to the actual organizing of an evaluation portfolio.

In general, the promotion process is often considered complicated, time consuming, nerve wracking, and sometimes confrontational.[1] Applying for promotion is also considered a valuable process that provides affirmation of an organization's mission and validation of the applicant's professional activities, responsibilities, and growth that support the organizational mission and the library profession. It is important to realize you do have significant control over your promotion process and you can make the promotion process less stressful with some strategic, realistic planning and organization.

Applying for promotion is a professional decision that should not be made in haste. All promotion applications require substantial time and effort from the applicant in order to create a compelling portfolio that effectively communicates why an applicant is deserving of promotion. It is also a process that typically requires both peers and supervisors to scrutinize, judge, and place value upon your professional activities over a specified period of time. No matter how fair the promotion process, or how many due process safeguards are available to protect the applicant, being reviewed and professionally judged by your colleagues is unnerving for most promotion applicants.

This chapter is designed to help you successfully break down the promotion application process into six practical and manageable steps. Each highlighted phase includes realistic tips to help you achieve success in that phase, while preparing you for the challenges of the next step. In addition to these six specific phases, information concerning the foundational concepts and purposes of the promotion process is also included.

HISTORICAL AND THEORETICAL BACKGROUND

The theoretical foundation for the appointment, evaluation, promotion, and, when applicable, tenure of librarians centers on the principles of utilizing standard criteria to fairly and accurately review applicants in an unbiased appraisal in order to create a shared vision and excellence in an organization. It is a process that is intended to help communicate what is expected, reward employees who meet or exceed those expectations, and provide assistance to newcomers to the organization in understanding the organizational expectations. It is also a process that provides avenues for improving the contributions of employees not meeting the professional benchmarks established by the organization. It is a complicated and interconnected process that includes much more than the occasional creation of a promotion application portfolio.

Evaluating employees and rewarding them through a process such as promotion is a common practice that has been occurring for many centuries. For example, in 350 A.D. in ancient Antioch, teacher performance reviews were directly linked to either rewards (such as increases in pay or better living arrangements) or disciplinary actions.[2] Like other human resource activities in today's library organizations, the promotion process is a cyclical system that includes many interrelated steps, including, but not limited to: accurate position description, periodic goal setting, continuous monitoring and feedback, and systematic reviews. It is a process that needs clear and consistent definitions, written criteria, and mutually agreed upon expectations.

PROMOTION VERSUS TENURE

Most public, medical, legal, school, academic, and special libraries provide promotional opportunities for their librarians. In addition to promotion opportunities, many academic libraries also provide tenure opportunities. Although closely linked, and often utilizing similar processes and criteria, the conceptual foundations of these two activities are unique.

The promotion process focuses more on the past merit of a librarian's contribution to an organization and recognition of professional growth and accomplishments. It is a process acknowledging the achievement of specific skills and the earning of organizational trust to merit additional authority and responsibility in an organization. Typically, librarians can be considered for promotion more than once in most organizations.

The tenure process is typically a one-time-only opportunity. It is a process that focuses on and acknowledges the belief in the long-term worth of the librarian to the organization. For academic librarians, the American Library Association (ALA) strongly supports the tenure appointment and review of librarians following similar procedures established for the tenure appointment and review for other faculty within an organization while also providing avenues that address the unique contributions made by librarians to the organization.[3]

Organizations that offer tenure often follow a schedule of several strategic reviews in preparation for the final tenure decision that is made after a specific number of years. Tenure criteria is typically linked to an organization's promotional criteria. A promotion and tenure study of academic libraries found that 80 percent of tenure-granting institutions use tenure criteria that are generally the same as those used for promotion. The remaining 20 percent use the promotion criteria as foundational bases but also include additional criteria that were uniquely used in the tenure decision-making process.[4]

SHOULD YOU APPLY FOR PROMOTION?

Whether you are a beginning librarian applying for your first promotion or a seasoned professional applying for one of the more senior professional ranks at your organization, deciding to apply for promotion is a critical decision.

For the beginning librarian, your first probationary period is a special professional phase when you are expected to learn a lot about your new professional duties and the relationship of these duties to your organization. Deciding to apply for promotion is your symbolic gesture expressing that you are no longer one of the entry-level librarians at your organization and that you have successfully taken the theories learned in library school and combined them with the day-to-day practicality of the real library world. By applying for promotion, you are expressing to other librarians in your organization that you have faith that your actions in the last few years indicate that you have made satisfactory progress to becoming a seasoned professional.

For the seasoned professional, promotion application comes in recognition of many years of service and professional development. It is your symbolic gesture expressing that you have developed excellence in some aspect of your profession at your organization. You are communicating to your peers that you are confident that your many years of consistent professional activities, responsibilities, and growth are evidence that you are now worthy to join the special rank of other senior-level professionals. However, like the beginning librarian, creating an effective promotion application that verifies that you are now ready for this advanced status in your organization is equally daunting. Like the beginning librarian, successfully breaking down the promotion application process into practical and manageable steps is the most effective way of surviving the promotion process.

STEP 1: BEGINNING THE PROMOTION CYCLE DURING THE JOB ACCEPTANCE/NEGOTIATION STAGE

One common question asked by many librarians contemplating the promotion process is "Where does the promotion process begin?" Many experts argue that the promotion process actually begins during the job offer or job acceptance stage. For the professional trying to obtain their first professional job, this might not sound reasonable. However, the seasoned professional realizes that the job negotiation stage has a critical connection with future promotion applications.

Each organization has specific criteria for promotion. Most organizations' promotion criteria include particulars concerning the number of years of professional service, the number of years at a specific rank, and specific types of duties necessary for successful promotion to an explicit rank. However, the interpretation of these criteria is not always easy or clear. Therefore, before accepting a job offer, many librarians negotiate with their future employer for the documentation of credit they will receive concerning specific criteria that they will use for future promotion applications.

This process of documenting promotional criteria on past accomplishments prior to accepting a position at a new organization is also sometimes referred to as grandfathering. It is not unusual for many professionals to want to apply for promotion at the first possible opportunity. Therefore, during the final stages of the job acceptance process, these librarians ask to see a copy of the promotion criteria. Prior to accepting the job, they negotiate with their future employer concerning such issues as time in rank, years counting for professional service, and number of years needed at the new organization before they can apply for promotion. Grandfathering is the appropriate vehicle to use in documenting how your previous years of professional experience completed outside of a traditional library organization will be recognized by your new organization toward meeting a specific promotion requirement.

STEP 2: GATHERING DOCUMENTS AND DEFINITIONS

Once you have accepted a job offer and have received written documentation concerning the agreed-upon specific issues relating to your future promotion application, the next critical step is to collect all the necessary documentation concerning performance and promotion evaluations at your new organization. This is sometimes easier said than done, since related information can be spread throughout many documents, with these documents residing under the administrative control of several offices within your organization.

You should not feel uncomfortable requesting copies of these critical documents, nor should you feel uncomfortable asking for clarification of terms used in these documents. Management has the obligation to help establish a successful foundation for the future promotion application for all librarians in an organization through assisting in the mutual understanding of job assignments and promotion criteria.

Promotion documentation typically includes criteria for promotion eligibility and timetables for the various promotion stages, such as the deadline for applying for promotion. Useful promotion documentation includes information concerning the roles, responsibilities, and rights of all parties involved in the promotion process; it also includes information that guarantees fairness and due process. If your organization's promotion documents do not address these critical concepts, it is wise to ask for clarification. Necessary documents for the promotion process include, but are not limited to, the following:

- An accurate and up-to-date job description
- Annual assignments/performance goals
- Documentation concerning annual reviews and their relationship to the promotion process
- Documentation concerning the promotion process
- Documentation concerning promotion criteria
- Copies of all forms used for annual evaluations and promotion applications (this includes self-evaluation, peer review, and supervisor reviews)
- Collective bargaining documentation if your organization is unionized

After collecting all necessary documentation and forms, it is critical that you review the information for interrelationships between documents. Now is the time to ask questions concerning these documents and their relationship to the promotion process. In order to receive a balanced viewpoint concerning your questions, consider asking both a professional peer who has recently been successfully promoted at your organization, and a supervisor who might be responsible for conducting an evaluation that is related to the promotion process.

Clearly stated criteria for promotion assist both the applicant and the reviewers. Most institutions prefer fairly simple criteria with wording that is specific but not restrictive. However, it is not unusual for documents to include specific terms without providing definitions. For example, if the term "Excellence in Librarianship" is a criterion for promotion, is this term specifically defined with an illustrated example? If not, you should consider documenting what the term means for you professionally, utilizing a national standard or benchmark when possible, and including this definition in your promotion documentation.

STEP 3: SURVIVING PROBATION AND THE PREPROMOTION PHASE

Once documents have been gathered and definitions have been established, a significant phase of the promotion process begins: surviving the prepromotion phase while building professional skills and completing job assignments necessary to support a future promotion application. Depending upon your organization, you can have both a probation period and a prepromotion period.

Librarians are professionals who are typically hired after extensive and expensive search and screening processes. Therefore, it is not unusual for librarians NOT to have a probationary period. Understanding the criteria and terms of the probationary evaluation period is especially important since ending a job appointment during a probationary period is much easier for the library administration and typically does not have as many due process rights for the working librarian.

Before promotion is granted, new librarians need a chance to prove themselves to their organization while providing their colleagues an opportunity to observe and evaluate them on the basis of their professional assignments. Therefore, it is not unusual for many organizations to discourage new librarians from applying for promotion until they have successfully completed several years of service. The wise library professional realizes the critical value of the prepromotion phase and expertly uses this time as an opportunity to aggressively learn new skills, learn about their organization, and consistently prove themselves to their peers and supervisor. This prepromotion phase also provides ample opportunities for the organization to fairly evaluate the new librarian. Even though the first application for promotion is several years away, now is not the time to relax!

According to the American Association of University Professors (AAUP), the prepromotion phase is especially important for academic librarians because beginning librarians frequently have no training or experience with actual professional requirements. They are moving from the theoretical world to the practical, day-to-day application world.

All evaluation periods, including the prepromotion period, should begin with a clear and consistent documented definition of job expectations and responsibilities. Your job description and expectations should not only serve as the key components of your annual evaluations, but they should also serve as the evaluation foundation for your future promotion application. It is your responsibility to fully understand your job description and responsibilities and to make sure you meet or exceed those expectations if you wish to apply for promotion in the near future. Effective job descriptions are specific and include information about how performance will be evaluated, who will be conducting the evaluation, and what due process procedures are available when professional differences in opinion occur.

It is also your responsibility to fully understand what type of job responsibilities are needed in order to qualify for promotion at your organization. It is not uncommon for the job assignments of beginning librarians to have fewer responsibilities with a direct link to the future promotion process. This is done to provide the new librarian opportunities to learn about the organization and to carefully acquire new professional skills. If you are concerned that your work assignments do not support your future promotion application plans, you have the responsibility to ask your supervisor to review your assignments and discuss your current progress toward promotion. Although management has the responsibility to make job assignments fairly among all qualified employees in order to ensure equal opportunities for promotion qualification, it is your responsibility to monitor your professional career and to speak up when you have questions or concerns.

All librarians have the right to expect truthful and constructive assistance from their peers and the library administration, especially during the prepromotion phase. Evaluation has evolved from being a threat to becoming a common and expected occurrence. If done effectively, evaluation is a method for communicating and enhancing performance. It is a means for strengthening the individual and the institution.

Performance appraisals are one significant way administration communicates with librarians about job retention and future promotion support concerns. Performance appraisals that include specifics concerning how a librarian is not meeting organizational expectations can prevent unnecessary time, energy, and emotion when denying a future promotion request. However, monitoring the development of a colleague and keeping that colleague informed concerning their progress toward promotion, especially when the librarian is not performing to expectations, seems to be regularly neglected.[5] Therefore, it is wise to find additional means of acquiring performance feedback within your organization.

One method of making sure you receive constructive and truthful assistance while surviving your prepromotion period is to utilize a mentor. Mentoring is a very effective way for a new organizational member to become familiar with the organizational rules and culture. Research shows that thse who utilize the assistance of a mentor can develop professional skills and expand their professional network more quickly than their peers. Unfortunately, most library organizations do not have an official mentoring program. Therefore, it is important to consider trying to create an unofficial mentoring relationship with a senior librarian at your organization who is well-respected and supportive of beginning professionals.

Finally, some organizations encourage new librarians to serve as junior members of promotion committees. While many new librarians wish to pass on this organizational duty, wise librarians realize it is a perfect opportunity to learn what are considered successful application practices for their new organization. Serving as a junior member of a promotion committee provides insight into how the committee conducts peer review and how the organization values specific professional activities. It is an opportunity to review submitted promotion applications in order to learn organizational and portfolio appearance tips.

In summary, the probationary or prepromotion period is a time of significant importance for the promotion application. This is a critical time when you need to make sure you develop the professional skills that will support your application for promotion. In order to make this period as effective as possible, you should take the following actions:

- Fully understand your job assignment, including how assignments are evaluated.
- Fully understand what type of job assignments are needed for promotion and begin to develop the needed skills that will allow you to receive those assignments.
- Begin to understand the unwritten laws of your organization.
- Utilize the assistance of a mentor for constructive feedback concerning your progress toward promotion.

STEP 4: GATHERING AND ORGANIZING QUALITY DOCUMENTATION

One additional task that needs to be accomplished during the critical prepromotion phase is creating a system for effectively gathering and organizing documentation that you will use later to assemble your promotion portfolio. Effective promotion applications typically include a wide assortment of documents in a professional portfolio. The creation of an effective promotion portfolio is the direct result of many consistent years of documentation gathering, the selection of the best examples, and effective organization.

Your filing system does not need to be complicated. An effective filing system can be created with very little money. The basic necessities include a simple filing crate, a few hanging folders, a few filing folders, and some organizational tabs.

The difficulty of a filing system is related to professional discipline. In order to make this process effective, you must be willing to commit some quality time to this filing system. However, a few minutes several times a month during the prepromotion stage is all that is required. Creating a filing system and only organizing the information into files a few times a year quickly defeats the purpose of this important step. Gathering and organizing quality documentation during the prepromotion phases includes thoughtfully reviewing completed documents and consistently asking yourself: "How does this document support my future application for promotion?" and "What else do I need to be doing to ensure a successful promotion process?"

Once your organizational system is created, it is time to look at some of the specific promotion requirements that will take careful planning and time to accomplish prior to applying for promotion. For example, many organizations require significant scholarship and service activities prior to applying for promotion.

Many librarians incorrectly assume that scholarship is strictly limited to conducting research studies and publishing the results in peer-reviewed publications. This is no longer true for many organizations, with a recent study revealing that 57 percent of organizations closely link their institutional mission and priorities to the final promotion decision for support.[6]

The definition of scholarship has changed significantly for library organizations since the 1990 publication of Ernest L. Boyer's book *Scholarship Reconsidered: Priorities of the Professorate.* Today, many library organizations have adapted their traditional views of scholarship, moving away from complicated research studies and toward action-based research and activities. In addition, scholarship can be defined by your organization to include professional presentations, subject guides, web tutorials, and other practical resources for your organization. Once again, it is your responsibility to find out how scholarship is defined for your organization and to begin working on projects that will support these promotion criteria.

Professional service, like scholarship, is an integral part of the promotion process for many educational professions, including librarianship, since the later nineteenth century.[7] Like scholarship, the definition of service has evolved over the years. Today, many organizations requiring professional service as a promotion criterion expect a direct link between the service activity and the primary mission of the organization.

Scholarship and professional service are promotion requirements originally established to provide effective methods for professional growth. Wise librarians realize that the current acceleration of change in today's society requires faster and more effective dissemination of information and research to potential users. Librarianship is a knowledge-intensive profession, with an enormous need for continuous professional development. Scholarship and professional service are two effective methods for librarians to acquire new knowledge. Librarians planning to apply for promotion should try to develop scholarly and service activities that will support their professional growth, support their organization, and also support criteria for future promotion application.

STEP 5: PREPARING YOUR PROMOTION APPLICATION DOCUMENTATION

When many librarians think about the promotion process, they concentrate upon the actual preparation of the application document. Many librarians consider the organization and preparation of the promotion application portfolio the hardest and most time-consuming aspect of the promotion process. This step is one of the easiest to complete if you have created a timeline and a strategy for meeting all of the promotion criteria at your organization. Your understanding that the creation of a promotion application is just one critical step of many interrelated steps will make this phase of the promotion process much easier for you than for many of your professional peers.

Your well-organized files created in the prepromotion phase will greatly support your current efforts to select the best examples for your portfolio application. If you have followed the earlier suggestions of this chapter, you will find that you now have an abundance of high-quality documentation that supports your application for promotion.

It is important to realize that many promotion committees have to evaluate several promotion applications per year. It is not unusual for the promotion committee members to perform this duty in addition to all other professional obligations for the organization. Therefore, your promotion documentation should be strategically selected to clearly communicate a strong case supporting your promotion application. You should not waste the time of the evaluation committee by filling your application with pages and pages of nonsignificant documents. Portfolios consisting of fewer documents of high-quality examples are more effective than fat portfolios filled with trivial activities and documentation of every single activity that was completed during the review period.

The organization of portfolio information is absolutely critical. Many promotion committee members will not spend time searching for a specific document or performance example. Try to save the valuable time of your reviewers by using organizational tools such as table of contents, indexes, tab divides, and color-coding to assist committee members in quickly finding relative information. Although many promotion criteria include instructions on the organization of documents, promotion committee members are especially appreciative of any additional organizational efforts you might include. Saving the time of the reviewer helps to create a positive impression for your overall promotion application.

As with other successful business practices, the final appearance of your promotion application serves as a reflection of you and your professional contribution to the organization. Take time to make the arrangement of your documentation visually attractive. Make sure the documentation clearly identifies you and the promotional rank for which you are applying. For your traditional paper portfolio documents, consider the use of graphics, white space, photographs, and color-coding to create an eye-pleasing and professional application.

In addition to culling your files for the best documents supporting your application for promotion, you also need to make sure that all compulsory items, as listed in your organization's promotion criteria, are included in your final application portfolio. The following is a brief list of additional items some organizations require of their promotion applicants:

- Variety of application forms requiring signatures from supervisors
- Self-evaluation
- Professional philosophical statement
- Future professional development plans
- Copies of published scholarly activities
- Acknowledging letters of future scholarly activities
- Lists of professional activities
- Letters of support from professional peers
- Letters of confirming professional service activities

A mentor or organizational peer who recently achieved promotion can provide great expert advice on how to effectively complete each of these necessary documents.

STEP 6: CONTINUE THE CYCLE OF PROFESSIONALISM

The day you complete all the necessary documentation and deliver your completed promotion portfolio you will feel a tremendous weight lifted from your shoulders. You no longer have to worry about which documents you should include as examples of your exemplary work performance, scholarship, continuing professional education, or service activities. Although a tremendous weight has been lifted, for many librarians, a new feeling of anxiety immediately begins. This anxiety results from the realization that many of your professional peers are now actually reviewing and passing judgment on your professional value to the organization and the library profession based upon the documents you submitted.

While you wait for the final decision on your promotion application, it is critical that you effectively endure the rest of the promotion process. Worrying about what the evaluation committee might be thinking is not an effective use of your time. Instead, concentrate upon other tasks. For example, are there additional opportunities for promotion in your future? If so, now is the time to gather information documents and review the criteria for that next possible promotion step.

Another effective strategy for enduring this part of the promotion process is to once again enlist the help of your mentor. Share your concerns and anxiety with this trusted peer. You will quickly realize that most librarians share similar feelings during this stage of the promotion process. Experiencing this common bond can help provide comfort and relief while you await the final decision.

The submission of your promotion portfolio does not release you from other professional obligations. For example, now is the time to prepare your list for future thank-you letters acknowledging the help you received in this promotion application. Even if you do not receive the promotion, everyone who supported you in some significant way should be thanked and apprised of the final decision, shortly after you receive the decision.

It is also now your turn to continue the cycle of professional support for others in your organization and profession. You should consider how you might be able to assist a new librarian at your organization by sharing what you have learned about the process and any successful tips and strategies that worked for you. Even when you have been promoted to the highest rank possible at your organization, you will always have a professional obligation to continue to provide support and input into the promotion process for your organization and for other library professionals.

CONCLUSION

Although there is much research concerning librarian evaluation processes and promotion guidelines, it is critical to realize that there is no such thing as a perfect evaluation process. Promotion is part of the cycle of reviewing job descriptions, evaluating performance, and rewarding efforts. All evaluation processes include the human element of review, and there will always be differences in opinion on what constitutes a fair promotion process, sound promotion criteria, and a successful candidate for promotion. These professional differences create uncertainties that result in added stress for any qualified librarian applying for promotion.

A skilled and caring professional staff is the most critical asset of any library organization. Without a professional staff, a good library collection languishes and loses the benefit of its investment. The goal of library human resources management is to make certain that all employees are treated fairly and that they remain motivated to perform good work that supports the organization's mission.

Preparing for promotion is a tedious task that requires sound judgment, strong communication skills, organized record keeping, and a sturdy character. However, it is not a process that is intended to create an ulcer for the candidate. The wise promotion applicant realizes that the process includes several strategic steps and requires many years of strategic preparation and reflection. A candidate who understands his or her organization's promotion criteria, utilizes mentors to learn the unwritten organizational expectations, explores opportunities for professional growth, and maintains a well-organized file of supporting documentation will find the promotion process not only achievable but also affirming.

NOTES

1. C. M. Coughlin and A. Gertzog, *Lyle's Administration of the College Library*, 5th ed. (Metuchen, N.J.: Scarecrow Press, 1992), 468.

2. J. M. Bevan, "Faculty Evaluation and Institutional Rewards," *AAHE Bulletin* 33 (1980): 1–8.

3. K. Cottam, "Model Statement of Criteria and Procedures for Appointment, Promotion in Academic Rank, and Tenure for College and University Librarians: A Revision of the 1973 Model Statement," *C&RL News* (May 1987): 247.

4. R. I. Miller, *Evaluating Faculty for Promotion and Tenure* (San Francisco: Jossey-Bass, 1987), 96.

5. Bevan, "Faculty Evaluation," 7.

6. C. A. Trower, *Policies on Faculty Appointment: Standard Practices and Unusual Arrangements* (Bolton, Mass.: Anker Publishing, 2000), 180.

7. K. A. O'Meara, *Scholarship Unbound: Assessing Service as Scholarship for Promotion and Tenure* (New York: Routledge, 2002), 3.

RELATED READINGS

Bevan, J. M. "Faculty Evaluation and Institutional Rewards." *AAHE Bulletin* 33 (1980): 1–8, 14.

Boyer, E. L. *Scholarship Reconsidered: Priorities of the Professoriate*. Princeton, N.J.: Carnegie Foundation for the Advancement of Teaching, 1990.

——. *College: the Undergraduate Experience in America*. New York: Harper & Row, 1988.

Bukalski, P. J. *Guide to Faculty Advancement: Annual Evaluation, Promotion, and Tenure*. Los Angeles: California State University at Los Angeles, 2000.

Cottam, K. "Model Statement of Criteria and Procedures for Appointment, Promotion in Academic Rank, and Tenure for College and University Librarians: A Revision of the 1973 Model Statement." *C&RL News* (May 1987): 247–54.

Coughlin, C. M., and A. Gertzog. *Lyle's Administration of the College Library*. 5th ed. Metuchen, N.J.: Scarecrow Press, 1992.

Diamond, R. M. *Serving on Promotion, Tenure and Faculty Review Committees: A Faculty Guide*. 2d ed. Bolton, Mass.: Anker, 2002.

Miller, R. I. *Evaluating Faculty for Promotion and Tenure*. San Francisco: Jossey-Bass, 1987.

O'Meara, K. A. *Scholarship Unbound: Assessing Service as Scholarship for Promotion and Tenure*. New York: Routledge, 2002.

Trower, C. A. *Policies on Faculty Appointment: Standard Practices and Unusual Arrangements*. Bolton, Mass.: Anker Publishing, 2000.

ABOUT THE AUTHOR

Dr. Linda Marie Golian-Lui is the university librarian/director of the University of Hawaii at Hilo's Edwin H. Mookini Library and Graphic Services. Linda began her library career twenty-three years ago as a paraprofessional in the serials department at the University of Miami's Richter Library. Since receiving her MLIS, she has worked at the University of Miami Law Library, Florida Atlantic University, and Florida Gulf Coast University. Linda has also served as an adjunct faculty member for the University of South Florida Library School, FAU's College of Continuing Education, and FGCU's College of Arts and Sciences. She has a BA from University of Miami, an MLIS from Florida State University, an EdS from Florida Atlantic University, and an EdD from Florida Atlantic University. Besides being an active member of her state library associations, Linda has been an active member of ALA since 1990, serving on COSWL, LIRT, ACRL, LAMA, and NMRT committees. She is a past president of ALA NMRT and currently serves on the executive board of the Hawaii Library Association.

36

Library Management

Cindy Scroggins

When Priscilla Shontz first approached me about writing this chapter, I was more than a little surprised. My own management style defies classification (unless "unusual" is a valid classification), and I could not imagine why I would be deemed appropriate to advise others in an area where I have clearly forged my own path. But perhaps that is the point: There is no single "correct" way to manage, and people who consciously or unconsciously adopt a specific management style are likely to be dissatisfied in their jobs and have a staff of people dissatisfied with their manager. So this chapter is intended not as a primer on how to manage a library, but as a compilation of questions and observations that I have formed along the way. I hope the reader will find some measure of usefulness in my experience and perspective.

WHY DO YOU WANT TO BE A MANAGER?

This seems an obvious question for anyone considering a management career, but I have encountered an astonishing number of people who seem to view management as an expected and necessary step in the ladder of success, not as a field to be thoughtfully chosen. Of course, some aspects of "success" are bound to enter into consideration, including increased salary and a nice title. But I can tell you unequivocally that if those are the primary forces behind your desire to be a manager, you are not ready for the job. Salary increases and impressive job titles tend to have a strong impact when they are new, but very quickly they will be taken for granted. A successful manager's true commitment must be to the incumbent responsibilities of the management role, not merely a commitment to self-advancement.

The best reasons to consider a move into management, in my opinion, are a strong desire to effect positive change and a near-perverse sense of satisfaction at facing challenges. These drives are what help good managers transcend the mundane aspects of any job and fortify them to persevere in the face of budget cuts, staff reductions, and the many other "opportunities for change" they almost certainly will experience in their careers.

Having the right motivation is a good start to approaching a management career, but it also helps to possess certain personality traits. One thing good managers have in common is that they know themselves, know their strengths, and, especially, know their weaknesses. I am frankly less sure of traits that make a good manager as I am of traits that make a bad manager: people who love to say "no"; people who avoid change; people who must always follow A to B to C (as opposed to jumping from A to D on occasion); people who dwell on the specific in face of the larger picture; people who lack empathy; people without humor; people afraid of technology. If you recognize any of these characteristics in yourself, I strongly urge you to consider career options outside of library management.

PERSONNEL MANAGEMENT

The most important aspect of library management—of any management—is personnel management. I have witnessed dozens of managers with amazing skills in budget negotiation, grant writing, fund-raising, and the like, who fail as personnel managers in spite of these abilities—and, as a result, ultimately fail as library managers. This is because people are at the heart of any organization. Earning the trust and respect of your staff is essential if you want to be effective as a manger. A good library manager recognizes the individuality of her employees, takes the time to know the people working for her (yes, even if the staff tops 100), and takes an active role in ensuring that the library is a good workplace for all employees. The best personnel managers are approachable, involve their employees in the process of improving the library, and work to create an environment where library staff and users alike enjoy their library-related activities. One of my tenets is "Levity does not preclude efficiency." This is something we demonstrate every day in our library, where all of us are of the opinion that feeling happy is better than feeling sad (or angry, or resentful, or any of the ways people who feel "stuck" in their jobs might feel). It seems obvious that people who enjoy going to work will likely do better in their jobs than people who must force themselves to go in each day. Fostering such an environment is the manager's responsibility.

Easier said than done, you say? That's true. Most of us accept management positions in environments that are already staffed and firmly established in routine. Often we find ourselves surrounded by staff who do not like their jobs and library users who are dissatisfied with existing programs and services. The best advice I can offer someone new to a position is to make no changes in the beginning. The temptation to move in and "make a mark" is strong, but it rarely has the desired effect. The best thing you can do in the early weeks of a new position is to watch and listen. Determine why things are done the way they are done. Discuss with the staff and users what is good and bad about the library (and do this in person—don't form a committee, don't do a survey—speak to people). Look at the larger picture, get a feel for what changes should be made and what the impact might be, and, most important to personnel, communicate what you are doing and why. If you have watched and listened effectively, any changes you implement will be welcomed by most. You will not satisfy everyone—the world wouldn't need managers if that were possible. But the longer you hold the position, and the better you get to know your staff and users, you will likely develop an "informed intuition" that will guide your day-to-day personnel interactions.

While finding and utilizing the strengths of your existing staff is crucial to management success, hiring the right people is of equal importance. One thing I have definitely learned is that it is a mistake to hire a person based solely on that person's experience or knowledge. Those things mean very little if the person proves to be uncooperative with the rest of the staff, is resistant to learning new things, or has a personality that is simply at odds with the existing culture within your library. I tell prospective employees that I am more interested in how they think than in what they know. This is true for all positions, from high-ranking professionals to shelvers. Very often, I find that a person directly out of library school with limited work experience is better suited to a professional position than someone who has held a comparable position elsewhere. Much of what we do in libraries can be taught; how a person thinks, approaches problems, and works with others might be teachable, but I have yet to see it done effectively.

One other thing to keep in mind when hiring new people is to avoid the temptation to hire only people whose views and styles are similar to your own. Your library will quickly become boring and stale without a truly diverse staff. I think many managers who hire only one "type" of person are ultimately avoiding the job of management. After all, if everybody is more or less the same, it's relatively easy to treat everybody in exactly the same way. But the truth is that fair and equal are not one and the same, and what is fair to one employee might not be fair to another. Every parent knows this to be true: Just as one child might require more attention than another, at any given time one employee might require more attention than others. The key is to approach each staff member individually and to ensure that your entire staff knows that you will always be fair.

FISCAL MANAGEMENT

There is little to be said here except the following: If you do not have a solid understanding of fiscal management principles, get one. Read books, take a class, use whatever means you are comfortable with and learn it. You cannot be a successful manager without the ability to effectively manage budgets, demonstrate fiscal responsibility, and successfully compete for dollars in ever-tightening funding environments.

INFORMATION TECHNOLOGY

The line between library services and information technology (IT) services is blurring and will likely continue to do so. I envision a merger of library and information technology departments in many academic environments, where information content and access are of equally high importance. Unfortunately, I hear far more reports of battles between library directors and IT managers than tales of cooperative achievement. Like most librarians I know, I fully embrace the role of technology in libraries and am an enthusiastic supporter of electronic access to information, but I readily admit that my own experience in working with IT departments often has been less than positive. It is tempting (and easy) to place blame for difficulties between libraries and IT departments in the lap of IT managers, but that would be neither fair nor accurate, and it certainly wouldn't accomplish anything. Library managers have an obligation not only to be well-versed in information technology applications and issues, but also to work for development of solid, cooperative relationships with IT personnel toward the goal of excellent content and delivery for all users. How to do this could very well be a chapter (or even a book) unto itself. Recognizing the responsibility to develop and nurture relationships with IT managers is a good start; finding a workable path toward achieving this is a challenge the individual manager must address in the context of her own environment.

COOPERATION

Libraries have a long history of cooperating with one another, generally through formalized consortia or organizations designed specifically for the purpose of library cooperation. Library consortia have been extremely successful in negotiating licenses for the greater good of its library members, utilizing their collective purchasing power to acquire materials in bulk (and therefore at a more affordable rate), and generally serving as a support mechanism for individual libraries whose voices might not be heard without the affiliation to the larger group. I believe that such formalized consortia serve an excellent purpose, but I am concerned that many managers are missing other, perhaps less formal opportunities for cooperation that could be of equal or even greater benefit to their libraries. For example, several unrelated libraries within a geographic area (public, business, school) might join together to negotiate shared licensing for a costly resource they all need. This is rarely easy to do, given the various layers of bureaucracy inherent to the purchasing process (in publicly funded institutions, especially). Difficult or not, it is worth the effort to explore these possibilities, which can open the way for other, perhaps larger ventures. Given the many changes in the world of publishing, librarians will certainly be more effective in ensuring that information remains accessible and affordable if they are accustomed to approaching issues not only as individuals but as part of a cooperative with a single voice.

LEAD BY EXAMPLE

My parting words of wisdom are simple and often heard: Lead by example. Management and leadership are very different terms, but to be truly effective as a manager one must also be an effective leader. It is a simple matter of human nature that people do not want to work for someone they believe to be lazy or uninformed or weak. If you demonstrate to your staff that you know your job (and, better yet, that you know *their* jobs), that you will push up your sleeves and get to work alongside them, and that your behavior reflects the very work ethic and service orientation that you expect of them, you will be far more likely to have a dedicated and effective staff. With that, you're more than halfway there.

ABOUT THE AUTHOR

Cindy Scroggins has over twenty years of management experience. Since 1995 she has served as director of the Baylor Health Sciences Library in Dallas, Texas.

37

Staying Relevant: It's All Part of Learning

Birdie MacLennan

CURIOSITY AND THE SPIRIT OF BECOMING

La curiosité dynamise l'esprit humain [Curiosity powers the human spirit]."

—Gaston Bachelard

Much of the time, we don't consciously think about it. But staying relevant to the library and information science profession, as well as to our personal and organizational goals, is part of a regular, ongoing process. It begins at the start of your career, or even earlier, I think, with the idea of *becoming* a librarian or information professional, and progresses across a series of educational, training, and practical work experiences that lead to new and continuing opportunities for lifelong learning in what is, after all, a dynamic and ever-changing profession. The word "become" or "becoming" seems key here in that it signifies growth or movement in "coming to be," a process of continuous evolution. "Staying relevant" is crucial to remaining competent, effective, and dynamic in our work and to contributing to the well-being and relevance of the profession. "Staying relevant" means that we never stop "becoming" or evolving in our roles as librarians.

There are as many stories about the process of *becoming* a librarian as there are librarians. An Internet search using Google on the phrase "becoming a librarian" yielded more than 1,400 hits, many of which provide links to web pages that offer information about what librarians do and what types of training and education are appropriate for today's market. One noteworthy website by the Central Jersey Regional Library Cooperative, entitled "Become a Librarian" (www.becomealibrarian.org), offers profiles of some of today's librarians with a paragraph about why and how they entered the field. It also highlights excerpts from recent articles by Olivia Crosby and Linda W. Braun that chronicle the dynamic, changing nature of the field. Crosby writes that "Librarians [are] information experts in the information age . . . sorting data, finding answers, understanding what we need to know—these professionals are on the cutting edge. They use technology to manage knowledge" (2000–2001, p. 2). Braun reflects on the evolution of professional roles, particularly in light of the Internet and new and evolving technologies:

> Librarians are not just called librarians anymore. Increasingly their job responsibilities and titles provide a framework for the technological role that they play within the library. Professional journals and electronic mailing lists reflect these new roles. They are filled with openings for Technology Consultant, Technology Training Coordinator, Head of the Digital Information Literacy Office, Information Systems Librarian, Head of Computer Services, Webmaster, Cybrarian, and Internet Services Librarian. (2002, p. 109)

Priscilla Shontz interviewed several information professionals about career choices and career transitions. One of the questions that she asked them to respond to was, "How did I get here?"[1] Their responses, much like the narratives on the "become a librarian" website, give glimpses of what librarians do and how professional opportunities present themselves in ways that enable librarians to make transitions into new roles or new positions. The current job market, as Braun and Crosby note, reflects new roles and new titles for information professionals—"not just called librarians"—that incorporate new technological skills that are increasingly important in today's market. These narratives of what librarians do, how they transition, and how their job titles are changing suggest that *becoming* a librarian or information professional implies embarking on a career trajectory that unfolds continuously into a sequence of changes and opportunities that can lead in many different career paths. Librarians are continually "becoming" or metamorphosing into new areas, into multifaceted dimensions of the information realm.

This "becoming," a kind of ongoing transformation, is driven by changes that are taking place within and outside of the library profession. These changes may stem from new technologies or new tools and resources used to do our work, from the evolving nature of our user communities and their information needs, from new ideas gathered by working collaboratively with colleagues to realize projects or common goals, or from a variety of other internal and external influences that shape the environment in which we work. At times, the need to keep pace with change may seem overwhelming. Yet I think it is important to see change as a challenge and an opportunity for continuous learning and not as an obstacle. Attitude is everything! Making the most of change, viewing it as a positive force, can open new horizons by broadening your outlook on professional possibilities and by empowering you to expand your base of knowledge and expertise into new realms.

"Staying relevant" as a librarian is, I believe, a daily exercise. . . . I was going to say like eating and sleeping, but it is probably more related to staying professionally "fit." Staying relevant is akin to staying interested and informed, staying curious and enthusiastic, staying committed to learning, keeping an open mind, reserving time to spend for professional growth, and continually looking for ways to work creatively while providing quality service to our organizations and to the patrons that they serve. Staying open to new ideas, not being afraid to take risks and let go of old perspectives, and trying new methods for accomplishing objectives and meeting personal and organizational goals are all important aspects of staying relevant.

"*Apriamo le finestre* (Open the windows)!" Silvie Delorme, past president of the Corporation of Professional Librarians of Québec, cites the rallying call of Pope John XXIII when he convened the Second Vatican Council to bring about renewal in the Roman Catholic Church. Delorme uses this metaphor to challenge librarians to "open the windows" to professional renewal. She encourages openness to external influences, particularly to the expertise of colleagues from other professions, as well as to the ideas and changes taking place within our profession. She reminds us to communicate and collaborate with each other, to let ourselves be influenced to the very heart of our work by the spirit of change and transformation[2] that comes, like a fresh breeze, from maintaining an open attitude, letting new ideas infiltrate our perspectives. *Apriamo le finestre*! Open the windows! It is a good metaphor for the notion of transformation and renewal that is central to the ongoing process of becoming and staying relevant as a participant in a dynamic profession.

HORS D'OEUVRES AND ENTRÉES

Library and Information Science Schools

Education, training, and continuous learning are vital to the process of becoming and staying relevant as a librarian or information professional. Many of the websites that offer information about "becoming a librarian" suggest workshops, online courses, or other continuing education opportunities for practicing information professionals. For those who are considering entering or starting out in the field, particular training through educational or school media specialist certification programs or through a master's degree from a library/information studies program, preferably one that is accredited by the American Library Association (ALA), are suggested. The case for an ALA-accredited master's degree is compelling, I think, as the first step in *becoming* an information professional and in acquiring knowledge, skills, and a philosophy or work ethic for staying relevant professionally. The ALA Office for Accreditation responds to the question "Why should I go to an accredited program?" by offering the following observation: "Graduating from an ALA-accredited program provides greater flexibility in the types of libraries and jobs you can apply for and enhances your career mobility [since] most employers require an ALA-accredited master's for most professional level positions and some states require an ALA-accredited degree to work as a professional librarian in public or school libraries."

Yet obtaining the master's degree or other certification is just the beginning. This becomes apparent to most information professionals within a few months (if not sooner) after graduating, when they go out on the job and find that what was learned in library school has changed or been surpassed by new methods or technologies, or that skills needed on the job are not something they necessarily learned about in their library/information science school program. Faculty members in many reputable programs recognize this and teach students about the need for lifelong learning. For example, Ann L. O'Neill, former library/information science professor and current director of ALA's Office for Accreditation, writes about telling her students that the degree is "just the beginning of their education in librarianship. As such, they should think of [it] as an hors d'oeuvre that whets their appetite for more knowledge . . . not the end of a student's education, but the beginning of lifelong learning about librarianship." O'Neill reflects, "So if the M.L.I.S. is the appetizer, what's for dinner? And who is responsible for serving and preparing the main entrée of continuing education?"[3] She goes on to consider the role that American schools of library and information science play in continuing education.

Indeed, many library and information science schools offer vigorous continuing education programs on campus or through distance education, including online coursework using the Internet. For example, at the beginning of each new academic year, the library at which I work (which, coincidentally, is in a state that does not have an ALA-accredited library school program) receives brochures from several programs that offer courses and/or workshops that can be taken online. Several people at our library have updated their skills by enrolling in courses or workshops offered through such programs. Others have benefited from more in-depth coursework that has permitted them to pursue their MLS degrees online. Similarly, Christine Hamilton-Pennell, in her article "Getting Ahead by Getting Online," interviews several information professionals who have made creative use of the Internet to pursue professional goals through online education. She discusses many of the perceived pros and cons of online education and cites additional sources for "getting online." One of the key advantages to online learning is that many of the programs offer learning experiences that can be tailored to fit within the demands of a busy work schedule and home life. Online courses are valuable for gaining new skills, for staying abreast of ongoing trends and developments, for learning new methodologies and technologies to benefit the workplace, or simply to stimulate new thoughts and ideas for approaching your work more creatively.

While ongoing education and training, be it in a classroom or a workshop or online, is important for staying up to date, the library and/or information center, in tandem with the daily events of our professional lives, can be construed as a classroom in that there are a great many practical learning opportunities in our day-to-day work that are part of "main dish" librarianship and that offer endless possibilities for staying relevant with what we do in a quotidian sense.

WORKING RELEVANCE

"When I was younger I believed that by age forty-five or fifty I'd have mastered my craft, so to speak, and would have little left to learn. Instead, I have to work very hard to keep up with changes, in fact it's far more difficult than learning to become a librarian ever was. However, I'm grateful for the constantly changing workplace because I'm never, ever bored" — (Toni Lohman, collection management librarian, Virginia Beach Department of Public Libraries, quoted by GraceAnne A. DeCandido).

The Relevance of Professional Organizations

Montrese Hamilton and Joan O'Kane note on their website, the *Librarians' Career Manifesto*, that "professional development is so important that a commitment to continuous learning is stipulated in the codes of ethics of several professional associations." Indeed, many professional associations have goals and missions that are tailored to specialized needs or skill sets within the profession, depending on the career path that one follows or the region that one works in. Many state or regional library associations offer conferences or provide continuing education opportunities in their respective geographical areas. Other associations exist to provide forums for exchanging information or addressing concerns related to a particular specialty or area of work within the profession. For example, the Music Library Association, the Medical Library Association, American Association of Law Libraries, the North American Serials Interest Group, the Online Audiovisual Catalogers (OLAC), and the Society of American Archivists are examples of associations that offer resources, services, publications, conferences, and other tools for continuing education that serve the specialized interests of their members.

The vitality and relevance of professional associations depends on the participation of active, engaged members. To that end, professional associations offer many opportunities for members to become involved. Attending an association's conference or workshop is one way to stimulate thinking and ideas and to grow professionally. Volunteering to give a workshop or offer a presentation at a conference about a topic or area that interests you or that you've found to be particularly effective in your work setting, not only provides a greater opportunity for in-depth learning, it is also a great way to engage and connect with colleagues and peers who share similar professional interests. What better way to get up to date about a topic that interests you than to build on your current knowledge by preparing a presentation . . . or by writing an article? Many organizations send out calls for presentations or papers several months prior to their conferences. Indeed, many articles in library and information science literature begin with presentations or workshops and develop into formal publications.

Other ways to become involved in the activities of professional organizations include volunteering to serve on a committee or offering to stand as a candidate for an elected governance position within the organization. Working in committee and group structures permits opportunities for collaboration, developing interpersonal communication skills, and working toward common goals. The exchange of ideas and perspectives that take place in such groups permits cross-fertilization of experience and promotes professional enrichment while advancing the mission of the group, the association, and the profession as a whole. Being involved professionally enables us to develop a professional network of colleagues as well as greater awareness and understanding of what the major issues and concerns are and how we can react collectively to address them. Such engagement also permits us at the local level to move forward in our work in a more informed manner, knowing that we do not work in isolation but are part of a professional whole.

Organizational Relevance

How can you stay relevant at the institutional or organizational level? That is, at the place where you work? It is always a good idea before accepting a job to ask a potential employer whether or not they encourage or support professional development and/or what they can offer to help you keep your skills up to date. It is normal for employers to expect staff to keep pace with change and to master new tools and resources needed to work effectively. How much help or support are they willing to offer for continuing education, training opportunities, travel to professional conferences, and so on? If you move around much, through different organizations, you will probably find that circumstances vary from place to place. Many employers offer release time and/or varying levels of financial support to attend classes, workshops, and conferences or to pursue professional goals. Some employers may be equipped to offer continuing education opportunities in-house. For example, the University of Vermont has an innovative Training and Development program that offers employees the opportunity to enhance skills and enrich their work through a variety of special events, certificate programs, and classes (e.g., budget and financing, stress management, communications and customer services, computing and technology, health and safety, leadership, supervision and management skills, etc.).

Just as commitments to professional development and continuous learning are stipulated in the codes of ethics of several professional associations, many libraries and information centers stipulate codes of continuous learning as a condition of employment. It is not uncommon, particularly in the academic library sector, to expect (if not require for reappointment and promotion) that librarians, in addition to their "regular" library responsibilities, participate actively in professional service activities at the local, regional, or national levels. Such activities might include committee or task force work or other sorts of collaborative involvement, as well as research or publication. Such expectations should be clearly presented when a position is offered and can be thought of as a challenge and an opportunity that gives incentive to think creatively about your current skills and knowledge and where you can make professional contributions.

A commitment to professional development through active engagement has benefits for both the organization (employer) and the individual. The knowledge and skills of the individual are constantly being updated and expanded, while the organization benefits from the abilities of professionals who are knowledgeable and up to date in the latest issues, trends, and technologies needed to do their jobs well and to realize organizational goals. Innovative service and research also reflects well on the organization that supports it. Good employers recognize this and encourage employees to stay relevant by continually updating their knowledge and skills through professional engagement.

When I was in library school, I remember one of my professors offering a few words of friendly advice to a group of us soon-to-be-minted students about what to look for as we began searching for our first or "early career" professional position. She said, "*Look for an organization that has goals and a mission that most clearly matches your personal goals and mission.*" That advice still holds true. Finding the right organizational and individual mix will result in a harmonious blend of action, ideas, and motivation for tuning into mutual goals and staying relevant to overall personal and organizational missions.

Online Relevance

The Internet has revolutionized the way that librarians and informational professionals conduct their work. Its development over the last decade or so can serve as a metaphorical timeline for the advent of technological change and how it comes to bear on our work as librarians. In the late 1980s and early 1990s, when I was starting out as a librarian, the Internet was just a speck on the horizon and not part of most librarians' everyday repertoire. It was not something that my generation learned about in library school. I was not exposed to e-mail technology until 1990, after graduating from library school, when my employer gave me a BITNET account and sent me to a workshop to learn how to use it. Gopher and text-based web tools came along subsequently and we marveled. Beginning in 1993, I remember my excitement when we were given computers that provided a graphical interface to the World Wide Web using Mosaic, one of the early (now obsolete) web browsers. Today, I cannot imagine working in a library or information center without e-mail or Internet access . . . or what would have happened to my career had I, or the systems people at my workplace, failed to keep pace with the burgeoning array of Internet technologies that have now become so commonplace in our jobs.

I have already discussed some of the ways in which people are using the Internet to hone skills by taking courses or workshops online. Today, e-mail, along with Internet discussion lists and websites containing information from or about virtually every conceivable aspect of human knowledge, are integral to the way we communicate. The Internet exists as a primary tool for finding and delivering information, and keeping up to date professionally. Publishers, professional associations, scholars, and individuals are now putting their latest documentation and publications on the Web. Many associations are discontinuing printed distribution of their newsletters and journals in favor of providing them on the Web—either for free or through password-protected sites that require a membership affiliation for access. Many of the printed indexes that we used to find information in periodicals and journals have now become databases that are available only online. We, as information professionals, use the Internet daily to locate more and more of the reference tools needed for our work. Becoming familiar with a reliable web browser and one or more of the major Internet search engines (e.g., Google, AltaVista, AlltheWeb) and knowing how to use these tools effectively to locate information and resources for our jobs is crucial to maintaining professional relevance.

In addition to the Web, many Internet discussion groups have developed as "online communities" where informational professionals "meet" around particular interests or themes that are relevant to their work. Participants use such forums to regularly exchange thoughts, ideas, and perspectives, or to offer advice, or simply to read and maintain current awareness of the latest professional developments and trends in their areas of interest. Engaging in such forums enables participants to "meet" or to network with colleagues with similar interests to discuss issues, to ask questions, and to solve problems. Such lists may also be useful for monitoring job announcements from employers interested in recruiting someone with expertise or interest in a particular area covered by the scope or parameters of the list's discussion content.[4] Even if you are not in the market for a new job, monitoring Internet discussion lists for job postings or surfing the Web for job sites can provide information about what skills employers are looking for and what areas of expertise are relevant in the current job market. Indeed, you may find that some employers now only accept applications for employment online.

Knowing how to effectively use e-mail and the Internet to reach colleagues and to navigate the Web and various reference tools that are offered there is now central to the ways in which we communicate, collaborate, and provide quality services to our constituents.

SELF-EVALUATION: TAKING STOCK

In the course of our day-to-day work, dealing with a hectic schedule and many demands, it is natural to get caught up using tools and services that are already familiar to us to focus on tasks or projects that need to be completed, rather than to think about taking in more information to expand our skills. Yet every now and then, it is worth taking the time to step back and to evaluate where you are, where you are going, and whether or not you need to shift focus or change direction. The SOCAP (Society of Customer Affairs Professionals) website offers some useful advice for gauging where you are in your career and thinking about steps you can take to improve or to grow professionally. Their "Four Tips to Staying Relevant to Your Work" can be applied to librarians and information professionals:

> Take an honest look at your worth. Once a year, evaluate your competence and skills. If they don't match what's in demand in the market, determine how and where you need to improve. Use performance evaluations to help direct you.
>
> Stay on top of technical skills. Make sure you're competent on basic applications and have a command of available technology (the Internet and communication devices, to name a few) to make you more efficient. Stay abreast of technological change by reading relevant [print and online] publications.
>
> Make skills upgrading a priority. That means accepting lifelong learning as a principle. Take classes online, go back to school, attend a . . . conference or take continuing education classes that are applicable to your job—or to the [job] you want.

Interview your boss. Make sure you know where the company [or organization] is heading and whether your goals and the company's [or organization's] goals are in sync.

Keeping an open mind and maintaining a positive, upbeat attitude, thinking about what skills you have and where you can make contributions, or about new areas that interest you and how you might adapt current skills to meet demands in other areas are also ways of evaluating competencies in relation to where you are and whether or not you want to change course.

THERE ARE NO LIMITS TO LEARNING

The library connects us with the insight and knowledge, painfully extracted from Nature, of the greatest minds that ever were, with the best teachers, drawn from the entire planet and from all our history, to instruct us without tiring, and to inspire us to make our own contribution to the collective knowledge of the human species. I think the health of our civilization, the depth of our awareness about the underpinnings of our culture and our concern for the future can all be tested by how well we support our libraries.

—Carl Sagan in *Cosmos*

This chapter has attempted to touch on some of the ways in which a code of lifelong learning is central to the idea of staying relevant. Continuing education, professional engagement through service and volunteerism, reading professional literature, keeping up with technological changes, staying connected to colleagues, and developing interpersonal skills to work collaboratively are all important. When all is said and done, however, I believe that the key to staying relevant is most closely tied to attitude and the idea of approaching work with active interest and enthusiasm, as well as an inherent faith and belief in the value of what you do.

In her article "New Jobs for Old: Librarians Now," GraceAnne A. DeCandido "focuses on an issue that challenges the entire profession—how to help seasoned professionals stay current with their skills while integrating the talent and fresh perspective of a new generation."[5] DeCandido compiles and synthesizes the professional profiles of seven librarians who describe how they came into librarianship and how they have kept pace with increasing technological demands. She writes:

Over and over again, in the interviews with librarians that form the basis for this publication, they said that while the form of their work had indeed changed, the substance remained the same. Tools metamorphosed, but the ancient tasks of access, service, organization, and preservation remained. . . . Librarians see the vast changes in the workplace reflected in changes in their personal lives. There are many new professional titles, but librarians old and new, no matter how they described their jobs, strongly adhered to the basic ethos of librarianship, that of connecting people with ideas.

In considering a similar European model, the French term "*documentaliste*" refers to a category of information or research professionals who organize and provide access to information in general and specific subject areas.[6] Jean Michel, past president of the French ADBS (*Association des professionnels de l'information et de la documentation*), reflects that the origins of the term "*documentaliste*" come from the Latin, "*docere*," which means "to teach." He further reflects that the information-documentation profession exists in order to help society progress, develop, and be innovative; to help average individuals expand their knowledge and expertise[7] — much like any good teacher helps their students to learn, to develop, and to make contributions to society.

Libraries are wondrous places in that their collections and their services open doors and connections for individuals to the vast world of knowledge and information. In making recorded knowledge and information available and in giving assistance in locating and using that knowledge and information, libraries and librarians are making an immense contribution to democracy and social progress.[8] Just as libraries exist to offer access to information and knowledge, librarians are trained in a service tradition of helping people to find the information they seek to connect to ideas that help them and the society that they live in develop and evolve. We owe it to ourselves and our profession to maintain that perspective of service toward ourselves by taking the time to enable our own connections to new ideas and new professional knowledge as a means of staying vital and relevant to what we do — and to what we help others to do.

NOTES

1. Priscilla Shontz, "Career Planning," in *Jump Start Your Career in Library and Information Science* (Lanham, Md.: Scarecrow Press, 2002), 19–22.

2. Personal translation. Silvie Delorme writes in French, "*Apriamo le finestre! Que l'esprit et le souffle du changement, de la transformation et de la vie s'engouffrent au coeur de notre travail.*"

3. Ann L. O'Neill, "What's for Dinner? Continuing Education after the M.L.I.S," *Library Acquisitions: Practice & Theory* 22, no. 1 (Spring 1998): 35.

4. Two useful directories for locating Internet discussion lists that are of interest to librarians, scholars, and other professionals for use in their scholarly, pedagogical, and professional activities include *Library-Oriented Lists & Electronic Serials* (lib-

lists.wrlc.org/home.htm), compiled by Wei Wu at the Washington Research Library Consortium, and *The Directory of Scholarly and Professional E-Conferences* (www.kovacs.com/directory/), compiled by Diane Kovacs and the Directory Team at Kovacs Consulting (last accessed 12 September 2003).

5. DeEtta Jones, "Editor's Note," *Leading Ideas* 14 (May 2000). www.arl.org/diversity/leading/issue14/ednote.html (last accessed 5 June 2003).

6. *Le Petit Larousse illustré* (1998); for more in-depth discussion of how the term is evolving, see the debate at Le Centre National de Documentation (CND) "Débat: Définition d'un documentaliste?" (3 September 2002). webzinecnd.mpep.gov.ma/article.php3?id_article=68 (last accessed 12 September 2003).

7. Personal translation. Jean Michel writes in French, *"On fait de la documentation pour aider la société à progresser, à se développer, à innover, pour aider les individus simples citoyens ou professionnels à faire évoluer leur savoir, leurs compétences."*

8. Michael Gorman elaborates on this point in "Some Thoughts on Borders," his closing remarks at the X. Transborder Library Forum (25 March 2000). www.unm.edu/~foro/gorman_eng.html (last accessed 22 September 2003).

RELATED READINGS

American Library Association. Office for Accreditation. "Accreditation: Frequently Asked Questions" (see response to question: "Why should I go to an accredited program?"). www.ala.org/ala/accreditation/accredfaq/faq.htm#q2 (last accessed 17 May 2004).

Braun, Linda W. "New Roles: A Librarian by Any Name." *Library Journal* (1 February 2002): 109. libraryjournal.reviewsnews.com/index.asp?layout=articlePrint&articleID=CA191647 (last accessed 3 September 2003).

Central Jersey Regional Library Cooperative. "Become a Librarian!" www.becomealibrarian.org (last accessed 2 September 2003).

Crosby, Olivia. "Librarians: Information Experts in the Information Age." *Occupational Outlook Quarterly Online* (Winter 2000–2001): 2. stats.bls.gov/opub/ooq/2000/Winter/art01.pdf (last accessed 3 September 2003).

DeCandido, GraceAnne A. "New Jobs for Old: Librarians Now." *Leading Ideas* 14 (May 2000). www.arl.org/diversity/leading/issue14/newjobs.html (last accessed 5 June 2003).

Delorme, Silvie. "Apriamo le finestre!" *Corpo Clip: Le bulletin des Bibliothécaires Professionels du Québec*, n° 155 (mai à juillet 2003): 1.

Gorman, Michael. "Some Thoughts on Borders." Closing remarks given at the X. FORO, Transborder Library Forum: Beyond Our Borders: Interconnections, Albuquerque, New Mexico, 25 March 2000. www.unm.edu/~foro/gorman_eng.html (last accessed 22 September 2003).

Hamilton, Montrese, and Joan O'Kane. "Librarians' Career Manifesto—Professional Development." slis.cua.edu/ihy/sp2000/job/prodev.htm (last accessed 1 June 2003).

Hamilton-Pennell, Christine. "Getting Ahead by Getting Online." *Library Journal* (15 November 2002): 32–35.

Michel, Jean. "Formation, coopération et développement professionnel: la documentation en Roumanie" [this interview with Jean Michel—former president of the ADBS l'Association des professionnels de l'information et de la documentation in France—was originally written by Nicoleta Marinescu in October 1998 for the Romanian library science journal *Bibliotéca,* no. 12 (1998): 381–84]. michel.jean.free.fr/publi/JM313.html (last accessed 18 May 2004).

O'Neill, Ann L. "What's for Dinner? Continuing Education after the M.L.I.S." *Library Acquisitions: Practice & Theory* 22, no. 1 (Spring 1998): 35–40.

Shontz, Priscilla. *Jump Start Your Career in Library and Information Science.* Lanham, Md.: Scarecrow Press, 2002.

SOCAP (Society of Customer Affairs Professionals). "Four Tips to Staying Relevant to Your Work." www.socap.org/Publications/Quicktakes/stayrelev.html (last accessed 1 June 2003).

Vaill, Peter B. *Learning as a Way of Being: Strategies for Survival in a World of Permanent White Water.* San Francisco: Jossey-Bass, 1996.

ABOUT THE AUTHOR

Birdie MacLennan is library associate professor and coordinator of serials and cataloging at the Bailey/Howe Library, University of Vermont. She is founder of the SERIALST Internet discussion forum, an informal cyber-venue that addresses serials and continuing resources in libraries. As list-owner and moderator, she continues to maintain this forum for an international constituency of librarians, publishers, vendors, and other interested "serialists." She holds an MS from Simmons Graduate School of Library and Information Science in Boston. She is currently a candidate in the MA Program in French at the University of Vermont where she is researching the comparative cultural and historical contexts of public library systems in the state of Vermont and the neighboring province of Québec.

38

From Acorn to Oak: Transforming a Novice into an Expert

Carol Anne Germain

As you start a new job with your recently earned library degree in hand, you'll find plenty of possibilities for professional growth. Like the acorn that matures into a strong oak, you too will branch out and, over time, become an expert librarian. The steps to this destination may be set at your own pace or generated by job requirements. Often, tenure and promotions require demonstration of excellence in librarianship, service, and scholarship. Certainly, you will not be expected to write a book within the first year of your professional life, but you will need to be productive, and writing that book may come sooner than expected!

One of the joys of librarianship is the exchange of ideas, tips, practices, and theories with others in the profession. In your new career many opportunities will arise that allow you to share your invaluable experiences. If you are in a tenure or promotion-track position, you may need to publish, deliver presentations, and/or participate in professional organizations. Even if these are not requirements of your job, you will find yourself drawn to some or all of these activities to share your knowledge with other librarians. By engaging in professional activities, librarians get to share their expertise and during this process they grow. At first, this process may not seem very intuitive; however, you will discover that if you are resourceful, organized, attentive, and network carefully, your hard work will flourish.

GETTING STARTED

In the earlier stages of your career, you may find yourself overwhelmed with many of your routine assignments. You may wonder, "*How* am I ever going to be able to do more professionally if I cannot keep up with my regular work?" Surprisingly enough, after several months you will grow more comfortable in your new position and be ready to embrace new professional adventures and branch out.

As a new librarian you will be given plenty of work projects. Depending on your area of specialization, these may vary greatly. An instruction librarian may develop an information literacy program, a manuscripts librarian might produce a PowerPoint presentation highlighting finding aids for a rare collection, a business bibliographer could design a library exhibit at "frustrating tax time," a government documents bibliographer may initiate the creation of an interactive website for using government publications. Often, once completed, projects like these find their way to the back of a filing cabinet, are lost on a floppy disk, or are stowed away on a web server.

STOP!

WASTE NOT, WANT NOT

Instead of packing these projects and *your hard work* away, a better strategy is to take the time to develop them a little further. That information literacy program might be perfect for a best practices seminar, the PowerPoint presentation is an excellent outline for an article or the foundation for a local workshop, the tax exhibit could be the start of a poster session for a regional conference, and that government documents website might be award-winning instructional material. Poster sessions and PowerPoint presentations are outlines of your ideas. Take these and write articles. You might have to organize additional research, conduct a literature review, and develop the idea further for publication, but it is worth the time because you do not have to start from scratch. Remember, the oak sapling needs to stretch its branches to grow into a strong oak.

STRETCH!

Your resourcefulness in turning small projects into bigger successes will make the steps of your professional growth much easier. While a project may *seem* to be completed, your energy in expanding and further developing its content is not only vital for you to produce more, but it also offers you the chance to learn more about your library specialization. This wisdom will enable you to become the library expert you want to be.

CHARTING YOUR PLAN

Even though librarians are often described as compulsively organized, it seems that this trait is not always followed when guiding our careers. While it may seem overly obsessive to map out your professional aspirations and log your professional accomplishments, this process will help keep you focused. Start by laying out a multiyear plan and review it every six months or so to make sure you are on target. The plan will include library-assigned projects, as well as publishing, speaking, and service endeavors. Here is a sample plan a new reference librarian might draft:

Year #1
- Inventory current reference collection
- Review library literature for articles on weeding reference
- Subscribe to reference discussion list—participate
- Review reference books and databases for library publication(s)
- Assess peer-library reference collection development statements
- Update current reference collection development statement
- Weed current reference collection
- Present poster session on reference weeding project at local conference
- Outline research project comparing print/electronic reference sources
- Set up methodology
- Survey reference librarians at peer-institutions
- Conduct literature review
- Join reference section of state/regional library association

Year #2
- Attend conference/meetings of library association reference section
- Ask for "working roles" with the library association reference section
- Implement plan for updating and maintaining reference collection
- Compose grant for print/electronic reference source comparison
- Design library exhibit highlighting reference sources
- Write article about current reference weeding tips (use poster session)
- Begin research for print/electronic reference source comparison
- Produce print reference finding aids
- Coordinate a "reference" panel for the library association reference section

Year #3
- Create website for electronic reference collection
- Write and submit print/electronic reference source comparison article
- Present research (from article) at state library conference
- Run for an official position on the reference section of library association
- Code and mount print reference finding aids on the Web
- Analyze and report on current condition of the reference collection

After reviewing this plan, you will notice that many of the activities listed overlap. Several build upon each other; for example, the work project on weeding the reference collection provided the knowledge and opportunity for presenting a poster session at a conference. Then the poster session was turned into a publishable article. Though not listed, this initiative could be further developed into a workshop to be presented at regional library councils or systems. If you strategize well enough, you will find that your in-library and out-of-library professional activities combine your energies to create a well-rounded professional experience.

This charting out helps with the larger scope of your career goals, but you will also want to be organized at a microlevel. Too often we accomplish many noteworthy undertakings and then overlook documenting them. A good technique to avoid this is to routinely log your completed projects. Jot down items in a notebook, create an electronic file, or keep a folder with copies of activity-related handouts. If you work at a library that requires an annual employee update, this system will be invaluable. Otherwise, these records can be used when updating your resume or curriculum vitae.

These organizational skills will be beneficial in administering projects and preparing speeches, publications, and the like. They will allow you to concentrate on the more important aspects of your endeavors, such as content. These practices will help you feel more comfortable with the processes and build your self-confidence.

OVERLOOKING OPPORTUNITIES

It would be wonderful if librarians were born with an instinct for building their careers; however, we usually are not. To create a rich and full professional life you will need to pay attention to the surrounding library world. This is where you will pick up on opportunities to advance your career. Join discussion lists and participate in ongoing conversations. Lists regularly post calls for presentations, publications, and other professional activities. You need not jump on the first posting, but keep an eye out for calls that engage your interests. If nothing provocative shows up—*go out and find opportunity yourself!*

Browse through professional library journals and select a few that you would like to publish in. If you do not want to start off with writing articles, look into the possibility of writing book and software reviews. If you are still a little timid about writing, ask a colleague to coauthor; in the process you will learn the ropes of publication.

For presentation opportunities you will need to investigate upcoming conferences. Library organizations regularly sponsor conferences and provide details on their websites. If these are not enough, contact the chair or president of the organization for more details. Make sure you have a few topic ideas to discuss. You do not need to have a completed presentation, and in fact it is highly suggested not to, but you should have the basics so you can negotiate a proposal.

If your "career plan" includes grant writing possibilities you, will want some experience in this area. To get a behind-the-scenes glimpse of this process, hook up with an awards/grant committee. You can also sign up to be a member of ALA's award jury panel. These will provide experience with reviewing applications for specific awards/grants, and you will learn many of the dos and don'ts of the process. There's plenty of opportunity in the library environment. *ASK! ASK! ASK!*

Even if you have found the right venue for authoring or presenting, you may find yourself without a topic to write or speak about. Many new librarians are unsure about what to present. If you are attentive, the possibilities will be innumerable. At first, your work projects will generate ideas to share. As you start to research, write, and present, other themes will arise. The more you explore a particular topic, the more you will discover gaps and intricacies in your area. For example, while researching the stability of web resources in other library catalogs, the question of missing book statistics may arise. In reviewing the literature you will find little research in this area, and thus, the seed of your next paper is started. Or, while delivering a presentation on marketing libraries, a member of the audience may point out that there is a void in marketing special libraries. When you return home, you can explore this further. If you are still at a loss, a good fallback strategy is to look at library issues that irk you—themes of my research are often derived from my motto: "What drives me nuts drives my research!" By investigating these areas, you might discover solutions to share with others in the profession.

NETWORKING

An important aspect in your career will be the service component of librarianship. Joining and participating in library organizations will help you accomplish this criterion. Again, start small; you do not have to run for the presidency of the American Library Association! Instead, begin by taking part in a local, regional, or state organization or, if you prefer a national presence, begin with one of their committees, sections, or roundtables.

Select a library group that shares your library career interests. Since you have some background in the area, the learning curve will be smaller and you will build on your knowledge base. If you choose a group with differing interests, you may find yourself disinterested. An archivist might feel very out of place at a catalogers' roundtable, yet if he were looking to learn to personally catalog some of his collection, this might be a boon! Choose carefully to make sure it's a good fit for you.

After you join an association, attend regular meetings so you get a feel for the association's culture. Once you've gotten your feet wet, you can actively take on organizational projects. These activities will allow you to learn more about the organization and the library field. Select initiatives that spark your interests; if you detest asking others for money, the donations committee will be a poor fit. If you have chosen well, you will find that many of these projects will turn into larger professional endeavors and, as earlier noted, overlap with work-related activities. You should regularly review where you are with these professional organizations. At these times you can decide whether it is appropriate to take on more challenging roles within the organization or stay put. Most likely, you will find yourself reaching for more exciting responsibilities, and ultimately you may run for an official position.

One of the key benefits of joining an organization is not the projects you will add to your resume or curriculum vitae, the continuing education sessions in which you will participate, or the conferences you will attend, but the people you will meet. These personal contacts will provide career advice, give direction, discuss library issues, and, at conferences, recommend the best places to eat! It will be these people who help to guide your professional career. These will be the librarians who proof your articles, watch a run-through of a presentation, recommend you as a consultant, or coauthor that book! They will also be helpful with day-to-day library decisions. You will call or e-mail these individuals for suggestions on purchasing subscription databases, drafting policy statements, or weeding collections. These people will be your cheerleaders—encouraging you throughout your new professional experience. Take advantage of their expertise; they will be your best mentors.

CONCLUSION

Like the acorn, you will start small, but with thoughtful planning, motivation, and spunk, you too will grow professionally to a mighty height. Along the way you need to acknowledge your accomplishments: Reward yourself regularly! These treats do not have to be extravagant but help affirm your hard work and success. As the oak needs water, sunshine, air, and fertilizer to grow strong, you also need nourishment to thrive.

ACKNOWLEDGMENT

This article is the combination of work presented at three State University of New York Librarians Association (SUNYLA) annual conferences: "Getting

Tenure: Making the Most Out of What You Do" (2001); "The Dreaded Dossier: Making it Less Painful" (2002); and "Do the Write Thing!" (2003). These workshops were initiated as a part of my role as chair of the SUNYLA Professional Development Committee, which I discovered because I presented a poster session at the 1999 annual conference. I was appointed to this position because I had served on the University at Albany Libraries' Staff Development and Training Committee. *Get the picture?*

ABOUT THE AUTHOR

Carol Anne Germain received her MLS from the University at Albany in 1997. She is currently the networked resources education librarian at the same institution. This position includes reference, bibliographic instruction and information literacy, and development of Web-based instruction tools. She has written numerous publications, including refereed journal articles, book chapters, book reviews, and nonrefereed articles.

39

Flamed! The Burned-Out Librarian

Zahra M. Baird

Find yourself complaining that your work is just not fun anymore? Feeling irritable constantly? These days, does a smile hardly ever touch your face? Do you dread answering the next reference question that you will be asked? Do you worry about not knowing the answers to your patrons' questions? Do you jump and does your heart race every time the phone rings? Are you overre-acting to minor hassles, feeling terribly overwhelmed and worried? Or are you feeling lethargic and empty in your work? If you are no longer getting job satisfaction and are questioning the value of the tasks you perform, chances are that you are flamed, a.k.a. burned out.

ALL FIRED UP: BURNOUT DEFINED

According to New York psychologist Herbert J. Freudenberger, who in the early 1970s coined the term, "burned" is a state of fatigue or frustration brought about by the devotion to a cause, a way of life, or a relationship that failed to produce the expected reward.

Social psychologist Christina Maslach's definition of burnout as a multi-faceted state of emotional, physical, and mental exhaustion caused by chronic stress occurring when helping-professionals experience long-term involve-ment with other people in emotionally demanding situations stemmed from her people-oriented, helping-professions research. Her definition is most ap-plicable to the library profession.

There are two types of stress, *eustress* and *distress*. Positive stress (*eustress*) happens when you are in control of your stress, whereas negative stress (*distress*) occurs when your stress is out of control. If you find yourself experiencing cumulative, increased amounts of negative workplace stress, which can lead to the experiencing of a heightened sense of failure and a devastating loss of self-esteem and self-confidence, then beware: you could be headed for burnout.

SMOKE SIGNALS: BURNOUT SYMPTOMS

There are many indicators that you might be burned out, or on the road to burnout. Symptoms can range from physical manifestations such as headaches, nausea, weight gain, and insomnia to mental ailments including depression to emotional indicators including detachment, inability to concentrate, and boredom to social symptoms, like rudeness and feelings of isolation from colleagues or the library profession.

Warning signals that you are headed toward burnout (or are burned out) can include any of the following:

* Excessive absenteeism and frequent tardiness
* Decreased job performance and a poor attitude
* Feeling a lack of control over your commitments
* Tendency of thinking extremely negatively
* Loss of energy and focus, coupled with an unclear sense of purpose
* Increase in feelings of detachment from all relationships
* Feeling of alienation and deep cynicism
* Believing (incorrectly) that you are achieving less

When we are in the process of burning out, it can be difficult for us to identify the symptoms in ourselves. Often, we simply miss the warning signals. Until we become more vigilant, our friends, family, and colleagues are more likely to identify and recognize us as potential burnout candidates.

FACTORS THAT AFFECT OUR POTENTIAL FOR BURNOUT

The very nature of our work predisposes us to burnout. What is normalcy in our profession as far as workdays go? A normal workday can be described as a continuous round of interruptions. As the demands for our services (including reference questions and reader's advisory) roll in, we must focus ourselves on finding the answers and setting aside whatever else we have been working on. These incessant breaks in our day interrupt the flow of our concentration and make it hard for us to complete our work tasks. The repetitive nature of library work does not help either. The monotony and boredom of doing things over and over again makes us prime candidates for burnout.

In *Stress and Burnout in Library Services*, Janette S. Caputo (1991) identifies many work-related stressors, which are highly correlated with job burnout. Stressors include: budget cuts, educating away from librarian stereotypes, the quick response time to reference questions, censorship issues, heavy workloads, the overload of clerical duties, poor management and supervision, technology-related problems, the lack of time for (and no voice in) collection development duties, the lack of closure for ongoing projects, a shift in priorities, low pay, obnoxious public/patrons, and few opportunities for advancement.

Judith A. Siess (2002), in her book *Time Management, Planning, and Prioritization for Librarians*, tells us that overwork is the primary cause of burnout. Regardless of our job title, as budgets shrink and expectations rise, we are finding ourselves having to do more with less. We have gotten ourselves into the habit of accepting more and more work without having any of our duties reassigned or hiring more staff. When overloaded, we just can't seem to bring ourselves to stand up and say "No!"

Some of us have only to look at our own work habits and beliefs when it comes to burnout. Sometimes the source of stress can lie within us. Highly idealistic people, those of us who are perfectionists, people who overcommit, others who are single-minded, and people who have not set up a personal support network tend to kindle the burnout fire.

Many of us are experiencing high levels of role conflict in our current positions. We are being given conflicting responsibilities, which in turn are pulling us in too many different directions. When we pay attention to everything equally without setting priorities, then burnout is inevitable. Another cause of burnout is role ambiguity. Many of us don't have a clear-cut job description, so we don't exactly know what is expected from us, or we lack positive role models and mentors. Other possible work factors include a lack of autonomy; our constant, and more often than not, draining dealings with the public; receiving little or no positive feedback/praise from our supervisors; and experiencing decreased chances for professional/personal advancement.

Who you are (your personality), where you work (your job environment, physical setup, as well as bureaucracy), and what your job entails (tasks and duties assigned to you) all directly impact your potential for burnout.

FANNING THE FLAMES: DEALING WITH BURNOUT

So the fire is already out of control and you are well on your way to, if not already at the point of, burnout. Is there any hope for you? What can you do? Thankfully, there are myriad strategies tried and true that you can use to help get your burnout under control. It is important to note that what works for one person might not work for another. You just have to try different strategies until you reach a more balanced and harmonious existence.

Self-Strategies

Self-strategies are personal strategies that you can use to regain control of your work life. It is of paramount importance to raise your consciousness of work stress. Listen to your body; if you have aches and pains, then those are signals that something is not working for you. Be kind to yourself; slow down. Set realistic limits, and once you do, keep them. By lowering your standards you will be able to lessen the pressure that you put on yourself. Let go and stop being such a perfectionist.

Get to know yourself better by taking stock of your strengths and weaknesses. Be honest with yourself so that you can identify what pressures you. If you know what pushes your buttons, you can refuse to accept or take on undoable jobs. Study how you are using your time by taking inventory on a regular basis. Identify things that you want to spend more time doing and make time for them.

Internalize optimism. This is easier said than done. Your attitude is of paramount importance. You can't change attitudes overnight, but you can work hard to see the silver lining in situations. Regardless of which strategies you decide to try, there must be a reevaluation of your priorities. I found out the hard way that money is not everything. Sometimes it is worth taking a pay cut and/or a lateral change in position in order to work in a less-stressful environment.

Work Strategies

Work strategies are organizational strategies that can help you overcome and manage the stress from your workplace. Developing a detached view of your job so that you don't take things personally can really help with reducing the chronic stress that leads to burnout. Taking a stress inventory to identify key areas of your work life that generate stress is a starting point. After identifying what portions of your job cause the most stress, you can start to do something about them. Learning to compartmentalize, especially leaving your work at work when the day is done, is essential.

If at all possible, figuring out how to adapt your present job to better reflect your interests and actively seeking out challenges can help with feelings of boredom. Pace yourself; don't rush around like a chicken without a head. Whatever you don't get done today can get done tomorrow; that is why it's called tomorrow! Believe it or not, the world will not come to a dead standstill if you don't catalog that book or respond to that last e-mail reference question. Work hard and steadily, but when it is time to go, be *gone*.

Don't be one of those people who never takes any time off. Never under-estimate the value of vacation! Don't skimp on vacations; take the days that you are entitled to, regardless of whether or not you travel or stay home. Don't forget to use your sick days when you get sick, use your complete lunch hour, and take those short breaks. The time away will help your mind clear, and you will get a mini-boost from having a small break.

Professional Solutions

Sometimes you need to get outside help in order to get back on track after ex-periencing burnout. A good psychologist can help deal with feelings of de-motivation and disenchantment with your job and your life. A life coach can help you set up a wellness plan that will help you revitalize, recharge, and re-plenish inner energies that were depleted due to burnout. Focusing on exer-cise can work wonders on burnout and stress reduction. I made the investment of hiring a personal trainer at my local gym six months ago. Let me tell you, the payoff is phenomenal. Thanks to Frank's great fitness program, my mind is clearer, I feel better about myself, and the physical workout helps to ease any tension or stress that I accumulate during the day.

Professional library associations are a wonderful source of support and mentoring and can offer many voluntary opportunities to cultivate and use your unique talents and skills. Getting professionally active if you are not ac-tive, and tempering your involvement if you are overinvolved, can really change your course if you are on the road to burnout. Many professional or-ganizations offer continuing education courses on topics like stress manage-ment, time management, and skill building that can help to alleviate stress.

DOUSING THE FLAMES: HOW I
GO ABOUT PREVENTING BURNOUT

Burnout is a process, and during this process we can recognize symptoms and take the necessary steps to prevent it—the first step being to stop denying that we are exhibiting burnout symptoms. Awareness and admitting that we are in danger of burning out is key to recovery. Finding a sense of fulfillment in your work can prevent burnout, so start rekindling your sense of enjoyment one step at a time.

I used to be guilty of allowing my job to invade and literally overtake my life. After traveling to Europe this past spring, the point was driven home for me. While exploring Amsterdam and Paris, I met many interesting people. I always wanted to know what they did for a living and I constantly focused on their work. But they never wanted to know what my job title was or how I earned a living; they were more interested in what I did *outside of work*, what I spent my *free time* doing. For me, this attitude stressed that work is work, but life out of work is important as well. Thanks to my trip experience, I have started to make sure that the world I have created for myself reflects the breadth and depth of *who* I am. It is easy to fall prey to the idea of investing too much of our personal self-image into our jobs. We must quit thinking of ourselves simply as our job titles—in my case, "I AM A LIBRARIAN"—and branch out to investigate and view ourselves from the other roles and interests that we have.

Renewing myself daily, connecting with sources of joy, practicing mindfulness meditation, and developing healthier eating and sleeping habits are all commonplace elements of life that help me slow down and reduce the rate of progression along the path to burnout. Cinematherapy (i.e., going to see movies) is one of my favorite ways of dealing with stress. There is nothing better than watching a movie to temporarily get away from it all. I have found that establishing very attainable short-term and long-term goals in both my personal and professional lives helps me to combat the feelings of hopelessness and helplessness that are the fuel that burnout runs on.

Allowing myself the luxury of having enough *down time*, time I use to reflect and think about things, has made me feel less stressed. When I am on the go constantly, there is little or no time to evaluate and rethink ideas, so my creativity stagnates when I don't take the time to just *be*.

The winter holidays always remind me to take the time to renew my friendships, both personal and professional. The message that *people are more important than things* rings true. Friendships can boost even the saddest heart and create energy. Finding mentors in and out of the profession has helped to nurture and develop my talents and skills. I would not be where I am today without the help and guidance of my many mentors.

I avoid bottling up anger; when feeling upset, hurt, angry, and annoyed, I let it out by journaling, talking out loud, and sometimes speaking to the person with whom I am experiencing difficulty.

When analyzing how I spent my time, I realized that I needed to work on developing better time-management skills and also that I needed to learn how to delegate. Delegating was a very hard thing for me to do, as I am one of those people who have micromanaging tendencies. Giving up control is not always an easy thing to do.

Rediscovering and/or finding my sense of humor is essential in my burnout prevention equation. Laughter can make any situation seem less serious than it really is. Being able to laugh either at yourself or at a situation can help diffuse tension and stress. Not all is lost and nothing seems as bad if we can giggle and see the fun in the situation.

Whenever possible, I create job diversity in my repetitive tasks. By alternating between my assigned tasks, I am breaking up the monotony and allowing for creativity, and there is less of a chance that I will become bored.

PUTTING OUT THE FIRE: RIDDING YOURSELF OF BURNOUT

As hard as it might seem, there comes a time when you have to eliminate and, if necessary, resign from commitments that do not fit in with your goals and abilities. Life is too short to be serving on unpleasant committees, spending time with people who are high maintenance, or engaging in volunteer work that causes chronic stress. There is a certain satisfaction of seeing things that you start through until the end, but enough is enough; know when to cut your losses and simply back away.

There are some instances when job rotation, job switching, retraining, or changing jobs is not possible, so you must basically see with new eyes. Keeping your options open by developing a positive perspective can make all the difference. As the famous saying goes: *Is your glass half-empty or half-full?*

RECLAIMING THE FIRE:
RISING FROM THE ASHES OF BURNOUT

Tired of feeling frustrated? Then give yourself permission to refocus your energies. Be sure to rest, relax, and, above all, resist the temptation of falling into old stress-inducing habits such as taking work home. With readjustment of your goals and aspirations, you will be able to better create balance in your life by investing in family, friends, social activities, and hobbies. Cultivating a taste for the simple pleasures in life will result in your leading a rich, fulfilling life outside of the library. It is important to note that outside pursuits cannot replace job fulfillment. If you have tried many of the burnout strategies listed above and still feel that you are totally burned out, it might be time to look for a new job and/or change careers.

Recognize the differences between building versus sustaining a career. It is easy to embark upon the road to burnout when we are beginning a career; we want to try everything! You don't have to do every big or little thing that comes your way. Weigh options and use your opportunities as stepping-stones. Once you have established a professional reputation, it is time to start strategically selecting the opportunities you choose to accept. When declining opportunities, you can recommend other people for opportunities that don't match your aspirations, talents, and goals. Saying "no" is easier when we can help people find a solution. Giving an alternative person's name will it take some of the guilty feelings we experience away and will help the person who has asked you to participate. You can rise like a phoenix from your burnout experiences if you take the time to investigate why you became flamed and take measures to not only correct but prevent more burnout.

CONCLUSION

Not all stress is bad. *Eustress* from stimulating challenges or circumstances can help you grow. In order to refrain from being flamed, you must become a well-rounded individual by investing time to craft a life outside of work. Burnout is an extreme consequence of workplace stress. Fortunately, burnout can be not only overcome but also prevented. For optimal results, it is imperative that you use your burnout crises as turning points or opportunities for change. Stress and burnout thresholds are different for each person. I urge you to take the tips and strategies covered in this chapter and incorporate those that can keep you from becoming *burned*!

RELATED READINGS

Arden, John B. *Surviving Job Stress: How to Overcome Workday Pressures*. Franklin Lakes, N.J.: Career Press, 2002.

Caputo, Janette S. *Stress and Burnout in Library Service*. Phoenix, Ariz.: Orynx Press, 1991.

Maslach, Christina, and Michael P. Leiter. *The Truth about Burnout: How Organizations Cause Personal Stress and What to Do about It*. San Francisco: Jossey-Bass, 1997.

Sheesley, Deborah F. "Burnout and the Academic Teaching Librarian: An Examination of the Problem and Suggested Solutions." *The Journal of Academic Librarianship* 27, no. 6 (November 2001): 447–51.

Siess, Judith A. *Time Management, Planning, and Prioritization for Librarians*. Lanham, Md.: Scarecrow Press, 2002.

ABOUT THE AUTHOR

Zahra M. Baird is a children's librarian at the Chappaqua Library in Chappaqua, New York. During her library career, she has had extensive experience dealing with and researching the subjects of stress and burnout. Zahra is coauthoring a book for Scarecrow Press called *Librarian's Guide to Managing Job Stress,* which will hit bookshelves in 2005.

40

Batteries Included: Ten Tips to Supercharge Your Library Career

Janet Foster

Nothing great was ever achieved without enthusiasm.

—Ralph Waldo Emerson[1]

Enthusiasm must be nourished with *new* action, *new* aspirations, *new* efforts, *new* vision. It is one's own fault if enthusiasm is gone.

—Ancient Papyrus

Enthusiasm is contagious—catch it! Those five words epitomize an ideal that is highly regarded in both our personal and professional lives, a concept that most people strive to achieve. Contrary to popular belief, enthusiasm may not be an inherent quality; however, it is a desirable trait that can be acquired. Getting and staying motivated is a quandary faced by people in all facets of life as evidenced by the ample amount of literature devoted to the subject. Each week the *New York Times* Bestseller List includes titles such as *The Five Patterns of Extraordinary Careers: The Guide for Achieving Success and Satisfaction* and *The Power of Full Engagement: Managing Energy, Not Time* books that depict methods of enhancing and energizing personal lifestyles.

This chapter offers a list of various strategies that can be used to exploit your intrinsic motivation and reenergize your enthusiasm for librarianship. However passionate you may be about your career, an occasional jumpstart can prove to be beneficial and rewarding. The ten tips range from traditional topics such as engaging in committee work to some unconventional strategies such as "trading places," and they offer brief, illustrative, and often-humorous anecdotes. A list of resources, books, readings, and websites is also provided to augment these tips.

When the Public Library Association (PLA) launched a campaign geared to attracting prospective new librarians to the profession, I was invited to write an essay about "Why I Love My Job." During the process of writing this testimonial, I experienced some unanticipated and pleasantly serendipitous effects. Reflecting upon why I had chosen to become a librarian provided me with valuable insights and renewed my own enthusiasm for the profession. Writing is an important way to visualize your career from a different vantage point—just one of the various methods to rekindle and sustain enthusiasm in the workplace. "Batteries Included" may be used by people who want to revive their enthusiasm for the profession of librarianship. For others it may be a creative way to supplement an already vigorous career. After perusing these tips, you may choose to try one or more or devise some unique strategies of your own.

TAKE A COURSE

One of the most invigorating ways to revitalize your career is to take a course—any course. It may or may not be in the field of library science; it might even be a continuing education seminar. A few years ago, as part of my job as web librarian at Danbury (Connecticut) Public Library, I was encouraged to learn a digital art program, Adobe Photoshop. Since I work in a technical environment, I eagerly embraced this challenge and registered for the class with an optimistic attitude. Before long, it was apparent that I was floundering in a sea of point-and-click commands. Accustomed to working in a PC environment, the Macintosh computer had me stymied. I would like to report that as the weeks passed, I became more proficient with the Mac and with Photoshop. However, suffice it to say that my digital art career was lackluster.

Months later, while dabbling with the Photoshop program, a veritable light bulb went off and I suddenly realized how to use layers, resize, adjust color, and manipulate images. What initially felt like an exercise in futility turned out to be a personal success story. An added bonus of taking the course was a heightened awareness of the experiences of students who attend Internet workshops that are conducted at the library. By becoming a student I had inadvertently become a better teacher and, in the process of taking a course, I recharged my enthusiasm and expertise in web design. Take advantage of opportunities in continuing education by checking the American Library Association (ALA) website or other organizational sites for listings of current and upcoming workshops, and explore colleges and institutions of higher learning for local courses.

JOIN A COMMITTEE

Participating in committee work, whether it be at the local, state, or national level, broadens your perspective of the library world. Opportunities to join library committees range from readers' advisories to web development to children's books and more. Meetings can vary from monthly to yearly and may not necessitate lengthy time commitments. Electronic committees for librarians who might not be able to attend committee meetings have recently been established.

After joining the PLA Public Libraries Advisory Committee, I found it such a rewarding experience that I continued in this capacity for the limit of six years. During that time, I revived a personal interest in writing and created the "Internet Spotlight" column, now a regular feature of *Public Libraries*. Since then I've participated in a variety of committees, all different, each one contributing to my personal development as a librarian. In addition to meeting new people and networking with librarians who share common interests and goals, volunteering on committees can be a career enhancing experience.

BECOME A MENTOR

Opportunities to mentor new and prospective librarians abound in the library world and provide mutually rewarding experiences. The ALA New Members Round Table (NMRT) sponsors a mentoring program that pairs novice librarians with experienced counterparts at the American Library Association's annual conference.

In addition to organized venues, a variety of other nontraditional mentoring opportunities exist. During the course of my career, I have been involved in job shadowing and have interacted with MLS students during their college internships. Participating in job shadowing allowed me to step back and envision the library from a unique perspective. The aspiring students who met with me ultimately enrolled in MLS programs and are looking forward to bright futures as librarians. The experience rejuvenated my own enthusiasm for the job by allowing me to view librarianship through the eyes of someone just entering the field, eagerly anticipating the challenges and rewards of the profession.

MAKE A MISTAKE

Failure may be an option. As a rule of thumb, people feel confident and possess a sense of well-being when life goes according to plan. Human nature dictates that we strive for excellence, go for the A+ endeavor in the classroom, and seek success in our jobs. In the world of librarianship, it is highly unlikely that a day goes by without some kind of error, especially in the current technologically oriented environment. As a novice web instructor, I found it frustrating that in each workshop I taught, a "404 error, file not found" message would appear or I would inadvertently type in a wrong web address by mistake.

One day as I was teaching Internet Basics it dawned on me that the students learned more by viewing mistakes and learning how to correct them than when the class was conducted flawlessly. The ability to be flexible, roll with the cyber punches, and overcome obstacles is a much more exciting path in work and in life. Making a mistake or two along the way acts as an energizer and may lead to a path of serendipitous discovery. In his book *Expectations of Librarians in the 21st Century*, Karl Bridges (2003) compiled essays reflecting the multifaceted field of information science. Being flexible and rising to the occasion when faced with obstacles is one of the earmarks of a successful librarian.

WRITE A BLURB

Like many bibliophiles, I've long nurtured a hidden desire to write the all-American novel, that highly readable, best-selling book that might catapult me into the category of super authors like John Grisham, Michael Crichton, and the others. That is not likely to happen (although I've been known to scribble sentence fragments on crumpled napkins in restaurants or riding in the car at stoplights).

While I will probably never write a best-seller, I may be able to write the all-American blurb. When offered the opportunity to write a book review, I jumped at the chance. Not only did I receive the satisfaction of reading for enjoyment and writing reviews, but I received a box of brand-new books to choose from in the process. A bibliophile's dream! *Library Journal, Booklist,* and other professional library journals look for people to review and write book reviews. It's a fun and creative way to participate in the world of librarianship. Put Rachel Singer Gordon's book *The Librarian's Guide to Writing for Publication* (2004) at the top of your reading list if you are a prospective or seasoned author.

FAST FORWARD

Where do you envision yourself in the next five years? Ten? After working in the field of librarianship for a while you may have explored a variety of different venues, from public or technical service to children's or medical fields or writing or teaching. As your career evolves you may even consider opportunities in management. Before taking the quantum leap to another library or a different position in your current library, picture yourself several years down the road. Talk with colleagues who have made career moves similar to those you may pursue. Use quantitative and qualitative measures to evaluate what career path is best for you.

As retirement looms for many librarians of the Baby Boom generation who now face the graying of the profession, decisions about where to live and about career moves become imminent. Sometimes remembering why you became a librarian in the first place is a valuable clue for the future. When I picture retirement, I envision myself around books, whether it be in a library or bookstore, or perhaps working in technical services, another area that I've thoroughly enjoyed during my career journey. Working part time or volunteering are also viable alternatives. The fast-forward technique helps me envision the future while taking stock of the past, a valuable and insightful technique.

TRADE PLACES

Once in awhile, if possible, take a vacation from your regular work routine and perform duties that are outside your area of expertise. Doing something extraordinary is a real energizer. Even though I'm a cyber enthusiast and spend 80 percent of my time online maintaining and creating pages for the library website, occasionally I'm "downloaded" to a service desk to assist at reference or teach an Internet workshop. Diversity is one of the keys to keeping enthusiastic about the profession in general and your position in particular.

If trading places can't be accomplished during regular work hours, try coming in a bit early or on a weekend on occasion to delve into unknown territory. Or volunteer for your library's summer reading program. Each year, I make a point of helping out at our library's summer reading party. Working with the kids and the librarians in junior services rejuvenates me. It's similar to refreshing the screen when you're at a website that seems to have stalled. Hitting the refresh button gets things moving again and energizes the spirit. Though it might not be feasible to do this on a regular basis, look for opportunities such as this to revive your enthusiasm.

READ THE WANT ADS

The Web is a great place to keep track of new and emerging jobs. Even if you're not in the market for a new job, it's fun to peruse help wanted ads and see what's available in the local area, state, or country. You also gain perspective about "what you're worth" by comparing different job descriptions, duties, and library salaries. The ALA website lists current librarian job advertisements across the country and is updated frequently. One caveat: Remember to take the cost of living into consideration if you contemplate relocation. You can calculate the cost-of-living factor using a salary calculator such as the one found at www.homefair.com/homefair/calc/salcalc.html.

Priscilla Shontz's (2002) book *Jump Start Your Career in Library and Information Science* is an excellent resource for both new and seasoned librarians. The chapter on job hunting is extremely valuable and includes a list of excellent websites, including LIScareer.com. The book offers insights and advice about defining your own personal success and taking advantage of unique opportunities that may arise.

ATTEND A CONFERENCE

Both state and national conferences offer a multitude of exciting experiences for librarians. Check the websites of your local library chapters for information about annual or other conferences. When I became involved with the Connecticut Library Association, chairing the New Members Round Table and setting up a booth at the annual conference, I broadened my horizons, met new people, and enjoyed the benefits of attending a statewide library event. As it turned out, John Updike was the guest speaker that year so I heard a mesmerizing and enthralling speech, an unexpected bonus of attending the conference.

Grants are available in many instances to help defray the costs. Check the ALA site for a list of grants and scholarships. One of the most rewarding experiences I've had since becoming a librarian was volunteering at the IFLA Conference held in Boston in 2001. People from all over the world convened in the United States and the spirit of camaraderie among fellow librarians was clearly evident. Lists of many current and upcoming conferences and meetings can be found in *American Libraries* or on the ALA website.

HAVE FUN

Being a librarian is synonymous with having fun. Each day, I see librarians engaged with customers, smiling, laughing, and talking about books, jobs, the news, and whatever else seems to be newsworthy. Public libraries are unique community-gathering places, and it is not uncommon to see babies, dogs, and people from all walks of life coming together to read, research, learn, or just peruse best-sellers or thumb through magazines. Working in a people-oriented environment is compelling.

Each day is different. In the testimonial that I wrote for PLA about "Why I Love Being a Librarian," I quoted a phrase my colleagues and I use frequently when reflecting about the field of librarianship: "I can't believe I'm being paid to have this much fun." It's the best-kept secret in the library world. Pass it on!

CONCLUSION

Experienced librarians can revitalize their enthusiasm for the profession in a variety of different ways from attending conferences to writing book reviews or taking courses. This chapter serves as a springboard and lists suggestions that may be tailored to fit your own personal lifestyle. Experiment with these ideas or invent some of your own. During the process of writing this chapter, states on the East Coast changed to daylight savings time and then in the fall returned to standard time. My computer automatically updated its settings, but the rest of the clocks at home and at work had to be manually reset. There was just no getting around it. Using the "Batteries Included" method as an analogy, you can update your own settings using your energy and enthusiasm. The good fortune of working in a job you find rewarding is the epitome of professional success. At times ideas for new projects arise, but inertia may prevent us from getting started or from carrying out the plans. Exploiting your own intrinsic motivation can result in a rewarding professional journey, one that exceeds your expectations and goals.

NOTE

1. Ralph Waldo Emerson, "Circles," in *Essays—First Series* (Boston, Mass.: J. Munroe and Company, 1841), 303.

ONLINE RESOURCES

American Library Association—www.ala.org
ALA Events and Conferences—www.ala.org/events
Booklist—www.ala.org/booklist
ALA New Members Round Table—www.ala.org/nmrt
Danbury Library—danburylibrary.org
LIScareer—www.liscareer.com
PLA—www.pla.org
Library Journal—ljdigital.com
Salary Calculator—www.homefair.com/homefair/calc/salcalc.html

RELATED READINGS

Bridges, Karl. *Expectations of Librarians in the 21st Century.* Westport, Conn.: Greenwood Press, 2003.

Citrin, James M. *The Five Patterns of Extraordinary Careers: The Guide for Achieving Success and Satisfaction.* New York: Crown Business, 2003.

Gordon, Rachel Singer. *The Librarian's Guide to Writing for Publication.* Lanham, Md.: Scarecrow Press, 2004.

Foster, Janet. "Why I Love My Job." www.pla.org/Content/NavigationMenu/ PLA/Projects/Public_Librarian_Recruitment/Public_Librarians_Talk_About_the_ Profession.htm (last accessed 17 December 2003).

Shontz, Priscilla. *Jump Start Your Career in Library and Information Science.* Lanham, Md.: Scarecrow Press, 2002.

Loehr, Jim, and Tony Swartz. *The Power of Full Engagement: Managing Energy, Not Time, is the Key to High Performance and Personal Renewal.* New York: Free Press, 2003.

ABOUT THE AUTHOR

Janet Foster is currently the web librarian at Danbury Public Library and has served on a number of library committees including the Public Libraries Advisory Subcommittee, New Members Round Table, PLA Electronic Committee, and RUSA Web Sites. She received an MLS from Southern Connecticut State University and an MS and BA from Western Connecticut State University. She is the recipient of library awards including Association of Connecticut Library Boards Scholarship, Wilson Grant, EBSCO Grant, and the NMRT/3M Grant to attend the ALA Annual Conference. Editor's note: Janet passed away after suffering a heart attack on August 8, 2004. Her enthusiasm and many contributions to the the profession will be missed.

6

SKILLS

41

Through the Mouth, the Fish Dies: The Importance of Good Interpersonal Communication Skills

Juanita Benedicto

It often seems that interpersonal skills are underrated. For the most part, there isn't a class in graduate school where we learn about the enormous impact these skills have on our work and potential advancement. We aren't given the tools for successful communication unless we pay for it or take the initiative to homeschool ourselves. Yet interpersonal skills, or the lack thereof, factor into our work environment every day. Not surprisingly, when asked to rate the most essential business skills, a survey of 900 business professionals listed interpersonal communication as the first.

I graduated from library school seven years ago. Since that time, I've learned the value of good interpersonal communication skills and that if I employ them, not only do I benefit, but the system I work in benefits as well. Good interpersonal communication skills foster a healthy work environment as they work to clear the debris that misunderstanding and resentment lodges in our interactions with each other. While working as a librarian, I've been given several pieces of good advice that resonated with me. It's this good advice that I would like to pass on to you.

DON'T FORGET THE SOFTWARE
WHEN ADDRESSING THE HARDWARE

Everyone in the library loves our systems department. They're constantly busy putting out fires, fixing our problems, and generally dedicated to making our lives easier. They're the superheroes of the library system. One of the guys in particular, Travis, has easily won the popularity award for a keen mix of charisma and professionalism.

When my job morphed overnight into a position that required much more communication with individuals and coordination across departments than I was used to, I found that I was repeatedly challenged by difficult interactions, frustrated because of it, and unsatisfied with how I was interacting with folks. There had to be a better way. Looking to the systems department as a model, I asked Travis out for coffee, thinking that a few key questions would release his charismatic superpower secrets directly into me. I, too, could be successful with colleagues if I could incorporate his advice into my affairs.

What Travis told me made a lot of sense: "When people have a problem, often times they're reporting [only] half of it. The other half is the way they feel about the problem. Acknowledge their frustration and factor it in when you're dealing with them." This was brilliant! His advice made immediate sense to me. I began viewing projects and requests as the hardware that needed handling and my colleague's emotions as the accompanying software.

HOW TO HANDLE THE SOFTWARE

In team settings, such as committee work, project management, or simply collaboration with another librarian on a project, I have found that people often feel threatened, defensive, and protective of their time and their portion of responsibility. If you attempt to encroach on their space, they'll react instead of act with you. What you want to aim for is working together as a system instead of separate, defensive entities. Peter Senge (1990) has written a brilliant book entitled *The Fifth Discipline*. In it he writes of "learning disabilities" within organizations. One of the greatest learning disabilities people learn within organizations is to focus on their position rather than the overall system and how the positions interact. Taking this one step further, if we begin to realize that it's not *my good* or *your bad* but that we are both contributing to the evolvement of the organization, than we begin to see how we contribute to our own problems.

This insight never proved stronger than when one of my coworkers was assigned on a committee I had been appointed to. Over the years, I have been on a number of projects with this particular individual and always dreaded to see her name on the roster. She never volunteers for assignments, misses half the meetings, and essentially, I viewed her as dead weight. When the committee work began, she remained true to form and took on precious little responsibility while the rest of the group labored intensely with a major project on a short deadline. As assignments were dispersed from week to week and our loads became heavier while hers remained perpetually unencumbered, I began feeling frustrated and aggravated. Couldn't she see how much we were doing? Why didn't she take on some of the responsibility? Why was I always assigned on the same committees as she was? While these thoughts were clamoring in my head, a single pervading sentence dubbed over all of them with, "How are you contributing to the problem?" I realized that not only was she sitting there and doing nothing, I was, too.

PRETEND IT'S A MATH PROBLEM

You can't exactly tell someone they are a slacker and you are tired of working with them. Under duress, resort to creative diplomacy. In *Dealing with People You Can't Stand*, Rick Brinkman and Rick Kirschner (2000) point out that *no one cooperates with anyone who seems to be against them*. If you can find a way to state your truth so that it builds a person up instead of tearing him or her down, you're going to be tremendously more successful than by stating the obvious. Scott Hunter has an interesting concept he calls "files." Essentially, he writes, since we've been taught to keep disappointments to ourselves instead of communicating them to the people we work with, we open files on these people, storing evidence against them whenever the opportunity arises. Over time, these files grow as we become masterful at detecting corroborating evidence on the files we've been keeping. Eventually, these unspoken resentments create a mind-set of discrimination, making honest communication and healthy collaborations with certain colleagues nearly impossible.

In order to break this cycle, be clear, honest, and nondefensive with people when you find yourself beginning to harbor resentment. Empty the files and speak without blame. Have a trusted colleague proofread your e-mails for emotional language before sending them. Wait until frustration settles and objectivity sets in before attempting to communicate. Create new scenarios that cancel out previous assumptions. An influential colleague once advised me to envision obstacles as math problems. When your high school algebra teacher divided the class into teams and gave each group an assignment, people worked together. They all wanted to complete the problem successfully. In the same way, when confronted with a challenge and a need to rewrite over crippling scripts, invite your colleague to work with you in completing it. Try and quarantine any negative feelings for a moment, objectively valuing him or her as a team member. If you can do so, true progress will begin and it will be a first step to healing the system in which your positions interact.

IF SILENCE IS GOLDEN, LISTENING IS PLATINUM

Flaxen D. L. Conway (1999), an extension community outreach specialist at Oregon State University, has written a powerful guide on effective communication. She asserts *that when you confront difficult issues, listening is more important than speaking or any other form of expression*. She lists the benefits as such:

- It saves time because you cut through people's defenses and get more information without having to repeat the same conversations over and over.
- It helps you assess a situation accurately.
- It enables speakers to clarify what they're saying and makes them feel they're being heard.
- It reduces emotions that block clear thinking.

As an experiment, I began actively listening to colleagues. When a colleague whom I respect but frequently disagree with held a different opinion than mine, I invited her to tell me why she felt as she did. Rather than formulating a response while she spoke so I could readily shoot holes through her argument the moment she completed it like I had on a number of occasions in the past, I held back my defensiveness, suspended all judgment, and attempted to understand the situation from her point of view. I listened with compassion for her stresses while keeping in mind that this person represents an integrated system of which I am part rather than a singular function distinct from myself. Her success is my success.

When it was my turn to speak, I began by reiterating my colleague's main points and addressed them. Then I introduced my own concerns in a nondefensive way, inviting her to step into the circle with me so we could objectively view the challenge from a united rather than divided perspective. This vantage point allowed us to brainstorm on a mutually acceptable solution. This strategy has fared far better in resolving conflicts than the one I used before, which essentially centered on bringing folks to see the paucity in their thinking and the sagaciousness in mine. In fact, I have repeatedly found that careful negotiation can wield the sword of conflict to carve out a better resolution than if there were no differing of opinions in the first place.

I found that when my colleague felt she had been heard and that I was willing to address her concerns, she reciprocated. Key to this dynamic is staying neutral. You can hold strong opinions, but the moment you become emotional and heavy-handed, you lose credibility. In *Crucial Conversations: Tools for Talking When Stakes are High*, Kerry Patterson and colleagues emphasize that *the more you care about an issue, the less likely you are to be on your best behavior.* Backing off when we feel strongly about an issue may seem counterintuitive, but it's exactly what we need to do.

WHAT DID SHE SAY? I DON'T KNOW . . .
BUT DID YOU SEE THE LOOK ON HER FACE?!

Back in 1967, UCLA professor Dr. Albert Mehrabian conducted a study, published in 1968, on the relative importance of verbal and nonverbal messages.

He wanted to determine if what people said was more salient than how they said it. What he found is crucial in terms of interpersonal communication:

- 55 percent of interpretation was based on what people saw.
- 38 percent was vocal (intonation, tone, volume, and speed).
- 7 percent of meaning was derived from the actual words people said.

His formula looked like this: "Total Impact = .07 verbal + .38 vocal + .55 facial." Mehrabian's percentages are hugely important to remember as you negotiate, compromise, and seek solutions. When you walk into a meeting feeling frustrated and emotionally charged, your nonverbal messages will override your words by 93 percent! Better to wait until the emotions have been reigned in and your approach is objective and sincere.

However, if you find yourself in a situation where you are angry and do not have the luxury of time to deal with the situation, you can still remain open in conversation, avoiding judgment and blame. Conway identifies the following strategies:

- Number 1 rule of thumb: *Use I statements.* For instance, say "I feel as though I'm not being heard," rather than "You aren't listening to me." Beginning a statement with "You" often sounds reprehensive and puts the other person on the defense. "I" statements communicate how you are feeling.
- Avoid judgment and exaggeration. This is particularly important when crafting an e-mail. Often, what doesn't sound overblown to you will read accusatory to your recipient. Have a trusted colleague review it first for unintentional heat.
- In dealing with an angry person, acknowledge their feelings, rephrase what they are saying, listen without interrupting, and together pinpoint what the issue is. You can deactivate a potentially fervid conversation by remaining calm and listening.

CONCLUSION

Treat a man as he is, and he will remain as he is. Treat a man as he could be, and he will become what he should be.

—attributed to Ralph Waldo Emerson

In the end, our beliefs, or "files" as Scott Hunter calls them, shape the way we interact with people. We change our environment by changing our perceptions. If we believe our colleagues and the folks we interact with are good people, willing to work with us and grow together, that our libraries are gratifying places to work in, and that we are valued, we will reflect this in the way we listen and talk to each other. Our assumptions about personal merit within the organization and the willingness of others to work in accordance with one another are the operatives that drive us to inspiration or to despair. These assumptions take root and grow every day. It requires constant pruning and discernment to maintain clear pathways and healthy relationships and to keep our perceptions in check. It's hard work to listen and speak genuinely to people when you are frustrated with them. But if you operate from the assumption that you can communicate and that situations will improve, you will be one step closer to realizing that end.

RELATED READINGS

Brinkman, Rick, and Rick Kirschner. *Dealing with People You Can't Stand: How to Bring Out the Best in People at Their Worst*. Rev. ed. New York: McGraw-Hill, 2000.

Ciesielka, Thomas. "Research Reveals which Lifelong Skills are Needed from Kindergarten to the Working World," The Nierenberg Group. www.selfmarketing.com/release6.html (last accessed 26 September 2003).

Conway, Flaxen D. L. "Effective Communication." Part of the *Working Together* Publication Series, Oregon State University Publication. EM 1510. Corvallis, Ore.: Oregon State University Extension Service and Oregon Sea Grant, 1999.

Hunter, Scott. "Productive Workplace." *Executive Excellence* 19, no. 1 (2002): 11.

Mehrabian, Albert. "Communication without Words." *Psychology Today* 2, no. 4 (1968): 53–56.

Patterson, Kerry, Joseph Grenny, Ron McMillan, and Al Switzler. *Crucial Conversations: Tools for Talking when Stakes are High*. New York: McGraw-Hill, 2002.

Senge, Peter. *The Fifth Discipline: The Art and Practice of the Learning Organization*. New York: Doubleday, 1990.

ABOUT THE AUTHOR

Since authoring this chapter, Juanita Benedicto has moved from her position as web coordinator for the University of Oregon Libraries to reference librarian at Lane Community College. She lives in Eugene, Oregon, with her two daughters, her running shoes, and her music collection.

42

Talk, Listen, Repeat: Some Thoughts on Communication Skills

Bob Persing

There are thousands of books on how to develop good "communications skills" in business. Your library may even have a whole section of them. So what makes these skills any different for librarians? Certainly, all librarians learn about the Socratic "reference interview" in library school, and the need for careful, probing, evocative questioning. But there's more to the communication skills of a good librarian than that.

What makes the art of communication unique for librarians is not the categories of people with whom you will interact. These will basically be three: patrons, peers (other librarians, either from your own institution or elsewhere), and support staff. This is no different than for most businesses, though they may call their patrons "customers" or "clients" instead.

A few factors make the librarian's situation unusual:

- Unlike most professionals, you will often be discussing subjects about which you have no intrinsic knowledge.
- You will be working in a range of situations: one on one in formal settings, both planned (such as consultations) and unplanned (such as at the reference desk), group or classroom presentations, staff meetings, even speeches before larger groups.
- In most libraries, supervision is not close; rarely will someone be looking over your shoulder. This means you must take most of your actions independently, relying on your own judgment. Fundamentally, how well you communicate your thoughts is up to you.

Librarians have one strong advantage over other professionals in these situations. There is no adversarial relationship, no dialectic between the librarian and the other party. Usually, both you and the person you're talking to have a common goal: to get that person the information he or she needs. Your interlocutor has no inherent reason to mistrust your motives; he or she knows you aren't selling anything. This is even truer for librarians than other service professions. Unlike doctors or lawyers, our interactions carry few overt overtones of money; unlike priests, we are not constrained by adherence to a predetermined ideology.

Taking advantage of that trust can be a librarian's best advantage. It can be squandered, though, if the librarian does not communicate intelligently and professionally in everyday interactions.

TELL ME WHAT YOU WANT, WHAT YOU REALLY, REALLY WANT

Though library school curricula have changed in recent years (often dropping even essential courses like basic cataloging), most of them still require a course on reference. Included in it is a discussion of the active listening and questioning skills needed for eliciting information from reference desk patrons. You will have learned to ask variations on the questions: "What are you really looking for?" and "Is that really what you need for your underlying purpose?"

This active-questioning technique is a vital skill for public service. The surprising part, though, is how important it is for relations with other library staff. Oddly enough, librarians and library staff are sometimes no more capable of asking a straightforward question than the patrons they serve. When it comes to asking questions, many librarians suffer from the same syndrome that affects doctors when they need medical attention. Though they know how vague, incomplete, or misleading answers frustrate them behind the reference desk, they forget this when they're in front of it. You may find yourself using your "reference interview" skills much more of the time than you are scheduled on the reference desk. Don't waste your time trying to reform all your colleagues or teach them better "asking" skills.

Another very important skill new librarians need to develop is knowing how to say "I don't know." The old adage is that librarians don't know everything—they just know where to look everything up. Even that is not true for all librarians, though, especially young ones. It can feel acutely embarrassing to be continually showing ignorance, either to colleagues or to patrons. And yet learning to express ignorance well is a crucial element in being a good librarian, though not one necessarily taught in school.

Sometimes the simplest method is best. If a patron asks you how to find research articles on zeolite structure, you should not feel ashamed to ask what a zeolite is. Most patrons will not be offended by the question, unless your library specializes in physical chemistry. The key is to ask politely and then use the information they give you as best you can. The innate feeling of sympathy that many patrons feel toward librarians, which I mentioned earlier, may make them more amenable to this honest approach, more willing to work with you in the knowledge you sincerely want to help them with their problem.

Be careful not to assume your patron or fellow staff member knows everything, either. The lacunae in the knowledge of otherwise bright people can be unexpected. I have ten employees reporting to me, and I was surprised to find that several of them did not know how to read Roman numerals (still an important skill when dealing with journal numbering). That they might lack this knowledge had never crossed my mind, but once discovered, was easily handled.

It's important to master the nomenclature of your area. Particularly in this age of commercial Internet services, you will run across a lot of brand names, acronyms, and nicknames in your work. Keeping them straight, and using them appropriately, will add useful precision to your work. Science Online (the online version of the journal *Science*), Science Direct (Elsevier's e-journal platform), and Borrow Direct (a private ILL network in the northeast United States) are very different products; if you confuse their names, you'll probably confuse your listener, too. "Interlibrary loan" and "document delivery" are sometimes used synonymously, but when the latter involves paying a fee, using the right one can be very important. Another good example is computer technical assistance. Calling a program "Word" when you mean "Word-Perfect" can send a user down the wrong path altogether.

"THERE WILL BE A MEETING TO DISCUSS THE NUMBER OF MEETINGS . . ."

If your library is more than a one- or two-man operation, you'll be having meetings. They are as unavoidable as death, taxes, and questions about the location of the restrooms. Libraries tend to be less hierarchical than many other organizations, less likely to have top-down management. One result: more meetings, so that more people can be involved in the management process.

Being a good library meeting participant is fairly easy, but it requires a little preparation. The keys are:

- Don't go into a meeting cold. Whenever you are invited to a meeting, you should try to find out what's going to be discussed. If there's no formal agenda, you can canvass the other attendees to see what they know. Once you know the topic, try to anticipate what questions might be asked of you or in what direction the convener might drive the discussion. Anticipating the meeting's path can help you reach its destination more quickly—and brevity is usually a good thing for any meeting.

- Speak up when you have something to say. Our profession does attract its share of shy or introverted people (though not as many as public opinion thinks). It is very easy to sit quietly through meetings, not making trouble, but also not contributing ideas. Some people even enjoy critiquing the meetings later, criticizing them if ineffective or inconclusive. This may make them feel superior, but it is not a productive strategy for the organization as a whole.
- Sometimes you'll even be running these meetings, regardless of your position. This can be better or worse than just participating in them, depending on your personal style and how well you do your homework. Even natural introverts can run an effective meeting, and hopefully they derive some satisfaction from that fact. The key is respecting the time and intelligence of the participants.
- Everyone is busy, and many staff will see meetings as an interruption to their regular work. You can help validate your meetings by only holding them when necessary. I have seen "planning committees" formed to dig up topics for monthly meetings because there were not enough arising naturally. Instead, why not cancel the meeting in months when there's not much to say?
- When you do have meetings, have a prepared agenda—not necessarily printed and distributed, but for your use. Make sure you get through at least the most important items on it. Don't be afraid to politely cut people off when necessary. Try to come to decisions where possible, and then write them down. Winston Churchill always sent meeting participants a memo summarizing what was decided; he said it prevented a great deal of confusion later.[1]
- Be sure to ask questions, too, that will help others know as much as you do. I was once surprised when one colleague asked another, in a well-attended meeting, when she planned to retire. I thought he was implying that she was getting too old for her position. When I questioned him later, though, he said, "I wouldn't have asked her the question had I not *already known* the answer. I wasn't asking for my own information; I was helping her to share the information publicly."

Likewise, you should make sure you share your knowledge with your colleagues. I am surprised sometimes to meet librarians who take the old saying "knowledge is power" seriously. They attend conferences (sometimes even at their library's expense) but hoard the information they learn there, as if it gives them an advantage over their coworkers. This is both selfish and counterproductive. If you are sent to a meeting, you should make it your responsibility to share what you get from it. Nor is it reasonable to say, "No one else is interested in my specialty." Many librarians are interested in the field as a whole, not just in their current area of concentration. I know reference librarians who find cataloging rules fascinating, and vice versa.

THE CLICK OF THE KEYS IS A MUSICAL SOUND

In olden days, many reference questions were sometimes submitted and answered by letter. Nowadays, letters have become much less common, and yet librarians probably do more writing than ever before. E-mail has replaced much formal letter writing. The net result is similar in either case, though, despite the difference in delivery device. You will find yourself sometimes writing memos to other staff, preparing budgets and annual reports for superiors or boards, and even writing letters to the local newspaper.

Using a proper business writing style can be a real advantage in many situations. The informality of e-mail can be seen as too familiar. I work primarily with serial vendors and publishers, sending several dozen e-mails in an average week. I rarely chat in these e-mails, limiting myself to a polite salutation at the beginning. While less satisfying as a memento of my personality, I feel the messages are more likely to be taken seriously by their recipients. Likewise, I make a point of never yelling at vendors (either literally or figuratively) when something goes wrong. Firm and insistent messages are useful, but venting usually will not help get you better results. If you didn't learn proper business writing in school, find a book or website and refresh your skills.

You will often find less formal avenues of online communication than memos and meetings useful. I know one reference department that uses an instant-messaging service. Staff working in their offices keep their instant message program open on their computers. If any of them (on the desk or consulting with patrons) have a question they can't answer, they message the others. Any of the staff who can help respond. This clearly only works if (a) all staff have computers, and (b) you have a large enough department to make such consultation worthwhile. But the general concept of not being afraid to use your colleagues as resources holds true.

Discussion lists, weblogs, and even chat rooms have become important venues for professional development in recent years. There are well-established lists covering most specialties within our field, and I would urge all new librarians to read one regularly. When you post to a list, try to be on topic and have something useful to say. Informality here is more permissible, though messages should still never stray too far from the professional realm.

You will quickly see how the lists vary in terms of "signal-to-noise" ratio. Some lists stay firmly on topic, while others drift off into peripheral topics, philosophical musings, infighting among members, and other less useful avenues. There are librarians who succumb to the temptation to post messages constantly, leading others to wonder how they find time to do anything else. Such name recognition is not necessarily a good thing. Ours is a relatively small profession, and librarians frequently know their colleagues and counterparts at other institutions. Being known as a compulsive e-mail writer may not help you at your next job interview.

KNOWING WHEN TO SAY "WHEN"

Formality can be seen as distancing, but I truly believe it still has a place in professional communication. Oddly enough, some formality can also be helpful in interpersonal communication as well. Some people simply prefer more separation between their coworkers or superiors and themselves, and respecting that wish can make them happier, more productive workers. A staff member recently retired from my library after thirty-two years of service, during the last eight of which he reported to me. When he retired, I did not know if he was married, whether he had children, where he lived, or many other details of his personal life. He preferred to maintain that distance, and I saw no reason to force his confidence. I doubt if doing so would have achieved any end other than gratifying my curiosity—and I don't think that's a sufficient reason.

There is a much older network for informal information sharing: gossip. Many libraries, like other organizations, have a whole informal network for passing news around. This can be useful, if approached with caution. I have intentionally sent messages through the "rumor mill" sometimes, when an official announcement was premature or awkward. Where it becomes unprofessional, though, is in the passing of purely personal opinions. I have worked with people I heartily dislike, sometimes for years, without saying anything personally against them to my colleagues. It does not devalue your opinions to keep them to yourself or to wait to express them until you get home at night.

Societal changes since the 1960s have encouraged us not to give innate respect to authority figures. You will likely work in situations where you feel more intelligent than your boss, or better prepared, or that you have more relevant experience. An unfortunate side effect of this is to devalue organizational structure, equating it with authoritarianism. "I'm innately as smart as my boss" may be a true statement, but it should not be followed by "There's no reason I shouldn't do his job." Structure can be both useful and important, and using it can make your job easier. Referring a salesman hawking photocopier toner to the business manager doesn't lessen your abilities in anyone's eyes; all it does is free you to concentrate on the next question of your day. Likewise, refusing to circulate a reference book without the head librarian's approval does not make you a peon. It means you recognize the importance of having policies and the utility of centralizing the right to make exceptions to them.

LISTEN UP, EVERYBODY

While it's important to sometimes speak up (when you have something to say) and to sometimes keep quiet (when some discretion is required), the complementary skill, listening, is crucial all the time. Having a voracious interest in your work, and your work environment, usually brings positive results.

One important reason to hone your listening skills is the need for self-training. Librarianship is a chronically understaffed profession. When you start a new job, you will be taught the basics, but it's likely you'll be expected to "pick up" many of the finer points on your own. The only way to do that is by keeping your mind and ears open. This need doesn't end after three months, either. It often takes years to learn all the intricacies of an organization and to earn the respect of your more experienced colleagues. I spent ten years at one library before a more senior library staff member stopped referring to me as "young Bob." (My graying hair may have helped change his mind.)

You never know what information will be useful to you. An example: The sales representative for a commercial bindery recently dropped in on me unexpectedly. I had just been put temporarily in charge of my library's binding operation, so I did my best to ask pertinent questions about his company's services. I would have sounded quite naïve had I not made mental notes about a similar sales call I had attended—*sixteen years earlier.* My memory is not especially sharp, but I had realized at the time that this information might prove useful some day. That simple thought helped me retain the key points of the earlier discussion.

AND IN THE END

Librarianship has a strong body of theory behind it, but in many ways, ours is a practical profession. Having good communication skills is not just desirable philosophically, it can have definite, tangible effects. When hired for your first position, you probably will know few details of your duties. On what else will you be judged, then, after your first three or six months on the job? Many times, when interviewing applicants for entry-level positions, I form my judgments chiefly on how well I think the applicant will interact with other staff. Likewise, the only librarians I've seen fired after short tenures have been those who could not express themselves well or who seemed not to be interested in listening to and learning from their colleagues.

Good listening and speaking skills also open up new possibilities in your career paths. I have known several librarians who moved from traditional librarian positions to working for book dealers or library systems vendors. These were people who found professional interaction with colleagues the most interesting part of their work. The best of them used the attention they had paid to their library work to inform their interactions with librarians.

Your career path may lie in a traditional library, with a vendor or publisher, or in some nontraditional role. Wherever it takes you, honing and developing good communication skills will serve you well. Other skills may become obsolete over time, but the ability to listen and talk effectively to your patrons and colleagues will always be useful.

NOTE

1. Winston S. Churchill, *Memoirs of the Second World War* (Boston, Mass.: Houghton Mifflin, 1957), 240.

RELATED READINGS

Many good books on communication skills, not specifically related to librarianship, can be found at your local library (naturally).
One specific to our field that I have found useful is:
Ross, Catherine Sheldrick, and Patricia Dewdney. *Communicating Professionally: A How-To-Do-It Manual for Library Applications.* New York: Neal-Schuman Publishers, 1989. Its only drawback is its age, since it does not cover the online revolution.

A good book on speaking and listening skills in the workplace is:
Sonya Hamlin. *How to Talk So People Listen: The Real Key to Job Success.* New York: Harper & Row, 1988.

ABOUT THE AUTHOR

Bob Persing is head of serials and currently acting director of the Goldstein Information Processing Center at the University of Pennsylvania Libraries. He has worked as an academic librarian for over ten years, focusing on serials and electronic resources. He is active in ALCTS and NASIG, currently serving on the latter's executive board. Talking and listening are two of his favorite activities, along with sleeping and eating.

43

Computer and Technology Skills for the Twenty-First-Century Librarian

Leo Robert Klein

Welcome to the world of computers and technology in the twenty-first century. In many ways it's a world you're already familiar with. You'll have heard of many of the tools — even used some. What might be different is how these tools are applied in the context of a library. That's the interesting part. That's what we'll be investigating in the course of this chapter.

Of course, technologically speaking, a lot goes on in the average library. Cataloging every possible use of technology might take up a whole encyclopedia. For that reason, we'll concentrate on the big things — on the things you're most likely to encounter as a general librarian in this day and age.

AFTER THE REVOLUTION

If you're just entering the profession (or just coming back), the great news is what you've missed. The standard library of a decade ago had much of its electronic resources on networked CD-ROMs. What wasn't available on CD-ROM more than likely was available only in print. Research was still very much a print-based activity. It's one of the major differences between our time and that time that most of the indexes have migrated to the Web. The journals themselves are on the Web. The advent of the Web has played a major role in how we deliver library services both in house and remotely. Just getting everyone connected and (reasonably) comfortable with the technology is a major achievement of the late1990s.

The late 1990s also saw the final conversion of many libraries' "manual" catalogs to electronic form. There may still be collections out there that haven't been cataloged — archival collections, foreign language items, and so

on—but for the most part, the average user walking into the average library
in this day and age is almost guaranteed to run into an OPAC and not a card
catalog. Most of the grief in getting to this point took place in the preceding
decade and is therefore happily behind us.

LEGACY TECHNOLOGY

Of course, we can't get rid of everything.

We can't get rid of the old stuff even if the new stuff beats the pants off the
old stuff. We can't do it even if we wanted to—even if we could afford it.

Legacy Formats

For starters, new formats may not offer the same wealth of material. It took
years for audio CDs to catch up with vinyl in terms of what was available. In
some cases, there still are things available only on vinyl, or on laserdisc, or
on 3/4-inch videotape. On the way out is VHS tape, yet libraries are unlikely—for years to come—to do away with the format simply because of the
wealth of their collections in this area.

Then there are our users to think about. There's just no way we're going to
discard an item no matter how old it is if we have an instructor who's built
his or her course around it. This might include an old piece of software, a set
of audiocassettes, a filmstrip—slides even. In the public sphere, we'd face a
revolution if we suddenly replaced all our books-on-tape with CDs; the same
goes for replacing VHS with DVD.

Realistically speaking, the formats most librarians will have to deal with
are ones they probably already know the best. This would be VHS, DVD, audio CD, and audiocassette.

Legacy Systems

Of course, there's more to technology than formats. There are whole systems still in existence that look like they date from the caveman era. These
clunker systems are usually part of a larger institution's information system
and typically hold critical data such as personnel or budgeting information.
Libraries that haven't moved over to a new ILS may have old command-
style interfaces. In certain cases, a vendor may offer two versions of the
same product, a web-based version and a command-driven one. Since the
command-driven one probably came first, many of the old timers may be
used to using that.

On the bright side, it's amazing how quickly you can master one of these systems—especially when it's the only way to look up your materials budget! Just keep that list of commands handy.

THE COMPUTING ENVIRONMENT

Much of computing in libraries will be familiar to anyone who's stepped into any kind of office for the past ten years.

Computer Accounts and Security

There's your own computer—or at least a computer you're able to use when not at the reference desk. Typically, this will require a log on and password. An account will have to be set up. Exactly what you can put on the machine—in other words, what you can download or copy to the hard drive—is decided by the IT security people. Most institutions will allow you to download various files, but they may not allow you to download or install programs. Almost all institutions have options to back up your work.

LANs

Part of computing for several years is working in a networked environment. In many cases, the networked LAN came way before the Internet. There'll be various shared directories that you'll have access to on the network—places where you can store files, reports, stats, and so on for others to see—for your group, department, school, university. Some of these internally shared resources may be formalized into an Intranet. Likely candidates for an Intranet include documents on library policy and procedures, systemwide forms, schedules of one type or another, a news function and information on career development.

Discussion Lists

In conjunction with the Intranet, there generally is an internal electronic discussion list—in fact there may be more than one. Larger institutions may have several according to various job categories (i.e., administrative staff, professionals, etc.). Lists like this can be a good source of news not simply for internal events but for professional development opportunities and current awareness. They're also a good way of interacting with others in your organization.

Local Computer

Looking at your local computer, your operating system is likely to be some version of Windows. They might have Linux or some form of Unix on the servers and they may be using a Mac in the media lab, but locally, it's probably going to be Windows 2000 or XP. Any earlier version of Windows, and your IT people deserve the procrastination award of the year. Your hardware should be good enough to run all the applications you need. If something's too slow or if it won't install at all, that's a good sign that it's upgrade time at the old corral. If you suddenly notice that away from the job none of your files or applications are supported—say, a Word 95 document or something done in MacPaint—that's a good sign that it's upgrade time as well.

Upgrade Plans

Typically institutions upgrade their equipment at set intervals. Every three years or so, the whole section or department will get a new machine. The process can be very formal: Specs are drawn up covering minimum hardware and software requirements for both staff and public workstations. Institutions then work with a vendor (e.g., Dell or Hewlett-Packard) to supply the hardware. At the same time they buy the site licenses for whatever software they need.

Tech Support

Tech support is who you contact when something goes wrong. Typically there's some form of "help desk." These are the people who will get into the nitty-gritty of a broken keyboard or uncooperative printer. The function is usually part of central administration, though depending on the size of the library there may be a number of people assigned locally. Equipment is usually covered by a service contract. If a Dell computer conks out, it's the Dell repairperson who comes to bring it back to life. Copiers are usually outsourced.

Software: Productivity Applications

No surprise here. The kind of software applications you're likely to encounter are ones you're probably already familiar with. Basically this would be the Microsoft Office Suite plus a few extras.

As said earlier, it's not the tools themselves that are interesting—it's what you potentially might use them for. For example, people do reports all the time, but in a library they also do pathfinders and subject guides. These require a certain level of knowledge of Microsoft Word's layout tools. You might have to do a floor chart showing where all the call numbers are or put together a newsletter including photos. Signage is important. You might have an author coming in as part of your reading program. There might be some other event you want to advertise. The promo you can do in Word. What's more, if in addition to Word you've also got the full version of Adobe Acrobat, you can take that promo or newsletter and easily convert it to .PDF for distribution on the Web.

Microsoft Excel also comes in handy. There isn't an activity taking place in the library that doesn't have its own set of statistics. You've got gate counts, workshop attendance, circulation, ILL requests, reference questions both in person and online, Web stats, database usage—the need to document what you and your institution do is never ending. Plus there are the various budgets or funds that you may have to administer or at least keep track of.

PowerPoint can also be useful. It's not unusual to give a workshop or some other form of bibliographic instruction. You might go to a professional conference and give a presentation. In either case, PowerPoint can help anchor what you're telling the audience. Students are so used to it, in many cases they've come to expect the slide show as a routine handout for their notes.

Not everything you're going to use is a Microsoft product. When it comes to e-mail clients, you're just as likely to use Qualcomm's Eudora as you are Microsoft's Outlook. In fact, you're just as likely to use Lotus Notes as either of the other two. Both Microsoft's Outlook and Lotus Notes come with calendars and schedulers. If Lotus Notes is set up properly (not always a given), you can tell when someone is free for a meeting. You can then send out an invitation and if the person accepts, the meeting will show up automatically in his or her calendar.

Web Page Construction and Images

Then there are webpages. The pages themselves can be constructed in a number of ways: The simplest is to save them out as a "webpage" in Word or Excel; better still is using FrontPage or Macromedia's Dreamweaver. The page itself might be a bibliography of library resources that you're compiling in collaboration with an instructor for his or her class. The page might be something you need to put up as part of your work with a local professional organization. The page might be something that you have in print that simply needs to see the light of day on the Web as well.

In most cases, there will be some kind of HTML template for the organization's website as a whole that you'll need to follow. Next there's a vetting process, and eventually the thing goes up courtesy of whoever has direct access to the Web server. Images can be scanned in or transferred directly from a digital camera. There are a number of great programs out there for dealing with graphics, including one by Macromedia called Fireworks. Nevertheless, for the most basic kind of work, you can usually get away with whatever graphics program comes with the equipment.

NETWORKED RESOURCES

It's hard to imagine a time before networked resources—a time when "go and look it up" really did mean go and look it up. Nowadays, the only thing you have to leave your office or cube for is paper for the printer.

Integrated Library Systems

Of course, not everything is on the Web, and not every networked resource has a Web-based interface. A prominent example is the Integrated Library System (ILS). The average heavy duty ILS is composed of a number of modules—acquisitions, cataloging, circulation, and so on—that taken separately can fill up whole job categories. Few people are expected to master more than one module.

Of course, if your operation is on the small side or if your job responsibilities cut across a number of library functions, you may have to learn just enough from several modules to get your job done. It's not unknown for the same person to charge out a book, look up an order, set borrowing periods for the school year, and tweak the odd monograph or serials record. At the other extreme, vendors like Fowlett will do the entire OPAC for you. Happily, most books come with camera-ready cataloging records. In fact, most processing is handled by the central office.

An ILS comes with a ton of "extras." Say you need to generate a list of all the titles in reference because you're going to do an inventory/weeding project this year. Say a professor from the film or drama department needs to know all the video titles you have in your collection. Say you've got a series of books that cost a pretty penny and before you order any more, you want to know whether they've circulated. These are the kind of things the "extras" in an ILS can do for you.

Collection Development

Most ILSs have a way for you to see how much you have left in your materials budget. To spend the money, you could go through the usually round of catalogs and "slips." Increasingly, many of the same publishers also have relatively sophisticated Web presences. In most cases, it's like ordering books from Amazon.com.

Subscription Databases

By far the most important institutional resources online are the subscription databases. They certainly cost the most. It goes without saying that you have to be an expert in those databases that people are most likely to use. This isn't simply a matter of knowing how to search them. You'll also need to know what kind of formats the search results come in—oftentimes text or .PDF, but occasionally Excel files or even more exotic things like RealPage or Mr. Sid. Library patrons will also want to know how their search results can be saved—to disk, sent by e-mail, and the like.

Each database vendor's approach to technology is different. What they require by way of browser or operating system will be different. What they require when they upgrade their design will be different. As a librarian, you're literally the front end of whatever they're putting out, so it's important to develop an awareness of how changes on their part will affect your users. Often vendors will have their own discussion lists. These are useful for learning about and commenting on their products.

Remote Access

Patrons love remote access. In survey after survey, the ability to access library resources at home or at the office is something they truly appreciate. On the other hand, very often they'll need a significant amount of hand holding to get the thing working. This amount of hand holding is directly proportional to which system the library is using. The less configuring that the system requires, the less hand holding. The best systems, such as EZproxy, only require you to type in your name/password or user ID.

Consortium Catalogs

One tool that's often forgotten is consortium catalogs. No one library contains everything. Often you'll have to refer a patron to some other institution. This requires a familiarity with one of the standard bibliographic utilities—OCLC or RLIN—or a regional union catalog if there is one, plus the local catalog of the partner institution for item status (i.e., "on shelf" or "checked out").

E-Reference Applications

Increasingly, many libraries are offering some form of e-reference to their users. This takes the form of e-mail or chat (or sometimes both). E-mail is simple: The user fills out a form on the library's website. The results are sent to an e-mail account that a number of librarians have access to. When something comes down the chute, the person on duty will either reply or forward the message to someone else.

Chat requires special software—at least on the library end of things. It's a form of communication that students know and that librarians are growing increasingly comfortable with. There are different types of chat software, some easier to use than others. The most popular among the public—AOL, Yahoo!, or MSN—are also the most basic. Administrators should bear this in mind when choosing among competing systems.

Course Management Systems and e-Reserves

It's hard to imagine a college or university that doesn't have a course management system like Blackboard or WebCT. Accounts are given out automatically to anyone teaching a course. Instructors use them first and foremost as a distribution system for class-related documents (handouts, readings, notes, etc.). The quiz function is also popular. Some also use the bulletin board function.

Librarians are involved first by having their own accounts as part of library instruction. Besides this, as part of their collaboration with the teaching faculty, they may be adding research and other support material to a faculty member's class account. This could take the form of a page of web links or an article from one of the library's databases. An option also exists for loading research material on an e-reserve system like Docutek. This is very similar to traditional reserve. In fact, it's usually handled by the same library unit. Why something ends up on one system as opposed to another is probably a mystery to most users. Integration between systems still needs a bit of work.

OTHER EQUIPMENT AND SERVICES

The moment you put a piece of equipment out there for public use, you are responsible for making sure not only that it works but also that people know how to use it. This goes for hardware, software, the network, everything. Major problems typically include printing, copying, and network connectivity. We can't fix everything, but usually we're the first line of defense.

Traffic Cop

Even when things are working perfectly, we may have to keep firm control over how a particular resource is being used. This is particularly true where resources are limited or in high demand. The librarian on duty at a public library has to make sure people are using computers with Internet access in an orderly way. Typically, people need to sign up ahead of time and sessions are limited to thirty minutes. It's up to the librarian to make sure the system works. In a school library, particularly K-12, where you may only have a handful of computers, the librarian may want to know ahead of time what exactly the student wants to do. Games are nice, but homework takes priority.

Specialized Equipment and Software

Libraries often have specialized equipment to accommodate special users and needs. There may be a Kurweil or Apollo reader for people with disabilities. There may be specialized software—CD-ROMs, for instance, that didn't make it to the Web, or courseware and other sorts of multimedia learning tools that are sitting on stand-alone computers. A librarian may not be an expert in all of these programs, but depending on the library and resource, they may need to know enough at least to get the patron started. In many cases, this may mean just knowing how to turn the machine on.

Smart Classrooms for BIs and Wireless Laptops

Getting a classroom "to work" used to mean turning on the lights. Nowadays there's more to classrooms than overhead lighting. Many of them are wired. The degree to which they're wired is usually set out by local or state authority and is defined as one of levels: having a workstation and projector at the head of the class is one level, having a workstation for each student is another. These "Smart Classrooms" may be part of the library; the equipment may be housed there. In any case, they provide powerful tools for library instruction where demonstration and hands-on training are so important.

An added degree of flexibility is provided by wireless laptops. A library may have a certain number of these that it can deploy for group instruction either in the library or, connectivity permitting, in some far-flung classroom. Once the instruction session is over, the laptops are collected and returned either to storage or loaned out as part of a laptop loan program.

Committee Work

All this technology is great, but someone has to go out and choose it. That's the function of a committee, and at some stage you may find yourself assigned to one. A committee will typically vet competing technologies or vendors; they'll either design or sign off on an interface. Committee work is a two-way street: You represent your local group on the committee, and in return, you represent the committee's work to your group. All parties need to be aware of the various stages in a committee's deliberations. Committee members need to listen. They also need to be articulate and tech savvy enough to explain their decisions.

CONCLUSION

Innovations in technology are happening all the time. Many have appeared so recently that their implementations leave considerable room for improvement. Many don't work so well one with the other. Many are duplicative.

Beyond these obvious teething problems, even mature technologies will be "upgraded" at one time or another. This isn't so much something we have to get used to as a routine part of the job. Routine as well is our need to provide informed input on these changes. Databases will go on trial or we'll be asked to look at a new piece of equipment. We may notice an innovation done at some other institution and propose it for our own. In short, we can't simply be consumers of technology; as librarians we need to be articulate evaluators of it as well.

ACKNOWLEDGMENTS

This chapter is partially based on interviews from several librarians in the Chicago area. The interviews provided background material for the text. I'd like to thank Kathy Ryan and Paul Whitsitt of the Chicago Public Schools, Jo Cates of Columbia College, and James Pletz of the Chicago Public Library for suggesting people I might interview. I'd particularly like to thank interviewees Harry Hoynes of Lakeview High School, Jessica Alverson of Columbia College, and Tony Powers of CPL Austin-Irving for their wonderful insight without which this chapter would not be possible.

ABOUT THE AUTHOR

Leo Robert Klein has been library web coordinator at both NYU and Baruch College (CUNY). In addition to his MLS from Queens College (CUNY), he has a master's from NYU's Interactive Telecommunications Program (ITP). He currently lives and works in the Chicago area.

44

How to Pass the 4:55 Friday Afternoon Test: The Importance of Being Organized

Ladd Brown

Do you make daily or weekly To-Do lists? Do you use some sort of planning calendar? Are all your files—paper and electronic—in reasonable order? Is your sock drawer straight?

If you answered "yes" to all of these questions, then you are already well on your way to earning the Good Housekeeping Seal of Organization. If not, then just where are Organizational Skills on your Value System ladder? You, my Chaotic Friend, may have problems passing that dreaded 4:55 Friday Afternoon Test.

Why is organization valued? There are those who claim that being organized increases productivity; that organization makes teams, departments, and units easier to manage; and that being organized generally contributes to a positive working atmosphere: all good things for a library, right? If you stop and think about it, libraries have traditionally been classic examples of institutions that have been closely associated with organization, being organized, and supplying an "organized product" in the form of our collections and services. We, of all people, should value organization.

What is organization? Merriam-Webster uses terms like "systematic planning" and phrases such as "to form into a coherent unity or functioning whole" to describe the term. I like the definition I heard years back: "We can't tell you what organization is, but we'll know it when we see it." You also know it when you *can't* see it.

What are the key components of being organized, of organization? There are physical aspects of organization, such as using workspaces wisely and choosing good tools (like a planning calendar). There are cerebral aspects of organization: using time-management techniques, getting into a routine of good habits, and spending time on planning.

Discussions on organization may also include variations of Pete Drucker's familiar explanation of how we do things ("efficiency is doing things right") and what we do ("effectiveness is doing the right things").

Organization is efficiency: Do you have your archived spreadsheets clearly labeled and easy to find?

Organization is effectiveness: "Hello, this is the Dean calling. I realize that it's 4:55 P.M. on a Friday afternoon, but could you resend me that one spreadsheet with publisher info you sent me last month, or maybe you sent it last fall?" "Yes, Dean Doe, I have that exact spreadsheet right here and I'll attach it to an e-mail, pronto!" (Note the exclamation point, which represents the joy you will feel when your Organizational Skills triumph over the evils of Embarrassment and Unpreparedness.)

My job title is Acquisitions Librarian, but my everyday duties lie in the ever-dynamic world of managing online resources. I thought I was pretty organized before I started working full time with e-resources, but I was wrong. Some of the examples provided here come from my experiences dealing with, living with these hydralike e-beasts, but don't let that mislead you: This chapter is for all of us, whether we're in technical or public services, working with spreadsheets or patrons. We all have ample opportunities to exercise and hone our organizational skills daily—even hourly—to fulfill our missions, to complete our assigned tasks, and to generally cover our . . . I mean, keep our noses clean.

I've chosen to break down this short piece on organizational skills into the physical aspect of organization and the mental approach to being organized and being prepared. Don't worry, you won't get a Checklist, neither will you get a list of twenty Sure-Fire Tips, nor will you learn any Great Secrets. Instead of memorizing rules, you can take a look at your own environment and your own habits, identify the strengths and the weaknesses, and come up with your *personal approach* to organization. No matter how you achieve it, being organized pays off, especially on Friday afternoons.

LOCATION, LOCATION, LOCATION: THE PHYSICAL APPROACH TO ORGANIZATION

Before we delve into the details of the physical side of our topic, let's discuss some of the very broad aspects. Is your office or workstation near the photocopier, across from the departmental mailboxes, adjacent to the student assistant's time clock computer, or next to the administrative assistant, like mine is? These are noisome areas, full of distractions, and you are liable to acquire copier repair skills, become a campus mail expert, help new student workers clock in, or be a walking (or sitting) departmental directory if you are not careful.

Do you have an office to call your very own? Does it have a door? If so, you may want to use it on occasion. (The door is an excellent time-management tool; I'll discuss more about time management later on.) Do you have your monthly calendar printed out and taped on that door? Is your office or workspace small and easy to keep organized? Small offices—like ship's cabins—force you to make a place for everything and clutter is harder to hide. If you have a large office, fill it with semicomfortable chairs and your staff or your project group can stop by for a productive fourteen or fifteen minutes. (I address more on meetings later).

How about your desk or work surface? Is it kept neat, even during the day? Is it tidied up, or even cleaned off, when you leave? I have thirty-one stackable trays (including one In Box and three Out Boxes) for current work and projects within reach of my desktop and twenty-two other stackables for things like procedures and not-so-current projects on the far side of my office. I have two bulletin boards: one for current material, like calendars and new policies, and one for not-so-current documents, like lists of our state contracts and the campus map. Material is binder-clipped and then hung over push pins stuck in the bulletin boards for easy-on, easy-off access. I stick a label in the binder clip for instant recognition.

I have a surplus book cart in my office for those projects that need lots of surface space. So, next time I want to put together an RFP, I have about nine square feet of paperwork I can wheel back and forth. Add that to the three ranges of bookshelves I have, and you can see that I have plenty of open spaces—not drawers—to organize my work.

In my personal style, my approach to organization is "out of sight is truly out of mind." All pertinent documents, current projects, everything I need to conduct daily business is clearly able to be seen. What is in my file cabinets is essentially archival material, original documents, or personnel files. Therefore, one of my personal requirements for office organization is visibility, and lots of it.

To enhance this visibility, all current work in the thirty-odd trays is marked with a yellow sticky with the bright-orange-highlighted name (usually the publisher) and a keyword describing the work (e.g., "ManyGuilders Press, 2004 terms"), and these trays are stacked up according to broad themes: Cancellations, Print to Online, Licensing, Waiting for Publisher's Response, Still Waiting for Publisher's Response, and so on. Theoretically speaking, my goal is to be able to lay my hands on almost anything current within a moment's notice, or, if I were away from the office, someone would be able to come into my office and find what they were seeking.

Even if they are looking for extra clothes, they would find them: I keep a blue sports coat in the office for high-level meetings and visitors; I often stash a clean shirt and tie in a desk drawer; and I keep an extra pair of dress shoes in the office in the wintertime.

Now that we have our work surface all prepared, are all of your paper files in order? Have you cleaned them out lately? Pull up the recycling box and take a stab at it. Know what you have to keep (e.g., personnel records, fiscal documents) and for how long. Most institutions have storage or records units where you can send important documents; all institutions have cardboard boxes for recycling.

Let's talk about electronic files. I want to see mailboxes, mailboxes, mailboxes, mailboxes in your e-mail system: remember what happens on Friday afternoons. Do you make it a goal to clear out your incoming e-mail every day? I stopped whining about it and now I clean it out at least three days a week. Yes, it can be done. Run your daily e-mails through something like the Delete-Forward-Print&Do-File It routine or whatever works for you. Save time on spam and junk e-mail: Take advantage of your filtering and blocking mechanisms in your e-mail program.

Despite a popular conception, it's really OK to handle an e-mail or document more than once. You also have to be concerned about getting the job done, and if you have to handle a particular e-mail or other document twenty times to do that, then that's part of the game. Despite another popular conception, it's OK to print out e-mails if you're going to use them as working documents. I frequently cover the front of e-mails with handwritten notes in the course of a project. These can always find their way into your paper files if they contain useful notes, phone numbers, and other important notations.

For everyday correspondence and logging or record-keeping purposes, I use a high-tech/low-tech approach. I try to make it a high-tech habit (and encourage my staff to do likewise) to communicate as much as possible via e-mail. That way, I can forward messages to stakeholders, keep correspondence organized in e-mailboxes, or cut and paste or transcribe info into one of our principal serials management tools, our continuations payment database. Low-tech-wise, I do make a lot of old-fashioned, pencil-and-paper notes to myself during the course of the day. These working notes, invaluable to a worn-out, old brain like mine, are usually on recycled office paper quartered into a nice, usable size. Try not to make a practice of writing on the back of them. Remember my *visibility* requirement from earlier? What is on the back of papers or documents may not always be seen at first glance; losing that info, even temporarily, may cause you unnecessary delay or even momentary panic.

I have even recorded relevant info from phone conversations, faxes, and other communication channels into an e-mail message, and then sent it to myself for filing in the appropriate e-mailbox. Sound weird? Maybe, but I really did believe all those Paperless Office prophecies back in the 1980s. E-mailing yourself with germane information and relevant data does create a fairly permanent record, easily forwarded, easily organized.

How about word-processed documents, spreadsheets, PowerPoint presentations, images, and other e-files? Are these organized and clearly labeled? Take time to clean these out and make e-file navigation easier; your electronic files are likely to grow and grow, so get them managed now.

Since I work with publishers and information providers, both my e-mailboxes and e-document folders follow basically the same filing scheme: alpha by publisher. Some documents, such as promotion and tenure material and annual reports, may be best filed by date. Since my e-mailboxes sort in reverse chronological order, I do the same with my paper files and put the most-recent filing up front in the folder.

Browser bookmarks should also follow a logical, organized pattern. Set up the Top of the Screen toolbar with your most-used (work-related) bookmark folders. For library work of all types, the Internet is probably the Workhorse Tool. Like all electronic files, your Internet bookmarks are likely to grow, or at least be very dynamic, so take time to get these in order.

TO PALM OR NOT TO PALM

One of the essentials of organization is some sort of calendaring, scheduling, or personal notation system or device. Although many of my friends and colleagues swear by the handheld PDA or similar device, my vision prevents me from seeing the screen easily or using the stylus properly: I need bifocals. Personally, I use a three-ring calendar notebook (printed from my e-mail software package) for central planning activity and a portable clipboard with Project Notes, my Master To-Do list, and a Gantt chart thrown in to manage deadlines. For those of you less vain about your eyewear, the handheld machine may work best for you.

"IT'S OK, I KNOW WHERE EVERYTHING IS . . ."

Who among us can resist the sirenlike attraction of an orderly workstation or office, desk area precisely arranged, with all those little yellow stickies neatly sorted according to size? Despite what you may have heard or read, neatness counts and, yes, organization is also about *appearance*. I am not talking about handwriting here, I am mainly referring to what we'll call Cellulose Transition and Integration Management. Clutter rarely inspires confidence or conveys competence. You may be able to fish a document out of a pile quickly, but you will probably not be able to do it on a consistent basis, especially under pressure on Friday afternoon. Want to see sublime organization, a prime example of a clutter-free environment and awe-inspiring neatness? Drop in on Shakertown at Pleasant Hill near Harrodsburg, Kentucky, sometime; it is the Mecca of Tidiness.

"SIMPLIFY, SIMPLIFY . . ."[1]

Let's get to the mental part of being organized in the workplace. Everyone turn to their Organizational Statement of Philosophy in their Organizational Skills Workbooks . . .

Yeah, why not? Let's pretend our OSP would include a phrase like "my mission includes client-centered service" or "my mission is based on customer-oriented decision making." That's not a bad thing to keep in mind as we practice our organizational habits. Let's be efficient and effective for our clients; isn't that what they've traditionally expected of us? Organized responses to their inquiries and needs?

Organization is client-centered efficiency: Do you have e-mail and other files logically arranged? Are payment and other important records easy to access?

Organization is client-centered effectiveness: "Hello, this is Bob down at Reference. Listen, I know it's 4:55 P.M. on a beautiful Friday afternoon, but I have a patron down here who needs the log-in info for the ManyGuilders Press e-journals." "Right, Bob, I have it right here in my ManyGuilders Press e-mailbox!" (Note the exclamation point.)

Like the arrangement of your own physical spaces and your choice of organizational tools, time management is also a personal challenge, and this challenge is best approached in a personal style. Ideally, time management should allow you to paint a realistic picture of the relationship between the fixed number of hours in a day or week and a collection of prioritized tasks. Time management is sometimes more of a gut feeling than an absolute science, so don't go out and buy a stopwatch or hourglass right away.

Try to find out if you are a high- or low-pressure performer. High-pressure performers can't really do their best until the deadline is very near; their time-management style can be fairly loose because they react positively to pressure and thrive in a stressful situation. The opposite is true for low-pressure performers. Don't create unnecessary anxiety for yourself and try to plan for 100 percent of your time in any given day: 80 to 85 percent is usually the most time you can really account for in a job-time survey. Be prepared to be flexible, or as we say around here, "exercise a high tolerance for ambiguity." Interruptions and other snags are a fact of work life: You may have to bump deadlines or projects back a few days. Everybody has had those perfectly planned days fly right out the window when some disaster, some bigger project, or some request from the Dean comes along.

As you begin to take a closer look at your own work time, don't forget to show some Golden Rule respect for other's time, too. Don't fall in love with calling meetings or end up being responsible for involving others in unproductive time or gaps in their day. Treat their time as you would your own. There are a lot of good meeting helps out there, and they are all useful. Everyone appreciates a productive, fast-paced meeting with structure and a clearly defined agenda or pathway to the meeting's objectives.

Conversely, if you are working with colleagues who are not as focused (or as organized) as you are, this may hamper your own productivity or the success of the project. You may want to consider other pathways or alliances or even a creative approach to the project in order to get back on track. Are you attending standing meetings where you always listen and never contribute? Reconsider what you gain from that exercise.

Even though planning takes valuable time, set aside a few moments to make some decisions or draw up some lists, whether it is a quick triage of the most pressing problem or pile of paperwork morning or something long term that you can diagram into a deadline management display like a Gantt chart. Even the simple activity of creating a to-do list for the next day or week is an effective time management move.

Naturally, in the course of the workweek, there will be some inevitable and unpredictable stretches of mental downtime—we'll call it Organizational Block—where you just cannot give the usual 110 percent. Have some professional reading, a crossword puzzle, or something humorous (this book?) handy to rejuvenate the blood. Or, better yet, go for a walk and get a cup of coffee.

Perhaps an overlooked result of some time-management activity is the actual accomplishment of tasks on your lists. Put an easy task as Number One on the to-do list; why not start the day off—especially Mondays—with a bunny and get it going on a good note? As far as daily habits and practices go, Ol' Henry David was more right than wrong: Don't load yourself up with too many daily or weekly items on your to-do list; break those big tasks down into manageable sections; segment the day into logical chunks; keep your focus; and don't forget to laugh once in a while, especially as it nears Friday afternoon.

One of the end results of organizing your day, your work, your space is the attitude of readiness or preparedness to either take on what you've assigned yourself or cope with whatever the workday brings. What bears repeating one final time is that the acquisition and development of organizational skills is mostly personality-based: it depends upon learning style, individual strengths, and how tasks and projects are perceived and prioritized.

LET'S GO A-CONFERENCING!: BEING ORGANIZED AWAY FROM WORK

When away from the office on library- or institution-related business, it's not really a vacation from being organized. Days at conferences and meetings are usually a little longer than your normal workday, so pay attention to the conference schedule and do a little time management with your daily—and evening—schedule. Give yourself plenty of time to get from that 4:00 session on Shelflisting to the 6:00 meeting of the Another Round Roundtable.

Are you doing a presentation? The smart presenter takes along two backups: an overhead version and a paper version (handout). Yes, Virginia, even in the twenty-first century things do go horribly, horribly wrong minutes before your scheduled presentation, or even right in the middle of your presentation; so be ready, be prepared.

Speaking of being prepared, you must have a Boy Scout Camping Mentality when on the road. Carry everything you need around with you: flashlight, writing equipment, reading material, duct tape, a current conference schedule, water, and a bunch of your business cards. Those cute, fashionable business card carriers may be too small. You will want to be a good networker and collect as many cards as you give out. You may want to take along your own nametag holder to accommodate business cards, meal tickets, keys, and so on. And remember, Scouts: leave your campsite cleaner than you found it.

Don't forget to touch base with the folks back in the office: If possible, get a remote e-mail access at the conference and clear out your incoming messages. Answering any staff or colleague's e-mail while you are away at a conference is worth two Organizational Skills bonus points.

THE LONG HAUL: STRATEGIC ORGANIZING

Seems like we never stop organizing, do we? Long-range plans are a part of your annual report, the department's future, and the library's vision. If it exists in readable form, get a copy of the library's master plan, or vision, or strategic document, or whatever it is called, and work backward. Where are they trying to go? What does it mean for my department, unit, team? Where does my team fit in at the present time and five years down the road? Hopefully, you see yourself as having a prominent position in the future of the institution, or at the very least, still drawing a paycheck from it. If you have trouble seeing yourself or your team in the strategic plan, then you have a chance now to change direction for yourself and/or your team.

Are there any "life-changing library events" on the horizon? Does your workflow or information flow need revamping? If you are in the market for a new ILS or new module in the next couple of years, then that will require some long-range planning. Does your institution use state contracts for services such as serials and binding? Enter their expiration dates in your long-term calendar or planning system. No use having those RFP deadlines sneak up on you!

What are your personal goals at work—promotion, tenure, a better parking space? Then put some of those milestone-type dates and deadlines in your strategic planning system. What about continuing education or future meetings and conferences? Keep those charted, too; you may need to make early travel plans in those lean-budget years. If your institution offers an employee tuition waiver or discount, plot out how long it would take to get that next degree. Don't be afraid to plan two, three, or five years out; that type of planning translates very well over into your personal life, where planning five, ten, or twelve years in advance is not uncommon.

"WE'VE REACHED A SPECIAL PLACE. . . . SPIRITUALLY. . . . ECUMENICALLY. . . . GRAMMATICALLY." [2]

Organizational skills are really just another tool to help you cope with the challenges of the workday, to help you become a little more productive, and to help you reach that special place. Ideally, the structure achieved from those well-developed skills and good habits should reduce some of that on-the-job (and off the job!) stress.

Like me, you've probably come to the conclusion that this is the most enchanting and spine-tingling chapter in the book. Being organized—and being proud of it!—is not just a statement of your prowess over the anarchy of Modern Society; being organized is not merely your courageous stand against the Vast Emptiness of the Universe and Beyond; being organized is not just super-sexy: It is also darned practical.

NOTES

1. Thoreau, Henry David, *The Mental Approach to Organization.*
2. *Pirates of the Caribbean: The Curse of the Black Pearl*, 2003.

ABOUT THE AUTHOR

Ladd Brown is the head of acquisitions at Virginia Tech, but the only thing he really acquires anymore are headaches from the day-in, day-out struggle to stay on top of all those damn e-resources. As an avid baseball fan, Ladd believes the only reason we do not have a twelve-month baseball season is because of all the Communists in the federal government; he is also familiar with many aspects of the Infield Fly Rule.

45

It's About Time: Time-Management Skills

Beth Thornton

You dash through the door of the library—eleven minutes late for work—and think to yourself, again "Why am I always rushing?" Already there is a new problem on your chair and a note on your desk from your boss. She wants to see you. Looks like yet again you won't get any time to work on the big project that's due . . . tomorrow?! What's left to be done? Why haven't you heard from the other committee members? Stress attack! The phone rings, you have e-mails to read, staff with questions, material to move. You'd like to spend some time with your spouse, but it looks like another late night at the office.

If any part of the above sounds familiar, then read on.

Time management. The words imply that you can actually manage and control time. In fact you cannot control time, but you can control your conception of, and what you do with, your time. On first consideration, time management conjures thoughts of to-do lists, prioritization, and other tools. These are valuable, to say the least, but there is another dimension to time management that goes deeper than your to do list and your day planner. In her book *Managing Time: A How-To-Do-It-Manual for Librarians*, Dian Walster (1993) says that time management can also be a voyage of self-discovery, an attempt to make life more meaningful and work more important.

What is your relationship to time? Do you fight the clock trying to accomplish everything while the seconds tick away? Or is your day a vast expanse of unorganized time where you spin and spin and still nothing seems to get done? Do you manage your time or does your time manage you? Whether you are just beginning your career, becoming a first-time manager, or are a seasoned librarian, you can benefit by improving your time-management skills. Effective time management can greatly reduce stress. In his book *Timeshifting*, Stephan Rechtschaffen (2002) says that 95 percent of the stress we feel most likely relates to our feeling of time poverty; it's the feeling that we cannot possibly accomplish all we have to do. A recent job ad lists flexibility in prioritizing multiple projects in a demanding environment as a highly desirable qualification. Project management requires excellent time-management skills. Supervising people, especially if you have production expectations yourself, requires time-management skills. Being as productive as you can at work or at school requires time-management skills. An amicable relationship with time, as well as an arsenal of tools and techniques to increase your efficiency and effectiveness, can improve the quality of your work day and professional life.

TIME

Time is measured in seconds, minutes, hours. . . . it ticks away and is so quickly gone. We divide our life into segments of time. Rechtschaffen (2002) says that a day holds both twenty-four hours and an infinity of time. He says that we can create time by shifting our rhythm and living in the present moment. Time expands in the present moment.

Living in the moment can improve the quality of your work and help you enjoy your day a bit more by allowing you to fully experience it. Staying in the present moment, we can practice mindfulness, focusing on the task at hand and giving it the full attention it deserves. We can also focus on the people in each moment. If I am in the moment, I am better able to really listen to someone, answer a question, or solve a problem. If I am worrying about what I'm going to do next and someone is talking to me, I find myself half paying attention, nodding at the appropriate (I hope!) times, and making mental lists. This is not fair to the person with whom I am talking, nor is it fair to the future problem or activity on which I am half-concentrating.

Regardless of how adept one becomes at expanding each moment, the truth remains that there are only twenty-four hours in a day. Hopefully some of those hours will be spent at work, and others will be spent pursuing different aspects of your life. How can you make the most of the hours spent at work? Literature on time management talks about efficiency and effectiveness. In *Time Management, Planning, and Prioritization for Librarians*, Judith Siess (2002) defines efficiency as completing a task with the least amount of wasted labor, money, or time. Effectiveness is examining a range of tasks and selecting the most appropriate and important. In other words, effectiveness is doing the right job and efficiency is doing the job right. Good time management means being both effective and efficient. This applies in your everyday work life, as well as when you are planning projects and working on other professional activities.

BE EFFECTIVE

Effectiveness means doing the right job. You must choose from the many things vying for your attention and time. In order to be effective you must become adept at planning and prioritization. Planning happens at different levels. You can have a big-picture plan for your life, a plan for the next five years, the next year, a project you need to complete in six months, this week, each day. All of these plans should be related.

Wesley Cochran's *Time Management Handbook for Librarians* (1992) has some good ideas about planning. He says that in order to plan, you must identify unifying principles in your life and set long-term goals to support them. Take into account your personal values. When considering your personal values, think about your work, career, family, the life of the mind, and your social, spiritual, and physical life. For example your career principle may be to strive for excellence in the library profession. Then you should identify goals that support your principles. A goal to support striving for excellence might be to contribute meaningfully to your profession. Next, develop objectives. Objectives to reach the contribution goal might be to teach a workshop in the next year or serve on a national committee. Finally, develop an action plan toward your objectives. Include a list of major accomplishments you want to achieve in the next month, year, and three-year period. Review this periodically. Always try to keep these goals and objectives in mind when working on your short-term planning. Cochran reminds us to make sure our daily plan reflects our goals and objectives.

Daily planning is tending to the trees that make up the forest. It begins with your to-do list, prioritization of your list, and scheduling your time. Your to-do list can be like mine—a list on a piece of paper. Or perhaps you prefer software, such as Microsoft Outlook, or an electronic organizer. Use what suits you.

Use your list as a guide but don't be a slave to it. It is inevitable that things will come up. Some people advise updating your to-do list at the end of each day. This way you can see what you've accomplished and set yourself up for tomorrow. I update my list throughout the day. As things come up, I jot them down in no particular order, and I prioritize at the beginning of the next day. Again, experiment and see what works for you.

What, exactly goes on a to-do list? How helpful is the entry "Write task force report"? Dividing tasks is the first step in planning. Perhaps you can delegate some of the parts. If, for example, you are chairing a task force, you will need to delegate tasks as well as solicit input from your other members. What helps me divide tasks is to work backward from the desired outcome. If the task force is required to submit a report, what goes into the report? Results of a study? How will we conduct the study? Who can gather information? Analyze it? I keep project to-do lists separately and work those tasks into my daily to-do list. For example, as a task for Monday I might have to e-mail a colleague to touch base about a project. These coexist on my daily list along with checking student inputting and exporting my cataloging from yesterday.

List and divide tasks in a way that makes sense to you. Some people divide tasks by the amount of time it takes to do them. You can have one list of tasks that are long term (for example my projects list), another of things that will take an hour or two, and a list of ten-minute tasks. The ten-minute tasks are good when you have a small amount of time before you need to leave for a meeting or at the end of the day.

If you are a visual person, Mind Mapping might work for you. Mind Mapping was developed by Tony Buzan as a tool for note taking, but it can be used for many things, from project management to writing to your to-do list. A mind map consists of a central idea with related ideas radiating from it, like spokes on a wheel. Each related idea may also have related ideas radiating from it. This allows you to quickly make a list of related ideas that flows.

In the case of project management, it is a wonderful tool to help you divide tasks. The task force example I mentioned earlier is a good candidate for a mind map. The central idea on the page might be "complete report." What do I need to do in order to finish the report? Do a study, analyze results, and come up with recommendations? Each of these things would be in their own bubbles connected to the central idea of finishing the report. What to I need to do for the study? I need to gather data, do experiments, gather input from task force members on how well it worked. Those ideas would radiate from the study bubble. Tony Buzan's website (http://www.mind-map.com/) has wonderful examples of mind maps. They look like art!

PRIORITIZE!

Once you have your list or your picture, the next step is to prioritize the tasks. Prioritization is really the key to effectiveness. Your priorities should be based on your values. They also should dovetail with those of your boss and your organization. Do you know what your boss's priorities are? Communication is very important here, both for learning priorities and keeping abreast of them. Priorities can change.

Prioritization involves making decisions about your tasks. First and foremost you must distinguish between what is important and what is urgent. Rechtschaffen (2002) draws from *Covey's Seven Habits of Highly Effective People*, telling us that urgency has to do with events that intrude upon us and demand immediate attention. Importance refers to things that go beyond the immediate and are aligned with our plans and goals. Crises and interruptions are examples of urgency. Sometimes an urgent task makes a lot of noise. Do not automatically assign a high priority to something that is urgent, as it may not be important. Planning is not necessarily urgent, but it is extremely important. Planning can avoid crises, perhaps reducing some urgency in your day. Urgent tasks can crowd out your important ones. Urgency can make the day go quickly, and at the end, you can have accomplished little of what you set out to do.

In terms of important versus urgent, you want to accomplish the tasks that are both important and urgent first. Next you want to tackle those tasks that are important and not urgent, though sometimes tasks that are urgent but not important may intrude. Another approach to prioritization is to look forward to the end of the day and think about what you will have accomplished. Which tasks make you feel like you have made progress toward your goals? Those tasks should be your higher priority task. There are many other ideas for prioritization in the sources listed at the end of this chapter, particularly in Siess (2002) and Cochran (1992).

YOUR SCHEDULE

Once you have your plans and priorities set down, you need to make your schedule. For projects, especially if there is a strict deadline, I schedule by weeks. After breaking down what needs to be done and estimating time, I count backward from my deadline and in my calendar write down what I need to accomplish each week. In addition, I always try to leave a little time at the end to account for the unexpected. This is important if you are depending on input from other people.

When making your daily and weekly schedule, there are several things to consider. You may want to schedule your high-priority tasks in the morning, or you may prefer to schedule the things you don't want to do in the morning, so you don't worry about them the rest of the day. Become aware of your energy pattern. I have more energy and concentrate better in the morning, so I make sure to schedule my difficult tasks then, and I save easy and fast things for the late afternoon, when my energy and concentration wane. If there is a time of day when you tend to get more interruptions, you may want to schedule low-concentration tasks at that time.

Cochran (1992) suggests setting aside a certain day to work on various library routines so things don't pile up. He uses the example of technical services. Original cataloging tends to pile up, so for example, you might want to set aside Monday mornings for original cataloging so that some is done each week. While this will not likely prevent a backlog from developing, it could certainly avoid feelings of hopelessness because, though we cannot necessarily keep up, we are doing the best we can.

When allotting time for various tasks, meetings, and the like, try to allot more time than you think necessary. Generally, tasks take longer than you think. Even if it is a routine task and you know how long it will take, Cochran (1992) says to add an extra 20 percent of time to account for interruptions. It is a good idea to arrive at meetings and appointments early. Schedule this time. If you have a doctor's appointment at 3:00 and it takes fifteen minutes to get there, enter it in your schedule for 2:30. Also, while you are scheduling, schedule some personal time. For some people, if it's not scheduled, it will never happen.

BE EFFICIENT

Efficiency means doing the job right. "The job" can mean the job in specific sense, such as a project. It also can mean the job in a general sense, accomplishing what you need to in a day at work. Efficiency is about being as productive as possible in a given situation.

Before you plan for improving your productivity, it is helpful to know where you need to make improvements. Exactly how do you spend your time at work? A time-analysis log is a good tool to ascertain how you spend your day and where you can make improvements. Siess (2002) has a good section on time-use analysis. First, write down all the activities you do throughout the day and estimate how much time you spend on each. Then, keep a log to determine how much time you actually spend on each activity. Activities on my own log included cataloging, answering questions, training, revising, checking e-mail, delegating, chatting, and attending meetings. In my own study I was rather surprised. My job consists of production as well as supervisory responsibilities. I'd always felt that I don't get to spend much time actually cataloging. I learned, by actually charting my time, that I spend more time cataloging than I thought. Keep a log for at least two weeks and you will begin to see patterns. Then you can slowly begin to make improvements.

ROOM FOR IMPROVEMENT?

There are many ways to improve your efficiency. What follows is a brief discussion of some common "needs-improvement" areas, and some suggestions for making improvements.

Too many papers; too many e-mails! One of the most common time-management problems is too much information. Cochran (1992) says that librarians can take their training to organize and place material where it can be retrieved to an extreme, and paper shuffling can be a serious time-management problem because it distracts from the task at hand. Try to handle paper only once, or each time you handle it, take some action toward its final disposition. Sort your mail near a trash can. Toss items you don't need right away. Sort other items into folders. I have three folders on my desk. One is labeled "Now." It contains items that I need to take care of as soon as possible. The other is labeled "Hold." It contains items that will require action in the next several days. The final is labeled "Forms." It contains forms I frequently use.

Siess (2002) says there are 4½ things to do with a piece of information:

- Toss it
- Refer it
- Act on it
- File it
- Read it

To decide what to do with a piece of information, ask yourself whether it requires action on your part. Do you need it? If the information is available elsewhere, toss it. If not, then file it. If someone else needs to see it, then refer it. Do NOT put it back in your inbox or set it on your desk!

E-mail may be an even bigger source of incoming information than your inbox. Not only is it a constant influx of information, but it can also become slightly addictive. That alt-tabbing habit can be hard to break! If you are an e-mail junkie, it is possible to moderate. Set limits for yourself. Tell yourself you can check your mail once each hour. You need to check it often enough so you don't miss urgent messages, but too much checking is very distracting. Otherwise, treat e-mail as you do your paper inbox. Triage by subject. Set up action and hold files. Read your lists at home. If you are going to be away from work awhile, check your e-mail remotely. This will save time and anxiety on your first day back at work.

Another time-management problem is interruptions. There are many techniques for handling interruptions so that they do not become a time-management nightmare. In some cases, interruptions can be avoided by careful planning. If you plan frequent-enough meetings with your staff, for example, they might be less inclined to interrupt you, knowing that they can bring up their issue at your next meeting.

Even with careful planning, however, interruptions happen. If you are working on something and don't want the flow of your concentration to be broken, there are things you can do to discourage interruptions. You can create boundaries. If the telephone is an interruption, simply don't answer it. If you have an office, close the door. I work in an open environment, and it's understood that if one of us has her headphones on, then it might not be a good time to interrupt. You could also stack books on your visitor's chair to discourage long conversation. If subtlety isn't part of your office culture, you could make a sign to the effect of "do not disturb." Or perhaps designate the hours of 8–10 A.M. as concentration hours, and all questions wait until after 10 A.M. It is possible to nicely let someone know that it isn't a good time. You can say that you're in the middle of something, but you have twenty minutes free, say, at 2:30.

Trying to do too much can also be a time-eater. Too many things on your list can lead to a number of problems. You may get discouraged at your impossibly long list and become tempted to procrastinate. You may try to finish it all, not giving each task the proper attention it deserves and letting the quality of your work suffer. There are several things you can do to avoid this problem. Careful planning and prioritization, again, can be of help. If you prioritize, then you will know what you really need to accomplish. You can also learn to say no. Finally, you can delegate.

Cochran (1992) says that librarians tend to be some of the most overcommitted service professionals. In my own experience, I find myself overcommitted both because it is difficult for me to say no (I want to please people) and also because there are so many cool things to do! Keep in mind that if you overcommit, you risk not having enough time to devote to the things you are already committed to. I have learned to say "I'm honored to have been asked, but I don't feel I can give this project the time it deserves." If you need to refuse, answer promptly so that the asker can find someone else. Perhaps you might even know someone else who might be interested.

Saying no and not overcommitting also applies to job duties. With cutbacks, libraries must do more with less money and staff. When you are asked to take on more responsibilities in your job, be realistic. Can you really handle it? If not, ask your boss how high a priority the new responsibility is. If it is very important, perhaps there is something you can let go of or let slide down the priority list.

Delegation also is a way out of the "too-much-to-do" nightmare. It keeps you focused on what you do best. Knowing what and how to delegate helps improve your own efficiency. Delegation also is crucial for project management and running a committee. Delegation can be difficult. We may think we are imposing on someone, or we don't want to seem as if we are too lazy to do something ourselves, or we simply may not know how to delegate.

If you think you are imposing on someone, consider, as Siess (2002) says, that not delegating is also selfish; it does not let others learn the skills they need to succeed. Think of delegation as giving others an opportunity. If you are chairing a committee, delegating tasks is giving committee members an opportunity to participate. If you are delegating to a subordinate, you are giving them an opportunity for job variety and learning another skill.

What sorts of things can be delegated? Siess (2002) says you should never do something that someone else could do better or that could be done by someone making less money. I work with someone who is an expert with the MARC format for holdings. If someone comes to me with a horrific problem with a holdings record, I delegate it to her. She will do a better job than I could, and faster. You must decide whether delegating a particular task is worth the time you spend training someone else to do it.

Siess (2002) has some good tips for delegating. Once you've decided to delegate something, make sure you delegate it to the right person for the job. Delegate in advance. Waiting until the last minute is not a good idea. Delegate gradually. Do not transfer everything in the first fifteen minutes. Be specific about the outcome you have in mind. Give the person or people to whom you are delegating the big picture and the why behind the what. Give them a say in what they get to do. This is particularly important when delegating to colleagues on a committee. Divide the work up, present it to them, and ask for comments.

If delegation requires training, provide it. Take time to be sure the person has learned and is fairly confident. Be available for questions. Periodically review the project's progress. Finally, give credit to the person or people who did the work.

WHERE TO START?

Learning to manage your time may seem like an overwhelming undertaking. It's not. Reading this chapter is a good start. The sources listed below address the ideas I've presented in more depth and contain many good ideas and strategies for effective time management. You cannot change everything overnight. Think about where you would like to make improvements. Start small and, most of all, be patient with yourself. The payoffs? Better efficiency, a sense of purpose and accomplishment, and less stress are well worth the effort of rethinking some old time-management habits.

RELATED READINGS

Cochran, J. Wesley. *Time Management Handbook for Librarians*. Westport, Conn.: Greenwood Press, 1992.

Kolberg, Judith, and Kathleen Nadeau. *ADD-friendly Ways to Organize Your Life*. New York: Brunner-Routledge, 2002.

Masterton, Ailsa. *Getting Results with Time Management*. London, UK: Library Association Publishing, 1997.

Nhat Hanh, Thich. *Peace Is Every Step: The Path of Mindfulness in Everyday Life*. New York: Bantam, 1991.

Peterson, Lisa C. "Time Management for Library Professionals." *Katherine Sharp Review* 5 (Winter 1997).

Rechtschaffen, Stephan. *Timeshifting.* New York: Broadway Books, 2002.

Siess, Judith A. *Time Management, Planning, and Prioritization for Librarians.* Lanham, Md.: Scarecrow, 2002.

Silber, Lee. *Time Management for the Creative Person.* New York: Three Rivers Press, 1998.

Walljasper, Jay. "Our Schedules Our Selves." *Utne* (January/February 2003): 61–63.

Walster, Dian. *Managing Time: A How-to-do-it Manual for Librarians.* New York: Neal-Schuman, 1993.

ABOUT THE AUTHOR

Beth Thornton has been at the University of Georgia, where she is head of serials cataloging, since 1996.

46

Public Speaking Skills

Trudi E. Jacobson and John R. Vallely

You have just found out that you will need to speak publicly. You may have been asked to take part in a presentation at a conference or speak to a group of patrons or trustees. If you have not done much public speaking (or even if you have!), the thought of speaking in front of a group of people may make you feel nervous. Unless the responsibility is clearly a part of your job, you may wonder why you in particular have been asked to speak. Public speaking may bring back unpleasant memories of speaking in high school, with all the attendant worries of how you will be received.

Speaking professionally, however, is a very different experience. You will be speaking to people who are interested in what you have to say. Conveying information is the key point—information that you have and others would like to know. There is a good reason why you have been asked to speak, and that reason is your knowledge or experience in a particular area. It is very rare that someone is asked to speak on something about which they are not knowledgeable. You may not feel that you are an expert in a particular area. In some speaking situations, a full-fledged expert may not be what is needed. Perhaps a discussion starter, someone who can raise pertinent issues, is just the ticket. However, in situations where greater knowledge is called for, you can use the time before the speaking engagement to increase your own expertise, if you feel uncertain. Another tactic might be to include a cospeaker, if that is acceptable to the organizers of the event. If you and someone you know have complementary knowledge, you can work together on a more comprehensive presentation.

This chapter addresses key issues connected with public speaking and presenting: preparation, content, and the day of the presentation. While we cannot guarantee that you will conquer your nerves completely by following the advice in this chapter, we can assure you that you will feel more confident about your ability to speak publicly.

PREPARATION

In most cases, an audience will expect you to speak with authority on the topic in question. They hope to be exposed to new ideas and concepts so they can leave the presentation with a better understanding of the topic than they had before you stepped up to the podium. No one really expects you to be *the* authority on the topic at hand, but everyone will expect you to be capable of addressing salient points on the subject and introducing them to one, or several, critical aspects of the subject.

RESEARCH

This means, of course, that you will have done your homework ahead of time. One of your first steps will be to spend some time researching the subject matter. While you will have your own knowledge of the topic to draw upon, you will also want to read or reread recently published or key materials on the topic. These will increase your awareness of current viewpoints and interpretations. Do not put off investigating your topic until the last minute. Procrastination will typically result in a less than adequate job.

As you are researching the topic, its central points will become obvious. These key issues can be used to structure your presentation. They will also point to the areas about which your audience will typically have questions. Concentrating on these topics when doing your research will enable you to quickly respond to many questions from the audience.

KNOW YOUR AUDIENCE

Do not fail to do research on your audience as well. You will need to know:

- *Size.* A small number of people settled around a conference table calls for a radically different approach than speaking in a large auditorium setting.
- *Background.* Consider professional, educational, and cultural characteristics of the audience. Addressing a group that has limited or no knowledge of the subject requires a totally different presentation than one you would give to specialists in the field.

- *Age*. This information may help you tailor your references to people and events. For example, an older audience might be lost if you mention MTV personalities.

Your primary source for this type of information will generally be the individual who invited you to speak. Ask this person about your expected listeners. Find out, if applicable, who has spoken to them before (you could then contact these people), how many usually attend, information on what the audience's concerns and interests are, their awareness of the subject, and whether your source knows of any recent changes that have had an impact on the organization.

TIME FRAME

One of the details you will be given when you are asked to speak is how much time you have. Ask if this time includes a question period or if extra time has been allotted for that purpose.

CAPTURING AUDIENCE INTEREST

As you prepare, think about how you would like to convey your information. What would be the most effective method? Remember that typical attention spans are about fifteen to twenty minutes. You might want to break up what could be straight lecture with visuals or audience participation, particularly if you have been allotted more than fifteen to twenty minutes. You can involve the audience in a number of different ways, including asking them to brainstorm answers to a question or to reflect on a particular issue or problem and how it might affect them. The topic of your presentation, your audience, and your own style will determine what methods might be useful during your pre-sentation. Decide which techniques you might like to use during this early preparation stage so you will be able to fit them seamlessly into your presentation.

GAINING SPEAKING SKILLS

If you are concerned about your public speaking skills, there are a number of ways to increase them. Look for an appropriate course, read more about the subject, or ask friends or colleagues who are accomplished speakers for some key tips. Observe other public speakers: What do they do that works well and what doesn't? However, one of the best ways is to practice speaking! Look for opportunities in your job to give presentations, even if they are short or informal. Ask colleagues to critique your presentations or your practice runs. The more you speak publicly, the more comfortable and adept you will become.

CONTENT

Once you have determined the crucial points of subject matter, audience, time frame, and format, you will be ready to start organizing your content and then begin writing.

Key Points

Determine the most important information to convey to the group. Almost always, there is more material than you will have time for. In addition, there is the issue of how much listeners can absorb. Teachers are told that they should focus on three main points during a class, and this is also useful advice when presenting or speaking publicly. An excellent way to focus on the most important elements is to identify your goals and objectives for the session and then to develop a corresponding outline. This outline will help you to determine what to include and what to cut. The presentation goals and objectives can be shared with audience members, letting them know what to expect and how the various pieces fit together and helping them to follow where you are in your presentation. As you become more experienced as a public speaker, you may want to take this one step further. If you feel comfortable being flexible about what you present, you can ask the audience to develop their own list of goals and objectives for the session or to critique the list you have developed. This strategy requires that you be able to change direction with little notice and thus is not recommended for novice public speakers.

Opening

Once you have decided on the main points, you will need to develop an introduction or opening. Richard Dowis (2000) suggests that you consider the following six purposes for your opening:

1. Establish a common ground between speaker and audience
2. Set the tone for the speech
3. Reinforce or establish the speaker's qualifications
4. Arouse interest in the subject

5. Take advantage of the speaker's "grace period" (the period when the audience is most attentive)
6. Segue smoothly into the subject

Openings are crucial and often require a level of work out of proportion to their length. Don't stint when working on your opening.

Core of Your Presentation

Use the tone you have set and the goals you have developed for the session to select your material. Include any activities you have developed to engage the audience. Make sure that these activities fulfill a genuine purpose (challenge audience members to think more actively, change of pace to address attention span issues or long periods of sitting, etc.) and that each one you propose to include meets the goal you have set for it. If you plan to use humor, use it with care. Everyone's sense of humor differs, and what might be funny to you may fall flat with others. Be certain that you are not using humor at anyone else's expense. It is a good idea to run your humorous material by two or three others, just to make sure it has the effect you think it does.

Conclusion of the Presentation

Once you have decided upon the core material, you will need to write your conclusion. You will most likely summarize your key points. You might also throw out a challenge or call to action to the audience. And don't forget to ask if there are any questions or comments!

TO WRITE OR TO OUTLINE?

In most cases, you will not need to memorize a speech. You will be able to bring material with you to the lectern or table. The question becomes, should you write your speech out in full, or should you outline it? Most people will know immediately which option makes them feel most comfortable. If you need to have the complete contents, make sure that you use a large font so that you can read the pages easily. Do not forget that it will be more challenging to maintain eye contact with the audience if you are reading verbatim. If you intend to use an outline, be certain that there is enough information included so that the points are meaningful to you when you give your presentation. If you think you may freeze, use an outline with more details to ensure you have enough material to prompt yourself.

EQUIPMENT

As you make final decisions about your content and how you would like to present it, request the appropriate equipment from the organizers of your presentation. These may include:

- table, podium, or body microphones
- a whiteboard or flipchart and markers
- an overhead projector
- a computer with appropriate software
- an Internet connection
- a projector system with appropriate cables
- a screen
- a laser pointer

A great deal will depend on the type and size of the room in which you are speaking, the size of the expected audience, and what the organizers are able to provide. You may need to be flexible based on what they have available. Make certain that you have a backup system. If you intend to connect to the Web, for example, download website screen shots to a disk or produce overhead transparencies of the screens in case the Internet connection is not working. There is nothing worse than having no contingency plan if equipment fails.

A note on the use of PowerPoint: It has its advantages, such as providing written material for those audience members who learn best through text and providing visual markers for the progression of the presentation or speech. However, PowerPoint is often overused or used poorly. Do not clutter your slides with text. Do not read your slides. And do not include too many slides. PowerPoint is most effective when it serves as an organizer for your comments or when it presents visuals such as graphs or charts. Audience members may consult the slides as you provide expanded material, but they do not want to slog through extensive text or, worse, have it read to them. Consider taking advantage of PowerPoint's ease in creating handouts containing the slides with space for comments. Audience members generally like to take something away from a presentation as a refresher on the content.

PRACTICE, PRACTICE, PRACTICE

It is critical to practice your presentation for a number of reasons:

- *To become thoroughly familiar with the material.* When you practice your presentation out loud, you will be able to tell if it flows smoothly. If you are using notes rather than a written speech, you will particularly want to make sure that you know exactly what you plan to include and where. You will also want to make sure that segues between sections are smooth.

- *To make sure you have a good opening.* Audiences often judge a speaker by the first few minutes. While the rest of your content may be logical and clear, openings can be more problematic, and if you haven't decided on and practiced how you will begin, you may find yourself stumbling during the critical first few minutes.
- *To time yourself.* Keep in mind that actual presentations may take longer, particularly if audience members ask questions during the presentation rather than at the end. For this reason, you may want to ask them to hold their questions until you finish. This allows you to factor in a set amount of time for questions. Occasionally, actual presentations take less time than your run-throughs if you become nervous and speak very quickly.
- *To hear your tone and inflections.* To do this, you will need to audiotape yourself. You want to make sure you are moderating your voice throughout the presentation, emphasizing key points. Make sure you aren't speaking in a monotone. As an alternative to taping, you might practice before one or two colleagues or friends, asking them to provide you with feedback.
- *To see your body language.* If you videotape your rehearsal, you will have a chance to see how you will appear to the audience. Do you look stiff? Nervous? Not all speakers videotape themselves during their trial runs, but doing so will provide useful feedback.
- *To determine where you can cut or expand material.* As you hear your presentation, you will find it easier to note places where you can cut material, if you are running out of time, or add material, if you find you are moving through your presentation more quickly than expected. Develop a system that works for you and annotate your outline or speech accordingly.

DAY OF THE PRESENTATION

When the day finally arrives, you'll want to attend to a number of items that will help you feel more comfortable, secure, and in control of the situation.

Nerves

While nerves certainly do not contribute to feeling more comfortable, neither is nervousness a condition that should frighten you. Most accomplished speakers feel nervous or uncertain in the moments before they speak. Be aware of this and when a touch of panic sets in, you will have expected it and can better deal with it. If nerves hit during the presentation, take a deep breath or a sip of water and give yourself a chance to focus. Your audience isn't going anywhere, and taking a moment to relax allows you to get back on track before continuing.

Dress

You are a professional. You spent a great deal of time and a substantial amount of money in fulfilling the requirements for a graduate degree in librarianship. You expended a fair amount of psychic energy in interviewing for your current position and you have worked long and hard to perform your job at a consistently high level. Further, you are held in such high regard that you have been asked to speak at a public forum. Does this mean you have to worry about what color tie to wear or the length of your skirt? Why, yes, as a matter of fact it does. Like it or not, we are judged by our appearance. You may wear jeans, sandals, and a casual shirt in your job, but spending more time on your clothing is a requirement a speaker should accept as a natural part of public speaking.

A speaker should always strive to treat the audience with respect. If you are to speak before the library's Board of Trustees, you should dress in a manner appropriate to the occasion. If you are speaking at a summer camp for high school students, you would obviously dress in a more casual manner. If you are uncertain as to how formal or informal the event is, ask the individual who invited you for advice. A good rule of thumb is to wear the same type of outfit you would wear to a job interview. If in doubt about your selection, ask your spouse or a friend for their opinion. Wear clothes in which you are comfortable.

John, one of the authors of this chapter, recalls a conference where a speaker's pants were at least two inches too short. Quite a few people spent more time giggling at the poor guy than listening to what he had to say. He also remembers a speaker whose new shoes were so uncomfortable she told the audience that the only way she could make sense was to first remove the "shoes from hell." The crowd loved it!

The Room

John once served on a panel that spoke at a restaurant known for its conference facilities. Unfortunately, the panel's room was right off the kitchen, with wait staff rushing to and fro. Can you control this type of factor? Usually, this kind of problem is outside your control. You rely on the conference organizers and the building staff to troubleshoot problems. Knowledge is power, however. Get to the room where you will be speaking ahead of time to assess the following:

- *The acoustics.* Stand at the lectern and speak in your "lecture voice." Ask someone to stand toward the back of the room and tell you if they can hear you.
- *The microphone.* If it doesn't work, speak to someone connected with the event.
- *The lighting.* Put your notes on the lectern and see if you are able to read them without bending over and squinting. If there is a problem, talk to the organizer.
- *The equipment.* If you are projecting data on a screen, walk to the far corner of the room and make certain the people in the back row can see it.
- *Need for assistance.* If you need someone to assist you with the equipment, work out your needs ahead of time. Also, be certain to introduce your helper to your audience and thank him or her at the end. Your audience, and your helper, will be impressed by this simple courtesy.

Handouts

Bring a sufficient number of copies if you intend to distribute handouts. You can place your handouts by the door so people can pick them up as they come in or you can pass them out before you speak. The former method, which is less time and labor intensive, is preferable. It also avoids the problem of your taking time away from your presentation to pass out the handouts. If you do choose to pass them out before your talk, think about asking a conference organizer or colleague to do it for you. You are there to speak, not to count handouts. Also, remember to wait until everyone has copies before you refer to them. Organizers of your event can give you an estimate of the number of participants as a basis for making sufficient handouts. However, they may under or overestmate. Bring extra copies. If possible, put your materials up on a website and have the URL available to announce during your talk. Another option is to have a sign-up sheet so you can send handouts to those who don't get copies.

Body Language

A speaker does not have to be incredibly dynamic to be successful. Fluid and measured body movements are far more successful than striding around the podium. Strive to have your body movement fit in with the material you are discussing. Pounding the lectern may work in a political debate, but a calmer approach is usually more appropriate. Always remember that excessive body movement distracts your audience. You want them to hear your remarks, not to watch your hand movements. Practice your speech in front of a mirror or videotape it.

Eye Contact

Many years ago John was made aware of an obvious but frequently ignored aspect of public speaking by a foul-tempered U.S. Army sergeant. As he was briefing a class, the sergeant yelled (in a manner of speaking practiced only by sergeants!), "You #x!!#! Why are you talking to the x!!# board and not to the class?" Although he would have preferred a more moderate response to his speaking abilities, he nonetheless will never forget the sergeant's observation. The whiteboard and the lectern are most assuredly *not* your audience. A speaker who only looks at the board, the screen, or their notes is a speaker who has lost his or her audience. If you intend to write on a whiteboard, overhead projector, or flipchart, remain quiet until you have finished writing, and then turn and speak directly to the audience. People with hearing difficulties will be especially grateful if you follow this advice. Who knows—there may even be a sergeant or two in attendance who will smile in appreciation!

Establish rapport with those people who took the time to come hear you. Do not simply stare at a particular individual or a certain section of the room. Include everyone in your remarks by making eye contact with each section of the audience.

Time Warning

Keep a close eye on your watch. All of us have attended conferences and workshops where the speakers have droned on and on until their time has run out. Those in the audience with questions have to hope they can ask people sitting near them or collar the speaker after the speech. On behalf of audience members everywhere, we implore you to leave time for questions. Audience members are there because they are interested in your topic and they frequently have questions or would like clarification about a particular point. Allow for this. You should have timed your remarks during your preparation, but keeping track of your time is critical so you can cover your material with time to spare for questions. If you find this difficult to do, ask the event organizer to have someone flash you time reminders as you get close to the end of your allotted period. And if the questions go beyond the time available, provide your e-mail address and encourage audience members to contact you.

CONCLUSION

Speaking to a group can be an incredibly rewarding experience. If you are well prepared, you need not have anything to fear about the experience. The tips in this chapter will get you started. You may find yourself seeking out presentation opportunities, and you will soon find that your preparation becomes second nature. Don't be surprised when you are asked to speak again, and again, and again!

RELATED READINGS

Dowis, Richard. *The Lost Art of Great Speech: How to Write One, How to Deliver It.* New York: AMACOM, 2000.

ABOUT THE AUTHORS

Trudi E. Jacobson is the coordinator of user education programs at the University at Albany, SUNY, and an adjunct faculty member at the School of Information Science and Policy at the same institution. She coordinates and teaches the undergraduate information literacy credit courses, which reach approximately six hundred freshmen and sophomores each year. She also teaches numerous course-related instruction sessions. Her professional interests include the use of critical-thinking and active-learning activities in the classroom. She is the coeditor of *Teaching the New Library to Today's Users* (Neal-Schuman, 2000) and *Teaching Information Literacy Concepts: Activities and Frameworks from the Field* (Library Instruction Publications, 2001) and editor of *Critical Thinking and the Web: Teaching Users to Evaluate Internet Resources* (Library Instruction Publications, 2000). She has published articles in a number of journals, including *The Journal of General Education, College & Research Libraries, portal, Journal of Academic Librarianship, Research Strategies, College Teaching, The Teaching Professor*, and *Education*.

John R. Vallely, MA, MLS, is a librarian at Siena College in Loudonville, New York. His main responsibilities are in cataloging, but he plays an active role in the library's extensive instructional programs. He is also an adjunct professor in the Siena College history department where he teaches an upper-level course in U.S. military history. His public speaking experience includes classroom teaching, library instruction, serving as a guest lecturer, conducting battlefield tours for faculty and students at the Gettysburg National Park, and appearing before audiences ranging from high school students to professional military historians to the Daughters of the American Revolution.

47

Librarian as Educator, or Dewey, Dewey, and You?

Gale Hannigan and Kathleen Dalton

Librarianship and education go hand in hand, thus our acknowledgment of the two Deweys. Melvil Dewey was a reformer and librarian; John Dewey was a prominent philosopher-educator. Both made notable contributions to their respective fields: one to classification, the other to progressive education. Librarian-educators blend their two worlds. The word "educate" comes from the Latin *educere*, to lead forth or bring up (a child) (*Webster's International Dictionary*, 2nd ed.). As librarian-educators, we show the way to needed information and teach people of all ages the skills of information literacy.

GENERAL CHARACTERISTICS

Today's audience for library instruction routinely uses the Internet and has access to more information than any one library can hold. We no longer only teach people how to use libraries, but we also teach them how to navigate efficiently through a sea of information that is neither organized nor filtered for quality or accuracy. No wonder the catch phrase has become "information literacy," defined by the ACRL Standards Committee and approved by the Board of Directors of the Association of College and Research Libraries (ACRL) "as a set of abilities requiring individuals to recognize when information is needed and have the ability to locate, evaluate, and use effectively the needed information" (http://www.ala.org/Content/NavigationMenu/ACRL/Standards_and_Guidelines/Information_Literacy_Competency_Standards_for_Higher_Education.htm). Our students may be more computer literate than information literate and may confuse the two—what, they wonder, do librarians have to teach them? They may not see the need for information seeking skills; after all,

Google does a pretty good job of locating relevant websites. Or, they may be befuddled about where to begin, how to define a topic, and how to logically search for reliable information. Increasingly more curriculum initiatives stress the importance of information management and lifelong learning. Librarians find themselves working with other faculty to develop assignments because the discipline-based faculty are not as confident about their own information skills and also because they value the librarian as a partner in teaching. As more professions acknowledge that much of their work relates to information management, entire courses about the information aspects of a discipline will be introduced. Librarian-educators bring considerable expertise to these activities and achieve the satisfaction that comes with conveying the knowledge and skills that develop the confidence of knowing you can find, if it exists, any information you might need.

We all remember favorite teachers. Whether it was the passion for their subjects, their amazing expertise, or the ability to make us want to learn, the best teachers are knowledgeable and engaging. Not everyone can be a memorable teacher, but there are characteristics that effective educators need to have or develop. Among these are subject expertise, self-confidence, the ability to organize and distill information for a specific audience and make it meaningful, and effective presentation skills. Flexibility and a sense of humor help, especially when a session doesn't go as planned.

What follows are examples of common librarian-educator roles, representative situations, general characteristics, and questions that might help you decide if this is a career option that suits you.

REFERENCE SERVICES

Scenario: It is midmorning and you've helped several students working on an assignment to find biographical information about contemporary African American writers. At 10:30 a harried-looking student rushes in and asks if you can help him find a photograph of a UFO for an 11:00 class.

Characteristics

Education is a process and the librarian at the reference desk may not have the luxury of time for that process. The student in a hurry who approaches the desk should be commended for knowing where to go for information, but he is not a receptive audience for instruction. Effective educators recognize opportunity, and this is an opportunity to demonstrate expertise and helpfulness, not a teachable moment for explaining how to search databases or catalogs, what terms to use, or even to explain the location of materials in the library.

This student will be a repeat user if the librarian meets the immediate need within twenty minutes.

The more typical interaction at the reference desk often evolves into an opportunity to instruct users. For example, the student approaching the librarian for help with researching the death penalty does provide the opportunity for a mini-lesson. Searching the catalog together, reading entries, looking at classification numbers, locating the book, using the index or table of contents demonstrates a repeatable process. According to the U.S. Department of Education National Center for Education Statistics Integrated Postsecondary Education Data System *Academic Library Survey 1998*, more than 12,000 transactions like this occur every *week* at the Harvard University libraries.

The reference interview enables the librarian and the student to establish rapport and define the task. Formulating the right question is as important a skill as knowing where to find information. When asked what skills undergraduates should learn about using libraries, librarians at a large corporation said "knowing how to ask the right question—time is money." Asking what class the information is for (e.g., sociology, religion, rhetoric) helps the student realize there are different ways to approach a topic and possibly different sources to use for each approach. This perspective leads to the choice of appropriate databases. Many library websites organize their databases by subject or have pathfinders directing users to the appropriate sources. Reference librarians play an important role in developing these tools, as they are closest to the end-user.

Unlike classroom teachers, reference librarians are less in control of the parameters of instruction. The user defines the topic and it may be something unfamiliar to the librarian. Time is limited by the user's schedule and motivation as well as the needs of others waiting for reference assistance. A good reference librarian likes helping people and the challenge of finding information quickly. A busy day can be both fun and exhausting. There is an element of performance to be at a reference desk, willing to take on all comers. One librarian we know would start her shift at the reference desk by declaring "SHOWTIME!"

Questions to Ask Yourself

Do you like the unexpected and working "on demand?" Are you service-oriented and good at establishing rapport with strangers? Reference librarians do a quick assessment of personality and educational level. Do you mind being the expert in the process, but maybe not in the subject? Providing reference service requires a good working knowledge of resources and the ability to learn enough about a topic to help the user or make an intelligent referral. Not everything is about content. Tenacity and patience are key. It took several iterations by a persistent librarian to realize that the user who kept asking for a larger picture of the Mona Lisa really wanted the "full body view!" Are you able to multitask, be interrupted, and remain unflappable when faced with the unexpected? Reference librarians are expected to be experts in all aspects of word processing, know how to print from any software, clear paper jams, and fix equipment problems, not to mention give expert opinions about copyright, plagiarism, and citation formats. Do you believe that no question is stupid and that confidential inquiries are just that? Do you love to know a little about a lot of things? Good reference librarians are truly the experts when it comes to finding information about anything!

CLASS ASSIGNMENTS

Scenario: Eighteen freshmen arrive in the library for scheduled bibliographic instruction. Earlier in the semester, you were asked by their professor to present sources using female genital mutilation as the topic because the students would be reading Alice Walker's *Possessing the Secret of Joy*. The professor is unexpectedly unable to attend the session and you discover that the students have not yet been assigned the book.

Scenario: A hog factory farm is being built in the town. Local groups are up in arms. A faculty member works with you to identify sources that his students could use in researching the local situation and its global context. The class comes to the library following a discussion of the issues.

Characteristics

Every college student completes at least one research assignment. Faculty recognize that finding, evaluating, and using information are fundamental to learning. How they teach these skills varies: Some are creative in their assignments, some assign the traditional scavenger hunt. Many, but not all, involve the library. Fifteen years ago library instruction often consisted of compiling bibliographies and displaying books and periodicals relevant to assigned topics and discussing these with the class. Then came the Internet, Google, and Yahoo! Students used Joe's homepage for their research, never setting foot in the library. Faculty recognized what was happening to the research process and turned to librarians, who were somewhat responsible for making the Internet so easily accessible, to include Internet searching and critical thinking in their repertoire.

The library instruction session is often a one-shot, fifty-minute opportunity. An assigned research project is usually the impetus. Librarians may assist in developing the assignment, but they also may not. Either way, they are the ones who deal with novice researchers who don't know where to look, need ten sources, and "need them by tomorrow." The instruction session, geared to teaching search strategy and identifying quality resources that satisfy the requirements of the assignment, is expected to meet those needs, as well as allay anxieties about doing research in the future.

Librarians contribute important strengths to these assignments. While subject faculty often have expertise in specialized areas, librarians usually work across a wide range of disciplines and frequently see connections between them. The class researching the hog farm could look at resources from the domains of politics, science, journalism, economics, psychology, and sociology. Relevant materials may be found in popular magazines, scholarly journals, newspaper articles, government documents, and in primary sources such as interviews and meeting minutes.

But therein lies the challenge: so much information, so little time. A session in the library is efficient and allows the librarian to address the class's needs once rather than eighteen individual times. But the fifty-minute challenge is to reach all of those students with information they can use. Most instruction librarians talk fast and every sentence is a nugget of knowledge. Involving students is critical, with lots of "hands-on" activities—on indexes, on encyclopedias, on computers! Introducing novice researchers to an array of disciplines and sources, while making sure that all computers are working and everyone is "on the same page," requires solid, prior knowledge of the sources, searches, and results. Doing all of this well takes planning, creativity, public speaking skills, and stamina. Some students may be bored by the topic and process; others might be experts. As with all classroom teaching, instructor control and enthusiasm are important to success.

In some academic institutions, librarians have faculty status; in others they do not. But in either case, librarians who demonstrate knowledge of their resources, who actively market their instruction programs, who work on a daily basis with the faculty either in library liaison programs or campuswide committees, are usually recognized as peers by the teaching faculty. They work with faculty, encouraging them to assign research, to schedule instruction sessions, and to feel comfortable walking into the library for a spontaneous instruction session.

Questions to Ask Yourself

Can you present material in a clear and logical manner, showing progressive steps such as in a search strategy? Do you have a classroom "presence?" In some situations there may be discipline issues; do you want to deal with these? Are you collaborative and diplomatic? After all, you are an invited guest in someone else's course but also an expert in your own right. You may have to negotiate content so that both you and the course instructor are satisfied that each of your goals will be achieved.

TRAINING SESSIONS

Scenario: Your flight was late. It's 10:00 P.M., and you are just now checking into the hotel. There is just enough time to get some sleep and spend thirty minutes on the hotel's treadmill in the morning before you are due to arrive at the library at 7:45 to meet your host and check out the equipment for an all-day training session that starts at 9:00.

Scenario: It's 10:00 P.M.. It's dark. It's cold. You are trudging across campus pushing a cart laden with a laptop and a projector. For the past few weeks you have been negotiating with a residence assistant to schedule a dorm visit. This is it. Twenty students should be waiting. If they all have questions, this session could last a couple of hours.

Characteristics

The widespread use of library systems, specialized databases, and information management applications means there are many people who need to learn to use them. Here we distinguish training from other types of teaching, although they may overlap. The trainer's goal is to concisely communicate the skills to use a specific resource. Training is often presented as step-by-step instructions to a willing audience of users and potential users of that resource. Unlike a session designed around an assignment where using the resource is a means to an end, not the end itself, training is often "context free." Trainers may only meet their audience once. Attendees may be professionals, including other information specialists, as well as end-users. Career trainers usually work for companies that sell an information product; their goal is to attract and retain customers for that product.

Working as a trainer means developing and delivering an engaging session that accomplishes the task of transmitting specific skills. Audience expectations are high; technical problems or the inability to satisfactorily answer questions will alienate an audience. Trainers must project confidence and expertise, as well as poise under the pressure of whatever thing (small or big) is bound to go wrong.

Trainers typically travel, which means long days and nights away from home. Considerable preparation is required—both personally and professionally. Appropriate clothes, copies of handouts, equipment, and contact information make up most trainers' essentials. As a trainer, you may finally meet people who have been phone contacts for a long time. It is a social role at work, meeting many people all at once and being "center stage" from the beginning to the end of the training period. The pay may be higher in private industry.

Although the trend is to incorporate library instruction into the curriculum, many libraries offer stand-alone sessions about searching the catalog, major databases, and new information technologies such as PDAs. These may be held in the library or in outreach sites, such as dormitories, community centers, hospitals, and so on. Characteristics are similar as those for commercial trainers, but with less travel, better familiarity with the audience, and, perhaps, more control over the technology. These are usually one- to two-hour sessions, scheduled at a time convenient for the attendees. That may mean 7:00 A.M. in a hospital or 10:00 P.M. in a dorm.

Questions to Ask Yourself

Do you like working in different places, meeting new people, and being the center of attention? Do you enjoy giving the same presentation time and time again? Can you organize materials logically and develop polished presentations, handouts, and exercises? Are you an effective public speaker with good voice projection—or willing to develop these skills? Do you perform well under pressure and handle the unexpected with composure, such as when the equipment doesn't work and there are no IT staff available? Is traveling for work something you would enjoy? Do you function well at all times of day? Are you effective at marketing a resource or service?

COURSES

Scenario: Next week you have three medical students scheduled for an evidence-based medicine rotation (ten contact hours); one medical student enrolled in your two-week, Web-based computers and medical information elective; and twelve MLS students in the three-credit course, introduction to health sciences information management, which is a combination of in-class and Web-based curriculum. You've just spent two hours grading last week's assignment for this course and are preparing to post the next assignment.

Characteristics

The recognized importance of information management creates significant opportunities for librarians to assume a more formal teaching role. A growing number of librarians are responsible for teaching entire courses. With that responsibility come the more traditional roles of teaching, such as developing curriculum and grading. The opportunity to work with a group of students over time can be quite different from the "one-shot" workshop or session. Feedback flows both ways and students can be quite grade oriented. The semester schedule imposes its own constraint and students juggle courses and personal situations.

Conscientious faculty members are busy people. Full-time faculty in schools of library and information science are also expected to conduct research and publish. Faculty librarians based in libraries are still part of a service organization and are expected to contribute to the overall goals of the library. If under a tenure system, they are also required to do research and publish. These librarians may not have another departmental affiliation and may be isolated from teaching faculty in other academic departments. With joint appointments, they have responsibilities in more than one department. No one easily escapes myriad meetings associated with any organization.

Teaching an entire semester course is labor intensive and involves developing educational objectives, creating a syllabus, making assignments, grading, arranging for guest speakers, and managing classroom logistics. These efforts, plus the time spent actually teaching, take time away from other responsibilities. For practicing librarians, teaching a course—especially an online course, which is less visible to others—is an addition to, instead of in lieu of, other activities.

Web-based courses and distance education represent two popular trends in teaching. Librarian course directors have advantages when it comes to using educational technology simply because they have been computer systems users for so long. Promoting interaction among students can be a challenge, but few will disagree that student-teacher interaction soars when mediated by e-mail. Enrollment numbers can explode, too, when not limited by classroom seating. As a result, many instructors find that they spend much more time teaching than they did in the past, even if some of it can be at home and in your pajamas!

The relationships between students and teachers can be energizing and draining at the same time. It is a delight to be around motivated learners, but what about the indifferent student enrolled in a required course? Many students share information about their personal lives and view the teacher as a mentor and advisor about matters outside the scope of the course. Long after a student is gone, you may be asked to write a letter of reference.

A major reward of teaching a course is the potential for making an impact on someone's knowledge and point of view. Effective teachers select and organize content from an overwhelming amount of available information. There is bias in selection. How you develop and deliver the curriculum speaks volumes about what you believe is most important about the subject.

Questions to Ask Yourself

Can you conceptualize and implement an entire course or successfully plan one with other instructors? Are you comfortable giving feedback, advising, and assigning grades? Do you communicate clearly and enthusiastically? Are you ready to assume the authority and influence that comes with the position? Are you interested in pursuing an advanced degree or subject specialization that is typically required for a career as a full-time teaching faculty member?

TRENDS

You've probably heard that one trend is for educators to be "guides on the side" rather than "sages on the stage." This bodes well for librarian-educators, since so much of our tradition is working with people to help them find what they want rather than what we decided they want. Another significant trend is distance education, which creates challenges for traditional library support as well as providing us with the opportunities for using videoconferencing and Web-based technology to deliver curriculum.

Lifelong learning is essential for everyone as career opportunities change and new skills are needed. Librarians have to be lifelong learners. No sooner are we expert in one search interface, when another one comes along. We often have to teach what we have just ourselves learned to do, and sometimes we are learning along with (or from) our users. Many of us who teach did not start with formal training in education but learned on the job, through continuing education courses and conferences, and reading and hearing about what others do. We are probably ahead of the curve as far as teaching adult learners and teaching process instead of content—growing trends in education.

Assessment is a current hot topic in academe. Librarian-educators can expect to be assessed in annual reviews by their supervisors and in formal and informal feedback from students and faculty. It is no longer sufficient to count the number of sessions, contact hours, and participants, there is now increased interest in objectively measuring the impact of library services, including user education.

REWARDS

If you love learning and believe that education is an answer to the world's woes, you will probably get great satisfaction from being a librarian-educator. If you are energized by the hunt for information and want to lead, that is, to educate others in their quests, you will enjoy your work. When a student says you are the reason he made it through college, or a professor tells her students you know everything, or a physician sends an e-mail praising the search skills of a student, or an alum calls to ask the name of a database you showed her because she wants to recommend it to her boss, when you see people competent in using information resources—then you will know that you have done your job well.

RELATED READINGS

Hanna, D. E., M. Glowacki-Dudka, and S. Conceicao-Runlee. *147 Practical Tips for Teaching Online Groups: Essentials of Web-Based Education*. Madison, Wisc.: Atwood, 2000.

Meulemans, Y. N., and J. Brown. "Educating Instruction Librarians: A Model for Library and Information Science Education." *Research Strategies* 18 (2001): 253–64.

ABOUT THE AUTHORS

We are sisters as well as librarians and university faculty. Some of our earliest memories have to do with playing school—an enthusiastic seven-year-old teacher with her eager four-year-old student. No wonder, to this day, teaching and learning are significant aspects of our job responsibilities and satisfaction.

Kathleen Dalton began her career as a classroom teacher and now works at Susquehanna University where she provides reference service and workshops, and works with other faculty in designing course assignments. Gale Hannigan teaches at the graduate level in medical and public health informatics at Texas A&M University and as adjunct faculty in library and information science at the University of North Texas. Both are tenured faculty.

48

Effective Writing for the Career Librarian

Bob Schatz

WHY WRITE?

Writing is important. It provides for posterity a record of thoughts, plans, and actions. During the course of your library career, you will write any number of documents, some of which may include:

- E-mails
- Letters
- Employee evaluations
- Training manuals
- Announcements
- Reports
- Recommendations
- Solicitations
- Policies
- Brochures

. . . just to name a few.

Your writing will make the difference in the library in how efficiently things work. In extreme cases, it may affect your library's legal standing in matters of importance. From an individual standpoint, the documents you write will reflect on you personally and professionally. As with other matters of presentation and conduct, you will want to present your best effort when you are asked to write as part of your work-related responsibilities.

Writing well is made up of various components: using words correctly, framing your text in a logical sequence, knowing when to bring things to an end. Writing effectively is trickier. It relies on your understanding the various vested interests that may be at work and incorporating those interests into what you write. It may sound simple, but in reality it can be quite complex.

Take, for instance, a letter you are asked to write to an angry patron who wants an "offensive" book removed from the library's collection. Most libraries have written policies outlining the specifics for accepting and rejecting materials, so your response should be fairly easy to craft, at least in terms of its factual content. Imagine, though, that the patron in question is the library's most significant financial donor and a friend of your director. Suddenly, your effort to write effectively may become more complicated. Adhere to official policy, and you run the risk of offending this important library contributor. Bend to this patron's demands, and you may leave the library open to criticism from other quarters, including your own conscience.

SETTING OBJECTIVES

It will be helpful, before you begin any professional writing task, to clarify such things as:

- Who are the "stakeholders" within the library, and where do their needs lie? Do your supervisors have a vested interest in seeing certain information included or excluded in your work? Do they need the information presented in a certain way? What do they stand to gain or lose?
- What is the primary audience of the piece?
- Is there more than one audience?
- What are their objectives, and do they need to be addressed in what you write?
- Do they have preconceived opinions that need to be factored into your writing?
- What are their language skills? If you use jargon or technical terminology, will they understand?
- What are your language skills? Do you have command of the right words to express the information you need to present? Do you have access to expertise you may be lacking?
- How will the final "product" be presented? Are there space or format limitations that will affect how you present your material?
- Will graphics be included? How will you acquire these, and will their presentation affect what you need to express in words?
- When is the piece due? Are there time constraints that will affect your ability to present your material as planned?

It is helpful to consider all of these factors before you start pulling together the actual information you will be presenting. At the informational stage, you'll need to determine the sequence of presentation. While your facts should flow in a logical sequence, there are other things to consider as well.

Determining your end objective is essential to knowing what information is important and how it should be presented. In other words, begin any writing assignment by analyzing the situation, identifying outcomes, and validating those objectives against the library's overall needs. Where the situation lacks clarity, get input and information from colleagues and supervisors. If the outcomes carry some risk, make sure you have a clear picture of where you need to be at the end to avoid bad results either for the library or yourself. Whether you are writing official correspondence, creating training materials, or crafting a descriptive brochure, your writing will benefit by having a clear understanding of the purpose to which you are working.

THINKING STRATEGICALLY

Once you know what your writing needs to achieve at its end point, you'll need to analyze how best to get to that outcome. Consider this your road map. Just as in the planning for a trip, you'll have to take into consideration the possible routes you might take to achieve your identified objectives, the condition of the roads, the weather you'll encounter, and the terrain.

What sequence of presentation will make your writing more understandable? What conceptual or informational hurdles will come between you and an outcome that will be understood and appreciated by your readers? How will you surmount those hurdles? Do you have to factor in audience expectations or preconceived biases? (Never forget that writing in the professional context always has an audience. Success depends on their understanding and acceptance of the information you present.)

When your audience may be resistant to an idea, don't present your key arguments too directly. Soften that resistance with broad background information that will give them a fuller understanding of the larger issues at hand. Imagine you have to present a request for funding to acquire increased security services within the library. Perhaps the body to whom you will be presenting this request (your city or state government, the university administration, a board of trustees) does not want to provide any further funds to the library. Rather than jump too quickly to the specifics of the request, give a background view of the situation or events that are behind the request. By providing a fuller understanding, you may reduce the level of resistance that remains by the time you present the specific request for funds.

THE ACTUAL WRITING

When you have gathered and analyzed all the "context pieces" that relate to your assignment, you will finally be ready to write. Starting can sometimes be difficult. Here are a couple of suggestions. When replying to some kind of correspondence, start with a thank you. Even if the letter/e-mail you received was unfriendly, you can thank the writer for sharing his or her thoughts. Thanking someone sets a respectful tone to your reply. From there, you can take the correspondence any direction you need, but at least you've begun on a positive note.

In other situations, beginning with a statement of purpose will be helpful to both you and the reader(s) of the piece. "The purpose of this brochure is to describe new library services in the area of . . ." or "The purpose of this report is to provide an overview on the library's current financial crisis," and so on. By identifying the purpose of your writing, the reader has a chance to adjust his or her attention toward that end. You have also provided yourself with a mission statement for the piece on which you are working. When you complete your writing, you can use this statement to measure whether you achieved your objective.

From your initial statements, try to keep the flow of information logical. One of the great features of word processing is the ability to pick up sentences or paragraphs and rearrange them. Sometimes you'll have the right information, but in the wrong sequence. Keep in mind that your readers are viewing your work for the first time, so you need to make sure they understand the flow of your presentation. As you are writing, think of the word "therefore" to maintain a logical flow. When there is no "therefore" sentence that follows the one you've just completed, your paragraph will likely be at an end. When there is no new "therefore" paragraph that follows the one just composed, your piece may be at its end.

When you write, use language you can control. If you try to throw in technical terms or jargon with which you are not entirely familiar, you may misuse those terms or make your writing less comfortable for your readers. It is even more important to understand the likely language skills of your audience. As much as possible, craft your writing to the level at which those people will be most comfortable. If your readers are nonprofessional, be sure to provide definitions for library terms you use. If they are experts, don't make your writing too simplistic; it will insult them. And keep a thesaurus handy. Find a variety of words to express your thoughts, to avoid boredom and redundancy.

Remember that time is valuable in the workplace. Your readers may not have much of it to devote to the reading of your piece. There's nothing that guarantees your audience will read all of what you've written. As such, keep your presentation brisk and interesting, though not abrupt. Where ten words will make your point, don't use one hundred. Where you are presenting complicated information, break up your writing into more easily read short sentences. Long, winding sentences and paragraphs lose readers' interest and create confusion. When in doubt, read long sentences out loud. Usually, you'll be able to hear when they need to be made shorter.

When you are writing long documents, take "brain breaks." Over time, your mental acuity will become dull. Taking a coffee break or going for a short walk can revive you and help make your writing crisper.

THE IMPORTANCE OF PROOFREADING AND REWRITING

When you have finished, reread what you've written, preferably the next day when you can look at your results with fresher eyes. It won't be as good as you remembered, but that's OK. Good writing requires numerous rewrites, even for the best writers. Be prepared to edit and rewrite portions of your work until all the words make sense and all the pieces fit together properly. Be sure to validate your work against your initial objectives and what you know about the audience for the piece and their objectives.

For serious writers, proofreading is about much more than correcting misspellings. Look at the individual words you've used to describe things. Are they the best ones for the purpose? Does your phrasing grab the reader's attention? Are your arguments and explanations clear and compelling? Be demanding on yourself when you proofread and edit your work.

Before you declare your work completed, proofread it in its final physical form. If you are presenting information as a printed report, don't review your work on a computer. By printing a copy for yourself, you may spot problems that would not be apparent on a screen. Since part of effective writing is the presentation itself, it will be helpful to see how your work looks on the printed page, where breaks or section titles may make the information more accessible, where graphs and charts should appear, and so on.

Ideally, have another person proofread your work. They will spot concepts that lack clarity or typographical errors you might miss. They can also tell you whether your presentation was convincing. The more attributes your proofreader shares with your final audience, the more they'll be able to help you determine whether you've crafted an effective piece.

LESSONS LEARNED

Understanding why some writing fails can help make your writing even better. Here are a few reasons why your writing may not be as effective as you'd like:

- Your work is factually in error. Sometimes in the rush of getting a piece written, you can fail to gather correct information. In a professional organization, the factual accuracy of your work is essential.
- You misuse words. When in doubt, look up words and definitions in a dictionary. By doing so, instead of relying on the spell-checker on your computer, you will acquire a better, more useful vocabulary.
- Your writing rambles or is disorganized. This is usually caused by rushing through your work or not proofreading your results. Be committed to rereading and rewriting your work until it is right. In the library setting, your work is a reflection of your professional values.
- The presentation is good, but you failed to meet the objectives of your assignment. Always validate the final product against your original goals. If you haven't met those goals, you need to recraft your work or alter the expectations of your audience. This is another example of the need to reread and rewrite until the outcome is correct.
- Your presentation is too text-heavy. Visual images can help express concepts in ways that are too ponderous for words. They also help break up the monotony of the written page. Where your work is lengthy, look for ways to break up the content so it will be more approachable for your readers.

GOOD HABITS

Since writing will be part of your professional activities, there are certain habits that will help make you a better writer:

- Practice. Like any other skill, writing develops over time and through usage. Don't shy away from opportunities to write. It will become more comfortable each time you do it.
- Be a discerning reader. Notice others' writing and what excites or offends you. News articles, advertisements, pleasure reading, and professional reading all afford you an opportunity to see how others have tackled the task of writing. Look for guideposts within their work.
- Seek feedback. Other people can help you track your progress as a writer. Seek out their opinions, and don't let negative feedback scare you off; they are doing you a favor by pointing out areas that need improvement.

Plentiful outside resources are available for anyone serious about writing. Large bookstores usually have whole sections devoted to writing tools, ranging from the "For Dummies" series to monographs with a more scholarly viewpoint. Since different writing projects will bring different demands, you may find a variety of these tools useful to you over time.

Most universities and community colleges offer writing courses that can be helpful. Even courses on creative writing can help you hone skills that you apply in the workplace. Outside of the academic setting, business-related courses on writing are offered by companies specializing in professional seminars. These, too, can help improve your writing capabilities.

If you are looking for a more private setting in which to practice writing, consider keeping a journal. Daily practice, even if you are only jotting down personal thoughts, can help you become a better writer in all applications. For a fun way to expand your vocabulary, fill in the crossword puzzle in your daily newspaper. Whatever approach you take to practicing writing, your efforts should help you in ways that will be useful in the library.

Writing is an essential part of professional librarianship. Each writing task you undertake is an opportunity to demonstrate the seriousness with which you take your work as a librarian. Embrace that opportunity. Your efforts will be rewarding and will help make your career as a librarian even more fulfilling.

ABOUT THE AUTHOR

In addition to an MLS, Bob Schatz has a degree in communications and is a graduate of the publishing procedures course held annually at Harvard University. For the last twenty-five years, he has worked with libraries as a bookseller in several different organizations. He currently works as president of Franklin Book Co., Inc. Bob is a frequent speaker at conferences and has made numerous contributions to library literature. Among his other professional activities, he serves on the editorial board of a major library journal and recently served on a task force for the North American Serials Interest Group.

49

The Core of Leadership: Skills for Emerging Leaders

Teri R. Switzer

The study of leadership brings about several discussions ranging from what leadership is to the roles leaders play and what skills an effective leader should have. There is no doubt that the concept of leadership is as deep as it is broad. However, as we examine the core of leadership, it is important to look at the roles a leader plays in order to have a better idea of the skills necessary to fulfill those roles.

ROLES OF LEADERSHIP

According to Henry Mintzberg (1973), there are three primary roles that form leadership: interpersonal, informational, and decisional. Interpersonal roles are those that surface from formal authority and status. In other words, interpersonal roles are typically thought of as those of a figurehead or authority figure. They define the structure in which the work is accomplished, and they oversee the tasks. The informational role has responsibility for monitoring internal operations and external events, providing an analysis of the events, looking at ideas and trends, and disseminating the information as needed. The decisional role initiates and designs the actions to be taken as well as serving as the heart of the organizational strategy and acting as the organization's representative in major negotiations.

Within each of these three roles are other roles that effective leaders find themselves in. Although these roles are the more traditional ones, they provide a broad outline of the direction that a leader's responsibilities can take. It is all of these roles that form the core of leadership and upon which skill sets are created.

COMPONENTS OF LEADERSHIP

As today's library leader looks for tools and solutions in the efficient administration of the organization, the concept of leadership skills becomes important. However, separating the skills from the traits is difficult. Synthesizing the skills a leader should possess is a task that has been the subject of several dissertations.

Perhaps one of the most straightforward approaches to determining essential leadership skills is examining James M. Kouzes' and Barry Z. Posner's (1995) five leadership practices common to successful leaders. These five practices will be used as a foundation for our discussion on leadership skills.

According to Kouzes and Posner, leaders who are at their personal best make a commitment to a vision while maintaining a high level of integrity by following five practices:

- Challenge the process
- Inspire a shared vision
- Enable others to act
- Model the way
- Encourage the heart

Within each of these five practices are behaviors that form the basis of effective leadership. These behaviors make up what Kouzes and Posner (1995) call the ten commitments of leadership. When looking at the skills associated with these behaviors, it is necessary to examine each behavior and extract those parts that are critical to accomplishing the practice each is associated with, thus providing a list of the skill sets exemplary leaders should possess.

CHALLENGE THE PROCESS

The two behaviors associated with this practice are:

- searching out challenging opportunities to change, grow, innovate, and improve; and
- experimenting, taking risks, and learning from the accompanying mistakes.

Leaders who challenge the process are not complacent. They welcome and proactively analyze change. They recognize the importance of risk and the failures that often accompany these risks. Many people are uncomfortable taking risks because of the fear of failure. It is vital that leaders alleviate some of this fear and instill a sense of creativity and innovativeness. Leaders foster a desire to try the untried, analyze what occurred, and then make changes as needed.

Some of the characteristics leaders exhibit when expanding their "comfort zones" include imagination, inspiration, forward-looking, courage, ambition, and determination. These leaders are fair and model risktaking in their own lives.

INSPIRING THE VISION

The two behaviors associated with this practice are:

- envisioning an uplifting and ennobling future; and
- enlisting others in a common vision by appealing to their values, interests, hopes, and dreams.

Inspiring employees should be looked at as a reciprocal process. In order for leaders to inspire their employees effectively, they need to have a well-grounded belief for the organization's vision, mission, and goals within themselves. To do that, they continually examine these beliefs and test these beliefs. These leaders envision what the future can and should look like. They see the invisible. They transmit their beliefs and visions to others. These leaders are passionate, supportive, believing, caring, imaginative, and cooperative. They use their experiences to inspire and motivate.

ENABLING OTHERS TO ACT

Behaviors connected with this practice are:

- fostering collaboration by promoting cooperative goals and building trust; and
- strengthening people by giving power away, providing choices, developing competence, assigning critical tasks, and offering visible support.

A good leader realizes the importance of letting others take an active role in creating and reaching the organization's vision, according to Margaret J. Wheatley (1999); a good leader also fosters accountability while encouraging others with truthful and meaningful information. The practice of silo-ism, or keeping one's work knowledge to oneself and using it to build power, is not one that the exemplary leader follows. Instead, leaders share the power and, in doing so, build trust within the organization's ranks. These leaders are co-operative, broad-minded, supportive, inspiring, and fair-minded. They mentor, coach, and train their employees.

MODELING THE WAY

Leaders who are not afraid to go first

- set the example by behaving in ways that are consistent with shared values; and
- achieve small wins that promote consistent progress and build commitment.

Mentoring and modeling are important tools in the leadership academy. Exemplary leaders show the way and know the importance of being successful in one's job. They give their staff concrete examples to follow. They are specific and realistic when offering suggestions for improvement. They impart to their staff the meaning behind the organization's values. They build confidence by recognizing progress. These leaders are competent, inspiring, supportive, straightforward, mature, and forward-looking.

ENCOURAGING THE HEART

There is nothing more important than a leader who can maintain high spirits and encourage employees to go that extra mile. The behaviors associated with this practice are:

- recognizing individual contributions to the success of every project; and
- celebrating team accomplishments regularly.

Exemplary leaders not only believe in the vision but also see the possibilities of the future and instill that excitement in others. They encourage motivation and publicly acknowledge all successes. Leaders who recognize the importance of celebrating successes and people's accomplishments are caring, supporting, broad-minded, honest, and fair-minded.

DEVELOPING LEADERSHIP SKILLS

There are several individuals considered to be great leaders. One of the more recently recognized leaders is the Antarctic explorer Ernest Shackleton.

Shackleton led twenty-seven crew members on a failed Antarctic expedition in the early 1900s. Although the expedition was, by all accounts, an utter failure, the mere fact remains that in spite of becoming stranded with few supplies, inclement weather looming, and death imminent, Shackleton refused to give up and safely returned every one of his men to home port.

According to Margot Morrell and Stephanie Capparell (2001), Shackleton's leadership skills consisted of ten concepts. These concepts directly coincide with Kouzes and Posner's ten commitments of leadership. They include:

- Cultivate a sense of compassion and responsibility for others.
- Commit to sticking through the tough learning period.
- Do whatever is needed to maintain a positive and cheerful work environment.
- Broaden your cultural and social horizons, and learn to see things differently from how you normally would.
- Seize new opportunities and learn new skills.
- Use failures to your advantage.
- Try something new, but make sure you plan well.
- Learn from your mistakes.
- Never insist on reaching a goal at any cost.
- Engage in respectful competition and do not be drawn into public disputes.

Underpinning all of these skills is one concept that is not explicitly mentioned but that is far-reaching—communication. Unfortunately, many libraries, like many business organizations, have communication failures. One of the most important skills a leader can possess is being able to effectively communicate to his/her employees and other colleagues. So much of what a leader is responsible for depends on being able to communicate effectively.

Communication has different forms and includes verbal, nonverbal, and listening skills. Of these, listening is the most important, and most difficult, skill a leader can possess. Good listeners use their body when they actively listen. They generally look at the person talking and will use facial expressions to show interest and comprehension. However, hearing and listening are two different concepts. Good listeners concentrate on what is being said. Their minds are focused on the present rather than what the day's activities are or what was done the day before. They not only hear the words but they also understand the words and the message that is being sent.

Nonverbal communication is used to heighten the process of verbal communication. Facial expressions, hand gestures, body posture, and proximity to the recipient(s) are all nonverbal behaviors effective leaders exhibit. As a leader, it is important to have an understanding of the roles verbal and nonverbal communication play when interacting with other people in a work setting.

CONCLUSION

Leadership involves many different roles and many different tasks including committing to a vision, imparting that vision to others in the organization, and maintaining a high level of integrity. These tasks, as well as the dozens of other tasks a leader is responsible for, are accomplished by utilizing the skills learned and perfected over the course of one's lifetime. The leader inspires, models, enables, and encourages while not losing sight of the organization's vision and mission. A leader's skills are not stagnate. Instead, a leader's skills are in a continuous process of improvement. It is through this process of continuous learning and refining of one's skill set that the core of good leadership is found.

RELATED READINGS

Kouzes, James M., and Barry Z. Posner. *The Leadership Challenge*. San Francisco: Jossey-Bass, 1995.
Mintzberg, Henry. *The Nature of Managerial Work*. New York: Harper Row, 1973.
Morrell, Margot, and Stephanie Capparell. *Shackleton's Way*. New York: Penguin Books, 2001.
Wheatley, Margaret J. *Leadership and the New Science*. San Francisco: Berrett-Koehler Publishers, 1999.

ABOUT THE AUTHOR

Teri R. Switzer has been a librarian for thirty years and is assistant director for research, operations, and document delivery at the Auraria Library, University of Colorado at Denver.

7

PROFESSIONAL DEVELOPMENT

50

The Art and Science of Professional Behavior

Nancy George

Knowing how to act, or behave, in a job is an art. When you think of it, we spend more waking hours at work than at home. Pretty crazy. But this means that our behavior at work, or our professional behavior, is all the more important because we are going to be stuck with these people, our coworkers, for literally hours and hours each day and week. And don't forget our interactions with those pesky patrons who interrupt us at the most inopportune times!

All professions have some sort of guidelines for how to act on the job. For example, in my reading I came across something from, of all things, *Modern Machine Shop* that was appropriate for most professions: "I believe professionalism is earned by behavior, not bestowed. It's earned by taking care of business in a manner that is commensurate with one's vocation. There are ethics and morals involved in professionalism. There's also a big dose of competence."

So, if librarians are supposed to act in a certain way, how is it we're supposed to act? Do we fashion ourselves after the old, stereotypical librarian—you know, the old maid, pencil through bun, reading glasses perched on nose? Gee, Donna Reed in the dream scene of *It's a Wonderful Life*. I would hope that those days are long gone—although unfortunately, I've had some colleagues who would fit that visual bill. Or do we want to be like the *Lipstick Librarian* of Web fame? Outfitted in a slinky outfit, teetering on some flaming stiletto heels? Using your time at the reference desk to achieve beauty and fame? I've not worked with any *Lipstick Librarians*, but I had an interview with a wannabe librarian who showed up for the interview wearing a little tank top, revealing tattoos. It was visually pleasing, for those into body artistry. We certainly remembered this candidate and thought that perhaps she'd relate well with our similarly festooned student patrons, but wondered if she'd get along with colleagues. (We are unfortunately of a certain age, with gray hairs outnumbering tattoos and body piercings.)

A librarian who has been at a job a long time might be getting a bit relaxed in her professional behavior. Dressed in super casual clothes and slumped down in her chair, she's spending all of her energies working on her cat fancy club's web page, bidding for items on eBay, pointing to items on the reference shelves, and dusting off those old mimeographed bibliographic instruction handouts. With whiteout on the sections labeled *card catalog*, no one can tell what's going on—or can they?

Librarians new at a job have an especially rough time figuring out how to behave in an organization. One hurdle has been reached—that is, getting the job. Obviously, the new librarian did something right—otherwise she or he'd still be looking for a job. Something must've clicked between the interviewed and interviewers. But once the newbie starts the job, then what? How does one navigate the minefields in a new library? And there are minefields! This is especially true if the library's librarian population has been working there for ages. Twenty-five years, ten years, thirty years. Whatever. There's bound to be "bad blood" between some of them, a general feeling of how things should be done and have been done for decades, and a general feeling of distrust toward a youngster joining their ranks. This new employee is becoming a part of their comfortable or uncomfortable family, and some of them are not going to like it. Not one bit.

And what about those patrons?

SURVIVING BEHIND THE SCENES

The Boss

First off, figure out who your boss is. In a public library setting, you might have a number of bosses—the library board, the library director, and a department head. School librarians may report to a library director and principal. In an academic setting you may report to a library director and a department head. Be careful. Your colleagues serving on a Peer Evaluation Committee may do your annual evaluations instead of the director or department head. So, in essence, they are all your bosses. Yikes!

In Will Manley's very funny book *Unprofessional Behavior: Confessions of a Public Librarian*, he describes a number of his jobs and the characters he encountered. In the chapter "Learning to Love Prime Rib," he states:

> Get along with your boss. If you can't get along with your boss two things will happen: you will end up being very miserable, and you will end up being very

unemployed. . . . Once you have mastered the art of not calling your boss a jerk, you need to learn your boss's idiosyncrasies. . . . Most bosses have three strong beliefs, usually in the areas of religion, politics, and sports. For instance, if your boss is a Roman Catholic Democrat who loves the Chicago Cubs it would be very intelligent of you to (a) convert to Catholicism, (b) say some derogatory things about lame-brained Republicans, and (c) start wearing a Cubs hat. Sooner than you think, your value in the eyes of the boss will go up immeasurably. (1992)

He's going a little over the edge on this one, but at least try to fit in. If you notice your boss and colleagues are dressed in casual wear, don't come in dressed in a suit. If the atmosphere is casual and relaxed, socialize with your colleagues at the break table. Go to birthday parties and luncheons. You'll find that most of the information you can learn about an organization comes from informal conversations and situations. But don't overdo it because your colleagues may think you're a slacker! If, on the other hand, your colleagues look like the *Lipstick Librarian*, you might want to invest in some fancy clothes that you feel comfortable in and are dressier than your casual shirt and jogging pants. Follow patterns of behavior for where you are employed. Don't burn any bridges or annoy anyone. Be observant and flexible and act appropriately.

When I Was at Princeton . . .

An easy way to annoy everyone is to constantly compare a previous institution with the new institution. The new place, of course, always comes up short. Things were always done better at the previous institution. I worked with a librarian who constantly said, "When I was at Princeton. . . ." She used that phrase enough times to make me want to drive her back to Princeton; no easy feat considering I was living in Indiana at the time. Make most of your comparisons in your head and suggest change based on these mental comparisons. Don't say, "When I was at University X." And don't say it in a snooty way. This is no way to win friends!

Rome Wasn't Built in a Day

Something that new and seasoned librarians forget is that Rome wasn't built in a day. Many librarians new on a job like to work really, really hard. You know, write a collection development plan for the library after arriving three months ago, retool an instruction program with little idea as to what sort of program is in place, give fifty-minute instruction sessions filled with two

hours worth of information, suggest a total reorganization of the library organizational structure—based, of course, on his or her previous institution. In
general, they go about eighty miles an hour in a twenty-five-mile-an-hour
school zone. I was the new librarian who wrote a professional development
policy after arriving three months before that. Crazy. All I managed to do was
infuriate colleagues who were busy not working due to various states of personal mental anguish and mental illnesses.

Don't Be a Naughty Johnny

Don't exaggerate on resumes. When I was growing up, my mother loved
to talk about her father. A scrappy fellow, he was hardly ever without a job
due to his skills at filling out job applications. Butcher, mechanic, engineer, there wasn't a job he couldn't take on. Filled with a great deal of self-
confidence and the ability to charm anyone, he would learn skills after getting a job. He never admitted a lack of skills, but would ask questions and
bluff his way through situations. It's amazing how many librarians exaggerate on resumes or job applications, but are horrible at the bluffing part
of the game. If you have stretched the truth on a resume, try to pick up a
few of these exaggerated skills *before* the job begins—or be good at learning on the job.

I had a librarian apply for a job requiring Web skills. Let me refer to him
as Naughty Johnny. Naughty Johnny stated on his resume that he had experience putting up web pages and even provided URLs for the web pages he
produced. However, when Naughty Johnny began the job, it became obvious
he had no Web skills, and, in fact, he even admitted to having few skills in
this area. What?! I couldn't believe what he was saying. I felt betrayed by
Naughty Johnny who obviously exaggerated (lied) on his resume and during
the interview. In addition, I was amazed he was too lazy to get some Web
skills between the time of the interview and his first day on the job. It's a
small librarian world out there and librarians love to talk. It's not in anyone's
best interest to behave like this.

Keep Up with the Profession

Do your homework. Don't know how to use those new-fangled electronic resources or how to use a print reference tool? Take the time to learn the skills.
Read manuals, ask questions, and attend workshops. Constantly update your
skills. It's part of the job and being a professional. Fall behind with what's
happening in the profession and you might as well be that librarian with the
bun. Keep up with the action and have fun!

Do Lunch

Network with your colleagues, the teachers at your school, your library's Friend's group, a Rotary Club, the teaching faculty at your college/university, other librarians in the area, and librarians everywhere. And keep things pleasant. No flaming allowed! The more you network the better; this will serve you well in future job hunts, professional activities, and requests for professional advice. You might participate on Web discussion boards, go out to lunch with a couple of people from your library board, meet with teachers in the break room, and go to conferences and workshops. And if you attend conferences and workshops, don't just sit in the back of the room looking alone and forlorn. Sit with someone. Talk. Get out of your shell. Schmooze. Remember, networking is not a solitary activity!

Kill Them with Kindness

Eventually you will have to work with people, both patrons and colleagues, who make you feel uncomfortable or are simply unpleasant to be around. You don't have to be friends with them, but try to be as pleasant as possible, even when it's difficult. As my father always told me, "kill them with kindness." As I said before, it's a small world out there. Often, bullies will try to get a person upset just for the game of it. I had a music teacher once who was verbally abusive toward his students. A bit of a sport for him. At one point he was screaming at me, ready to burst with anger, and I smiled at him, keeping my cool. This absolutely infuriated him! It was beautiful. The same will work with nasty colleagues or an irate patron screaming about an overdue fine.

WORKING WITH PATRONS

OK. So you're doing great with your bosses and colleagues. Then how should librarians behave as professionals while working with sometimes-unpredictable patrons? If you're in a corporate, academic, or school library setting, you'll find that the clientele are fairly consistent. Students, staff, or faculty of the institution frequent the library to fulfill their information needs. Those outsiders who come to these libraries are usually working on a legitimate project and not just looking for a place to crash while the homeless shelter is closed. Librarians who work in public libraries are helping individuals of all segments of the population, including those living in the shadows of society.

Here's a simple fact. Most people who go to a library need something: a book, a journal article, an answer to a question, a place to get onto the Internet, or a place to read the newspaper. It is your job as a professional to help them find what they need. If patrons are in the library for a library instruction class or workshop, it may be your job to lead the workshop and instruct patrons on the topic of the session.

Some patrons make things easy. They have information/library needs and can communicate their needs to a librarian. But how do you react to the older woman at the reference desk, mumbling and muttering to herself, wearing a peek-a-boo blouse? Or an irate patron who screams profanities at you because he can't find the information he needs? Or the woman who attends library instruction classes with her ill-mannered child? In difficult situations, take some deep breaths and concentrate on the task at hand. What do they need? Can you help? Establish boundaries. You are a librarian, not a social worker, psychiatrist, or security guard. Keep your cool. I had a colleague who used to move slowly and quietly when faced with a difficult question or request. No need to exclaim to the patron, "Gee, I have no idea what you're talking about!" Give patrons your attention, attend to in-person patrons before answering the telephone, and don't bury yourself in work while at the reference desk. Work if you can on duty, but do not appear to be unapproachable. Listen. When dealing with bullies of any kind, whether they are uptight executives at a corporation or the local neighborhood loudmouth, it's better to excuse yourself from a situation than to contribute to the patron's explosive behavior. And remember the golden rule: treat others as you would like to be treated.

So, there you have it! Librarian behavior is an art most can master. You don't need to act like a trained monkey in the boss's shadows or be so busy pleasing everyone that your individuality is gone the minute you enter the library. Be yourself—but only to a certain point; no one really needs to know about your obsession with UFOs. Be bold enough to be a trendsetter within the institution's behavioral environment. Approach your library world with flexibility, a sense of humor, imagination, sensitivity, and the ability to mirror positive patterns of behavior. And, most importantly, *have fun*!

RELATED READINGS

Absher, L. *The Lipstick Librarian.* www.lipsticklibrarian.com (last accessed 7 August 2003).

Dirks, T. *It's a Wonderful Life.* www.filmsite.org. www.filmsite.org/itsa3.html (last accessed 7 August 2003).

"Guidelines for Behavioral Performance of Reference and Information Services Professionals." *RQ* 36, no. 2 (1996): 200–3.

Koepfer, G. Chris. "What Makes People Professionals?" *Modern Machine Shop* 74, no. 3 (2001): 10.

Manley, W. *Unprofessional Behavior: Confessions of a Public Librarian.* Jefferson, N.C.: McFarland and Company, 1992.

Rodger, Eleanor, and Charles Robinson, "Purveyors or Prescribers: What Should Librarians Be?" *American Libraries* 29, no. 5 (1998): 66–69.

Shontz, Priscilla K. *Jump Start Your Career in Library and Information Science.* Lanham, Md.: Scarecrow Press, 2002.

Yucht, Alice. "Degrees of Professionalism." *Teacher Librarian* 27, no. 3 (2000): 29–30.

ABOUT THE AUTHOR

Nancy George has been the electronic resources librarian at Salem State College Library in Salem, Massachusetts, since 1996. Prior to coming to Salem, Nancy worked in academic and public libraries in the Midwest and East Coast and is active in national and regional library/academic organizations. In her free time, Nancy enjoys spending time with her family, skiing as much as possible in the winter, and spending time outdoors.

51

Click to Connect! Successful Online Communication

Kate Sinclair

In the information age, we inhabit a world without boundaries. I live in Australia, where it takes a day to travel to London or New York by plane, but now the world is a mere mouse-click away. I can sit in my office and lean sideways for a blue glimpse of the Southern Ocean through my window, while browsing Librarian.net, sending e-mail to the UK, or reading a post from NEWLIB-L on my computer. The limits of geography have been transcended by technology.

In this environment, the Internet is one of the core tools in the librarian's career development kit, expanding—on a global scale—the opportunities available for networking, promotion, and self-development. The savvy information professional knows how to develop and utilize the available resources to establish a strong online presence. The key skills required? An understanding of the forums for online communication, such as e-mail, discussion lists, or web page design; an awareness of how they can be used for networking, profile-raising, and career development; and the ability to successfully communicate with others in the online format.

BUILDING YOUR ONLINE PRESENCE

When you interact with others online, as in the real world, they form an impression of you based on the way you conduct yourself, treat others, and express your opinions. That's why it's important to have a clear idea of the image you wish to establish and consciously use it to develop your online presence. In his article "Networking on the Network," Phil Agre advises, "The most important thing [in online communication] is to employ electronic media consciously and deliberately as part of a larger strategy for your career."

Your online presence encompasses a range of behavior, from e-list participation to other forms of online communication, such as personal web pages and weblogs (blogs). A quick way to ascertain whether you have a strong online presence already is to search for your own name in a couple of major search engines. Does it come up in the results? In what context? What organizations, ideas, or professional concepts do you seem to be associated with? If your name doesn't appear, why not? If you are active in the profession, you should expect some mention of your name in an online forum, list archives, or professional association web page.

Be aware that some potential employers will conduct this same exercise when considering your application. What kind of online picture would you like to present as a prospective applicant?

PROFESSIONAL BEHAVIOR

The most important thing to remember when you are online is that you should remain professional at all times. The online medium is a different way to communicate, but the principles that govern your real-life interactions as a professional should apply here, too. If anything, you should be even more careful of your behavior online, where you are unable to read nonverbal cues and situations may be easily misinterpreted. The fluidity of the medium, where one e-mail or web address can be forwarded to hundreds of people within minutes, means that few online interactions can be considered "private." Don't assume you are anonymous or that no one read that e-mail or blog!

Begin with your e-mail account. Choose a standard text font and color that will display clearly in the most basic of e-mail programs. Avoid unusual fonts that may display in annoying, hard-to-read HTML markup in less sophisticated programs.

For the same reasons, keep your signature file simple! Keep quotes and other displays of personality, such as graphics, to a minimum.

Show respect for other people. Don't "shout" or "flame." To maintain a professional online image, make sure you know basic Netiquette:

- Networking on the Net—www.easytraining.com/networking.htm
- The Net: User Guidelines and Netiquette—www.fau.edu/netiquette/net/
- Netiquette Guidelines—www.albury.net.au/new-users/rfc1855.txt

Don't post material that is obnoxious, obscene, or inappropriate to the forum. Swear words and obscenities should be avoided at all times.

When using e-lists, don't send posts that don't contribute anything to the discussion. E-mails that simply add "Me too!" or "I agree" to previous posts are annoying and unprofessional. If you simply wish to agree with a previous e-mail, reply to the sender only. Don't waste the time of other subscribers.

Discussion lists are a great resource for students and also function as a gentle introduction to professional networking. However, as a student, try not to use the list as your first point of call for information for assignments. We all know the type of post: "Hullo, I am studying at College X and am doing an assignment on Y—can anyone suggest some resources?" This can give the impression of laziness, especially in an industry where research skills are essential. The best way to use discussion lists during study is to seek clarification on a point or to access practical information that you have been unable to gain through other sources. When e-mailing a list with such a request, indicate the reading you have done already and what aspects you need help with.

NEVER criticize your employer, boss, or coworkers on a public list. If you must ask the list for advice on a difficult situation in the workplace, try to disguise the identity of those involved and use a personal e-mail address, not the address that identifies where you work. E-lists can be an amazing source of peer support and constructive advice, but remember that the library world is relatively small and your words may rebound on you. Negative comments might not only come to the attention of your current boss; potential employers on the list may note your attitude as well.

E-NETWORKING

We all know the importance of networking skills to continuing professional development. The personal contacts you make through networks can help you find a mentor, glean advice, assist with job applications and employment, introduce you to new challenges, and, most importantly, develop your confidence as a professional. The online environment offers further opportunities to develop your professional networks, not just locally but on an international level, reinforcing the global community of information professionals. Online networking is basically any communication in an online environment, whether one to one or one to many. It is a core aspect of your professional development and especially benefits librarians who live in a remote location or who are otherwise isolated physically from other information professionals, such as stay-at-home parents, distance education students, or those who are mobility impaired. E-networking forums, such as electronic discussion lists give librarians the chance to access online communities that they would otherwise not have known. However, the essence of networking is still about developing relationships between people.

E-NETWORKING ON ELECTRONIC DISCUSSION LISTS

Whether you are a student, recent graduate, or established professional, you should subscribe to at least one or two electronic discussion lists. They offer an opportunity to participate in a vibrant online community. Subscribers use the list to post thoughts, opinions, and questions; share interesting links or articles; and discuss topical issues. Lists facilitate the sharing and exchange of information and can vary greatly in activity and tone.

For the new librarian, there are a staggering number of lists to choose from. Sometimes a friend or colleague will recommend an e-list to you, so you can find out from them how the list actually works in operation, as opposed to the promotional blurb on the list subscription page. Choose lists based on your professional interests, work responsibilities, and location. I always make a point to subscribe to at least one overseas discussion list—it's a good way to gain a different perspective and broaden your understanding of the current issues in the profession.

If you want to go hunting for potential lists to subscribe to, here are some good directories for electronic discussion lists in the library field:

- Library-Oriented Lists and Electronic Serials—liblists.wrlc.org/home.htm
- Library E-mail Lists and Newsgroups from the Internet Library for Librarians—www.itcompany.com/inforetriever/e-mail.htm
- CataList—www.lsoft.com/lists/listref.html
- SLA Discussion Lists—www.sla.org/content/interactive/lists/index.cfm
- AALL Discussion Lists—www.aallnet.org/discuss/
- National Library of Canada, Canadian Discussion Lists—www.nlc-bnc .ca/services/ecanlist.htm
- Australian Lists— www.alia.org.au/e-lists/

Don't restrict your search to library and information sector lists. Other professional lists may be useful to you, depending on your work, professional interests, and career path. If you can't find a list that meets your professional needs, then create your own! Initiating, marketing, and managing a new discussion list gives you valuable experience that you can add to your CV or resume. You can create a new list under the banner of your professional association or use a web-based provider like Topica (www.topica.com/)

When you subscribe to a list, don't forget to save the list details, including instructions on how to unsubscribe or change your subscription. Sending plaintive "unsubscribe" messages to a list is unprofessional and annoying to the other subscribers. Keep the original list instructions for all of your e-lists in a special e-mail folder, or save them on a floppy disk, or file a printed version away. Either way, ensure that whenever you subscribe to a list, you have the list details saved and easily accessible for future use.

Protect yourself against information overload. Be selective. Don't subscribe to every list or e-newsletter that looks interesting. If your mailbox is flooded with overwhelming amounts of information, you won't have the time or the inclination to read any of it, let alone absorb it. Make your choices carefully based on your professional needs so that your Inbox is a source of information and enlightenment, not stress and frustration. If you are an information junkie, protect your work time by using a home e-mail address to subscribe to some online services. An active list with many posts each day may disrupt your work, so access it at home so that you can still keep up to date at your leisure. Another good tactic is to select the Digest option when subscribing, so that you just get one big daily digest rather than lots of individual e-mails.

Before posting, read the list rules. Does the list have clearly defined boundaries for discussion? You need to know the dos and don'ts before you start posting. "Lurk" on the list for the first couple of weeks to get a feel for the appropriate behavior and tone. However, don't lurk for too long! You'll get more out of a list if you make an effort to actively contribute. Give thought to each posting and make sure you are contributing intelligently to the discussion. As you become more confident, you will begin to establish yourself as a regular poster and your name will become familiar to list subscribers.

E-NETWORKING WITH INDIVIDUALS

When you have spent some time online, you will begin to identify possible mentors, advisors, or role models. Wherever you are online—participating in an e-list discussion, surfing the Web, or reading electronic current awareness services—look out for people who have similar professional interests as you. Maybe they wrote an article or presented a paper that you enjoyed, or they're on an association committee you would like to join, or they maintain a website that is focused on your specialized field. Most people, particularly if they are active in the industry, will make their e-mail address available online, either on their employer's website, their personal page, the website of the professional association they are involved with, or in a post to a discussion list.

Draft your e-mail very carefully, checking for spelling and grammatical errors. First impressions count! Make sure you have spelled their name correctly, and begin by introducing yourself and your reason for contacting them. Keep your e-mail short, polite, and to the point. Mention the aspects of their professional work that relate to your query or where you can see a correlation of interests. Under no account send your resume or any other unsolicited attachments.

When you have sent the e-mail, don't be impatient for an answer. Sometimes you may not receive an answer at all, in which case assume that they are busy or not interested. Once, when seeking information for a conference paper, I e-mailed ten people across Australia who were working in the same field. I received only *one* reply, but that reply came from someone who was amazingly helpful and enthusiastic, and we have remained in touch since. You will find that some people, even those with established reputations, will still be flattered by your approach and eager to give you a helping hand.

Don't forget to nurture an online relationship once it has been established. Make sure the members of your online network feel valued and appreciated. Keep in touch with occasional e-mails updating them on the project you were working on, asking about the new initiative they were implementing, or just to catch up and say hi! Be willing to help them out in turn and seize the opportunity to meet in person if you happen to be in the same city or attending the same conference.

YOUR WEBSITE

A personal or professional website gives you great scope to develop a strong online presence. It can serve as a fulcrum for all the other modes of online communication you may use—weblogs, discussion lists, and e-mail. First, you need to decide what you want to achieve by setting up the website. Do you want to fill a gap in a particular field of research or establish a new information resource for a subject? Do you want to advertise professional services as a consultant or freelance librarian? To begin, you may only see it as a good opportunity to practice your web design skills away from the spotlight. Think about the purpose of the website. Why do you want people to go to your site?

When designing the look and functionality of the site, use the KISS principle—Keep It Simple, Stupid! Don't overuse graphics or color. Most successful, easy-to-use sites have a lot of white space and an organized structure so it is easy to find what you are looking for. If you are new to web page design, the links below have some good resources:

- Microsoft FrontPage—www.microsoft.com/frontpage/
- Macromedia Dreamweaver—www.dreamweaver.com
- Web Developer's Virtual Library—www.stars.com
- Bare Bones Guide to HTML—werbach.com/barebones/

One of the purposes the website can serve is as a home to other professional development activities, such as your online resume and your weblog.

You can also link to presentations, PowerPoint slides, online articles, or any other online projects you have been involved with.

YOUR E-RESUME

Everyone should maintain an up-to-date resume outlining their skills and experience to prospective employers. It is a document required for almost all job applications. Developing and updating your resume also helps you to assess your achievements and identify gaps in your experience. The next step is to make your resume available in an online environment. An electronic resume is easily transferred via e-mail or placed on a web page to publicize and promote your skills to a wider audience.

You may not realize it, but you probably already have an e-resume! Most people keep their resume as a Microsoft Word document—an electronic document that can be easily sent as an attachment by e-mail. However, there are a number of potential problems that can occur here. Some organizations can't (or won't) accept attachments to e-mail. Viruses can be easily spread through attachments—when you do e-mail your resume, do a virus check first to avoid transmitting an electronic virus to your prospective employer! Very often, the formatting may display differently when it reaches its destination, especially if unusual fonts have been used in the original version. Entire chunks of your resume can be lost or garbled. However, sticking only to standard fonts and formatting when compiling the document should help to prevent this.

The alternative approach is to place your resume on the web in HTML format. You can create a basic document from the Word version and place it on your personal website, simply directing employers to the relevant address. In the web format, you can hyperlink to relevant online material, adding extra information that complements the content of your resume. You can also make your resume graphically interesting by adding color, although beware of using all the "bells and whistles." Scrolling text, animated cartoons, and rainbow colors are not recommended—remember, you are trying to create a dynamic but professional image. Keep it clean and simple.

If you choose to display your resume on your personal website, don't forget to remove some of the traditional print resume information in order to protect your personal privacy. This includes any personal information that may identify your home address, family, and hobbies, as well as the personal contact details of your referees.

BLOGS

A blog, or weblog, is a website that is updated frequently with links or commentary. Blogs can be journals, personal diaries, or just a collection of interesting links. Some popular library blogs include:

- Librarian.net—www.librarian.net/
- ResearchBuzz—www.researchbuzz.com/
- The ResourceShelf—www.resourceshelf.com/
- Neat New Stuff on the Net—marylaine.com/neatnew.html

Establishing a personal or professional blog is a way to express your personality, thoughts, and opinions online. You can have it linked to your personal web page so that it becomes a one-stop-shop for your online professional profile. Not everyone has the time or the inclination to maintain a blog, and not all blogs develop the "must see" reputations of those listed earlier. However, it is an opportunity to further extend your online presence and perhaps make a name for yourself within the industry. The following resources are very useful for the new blogger:

- Weblog FAQ—www.robotwisdom.com/weblogs/
- Blogger—www.blogger.com
- Weblogs.Com—http://www.weblogs.com
- Pitas.com—www.pitas.com

The blog will act as a two-way, online communication tool, giving you a forum for your views and enabling visitors to respond via e-mail or online to your ideas. It may also give you an incentive to think more about professional issues, read the literature, and conduct research on the topics that interest you.

CONCLUSION

Online communication is everywhere, but few people know how to do it well. Librarians who make the most of the career development opportunities available in the online environment will stand out from the crowd:

- Always maintain a professional attitude and outlook.
- Keep your sense of humor! Enjoy yourself and have fun while exploring the online world.

- Think globally. Make contact with librarians from different countries and share your experiences.
- Consciously develop and nurture your online networks.
- Be proactive. Use online forums to raise your profile in the industry.
- Work to establish and maintain an online presence.
- Seize opportunities as they arise. You never know what might happen!

RELATED READINGS

Agre, Phil. "Networking on the Network" (2003). polaris.gseis.ucla.edu/pagre/network.html (last accessed 22 May 2004).

ABOUT THE AUTHOR

Kate Sinclair is liaison librarian for law and legal studies at Flinders University Library, South Australia. She is a cofounder of SALIN, the South Australian Library and Information Network, and has been list administrator for the SALIN e-list and AliaSASPEC, the e-list for the ALIA Special Libraries Group (South Australia). She is also a member of the ALIA New Generation Policy and Advisory Group, a national committee that advises the Australian Library and Information Association Board and communicates largely in the online environment.

52

Conference Attendance

Jeff Bullington

If you are new to "conferencing," there are probably many questions you may have about conferences and how you should approach them. You have likely started to determine that there are many different professional organizations or societies in the field, such as the American Library Association (ALA), the Special Libraries Association (SLA), the International Federation of Library Associations (IFLA), the Medical Library Association (MLA—not to be confused with the Modern Language Association), the Music Library Association (yet another MLA), the American Association of Law Libraries (AALL), the American Theological Library Association (ATLA), the Art Libraries Society of North America (ARLIS/NA), the American Society for Information Science and Technology (ASIST), the Canadian Library Association (CLA), state library associations, regional and local library associations, and many other subject- or function-oriented associations.

Many of these organizations hold periodic conferences where members gather together for several days and spend the time discussing issues in the field, current developments in libraries, services, resources, patrons and information seeking, what libraries are, or should be, among other topics. If you take a look at the Events & Conferences section of the American Library Association's website, you will see that ALA has posted dates for various conferences, including their own, those of ALA's many divisions, as well as conference dates for other associations such as those listed earlier. And this listing is not even close to being comprehensive! There are numerous other associations such as the North American Serials Interest Group (NASIG), another member association with its own annual conference. And then there are many topical conferences such as the Internet Librarian, the Virtual Reference Desk Conference, and various other conferences, workshops, meetings, or seminars where people in the library and information field get together to mingle, so-cialize, and learn from each other. Where to begin with all these options? It can be overwhelming; just trying to figure out what one or two events you might try to attend in any given year.

YOUR EMPLOYING INSTITUTION'S TAKE ON CONFERENCES

The first piece of advice is this: take some time to determine your employing institution's position on the role of conferences and similar events as they re-late to librarians. You will find that each organization has some unique mix of expectations regarding conferences. In many academic libraries, librarians go through a promotion process (which may be called tenure, promotion, con-tinuing appointment, or something else). For success in this promotion process, it may be quite important for librarians to establish a track record of active involvement in the profession, including membership in professional organizations, attendance at conferences, and activity in the organization and conferences (serving on committees or task forces, participating in confer-ences by giving presentations). In many other library organizations, such ac-tivity may not be explicitly required, but showing active involvement in the profession may still be considered important as a way of continuing to grow as an individual and to provide for the overall growth and development of li-braries and the field. There may be some libraries and organizations where conference activity is not considered important, and is even perhaps a dis-traction from "real work," but this is uncommon—our field is simply too dy-namic and changes too rapidly for many libraries, or the people working in them, to remain inside of their own little bubbles and continue to be success-ful. We need to speak to our colleagues in other libraries to learn what they are doing, how they are managing information, working with ever-changing patron needs and preferences, and just trying to keep up with it all!

The point is, knowing your own local climate regarding conferences will help you figure out how to handle this aspect of your career. If such activity is rou-tinely expected, then great—now you can move on to deciding how to get go-ing. But if support for this is tepid, or maybe even negative, you may need to think more strategically about how you might want to proceed. In any event, take conference attendance and activity seriously. It is a great way to network in the field, get to know many people, learn what is going on, and hear what other li-brary organizations are like. Find a way to attend at least one such event a year, if for no other reason than pure self-interest. You are likely to change jobs, if not careers, several times in your working life. Knowing what is "out there" helps you make better choices when you are looking for new employment.

CONFERENCE ATTENDANCE AND TRAVEL

After you learn about your library's general stance on conferences, your logical next step is to familiarize yourself thoroughly with your employing institution's professional development and travel policies. As you already know if you've traveled, there is a tremendous number of logistical pieces involved in planning a trip, such as securing transportation and lodging, figuring out how to carve out time in your hectic schedule, and deciding how to pay for it all! There are many important questions that you need to research. Ask your supervisor or another colleague where to find this information. Quite often, it is someone in your administrative office, perhaps your human resources staff or your procurement staff.

Release Time for Conferences

Are you allowed any formal release time to attend conferences, or would you be required to use personal time (vacation) to attend conferences or workshops? In either case, what procedures must you follow in order to take the time?

Funding Resources and Models

Are any funding sources available to you? Do you have access to any additional institutional funding to help underwrite professional activities? What would be available? Institutions have different structures for what is often called "Professional Development Funding." Presented below are some common models.

Lump Sum Allocation: Professionals and other staff may be allocated a lump sum, say for example, $1,000 per fiscal year for professional development activities. Within the specific criteria your institution has set up to define acceptable use, these funds can be yours to use as you wish toward conference attendance—you could use all of it for one event, or split it up across several events.

Funding Per Event: There may be some formula to determine how much funding would be available to you for any event you may wish to attend. This can quite often be some percentage of the standard expenses for attending an event (registration fees, travel costs, lodging and subsistence, and miscellaneous). Again, there may be a maximum amount you could use in any given year. Your level of activity at the conference may influence the amount of funding that you qualify for, for example, attending the conference, serving on a committee, giving a presentation.

Funding by Application: You may be expected to put together an application for funding and state why attendance would be beneficial to you and the institution. Again, the actual amount you are allocated may depend on a variety of factors as specified by your employing institution.

Additional Funding Resources

In addition to professional development funds managed directly by your library, there may be additional possibilities you could pursue. You may be able to make a case to your administration to get administrative funding for a particular conference, perhaps as a result of your involvement in that conference or perhaps if the administration itself decides that your institution needs a representative at that particular event (the event topic may be of strategic importance to your library). Finally, there may be additional funding sources outside of the library that you could pursue. In academic libraries, there may be funds from the institution's central research unit to underwrite attendance, particularly as it may relate to research you are conducting or presenting at a conference. It can really pay off to invest some time asking around to see what might be available.

You may also be able to get funds from your local, regional, state, or national professional associations. For instance, the Association of College and Research Libraries has offered competitively awarded scholarships to new professionals to underwrite attendance at the semiannual ACRL National Conference. Such an award may only cover a portion of the total costs, but it helps augment your own professional development funds, and your administration may grant you matching funds as a result of winning a scholarship. It makes the institution look good to have an award winner on staff, so they may put some additional funding toward your attendance.

Other national organizations may have similar scholarship opportunities. The North American Serials Interest Group (NASIG) makes similar scholarship grants to library school students for attendance at their national conference. Your state, regional, or local library association may make similar awards for its annual conferences or meetings. These may be particularly geared toward new professionals, but there are also midcareer possibilities, awards for other kinds of meritorious accomplishments, and various other awards. Again, it can greatly benefit you to investigate possibilities with any organization you are affiliated with.

Personal Professional Development Funding

Even with all of these possibilities for professional development funding, you still must often be prepared to supplement any funds you may receive with some of your own dollars. With few exceptions, no institution is able to fully fund all professionals for all the events that they may wish to attend. So be prepared to budget a portion of your own salary for your professional activities. It's your own career; I would argue that you should be prepared to provide some of the support for your own professional development. Try to plan ahead and stash some money away over the year so that you will always have funds to dip into for conferences and travel.

Travel Logistics

Once you have figured out how much money you can pull in from all the various sources you may have, make sure you thoroughly understand the regulations on what you can use it for and procedures for how to use it.

Can your institution prepay some costs such as registration fees or airfare so that you don't have to take care of these out of your own pocket? You may be able to work with a designated travel agent, book your airfare, and have the bill sent to your administrative office to be paid. You may be able to book your own airfare but may be required to meet certain criteria in order to get that airfare reimbursed (one such model is to document that you chose the least expensive of three alternative itineraries).

Many conferences will prearrange housing with hotels near the conference site, negotiating special rates for conference attendees. You may need to book these hotels directly with the conference organizers or their designated agents. Again, your own institution may have particular rules about what you can do in order to get reimbursed for those expenses—that is, book through a designated agent or book your own hotel up to a designated limit (meaning if you are allowed up to $100 a night for hotel, but your room rate is actually $125, the balance comes out of your own pocket). Although conferences want you to use the hotels they have already lined up, if they are simply out of your price range (even with a conference roommate), then you should research the area and find a rate that fits with your budget. Using travel sites and online booking resources and online map sites, you can find a "nonconference" hotel close to the conference site that will serve your needs.

Subsistence costs, such as meal expenses, are another element of your expenses for a conference. Many institutions simply allocate a per diem amount (i.e., you can get up to $35 a day) where you don't need to present all of your receipts for submission to get reimbursement. Some places do require that you have a receipt for each item you claim for reimbursement.

You will have other incidental costs, such as shuttles to and from airports, mass transit costs, and the like. Again, depending on your employing institution's policies, you may or may not be able to apply any funds allocated to you for these expenses.

Travel Advances

Having $1,000 or more at your disposal to fund a conference trip can be a challenge, even if you will get a large portion of that money reimbursed to you after the event. Again, there may be help available to you besides racking up charges on a credit card. You may be able to request a travel advance from your employing institution. You can fill out the appropriate paperwork and have a check issued to you before you travel to pay for your expenses. When you get back, you total up your actual expenses and submit the claim form; if you spent less than your advance, you pay back the difference, and if you spent more, then you don't have to return any of the advance. There may be different ways of getting advances—for example, directly from your administration or through an arrangement with your institution's endowment association or other fund-raising organization. This may or may not be a possibility for you, but you will never know if you don't ask.

GETTING THE MOST OUT OF
CONFERENCES ONCE YOU ARE THERE

Deciding What to Attend at the Conference

Conference program booklets are an invaluable resource for figuring out what specific programs or meetings to attend at a conference. Read the program information carefully to learn more about what will actually be going on and to decide where you want to invest your time. Many conferences will have at least some level of conference programming information available to you on the Web months in advance. Note what programming appeals to you, or what programming is covering things you know you need to learn. You may also be interested in something because of "names" (people you have heard about or have heard are experts on topics that interest you).

Once you are on site and have the final conference program in your hands, go over your preliminary list and make your final decisions about what to attend. Don't be concerned if your plans change dramatically once you are at the conference; different information may have come your way to alter your original interests. Just make the changes in your own schedule and pursue what interests you. The whole point is for you to explore various aspects of the work of libraries and to learn new things. One frequent comment about conference programming is that the actual program was different than it sounded in the program. This can happen and may be a disappointment ("If only I'd known it was going to be like that, I'd never have bothered to attend"). On the other hand, that program may be even more interesting and useful than you expected.

Committees at Conferences

At the conference, there may be committee meetings in addition to conference programming. Working committees often use the conference time for business meetings. This may be the one time of the year when committee members are actually in the same place. Committees may be working on things such as preparing programming for upcoming conferences or planning for other activities and initiatives for the organization. Committee meetings are a great way to learn more about the inner workings of an organization, and depending on your own situation, you may want to get an official appointment to a committee. If you have an interest in that committee, then go attend the meeting. Unless a particular committee meeting or session is designated as "closed" (usually for awards or nominations committees), most committee meetings are open and visitors are welcome. If you attend a committee meeting, even as a guest, introduce yourself to the committee chair, members, and other guests. Sit in on a meeting, listen as they conduct their business, and learn more about what the committee is doing and how they are doing it. If you have something to contribute and feel your input would be welcome, don't be afraid to speak up. Your observation or contribution could be very helpful, and you will never know if you don't try. Be persistent if a particular committee interests you and you want a committee appointment; keep attending that committee's meetings at subsequent conferences. In organizations, the appointing officers often ask committee chairs to suggest names for appointments. Making a positive impression by attending meetings and expressing interest can get you noticed and mentioned for an appointment.

Social Events

Most conferences have some organized social events such as receptions, organized meals, tours, or other activities. These can be very good places to meet new people, enjoy food (which can help you stretch your travel dollars), and get a good idea of what is going on. These could be conferencewide events, or events for particular groups within an organization; for example, the ACRL Instruction Section Dinner, which takes place at every ALA Midwinter Meeting and Annual Conference, is a good place to meet others with an interest in instruction. Other groups have similar events, and if you are on topically oriented discussion lists, you will hear of these activities. Also, it seems that library people just love to get together and socialize. People are always gathering together in groups to go eat, have coffee, or do some other activity, and talk "library." Look for these opportunities to mingle, socialize, and meet new people.

Exhibits and Exhibitors

Many of the conferences in our field have an exhibits component. Exhibits are an important part of conference attendance. The exhibitors invest a significant amount of money to come to the conferences and display their products and services. Yes, they are interested in acquiring new customers, and when you are walking through exhibits you can feel inundated with information and offers to look at the latest and greatest thing in the world of libraries. But that is what can be so useful about exhibits. Devoting some of your time, attention, and energy touring the exhibits can be a good opportunity to learn what is going on in the field, see a demonstration of that great resource you've heard about, and ask questions. You might even be able to go back to your employer and provide some good information that could help in decision making. The exhibits are one of the best ways to learn about all the variety of information resources and services that are out there for potential use in your library. Finally, exhibitors frequently host sessions at conferences as another venue for demonstrating their products and services; for example, you may get invited to a vendor breakfast where the vendor provides a more in-depth review of their products, and you get breakfast to boot! Once you are registered for a conference, you may start getting such invitations or these invitations may come to other colleagues at your institution who may pass them along to you. Again, these are great ways to both stretch your own conference dollars and further explore particular resources, services, or vendors.

ONCE YOU ARE HOME FROM A CONFERENCE

Once you are back, you are probably going to feel an interesting state of exhilaration and exhaustion. You have spent several days in this heady atmosphere full of new possibilities, ideas, and people. What a rush—people refer to it as "conference high." You probably got up and began moving far earlier each morning and got to bed far later each night than you usually do. In between you walked, talked, listened, learned, met new people, and raced around more than you usually do in any given day—and kept doing it for several days in a row. How to make use of all the information and ideas you collected at the conference? Where to start? Of course you are tired! But on your way home, take some time to reflect quietly on your conference experience. What are the things you want to make sure to tell a colleague back at work? What do you want to explore further or learn more about? Make some plans to do some of that as soon as possible. Don't let the "conference high" just melt away entirely. Keep some of the best experiences, information, and ideas in the front of your mind, and keep working on them. Then start the planning for your next conference. It's coming up sooner than you expect!

ABOUT THE AUTHOR

Jeff Bullington is a reference librarian and subject specialist with the University of Kansas Libraries. He earned his MLIS from the University of Illinois at Urbana–Champaign and has worked in academic libraries in Illinois, Texas, and Kansas. Jeff is professionally involved in the American Library Association, the North American Serials Interest Group, and in the Association for Research Libraries. Conferences are one of his favorite ways to reconnect with colleagues and friends he already knows, meet new ones, learn about developments in the field, see new places, and discover new music (one of his abiding passions).

53

Association Work: What's in It for Me?

Ann Snoeyenbos

Library associations are the glue that holds us together as a profession. Our associations play a key role in many of the legal "events" that shape our daily work. They coordinate the creation of standards that make it possible for us to communicate effectively among ourselves and with our patrons. They help us form the personal bonds that keep us moving forward when technology and the public seem to conspire against us.

What do I mean by professional associations? I am thinking mostly about the influence of large overarching organizations that make room for all job types, all library types, and all political types. Two very well-known examples are the American Library Association (ALA) and the Special Libraries Association (SLA). State and regional associations also qualify, as do the more specialized associations, such as the Progressive Librarians Guild, North American Serials Interest Group (NASIG), and the Theatre Library Association, among many others. Most of my experience has been in the ALA, so I will refer to that in this piece, but I value the experiences other associations offer just as highly.

WHY JOIN WHEN THE BENEFITS ARE FREE?

Yes, we all win when the ALA fights our intellectual freedom battles for us, or when an association-funded advertising campaign results in greater awareness of libraries and librarianship. So why pay big bucks to join if these benefits will trickle down to you even if you don't? I do cry a few tears each year when I write the check for my ALA membership dues. And I will admit that I cut short a period of active involvement (and great fun) in my state library association because I couldn't afford to write two large checks for membership dues each year. If you do not have your employer's support, it can be expensive to go to workshops or attend meetings sponsored by your association. Committee work does take time and energy. Nonetheless, I firmly believe that my experiences as an active member of a library association have made me a better librarian.

Join for Yourself

My involvement in the American Library Association has given me the opportunity to do things that I would never be able to do in my current job. I've done party planning on a financial scale that I will never see in my personal life. I've learned how newsletters and other publications are put together from start to finish. I have been able to talk to colleagues about the shared values of librarianship in a way that I rarely have occasion to do on the job.

The things I've done in the ALA give me confidence to embark on new projects and skills and experience to add to my resume. ALA has provided high-quality training that I would normally have to purchase from a continuing education provider. A few examples of this include: facilitation skills training, financial planning and budgeting, leadership development, and media training. In my day job I am not an administrator, but in the ALA I can be the boss, the leader, the coordinator, and the facilitator. I can try on different types of library work without leaving my current position.

Serving on award committees exposes you to new worlds of opportunity. Every time I read an award application I come away with some piece of knowledge I can use in my own career. I have learned that when you are asked to address specific things in an application, you must do so, and you must make it clear to the reader which item you are addressing. It sounds simple, but don't underestimate the need to answer direct questions directly. Now when I write a grant or job application, I think back to all the different examples of presentation and self-description people have used. Serving on a grant or award committee teaches you to write better applications yourself because you have seen how the evaluation process works and how comparisons are made among candidates.

Perhaps most importantly, the personal connections I've made through association work give me courage when my own circumstances seem bleak. I know there are a lot of libraries that do not support the professional involvement of their librarians, that there are worse administrators than some I've known, and that some institutions haven't given raises several years in a row. I have observed the circumstances under which librarians flourish, and I can find out from colleagues which are the best employers.

Committee work has given me the opportunity to learn things that are useful in my private life. Again I mention the large-scale party planning, budgeting and financial planning, and the leadership skills. I have learned to ask for help, for money, for favors, and for apologies. I have served on committees with leaders from across the profession; doing so has allowed me to observe how they work, and I have learned a few things about what it takes to stay at the top of your field year after year.

Join for Your Employer

Committee work has provided opportunities for me to do things that are directly related to my job. Through committee work I've been pushed to develop my skills and try things that are more complex than I would normally experience on the job. These kinds of challenges help me stay on top of new developments, and they have helped me anticipate some of the changes in our profession. The committee work that I've done has helped me learn how to build coalitions, how to lobby, and how to defend my own views as well as the opinions of those I represent.

On days when you're fed up with a troublesome situation at work, it can be nice to have other projects to turn to, like your committee work. For me, switching gears in this way usually recharges my interest and makes it easier to go back to a tough project with a positive attitude. Things tend to move at a slower pace in association work because the meetings are widely spaced on the calendar; six months to a year can go by with just a small project to complete. This allows you to dip into your committee work a little at a time, as needed for diversion.

Certainly there are some very demanding committee assignments for which a small group of people must accomplish a lot of work in a short amount of time, but you are made aware of that when you sign on as a member. Committee chairs are mindful that member-volunteers are the ones doing the work; they are aware that without their help very little could be accomplished. The chair and the members of any committee will be busy people themselves, so they know to allow time for questions, opinions, and additional research.

For me the real value in these experiences is that the learning and experimentation are done away from my direct supervisors. I feel less performance pressure because my annual review and salary increase don't depend on the outcome. This leaves me free to try new approaches and even make mistakes. In my day job the pleasure of learning new skills is often diminished by pressure to learn those skills quickly and definitively. The lower-stress approach results in greater creativity, and I actually make fewer mistakes and learn more quickly. I enjoy committee work because it is similar to the work I do in my day job, yet different enough to be refreshing. It can be very liberating to practice librarianship without a boss.

Join for the Profession

When I grow up I would like to teach a class on the role of library professional associations in the growth and development of librarianship in the

United States. I'd teach about the political impact of our associations, about the social impact, and above all about the impact our associations have had on the profession. I'd teach an entire class on the pros and cons of standardization, collaboration, and competition, and how the associations figure in those debates. I'd like to teach a separate course on national and international library associations around the world and their role in international politics. That is an example of how important I think library associations are, and how influential they are within librarianship.

I honestly do not know how this profession could be as strong as it is if we did not have the associations working on our behalf day after day and year after year. The time and energy of dedicated professionals have resulted in performance standards and a unified professional image across the United States. Without the help of the many friends and acquaintances I've met throughout ALA, I wouldn't be able to answer many of the reference questions I receive. Without our professional associations, I wouldn't have an instant connection to hundreds of people doing the same type of work that I do in a variety of contexts. I would have burned out a long time ago if I weren't able to attend professional meetings and refresh my enthusiasm.

I believe that if we reap the benefits of the work our professional organizations do, we have an obligation to give back by serving those organizations ourselves. I had several mentors as I was "growing up" in the ALA New Members Round Table, so I know how valuable mentoring relationships can be. I believe I have a responsibility to provide the same support for newcomers as my mentors did for me. Keep in mind that library associations are membership-driven organizations, and our profession functions in a collaborative structure, not a competitive one. If active professionals don't do a large portion of the association's work, it simply will not get done.

GETTING STARTED

Now that I've convinced you that you have something akin to a *moral imperative* to be involved in a library association, how do you turn that interest into involvement? Before you join any organization, do some research on it. Talk to your friends and colleagues about the organizations you're considering. People who know you and the different organizations should be able to help you make a good match. Join their electronic discussion lists if you can in order to get a feel for the work that's being done and the approach taken. Read their publications. Is communication among members formal or informal? Do they actively solicit member participation? If they don't actively solicit, then do they at least let you know what the committee structure is and provide a contact name for each one?

Once you've joined the library organization of your choice and paid your (monetary) dues, you're ready to move forward toward full participation and involvement. Again, ask your librarian friends and coworkers about how to get involved in the groups they belong to. Groups can function in very distinct ways within the same organization. ALA's New Members Round Table guarantees a committee position to anybody who requests one, and new members are invited to contact the president directly. Other groups want to know you and see your face for a year or more before they trust you with any work. Sometimes you need to ask a committee chair or executive board member for a formal introduction to the group. Some units will immediately create an "internship" on an existing committee (sometimes formal, sometimes off the books) so you can get started even though they're still evaluating you.

Generally once you get started with a particular unit within a larger organization, momentum will carry you forward from one committee appointment to the next. Members often start with a small assignment on a not-so-important committee or task force, and then work their way up to be a committee chair, an executive board member, and then maybe president of the group. This might take years of faithful meeting attendance and regular participation in discussions. From my experience with ALA, I can tell you that just showing up is more than half the battle. You would be shocked to know how many times I've seen people agree to serve as chair of some committee and then drop off the face of the earth. No apologies and no compunction. So if you are one of the good people who show up (on time) to meeting after meeting, year after year, the odds are good that you'll be chosen to work on some very meaty assignments.

A sage once counseled me not to change my appearance very much from year to year, or from day to day, during a conference. If people don't recognize you, they are less likely to talk to you, and thus less likely to ask you to work on a project with them. One of the problems with the amount of electronic communication we conduct as professionals is that it is hard to recognize each other when we're face to face. Sometimes it's a relief to go back to written communication so I can know who's done what. Of course, before the days of committee work conducted by e-mail, people had to rely on infrequent face-to-face contact, phone calls, and paper mail.

There are increasing numbers of committees and working groups who do their work by e-mail, supplemented as necessary by telephone and fax. If you want to be involved but can't physically attend meetings, let the president or committee chair know, and they'll try to assign you to an activity that doesn't require your live presence at meetings. Not everything done by our associations requires long-distance travel.

My favorite approach to leadership is one I call "going in the back door." This is the one I'm best at, and I'm not too proud to admit it. The first time I ran for president of the ALA New Members Round Table, I was defeated. It was a painful defeat because I really did want to be president (by the way, if you don't want the responsibilities of an office, don't run for one), and I felt like I only had one chance. Then six months into the three-year commitment (vice-president/president-elect/past-president), the person who beat me had to step down, and I was the first runner up. I was still interested in being president, so I said yes, and the loser was suddenly the president. I have had the privilege of working on several other great committees just because I was in the right place at the right time; something needed to be done and I got drafted because I was the only one in the room at the time. A sure way to get an assignment is to complain loudly about something the group does. Just to shut you up you'll be put in charge of fixing whatever it is you didn't like.

STAYING INVOLVED THROUGHOUT YOUR CAREER

The key word here is *pacing*. Do a little bit of committee work every year and don't be afraid to mix in some periods of more intense commitment. In association work, name recognition counts for a lot, even if it is negative publicity that you've generated, so your goal is to keep your name in the rotation. This is a case where having an unusual name (like Snoeyenbos) makes it more likely people will remember you from year to year. Once you gain a reputation as a good worker, the association's various leadership circles will get to know you and you might get an invitation to work on projects you didn't even know existed.

Try not to walk away from opportunity. Say yes as often as you can, even if the offer is not the one you had hoped for. It does take time to land the plum assignments because often there is competition for them. That said, I must caution that one shouldn't accept more responsibility than you can realistically handle. Our day jobs vary from season to season and from year to year. If you hit a very busy or stressful point in your life, it is better to ask for help with your association responsibilities, or even step down from them, rather than allow your negligence to create a bad situation for others.

Steady involvement builds momentum, but you should also take charge of your trajectory within the association. It is possible to get stuck in a rut doing only one type of work in one unit, but for association work to serve you in all its many ways, you need to let people know what it is you'd really like to be doing. Ask for appointments to the committees you want to work on, and propose your own name for an elected office. Keep in mind that some parts of the association, such as NMRT, work on committee appointments six months to one year in advance; others, such as the ACRL division, work two years in advance; and still others can work as much as three years out, putting together their slate of candidates. The term of commitment can be as short at six months for an ad hoc committee or task force, or as long as three to four years for standing committees, executive boards, or elected offices. Of course it is difficult to know what life will bring, but try not to take on commitments you will be unable to fulfill.

WHEN SHOULD YOU BE INVOLVED IN ASSOCIATION WORK?

You should be involved in library association work when you know you need it and when you think you don't. At the start of your library career, you need committee work because it helps you build connections in the profession—it teaches you things, it helps you gain perspective, and it connects you to your professional cohort (those who joined the profession at the same time you did). In the middle of your career, you should be involved in association work because it will help you keep your networks strong; it can help you identify potential employees or employers; and it keeps you on top of developments in your field.

At those times when you don't need library associations for their networking potential or for the learning opportunities, you should still be involved because ours is a profession in the midst of profound change. Technology is impacting on the way we do our work and the types of services we can provide. Budgets are in turmoil and there are challenges to intellectual freedom on every corner. Your association connections can support you in all of these areas, and you can support your association by providing context and historical perspective on the changes taking place.

WHAT'S THE PAYOFF?

I can't promise you fame and fortune, because after all this is librarianship we're talking about. However, I think you'll find that your professional satisfaction will increase as you become more engaged in association work. You will find opportunities you didn't even know existed. You will gain understanding about the role that libraries play in our society and the role that society plays in our libraries. You'll meet a diverse group of people who share many of the same passions and challenges you do as a librarian.

ABOUT THE AUTHOR

Ann Snoeyenbos has been a member of several library associations since she completed her MLS in 1991 at the Indiana University–Bloomington School of Library and Information Science. In twelve years she has served on over thirty different library association committees. She currently works coordinator for international sales and special markets for Project MUSE at Johns Hopkins University Press. This chapter was written while Ann was librarian for West European Social Science at New York University, a job she held from 1991–2004.

54

Mentoring: A Primer

Carol Ritzen Kem

Last year I participated in a discussion session held as part of the University Minority Mentor Program (UMMP) at the University of Florida. The UMMP matches African American and Hispanic students with a faculty member or administrator for their first year at the university. One group activity brings mentors and mentees together to discuss the connection process while sharing strategies to improve the program. In this session, the chair of the council that organizes and evaluates the program served as discussion leader. She began by asking the mentors three questions: *Why did you volunteer to serve as a mentor; were you ever mentored; and, if so, by whom?* The answers were highly instructive and are particularly useful in framing this discussion of mentoring and career development.

Almost without exception, the mentors believed they had been mentored at some point in their life and, in some cases, had experienced multiple mentoring relationships. Again, almost without exception, the experiences were positive and considered valuable. The timing of a mentoring event and the responses to the question *"Who mentored you,"* however, revealed many different types of mentoring and many different understandings of just what mentoring actually is. More than one mentor mentioned an advisor in college or graduate school who took interest in them, acculturated them to their prospective profession, and facilitated their progress toward a degree or first job. Others remembered a teacher in high school or middle school who had shown an interest in them and encouraged them to pursue some particular interest. One mentor said the librarian in his small town public library encouraged his reading and intellectual growth by recommending books to him and directing him to things he would not have found on his own. Another faculty mentor said her father had been her first mentor. At a time when professional opportunities for women were limited and women in graduate and professional programs were few in number, he always made her feel she could and should do what she wanted and that she should go as far in her training and profession as possible. She had brothers but was not marginalized in either parental expectations or support because she was a daughter. I found this particularly interesting, as research has shown that bright young women sometimes "turn off" to academics in their early teens, bowing to societal pressure to conform to some expected role. Research also indicates that young women in particular can be empowered by a supportive older male such as a father, a brother, or a mentor who shows confidence in their ability to frame their own future.

This summary of responses to the question *"Were you mentored and, if so, by whom?"* demonstrates that mentoring can occur at many times in one's life and that a mentor is often defined as such by the mentee or protégé. As more than one of the UMMP mentors stated, their mentor may not have even realized that they were considered to be in that role. Finally, their *"reasons for volunteering"* to serve as a mentor to a university freshman were more consistent. The mentors appreciated what they had gained from their personal experiences, and they wanted to share this. Some of them serve as academic advisors to undergraduate or graduate students, but they saw the structure of the UMMP as one that would allow for a different type of mentoring. Without exception they expressed commitment to diversity in the university and wanted to participate in one of the oldest and most successful of the various programs designed to enhance diversity and success. Finally, there was almost an attitude of obligation to participate in the life development of these students as part of the mentor's own professional development and accomplishment. As you continue to read, ask yourself how you would answer the questions asked of the UMMP mentors:

- Have you ever been mentored?
- If so, by whom?
- If you have served as a mentor, why did you take on that role?

MENTORING: WHO, WHAT, WHEN, AND WHERE?

Who Is a Mentor?

The word "mentor" has been defined in a variety of ways. For example, the *Century Dictionary and Cyclopedia* (1901) states that a mentor is "One who acts as a wise and faithful guide, especially for a younger person; an intimate friend who is also a wise counselor." Other descriptions of a mentor emphasize the importance of serving as a role model, guide, tutor, coach, or confidante. Mentoring for career development may involve teaching, counseling, psychological support, protecting and promoting, or sponsoring. Ideally, then, a mentor is a trusted person who can help facilitate a dream by believing in and supporting a mentee through advice, resources, research, caring, and the sharing of self and experiences. The mentor usually establishes the agenda for the relationship and controls the elements, that characterize of the actual connection. If you are considering serving as a mentor, consider the following: (1) Do you like having others seek you out for advice or guidance?; (2) Do you find helping others learn to be personally rewarding?; (3) Do you have specific knowledge you want to pass on to others?; (4) Do you like collaborative learning?; (5) Do you find working with others who are different from you to be energizing?; and (6) Do you look for opportunities to further your own growth? If your answers are positive, you may be an excellent mentor to someone.

Who Is a Mentee?

The terms "protégé" and "learner" are used in much of the literature on mentoring to describe the person being mentored. My preference, however, is for the term "mentee," and that is what I will use in this discussion. The mentee is an individual, selected by personal choice or through placement in a formal mentoring program, who is designated to receive the assistance of a mentor. However, a potential mentee should not wait to be selected but should be proactive in seeking a mentor. This is one way to increase your visability and become viewed as someone with potential in the profession. Usually younger or new to a situation, mentees are considered candidates for the role modeling, training, support, and sponsorship a mentoring relationship may provide. The mentee is the potential recipient of all the resources and nurturing the mentor may be able to provide. However, the mentee should not be a passive participant. He or she should work on developing goals for the process, be willing to accept candid feedback, and understand that the mentor also wishes to gain something from the connection.

What Is Mentoring?

When thinking about the process of mentoring, it is important to consider the variety of activities that are called mentoring. They range from the most informal and brief of connections to highly structured, thoroughly planned, and extensively evaluated programs. Participants may choose to participate in some type of mentoring scheme, or they may be required to participate for a set time period and to seek defined results from the process. The UMMP mentors who reflected on their personal experiences as mentees primarily described informal contacts and relationships based on their academic programs. By volunteering to be a mentor for the UMMP, however, they volunteered to be part of a structured program with eighteen years of history, planning, evaluation, revision, and success. For them, as for many individuals who have been part of some mentoring relationship, there is no single way for the mentoring process to occur. At its heart, however, mentoring is a one-to-one process. Participants may volunteer to participate in mentoring activities, they may be required to participate in a structured program, or a mentor or mentee may self-select a mentoring relationship. In all cases, the mentoring connection involves one mentor and one mentee. Even if a mentor, such as a faculty mentor, is mentoring more than one person at a time, each relationship is unique and each connection includes a single mentor and a single mentee.

Informal Mentoring

The first time you attended a professional meeting such as the American Library Association Annual Conference or the Public Library Association Conference, for example, did someone help you understand the structure of the conference, show you how to make sense of the conference book and schedule of events, give you tips on navigating the exhibits, or just make sure you were included in some social activity? If you answered yes, you were exposed to *informal mentoring*. Without this assistance, how effective would attendance at the conference have been for you? At my first American Library Association conference, a midwinter meeting about twelve years ago, I picked up the conference book and thought, "What do I do with this?" A colleague who was an experienced conference attendee noticed my expression and in a brief but important encounter told me what I needed to know to make sense of the book and consequently the conference. She also introduced me to the exhibit floor, an integral part of the meeting that requires a totally different orientation from that required to navigate the conference itself. I could have done this on my own, but the time saved, the frustration avoided, and the realization that a colleague was willing to take some of her limited time to make my conference experience a better one added up to an excellent informal mentoring connection. Informal mentoring may be confused with a supportive personal relationship, especially when a woman assists another woman. The one-to-one relationship in a professional setting, rather than a relationship based on a supportive social or professional group, is more appropriately called informal mentoring. To summarize, *informal mentoring* may be brief, specific to a particular need or event, and may be similar to orientation in an organization, a work situation, or a group. Informal mentoring may, however, extend over a period of months or years. It may eventually become a different type of relationship or it may come to a natural end.

Peer Mentoring

One-on-one *peer mentoring* is usually characterized by commonality rather than difference. That is, an upperclassman at a high school or college may be part of a peer-mentoring group whose function is to orient younger students to a class or organization. An employee who has been in a position for a year or two may be asked to serve as a peer mentor to a newly hired person in the belief the mentee will have needs and questions during the first few months of employment that an individual close to the situation can better anticipate and answer. Another aspect of peer mentoring is peer tutoring, which can be described as mentoring with an anticipated specific outcome. Peer mentoring can be comfortable, nonthreatening, and useful for specific situations. Peer mentoring may be one component of a larger mentoring program, and peer mentors may themselves be supervised and/or mentored as part of the program.

Structured Mentoring

Formalized programs that pair an experienced individual with someone new to a situation are examples of *structured mentoring*. Defined by organization, established goals, timelines, required or encouraged participation, and assignment of roles and relationship pairings, these programs can be useful in a variety of professional and academic settings. For undergraduate, graduate, or professional students, a planned faculty/student mentoring program can be critical to academic retention and success, orientation to a major or professional career, and full participation in the life of a department, school, or university. For a new employee in any library setting, a formalized program may be required and may include not only typical mentoring activities, such as support and career coaching, but also training in specific job related tasks, such as one would attain through an internship or practicum (Kuyper-Rushing 2001). Academic librarians may be mentored specifically for tenure and promotion, depending on their institution and its faculty requirements (Colley and Thorson 1994). Although structured programs generally include reporting requirements, meeting expectations, established goals, and evaluation components, the best ones allow flexibility as each specific mentoring relationship still involves two people working one to one.

When Does Mentoring Occur?

As the previous description of three common types of mentoring indicated, actual mentoring can occur at any time in an individual's education or career. The optimal time is when the need is present. This probably accounts for much of the informal mentoring and event-specific mentoring that may be observed.

Even in structured mentoring programs, actual meetings between mentor and mentee are generally arranged by the two individuals involved, although there is some timeline provided for the completion of the program. For example, as with the University Minority Mentor Program described in the introduction, a structured program may be planned for a first year in college or graduate school or for a first year in a new professional position. Certain activities may be planned at particular points in the year, and group activities may be held, but the best programs also allow for less structured encounters or for the development of parts of the program based on the interests of the mentor and the mentee.

Where Does Mentoring Occur?

This question may seem so obvious that you wonder why it is even included. If mentoring is a one-to-one relationship, then it must follow that the individuals involved will meet face to face. This is the case in many mentoring relationships, and some actual meetings are desirable for any mentoring connection. It is not, however, the only way an effective mentor can serve the needs of a mentee (Owens, Herrick, and Kelley 1998). Telephone counseling, e-mail contacts, and other written communication may be used as part or all of a mentor/mentee relationship. What is more important is the commitment the participants bring to the process and the determination they have to make it work and succeed.

ELEMENTS OF SUCCESSFUL MENTORING

There is agreement, both in the literature and in discussions about mentoring, that certain principles should be the foundation for any mentoring process. The first requirement for a successful mentoring relationship is trust between the two primary participants. They need to be able to count on honesty, accountability, and mutual respect. Mentees should accept the fact that the relationship is intended to assist their professional growth and development, that they will need to listen to advice, that the relationship is not one of equals, with the possible exception of peer mentoring, that they need to participate in defining the relationship, and that they should expect and accept sometimes candid evaluations. Developing a friendship may result from the mentoring connection, but this is not, nor should it be, the focus of the process. To be really effective, a certain level of objectivity on the part of the mentor is important. As a method of understanding successful mentoring, imagine you are a mentee. What would you expect from a mentee/mentor relationship? Now imagine you are the mentor. What expectations would you have for the mentor/ mentee relationship?

The element of trust has already been mentioned, as has the importance of accountability. In any but the most casual and short-lived of mentoring relationships, some preliminary discussion of just what is expected or desired from the relationship is important. This goes to the heart of the question you just considered. There needs to be a clear understanding of and agreement on the purpose of the relationship between the mentor and the mentee, even allowing for the natural evolution of the relationship over time. Regular contacts, in person, by telephone, or through e-mail need to be planned for and completed. What is important is that commitments of time are met. That is, if a weekly meeting is set, both parties in the relationship honor that agreement by reserving the time and preparing to the extent that the time is well spent. Failing to meet commitments, on the part of either participant in the mentoring relationship, should not be part of any type of mentoring from the most informal to the most structured. By some estimates, half of all mentoring arrangements end within a few months. Lack of commitment on the part of the mentor and the mentee, failure to define and understand the potential relationship, and, sometimes, a simple failure of the two parties to "click" are given as reasons for this failure. Evaluation or a revisiting of goals, which are important components of any relationship, could help make more connections successful. For example, the mentor may feel everything is going along well, but the mentee may be uneasy, frustrated, or confused. Obviously, this can be reversed and the mentor may be the one who wishes to revisit the basis of the mentoring relationship, revise goals, or evaluate progress. Each participant needs to feel they are receiving a real benefit from the process. For example, mentors may feel a renewal of professional purpose, appreciate the support of the mentee, enjoy recognition for their contribution to the future of the profession, and have a sense of personal satisfaction. They may find they are considered to be visionary, knowledgeable, and skilled as they are recognized as an effective mentor. Mentees receive support, encouragement, information, and, possibly, training or skill development. In some organizations, they may be on a faster track for promotion, salary increases, or other tangible benefits from participating in a mentoring relationship.

Mentoring can have some potentially negative elements, which should be considered before you embark on the path of being a mentor or a mentee. These cautions are not intended to discourage you from participating in what is usually a rewarding and beneficial experience, but it is wise to be aware of some of the pitfalls. By definition, mentoring implies a special relationship. Those who do not participate in this kind of relationship, even if they do not seek it out, may be jealous. It is especially important for the mentee to realize that this may occur so he or she can be prepared for any possibly negative encounters. In addition, mentoring programs should strive to include anyone who wishes to participate. If all mentoring is based on self-selection, those who are "different" from the majority group may be excluded. This is usually not intended, but it is no less hurtful and harmful than if it were planned. Bernice Sandler said, "[As a mentor, you should] be willing to provide support for people different from yourself. I have always believed that it is far easier for women than it is for many men to cross boundaries such as race, color, ethnicity, class, and religion in working with others. But we all need to practice this skill and avoid the temptation to assist only those with whom we feel the most comfortable, those who are the closest to being clones of ourselves" (1993, p. B3). Finally, to avoid any misunderstandings, be sure the boundaries of the relationship are clear from the beginning to both the mentee and the mentor. As an exclusive and possibly intense relationship, the end of the commitment may lead to disruption and even damage to the participants if objective goals and regular evaluation have not been part of the entire process. Marci McDonald quotes Stacy Blake-Beard, a mentoring expert at Simmons College, regarding the end of a mentoring connection: "Once you formalize the relationship, you also politicize it. I get calls all the time from women saying, 'How do I get out of this without ruining my career?'" (2003, p. 38). Remember, the relationship being established is intended to be a mutually beneficial connection. Common expectations, honesty, and mutual commitment to this primary goal should help avoid some of the potential problems outlined above.

CONCLUSION

According to Clare Nankivell and Michael Shoolbred (1997), six key types of mentoring are of importance to library or information science professionals: (1) Mentoring for management skills; (2) Mentoring for professional support and development; (3) Mentoring for specific skills; (4) Mentoring or acclimatizing for a new employee; (5) Mentoring for professional contacts; and (6) Mentoring for career development.

If you can provide guidance in even one of these areas, you have the potential to serve as a mentor. Participating in a mentoring relationship can be one of the most rewarding activities in your career. In her "10 Commandments of Mentoring," Sandler wrote, "Don't be afraid to be a mentor. Many people, especially women, underestimate the amount of knowledge that they have about the academic system or their organization, the contacts they have, and the avenues they can use to help someone else. A person does not have to be at the absolute top of his or her profession or discipline to be a mentor." She continues, "Remember that you don't have to fulfill every possible function of a mentor to be effective, but let your protégés know where you are willing to help and what kind of information or support you can give that you believe will be particularly helpful" (1993, B3).

Keep in mind these guidelines and tips, be aware of some possible pitfalls, and then ask yourself again the three questions that began this discussion: *Have you ever been mentored; by whom; and have you ever been a mentor to someone?* I hope you can answer "yes" to the first and that you will also be able to answer "yes" to the last. For both mentor and mentee, the rewards far outweigh any drawbacks.

RELATED READINGS

The literature on mentoring is rich and varied. A current Internet search on the term will lead to several hundred citations. Journal articles, book chapters, dissertations, best practice documents, abstracts of conference presentations, and other types of publications all provide information on some aspect of mentoring. The literature of human resources is one major area where relevant and useful material may be found. Programs that prepare new teachers for success in the schools are also well represented in the available literature. Another area of concentration in the literature is related to academic mentoring connections between student peers or between post secondary faculty and students. The suggested reading list, which follows, is more general in nature but should serve as an introduction to the material available to the reader.

Campbell, David E., and Toni A. Campbell. "The Mentoring Relationship: Differing Perceptions of Benefits." *College Student Journal* 34, no. 4 (2000): 516–23.

Colley, Joanne, and Connie Capers Thorson. "Mentoring along the Tenure Track: Helping New Library Faculty Members Meet their Goals." *College and Research Libraries News* 50, no. 4 (1990): 297–300.

Emerson, Diane M. "Mentoring as Metaphor: An Opportunity for Innovation and Renewal." *New Directions for Teaching and Learning* 85 (2001): 7–13.

Goodwin, Laura D., Ellen A. Stevens, William L. Goodwin, and E. Allison Hagood. "The Meaning of Faculty Mentoring." *Journal of Staff, Program, & Organizational Development* 17, no. 1 (Spring 2000): 17–30.

Hansman, Catherine A. "Mentoring as Continuing Professional Development." *Adult Learning* 12 (2001): 7–9.

Kuyper-Rushing, Lois. "A Formal Mentoring Program in a University Library: Components of a Successful Experiment." *Journal of Academic Librarianship* 27, no. 6 (2001): 440–46.

McDonald, Marci. "The Mentor Gap." *U.S. News & World Report* (3 November 2003): 36–38.

Munde, Gail. "Beyond Mentoring: Toward the Rejuvenation of Academic Libraries." *Journal of Academic Librarianship* 26, no. 3 (2000): 171–75.

Nankivell, Clare, and Michael Shoolbred. "Mentoring: A Valuable Tool for Career Development." *Librarian Career Development* 5, no. 3 (1997): 98–103.

OP-ED. "Look for a Mentor You Can Work With, Not Just Listen To." *PR Week* (27 October 2003): 6.

Owens, Brenda H., Charlotte A. Herrick, and Jean A. Kelley. "A Prearranged Mentorship Program: Can It Work Long Distance?" *Journal of Professional Nursing* 14, no. 2 (1998): 78–84.

Reinarz, Alice G., and Eric R. White, eds. *Beyond Teaching to Mentoring*. San Francisco: Jossey-Bass, 2001.

Robbins, Jane Borsch. "Building a Power Base in the University." In *Aspirations and Mentoring in an Academic Environment: Women Faculty in Library & Information Science,* ed. Mary Niles Maack, 172–74. Westport, Conn.: Greenwood Press, 1994.

Sandler, Bernice R. "Women as Mentors: Myths and Commandments." *Chronicle of Higher Education* (March 10, 1993): B3.

Snow, Marina. "Librarian as Mentor." *Journal of Academic Librarianship* 16, no. 3 (1990): 163–64.

Young, Clara Y., and James V. Wright. "Mentoring: The Components for Success." *Journal of Instructional Psychology* 28, no. 3 (2001): 202–6.

ABOUT THE AUTHOR

Dr. Carol Ritzen Kem is a library faculty member in the department of collection management at the University of Florida. She is also an affiliate faculty member in the Women's Studies and Gender Research Center at the University. Dr. Kem is a member of the Council that organizes and evaluates the program of the University Minority Mentor Program. She has served as a panelist and has presented research on mentoring at national conferences. Dr. Kem's primary research area is related to work behavior type and personality type of librarians, generational change, and diversity in the profession.

55

Keeping Our Heads above Water:
Staying Current with Professional Issues

Denise Landry-Hyde

In this day of the Internet, it is easy to become overwhelmed by the amount of information and the number of information resources at our disposal—both traditional formats and electronic formats—all designed to help keep us up to date in an ever-changing world. Ironically, it is the technology itself that changes most rapidly. Keeping up with all of this information can be a daunting task, but a great deal of help is available to make the task easier.

DISCUSSION LISTS, ALERT SERVICES, WEBSITES, WEB LOGS, AND E-PUBLICATIONS

Lists, or electronic discussion lists (particularly moderated ones since they reduce extraneous posts and keep members' discussions on track), are a great place to start. Thousands of e-mail lists exist to address all manner of needs. *Catalist* (www.lsoft.com/lists/listref.html), the official catalog of LISTSERV lists from LSoft, the manufacturers of the LISTSERV software, counts 308,125 LISTSERV lists—72,332 being public lists. While the Web has garnered worldwide attention as an academic tool, LISTSERV has been quietly dominating academic discussions for at least twice as long. As Avi Hyman states, each list is "a virtual neighborhood defined by common interest, not geography" (2002, p. 17). Rather than Marshal McLuhan's "global village," the phrase "virtual tribalism" better describes these groups; among them, there is a special version frequented by scholars, often referred to in the literature as Scholarly Electronic Forums (SEFs) or Scholarly Discussion Groups (SDGs). LISTSERV has been "the great equalizer," giving all parties a forum, regardless of their technological level or bandwidth capability. The beauty of

LISTSERV is that every participant is both teacher and student (Hyman 2003, pp. 17, 19–20).

For quick, up-to-the-minute updates on priority and legislative matters, some of the best are lists such as the American Library Association's *ALAWON* (Washington Office Newsline), *Library Journal Academic Newswire*, and *ACRL* (Association of College & Research Libraries) *Update*, and on the state level, something equivalent to *TexLine*, the legislative update list for the state of Texas.

For keeping up with the latest practices in one's day-to-day work life, lists focusing on a subject or functional area are invaluable. In the reference/ instruction areas, for example, *LIBREF-L* and *ILI-L* are two of the best. Serials librarian Sarah Sutton recommends *SERIALST: Serials in Libraries Discussion Forum* and the NASIG (North American Serials Interest Group) website (www.nasig.org). She also has an alert service activated in Elsevier's *ScienceDirect* database so that she can read *Serials Review* online when it becomes available. Another kind of alert that can be set up in *ScienceDirect* is the Search Alert. A search is scheduled to run automatically at a chosen frequency and to deliver an e-mail notification of search results. This can be an extremely valuable way to keep up with major topics important to the individual. Other document delivery vendors, such as Ebsco, offer similar alert services. Interlibrary Loan/Document Delivery manager Jose Gonzalez noted the *Ariel, ILLiad* (for OCLC's totally integrated system), and *ILL* as useful lists for ILL staff members.

Vendors are offering many lists designed to help keep customers abreast of changes in search features, interfaces, and so on. Ebsco, Gale Research, Cambridge Scientific Abstracts, OCLC's FirstSearch, and ProQuest are all examples of vendors following this practice. *INNOPAC- III Online Public Access Catalog Distribution List* is the discussion list for Innovative Interfaces. An example of a statewide consortium list is the *TexShare-Users* (for the state of Texas) list that keeps members abreast of resource sharing and commonly accessed databases.

Two favorite websites of mine are *Librarians' Index to the Internet* (www.lii.org) from the Sate Library of California, and ResourceShelf.Com (www.resourceshelf.com) from Gary Price, a former reference librarian at George Washington University and currently a writer and compiler of the *ResourceShelf*. Both sites send out e-mail updates as new, quality websites appear. Librarians assess each of the sites.

E-Publications

Current Cites, edited by Roy Tennant and distributed by the library at University of California, Berkeley, is a monthly gem that gives annotated listings of key articles coming out in the field or in related fields such as in networking. The *PACS-L* list automatically distributes this title when it is published, or one may directly subscribe to it for free. *Cites & Insights: Crawford at Large* (cites.boisestate.edu/civ3il2.pdf) is a lengthy monthly newsletter on current library and technology issues with incisive commentary from Walt Crawford, a senior analyst at Research Libraries Group (RLG). For those interested in higher education, the *Chronicle of Higher Education* online is a "must." *ACADEME TODAY: The Chronicle of Higher Education's Daily Report* for subscribers gives summaries of key stories and links to fuller information. *The Informed Librarian Online* (www.informedlibrarian.com) consists of three sections: Guest Forum, which includes a specially written article for Web publication; a Featured Article; and a Featured Book. Periodicals included are *Byte, Choice, College & Research Libraries, D-Lib Magazine, EDUCAUSE Review, First Monday* (a peer-reviewed journal on the Internet), *Library Hi Tech News, The One-Person Library, Publishers Weekly,* and many more. This is a wonderful site for keeping up with current, professional issues.

"Lawrence Looks at Books" is a monthly review of reference sources. It is a free column available at the Gale Group website, www.galegroup.com/free_resources/reference/lawrence/index.htm. The column is written by John Lawrence, associate director, Joyner Library, Eastern Carolina University, Greenville, North Carolina.

Education Review, edited by Gene V. Glass at Arizona State University, is an open access electronic journal that publishes reviews of books in education. All reviews are freely accessible on the Web at edrev.asu.edu. The journal publishes reviews in Spanish and Portuguese as well as English. The publishing of new reviews is announced through a list, *EDREV*, which can be subscribed to through the website.

The *Scholarly Electronic Publishing Bibliography*, by Charles W. Bailey Jr. of the University of Houston Libraries, selects English-language articles, books, and other printed and electronic sources that are useful in understanding scholarly electronic publishing efforts on the Internet. Announcements for new versions of the bibliography are distributed on the *PACS-L* mailing list. A *Scholarly Electronic Publishing Weblog* (info.lib.uh.edu/sepb/sepw.htm) now also updates the bibliography. The weblog announcements are now available via e-mail as well. The *SPARC Open Access Newsletter*, a monthly newsletter edited by Peter Suber at Earlham College, is distributed by the *SCHOLCOMM* (scholarly communication) list based at the Association of Research Libraries (ARL) (www.arl.org/sparc/soa/index.html).

TGN (*Technology Grant News*) is a new website (www.technologygrant-news.com) with a Free Grant Index and Grants Index-by-Type Sampling that makes it easier for librarians to see what type of grants are available.

Library Support for Distant Learning (alexia.lis.uiuc.edu/~b-sloan/libdist.htm) is a site maintained by Bernie Sloan, Graduate School of Library and Information Science, University of Illinois at Urbana–Champaign, and Sharon Stoerger, MLS, MBA. General information on distance learning, planning/

policy documents, state and regional websites for library support of distance education, and selected resources on virtual reference service and evaluating Web resources are all included on this website. All resources listed are available on the Web. *Digital Reference Primer: a Basic General Introduction to Digital Reference Services* (www.lis.uiuc.edu/~b-sloan/primer.htm) and *Digital Reference Services Bibliography* (www.lis.uiuc.edu/%7Eb-sloan/digiref.html) are two important sources listed on the distance learning site. *DIG_REF* is a forum for the growing number of people and organizations answering questions via the Internet. It is maintained by the virtual reference desk (VRD), which is sponsored by the U.S. Department of Education (vrd.org/DIG_Ref/dig-ref.shtml).

Amigos Agenda & OCLC Connection (www.amigos.org/aaoc/), a monthly technical bulletin, answers frequently asked questions and offers timely tips and advice on a variety of subjects, such as "Internet Tips." Another useful e-publication is *EDUCAUSE Online*, a publication of EDUCAUSE (www.educause.edu/), a nonprofit association whose mission is "to advance higher education by promoting the intelligent use of information technology."

For those interested in library instruction, the publications of the LOEX Clearinghouse for Library Instruction (www.emich.edu/public/loex/loex.html), based at Eastern Michigan University, include *LOEX News*, a quarterly publication for members only, and *LOEX_Currents*, an e-mail current awareness service that contains time-sensitive information in library instruction.

TELECONFERENCES, WEBCASTS, AND E-LEARNING

The College of DuPage in Glen Ellyn, Illinois, has a long track record for presenting an annual award-winning series of quality teleconferences on library issues, such as its "Soaring to Excellence" series (www.cod.edu/teleconf). Recent teleconferences have covered topics such as reference service in all its manifestations—traditional, digital, and virtual, web design, and many others.

Vendors such as ProQuest and OCLC are utilizing webcasts as an efficient way to present database training and/or product updates to their customers. Usually these sessions are brief and are extremely cost-effective ways for libraries to provide needed training to their staffs.

Amigos (www.amigos.org/), one of OCLC's regional networks, offers various e-learning workshops. Live, online learning from learning@amigos.org involves instructor-led training at one's own computer. A complete, live, online training schedule, course descriptions, technical requirements, and so on are available online at www.amigos.org/learning/calendar/index3.php. Self-paced courses are available anytime. Learning without the expense and inconvenience of travel is especially appreciated when budgets are tight. Currently, topics for self-paced courses include cataloging, interlibrary loan, preservation, and Web publishing, with more to come. Complete details, course descriptions, technical requirements, and the like are available at www.amigos.org/learning/description.html.

HorizonLive (www.horizonlive.com/try_product/desktop_lectures.php) has now been offering its Desktop Lectures Series for three years. Topics for these lectures include those of interest to educators, such as "Best Practices in Online Instruction" and many others.

PROFESSIONAL ASSOCIATION MEMBERSHIPS, SUBSCRIPTIONS, AND CONFERENCES

Membership in professional organizations, which carries with it subscriptions to a wide variety of journals, has always been an excellent way to keep abreast of professional issues. Membership in the American Library Association (ALA) (www.ala.org) includes a subscription to *American Libraries*. Divisional membership in ALA includes receipt of even more specialized periodicals, such as *College & Research Libraries* and *College & Research Libraries News* for ACRL (www.ala.org/acrl) members. ACRL also publishes *Choice: Current Reviews for College Libraries*. Reference and User Services Division membership includes a quarterly of the same name. The Public Library Association (www.pla.org), also a division of ALA, distributes *Public Libraries* to its members. The American Association of School Libraries (www.ala.org/aasl) publishes *School Library Media Research*. The Librarians Administration and Management Association (LAMA), Library and Information Technology Association (LITA), and Association for Library Collections & Technical Services (ALCTS) also distribute specialized publications to their members.

Special Libraries Association (www.sla.org) is an international group of information professionals serving business, research, government, universities, newspapers, museums, and so on. *Information Outlook* is circulated to its members. *Law Library Journal* is the quarterly publication of the American Association of Law Librarians (www.aallnet.org). The Medical Library Association (www.mlanet.org) publishes *Journal of the Medical Library Association*.

For very specialized areas, such as Marine Science, relevant associations such as the International Association of Aquatic and Marine Science Libraries and Information Centers (IAMSLIC) (www.iamslic.org/index.html) exist. In any professional community, networking, mutual support, and resource sharing are more important. Most organizations put out newsletters, publications, and websites to inform members. Associations usually hold conferences as well as regional annual meetings.

ANNUAL CONFERENCES

Most professional associations hold annual conferences—some even hold more than one meeting per year. Conferences offer librarians the chance to circulate and network, face to face, with peers. Instantaneous communication via e-mail and the Web is wonderful, but nothing can take the place of human interaction. From ALA's Annual and Mid-Winter Conferences to ACRL's national conference, to more specialized gatherings such as the LOEX-of-the-West Conference or NASIG's Annual Conference, there are many opportunities to network with peers on all levels.

OTHER CONTINUING EDUCATION OPPORTUNITIES

In-House Opportunities

Often, lifelong learning opportunities can be found right at your doorstep. On university campuses, for example, there is typically some kind of center for the promotion of teaching excellence. The names of these centers vary, but the purpose is to provide faculty with the support and resources they need to enhance their teaching skills. Usually this involves helping them integrate technology into the curriculum. Computing centers also typically offer short classes on everything from Microsoft Word and Office training to e-mail and list management training. The library itself is often a gathering point for seminars on database searching, website evaluation, creating successful research assignments, and so on.

Workshops and Institutes

Every once in a while, outstanding opportunities arise that introduce us to issues of current importance. One such opportunity is the Building for Tomorrow Program (www7.twu.edu/~f_westbrook/iM.L.S.) funded by the Institute of Museum and Library Services and supported by the Texas Woman's University School of Library and Information-Studies. The program focuses on three pressing staff development needs of librarians: user education, digital reference, and community needs analysis. The program is made up of three segments: subject-specific institutes, locally conducted projects that build on each institute, and web support for each subject area. The overall program website provides the resources, including links to Institute participants' Web-based projects, and information necessary for the program to be replicated by libraries, consortiums, and state associations.

Another excellent regional institute is the Tall Texans Leadership Development Institute. It is a high-quality, five-day, intensive learning experience held each summer in a retreatlike environment in the Texas hill country. The Institute has been facilitated since 1995 by noted consultants Maureen Sullivan and Jack Siggins. Participants are midcareer library and information science practitioners (degreed and nondegreed) who are currently employed in the field and who have at least five years experience in library and/or information science. Library laypersons with at least three years of service to the library community are also eligible.

Print Sources

Stepping back into the print world, the *Bowker Annual of Library and Book Trade Information* is a trusted source for keeping up with developments and trends in the field. News and trends of the year, federal agency and federal library reports, national association and organization reports, international and special reports, such as those on "Homeland Security and Information Management," "Digital Rights Management," and "Recruitment and Retention—a Professional Concern," are all part of this annual. Also included are legislation, funding, and grants information; library/information science education, placement, and salary information; research and statistics on the library and book trade industries; reference information; and a directory of library and related, as well as book trade and related, organizations. In this age of the World Wide Web, discussion lists, e-publications, webcasts, and e-learning, it is good to remember trusted print sources such as the *Bowker Annual* to help keep us up to date in our professional lives.

ONLINE RESOURCES

Amigos Agenda & OCLC Connection—www.amigos.org/aaoc/
Between the Stacks, Library and Information Science Discussion Forums—www.betweenthestacks.com
Building for Tomorrow Program—www7.twu.edu/~f_westbrook/imla
Catalist—www.lsoft.com/lists/listref.html
Chronicle of Higher Education—chronicle.com
Cites & Insights: Crawford at Large—cites.boisestate.edu/civ3il2.pdf
College of DuPage Soaring to Excellence Series—www.cod.edu/teleconf
Digital Reference Primer—www.lis.uiuc.edu/~b-sloan/primer.htm
Digital Reference Services Bibliography—www.lis.uiuc.edu/%7Eb-sloan/digiref.html
Education Review—edrev.asu.edu
EDUCAUSE Online—www.educause.edu
High School Teachers Support—groups.yahoo.com/group/highschoolteacherssupport
H-net, Humanities, and Social Sciences Online—www.h-net.msu.edu
The Informed Librarian Online—www.informedlibrarian.com

"Lawrence Looks at Books" — www.galegroup.com/free_resources/reference/lawrence/index.htm
Librarians' Index to the Internet — www.lii.org
Library Support for Distant Learning — alexia.lis.uiuc.edu/~b-sloan/libdist.htm
LOEX Clearinghouse for Library Instruction — www.emich.edu/public/loex/loex.html
ResourceShelf.Com — www.resourceshelf.com
Scholarly Electronic Publishing Bibliography — info.lib.uh.edu/sepb/sepw.htm
SPARC Open Access Newsletter — www.arl.org/sparc/soa/index.html
TGN, Technology Grant News — www.technologygrantnews.com
Virtual Reference Desk (VRD) — vrd.org/DIG_Ref/dig-ref.shtml

RELATED READINGS

ARL Directory of Scholarly Electronic Journals and Academic Discussion Lists. Washington, D.C.: Association of Research Libraries, 2000. Also available online at db.arl.org/dsej/start.html.

Bowker Annual of Library and Book Trade Information. New York: R. R. Bowker, 2003.

Cohen, Stephen M. *Keeping Current: Advanced Internet Strategies to Meet Librarian and Patron Needs.* ALA Editions, 2003.

Hedblad, Alan, ed. *Encyclopedia of Associations.* New York: Gale, 2003.

Hyman, Avi. *Twenty Years of ListServ as an Academic Tool.* 2003. 0-www.sciencedirect.com.portal.tamucc.edu/ (last accessed 10 October 2003).

Rafaeli, Sheizaf, Fay Sudweeks, Joe Konston, and Ed Mabry. "ProjectH: A Collaborative Quantitative Study of Computer-mediated Communication." *ProjectH.* 1998. www.it.murdoch.edu.au/~sudweeks/papers/techrep.html (last accessed 10 October 2003).

Tennant, Roy, ed. *Current Cites.* Berkeley: The Library at the University of California, Berkeley, 2004. sunsite.berkeley.edu/CurrentCites/ (last accessed _____).

Ulrichsweb. New Providence, N.J.: R. R. Bowker, 2003. Available online at www.ulrichsweb.com

ABOUT THE AUTHOR

Denise Landry-Hyde is currently serving as reference distributed learning librarian at Bell Library, Texas A&M University–Corpus Christi. Most of her library experience has been in university/research libraries, but she has also worked in an online newspaper library, as researcher for development in a university foundation, and as a one-person library in a Marine Science Center. Along the way, she worked part time on the retail side of the book trade and as an intern at a public library, and she fulfilled a practicum in a business and industry association library. She began her professional life as a teacher.

56

Publish the Thought: Writing for the Professional Literature

Wayne Jones

WHY WRITE?

Like most other fields of human endeavor, library and information science (LIS) has a substantial and always-growing body of professional literature behind it. People work in libraries or teach in information-studies program, and somewhere along the line they are compelled to write about practices and theories. Books and articles get published, other librarians and teachers read them, and in the midst of their own careers they decide that they want to write something, too.

There are many reasons *not* to write. It can be hard work. "Hard work?!" you ask incredulously. "Don't you just have to jot a few things down?" Well, yes, it is only writing and not playing linebacker, but it can be taxing, and frankly it is not something that everyone can do or enjoys doing. It can also be very time consuming. Many people don't want to spend their free time writing about the same stuff that they are working on during the rest of the week.

So, why should you be writing for the professional literature?

The main reason is that writing forces you to synthesize your thoughts, to figure out what you really think (and know) about issues in your corner of LIS. It's a busy profession with many different specialties and with changes happening all the time. If you are caught up in the day-to-day work of, say, dealing with vendors, or figuring out the pros and cons of virtual reference, or adjusting to the latest changes in the cataloging rules, you may not have much time to become familiar with the broader trends. You attend conferences, yes, but those can be harrying (harrowing?) affairs during which there are too many sessions to attend and too many people to see, and you sometimes feel lucky that you at least came away with a reading list or summary of the main points.

The requirement to actually *write* about a particular topic slows things down. You'll need to do some research to determine whether someone else has not already written about your idea (see more about that later). But perhaps more importantly, the actual sitting down and marshalling of facts and thoughts into a cogent argument has the effect of exposing to yourself just what you know and just what you want to say. You can't just think or feel something in an article: You do need to demonstrate or prove it, and writing (or, at least, *good* writing) channels the content. What exactly do I know? What have others said? How can I make this article the clearest it can be?

Another good reason to write is highly practical, and maybe a little crude, but true: Having a record of professional writing looks good on your resume. If you are a beginning librarian or information professional, that potential second employer might list "evidence of involvement in the profession" (or words to that effect) as a necessary or desirable qualification for the job. Having published an article or two demonstrates not only that you have thought about the issues, but also that your thoughts have been reviewed by peers who considered them worthy of publication. A future employer—or whoever is reviewing your promotion potential at your current institution—will look favorably on that.

SAY SOMETHING NEW

Of course, if you are thinking about writing, you likely do already have something to say or report on, but there's always a possibility that someone else beat you to it. You should be generally aware of what's going on in your particular corner of library and information work anyway. Keep up with the professional literature: You don't have to read every new monograph or every article and book review in every journal, but you definitely need to be aware of trends and major issues. "Oh my God! He's read *LRTS* and *The Serials Librarian* cover to cover, and I just saw him heading to lunch with *International Cataloguing and Bibliographic Control* tucked under his arm!" You don't have to fret like this, but you do need to be generally informed.

Before writing an article (or anything else for the LIS literature), as before any small or large project, you need to do research. Most journals and books are indexed in databases, and you need to get access to those databases before you start (see appendix B for a list of the main ones). Your own current library may already subscribe to them, but if not you will need to check out a library in the biggest city closest to you, or in the library of the information-studies program nearby. It is absolutely essential that you orient yourself in this way. The rationale for the research is not only to find out whether your topic has already been "done," but also to find citations to works on similar topics or with relevant takes on what you'd like to write about. If you end up deciding that there is something for you to write about, you want to be sure that you credit previous writers, and maybe even quote them directly.

That said, you really should be encouraged because there are lots of journals out there—printed, online, and available in both formats—that may be to some extent competing with each other, and so they are anxious to get your article before someone else does. That's not to say that there are no standards, or that the journals are desperate for copy, or that it is a nasty business of producing more widgets than the competitors—but just to say that there are markets out there for you.

WHERE TO PUBLISH

It might be nice to publish a full-length monograph that completely revolutionizes library science, but you need not (and probably shouldn't) aim that high, especially with your first writing efforts. The main sources for publishing your professional writing are:

Professional journals. The main possibilities are articles and book reviews, but some journals also publish brief reports and notices of various kinds.

Books. If you have an idea for a full-length monograph, there are publishers out there for that, too (some of them also publish journals). It is best to query the publisher first: that is, don't write the book and send the whole thing, but send a cover letter and a couple of chapters to the publisher, even if you have already written the whole thing. Many publishers have strict guidelines about the kinds of things they need to see in a query (e.g., cover letter, synopsis, sample chapters, outline). Your book can be either one that you write all by yourself or one like the one you are reading now, in which you may write a chapter or two, but mainly you bring together and edit contributions from others. A book is generally a huge undertaking that will cost you a lot of time: If you are a beginning writer, it's best to start with a piece in a professional journal.

Conference proceedings. Most professional associations in the library and information field hold conferences, and many publish the proceedings of those conferences. Furthermore, some of the associations call on members to volunteer as editors. The North American Serials Interest Group (NASIG) is an excellent example. It holds an annual conference in the late spring or early summer, and it issues a call for volunteers to edit (and other members to index) the volume. It's not writing per se, but it can be an interesting way to contribute to your association and to gain some insights into publishing.

Presentations and program reports. Sometimes getting published is a natural result of your participation in other professional activities. If you give a presentation at the annual conference of the American Library Association (to name just one example), you may be able to write a relatively brief report of that presentation for one of the journals. Alternatively, you may get the opportunity to expand the text of the presentation and make a full-fledged article out of it. Sometimes it doesn't even have to be your own presentation. The NASIG proceedings, for example, routinely include summaries of presentations delivered at the conference, and these summaries are written by people other than the presenters. It's another excellent way to participate in a professional association, and although they would not be your own ideas, you would be responsible for reporting and writing the ideas of someone else—not as easy as it might sound.

See appendix A for a list of some websites about getting published in the LIS field.

WRITE IT WELL

I've worked as an editor since the mid-1990s, and I've seen the whole range of quality in the manuscripts I've read. Most of them are well written, a small proportion are extremely well written and a joy to read (and a cinch to edit), and another small proportion are very badly written. Articles in this last category can sometimes be cases in which the editor in effect makes the thing readable and saves the author considerable embarrassment by preventing his or her work from being exposed to the public in shoddy form.

So, once you've written your article, set it aside for a while, and then reread it not so much for the ideas as for the clarity of the writing. Give it to friends or colleagues whose abilities you respect. Then read it again and submit it to the journal after having incorporated all that you have judged necessary to change. It is in your best interest to ensure not only that the facts are right in your article, but also that the writing is clear and the arguments are arranged logically.

One of the common mistakes—the thing that makes bad writing bad—is putting all the facts and details into the article and arranging them in a more or less logical fashion, but being careless or negligent or ignorant about the actual sentences, about what they mean, about how they say what you are trying to make them say. Sometimes this is a result of a fundamental problem with the research or with your knowledge of what you are writing about. It is sort of like the thing that some politicians do: unable to reveal the truth because it would be embarrassing or because they don't know what it is, the only solution is to present part of the truth, and sometimes even to obfuscate. The solution for writers is to know what you want to say, to do your research, and to be careful about the clarity of your writing.

More typically, bad writing is the result of knowing what you want to say (though perhaps only vaguely), but not really taking the time to ensure that your written words convey exactly what's in your head. It's therefore left to the editor to tease out your meaning. It's probably an exaggeration to say that anything badly written is summarily dismissed by journal editors. Part of the editor's job sometimes is to recognize the core of a potentially good contribution to the professional literature, even though it might be obscured by bad writing. However, you'll generally increase your chances of being noticed, and of eventually being published, if you work as hard on the composition of your article as you do on the content.

Finally, you should carefully follow what are called the "guidelines for submission" or "instructions to authors" (or some such similar phrasing) of the journal to which you submit your article. Virtually all journals have them: You can generally find them on the journal's website or tucked somewhere at the front or back of the printed issues. The guidelines generally provide explicit requirements about the acceptable length of articles, the format in which it should be submitted to the editors, the style of the notes and bibliography, and many other mechanical details. For example, the instructions to authors for *The Canadian Journal of Information and Library Science* specifies (among other things):

- three (hard) copies of the manuscript should be submitted
- a 50-100 word abstract should be included
- notes should be appended at the end of the manuscript
- writers should follow *The Chicago Manual of Style*

And the list goes on to specify the exact style for notes and references.[1] Most journals will provide guidance about how you should format those notes and references—all the niceties about whether it's a period or a comma, what goes inside the quotes and what doesn't, what's in italics, and so on (see appendix C for more information about citation). It can be pretty tedious for you if you are not the type who is fascinated by that level of excruciating detail. Instead of trying to work your way through the latest edition of *The Chicago Manual of Style*, for example, you might take your best guess and leave it to the editor to fret over and fix. And, indeed, editors do spend a substantial portion of their time poring over these details, but if you really want to impress a journal editor, take it upon yourself to get them right. It will also give him or her more time to check out what really matters, which is the text of the rest of your article.

DON'T BE INTIMIDATED

In a way I think this is the most important advice to new writers. Nicely laid-out articles in respected journals can positively glow with authority when you read them, and you might have trouble imagining that your own humble offerings should even dare to be so presumptuous as to vie for the same space. Don't think that. The writers of those articles have gaps in their knowledge and limitations in their work experience, just like you. They don't know it all, and yet they have written articles about what they *do* know. You should feel that you could do the same. Really.

NOTE

1. "Guidelines for Submission," *The Canadian Journal of Information and Library Science.* www.cais-acsi.ca/guidelines.htm (last accessed 18 July 2003).

APPENDIX A: GENERAL
INFORMATION ABOUT PUBLISHING AND LIS

BUBL Journals. BUBL Information Service. bubl.ac.uk/journals/ (last accessed 21 July 2003). A "collection of links to current library and information science journals/newsletters." Definitely not comprehensive, but a good starting point with an international focus.

Crawford, Walt. *First Have Something to Say: Writing for the Library Profession.* Chicago: ALA Editions, 2003. Contains comprehensive information on the writing and publishing process, with chapters on copyright, contracts, editorial boards, reviews, columns, drafts, and much more.

"Doing Research in Library and Information Science: A Guide." University of Washington Libraries. www.lib.washington.edu/subject/LibrarySci/guide.html (last accessed 21 July 2003). A good, brief beginner's guide with basic information, some of which is applicable only to the University of Washington Libraries.

Gordon, Rachel Singer. *The Librarian's Guide to Writing for Publication.* Lanham, Md.: Scarecrow Press, 2003. Also comprehensive, with information on proposals, marketing, and more, including interviews with library publishers and editors.

"Publishing in LIS: A Few Useful Sources." University of Illinois at Urbana–Champaign, Library & Information Science Library. gateway.library.uiuc.edu/lsx/lispubguide.html (last accessed 21 July 2003). Includes: Guides to Journals in LIS (with the caveat: "There is no current, comprehensive guide to journals in LIS"); Research and Advice on the LIS Publishing Process; Some General Guides; and Other (e.g., information about NMRTWriter, an e-mail discussion list "dedicated to supporting librarians looking to write and publish articles, books, grant narratives, or other scholarly communications").

"Serials Publications: Resources for Authors." NASIG. www.nasig.org/publications/pub_resources.html (last accessed 21 July 2003). An excellent selective listing "for NASIG members who are looking for outlets to publish their work," but with broad information that may be useful to all information professionals. Includes links to e-resources about style guides and publication guidelines, as well as a list of journals that publish articles about serials and other LIS topics.

APPENDIX B: THE MAIN ABSTRACTING AND INDEXING (A&I) DATABASES IN LIBRARY AND INFORMATION SCIENCE

Information Science & Technology Abstracts. Published by Information Today; covers about 450 publications from 1966 to present; updated nine times a year.

Library and Information Science Abstracts (LISA). Published by Cambridge Scientific Abstracts; covers about 440 periodicals from 1969 to present; updated every two weeks.

Library Literature & Information Science. Published by H. W. Wilson Company; covers about 230 periodicals from 1984 to present; updated monthly.

APPENDIX C: STYLE GUIDES AND CITATION

"APA Style Essentials." Vanguard University of Southern California. www.vanguard.edu/faculty/ddegelman/index.cfm?doc_id=796 (last accessed 25 July 2003). A condensation of the "common core elements" from the *Publication Manual of the American Psychological Association* (5th ed., 2001).

The Chicago Manual of Style. www.press.uchicago.edu/Misc/Chicago/cmosfaq/cmosfaq.html (last accessed 21 July 2003). Answers to frequently asked questions, from one of the main authorities on bibliographic style (15th ed., 2003).

"Citing Sources." College of Saint Benedict/Saint John's University, Clemens Library/Alcuin Library. www.csbsju.edu/library/internet/citing.html (last accessed 25 July 2003). Links to information on citing resources from various authorities.

Columbia Guide to Online Style www.columbia.edu/cu/cup/cgos/ (last accessed 25 July 2003). Excerpts from the book of the same title, with basic information on citing resources on the Internet.

"Style Manuals and Citation Guides." Duke University Libraries. www.lib.duke.edu/reference/style_manuals.html (last accessed 25 July 2003). An excellent annotated list of the main manuals, arranged by style and by discipline, with links to online versions when available.

ABOUT THE AUTHOR

Wayne Jones is head of central technical services at Queen's University in Kingston, Ontario. He has published over thirty articles and book reviews in library and information science (focusing on serials and e-resources), has edited five books, and is a member of the editorial board of the journal *The Serials Librarian*.

57

Marketing Yourself: Planning to Achieve Your Professional Goals

Christine Shupala

MARKETING IS NOT A DIRTY WORD

Businesses have understood for years that only by marketing themselves and their products can they expand their customer base and increase profitability. Libraries, on the other hand, have traditionally shied away from the concept of marketing, perhaps because of its association with profit orientation. The altruistic values of libraries and librarians seem at odds with the blatantly capitalistic concept of marketing. In recent years, however, libraries have begun to recognize the importance of marketing themselves. The American Library Association (ALA) and various state and local library associations provide materials and expertise to assist libraries in making the publics they serve aware of the products and services that are available within their walls. And librarians have increasingly accepted that whether they work in public, academic, school, or special libraries, they must be willing to borrow marketing concepts from the business world in order to make both current and potential library "customers" aware of the services and products they offer.

While librarians have demonstrated an increased willingness to market their libraries, most still struggle with the apparent conflict between self-promotion or self-marketing and service. Many view self-marketing as "bragging." While they are willing to work to ensure that their users understand and value the products and services offered by their libraries, they are less willing/able to ensure that colleagues, supervisors, and users understand and value the skills and knowledge that they—as individuals—bring to the table.

It is a fact that, whether you have been in the profession for a year or a decade, you have seen changes both in how people access information and in the services that librarians provide. Changes in technology and in information retrieval occur so quickly that it is difficult for us as professionals to keep up. We are constantly reeducating ourselves, refining our skill sets, and reinventing our services. Given the rapid pace of change in our profession, how can you expect your supervisors, your colleagues, and your users to know what it is you do—or can do—for them if you don't tell them?

There is no doubt that you have already had some experience in marketing yourself. Consider the marketing in which you engaged to obtain your current position. Your resume, your cover letter, your responses during your interview all were designed to present you at your best—in short, to market yourself. You also intend to continue to present yourself at your best. To do so, you will continue to engage in self-marketing—even if you do not recognize it as such.

Other chapters in this book focus on the importance of the well-developed resume and cover letter, of interview and negotiating skills, of developing your professional image, and of mastering a wide range of interpersonal and technical skills. These tools and skills are essential in the development of you as a professional "product." They belong in your professional toolbox. In order to use your tools effectively, however, you must have something to build and a plan by which to build it. Consider the master builder. He begins his building project with a blueprint or an architect's plan and his tools. The plan indicates what tools he will need and when he will need them in order to construct his building according to the plan. Similarly, you need a blueprint by which you can build your career. In your toolbox you carry the tools you will need to begin your building project. You will add other tools along the way. Your self-marketing plan is your blueprint for effectively marketing yourself.

This chapter focuses on how you can develop and implement your own self-marketing plan using the tools you have available. It will help you understand your "product" and know who your "customers" are. It will assist you in creating your own unique brand and promotional strategy. It will also provide some tips to make it easier to effectively market yourself and accomplish your goals.

DEVELOP YOUR SELF-MARKETING PLAN

The business literature contains many articles and publications devoted to the concept of self-marketing. Business writers have long recognized that opportunity favors those who are prepared. It is no different in librarianship. Ask a colleague whom you consider to be successful how he or she achieved success. The first response may be that he or she was just "lucky." But further questioning will reveal that preparation was at least as important as being in the right place at the right time. For each successful individual the formula is a little different, but at its core are preparation and self-marketing.

UNDERSTAND YOUR PRODUCT—THAT'S YOU!

No marketer can begin to sell a product unless he or she understands what it is about the product that makes it unique or desirable to others. Marketers use these characteristics to develop a branded package. Similarly, you cannot begin to market yourself—to create your own branded package—if you cannot tell others what you have to offer.

Begin by writing down what you consider your core strengths to be. These are the skills, knowledge, and/or expertise that you bring to the organization and that enable you to add value to it. Are you a creative problem solver? Do you work well with children? Are you able to explain technology to those who have little or no experience with computers? Do you relate well to older people? Do you have highly developed organizational skills? Do you adapt well in stressful situations? Do you function effectively in a team-centered environment?

Next make a list of your short- and long-term professional goals. What do you want to be doing in one year, in five years, in ten years? Compare your list of strengths to your list of goals. Reflect on what you are doing now professionally and why you are doing it. Does it meet your short- and long-term needs? Will it help you to achieve the goals you have set? If not, you must determine what you need to do now in order to prepare yourself so that you can achieve your goals.

Then list those skills you believe need further development in order for you to effectively pursue your goals. Are your technology skills up to date? Would you benefit from further training in public speaking? Do your organizational or interpersonal skills need some refinement? Actively seek out opportunities to develop these skills through workshops and professional organizations and with the assistance of mentors.

Finally, recognize that your product—you—changes and develops over time. Your goals, skill set, and knowledge base change. Revisit your lists frequently and note those changes so that you can continue to refine your unique brand and your marketing plan. Focusing on your product and understanding it as it changes are essential to your success in self-marketing.

UNDERSTAND YOUR CUSTOMER(S)

You are your product, but who are your customers? Of course, they are your library users. Indeed, the products and services that your organization provides are designed with these customers in mind. But your customers are also your colleagues, your subordinates, and your supervisors—both within the library and within the larger organization it serves. They may also be your colleagues within professional organizations and at other institutions similar to yours. In short, anyone with whom you interact as a professional is a potential customer. Within this large group of customers, there are a wide variety of needs and wants. To sell your product to them, you must understand both what they need/want and how you can help meet those needs/wants.

With such a large group of potential customers, though, it is difficult to pick out one or two needs/wants as most important. Marketers deal with this situation by dividing their potential customers into subgroups. They determine what it is about the product that will appeal to each subgroup, and they market those specific attributes to each group based on its primary and secondary needs/wants. Similarly, you can market yourself to different groups based on the needs and wants you are able to fulfill. In addition to those skills/attributes on which each group places the highest priority, there will be a host of secondary attributes that each group considers to add further value to the package. For example, your supervisor may place the highest priority on organizational skills, but he or she might also value team-orientation, the ability to communicate effectively, and the ability to make/explain decisions. Your colleagues, on the other hand, may place the highest priority on the ability to work in a team, but they also value communication, decision making, and organizational skills. Once you have clearly identified what it is that each group values most highly, you can focus on presenting that particular skill/attribute set when you are working with members of that group.

IMPLEMENT YOUR SELF-MARKETING PLAN

Select Your Target Market(s)

Marketers divide their potential customers into subgroups to create manageable marketing segments. They also determine if there are groups or areas in which they do not want to focus their marketing efforts. Once you have divided your potential customer base into subgroups, you must determine if there are subgroups within that base on which you do not want to focus initially. New businesses limit their advertising and marketing presence to the customer subgroup or geographic area in which they are most likely to succeed. Only after they establish a secure and loyal customer base do they expand their marketing plan to include additional subgroups or geographic areas. As a relatively new professional, you will also want to begin your self-marketing plan with one or two core customer groups. You should focus your efforts on developing relationships with those "customers" who are important to the achievement of your immediate or short-term goals and with whom you are most likely to succeed. Early in your career your primary customer groups will be limited (in most cases) to your immediate supervisor and the colleagues and/or subordinates with whom you work most closely.

Package and Promote Your Product

Whether you see your core customers in meetings, while working on projects, or in the performance of your daily duties, you should consistently and actively demonstrate the skills/attributes that you believe add value to the organization. How you choose to present the unique set of skills and experience you have acquired determines the package others will see when they consider the product that is you. You build your package as a part of your self-marketing plan and using some of the tools discussed within the chapters of this book. And the packaging is just as critical to the success of your marketing plan as the skills and experience that make up your product's attributes. If the appearance of the package is at odds with the attributes promoted in your marketing plan, it will be less successful.

Presenting the skills/attributes you have identified as most desirable to your customer groups is the essence of self-marketing. Once you have established your package and your product and presented it to your customers, you want to make sure that you continue to present it consistently. This means that you must be very comfortable with the skills/attributes you claim to possess. Your customers are buying you—that is, they are buying the product that you have advertised as you. So it is important that you strive in all packaging and advertising to present an accurate picture of yourself—your skills, your knowledge, your experience, your personality. To do otherwise will make both you and your customers unhappy. If you are a competent public speaker but dread each occasion at which you must speak, do not present yourself as one who enjoys and seeks the opportunity for public speaking. If you do not possess a skill or expertise and have no interest in acquiring it, then do not say that it is something you are willing to learn. If you do not possess a skill or expertise but are excited about developing yourself in that area, then present yourself accordingly. Acknowledging that you do not possess a particular skill/expertise but are willing and excited about developing it demonstrates secondary qualities that most of your customers will find desirable—honesty, enthusiasm, and courage.

Marketers stress the importance of developing a relationship with the customer. By developing a strong and positive relationship with your primary customer groups you build a foundation from which to expand your network of contacts and customers. Once you have established a solid and positive reputation with core groups, you will have the opportunity to develop further customer segments beyond this core. Your satisfied "customers" become supporters and advocates for your marketing in other customer segments. Your supervisor may recommend you for a project that involves multiple departments within the organization. Your colleague may suggest you for a position within a professional organization.

As each new customer segment is developed, your marketing plan should be revisited to review your strengths, your goals, and the areas in which you need further development. These can then be compared with the needs/desires of your new customer focus, and a marketing plan can be designed to attract the new segment. Remember, though, that any added skills or attributes should both attract new customers and enhance the value of your product for established customers. It is your established customers (your supervisors, your colleagues) who have supported your development and who are most likely to continue providing support as you advance in your career.

MARKETING YOURSELF: SOME TIPS TO MAKE IT EASIER

Continue Your Education

Your skills and your knowledge are what make you marketable—they are ultimately what any customer is seeking when they approach you. Rapid changes in technology and advances in knowledge make it impossible for us to look at education as anything but a lifelong pursuit. Look for opportunities to obtain additional training that will enhance the skills you have identified as necessary to achieve your goals. Seek mentors in your workplace and your professional organizations that can help you further develop your skills. Read, read, and read some more. Understand the current trends in librarianship and how they affect you, your goals, your library, your organization, and your profession. Attend conferences and learn from your colleagues. By keeping your skills up to date and continuing to enhance your knowledge base, you become more marketable—both inside and outside your organization.

Develop a Businesslike Attitude

In any arrangement or agreement, you assume obligations. In the workplace you may agree to complete a project by a certain deadline or under a certain budget. Always strive to meet those obligations. When problems arise, focus on finding and presenting solutions or alternatives. Always accept ownership for both your successes and your failures. In doing so, you demonstrate integrity and professionalism.

Extend your businesslike attitude to your appearance and behavior in the workplace. Dress in a manner that fits the environment in which you work. Keep conversations and interactions professional. While everyone enjoys personal contact, keep gossip to a minimum and avoid the negative aspects of office "politics."

Keep Your "Customers" Informed

Request regular meetings with your supervisor so that you can discuss your work and the progress you are making as well as your goals and what your supervisor can do to help you achieve them. Prepare for these meetings by listing the items you want to discuss. You might even prepare a brief agenda and deliver it to your supervisor before the meeting so that she or he has time to consider the items beforehand. Be positive in these meetings, but also discuss any difficulties you are experiencing and why you are experiencing them. If you have suggestions for improvement, use these structured meeting times to present them.

Beware of Bragging

Beware of bragging—there is a difference between informing your supervisor of your successes and detailing at length the many virtues you possess that enabled you to succeed. If you received assistance from a colleague on a difficult project, be sure to give credit where credit is due. By focusing on the project rather than on yourself, and by highlighting the efforts of others, you will earn more respect and credit than you possibly could by "tooting your own horn."

Seek Feedback Regularly

Annual performance appraisals alone are inadequate as a source of feedback if self-improvement is a goal. It is especially important in the early stages of your career when you are still learning the ropes that you have regular feedback from supervisors, colleagues, mentors, and subordinates alike. If you have scheduled regular meetings with your supervisor, ask for feedback during these meetings. Ask specific questions about your performance so that you receive specific suggestions or comments. If you are interested in feedback on a particular aspect of your work, ask about it directly.

Your supervisor is not the only source of information about your performance. Seek feedback from your colleagues, subordinates, and mentors as well. Mentors are usually happy to provide both praise and suggestions for improvement. Colleagues and subordinates may feel less comfortable evaluating your performance critically in a one-on-one situation. Many organizations now have evaluation instruments that allow these groups to rate your work and make suggestions for improvement without attaching their name to the comments. Regardless of the type of library in which you work, you are likely to find at least one colleague or subordinate who is willing to share his or her opinions openly and honestly.

Obtaining feedback is important, but it cannot help you unless you use it to improve your performance. Listen to what others are telling you. Don't be defensive. Take time to consider its merit. Then use what you learn to improve your performance. Those who have provided feedback in the past will be more willing to continue to do so in the future if they see that you take it seriously and act upon it. As a result you will be able to continue to improve as you advance in your career.

Maintain Your Focus

Your marketing plan was founded upon the goals you set for yourself, the strengths you possess, and the interests you would like to further develop. Keep these in mind at all times. Seek opportunities that enable you to further your goals, hone your strengths, develop your interests, and minimize your weaknesses. As a new professional in a rapidly changing environment, you will have many more opportunities than you can possibly accept. Be selective. Choose only those that you believe fit with your goals or that are so fascinating they have caused you to rethink your goals. While saying "no" is never easy, you can say it in a way that reassures others that you appreciate their consideration and would welcome their support for other opportunities that are more in line with your goals.

COMPLETING THE PACKAGE: EVALUATING YOUR PROGRESS

Understanding your product and your customers and developing your self-marketing plan takes both time and effort. Successful implementation of your plan requires still more time and effort. To ensure that it is time and effort well spent, you should periodically review your plan and determine if it has been meeting— and can continue to meet—your needs. It is a good idea to perform this evaluation when you revisit and update your lists of strengths and goals. It is, after all, these strengths and goals upon which you built your original plan.

Consider what you wanted to accomplish with your self-marketing plan. How successful has it been? Note your successes and congratulate yourself! It is important to celebrate your accomplishments—both small and large—and to recognize progress made toward your goals. Also note any goals that your marketing plan has not addressed adequately. Do not be discouraged if there are a few of these—there should be. Recall that you began by considering where you wanted to be professionally in the short term (one year), in the midterm (five years), as well as in the long term (ten years). As a new professional, your marketing plan will have focused primarily on your short-term goals. Your marketing plan evaluation is an opportunity to determine if you are ready to begin focusing on more of those goals that are midterm or long term.

If you have accomplished a significant number of your short-term goals, you may also wish to establish new short-term goals. Establishing new short-term goals is important for several reasons. Carefully designed short-term goals will help you stay on track as you work toward the longer term goals. They also make the task of achieving those longer term goals seem less daunting. Shorter term goals require more frequent evaluation, which means that you will revisit your lists of strengths and weaknesses more frequently as well. Each time you revisit your lists of strengths, weaknesses, and goals, you will see progress worth celebrating. Since each time you evaluate your goals you also evaluate and revise your marketing plan, your plan will always be current. A current plan will take advantage of your newly developed strengths and provide your customers with an accurate picture of the complete professional package that is you.

ABOUT THE AUTHOR

Christine Shupala received her MLS from Indiana University in 1994 and her MBA from Texas A&M University–Corpus Christi in 2003. She is currently the library director of the Mary and Jeff Bell Library at Texas A&M University–Corpus Christi.

8

ENJOYING YOUR CAREER

58

Decompressing the Overstressed Librarian

Timothy A. Baird

Many people do not think of librarianship as a stressful profession. They think that librarians have a relaxing job reading and ordering books in a nice, peaceful, and quiet environment. Unfortunately, this idea is simply a myth. Whether you are a solo librarian or a librarian at a small library in a friendly community, you will still have to deal with stress and stressful situations. This chapter offers suggestions about how librarians can destress. Before we can discuss solutions to help reduce stress, we need to identify stressors as well as stressful library situations.

IDENTIFY YOUR STRESS SOURCES

Day-to-Day Operations

Librarian stress can come in many forms. Many public librarians in urban settings have to deal with working through staff and budgetary shortages. There are only so many hours a week that a librarian can be on the desk dealing with patrons before he or she starts feeling overburdened. With fewer staff members, each librarian is expected to pick up the slack and do more. Often, they are held responsible for tasks for which they lack experience and training. Add to this equation the money factor, that is, having to complete tasks on a very tight budget, and you can see how difficult and stressful a librarian's work can become.

However, this feeling of being overburdened is not limited to urban libraries with small staffs. Academic librarians have to deal with the tango of tenure; corporate librarians must keep up with the fast pace of the business world; and school librarians fight the ticking clock, counting the extremely short periods during which they must deal with hundreds of students. Nearly any librarian in any library setting who shows competence and a willingness to learn will be asked to perform new tasks and duties. Sure, some people can juggle stressors and handle stressful situations with ease, but most of us will find we can be excited, challenged, overwhelmed, as well as overburdened and stressed at the same time.

Technology

There are also many librarians who feel the pressures of having to keep up with all of the new technology associated with our profession and who suffer from technostress. Being a computer-savvy librarian no longer means being a skilled searcher of the online catalog. Librarians are now faced with multiple databases in a wide range of subjects that have different interfaces, as well as all of the CD-ROM and software packages that people expect to find and be able to use when they go to a library. More and more, library staff are being asked to assist people with their resumes using Microsoft Word, or are asked how to add an image to their PowerPoint presentation. It is a very stressful feeling when you are called upon to help and you feel that you lack the technological know-how to perform the task. These feelings of letting the patron down and making the library look bad by not being able to provide adequate help when a patron is asking for it increases stress.

Pressure to Find Answers

Finally, our anxiety grows, wondering if the next question will be the one that stumps us and whether we will look foolish in front of our colleagues and the patron. Are you the librarian who is always the last one to reach for the phone when it rings or the last to volunteer for any kind of demonstration? Is your anxiety level growing because you feel like you should know all the answers but don't? This self-created pressure elevates our stress levels even higher.

MENTORING

What can be done to help these librarians both destress and improve their skills as professionals? One of the best answers is mentoring.

Mentoring in the library setting can come in many forms. Finding a mentor is easiest when a library already has a mentoring system in place. New librarians are assigned a mentor to whom they can go to to talk about difficulties they are having and with whom they can work out solutions to their problems. This can range from filling out their vacation papers properly to finding a person or resource that can help them in a newly assigned task. No one wants to run to their library director or direct supervisor each and every time they have a simple question or small problem. Meeting with your director can be stressful in itself! Having a colleague as a mentor will help the librarian find answers in a very low-key, informal manner.

Now what about libraries that do not have a mentoring system in place? Or what if a library director is having difficulty with some new project that they are responsible for? Where can they turn for help? This is where library associations can step in to help.

Long-Term Library Association Mentoring

The Connecticut Library Association (CLA) has a very formal mentoring program in place to help new librarians, students, or library personnel looking to advance their careers. The mentors and protégés are matched through the mentoring program, and they agree to commit to a one-year relationship. The participants meet once at an orientation and are then expected to be in contact at least once a month, either in person or by phone or e-mail. This one-on-one relationship is of real benefit to the protégé who now has someone to turn to for guidance and advice. And it is often easier to discuss work situations with someone who understands the library environment but does not work at the same library. This type of mentoring is very similar to having a mentoring program at your library, but the association does the work of matching up participants.

Short-Term Library Association Mentoring

The New Members Round Table (NMRT) of the New York Library Association has a different type of mentoring program in place to help all librarians and library staff in New York state. NMRT recruits librarians who are skilled in certain areas of the profession and who are willing to be listed on a Mentor Resource List mounted on the Web. If a librarian is having difficulty in a particular area, he or she can call or e-mail a mentor and receive guidance from an experienced librarian. This virtual assistance could be ongoing or could be for just that one stressful situation that has arisen. The benefit of this type of program is that no one has to commit to a long-term relationship. You can ask for help, receive advice, and be on your way. The other benefit is that if you have more than one problem, you can contact a different skilled librarian for each area that you need help with. An electronic resource librarian who can help you with databases and Internet searching questions will probably not be able to help you with your upcoming children's craft program for Halloween. The NMRT program's flexibility and large pool of mentors from varied backgrounds enables you to go directly to the right skilled librarian for help with your specific problem area.

Informal Mentoring

The third type of association mentoring that I have encountered is the least formal of all. The American Library Association (ALA) has many different discussion lists set up for librarians in various fields to join. I am on a Public Programs list, and quite often librarians pose questions asking for help with a new project that they have been assigned. This is the perfect example of reaching out for help when you do not know where to begin. Not surprisingly, in many instances another librarian may have been involved in the same type of program and he or she offers advice by posting messages through the lists. An even greater benefit is when the librarian receives more than one response, broadening the variety of sources to choose from when developing the program. The beauty of this list is that it encompasses subscribers from small to large libraries, academic to public, and from every corner of the country. This sharing of information and stories among colleagues is a great way to make a stressed librarian feel like they are not alone. There is help out there and he or she does not need to recreate the wheel to complete a task.

If you work as a librarian long enough, chances are you will run across many unfamiliar situations that you are unsure how to handle. Our training has enabled us to do the best that we can with the available resources, but by having some sort of mentoring available to us as librarians, our pool of resources grows substantially. Even if you are in a formal mentoring program or have access to a mentoring resource list, I strongly encourage all librarians to make use of mentors. Everyone can feel their stress dissipate when they find the answer to their work-related problems, and making use of mentors is a giant step toward becoming a happy, stress-free librarian.

OVER-COMMITMENT TO ASSOCIATION AND COMMITTEE WORK

Another area of stress for librarians comes from being overly involved in library association and committee work. I think that library associations are a great benefit to librarians individually and collectively. There is no better opportunity available for us librarians than to attend library conferences where we can learn about trends in the field, hear new ideas, discover new products, and hear about what other librarians in our county, state, or nation have been doing to improve library service. We can then return to our local libraries and implement these new ideas. At large conferences, we get to meet with library vendors, hear legislators and authors speak, and gather with colleagues from near and far. A conference is supposed to be an enjoyable time, but for many active librarians the stress of the conference outweighs the pleasure. Having a set plan, slotting out which programs you want to attend ahead of time, wearing comfortable shoes, and leaving some time to unwind and relax can combat the conference stressors.

GETTING INVOLVED: THE DOMINO EFFECT

Much like library management who will give an extra project to the librarian who shows enthusiasm and initiative, library organizations will do the same. If word gets out that you are very hard working and reliable, other groups will want you to volunteer for them, too. Next thing you know, you are involved in so many groups and committees that you are always faced with one deadline or another. No one likes the pressures of a deadline, let alone ones that they are not even being paid for!

I have a colleague who is president of a round table, is chair of a committee, is an officer in a section, has been asked to join another committee at the state level, and is also on two committees at the county level. Many would agree that this person is being spread too thin. He will not be able to devote as much time and energy as he would like to any one group because he is already so pressed for time. What can this person do to reduce his stress yet still remain involved and dedicated to his profession?

Learning to Say No

A librarian who I know felt that she was in the same situation of overcommitment. Her committee work and organization work were eating away at the time she should be spending on her library work, and even worse, she was devoting many evening and weekend hours to just stay afloat. Her solution was to learn the power of one, simple word: "NO"! Many of us cannot help but feel honored when a group wants us to join them and work with them. It is recognition of our good work and past performances. If we said "no" to one group or the other, many of us would feel guilty or would feel that we had let the group down. One cannot look at it that way or else we will be saying "yes" to every opportunity that presents itself. My colleague said that she now carefully chooses the projects that she becomes committed to and that, consequently, they are a pleasure for her to be involved in. Where is the stress when one is enjoying oneself? She no longer feels rushed, the quality of her work has increased, and she is a much happier librarian because of it.

Prioritizing and Being Selective

My recommendation is not to say "no" to library association work. Become involved in your local, state, and/or national organization(s), and do more than just pay your dues and attend a conference every now and then. By being an active member, you are giving back to your chosen profession and you are continuing your professional development. It looks very good on your resume to list that you were an officer or on the board of a group, and your library management will recognize your dedication to the profession. You will be the one coming to department meetings with new ideas and suggestions for improvement in library services, and it will make you feel confident in the work that you do.

The important factor here is to not overdo your involvement. If you are constantly tired from late nights and running from meeting to meeting, you will feel the physical, mental, and emotional effects of stress. If you are stressed, it will affect your job performance and your quality of life. Understand the power of prioritizing, being selective in your commitments, and learning to say "no" and you will be one step ahead of the pack.

RECLAIM YOUR LEISURE TIME

Now that we have looked at some of the sources of stress for librarians and how mentoring and limiting one's association and committee work can help reduce that stress, I want to mention one final tip for destressing the librarian. No matter how much we love our work or we want to stay one step ahead of the growing paper piles on our desks, it is not a good idea to spend all of our free time doing work, thinking about work, or worrying about work. We work our full forty-hour weeks so that we can enjoy our days off and our vacation time. Every person, regardless of profession, should have outside interests to enjoy in their spare time. Physical activity is a great way to relieve stress and to stay in shape. Whether it is playing tennis, golf, jogging, or working out at the gym, this physical activity will help release your stress, will relax your body, and will lead to a more restful sleep. Not everyone has the time or is able to do more strenuous activities, but even something as simple as taking a walk around the neighborhood with a friend, neighbor, or family member after dinner is a great way to get fresh air, a little exercise, and relax.

Besides physical activities, there are other leisure activities in which one can participate. Playing bridge is a great activity, whether you play socially or competitively. The game stimulates your mind while, at the same time, bringing you into a social atmosphere. Besides bridge, there are knitting groups, chess clubs, historical societies, and all kinds of other groups that meet regularly where their members can enjoy their special interests together.

Another activity that a lot of librarians could enjoy is joining a book discussion group. Now, you might say, librarians spend all day working with books, why would they want to spend their leisure time still surrounded by books? The answer is that most librarians really enjoy their leisure reading and getting together with a group on a monthly basis is an activity ideally suited for someone who loves good literature. The key is to do something that stimulates the mind or the body in an activity that is completely separate from work. By taking your mind off of the stresses of work, you will be able to relax, your body will be less tense, and come the next workday, you will be renewed, rested, and ready to face the challenges of our profession.

CONCLUSION

As librarians, we will never be able to escape the mounting pressures and increasing stressfulness of our profession. Whether we are administrators or department heads, in charge of programming or the new librarian out on the reference desk, we all face challenges and difficulties that we must overcome. The task is to learn to handle our jobs without letting our stress overwhelm us.

Any form of mentoring is a great forum for seeking help when we come across a stumbling block, big or small. Limiting one's association and committee work to what can be handled without overburdening one's self and making sure that both our work time and free time will not be taken over by these commitments is a difficult balance to maintain, especially for someone dedicated to their profession. The solution is to learn how to say "no" when you already have a full slate.

Finally, use your free time to exercise and relax. Make sure to dedicate your free time to rejuvenating your body and mind to recover from the rigors of work. If you do nothing else but follow these simple tips, you will find yourself well along the path to becoming a destressed librarian.

RELATED READINGS

Bankhead, Betty. "Power to the Librarian." *School Library Journal* 49, no. 12 (2002): 48–50.

Caputo, Janette S. *Stress and Burnout in Library Service*. Phoeniz, Ariz.: Oryz Press, 1991.

"CLA Mentoring Program." *Connecticut Library Association*. cla.uconn.edu/membership/mentoring.html (last accessed 3 September 2003).

Harrison, Lucy. "Stress Relief: Help for the Technophobic Patron from the Reference Desk." *The Reference Librarian* 69/70 (2000): 31–47.

"Mentor Resource List." *New Members Round Table of the New York Library Association*. www.nyla.org/index.php?page_id=214 (last accessed 26 September 2003).

Nawe, Julita. "Work-Related Stress among the Library and Information Workforce." *Library Review* 444, no. 6 (1995): 30–37.

Reinhold, Barbara. *Toxic Work: Overcoming Stress, Overload, and Burnout and Revitalizing Your Career.* New York: Dutton, 1996.

ABOUT THE AUTHOR

Timothy A. Baird received his MLIS from McGill University in 1998. He is currently an adult services librarian at the White Plains Public Library in White Plains, New York, and was also the 2002–2003 president of the New Members Round Table of the New York Library Association. Tim is coauthoring a book for Scarecrow Press Inc. entitled *Librarian's Guide to Managing Job Stress* that will be published in 2005. In his leisure time, Tim loves to play golf, tennis, and bridge; watch movies; and spend time relaxing at home with his wife, Zahra, and their two cats, MacKenzie and Tazmyn.

59

Adapting to Change

Mary Anne Hansen

> The greatest discovery of my generation is that a human being can alter his
> life by altering his attitude.
>
> —William James[1]

Is your cup half-empty or half-full? How you react to change in any given situation depends on your attitude and your way of thinking about the situation. Our life experiences as well as our personalities determine to a great extent how we perceive changes thrown our way. While no one can be prepared for every possible situation they might encounter, there are some key ideas and strategies to keep in mind for more effectively adapting to change. Adapting effectively to change in the workplace is a requirement for career survival, as for well as maintaining good mental health.

MOST PEOPLE FEAR CHANGE

The good news is that you're normal if you dread change. The bad news is that change is going to happen in our lives, over and over again. However, learning to anticipate and even welcome change will make change a much less disruptive force in your life.

Depending on our perceived difficulty in accepting any given change, we may experience any of the following reactions and more: fear, disquietude, uncertainty, loss of control, lack of self-worth, increased stress, confusion, blame, victimhood, or cynicism. Additionally, change at work that seems like a threat to us may result in a loss of respect for those in power, our supervisors and managers, who may or may not have made the decision for the change. Furthermore, these negative feelings can lead us to be highly resistant to the change, reducing our creativity and productivity.

What happens when you can't adapt to change successfully? You risk burnout, you may risk losing your job, and even worse, you risk health problems that might result from the stress of getting mired in negative thoughts such as "We've never done it this way!" or "This will never work!" You have some control over the level of stress in your life, because you have control over how you deal with stress, whether in your job or your personal life.

ATTITUDE IS EVERYTHING

> I am convinced that life is 10 percent what happens to me and 90 percent how I react to it.
>
> —Charles Swindoll

To a great extent, you create your own destiny through the choices you make in what livelihood to pursue and, more important, how you choose to comport yourself in both your personal and professional life. While we all go through periods in our lives where we feel like things are out of our control, we always have control over our attitudes and how we react to those feelings of having no control. Essentially, we do always have some control because we can control how we think about something and how we react to it; we have a great deal of power in our ability to make conscious choices about how we adapt to any type of change.

ARE YOU READY FOR NEW CHEESE?

In his book, *Who Moved My Cheese? An Amazing Way to Deal with Change in Your Work and In Your Life* (1998), Spencer Johnson conveys a simple, yet profound, message about adapting to changes in our lives. Through the metaphor of navigating a maze to find our cheese (cheese representing anything in life that we desire, such as our families, good health, our work, etc.), Johnson shares an amusing message about the need to be aware of what's happening around us, and the need to recognize smaller changes as they happen so that we can be prepared for bigger changes that might come along. His work also encourages us to be optimistic about change, not to fear it. The "handwriting on the wall" that we should all recognize in our lives includes these metaphors for adapting to change:

- Change happens: they keep moving the cheese
- Anticipate change: get ready for the cheese to move
- Monitor change: smell the cheese often so you know when it is getting old
- Adapt to change quickly: the quicker you let go of old cheese, the sooner you can enjoy new cheese
- Change: move with the cheese
- Enjoy change! Savor the adventure and enjoy the taste of new cheese
- Be ready to change quickly and enjoy it again: they keep moving the cheese

POSITIVE SELF-TALK

We are entitled to our feelings, but we're responsible for our behavior. When we're feeling negative about a change that is imposed on us, how do we move beyond the negativity? Look for the positive. Optimism can be learned! How do you make yourself think positively on a consistent basis, especially when you're bombarded with unforeseen, difficult changes time and again? How do you move beyond focusing on the difficult and negative aspects of life, especially changes that you have little or no control over? You practice, practice, practice, just as you would do to learn any other skill. A professor once told us the following simple statement about dealing with change: "Don't sweat the small stuff and everything is small stuff." He was encouraging us to keep things in perspective and to not make things bigger than they really are. I still repeat this mantra to myself through the more stressful times in my life, along with another of that same professor's sayings: "This, too, shall pass." These messages are simplistic; yet repeating them to ourselves, and even to others around us, can help us get into a habit of believing them, which can lead to more optimistic and flexible thinking.

When an unexpected, unwelcome change comes our way, it is easy to overreact and blow the issue out of proportion. Such behavior is a defense mechanism; it is also normal behavior, human nature. When something happens that we don't expect, we feel a loss of control. We lose sight of the bigger picture, focus on the negative, and we even might annoy other people who might otherwise help us deal with the situation. We can regain control by exercising positive thinking and regarding the change as a challenge and an opportunity for growth and even new beginnings.

Another important component of positive thinking is realizing that, most of the time, the frustrating events that have happened are not about you personally. Before you jump to conclusions or dig in your heels to resist the change, investigate and find out why the change was made, even if you have been notified in advance of the change. Initiating further communication before reacting negatively will demonstrate to your superiors your interest and investment in the organization. Be proactive rather than reactive. If you show resistance and resentment, you may be regarded as a problem employee. If you demonstrate curiosity and open-mindedness, your perspectives and opinions about a significant change will more likely be welcomed and considered. Your behavior in response to a change will leave a lasting impression on your supervisor and your colleagues. Do you want that lasting impression to be positive or negative? Do you want to be known in your organization as a team player or as a troublemaker? Teach yourself to respond to the unexpected with grace and humility; learn to disagree agreeably and respectfully, and you'll be a respected, trusted member of your organization.

HOW DO I ANTICIPATE CHANGE AT WORK?

We know that change is inevitable, but how do we prepare for it? As librarians, we have myriad information resources at our fingertips, and we need to use them for ourselves, not just our patrons, in order to keep abreast of impending changes. First and foremost, we should interact with our colleagues frequently, discussing, questioning, and learning about the latest ideas and trends in the field. This collegial interaction includes participating in professional discussion lists via e-mail. We should also make it a habit to read regularly at least one, and preferably several, professional journals in librarianship, as well as consumer news publications (*Time, Newsweek, Business Week, New York Times,* to name a few).

There are a plethora of continuing education and professional development activities available for learning about new trends in technology and librarianship. If your employer doesn't provide financial support and the price tag makes you gasp, think of professional development opportunities as an investment in your own career. If travel for the purpose of professional development is out of the question, explore alternative means for free or inexpensive professional development, such as the utilization of in-house experts—your own colleagues. If your library doesn't already encourage employees to train and mentor each other, initiate this effort. Each person has his or her own areas of strengths and expertise that can be shared with others in the organization.

If your supervisor or administrator is not in the habit of communicating frequently with staff about the vision for the library or strategic planning, be proactive and inquire about the possibility of initiating this practice. It doesn't hurt to ask, especially if you're tactful about how you inquire. Most of us prefer to know the reasoning behind any action, so it is logical to assume that preparing yourself with a well-thought-out rationale behind such an inquiry will more likely be received with an open mind by your superior and may even result in your desired outcome.

FROM THE TOP: MANAGING CHANGE AND MANAGING EMPLOYEES

Management can set the tone and positively influence the morale in the workplace by planning for change, guiding progress toward change, and steering employees, rather than waiting for change to happen and reacting to it. Planned change will result in less employee resistance, often the largest impediment to change.

What can supervisors and managers do to ensure a flexible workforce that adapts effectively to change? First of all, managers and supervisors must recognize their role as agents of change in the organization. Managing change is one of the most important components of any professional development program in any organization, and managers as change agents must give attention to specific skills related to change projects, states Lyndon Pugh in his work *Leadership and Learning: Helping Libraries and Librarians Reach Their Potential* (2001). In an earlier work, Pugh (2000) summarizes the necessary requirements of managers for guiding employees through each stage of the change process: awareness raising; communication skills; project management; team skills, including team learning; new operation skills; motivation; and handling resistance and conflict.

Communication skills overlap with each of the other management requirements. Without adequate communication, a manager cannot expect to succeed in the other areas. The successful manager will communicate frequently with all levels of employees about any issues, large or small, that will affect members of the organization. Furthermore, successful managers will communicate not only *what*, but also *how*, *when*, and, most important, *why* she or he has decided to make a particular change. It's not too much for employees to expect their managers to share their thinking, their rationale, behind the decisions they make, especially when employees are affected by those decisions.

Listening carefully to employees, no matter how they voice their opinions and ideas, is essential to any learning organization. Additionally, managers should recognize that not every objection is resistance; objections to change initiatives may be a sign of employees caring about the organization as well as their role within the organization.

Managers and supervisors can prevent a certain amount of negativity or resistance from entering the workplace by building specific behavioral guidelines into position descriptions, making it an expectation for continued employment to "contribute to a productive work environment." If an employee is disgruntled and resistant to change, he or she can be given constructive criticism about the specific behaviors expected of him or her, especially if these expectations are documented in the position description. Such employment requirements will make it easier for an employer to terminate an employee who refuses to adapt, learn new skills, or contribute to the growth of the organization.

More and more managers are recognizing the benefits of participative management over directive management. The great value in participative management lies in making wiser, more informed decisions. Involving employees, or gathering their input in recognition that they are the experts in what they do on a daily basis, also serves to empower employees. Granted, there will always be instances when a manager must make a decision without involving employees, but for the majority of the time, it is more advantageous to gather input from employees on decisions.

In addition to resulting in better decision making, involving and empowering employees serves as a motivational factor, an added benefit for libraries that usually cannot reward employees monetarily.

Marquardt (1996) states that managers can also enhance the management of change in libraries by replacing the traditional performance appraisal approach with performance planning. With performance planning, employees are empowered to collaborate in the formation of their own performance goals and objectives. This collaborative effort will result in employees feeling more vested in the organization. Employees who are motivated and feel that they are a vital part of the organization are less likely to resist changes and are more likely to be productive contributors to any changes.

Finally, successful managers will invest in the necessary training for their employees and will make certain that employees have the tools and equipment they need in order to do their jobs. Included in these tools are the personnel policies, the road map to the organization, so that employees have written guidelines to follow.

EXPECT THE UNEXPECTED

One of the few certainties in life is the inevitability of unexpected changes happening continually. Whether you're an employee in the trenches or a manager or supervisor, you can thrive in the workplace if you train yourself to imagine possibilities rather than drag your feet when faced with change. Envision what you and your organization will gain as a result of a change rather than what you might lose, and you'll feel more motivated and satisfied in your work.

NOTE

1. William James, *The Will to Believe*, 1897.

RELATED READINGS

Johnson, Spencer. *Who Moved My Cheese? An Amazing Way to Deal with Change in Your Work and in Your Life*. New York: Putnam, 1998.

Marquardt, Steve. "Managing Technological Change by Changing Performance Appraisal to Performance Evaluation." *Journal of Library Administration* 22, no. 2–3 (January–February 1996): 101–11.

Pugh, Lyndon. *Change Management in Information Services*. Aldershot, UK: Gower, 2000.

Pugh, Lyndon. *Leadership and Learning: Helping Libraries and Librarians Reach Their Potential*. Lanham, Md.: Scarecrow Press, 2001.

ABOUT THE AUTHOR

Mary Anne Hansen is an associate professor and reference/instruction librarian at Montana State University–Bozeman; she recently completed a one-year appointment as interim associate dean. She has a master of library and information resources from the University of Arizona's distance education program, as well as a master of education in adult and higher education, with a counseling emphasis, from Montana State University. Her undergraduate degree is a BA in modern languages, French and English, also from Montana State University. Her professional and research interests include leadership, mentoring, library instruction, information literacy, Native American issues, and distance education. Each summer she cofacilitates an annual weeklong professional development institute at her campus for tribal college librarians from the United States and Canada.

60

Positive Attitude

Dora Ho

It's Monday morning at 10:00; your colleague has just called in sick. You have seven people waiting in line to sign up for the Internet, an elderly couple is asking for you to help them with the catalog on the computer, a five-year-old child wants you to show him how to play a game on www.cartoonnetwork.com, and your clerk just informed you that we are running out of printer paper. Does this sound familiar to you? It is exactly what my days are like. How do you deal with an everyday situation like this? And how do you manage in crisis situations? A positive attitude is the key. With a positive attitude, we can accomplish things smoothly and sensibly, even in extreme circumstances.

Attitude is the disposition or frame of mind with which we approach our daily life and work. Maintaining a positive approach when the surrounding environment seems clouded with difficulties will be our real challenge. Holding a positive attitude in the face of adverse conditions does not mean simply repeating one of those familiar pieces of advice like "keep a stiff upper lip," "roll with the punches," or "just muddle through." Unless you are one of those very rare individuals blessed with total serenity, you must be able to adapt, think logically, manage your time, plan ahead, and communicate well.

LIMITED RESOURCES, STAFFING, AND BUDGET

Today, librarianship is practiced in a world of constraints. All librarians discover the realities of limited staffing, resources, budgets, and space. Our job is to serve the public effectively while working within those constraints. We have been hearing that librarianship is turning into a graying profession and new librarians entering the profession are scarce. As we face a shortage of librarians, we often have to wear many hats in our own institutions. Sometimes, we are requested to spend much of our time on "other duties as assigned," the catch-all phrase in our job descriptions. For example, I was asked to oversee the volunteers because many of the volunteers at the library are teens. On another occasion, I was given the task of scheduling for the messenger clerks (LAPL terminology for library aides or shelvers) when the library assistant retired. The phrase "other duties as assigned" is written in my job description. My boss even shows it to me from time to time as a reminder. We can't avoid doing these extra duties. So how we deal with them is the key. Take them on with an approach that you may learn something from the experience, and you might ultimately enjoy the new tasks as assigned. Instead of feeling that you are already overwhelmed with the many things you have to do, make yourself a better manager of your time and resources.

What do we do when our resources are limited? We need to rely on our reference skills and technology. It is important to be aware of the resources in our system, even if we don't have the resource in our branch, and know when to refer people to useful Internet resources and other local neighboring libraries. Someone else might have the information that you need. Your colleagues are sometimes your best resource. They may know more than you do. Two heads are better than one.

Often we have no control over the size of our budget. The amounts are set by administration or local government or the state. We need to find creative ways to stretch our limited budgets through each fiscal year. Planning is the key to how well you spend your money. Analyze your budgets from the last few years so that you can study your spending patterns and determine where your collection needs are before making expenditures. This way, you can confine your spending to things you really need for your collection.

Limited space in your library can be a problem. How you use space depends on your creativity. You can display your books from the shelves when there is no window display available. Sometimes the top of the shelves are very visible to users. Make sure signs or displays are big enough, eye-catching, colorful, and at eye level. These trips will definitely help you promote an event or a book.

WORKING WITH PEOPLE

We spend more than eight hours a day, five days a week, at work. That is probably more time than you actually spend with your own family. Our coworkers and colleagues are like our family. Learning to get along means sometimes having to compromise. Like a family, library staff is made up of different personalities. Harmoniously working together without creating personality conflicts or friction among the staff may not be easily done. The manager sets the mood for staff. However, if your supervisor is often out of the workplace or is indifferent to morale, there are sure to be problems. Compromise is a way to avoid conflicts. Sometimes, others' moods may be affected by family or personal problems.

Staff socials are good instruments to get to know your colleagues. This may help you understand your fellow staffers better. Try having lunch together with other staff members. Get to know them.

Whether it is with new people or a new work location, we need to be adaptive. I know someone who was temporarily reassigned to several different libraries when her branch closed for renovation. During a two-year period, she was moved four times. Her approach was to look at each new location as a learning experience and a way to get to know staff throughout the library system. She was never bitter and never questioned why administration kept moving her around, but instead she looked at how she could be helpful at these various locations.

Many times we need to adapt to others instead of trying to change them, especially if they do not recognize there is a need to change. When we change our ways of looking at things, we have a fresh perspective on things. For example, I know from past experience that one of my coworkers complains with vehemence about any new changes as soon as she hears of them. At times I have been the one to let her know about the changes and had to listen to her biting response. Instead of telling her not to complain, I understood that her negative feelings were not directed at me, and that griping is how she responds to new situations. Once I understood that I couldn't change her behavior, I realized that any rebuttal I might offer to one of her outbursts was pointless and that it was best just to let her vent.

Pleasant patrons or library users are what we pray for. Once in a while you will encounter patrons with certain unreasonable, demanding, or harassing attitudes. Whether these people treat us politely, rudely, or otherwise, as librarians we need to keep in mind that we are professionals. We need to deal with our public with professionalism and courtesy to help them find the information that they need. It is important that you remain calm and focus on the issues or questions at hand so that you can find the answer to that person's request. As long as you are doing your job professionally, most people will appreciate your efforts.

BALANCE BETWEEN WORK AND FAMILY

We are often faced with family and career dilemmas. If we must both work and care for our family at the same time, we need to strike a balance. The best rule is never take your work home, because you should always regard home as a place where you can relax from work and spend time with your family.

Setting priorities is the key to a balance between family life and work. We are often faced with a decision on priorities. Which is more important, your family life or your career? My answer is, they both are. Learning time management can be the answer to your frustrations. You can definitely spend more valuable time with your family and still get your work done. Often, quality time is what we should shoot for—for example, an hour well spent with your family is worth more than a day just juggling three or four different things.

OUTSIDE ACTIVITIES AND CAREER DEVELOPMENT

Those of us who are interested in getting more involved in our profession become active in professional organizations, such as the state library associations or a national one, such as the American Library Association (ALA). Keep in mind that you should only commit to what you can handle. That is why some of the associations have a limit on the number of appointments that you can hold. For example, ALA limits its members to three official appointments on committees or positions as an officer. We need to seriously think about how much we can contribute and what we can learn before holding a position. Because each position comes with responsibility, we should take great care to do our best, not just put our name on a committee roster.

EXTREME SITUATIONS

During extreme situations, we need to focus our thoughts on the matter at hand and not let our emotions govern us. Sometimes in difficult situations, our emotions can cloud up our judgment. Focus on the situation, think of ways to resolve the matter, lay out all the possible solutions, and consider whether we can share the problem with someone else to help us solve it. Keep in mind that the safety of the staff and users is our priority in the library, and we must face each situation with care and delicacy.

Sudden Changes

In the book *Who Moved My Cheese?*, Spencer Johnson (2002) writes about the different ways mice in a maze may react when the location of the cheese is suddenly moved. Hem and Haw are resistant to change and remain in the maze, unable to look for the cheese. However, Sniff is adaptable to change and is able to react quickly and look for cheese placed elsewhere. The point is, being ready for changes to occur will help you deal with them much more efficiently and

effectively. Change occurs every day. Our lives evolve and change in response
to a variety of circumstances. Being adaptive is another key to a successful way
of handling life. We need to prepare ourselves to face any situation and enjoy
the changes. If we build up our tolerance for little changes, then when a big
change comes, we will be able to respond more quickly.

Technology

According to "Digital Reference: Reference Librarians' Experiences and Attitude" by Joseph Janes (2002), reference librarians are using technology,
such as databases, the Internet, and e-mail, to answer questions. Public-use
Internet stations, while a boon to many, sometimes cause real friction among
patrons. People who favor the traditional library where they can read books
in quiet may complain about the noisiness of the computer users. Even worse,
the computer users sometimes get into arguments with each other when users
do not promptly give up their seat to the next scheduled user. Handling these
arguments and exchanges takes a delicate touch.

Occasionally, disputes between computer users over computer time can es-
calate into physical threats and violence—either directed against the recalci-
trant patron or sometimes even against the intervening librarian. Therefore,
we must be as courteous as possible when asking people to relinquish their
computer because another scheduled user needs to use it. Often we may need
to compromise and find a solution for those who still require more time on
the computer. Once a compromise is offered, perhaps the two people who've
been quarreling will recognize that the more time they spend arguing, the less
time they will have on the computer.

Staff

Most staff members do their work exactly as they are trained to do. But some
clerks decide that they are going to do it "their way." When your clerk is taking over or bossing you around, how should you react? You need to step back
and rethink the whole situation. Dealing with our staff requires tolerance and
acceptance. We need to recognize their potential and ability to help within the
library so that tasks will be carried out as efficiently as possible. So if they try
to take over the world, we must try to understand their reasoning. Make sure
communication remains open at all time. That way, information can pass back
and forth to avoid any misunderstanding. For example, suppose your clerk
decided to process your comic book collection without any library address labels and security stripes and places them in a hidden corner of the library. You
must inform the clerk that this is not the correct way of processing, even
though the clerk thinks that these comics will be stolen the minute they are
put out. Open communication between the clerk and yourself can help edu-

cate the clerk that even if things get stolen from the library from time to time, it is still very important to process the materials correctly and to display them in a visible location for the public.

HELPFUL HINTS

Teamwork: Teamwork is the key to success. Humans are social creatures. The sense of belonging is important. Whenever people feel that they are needed or they are part of a group, they tend to perform better. Working in a team helps to bring out the various abilities and talents in people. Demonstrate good leadership skills, and others will usually respond by demonstrating the ability to compromise and share when needed.

Mistakes: Don't blame others for your own mistakes. Mistakes help you learn so that you will not repeat them in the future. To free yourself from a mistake, you must accept it as your own; then the lesson you learn is valuable and can last a lifetime. We tend to make more mistakes when we are careless and clouded with emotion disturbance. Try to keep your mind from factors that will prevent you from thinking clearly and making the correct judgment and decision.

Perspective and priority: Time out is important for you. Don't forget that you are entitled to your vacation. If you are not the type who takes a long vacation, a miniature one will always work. Even if it is just a day of rest at home or a drive down to the beach, a break can help you to relax and refresh.

Unreasonable demands: Whether it is to your boss or users, learn how to say "no." You are not Superman or Superwoman. Know your limits. Saying "no" doesn't mean that we deny ourselves options, but instead that we are in control of the situation and can decide our own fate. For example, assume you have a research project due tomorrow and you have been working on it all week, but your boss asks you whether you will be able to write up a grant request for him right away. Even though you probably could whip up something fast, and he knows what a great writer you are, it may be better to decline his request. Rushing this new project to get it done quickly might affect the quality of both your project and his, and, at the same time it may increase your stress level significantly.

CONCLUSION

In the Chinese culture, numerology is a respected tool. Recently, I read an article in a Chinese newspaper called *Epoch Time,* which stressed the primary importance of one's approach to life—our *attitude*, which the author said was even more important than our *knowledge* and *hard work*. The author demonstrated that if we added up the numbers in these words (where A=1, B=2 . . . Z=26), we will get the following: *Knowledge* = 96, *Hard Work* = 98, and *Attitude* = 100.

How well you deal with things depends on your perspective and approach. We are always going back to the glass of water—whether it is half-empty or half-full. There are so many ways to deal with particular situations. Approaching situations with the viewpoint that we want to benefit ourselves and others is the best tactic.

A few lucky people seem to have been born with a placid personality, perhaps the result of a genetic predisposition. One of my coworkers is extremely relaxed in any circumstance. She is always in control. I have never seen her get mad or upset about anything. I marvel at her temperament, which enables her to handle adversity with grace. Her tranquility and calmness often reminds me to slow down and think carefully before reacting to any critical situation.

A positive attitude is a key to being happy at work. Many times in our life and work we are faced with numerous stressful situations, or sometimes crises; depending on our attitude, we deal with them well or poorly. Think back to the scenario at the beginning of this chapter. If we learn to deal with one situation or crisis at a time, our lives will definitely be much happier.

RELATED READINGS

Canfield, Jack. *Chicken Soup for the Christian Woman's Soul*. Dearfield Beach, Fla.: Health Communication, 2002.

Dodge, Chris. "Revolution at the Reference Desk." *Utne* 114 (November/December 2002): 32–33.

Janes, Joseph. "Digital Reference: Reference Librarians' Experiences and Attitude." *Journal of the American Society for Information Science and Technology* 53, no. 7 (May 2002): 549–66.

Johnson, Spencer. *Who Moved My Cheese? For Teens*. New York: Putnam, 2002.

Tenopir, Carol. "Educating Tomorrow's Information Professionals Today." *Searcher* 10 (July/August 2002): 7.

"The Mystery of ABC and 123." *Epoch Times* 196 (6–9 May 2003): 6.

ABOUT THE AUTHOR

Dora Ho is the young adult librarian at the North Hollywood Regional Branch of the Los Angeles Public Library. She received her MLS from UCLA. She is an active member of the ALA and was elected as councilor-at-large for 2003–2006. In 2002, she also served as the president of the New Members Round Table of ALA.

61

Balance

Ann Snoeyenbos

Balance is something we should all strive for. I'm also going to give you some ideas about how to find it. For me, maintaining separation between my librarian-self and my outside-the-library-self is one of the ways I maintain a modicum of balance in my life, but that is because I live across the street from my workplace. For others, a more integrated approach might be the thing they need. We each juggle a different set of stressing and relaxing elements in our life, so in this piece I'll offer some examples; but really it is up to each individual to assess his or her own situation and find the best mix. I'm not sure I have it all figured out myself. I have a good idea what my ideally balanced life would look like, but things don't always work out the way we want, even with extensive forethought and planning.

I should point out that I am single, never married, have no children, and most of my family lives 900 miles away. This makes a difference in a discussion of how to balance personal life and career. As a single person, I have more freedom in constructing my days and weeks than do people with spouses, children, and other family responsibilities. However, single people do face particular challenges. Single people are responsible for creating their own activities, their own social networks, and their own holiday celebrations. I'm not suggesting that all single people exist in a vacuum, but rather I'm pointing out that we have to make an extra effort to plan activities in a way that people who live in a family unit don't have to. Families, whether they be made up of two people or an extended family network, create their own momentum. This book includes another chapter on balance that will address issues related to seeking balance within a family unit.

WHAT IS BALANCE?

In the book *Thinking Body, Dancing Mind*, authors Al Chungliang Huang and Jerry Lynch cite the *Tao Te Ching*: "Unbalanced energies are unstable extremes that detract from personal power and performance. A balanced life enables us to perform with increased excitement and motivation, with the potential for higher levels of output" (1992, p. 280). This Taoist teaching sums up my beliefs very well. How do we get to this ideal balanced state? Human beings are multidimensional. Each of us has many facets that provide opportunities for adjusting the way we spend our energy.

Over a lifetime we all face many challenges to our emotional equilibrium. Living a full life means navigating high and low points, weighing competing interests, and experiencing the resulting rewards and disappointments. One of the ways we get through the difficult times is by distracting ourselves with positive thoughts and rewarding activities. Many of the librarians I've met have a significant activity focus in their life that does not involve library work, and I believe this is the key to living a happy, healthy life. I've met librarians who are writers, artists, dancers, athletes, inventors, volunteers, and other things in their "other" life.

When we take our nonlibrarian activities seriously, finding the right language to describe these things we do is difficult. Perhaps you remember when housework was first considered a job in its own right. Instead of being asked, "Do you have a job?" women were asked, "Do you work outside the home for money?" I don't consider my sports life to be a job, and I make very little money at it, but if you were to refer to it as a *hobby*, I'd be insulted and feel you were belittling the importance of sports in my life. Is it a *lifestyle choice* then, a *leisure-time* activity? I don't think so because these things we do outside of our library work also contribute busy-ness, responsibility, and obligation to an already full schedule. These things are a part of who we are. I *am* an athlete. I *am* a librarian. There are a lot of other things that I *do*, including working at two part-time jobs, but I don't consider those activities to be part of my fundamental being. We do these things to help ourselves maintain our mental and emotional balance.

HOW IS IT DONE?

In his book *Stress for Success*, Jim Loehr (1997) emphasizes that stress in itself is not damaging to us. In fact we could not grow physically or mentally, learn new skills, or become more generally capable if we did not have stress. The danger is in unrelenting stress all day long, day after day. While most people recognize the physical danger of long-term exposure to stress, the most common approach is to work hard for as long as you can—weeks or months, or even years—and then take a long vacation during which you do nothing but sit in a stupor and watch TV, drink alcohol, or engage in some other passive form of rest/recovery. Loehr's recommendation is that we restructure our lives so that work and recovery cycles are much shorter and more frequent, much like a runner might do an interval workout: a period of fast running followed immediately by a recovery period of easier running or walking. Work and recovery alternate in this way for the duration of the workout.

Loehr's concept is similar to another approach to physical training used by many endurance athletes: periodization. Periodization consists of microcycles, macrocycles, and mesocycles. To apply this concept to a work setting, one would divide the year into large chunks (mesocycles), such as a semester or a quarter; then each is broken into a smaller unit (macrocycle), which could be a month, a week, or even a day, depending on the activity patterns of your library. Each of these is further broken down into even smaller units (microcycles)—a week, a day, or a portion of a day. Within each of these cycles you strive for a repeating pattern of work followed by recovery. This might mean that you plan your day so that four hours of report writing is broken up into twenty to thirty minutes of focus, with a bathroom or water break in between. Even briefly standing up to stretch helps to refresh the mind. If the breaks are short, they don't interrupt the train of thought. Taking a thirty-minute break does interrupt the flow, however, so keep the breaks short—five minutes or fewer. Throughout your week you should strive for days of high output alternating with days of lower output. We cannot give 100 percent of ourselves all day every day. Rhythmic cycling of work and rest usually results in higher overall output, with less burnout. In my experience, this approach makes a world of difference in how I feel at the end of the day

Once you've built microcycles of work and rest into your workday, and the macrocycles of your workweek or month are similarly put together with the idea of ebb and flow in mind, then you can look at the mesocycle to schedule periods of work and play into your semester or year. Too often we grind through a project until it is finished, but this can take weeks or months, and upon completion we just feel drained. Often we feel that we cannot take a vacation until the semester is over. But for best performance we need to build miniholidays into our schedule: an afternoon off, a long weekend, a weekday morning sleep-in. Excellent recovery doesn't necessarily mean doing nothing at all. Once in a while I get to spend a half-day at a nearby library to work on a project with colleagues. I come back from those little adventures quite charged up, and we do get a lot of work done. All it takes is a few small changes to our daily work patterns, and the incorporation of rest breaks, and the result will be renewed enthusiasm.

At this point I must say something about chaos and multitasking—two concepts that every librarian understands very well. First of all, chaos is extremely stressful. Humans take comfort in routine, and if you don't have control over your workday or your home life, you are dealing with a very different set of circumstances than those I'm addressing here. Multitasking is also very stressful and ultimately frustrating on several levels. Surveys have shown that humans derive lasting satisfaction from deep focus on just one thing at a time. The Dalai Lama is reported to have said: "I ride my bicycle to ride my bicycle."

Loehr also divides our sources of energy into four categories: physical, emotional, mental, and spiritual. In striving for balance you don't have to create a giant grid with multicolored squares to sort out your micro-, macro-, and meso-cycles and see where they bisect your energy sources. That is not necessary at all, and it would probably end up being a stress-inducing activity. Rather, you should be mindful of how the different elements impact on your energy and your enthusiasm for the things that you do. The goal is to never deplete our energy in any one category, because then we still have the ability to rejuvenate that energy source. I think of it like mowing the lawn—as long as you just trim the new growth, the grass will be able to recover and grow again. But if you rip the grass out by the roots, that's the end of it. Once a person becomes burned out in their job, it is very difficult to recover and regain enthusiasm.

WHY IS BALANCE AN ISSUE FOR LIBRARIANS?

I've met a lot of people over the years from a wide variety of professions, and I think librarians are the most passionate professionals I've met. My mother was a children's librarian, and so her social circle was full of librarians. All the librarians I knew as a child continued to work in libraries after they retired from their jobs. They filed catalog cards at the public library in the evening; they organized books at the nature center on the weekend; they built their own special libraries at home and cataloged the holdings. If that doesn't speak to a passion for librarianship, then I don't know what does. In New York City, where I live, there are many librarians who take part-time jobs to help make ends meet. These librarians most often take part-time jobs in other libraries, even though they could make more money doing something else. I chalk it up to this passion librarians feel for their work. I doubt that it is the money, the fame, or the social standing that keeps us in the profession, so it has to be the passion.

This passion, however, makes it harder for us to balance our lives between work and play, activity and rest, giving and taking. The work we do is often detail-oriented and can involve a lot of reading. In a given day we make dozens of decisions that will have long-term impact, so the weight of future generations is constantly on our shoulders. We untangle knots and we solve problems throughout the workday. We frequently teach, and we constantly learn. Too frequently we find ourselves having to justify our existence to administrators (academic or governmental) who perceive libraries as bottomless money pits. The shared stresses, the shared social values, and the shared passion lead many librarians to hang out with other librarians outside of work. This is fine and good, but it doesn't provide the kind of recovery from work-life that we all need. We need variety in our transactions and in our interactions to stay fresh and productive.

The *Occupational Outlook Handbook* (2002–2004) describes the work librarians do with patrons as both "challenging and satisfying" and "demanding and stressful." This profile also states, "Librarians spend a significant portion of time at their desks or in front of computer terminals; extended work at video display terminals can cause eyestrain and headaches." A quick perusal of the library literature results in a long list of articles on burnout among librarians. We've all worked with a burned-out librarian at some point, and some institutions are packed full of these empty shells. In the end it is not good for our profession. Burned-out librarians often end up leaving the profession, and if they do stay they bring down the mood and the quality of work of their colleagues. Burnout seems to be contagious. Similarly, a happy energetic librarian can raise the mood of an organization.

BALANCE ON THE JOB

No matter what type of job you perform in your library, whether you work as a solo librarian doing a little bit of everything or in a large research institution where jobs are defined very narrowly, there is always room to adjust your mix of activities throughout the day. I try to intersperse mindless but necessary work (tearing apart vendor slips, sorting incoming mail) with work that demands focus and concentration. When I'm "warming up" in the morning, I start by reading e-mail, and I quickly answer the easy questions, leaving the complex stuff for later when I'm up to speed. After lunch I know that I'm always low on initiative, so I try to do difficult tasks before I eat. Learning to take breaks when I work on things that require extended concentration has helped me a lot. Go to the bathroom, get a drink of water, allow yourself to space out and daydream for a few minutes. We assume that the longer the "break" is the more effective it will be, but the mind only needs a brief change of activity to be refreshed.

When I do a lot of teaching in instruction sessions, or with patrons at the reference desk, I end up mentally drained; I find it hard to produce new content until I've had time to switch gears. To do this I'll run errands in another part of the building, make notes for the next time I teach, or flip through a vendor catalog. Also, after I've done a lot of teaching, I find it hard to sit still and listen, so I don't schedule myself for learning activities until later in the week, or later in the semester. When I am ready to learn, I truly take pleasure in listening and taking notes; when I don't feel I have to perform or produce, I am free to soak in the new material.

As an academic librarian working in a large research institution, much of the collection development work I do will not see the light of day for years and years. It can make the things I do seem kind of futile. It is important then for me to balance these future-oriented projects with things that will have an immediate impact, such as creating an instructional handout or writing a newsletter article listing new acquisitions. I have a tendency to put off the long-term projects until the last minute, but alternating work on long-term projects with work on short-term ones satisfies my need for tangible results.

When I spend a lot of time on writing projects, I have a tendency to spiral down in a negative thought pattern about all the things I could have included, should have included, or should have expressed more clearly. It helps me to stop and make a cup of tea or have a quick chat with a colleague about nothing in particular. Usually that is enough to shut down my inner critic and let me get back to work.

Librarians who work with the public spend a lot of time with their "game face" on. It is fascinating to watch a long-time reference librarian maintain an absolutely neutral expression while a patron makes an absurd request. It's hard to imagine that people can perform this act day after day and year after year without exploding. In psychology this game face is referred to as "flat affect," and it is not a good thing; it can also be the face of burnout. Think about how you deal with a tough patron. What are your most successful coping behaviors? In my department, we each make an effort to gather good jokes for the busy parts of the semester. We've found it useful to make up funny names for the difficult patrons, such as "Cheap Shoes" and "Zebra Head." Sharing the code names has been a surprisingly effective way for us to blow off steam. More and more public-service work is being done by librarians in isolation—through chat and e-mail reference services. It will be interesting to watch as we develop coping behaviors for difficult patrons who we cannot see or share with our colleagues.

In our work and play activities, there is an important balance to be found between leading and following. A wise person once told me that a good leader should also be a good follower. It took me a while to understand this, but I think it means that you can't provide high-quality leadership all the time, in all situations. You need to learn how to step back and let somebody else be in charge. And when you do participate, do so as an equal, not with constant reminders of your (former) status. Organizing and running a meeting can be taxing in and of itself, apart from the content issues being dealt with at the meeting. Letting somebody else handle the logistics can free your time and energy to work on creative solutions to the issues.

In libraries we have many opportunities to rub up against traditions, standards, and policies created by others. We do need to challenge these constructs because, if we don't, we will lose the ability to innovate. However, my mentor reminds me over and over again that nobody can fight every battle with full energy, and that trying to do so is an exercise in exhaustion and disillusionment. Focus on the things that are most important to you and the areas where you can make a real difference. Let the rest go. If the issues are truly important, they will surface again and somebody else will take up the fight.

BALANCE BETWEEN JOB AND HOME

I know a lot of librarians who either swim or do yoga regularly as part of their workday. Maybe this is because academic libraries often have a gym or a pool nearby, but I suspect there is another reason that most people aren't aware of. Swimming is a great stress reliever, because if you don't pay attention, you'll sink! There is nothing better for clearing the mind than a physical activity that demands total attention. For me, running or mountain biking on tough trails does the job pretty effectively in about one hour. When I run or cycle on paved roads, which require less skill and attention, it takes a lot more time for my mind and thoughts to become clear. For me, complex physical movement is the only way to shut off the constant ticker tape machine in my brain. Knitting and other handwork can also be very effective, but once you're good enough at it that you start reading or doing other things at the same time, you lose the zen benefit.

At the times when my job has been particularly frustrating, my sports performance has actually improved. I use sports for stress relief, and training time allows me to idly digest the thoughts in my head. In planning for a sabbatical year, I sketched out a stellar year of writing projects balanced by multisport training and racing. I didn't anticipate that without any work stress whatsoever, and no daily schedule to juggle, I had no motivation to train. It was one of my worst sports years ever. As soon as I went back to work, the stress resumed, and my training and sports performance improved. We all daydream about having unlimited free time, but most of us do better when we have boundaries and routines in place. That sabbatical year was also useful to me because it taught me how much I rely on my colleagues for social and intellectual support.

BALANCING A LIFETIME, BALANCING A CAREER

I used to think that having a "balanced" personality meant walking a thin line right down the middle. Now I realize that balance requires more than that. I don't know where this expression comes from, but I think it is apt: "Moderation in all things, including moderation." That pretty much opens the door to excess, which is something we all need a dose of from time to time.

I firmly believe in the need for both modest and spectacular failures in a lifetime. How can anybody claim to have lived a full life if they've never really blown it, at least once? If you're not regularly pushing your limits to failure, then how can you ever know how far you might go? I've had some terrific failures already in just ten years as a librarian, and I am still too ashamed to mention all of them. One was an unpaid teaching opportunity that I accepted eagerly, but the whole thing turned out to be so far beyond my understanding of the material (at the time) that I had to slink away when it was over. I still see the people I worked with on that class and am mortified, even though nobody said anything about my poor performance. Perhaps they are too polite, but sometimes when we experience a major "failure," we're the only one who knows how much better it could have gone. Like many things, failure is subjective.

Living through a big failure provides a very concentrated learning experience, and that's why we need to keep pushing our limits. I have written elsewhere about the need to actively court failure, and the example I give is of a woman who set a goal for herself of one failure a day. The idea is that in order to shake up our performance—as librarians, as human beings, as friends, siblings, artists, athletes, and so on—we need to push harder. Not harder in the sense of accomplishing more, but harder in the sense of testing our assumptions and giving ourselves the freedom to think in different ways and to try new things.

CONCLUSION

There is a saying that came up frequently in my childhood home: "Variety is the spice of life." Sometimes we would repeat it back and forth for fun, changing the emphasis: Variety *is* the spice of life; *variety* is the spice of life; variety is the *spice* of life; variety is the spice of *life*. I think that quote sums up this chapter on balance very nicely. We need to weave a mixture of experiences into our day. Routines are necessary and comforting, but sometimes we need to subtly rearrange our routines to freshen our outlook. Play and recovery time should be a part of every work activity. The work we do as librarians takes many forms; by mixing and adjusting the organization of our day, we can take advantage of more than one type of energy, depleting none. The result will be a more productive and rewarding life.

RELATED READINGS

Bureau of Labor Statistics, U.S. Department of Labor. *Occupational Outlook Handbook,* 2002–2003 ed. Bulletin 2540. Washington, D.C.: U.S. Government Printing Office, 2002.

Huang, Al Chungliang, and Jerry Lynch. *Thinking Body, Dancing Mind: Tao Sports for Extraordinary Performance in Athletics, Business, and Life.* New York: Bantam Books, 1992.

Loehr, James E., ed. *The New Toughness Training for Sports: Mental, Emotional, and Physical Conditioning from One of the World's Premier Sports Psychologists.* New York: Plume, 1994.

Loehr, James E. *Stress for Success: The Proven Program for Transforming Stress into Positive Energy at Work.* New York: Three Rivers Press, 1997.

Loehr, Jim, and Tony Schwartz. *The Power of Full Engagement: Managing Energy, Not Time, Is the Key to High Performance and Personal Renewal.* New York: Free Press, 2003.

Snoeyenbos, Ann. "Failure is Bad, Right?" LIScareer.com. April 2002. www .liscareer.com/snoeyenbos_failure.htm (last accessed 21 December 2003).

ABOUT THE AUTHOR

Ann Snoeyenbos currently works as coordinator for international sales and special markets for Project MUSE at Johns Hopkins University Press. This chapter was written while Ann was librarian for West European social science at New York University, a job she held from 1991–2004. She is a dedicated endurance athlete, competing in on-road and off-road triathlons and in single sport races, including swimming, biking, running, and snowshoeing.

62

The Juggling Act: Balancing Family and Your Library Career

Catherine J. Woodworth Wong

Finding a partner to share your life with, caring for an elderly parent, or starting a family are all aspects of life that can greatly impact on your career. Not having faced every conceivable aspect of family/career balance, I did not feel it would be appropriate to write this chapter without enlisting the help of fellow librarians. A survey consisting of primarily open-ended questions was posted to several librarian discussion lists and bulletin boards in order to gain the perspective of these family/career balance issues important to librarians. Seventy-six librarians, eighteen LIS students, and ten library support staff between the ages of twenty-three and sixty-three completed the survey. The majority of respondents (99 out of 103) were female and married or living with a partner (88 out of 103). Answers and tips from the survey are incorporated into this chapter.

GETTING MARRIED OR FINDING A PARTNER

Getting married or finding a partner to spend your life with can have a big effect on your career. In today's job market, finding a job often means moving to where the job is. Depending on your partner's career path, you may be faced with moving to a new area without employment. Finding a job when you are geographically restricted can be challenging.

Start early, even before you move, but give yourself time. Do not expect to find your dream job overnight when you are geographically restricted. Spend time before the move working on your resume or CV and your cover letter so that you can hit the ground running when you get out there. Network in your new area. Join the state library association and talk to as many librarians as you can. Let them know your qualifications and that you are looking for a position. If you do not land the perfect job right away, consider taking a part-time or temporary position. You never know when something might open up, and you would have your foot in the door. Most of all, try to keep a positive attitude about the move. If you have some time off, think of it as a little break so you can get your new life in order and get to know the new area.

BECOMING A PARENT

No matter how you become a parent, it is a major adjustment to your prechildren lifestyle. Time will take on new meaning. Deciding if or when to have children and if or when you will go back to work are major decisions that will take a lot of soul-searching on your part. There are no easy answers or quick advice to such monumental decisions.

Timing of Pregnancy/Adoption

Many survey respondents reported planning very carefully for when they would have children for both financial and career reasons. Some respondents delayed or are delaying having children in order to establish themselves professionally, or are waiting until after they have earned tenure. One respondent wrote, "My husband and I are delaying having children for another year or two until I have fulfilled my requirements for tenure. I hope to work from home several days a week and believe that having successfully made tenure will give me more bargaining power to negotiate this more flexible schedule."

Other respondents put having children first, primarily for age considerations. Ann Upton (Haverford College) writes, "When I was in graduate school for my first degree in my mid-twenties, I knew I wanted children soon and that career plans would follow later. I felt it was important to have my children while I was young."

There is rarely a perfect time for anything in life, and having children is no exception. Waiting for the perfect time can cause frustration. One respondent writes, "During my twenties I've delayed having children due to my career, but then the economy went downhill as I hit age twenty-nine. I was laid off, and found myself in a position of having to start all over again. I'm now making half of what I made when I was twenty-seven. Over the past decade, I could have had a child, raised him or her, and reentered the library profession in probably the exact same position I'm in now (minus less experience, of course). Instead, I'm still childless AND my career has not advanced in the way I had planned. I've decided now to just have children, regardless of the economy or my career. I've spent too much time waiting for the right time, but due to life's curveballs, the right time is when you are ready, not when the economy or your checkbook is. I wish someone had been more upfront with me about this. You can always have a career, but after you hit thirty, it's much harder to conceive children."

Managing Pregnancy and Leave

Once it is confirmed that children are coming into your life, or even before, it is a good idea to look over your library's policy and procedures manual, as well as current state and federal laws. Check to see what benefits are available to you before approaching your supervisor. Deciding when to tell people is a personal decision, and you may decide to tell earlier or later. Regardless, if you are pregnant, everyone will know once you start to show.

Some people prefer to wait to share the news of a pregnancy until after the first trimester, as there is less chance of miscarriage after that point. "After having a miscarriage, I was unsure of the stability of my pregnancy and did not want to share the news with anyone yet," wrote one librarian. However, waiting is not always feasible due to morning sickness. Coworkers may wonder why you are constantly eating and running to the washroom. "I had severe morning sickness and was not functioning very well. I would have waited until much later in the pregnancy (at least twelve weeks) otherwise," said another.

Many felt the need to tell supervisors and coworkers early, so they could begin planning for their absence or resignation. "I didn't want my supervisor to be caught short. I believe in giving advanced warning about leave whenever possible," said one respondent.

Negotiating Leave

It may be possible to negotiate a longer leave or a transitional period, but it is very important that you do your homework first. Arm yourself with knowledge of your employer's policies, state and federal laws, as well as a written proposal. One prepared librarian was able to do just that. "I presented a detailed proposal for what I wanted to do and how I would distribute any work I couldn't take on during the leave. I included goals, completion dates, and so on. Also, I was flexible and so were my employers. We all knew that it would take at least as long as my proposed leave to replace me and even longer to bring a new person up to my level of knowledge and experience, so it seemed sensible to allow the proposed arrangement. My supervisor was a mother herself and was very supportive."

Be creative with your leave if you can. One librarian was able to ease her way back to full time. "I turned my last month of leave into two months of part-time work. This allowed me to start work on the stuff only I could do a month earlier," she said. Additionally, it is a good idea to plan ahead the year before you would like to take leave by saving as much vacation and sick time as possible.

Arranging Coverage during Leave

Depending on your situation, various levels of involvement in arranging coverage during leave may be necessary. In some libraries a temporary worker will be hired to fill in, while in other libraries tasks are just spread around. If tasks are to be spread among your colleagues, it is courteous to be involved with arranging coverage during your leave. This can be as informal as discussing your plans with your colleagues. Leslie Farrell (OCLC) advises, "Outline all major activities and upcoming projects to your coworkers. Give them contact information, but be flexible if they need to call you during your leave."

You may even want to write out a detailed plan. Nancy Renfro (Milligan College) writes:

> The sooner you tell your supervisor, the sooner you can begin arrangements for coverage of work duties. Before you tell your supervisor, make sure you've worked out at least a tentative plan for how long you would like to be out or can afford to be out and coverage of your work duties. This is one medical event that can be planned for. You'll get lots of points from your supervisor if you come to the meeting with a plan. Make sure the plan is finalized well before the due date, as well. Many babies come earlier than planned (both of mine were several weeks early), and if the plan is not finalized early in the third trimester, you may run out of time.

If possible, complete any big projects that you know will need to be done. One clever librarian advised, "Plan ahead! I was able to have an entire summer reading program ready to carry on in my absence when my first child was due in early July." Do your best to plan ahead, but do not beat yourself up if you do not get everything done you had planned. Pregnancy can be unpredictable.

Keep in Contact with Work during Leave

Keeping in contact with colleagues while you are away, even if it is just socially, can be useful and can help you stay connected to work. Most respondents reported that they kept in contact somewhat via phone and e-mail, but the level of contact varied. Kathleen Casey (Western Oregon University) writes, "I made sure to stay in contact through phone and e-mail; my coworkers felt free to call me about any questions they had, and I loved feeling as if I were still connected to the library."

Heather Groves Hannan (George Mason University–Prince William Campus) writes, "I didn't stay in touch very much at all. I left someone in charge and I trusted their judgment—I felt if I communicated too much I would undermine the chain of command I had put in place." Remember your leave is your time to bond with your child. Stephanie DeClue writes, "I didn't stay in touch! I forgot all about work and focused on home!" If staying in touch with work starts to cause stress, it may be time to step back. "I stayed in touch the first week or so, and then it became too stressful. At that point I asked them only to contact me in the event of fire, flood, or hurricane," wrote another librarian. Whatever level of involvement you choose is up to you, work will be there when you return.

Returning to Work after Leave

Returning to work after your leave may be an adjustment. If possible, see if you can work it out with your employer to return on a part-time basis. Jacqueline Samples (North Carolina State University) was able work out such an arrangement. She said, "I returned to work half time for the first two weeks back to work, in order to make the transition away from our son less traumatic. The other reason was to regain my connection to work without feeling a great deal of stress about the amount of work I was able to accomplish."

Nancy Renfro recommends preparing all involved:

> I started working on getting the baby and myself on a schedule. I practiced getting things together in the morning so that I would know how much time to allow myself to get to work on time. I checked in with the office more frequently. The last two weeks of maternity leave, I would visit the office for a few minutes, not to do any work, but to mentally and psychologically connect myself and my coworkers with returning. It also allowed time for coworkers to admire the baby and talk about nonwork-related things. That way, when I actually came back to work, we already had all the baby questions out of the way. It made for an easier transition.

Another bit of good advice is to "be prepared for things to have changed a bit in your absence and be gracious. Likewise, when someone else must take leave and you are working extra hard to cover her duties, remember the same favor was done for you," noted one respondent.

Finding Childcare

It goes without saying that finding high-quality childcare is the highest priority before returning to work. There are many books, such as the *Busy Woman's Baby Planner* by Marla Schram Schwartz (1993), that give detailed questions to ask potential childcare providers, as well as things to look for when visiting. Many respondents recommended starting the search as early as possible before the baby arrives. Many feel the best option for childcare is a relative. One creative couple came up with a plan. "Work opposite schedules with your spouse if you have a partner and both agree on this plan. It can be stressful, but it's good for the child."

Some respondents felt that an in-home provider was best, while other parents were happy with a center. Many felt that it is best to have the provider closer to work than to home so you can check in on your child at breaks and during lunch. The most frequently recommended way to find a good place was through referrals. Jacqueline Samples said, "The tips I followed to find childcare when my son was an infant were to talk to colleagues who had been in the same situation, and ask who they used, how they felt about them, and so on. This was when I was still pregnant. I also had personal interviews with the providers, asked them about their philosophies, how they scheduled the children's day, and found out how open they were to meeting my concerns."

Breastfeeding and Work

Breastfeeding moms should read as much as they can and seek as much support as possible, especially when you first start. There are many books, magazines, websites, and organizations devoted to breastfeeding. William and Martha Sears (1991) recommend pumping every three hours in their book *Keys to Breastfeeding*. Most respondents said it is very important to buy a hospital grade pump, to find a quiet place to pump with a locked door, and to keep hydrated. Do not be embarrassed to ask for accommodation from your employer; there is no need to pump in a bathroom stall. Be familiar with your state laws. In Connecticut, for example, employers are required to give reasonable time and accommodations for pumping.

Some mothers reported success with working out a way to visit their baby at lunch. "Keep in mind your pumping times when scheduling meetings. Nurse right before you leave for work and as soon as you can after, and nurse as much as you can on weekends/days off," suggested one mom. Another recommends, "Keep a cardigan in your office; you will leak. People may make comments about me wearing a cardigan in the middle of summer, but it is better than trying to explain the leakage!"

Taking a Break from Work

If it is financially possible, many couples are choosing to have one parent stay home with the children for several years. When deciding if it is financially feasible, it is a good idea to make a list detailing costs of childcare as well as all the extras involved with working. Include in your list extra items you would not be purchasing, such as lunches out, coffee breaks, work clothing, and gas money.

The most pressing question most stay-at-home parents have is: How will it affect their career? It is possible to stay professionally active while staying home. Many respondents said that they kept active by keeping up with electronic discussion lists, reading professional literature, being involved with committee work, and attending conferences. Others continued to write reviews, give presentations, and make contributions to the library literature. Karen DeAngelo (Town of Ballston Community Library) said, "When I was a stay-at-home parent, I kept my memberships in ALA and the New York Library Association. I also volunteered at public libraries and created and ran a toddler time for a public library that didn't have a children's librarian and wanted to add to their programming."

Part-Time Employment or Working from Home

Some librarians have found that working part time or working from home are the best options for their family. One librarian noted, "I decided to be a half-time stay-at-home parent and half-time librarian. I need the income of the job, but don't think I could take being away from the baby all day long. This was a good balance. I also would really miss my coworkers if I stayed home full-time. They are a real source of moral support!"

If you decide to work from home, there are many challenges. It is not easy, as there are constant interruptions. Many respondents recommended setting up a separate area to work during nap times, while others recommended keeping a schedule. CM! Winters Palacio (doctoral student at the School of Information Studies, Florida State University) advises, "Arrange a work schedule as if you were working in the office. And, keep that schedule no matter what! Also remember to pace yourself by making a schedule for yourself, for example, goals for the week, per project, and so on. And always reward yourself when you complete a project or goal." It may be necessary to find someone to watch your child so you can have some uninterrupted work time. Karen DeAngelo recommends, "Join or start a baby-sitting co-op and use it so you can work that way. It doesn't cost anything, gives you people contact, and brings in playmates."

Older Children and Work

While the baby and toddler years can be all consuming, respondents with older children feel they require just as much supervision and attention as little ones. "Sometimes they need you a lot more than they're willing to admit. Take it one kid at a time: Some kids you can leave alone for long periods of time, while others must be watched vigilantly," noted Judith Mathews (National-Louis University). However, older kids can take on more responsibilities at home. "Give them responsibilities appropriate to their ages. Kids love to help. They can take out food to thaw, set the table, police the living room for toys, and so on. They may even be able to suggest other tasks they can do. Praise them a lot, tell them how important they are to the family, and let them have some down time, too, even though you might feel frazzled yourself," said Sandra Givens (Prince William Public Library System, Virginia).

Most respondents with older children noted the need to be available for their kids. Ann Upton suggests, "Know their music and make your home a welcome place for their friends. Respect them. Be careful while the children are in middle school and do what you can to monitor after school time. Being an adult happy in your work is a wonderful example." Another mom suggests:

> Be available to them. Talk with them and don't stop. Ask open-ended questions that force them to have to respond with more than a yes or no answer. Give them your phone number at work and let them know, they can call you anytime, but also make them aware that there may be times that you have to call them back rather than talk right away. Let them know that they are still very, very important to you. Try to be flexible in your schedule so that you can attend the school functions, activities, sports and art events.

CARING FOR OTHER FAMILY MEMBERS OR FRIENDS

Caring for children is not the only family issue that may affect you over the course of your career. There may come a time when you need to care for an elderly parent or to help a friend or relative in need. In times like these, your career may need to take a back burner. "Taking time off to care for an aging parent is so much more important than any job. My (and my employer's) attitude was that I would only have one chance to care for my father. I can work for the rest of my life. The biggest piece of advice that I would give would be to try to leave work and not return until the parent has reached a reasonable point of health, or until the end has come. It is much harder to come in and out of a position than to focus just on caring for a parent," said Gretel Stock-Kupperman (Benedictine University Library).

Sandra Givens suggests, "Let people know what is going on as soon as you know. Try to have some proposals ready to show you will have your job duties covered while you are away. (It helps if you have been flexible with coworkers so they will want to help you too.) Provide updates while you are gone if for more than a week; this also gives your coworkers/boss a chance to ask you a question about a project or give you information you might need to hit the ground running when you return."

MANAGING YOUR HOME

Every minute counts and everyone wants more free time to do fun things. Some ideas respondents had included using work breaks for errands, cooking and freezing food on the weekends, and getting the entire household involved with chores. Noted one busy mom:

> It is important to share the household chores. Try to get into a routine of daily picking up. Don't bring anything into the house unless you know exactly where it will live permanently. Synchronize calendars/planners on a regular basis. When finances allow, hire help. The eight hours you spent trouble shooting the leak in the bathroom is more expensive then paying a plumber. Your free time is valuable. Always, always carry a book to read while waiting in line or when you are on hold. Schedule free time for yourself. Recognize when you need a break and take it.

Nearly all respondents felt that once they had kids, their cleanliness standards were lowered in order to have more time with the family. "Don't worry about a spotlessly clean house. Encourage everyone to pitch in on some level. We managed to keep the 'common areas' decent and company ready. More leeway was given for personal space (bedrooms, my husband's study). Spending time on harmonious family life is more important than cleaning," said another busy mom.

Amy Kearns (Clifton Public Library) had this simple advice, "Make a schedule, share/divide tasks, communicate!" If you are organized enough to have a schedule, remember to schedule in time for exercise (your lunch break, perhaps), as keeping physically fit will help you in all aspects of you life.

GOING BACK TO WORK FULL TIME AFTER A LAPSE

Some respondents reported looking for employment after a lapse was challenging, while others found employment easily. It is best to be up front about a gap in your employment record. If the employer does not look at it as a good thing, then perhaps it is not the work environment for you. Many respondents reported keeping fairly active or working part time so the "employment gap" really was not an issue. "For many years I worked two or three part-time jobs to provide the flexibility I needed to schedule around the needs of the children. These jobs are poorly paid and there were lots, but I was happy to have the flexibility and the opportunities. These jobs provided excellent experience that allowed me to move up and on when I was ready. They provided ways to prove myself to employers and yet still allowed me to keep the needs of my family first," said Ann Upton.

Several respondents recommended that if you have been unemployed for quite some time, it might be a good idea to take some refresher courses. "Brush up on your technical skills. Join community and state library associations. Network with former coworkers," advised a former, stay-at-home librarian mom.

CONCLUSION

Balancing your library career with family is an ongoing juggling act. At times, one may shadow over the other and that is okay. The balance you succeed in having is not over the course of one day, but over the course of your life. Try not to have any regrets over decisions you make, and know that you made the best decision for you and your family at that point in your life.

RELATED READINGS

Sears, William, and Martha Sears. *Keys to Breastfeeding.* Hauppauge, N.Y.: Barron's Educational Series, 1991.
Schwartz, Marla Schram. *The Busy Woman's Baby Planner.* Paramus, N.J.: Prentice Hall, 1993.

ABOUT THE AUTHOR

Catherine J. Woodworth Wong has an MS in biological sciences and an MS in library and information science. She has worked as a biology instructor and as a reference and science librarian in various colleges and universities. Since becoming a mother, she is working from home, teaching online biology courses and serving as the executive codirector of the Phi Sigma Biological Sciences Honor Society.

63

Conclusion: Librarianship for the Love of It

Karla J. Block

There's a lot to love about being a librarian. One of the things I love most is that *so many* librarians are *so excited* about what they do. Librarians seem to delight in talking about why they love being librarians. It's not hard to find librarians who will tell you not only why they love being librarians, but also why you'd love to be a librarian, too!

Some might wonder, isn't the word "love" a little strong when talking about your job? Apparently not, since so many librarians use the same word when writing or talking about their profession. Montrese Hamilton and Joan O'Kane, creators of the website *The Librarians' Career Manifesto*, ponder, "So why would anyone want to be a librarian? For the authors of this web page, the bottom line is that we do what we do because we love it." Many professional organizations in librarianship—the American Library Association, the Medical Library Association, the Public Library Association, and the American Association of Law Libraries, just to name a few—include on their websites or in their brochures information about why their members love being librarians. For example, the Public Library Association sponsors a Public Librarian Recruitment project. Promotional material includes "Ask Me Why I Love My Job!" buttons along with testimonials about why public librarians love librarianship. There's even the *Become a Librarian!* website from the Central Jersey Regional Library Cooperative, which offers testimonials and a brochure titled *Why I Love Being a Librarian*!

Many librarians speak of librarianship as a calling. Some may take a fairly direct route to librarianship, while others may take a more indirect route to the profession. My story is probably not unusual. I've been an avid library user since childhood. I think I always knew in the back of my mind that I'd love to be a librarian, but I resisted the idea at first, maybe because it didn't seem glamorous. I worked as a student assistant in a campus library during my college years, and my first full-time job after graduation was as a paraprofessional at the Bio-Medical Library, University of Minnesota. I was fortunate to work with many talented librarians who not only excelled at their jobs but also obviously loved what they did. I was intrigued by the idea of combining my love of libraries with my interest in health and medicine. It didn't take long for me to realize that librarianship was my calling—something I felt deep down and had resisted—and a profession that I loved. With the support of many wonderful staff, I enrolled in library school and worked full time as a library assistant while taking a full load of classes. I still work at the library where I took my first "real" library position and uncovered my love for librarianship.

In preparation for this book chapter, librarians were surveyed about their jobs and what they loved most about them. The librarians who responded represent another thing that I love about librarianship—diversity and variety. There are so many different types of libraries and jobs for librarians that it's almost too good to be true. There are librarians working in traditional roles and those on the cutting edge. There are librarians working in hospitals, museums, public libraries, academic institutions, corporations, nonprofits, the military, government, and their own businesses. There are solo librarians and those working with many colleagues. There are librarians called informaticians, cybrarians, knowledge consultants, information specialists, information professionals, and, yes, even librarians. I think it would be possible for practically anyone to define what they love doing and find it somewhere in librarianship! The survey respondents were no exception. They work in a variety of settings, including academic (community college, medical, university, college, and virtual university), preK-12, public, corporate, and consulting. They hold diverse positions—including director, department head, librarian, consultant, and company president—and have diverse areas of responsibility—reference, serials, youth services, outreach, and teacher/librarian among them.

The survey asked several questions, including "What do you love about your job?" The librarians' responses, reproduced at the end of this chapter, illustrate many of the things that librarians love about their jobs. Though the responses are listed in no particular order, some common themes are woven throughout. These themes transcend job title, type of library, or area of responsibility. What *do* librarians love most about their jobs? The people (mentors, colleagues, and patrons); the variety and flexibility; being involved in teaching and learning; helping others; the pursuit of knowledge; the challenge of a good question; and, of course, books!

Are there things not to love about being a librarian? Yes. Does that mean you can't love being a librarian? Absolutely not! Librarian Terren Ilana Wein phrased it best in an online interview: "I don't love every minute of my job. But I love being a librarian." Dr. Linda Marie Golian-Lui, university librarian/director for the University of Hawaii at Hilo, professes that "this is the greatest profession you can ever choose. You can be mobile and travel the world, or you can stay home in a small town for your entire life. The profession allows so much flexibility that it is easy to find a dream job." In an online interview for the Public Library Association's recruitment project, where public librarians talk about the profession, librarian Bette Ammon enthused that "there is absolutely no finer work than putting a book or some other vital piece of information into a patron's hands. Every day I do meaningful work and have an opportunity to make a difference in someone's life. . . . So I guess I must be one of the luckiest people in the universe. I get to come to work every day doing a job I love, working with people I enjoy, and providing important services to a grateful community. Sigh."

In another interview for the same project, librarian Sally Decker Smith expressed:

> It's the most satisfying work I can imagine. Every single day I am privileged to touch someone's life. And I know this because they tell me so. One patron needed information on liver transplants because her daughter was having one. Even finding a recipe can bring tears to a patron's eye, if it's the meatloaf her mother used to make and the recipe was lost in a house fire. Few days are that dramatic, but every day is different, and every day brings people who need something to which I can be the conduit. . . . Even on the slowest or most hectic day, at least one person thanks me, and I can tell they mean it. I don't think that happens in many jobs. I thrive on immediate gratification, and the opportunity to perpetually be on a treasure hunt—and they pay me to do it!

The Central Jersey Regional Library Cooperative's brochure, *Why I Love Being a Librarian!*, says that "as a librarian, you can learn something new every day, design a web site, tell a story to a child, organize information so people can find it, and teach people to use and evaluate information. Nothing you know is ever wasted!" Who *wouldn't* love a profession like that?

And now, in their own words, some of my colleagues share what they love about being librarians.

SURVEY RESPONSES: "WHAT DO YOU LOVE ABOUT YOUR JOB?"

- Chrissie Anderson Peters, librarian, Basler Library, Northeast State Community College:

    "Almost everything! It's never the same thing two days in a row. I have incredible freedom and flexibility and have an amazing supervisor who supports and encourages his staff members to pursue their interests on the job. I really enjoy getting to do children's programs again, but I love the overall feel of our college campus environment."

- Linda Rowan, school library media specialist, Grey Nun Academy:
  "I love the fact that I am working with students and assisting teachers. I am lucky to be in a private school where the administrators let me manage the library independently. I don't think I would like the bureaucracy of a public school system."
- Suzan Lee, librarian at an investment bank in New York City:
  "It's a job that requires quick thinking and quick turnarounds. Deadlines are short and demands on my time are constant and continuous. I wouldn't have it any other way. I like what I do."
- Gale Hannigan, director, Informatics for Medical Education, Texas A&M University Medical Sciences Library:
  "I love to teach and feel fortunate to work with bright students. Life-long learning is a big issue in medical education now and I believe I am contributing to these students' ability to continuously learn throughout their careers. Information skills are so important for everyone these days—it still amazes me that I found a profession that is ethical, interesting, and encourages me to learn more. Also, and importantly, I work with nice people."
- Celia Carroll, librarian/branch manager, Santa Monica Public Library:
  "Empowering people with information and enlivening their lives with wonderful books and movies. I love the comparative autonomy to shape programs, utilize volunteers for special projects, and market the library to our vibrant community. I could not do anything else—I feel like my 'calling' is to be a librarian. I read avidly, see lots of movies, and belong to two book clubs. My mother was a middle school librarian for twenty-seven years. I just received my twenty-five-year award from the City of Santa Monica. I am glad the City does not have a mandatory retirement age!"
- Benita Wheeler, assistant librarian, Advertiser Newspapers, Ltd.:
  "Variety—the news is always changing. Insight into journalism and the workings of the media. Fairly steady hours but some rotating shifts to give me some more free time in business hours. A nice group of people to work with. Friends love having you on their team at quiz nights. Access to fascinating historical information and seeing how much newspapers and society have changed."
- Karen Goodell, information literacy/reference librarian, Palmer College of Chiropractic:
  "I love libraries and books. What else would I want to do? I think what I really want to do is be a professional student. Being a reference librarian lets me do that and earn a paycheck at the same time. The best

of both worlds. So I kept my full-time job (had to pay the bills, you know), and went to grad school half time (and went half-crazy doing it), but at the age of fifty, I had the MLS I had always wanted."

- Tanzi Merritt, senior reference librarian, Kentucky Virtual University:

    "Because KYVL acts as Kentucky's library consortium, I am allowed to work with librarians from all types of libraries from directors on down to library technicians. I work with new young librarians, new librarians who are making this their second or even third career, and seasoned veterans. From these interactions I learn about the issues that are most important in different types of libraries, and also am getting to know more of my colleagues in Kentucky than would be possible in any other job. I am also involved with a number of projects that have allowed me to learn more about distance learning technologies, adult education and literacy initiatives, and a state's plan to reform education from kindergarten to adult learners."

- Eleanor Cook, serials coordinator and professor, Appalachian State University:

    "I am never bored. I also love the people I work with."

- Judith Siess, president, Information Bridges International, Inc.:

    "Getting to meet other librarians, especially in other countries. Not having to answer to anyone but me. Not being tied to a 9-to-5 schedule. I figure with bookkeeping, fulfillment, writing, etc., it averages out to about twenty hours per week. However, that may be sixty hours one week and none the next."

- Sandy Williams, children's public services librarian, Plano Public Library:

    "I love the interaction with the public, the diversity of my job duties, and the challenge of making things better."

- Cathy Ziegler, library manager, Maribelle M. Davis Library, Plano Public Library System:

    "I love serving all the diverse people who enter our public libraries. I love being a generalist rather than a specialist. I love the stimulation of learning something new every day. I love working surrounded by educated professionals in a modern spacious library with up-to-date materials."

- Sarah Sutton, serials librarian, Mary & Jeff Bell Library, Texas A&M University–Corpus Christi:

    "There are so many things that I love about my job. What I love the most is that I do what I told my college career counselor I wanted to do. I'd read a book back then about a world where all of the information contained in all of the books in all of the best libraries in the world was available by computer (ok, this WAS twenty years ago when that really was science fiction). That's what I told the career counselor I wanted to do: help people find the information they wanted on a computer. Twenty years later I know it's not nearly that simple and it never will be. But it's a lot more fact today than it was then and I am thrilled everyday when I come to work and fulfill that dream."

- Michelle Fossum, teacher/librarian, Oakland Catholic High School:

"I love when I see one of my students pick up a book and get lost in it, and she picked up the book because of a display that I had created or because of my recommendation. I love when I can help them find an answer to a question that has been perplexing them or eluding them, and then the next time they are looking for an answer, they have learned how to do the search themselves. And finally, I love when they discover that the library is the coolest place in the school (figuratively speaking, as we have no air conditioning!)."

- Brian Gray, library associate, University of Akron Science & Technology Library/Corporate Services:

"I worked as a student assistant in the S&T Library during my years as an undergraduate student in chemical engineering. Upon graduation I realized I loved the information side of chemistry and engineering the most. I loved finding the answers, showing others how to find the answers, and presenting the information. I stayed on as a temporary staff member, and now am a full-time staff member. In my current position at the S&T library and polymer company, I can still use my engineering knowledge."

- Susan Colloway Nimersheim, head of adult services, Kenton County Public Library:

"First of all, I love libraries and books and people, so it is a good environment for me. When I think about it, most of all I enjoy teaching, and this is what public libraries are all about . . . providing access to information and showing the public/individual how to find it. What I love about my job is the variety. In a public library you never know what the day will bring! Ours is the main branch and is in an urban setting and we have the complete spectrum of clientele . . . kids/youth, homeless, professionals, elderly, etc. Something is always happening! Our Director, Wayne Onkst, is progressive and encourages his staff to be creative and innovative."

- Penny Scott, reference librarian, Business Liaison, Gleeson Library, University of San Francisco:

"I love the fact that my job encompasses the best of being in library school: continuous learning, research, and collegiality with colleagues. I really enjoy helping patrons find what they need, and I work in a very progressive and encouraging environment, so I feel completely supported to grow and try new things. I really love my work, my colleagues, and my library!!!"

- Valerie Nye, public library consultant, New Mexico State Library:

 "I love meeting librarians who have come to librarianship from a wide range of life experiences. I love visiting rural libraries and seeing what creative and job-loving librarians can do with very few resources. I like the fact that I can still 'do reference' and my subject specialty is library science."

- Linda Marie Golian-Lui, university librarian/director, University of Hawaii at Hilo:

 "I am always learning something new. I feel that I am making a difference in people's lives by empowering them to find, use, and evaluate information effectively."

- Isabel Byrne, reserve officer, University of South Australia:

 "Every aspect—Reserve work means working to deadlines and at times under constant pressure, particularly at the beginning of each academic year—this I find exciting and challenging. I enjoy working in a team environment, the support and strength from team members at times is quite amazing—both professionally and personally. In the library we meet some wonderful patrons and hear some wonderful stories, see their children grow from babes in arms to toddlers and then high school students. Above all what gives me the most pleasure is students coming up to me either in the library or more often or not in the Mall in Adelaide and saying thank you for all your help—that to me is the true measure of what I have really achieved—assisting someone to achieve their goal and reach their dream."

- Amy Kravitz, youth services librarian, Westfield Memorial Library:

 "I am very glad I became a youth services librarian. I am lucky because I have a boss who is very fair and reasonable. She's also very involved in the ALA. She's currently on the Newberry committee this year. She also has a good sense of humor and likes my jokes. The other women in my department are also lovely, and are very supportive of me, professionally and personally. When you have a great staff, it makes it a pleasure to go into work. I also like the children. I think the toddlers are very cute, as they are my favorite age group. I like working with children because they are very honest, open, curious, and they tell it like it is (I am the same way in personality). They often make me laugh. I enjoy doing the arts and crafts with the children, as I am artistic, and I like coming up with new craft ideas. I also love reading funny stories to them and making them laugh. The funny books are the best. My mother gave me the idea of going to library school after I couldn't find a teaching job. I think being a librarian was her unfulfilled wish. At the time there was a glut of teachers in my home state, and I needed something to do. After I talked with my mother, I went to library career information seminars, spoke with folks in the field, and visited different library environments. It's best to enter a field when you have a lot of information about it beforehand. After all, this is your career. I truly love what I do and I feel it's a perfect match for my personality. I don't think I'd enjoy doing anything more than working in the public library. I consider myself lucky."

- Bonnie Young, director, Lititz Public Library:

  "Here are some of the reasons: 1. The sense of satisfaction I enjoy just knowing that we are providing a fantastic life-long learning experience for the community. We provide opportunities that nourish the mind, enrich the community, and connect to the world. The community is appreciative and people tell us so. 2. Leading in such a way that the staff feels a sense of accomplishment and we enjoy a camaraderie and dedication to the work. 3. The joy I experience seeing people come and go in the library, enjoying our many innovative programs, activities, the beautiful building, and the books and other materials. 4. The delight of trying new things and seeing the success and growth of our library service."

- Alyson Dalby, administrative officer, History of Medicine Library, Royal Australasian College of Physicians:

  "The collection. We have very valuable and rare material here, some of it over 500 years old. There are old herbal remedies and bizarre surgical treatments, we have antique medical equipment (some of which I'm still trying to figure out what it is!), and it's all housed in a gorgeous heritage building. It's a collection to be proud of, and one I never knew existed."

- Philenese Slaughter, serials librarian, Felix G. Woodward Library, Austin Peay State University:

  "I love all aspects of serials, be they newspapers, magazines, journals, or continuations. They are a never-ending challenge to manage and the job is never boring."

- Matthew David, approvals/bindery assistant, DePaul University Libraries:

  "The product: information. The responsibility we are charged with. Being in a campus library and feeling the learning pulse through the walls of this building. Serving students, the leaders of tomorrow."

- Carla Robinson, associate university librarian, Florida Atlantic University:

  "I really love interacting with patrons, and with the university faculty."

- Tess Midkiff, library director, Shawnee State University:

  "Feeling needed individually and as a staff by our students and faculty and the fact that they really appreciate our collective expertise and our willingness to serve. Personally, I like running a small library, which allows me to know my staff, student employees, and the students and faculty we serve. I also like having the flexibility to work the reference desk one shift a week with students so I can keep in touch with the needs of users and the challenges my staff experience. I also love the opportunity you are provided in a library setting to experience and learn new technology and use it to expand services to users."

- Rebecca Kranz, reference librarian, Z. Smith Reynolds Library, Wake Forest University:

   "I just started a little over a month ago, but I love the challenge of answering all kinds of questions at the reference desk, and I enjoying using various types of resources to find the information that will be most helpful to students and faculty. I haven't yet begun instructing, but have taught a bit in the past and will probably enjoy working with students. I really enjoy the selection part of my job, as well as learning constantly (especially in terms of performing arts resources). Also, my library is comprised of a wonderful group of people."

- Shelly McCoy, head, digital user services department, University of Delaware Library:

   "The ability to make this department what I want to make it, including providing new 'digital' services to the public and moving ahead on my career."

- Jessamyn West, outreach librarian, Rutland Free Library:

   "It's different every day. I work really well with my boss and we share a love of getting things done fast and a goofy sense of humor. The patrons are nice and the library is generally well supported by the townspeople as well as the board. It really is a community library and it's busy and vibrant. It's an exciting place to come to work."

- Clint Chamberlain, e-access/serials librarian, Trinity University:

   "I love the fact that there's always something new. Sometimes it can be a bit of a strain as I have to shift gears between, for example, keeping track of our journals budget, handling access issues for a particular online title or database, adjusting a standing order, managing collection development in my liaison areas, and then providing research help to students who are taking classes in my liaison areas. On the whole, however, it's a near-perfect mix (for me) of tech services and public service work. Yeah, so I'm not an expert in some areas that I'd like to know more about because I don't have enough time for it, but that's okay. The variety of tasks I deal with every day keeps me on my toes."

RELATED READINGS

"Become a Librarian! Homepage." Central Jersey Regional Library Cooperative. www.becomealibrarian.org/ (last accessed 5 December 2003).

Hamilton, Montrese, and Joan O'Kane. "The Librarian's Career Manifesto." slis.cua.edu/ihy/sp2000/job/home.htm (last accessed 5 December 2003).

Houdyshell, Mara, Patricia A. Robles, and Hua Yi. "What Were You Thinking? If You Could Choose Librarianship Over Again, Would You?" *Information Outlook* 3, no. 7 (July 1999): 19–23. www.sla.org/pubs/serial/io/1999/jul99/houdysh.shtml (last accessed 5 December 2003).

O'Brien, Ellen. "What Are We Doing Right? Why LIS Students Have Chosen Our Profession." *Ex Libris*, 133 (1 March 2002). marylaine.com/exlibris/xlib133.html (last accessed 5 December 2003).

"People." *NewBreedLibrarian* February 1, 2002. www.newbreedlibrarian.org/archives/02.01feb2002/people.html (last accessed 5 December 2003).

"Public Librarians Talk about the Profession." Public Library Association. www.pla.org/Content/NavigationMenu/PLA/Projects/Public_Librarian_Recruitment/Public_Librarians_ Talk_About_the_Profession.htm (last accessed 5 December 2003).

Spear, Martha J. "The Top 10 Reasons to Be a Librarian (With Apologies to David Letterman)." *American Libraries* 33, no. 9 (October 2002): 54–55. www.ala.org/Content/NavigationMenu/Products_and_Publications/Periodicals/American_Libraries/Selected_articles/The_Top_10_Reasons_to_be_a_Librarian.htm (last accessed 5 December 2003).

ABOUT THE AUTHOR

Karla J. Block graduated with an MLIS from Dominican University in 1997. She is an assistant librarian and head of access and outreach services at the Bio-Medical Library, University of Minnesota–Twin Cities in Minneapolis.

Index

About the Editor

Priscilla K. Shontz is author of *Jump Start Your Career in Library and Information Science* (Scarecrow Press, 2002). She currently works as a freelance writer and webmaster/editor of LIScareer.com. She has worked in academic, special, and public libraries. Priscilla earned a BS in journalism from the University of Texas at Arlington and an MSLS from the University of North Texas. She is a past president of the American Library Association New Members Round Table.